The Life of J.W. Alexander

Forty Years of Familiar Letters

Edited by the Surviving Correspondent,
John Hall, DD

Volume 1
1819–1844

AUDUBON PRESS
2601 Audubon Drive
P.O. Box 8055
Laurel, MS 39441-8000   USA

Orders: 800-405-3788
Inquiries: 601-649-8572
Voice: 601-649-8570 / Fax: 601-649-8571
E-mail: buybooks@audubonpress.com
Web Page: www.audubonpress.com

© 2008 Audubon Press edition
All rights reserved.
Printed in the United States
Cover design by Crisp Graphics

ISBN # 978-09742365-6-8

Original Publication:
In Two Volumes
Volume 1

New York:
CHARLES SCRIBNER, GRAND STREET
London:
SAMPSON LOW, SON & COMPANY
1860

Original Publication Layout and Typography:
John F. Trow
Printers, Stereotypers, & Electrotypers,
50 Green Street, N.Y.

CONTENTS OF VOLUME I.

                                                        PAGE

CHAPTER I.
JUVENILE LETTERS, ... 1
1819—1822.

CHAPTER II.
LETTERS FROM THE THEOLOGICAL SEMINARY, . . . 13
1822—1824.

CHAPTER III.
LETTERS WHILE TUTOR IN COLLEGE, ... 42
1824—1825.

CHAPTER IV.
LETTERS WHILE A LICENTIATE, ... 88
1825—1827.

CHAPTER V.
LETTERS WHILE A PASTOR IN VIRGINIA, AND UNTIL HE LEFT THE STATE, 98
1827—1828.

CHAPTER VI.
LETTERS WHILE PASTOR IN TRENTON, ... 119
1829—1832.

CHAPTER VII.

LETTERS WHILE EDITOR OF "THE PRESBYTERIAN," 203
1833.

CHAPTER VIII.

LETTERS WHILE PROFESSOR IN THE COLLEGE OF NEW JERSEY, . . 208
1833—1844.

INDEX, ... 405

PREFACE.

The familiar letters of forty consecutive years, out of a life of fifty-five years, and addressed to one correspondent, furnish in themselves the best memoir of their writer. Over every thing in the shape of diary or autobiography, such a series has the advantage of presenting the man in the successive phases of his character and opinions, as well as in their final mould.

Such a correspondence, in the nature of things, must be of rare occurrence. Too many elements must concur to make it otherwise. The incidents of time, friendship, local separation, and the preservation of the letters, cannot be often combined in the circumstances of two persons. Horace Walpole and Sir Horace Mann kept up their intercourse in this way from 1741 to 1786—nearly forty-five years. Bishop Jebb, of Limerick, and Alexander Knox, maintained a "thirty years' correspondence," from 1799 to 1831. But though in both of these cases the exchange continued until the death of one of the parties, in neither was it begun in boyhood. In the collection now given to the public, the writer passes before us, in his own undisguised expressions, from the frivolities and crudities of fifteen, to the maturity of his half century. Those who take an interest in his career, have special reason to be pleased that the correspondence took place, and that of all the eight hundred letters which he wrote to his friend, none have been lost, because his own views and wishes on the subject of Memoirs have been so construed by his family, that they could not have consented to any other form of biography.

The highest advantages of the method adopted would have been sacrificed had the editor, for the sake of producing an appearance of uniformity in his friend's opinions and positions, suppressed the evidence of such fluctuations as every independent and investigating mind is open to. With this view I have suffered to stand some diversities of his judgment, at different times, or in different lights, on points of theology, church order, church policy, slavery, and other topics. His views on some important questions may have been modified, without any trace of the change appearing in the letters; and I have been particularly requested to notice, under this head, that in the last years of his life, he saw the importance of a far stricter rule in observing the Lord's day, and in the allowance of fashionable amusements, than would appear from some occasional statements in these volumes.

And I am sure that I should not have been excused had I at all subdued the light and playful tone in which many of the letters are written, or attempted any amendment of the abrupt transitions and off-hand phrases so characteristic of the unstudied, unrevised expression of the uppermost thoughts at the moment of writing. To have changed his manner would have been as great unfaithfulness to the full delineation of my correspondent, as to have concealed his sentiments.

It may reasonably be expected, also, that there will be accorded to these letters the indulgence almost as claimable for a correspondence of this kind, as for ordinary conversation, of strong, and even exaggerated, language; when every thing in the connexion and style shows that these allowances are due. It would be the highest injustice to throw the private writings of another before the world, if such a consideration as this could not be depended on.

Still, I would not have it understood that I have used no editorial discretion. Scarcely one letter has been given entire; and I trust that I have so far omitted the personal allusions, which were, of course, frequent in the intimate interchange of our observations, that no fastidiousness will be offended by those which have been suffered to remain. And here I must state that it is only in deference to a delicacy which commands the most sacred respect, that I have excluded many references to the happiness, the comfort, the spiritual benefit, which Dr. Alexander possessed and appreciated as a husband. His whole domestic life, indeed, was a trait in his character and biography, to which even the most unrestricted publication of the correspondence could not do justice.

When I consented to undertake this work, it was with much dependence on the promised assistance of Dr. J. Addison Alexander. But I had scarcely entered upon it, before the state of his health made it improper to communicate with him on the subject, and in a few weeks he had followed his brother to the grave.

I have not felt disposed to introduce into this publication demonstrations of my own personal feelings with regard to my friendship with these beloved men, and under the loss of them both, by almost the same stroke; yet it affords me a lively satisfaction to believe that the letters, besides their more important results, will be a memorial of that long and affectionate attachment.

The aim of the editor has been to insert only so many notes as were requisite to explain the text, or supply biographical details. The purposes of a memoir are so fully met in this manner through the early commencement of the correspondence, that it is only necessary to prefix, in this place, a sketch of the short period that precedes the first date.

JAMES W. ALEXANDER, the eldest son of Archibald and Janetta Alexander, was born March 13, 1804. The place of his birth was the residence of his maternal grandfather, the Rev. Dr. James Waddel, in Louisa County, Virginia, on an estate called Hopewell, at the junction of the three counties of Louisa, Orange, and Albemarle, and near the present site of Gordonsville. In the month of December, 1807, his father having resigned the presidency of Hampden Sidney College, and accepted the call of the third Presbyterian Congregation of Philadelphia to be their pastor, the family removed to that city, where their residence continued until July, 1812, when Dr. A. Alexander entered upon his duties in the Theological Seminary at Princeton. During the few years of their home in Philadelphia, James attended two schools—first (in 1809) that of Mrs. or "Madam" Thomson, then that of Mr. James Ross. His principal preparation for College was therefore made at Princeton.

The first school he attended there was the Academy, the principal of which was the Rev. Jared D. Fyler, who was followed for a few months, in 1813, by Dr. Carnahan, and then by the Rev. Daniel Comfort. Then he entered the school of Mr. James Hamilton, afterwards of the University of Nashville. He also had the benefit of the instructions of several private tutors; among whom were the Rev. John Monteith, since of Hamilton College, and the Rev. Thomas J. Biggs, now of Cincinnati. He entered the Freshman class of the College of New Jersey in the spring of 1817, and graduated there in September, 1820.

A portrait is prefixed to each of these volumes. The first is from a painting by Mr. Mooney, taken in 1845, at the age of forty; the second from a daguerreotype by Mr. Meade, in 1855.

TRENTON, NEW JERSEY, *May* 5, 1860.

CHAPTER I.

JUVENILE LETTERS.

1819—1822.

PRINCETON, *May 5th*, 1819.[1]

According to your desire, as soon as I was a little recruited and had got my pen, ink and paper together, I set myself down to scribble away a scrawl to let you know I was safely landed at "Princetown in the Jarsys" at ten minutes after ten o'clock A. M., without having sustained any material injury, except a cut of the thumb, and a little broken-heartedness at leaving—you know what—behind me. I frightened them not a little with my mask, and diverted them as much with my dandies. I have been diverting myself a little with playing on my flute. I must confess I was not fairly out of the city, before I wished to be back again, and I shall not soon forget the delightful hours I spent last week in Philadelphia. I wish you could persuade your mother to let you come up and spend some time here. As I have made you my confidant, I will not say I had a bad pen, &c., but will candidly confess it is the best I can posssibly write, and I repose on your honour that it will not be shown to anybody.

PRINCETON, *June 6th*, 1819.

REV. AND DEAR SIR,—For such I expect will shortly be your title both from the long faced and crabbed style in which you write, and your parson-like division of your sermon; but

---

[1] This and a few other letters of the same year are inserted because they are the first in the series of a correspondence which soon took a different complexion. At this date Alexander was a boy of fifteen, and his friend whom he had just been visiting in Philadelphia, was a few years younger. The former was in the Junior Class of the College of New Jersey, the latter was at school.

waiving this subject I proceed to unfold the dark mystery of my not writing to you. Imprimis, you attribute my silence to bashfulness, and you were quite right in your supposition that it was not on that account I had not written, for since my extremely pleasant trip to the city, I have but few grains of that commodity (at present) on hand. I say at present, for I know not in what luckless hour it may return. 2dly. You pretend to think that I have not esteem enough for you to favour you with an epistle. My dear fellow, I am tempted to think that you belied your conscience when you put that sentence down. 3dly. Your letter was so far from being illegible that I think you must have meant what you said as a sarcasm upon my wretched scrawl—but the true, only, and unsatisfactory excuse, which I have to offer, is pure laziness. How far this excuse may go, I know not, but I hope that this letter itself will supersede the necessity of any farther apology, and if you prize my poor scrawl, this will be a little more acceptable on account of its being delayed.

Five of your school-mates have entered College, viz., James Stuart, and Sharpe, the Sophomore class; J. B. Clemson, J. S. Miercken, and J. M. Savage, the Freshman.[1]

PRINCETON, *June* 28th, 1819.

DEAR JOHN,—I was very agreeably surprised this morning by your letter, which I began to fear was never to arrive, and which, as you certainly know, afforded me great pleasure, which I think is sufficiently manifested by my sitting down to answer it immediately. I shall answer what requires it in your own letter first, and then proceed to add something of my own. You ask me to suggest some subjects of debate for your society. I know of none at present except two which have lately been discussed in a club at college, viz.: Is a man bound (by the laws of equity) to fulfil oaths taken to save his life, or when his life is in jeopardy? and Should any one swerve from the truth to preserve his life, or estate? Both these are moral questions, and I should have no scruples of conscience, hindering me from saying No to the former, and Yes to the latter. I cannot think of any now, but if I fall across any I shall let you know of them. The health of my father is much better than it has been for some time, he is at present at Somerville in this State. I have not been very well for a week past, occasioned, I am led to suppose,

---

[1] Stuart died a Presbyterian clergyman, in 1829. James T. Sharpe is a physician in Salem, New Jersey. Clemson is an Episcopal clergyman in Pennsylvania. Miercken died Captain of a Liverpool Packet.

by going into the water too often. I have been to swim every day for a fortnight, in fact it is the only time when I feel comfortable. I hope to see you up here before the *Dog-days*, so that I may have the pleasure of teaching you how to swim. I have wished very much to see a Velocipede but have not been gratified, nor do I expect to be, till I visit the city again.

PRINCETON, *Sunday, August 1st,* 1819.

MY DEAR FRIEND,—As I begin to feel rather ashamed of my neglect, I have dared to face your displeasure with a few lines. I dare say you will think I am out of paper from this specimen, which is really the case, as it is Sunday and there is no other in the house. I expect that by this time you have waxed exceedingly wrothy with your humble servant on account of his long silence, of which he has no very plausible excuse to offer, except a certain—degree—of—laziness—which the extreme heat of the weather has tended to increase.

By the by, the mercury in Fahrenheit's thermometer was yesterday at noon, as high as 110° in the shade, and 112° in the sun, which, if I am not very much mistaken, is enough to give the yellow fever to every man, woman, and child in the country.

After all this preamble I will proceed to inform you that we confidently expect you up here, as soon as your holidays begin, which I suppose are now near at hand, and that I shall be extremely disappointed if you should fail to fulfil your engagement; I wish you could persuade your mother or some one of the family to accompany you, as I suppose the weather is very unpleasant in the city at this time. I must confess that I am not able to hold out any great inducement to come into this dreary, out of the way, dog hole, except perhaps change of situation and pity towards me who have to stay here five months, without seeing, hearing, or feeling, any thing worth being seen, heard or felt.

I cannot forbear mentioning the happy hours I spent in my short but delightful stay in the city last Spring. I am certain that if you promised yourself half the pleasure which I enjoyed there, you would fly up here as soon as your vacation commenced. But alas, I have no such enticements here for you, as Philadelphia has for me. If your mamma should fear to trust you with me and our Princeton boys, be so good as to inform her that we have some with faces a yard long, and moreover that I will insure your life and morals, for the small sum of one cent.

It is stated by our Princeton astronomers that two comets

are visible at once at 2 o'clock A. M. If it is a fact, I suppose you have heard of it before this; for my part, I think five o'clock is time enough for me to rise without getting up to view the comets. Velocipedes are beginning to be introduced here. I have not seen one yet.

The bell rings for church, and I am forced to go; remember me to all, &c.

P. S.—I had three beautiful flying squirrels for the children, but unluckily the old cat demolished them, and now enjoys a pleasing "otium cum dignitate" in the bottom of the mill pond with a stone round her neck.

PRINCETON, *August* 23, 1822.[1]

MY DEAR FRIEND,—The agreeable visit of your sisters to our village has forcibly reminded me of the duty, so long neglected by me, of writing to my old friend and correspondent. What I shall have to say will appear in the sequel, for as yet I feel so great a dearth of writing materials in my brain, that I must needs push forward, and let the thoughts arrange themselves *ad libitum*. Since I last saw you, many strange and unex-

---

[1] The only suspension of this correspondence that ever took place, was from April, 1820, to the date of this letter. It was in this interval that Alexander's mind became engrossed with the subject of his personal religion. The first relief he obtained is described by himself in the following record: "On September 3, 1820, walking across the field, hardly daring to ask for faith or repentance, these words burst upon my mind—'*Waiting for the moving of the waters.*' I saw myself the impotent man in a moment, and I thought that Christ had been saying to me, 'Wilt thou be made whole?' hundreds of times in my hearing, but now it seemed to be addressed particularly to me. From that moment I felt able to trust my whole hope and life upon the Lord."

At the end of this September he finished his college course, but delayed a public profession of faith until the next year; then the return of his birthday, and the death of a young friend, combined to make him feel the risk of further postponement. He was received to full communion by the session of the Princeton Church, March 30, 1821, and sat at the Lord's table for the first time on the following Sabbath, April 1st.

On the 13th of that month he made a private entry to this effect: "When I look forward to future life, a dreary darkness presents itself. What am I qualified for? I never can, in conscience, embrace any other profession but the 'gospel of Christ;' but alas, where are my qualifications? I *never, never* can be a speaker." In a note written some time afterwards he says: "I thank God for having shown me that this conviction was in some measure unfounded and hasty. Though I never can be eloquent, yet God's spirit may make me a useful preacher."

The three days, Sept. 15th, 1820, March 30th and April 1st, 1821, he ever afterwards commemorated as times of peculiar humiliation and prayer.

pected things have no doubt befallen each of us, and I have had a goodly share of vicissitudes, painful and pleasant, during the three years just elapsed, but whether any of them could give you any pleasure, I cannot say. I presume I need not tell you that my time spent in college ran sadly to waste; indeed, I cannot look back upon the opportunities of acquiring useful knowledge which I then abused without shame and regret. Like most brainless and self-conceited boys, I undertook to determine that such and such studies were of no importance, and made this an excuse for neglecting them, although the wise of every age have united in declaring their utility. I was foolish enough to suffer almost all my previous knowledge of classical literature to leak out *e cerebro*, and consequently I found myself a much greater dolt when I was invested with the title and immunities of an A. B., than when I entered as an humble Freshman. I had acquired, not a vast amount of erudition, but an insufferable budget of silly opinions, self-conceited views of my own abilities, and innumerable vicious habits, which alone are sufficient to neutralize all the good which a college course can give in the way of knowledge. The labour of the two last years has but slightly repaired these injuries, and I have hardly reached the point which I ought to have attained, at the term of my collegiate race. To proceed with my egotistical harangue, (for I have nothing better to give you,) I have devoted most of my time since to classical reading, and my eyes I think are opened in some measure to those beauties, which, blinded with ignorant self-sufficiency, I was unable to perceive formerly. It is the fashion of this superficial age to decry the study of ancients, and more so in America than in Europe, more among the idle and ignorant coxcombs of this day, than the men of science and taste. I had caught this song at college, and like other *graduated fools* I presumed to laugh at those authors who have been the models of taste, and fountains of polite learning, for more ages than we have lived years. Homer was a favourite butt for my ridicule. I have read the old fellow's Iliad twice through of late, with new pleasure at every opening, and it is my intention if my life be spared, to spend one hour *per diem* for the rest of my life in reading the classics. No doubt, this prosing must be offensive to you; my next letter shall be more taken up about present concerns, as I hope to receive something from you to serve as a cue for my response. If you are curious to know what I am now studying—I have been for some weeks upon metaphysics, another of my old despicables; I now am much enamoured with it. You know, doubtless, that I expect to enter the theological seminary this fall. I anticipate the course of theology with a great deal of pleasure; many of my best friends expect to enter with me, and the studies are such as suit my taste. Theology is certainly a noble science, inasmuch as its subjects are the most exalted in nature, i. e. the relations subsisting between man and his Maker. "This is that science," says *Locke*, "which would truly enlarge men's minds, were it studied, or permitted to be studied everywhere, with that freedom, love of truth and charity which it teaches, and were not made, contrary to its nature, the occasion of strife, faction, malignity, and narrow impositions."

I did not expect, when I began to write, that I should take up two sheets—but I am proverbially garrulous, and as I shall not put you to the expense of a double postage, I shall continue to run on. I remember with many pleasing associations the time which I spent in your city, about three years ago. The traces of sundry fair countenances remain indistinctly marked upon my memory, and sundry boyish freaks I remember sometimes with pleasure, and sometimes with a little shame. But why should I be ashamed? *Dulce est desipere in loco*, (and the 1st of May and thereabouts is assuredly the proper season if there is such a *locus* in the whole year,) and it is no less sweet to *remember* these *desipientias*. I might indulge in the usual mawkish reveries usual upon such occasions, such as talking about "halcyon days" and "departed joys never to return;" but I will not falsify, I hope to enjoy happier moments than these; I *have* enjoyed happier moments, rendered so by nobler and purer joys than those.

I think it probable, that I shall take a journey Southward in the Autumn, to see my relations in Lexington, Staunton, and other parts of Virginia; my travelling lately has all been towards the North. My health appears to me to call for a jaunt; I have not been *sick*, but my flesh runs from me by degrees, to my great sorrow. A year ago I had a very respectable portion of fat; at present my sharp bones poke out their heads, threatening to pierce the skin. Have I not talked long enough, and incoherently enough, and tiresomely enough, and nos-met-ipsically enough? Farewell. Write, I beg of you. Amicus usque ad aras.

PRINCETON, *September 7th*, 1822, *Saturday.*

I received, a few minutes ago, your very welcome letter; and I begin an answer immediately, because I think it probable that a private opportunity of transmitting it will occur during the day. I feel relieved from much embarrassment by the receipt of your goodly two-sheet epistle. You know that a man is in a situation rather awkward when he commences writing to a new friend, or an old one metamorphosed by absence and years. What shall be my topics? where shall I begin? are the questions which rise in his mind; there is no common ground upon which he may venture, but the ice once broken, all to be done is to seize the cue presented, and swim down the current of your thoughts, wherever they lead you. Now the current of my thoughts is very apt to lead me into dry prosing, or trifling, or some such shoal; still, at all risks, here it goes, neck or nothing. I pray you to be content with whatever may meet your eye, let the partiality of friendship blind you to all faults. And, as I was talking of letter-writing, let me say a few words more upon the same subject. A letter, as I take it, is intended to stand in lieu of an absent friend, to be his proxy in all things, to talk in his stead, and convey his own ideas, in his own style of conversation. Now, so far as the letter is a faithful representative, it is a fair picture of the disposition and sentiments of its author, and its value is to be estimated not so much by the intrinsic weight of the opinions expressed, or the intrinsic excellence of the style, (though these things give it new value,) but by its resemblance to the writer. If the writer be a festive mercurial fellow, and the letter be as sage as an epistle of Seneca, I would not give a groat for it; still I would always have a letter be a vehicle of instruction, (such I am afraid this will not be.) But even this instruction must be given in the same way that its parent would give it vivâ voce. That letter which is so characteristic as to present its writer to my eyes during the perusal, is worth its weight in silver. And to obtain this excellence, the writer of a letter must be exceedingly passive, and just pen down whatever comes next. So I intend to do, hoping that it will be as acceptable, as if I should indite a profound dissertation.

As this is almost my first letter, I hope you will pardon me for dwelling so long upon epistolary writing. I am not a friend to quotations in general, but as I intend to spin out a long sheet, I cannot forbear giving you one from the prince of letter writers, Cowper. It appears to me to be the very thing. "I am very apt to forget, when I have any epistolary business on hand, that a letter may be written upon any thing or nothing, just as that any thing or nothing happens to occur. A man that has a journey before him 20 miles in length, which he is to perform on foot, will not hesitate and doubt whether he shall set out or not, because he does not readily conceive how he shall ever reach the end of it, for he knows that by the simple operation of moving one foot forward first, and then the other, he shall be sure to accomplish it. So it is in the present case, and so it is in every case similar. A letter is written as a conversation is maintained, or a journey performed, not by preconcerted or premeditated means, a new contrivance, or an invention never heard of before, but merely *by maintaining a progress,* and resolving as a postilion does, having once set out, never to stop 'till we reach the appointed end." By quotation and otherwise, you perceive I manage *to maintain a progress,* if nothing more. "An interminable preamble," you may possibly exclaim, "What grand display is to be made after all this 'pomp and circumstance?'" I will tell you: I am endeavouring to explain to you the terms upon which this correspondence is to be maintained, upon my part. As my humour is, so will my letter be. If I am grave and sober you may expect at least a *dull* letter. If I have been reading poetry, Cowper, and Thomson, and Shakespeare, and Ovid, as I have been all the last week, you may look for just such a foggy, sublimated, ethereal production as the present.

You mention that your character has undergone little change. No man is the proper judge of his own character. The changes of our bodily frame, and of our mental part, are so gradual and imperceptible, that they appear nothing to ourselves. "Law John! how you have grown!" has doubtless met your ear ofttimes from the mouth of some good old dame; and the same exclamation was mentally ejaculated by me, in a higher sense, while perusing your letter. I must say something of my own habits and character. Without being guilty of the enormity of eaves-dropping, I have by various chances heard the opinions of divers persons respecting myself, and if I am to judge of myself by these, I am truly an odd compound of qualities. "He's a tolerably clever fellow," say some; "but very eccentric." I acknowledge that I am a clever fellow, and also eccentric. As to the last attribute, I heartily wish I had none of it, and that my orbit were less elliptical. Like a comet, I am sometimes heated, and extravagant, indulging in untimely mirth; and soon, as you might prophesy, chilled with melancholy. Sometimes I am accused of unseasonable levity, and oftener of moroseness and obstinacy; so that, if I take all the advice which my kind friends so liberally bestow, I shall soon find myself in the predicament of the old man, who with his son carried the ass to market; you remember the fable. I have long since determined to shape my own course, without reference to the opinions of every counsellor; if I can discover the path of duty, I hope I shall muster up courage to tread it. The advice of my parents, and those who have a right to counsel, I shall always deem invaluable. As to my habits, there are some which I cannot but deplore, but which I fear will cleave to me *usque ad canitiem:* among these I rank first, an unconquerable spirit of trifling, and levity; my natural temperament makes me ready at all times, upon all occasions, for any silly jest—(verbal jokes, I mean, I have no taste for 'practical jokes.') Habits of idleness appeared deep-rooted in me when I left college; I have, however, happily acquired a taste for study; so that, as it is my greatest pleasure, I wish I could say that my improvement has been proportional to my labour; I seem to have been very laboriously doing nothing.

I concur with you in your *general* remarks upon education; still I would amend your proposition, by saying that boys are sent too early to *colleges,* instead of "*schools.*" The three or four years spent in college are usually looked upon by the student, and the world, as the top-stones upon the structure of his education. A structure so soon erected, and so slightly, must needs totter under every hurricane. As far as I am enabled to judge from my own experience, I think that boys should leave school, about the age that they usually leave college, i. e. about 18. This indeed does not accord with our present collegiate system, for in that time they would have made a greater progress than boys do in their whole college course. But let the standard of college attainments be elevated far above its present degree. Let the servile work of learning *to read* Latin and Greek be kept to the schools, and even there let it be taught upon some plan which shall not disgust the scholar, and make him loathe those noble authors, which are prostituted to the base purpose of teaching boys their accidence. Let boys be thoroughly versed in the learned languages before they enter any college. This is the plan pursued in most of the European universities. It is absolutely necessary that the student should be able not merely to read, but to talk Latin, before he can enter them. Let the studies of the schools be so diversified, and so suited to the taste of the learner, that he may take some pleasure in them. A school thus conducted, would not, I think, cramp the genius of any boy, but rather add wings to it, and assist its discursive flight. I think it necessary that boys should be sent *early* to school. Habits of idleness soon become inveterate; still, let the studies be proportionate to the scholar's capacity. Another reason I have for this is, that boyhood is the time when we receive with most pleasure, general knowledge; the lighter kind of knowledge obtained by indiscriminate reading, and which then amalgamates itself with the boy's previous knowledge, and sticks by him through life. Now where is the person who has much taste for this knowledge, whose education was not commenced early?

To go on with my Utopian scheme. I would have the student learn in college, the higher branches of education—the higher mathematics, if his taste led him to pursue it, the philosophy of the mind, ethics, natural law, political economy, and the *classics;* not construing and parsing, (for I would have him familiar with them,) but investigating their beauties, drawing from them rules of pure and correct criticism, and thus improving his taste and judgment. Above all, I would have Shakespeare's rule adopted:

> "Talk logic with acquaintance that you have,
> And practise Rhetoric in your common talk:
> The mathematics and the metaphysics
> *Fall to them as your stomach serves you.*
> *No profit grows where is no pleasure taken.*
> In brief, sir, *study what you most affect.*"

September 10*th, Tuesday.*

I was unable to obtain an opportunity of sending what I had written on Saturday, and therefore I shall continue to scribble as I have leisure until such an opportunity presents itself. My father returned yesterday, quite ill, from Newtown, Pa. He went on Saturday for the purpose of assisting Mr. Boyd in the administration of the Lord's Supper. He preached in the morning, and attempted it at night, but fainted away. We were very much alarmed when he returned. His disorder is the dysentery. We hope that the disease is subdued by the administration of very powerful medicines yesterday and to-day. He is, however, still extremely weak, and keeps his bed.

I was going on in answer to your letter on Saturday. Your disgust for the ancient classics is by no means wonderful. The method of teaching them in our institutions of learning, is calculated admirably to have that effect. When I commenced studying them after I took my degree, it was merely from a sense of their importance, and not from any love to them. I detested them as most nauseous, and felt disposed to esteem all their admirers arrant pedants, and crack-brained fools.

The words of Byron suited me well,

> "May he who will, his recollections rake
> And quote in classic raptures, and awake
> The hills with Latian echoes; I abhorred
> Too much, to conquer for the poet's sake,
> The drilled dull lesson, forced down word by word
> In my repugnant youth, with pleasure to record
> Aught that recalls the daily drug which turn'd
> My sick'ning memory; and tho' time has taught
> My mind to meditate what then it learned,
> Yet such the fixed inveteracy wrought
> By the impatience of my early thought,
> That with the freshness wearing out, before
> My mind could relish what it might have sought,
> If free to choose, I cannot now restore
> Its health, but what it then detested still abhor."

But I still persevered. Mr. Hodge and I devoted an hour each day to the study of the Latin and Greek writers, and continued this practice for eighteen months, during which time we had read several authors: and the effect has been a thorough revolution of my taste. I could now obey Horace's exhortation, and spend my days and nights in perusing these authors, but I do not think the time would be profitably spent. Of late, I have been engaged in reading our English poets, for whom I have a GREAT esteem. Cowper is my favorite among them all. He resembles very closely my other favorite Horace. As it regards pungency of satire, and close and powerful argument, I think these poets are unequalled by any of their own nations. If I except the odes of Horace, and a few blots in the satires, I think they are also parallel as to morals: I mean, of course, to measure each by the standard of the age in which he lived. Their faults are somewhat alike also; an apparent contempt of harmony of verse, where an idea would lose one morsel of strength by gaining in elegance. I hope you will determine not to forswear the reading of these authors as I did when I left college.

Thursday, September 12th.

You talk about my crying you mercy on your fourth page: what shall I say upon my ninth? May I presume that you have had patience to read thus far? For want of any thing to say, I tell you as another item in our domestic annals, that as I have not been well, I have been threshing in our barn for an hour, and consider it a very excellent kind of exercise, for cold weather especially.

Monday, 16th.

I see no reason why I should not continue to write, even though I have nothing to say, until I am able to send this to you. I have avoided saying any thing of my father's health for some days, because I wished to inform you that he was recovered. This I am not yet able to do; he has been becoming weaker and weaker, and though the disease appears to be checked, yet his strength is completely prostrated; he has not sat up since his illness commenced. We believe that he will gradually recover now; but we have been much alarmed. We have, however, had the satisfaction of seeing him at ease under all his pain, perfectly willing to live or die, as the will of God might be.

TRENTON, *November 4th*, 1822.

I came down to this place on Friday last, and the solicitations of friends and other attractions, have kept me thus long, and shall keep me probably some days longer.

I rode down on Saturday with a friend to Point Breeze, the seat of his Ex-Majesty Joseph, or to use his proper title *Le Compte De Survilliers.* We spent a long time very agreeably, in strolling about his elegant villa and grounds, gazing upon his buildings, and lakes, and bridges, and splendid statues. I felt transported to some of those European palaces which we poor Americans are forced to hear of, with itching ears, without the pleasure of seeing them.

The improvements which are still almost in embryo, display much taste in the planner, whoever he was, and are in a style entirely new to me. He has a daughter lately arrived from Europe, *La Comptesse, &c.*

To go on in the journal style. I heard Mr. Armstrong[1] preach a most eloquent sermon yesterday morning; he is one of my favorites. At night, Mr. Lybrand, the Methodist,—a very good preacher,—the coolest Methodist I ever heard. The Trentonians say that the Presbyterians have got the Methodist preacher, and the Methodists the Presbyterian.

My studies[2] begin on Thursday, then I am in for a six months' siege. I am rather afraid that my health will fail. The college commences at the same time; a great accession is expected.

My father has entirely recovered his health; and rides about the country.

[1] The Rev. William J. Armstrong, pastor of the Presbyterian church.
[2] In the Theological Seminary at Princeton, which he entered at the time specified.

CHAPTER II.

LETTERS FROM THE THEOLOGICAL SEMINARY.

1822—1824.

PRINCETON, *November* 22, 1822.

My studies and interruptions and engagements are so numerous as to leave me little time for exercise and recreation, and still less for the less imperative duties of correspondence, &c. Besides, our institution has been in a state of painful suspense and anxiety with respect to the case of Krebs for some days;[1] he is at last taken away, and this left a gloom upon the minds of all of us. On Monday the 18th instant he was first confined to his bed; about Thursday he was seized with a delirium, his fever raged from that time with the utmost violence, and all hopes of his recovery were relinquished. On Friday night the Debating Society was adjourned, and an hour was devoted by the students to prayers for his recovery or his restoration to reason and happy deliverance from this life. During this hour, strange as it may appear, he enjoyed a lucid interval, and though unable to speak, yet by looks and signs he manifested to my father and all who surrounded him his entire resignation to the afflicting hand of God, and his joyful expectation of a happy eternity. Saturday was spent in religious duties in his behalf; on Saturday night his fever abated and left him prostrate as to animal and mental strength; his father and mother arrived on Saturday night, but were not recognized by him until the next day. On Tuesday morning at 1 o'clock A. M., I was called up to see him die, but I declined going into his room. He melted away without a groan or a struggle.

On Tuesday afternoon his corpse was taken in a carriage to

---

[1] William George Krebs, of Philadelphia, a classmate of Mr. Alexander in College as well as Seminary. He was a member of the Lutheran Church. A biographical sketch, written by his fellow student Mr. Joseph S. Christmas, (himself afterwards so celebrated in the ministry,) is in Dr. Green's *Christian Advocate* for October, 1823.

Philadelphia, accompanied by seven or eight of his fellow students. Perhaps I am wearying you with what dwells so heavily upon my own mind; it may not interest you. I feel it to be a loud call to me to be also ready for this great change. Within three weeks, three of my college classmates have left this world; all of them far more robust, and having the promise of longer life than myself.

My studies are overwhelming, and as we study subjects rather than books, they are unlimited. I feel disposed to read all that I can on each subject, and when I have spent all my time thus, I find that I have only stepped upon the thresholds of these various apartments of science.

I thank you for your intelligence respecting the literary improvements in your city. I shall always rejoice to hear good tidings from the place where my early scenes of pleasure and pain were chiefly laid, and where I received the rudiments of my anomalous education. I always side myself with Philadelphians when New York is brought in competition with it, though I hardly know why. The associations of infancy ought not to bias the reason of more mature age.[1]

PRINCETON, *Theol. Sem. Last day of* 1822.

I wish you all the good wishes which are suggested by the return of this season of festivity, a happy and profitable New Year to you and all your family. You ask for particulars respecting the Seminary, our studies, &c.; and there is no request that I would grant with greater pleasure, for these several reasons: Imprimis, I love our institution so much, and am so happily situated in every respect, that I shall not be soon weary of my subject. Secondly, it is an inexhaustible subject, and therefore I shall have no difficulty in filling up this immense sheet. Thirdly, it is a subject on which I am at home, and therefore I shall write with more ease and pleasure. You shall be satisfied as to minutiæ, and so you have upon the third page of this epistle a brief but minute register of the members of our Seminary, in print too.[2]

I said I was happy,—never more so in my life. I enjoy good health, good spirits, and I have a most comfortable room, and a most delightful room mate.[3] I never had so great a variety of

---

[1] His residence in Philadelphia extended from December, 1807, to July, 1812—from his fourth to his ninth year. This gave him a short time to enjoy the exact and thorough initiation into Latin Grammar, for which the school of JAMES ROSS was so deservedly famous.

[2] The annual catalogue, on a folio sheet.

[3] Jared B. Waterbury, now D. D.

excellent company before: Metaphysicians, Wits, Theologians, &c., &c. I have here dearly prized friends, who endear Princeton to me. Books in the greatest abundance, as I have access to six public libraries, as well as my father's. Our studies are not burdensome, and far from being irksome. I saw a letter the other day from an alumnus of this institution to a member of it, in which he says: " My dear C——, you are now enjoying your happiest days, and whether you realize it now or not, you will feel it deeply when you are cast out upon the world." These sentiments are not peculiar to this individual, I hear them from every one who has ever been here. Indeed, the greatest cares I experience, are such as arise from an oration to be spoken, or a tedious lecture. Will you not say with Virgil, *O fortunati nimium sua si bona norint.* I will now proceed to give you some account of my course of life. I rise at half after six. Public prayers in the Oratory at 7. Breakfast at 8. From 9 to $9\frac{1}{2}$, I devote to bodily exercise. From $9\frac{1}{2}$ until 12, Study. 12—1, Exercise. Dine at one. 2—3, I usually devote to works of taste, and to composing. 3—$4\frac{1}{2}$ at Lecture. $4\frac{1}{2}$ Prayers. Until tea, at Exercise. After tea, until 12 (at which time I close my eyes) Societies, study, &c.

Perhaps you think I exercise my *body* sufficiently. I find it absolutely necessary to my well-being, or almost to my being at all. You may think, too, that I do not study a great deal; true—and moreover that I need not complain of want of time for correspondence; true, at present I need not complain; I have plenty of time for writing, and general reading. At the beginning of the term, before I had fairly got into the harness, our business appeared too much to grasp; but it is now methodized, and I find that I am quite a gentleman of leisure. To proceed: we recite twice in the week on Hebrew, once on Greek, once on the Confession of Faith, once on Biblical History. Hear Lectures once on Theology, (preparatory to the full and regular theological Lectures,) twice on Biblical history, once on the Criticism of the Original Scriptures, once on Jewish Antiquities. On Monday night, I attend a society for improvement in the criticism of the Bible; President, Mr. Hodge. On Tuesday night, the Theological Society, where every student delivers once in six weeks an original oration. On Thursday night, I am at liberty to attend an evening lecture at the college. On Friday night, Theological Society, where questions in ethics and divinity are discussed. On Saturday night, a weekly prayer meeting. On Sunday we have sermons from our three professors, and Prof. Lindsly,[1] in rotation.

[1] Philip Lindsly, D. D., the Vice President of the College of New Jersey.

The greatest advantage which I experience from being in the Seminary, and this is increased by my being an inhabitant of the house, is, that we live in a kind of literary atmosphere; all the conversation carried on here is of a literary kind; at table, in our walks, and wherever a cluster of us assembles, some lively discussion takes place which causes our time to fly very rapidly and pleasantly away. All our opinions are brought into the arena of free discussion, and we must defend them or relinquish them. Opinions founded upon ignorance, or prejudice, habits and manners which are unpleasant, and almost every eccentricity which is fostered during the course of a private education, is here likely to be rubbed off. So pleasant is my whole course of life here, that I feel not the least desire to go out into the great world.

But amid all my comforts, I am miserable unless when I am enabled to found my satisfaction and contentment upon a broader basis than any thing temporal. I find no substantial unmingled pleasure except in a conscience void of offence; which that I may always possess is my earnest and reigning desire. I know very well how repugnant it is to any one of nice feelings to have religion drummed into his ears, but I feel assured that a *word* in its favour will not offend you. I should be unworthy of the title of friend, if I did not endeavour in some feeble measure to make my friends partakers of the greatest happiness I can conceive of.

My habits have changed considerably since I entered the Seminary. I have bidden farewell to ennui, spleen, hyp., and all that class of old hangers on: also to the flute, to romantic air-castles, and walks in groves, to the company of ladies—item, to poetry, magazines, novels, &c., &c., too tedious to mention.

THEOLOGICAL SEMINARY, *January* 30, 1823.

Another month is tapering off to non-entity, and with it closes the first half of our winter term. On Monday next commences a recess from study of two weeks' duration; and, as you know that feelings of leisure and disenthralment are wont to creep over one before the vacation makes such feelings strictly allowable, you will not be surprised to hear that I am doing nothing about this time. Beware of dreaming that I have nothing to do; for since that unwarrantable boast in my last, that I was almost master of my time, I have been punished for my temerity by an influx of duties innumerable. The "pressure of business" upon me has been so mighty for two or three weeks, that my system has been considerably deranged in its bodily as well as mental parts. When I speak of business, I do not mean to convey to you the impression that my studies, &c., have been the only absorbents of my time, for the pursuits of the class do not necessarily consume many hours of the day; but my mind has been harassed by a multitude of questions in daily agitation, in these metaphysico-theologico-literario walks of science; questions from which I could not in justice to myself turn away my attention, but which have, at the same time, eaten up my vacant hours, and caused a host of unanswered letters to lie in my drawer praying for audience. At the present moment, being 10 o'clock P. M., (more or less,) I feel fit for no severe exertion; my animal spirits have been sucked up by a difficult Hebrew passage, a difficult mathematical query, and a difficult point in morals since tea, so that I am in a very proper state to utter that farrago of floating ideas commonly called when taken in a body, and put on paper, "A Letter." These ideas have been swimming *in cerebro*, I know not how long, crying for enlargement, and I am now arraying them before me on this piece of coarse foolscap, (by the way, the only connecting link between them, so incoherent are they and unsocial.)

My room mate left me this evening. I am now sole proprietor of this my little chamber. View me in imagination, seated in my chum's immense elbow chair, writing by the light of a shaded lamp, heated by a funereal looking stove just before me. Beginning at the south corner of my domicile, you observe first a row of shelves, containing all my little store of books, and many not my own, modestly covered by a gingham veil. In the same corner you may discern my spacious literary throne with all its appendages of drawers, &c. I need not direct your eyes to my scanty stock of chairs. A red desk standing in solemn guise among the sticks of fuel which lie in a capacious box, ready to feed the aforesaid stove. A high stool. A table. A mirror large enough to reflect my haggard features. An assortment of trunks, my own and Waterbury's. Three maps. A wash stand and appurtenances. A solitary picture to decorate my naked walls. A cluster of pantaloons in suspense. An axe and saw wherewithal our wood is cut. And finally, (though not least precious,) near to my room mate's couch is placed my lowly cot, into which wearied nature bids me presently creep. Pardon the vagaries of a half-crazed student. Good-bye, for this night.

Friday Morning, — 11 A. M.

I can assure you that I am in no humour for joking this morning. My old complaint the *blues* has come upon me like a strong man armed. Misanthropy is a sin which threatens at times to destroy not my own comfort only, but that of my friends around me. I despise it, and I loathe it, and yet, paradoxical and inconsistent creature, I hug it to my heart. I cannot say in truth that I hate any thing just now; but truly I am depressed; devoured by spleen, and fostering a crabbed, morose, churlish, silly, girl-like, sinful despondency.

Excuse my never-ending egotism. It is human nature to dwell upon our own real or imaginary misfortunes. It is still unreasonable when so many more luxuriant prospects present themselves for my contemplation.

I rejoice at the hint that you have given me, that you do not feel that unmanly and dastardly antipathy to the contemplation of the noblest of all objects,—the Great First Cause, and of the relations subsisting between Him and us. Why is it that the most sublime of all sciences, the science of man considered as an immortal being, and of God as the author of that immortality, and the only being powerful enough to make it blissful, should be shoved aside on all occasions from the mind's view, and thrust, whenever practicable, into oblivion? Is it because our interest in this subject is small—our personal interest? because these truths are merely speculative, and have no bearing upon our future and present happiness? because the importance of the subject is small? because life is so long as to warrant the hope that a better occasion for considering it will occur? because the addition of years is likely to take away our reluctance to consider it candidly? because we are not at all criminal in neglecting it? because our criminality is lessened by delay? I think that none of these are the arguments which keep us from its investigation. A real though hidden hatred of those truths which condemn us, and curtail our pleasures; a feeling that the gate to heaven is a strait, a narrow gate, and that few enter it on account of various encumbrances, these things keep our minds from viewing the truth aright. Till we are willing to sacrifice pride, vanity, love of fame and pleasure, and all love of created things to the pure unalloyed love of God himself, we must remain without the gate; an agony is requisite to enter it. This is a hard doctrine; but the kingdom of God suffereth violence, and so we are informed from the source whence all our knowledge of these things flows. The Scriptures represent man as a rebel, a lover of himself rather than of God; they command him instantly to repent, and all means are provided to enable him to know God's will. But it is useless to speak of means to attain any end when that end itself is hateful. The man of the world desires to be happy, but he does not desire to be happy in the way of God's commandment, in the way of self-denial, humility, and godly sorrow and fear. I am not at liberty to say that it is an easy thing to become a Christian. It may be easy to a being, if such there be, who has no sins to forsake, no pride to vanquish; who can, without any reluctance, crucify every evil affection and unruly desire, and live agreeably to the gospel. Some one may say, "Who does this? no man is sinless" granted, but none was ever a Christian who did not *desire* to do it.

Many are prejudiced against the Gospel without knowing what it teaches. No man ever CANDIDLY and PERSEVERINGLY studied the system of truths presented in the Old and New Testaments without finding his belief in them follow. Where there is belief, *real, firm belief*, that belief will result in corresponding *affections;* these affections necessarily lead to a holy life.

THEOLOGICAL SEMINARY, 1823, 1*st of March.*

I was about to congratulate you upon the prospect of your speedy emancipation from college restraints, but when I look back on my own academical career, I can see no ground for congratulation upon leaving it. I cannot picture to myself any situation in which a young man has so much happiness within his grasp as at college, whether I take into view the season of life, the nature of his pursuits, the variety and congeniality of his associates, or the fewness of his cares. You have not, however, had experience of the peculiar cares and pleasures of a genuine college life, but you can no doubt conceive it.[1] I did not myself enjoy it fully, as I lodged and boarded at home during my three and a half years; but so much of my time was spent within those loved old walls, and so delightfully spent that I can never forget it, or think of it, without a melancholy pleasure. I am constrained to own that many of my most jovial hours at Nassau Hall, were spent in a manner not exactly conformable to strict morals, but nevertheless I have there spent what I shall always consider my happiest hours. I often recall a merry circle of careless college blades seated about "the witching time of night" around a Nassau fire, by the way a pre-eminently good one, enveloped in fragrant clouds, enjoying all that flow of youthful hilarity and good humour, which a release from irksome duty engenders. Perhaps I feel too much pleasure in contemplating these old scenes; but in my hours of twilight musing, and castle-building, I often read in a bed of glowing coals, the almost faded story of these old times, and picture to myself the future various destinies of my old friends and classmates. But these joys

[1] His correspondent was in the University of his own city and home.

though they were sweet when I was in the midst of them, vanish in comparison with others which I experienced within those same walls.

It was there that, I humbly trust, my eyes were first opened to see the true value of eternal things; there I first saw with clearness, the awful nature of the rebellion which I was waging against my best friend and sovereign; and I there first determined to give up all hopes of happiness from the world, and to seek it in religion. I need not tell you that my determinations and resolutions have been broken, and unfulfilled, and that I find every day the truth of that solemn declaration, that the carnal mind is enmity against God, and is not, nor can it be, subject to his law. At the time of which I speak, I enjoyed happiness which I can find no words to express, and which has been lost only because I have so often returned to seek my consolation from mere earthly enjoyment. There cannot certainly be on earth any greater pleasure than to see without doubt, oneself condemned justly by God's law, and at the same time saved *freely* by the sovereign mercy of God in Christ. The satisfaction which I then felt in committing all my cares and concerns, my soul and body, into the hands of a Saviour whose infinitely lovely character I then saw, I never expect to receive from any other source. I remember that at that time, I looked back with unspeakable astonishment at the carelessness and indifference with which I had viewed the realities of another world; with what calmness I could contemplate all the particulars of my unfeeling ingratitude to God, and I remember that I then thought, that if at any time I had seriously and soberly considered these things for one hour, I could not have viewed them any longer with apathy. The friendships which I formed under these circumstances, are the closest and most tender I have ever known; and I feel attached to these friends in a way which I never knew any thing about before. Perhaps you may ask, "Does religion make you happy?" Alas! If I possessed religion in its purity, unalloyed, I should be perfectly happy; but I do not; my soul is still attached to the beggarly elements of this world, and I fear to say that I am a Christian. But this I can say: When I feel most deeply the force of divine truth, that is, when I feel myself most deeply a lost sinner, when I see the hellish blackness of sin, and the infinite loveliness of the divine character, then I feel most happy. I have known seasons when I could willingly have given up my life, and departed to enjoy the most unspeakable raptures of the heavenly state; when I could so unreservedly devote myself to God as to be willing to live or die, to go to the ends of the earth, or dwell in obscurity just as he pleased, to say ex animo, Thy will be done, and at such times, I have felt more unmixed bliss in one half hour than in a month as I commonly spend it.

No reasonable excuse can be given by any man for not loving supremely the most adorably perfect being in the universe. God calls upon all men now to repent, and has sanctioned his command by most terrific threats, and alluring promises. But I need not tell you these things. You have doubtless heard them urged powerfully and repeatedly, and I am but trespassing upon your patience.

THEOLOGICAL SEMINARY, *April* 10*th*, 1823.

I should commence by making an apology for writing on so ungain a piece of foolscap, if I had not a kind of dim remembrance of having sent you my ideas in the same homely vehicle once before. It is large, it suits my unmanageable pen, and above all it is at hand; so that you may consider it as a predilection of mine, and judge of the letter by the contents. And judging of it even in this way, I fear that you will have to exercise much clemency to suffer it to pass. I can assure you that after having spent a day in investigating Hebrew roots, one feels little energy of mind or body; and moreover there is such a stagnation hereabouts at this time, that I can promise you nothing interesting. The trustees of the college met yesterday and on Tuesday, for the purpose of electing a president.[1] Professor Lindsly was chosen President, and the Rev. Jared D. Fyler, of Trenton, Vice President in case Mr. Lindsly should accept his appointment. Mr. Lindsly requests four weeks for deliberation, which the Board have granted. They will meet at the commencement of the ensuing session, to receive Mr. L.'s final answer. It is generally supposed in this place that he will not accept the office. You probably know that he has lately received an invitation to the college at Nashville, Tennessee: they have made him very good offers, and many of his friends think that he will go to that institution.[2]

The college has dragged along rather lamely during the past winter. It has had no president, no regular professor of Mathematical and Physical science, and the tutors are young and inexperienced. Mr. Lindsly's administration has gained universal approbation, as far as I can learn, but what could one man, even of Mr. Lindsly's talents, do when clogged by so many

[1] Dr. Ashbel Green had resigned the presidency in 1822.
[2] Dr. Lindsly having declined the appointment, Dr. Carnahan was elected, and filled the office for thirty years.

disadvantages ? The college has scarcely ever, during the last fifteen years, received a greater addition to its numbers than at the beginning of the last session. I scarcely ever visit the college —indeed there is nothing there to interest me except the *Whig Society*, to which I pay an occasional visit. My time passes so happily and so busily up here, that I feel not the least disposition to leave my domicile. When I walk for exercise, I usually plunge into the thick woods to the east and south-east; I am fond of such roaming, especially at this season, when nature is beginning to resume her verdant drapery. I have indeed lost much of the *romance* which formerly entered so deeply into my character; but I still like to indulge sometimes in moonlight reveries, and rambles through dark and melancholy groves, or to catch the sweet breath of rising morn upon some gentle hill; but I am soon ejected from any such elevations of fancy by the sober realities of *life as it is*. The great pressure of studies, and the solemn prospect of the responsible duties which I expect before long to assume, dispel those airy visions which will sometimes rise before me in the shape of multiform delightful scenes of "fairy-land." A dark cloud of melancholy sometimes casts a shade over my horizon, but it is only for a moment; my greatest struggles are with a childish levity, and love of joke, and quip, and jollity, which I would gladly leave behind me in the regions of boyhood. My native loquacity leads me to give you a long letter, even full of egotism, in preference to sending you a short abstract of the floating news; all that floats here has been afloat until it is putrid and unfit for transportation. A few days since, we had a visit from David Brown, a Cherokee, who is one of the new converts from Paganism; he has been two years in the foreign mission school at Cornwall, Connecticut, and is now taking a course of theological lectures at Andover. He is genteel in his manners, has an agreeable expression of countenance, his face about the hue of my own, not quite so mahogany as most of his tribe. His attainments in literature are truly astonishing, when his opportunities of acquiring knowledge are taken into consideration. He expects in about a year to return to that part of his tribe which lives upon the Arkansas, where he hopes to preach the gospel. He manifests great zeal in the cause which he has espoused, and his piety is apparently such as to put to shame the majority of white professors. When I look upon such a person, changed so radically in opinions, and temper, and practice, and consider how little could have been effected in this way by mere moral suasion founded on natural principles; I am constrained to say, that the gospel is the wisdom and the power of God. To civilize these wandering tribes in any other way, than by Christianizing them, I am more and more convinced would be impossible; and I rejoice in the hope that every relic of barbarous idolatry and superstition will soon be extirpated by this holy religion.

Do you read Dr. Green's *Advocate?* He has devoted a large portion of its pages to the productions of our students. In the last number " the Dissertation on Types," on " the Style of the New Testament," and the " Death of Rebecca," are the effusions of some of my acquaintances. As for me, supposing that I could produce any thing not intolerable, my time is so engrossed by study, that I have no leisure for such attempts. I have bidden a reluctant farewell to poetry, classical reading, and indeed every department of general literature.

PRINCETON, 12th July, 1823.

Since the close of the vacation I have been striving hard to find a little recess from stated engagements, in which I might answer the communications of my friends. But our studies, now much increased, and the press of business on me as an individual, and a very variable state of health, have not left me one hour in which my mind was sufficiently disengaged to sit down at writing. This letter, if I am not greatly mistaken, will be eminently dull, and in that respect be a good representative of its author, who is superlatively so just now, in consequence of being pent up all last evening in a close, crowded, hot room, in attendance upon our Friday night debate. The discussion was peculiarly interesting, and ably conducted, and engaged my close attention for nearly three hours; which was so much the worse for me, as the excitement produced by it has been now succeeded by its usual consequent, a grievous stupidity and head-ache. In our societies, one of my greatest pleasures is to observe the development of uncommon characters, a satisfaction which our institution affords in a high degree, as it embraces specimens of every variety of American temper and manners which is not inconsistent with religion. We have the Yankee and the Kentuckian, the clown and the cit, the baccalaureate and the backwoodsman, the fastidious critic just emerged from a long confinement in the schools, and the rough unshapen child of nature fresh from the plough. Few countries whose inhabitants have branched out so generally from one stock as ours, have their different provinces marked as strongly by characteristic peculiarities as the United States. Politeness is a thing known only nominally among students—I speak of the formulas of the *bon ton*. By mutual consent, we deal plainly with each other, and waive the observance of fashionable etiquette. This gives us a better opportunity of discovering character. The garb of worldly politeness is so uniform as to hide in great measure individual peculiarities. Were I to seek for the soul of true politeness, I should look towards the South, but it would need the external polish of our own Middle States to make it perfectly suitable to fine taste. Nothing new in this stagnant pool. I am almost deliquesced by the oppressive heat; if I am suffering so much at a window in a current of air, what must the reapers suffer whom I see in the harvest fields around, all this day? I sometimes wish I had the Schuylkill here for the purposes of bathing; in lieu of it, I have to walk a great distance to swim in a little turbid stream, or to be content with the shower-bath. I am glad to see a new edition of Erskine's evidences; for clear and irresistible argument, and for elegance and originality, commend me to Erskine.

PRINCETON, 29*th August*, 1823.

You have begun to think, if I augur rightly, that your Princeton correspondent is either strangely indolent, or wilfully neglectful, or perhaps both. Neither, I can assure you, if he knows himself. An imprudent application to study during the first weeks of this summer, and a neglect of regular exercise, entirely unnerved me, rendered studying highly perilous, and drove me from my books to wander hither and thither in quest of health and spirits. This has been my business for a month or two past; and if you know any thing of the feelings of a genuine hypochondriac either by report or experiment, you need not be informed that I felt little like handling a quill, and least of all like writing a tolerable letter.

The amusements of several little excursions have, by the permission of a watchful Providence ever kinder than I deserve, restored me to my usual health, and I am just beginning to resume my regular studies. I was upon the Atlantic, and perhaps laved by its surges at the same time with yourself, and heartily concur in all your praises. I know no recreation comparable to a sea-bath; the excitement produced by the conflict with the surf, the stimulating effects of the salt water, and the healthful invigorating sea-breezes, have a better effect on me than all the nauseous potions of all the quacks in Christendom. My visit to Long Branch was peculiarly agreeable from the concurrence of a number of circumstances. We had fine weather, fine company, good accommodations, a season unusually fresh and verdant, and a spot of country (about Shrewsbury) which for richness and fertility is second to none in this state. I was surprised to find upon the high ridges of the Middletown hills, which are a continuation of the Navesink chain, numerous beds of marl, abounding with shells and other marine remains which indicate the alluvial nature of even those lofty eminences. But in connection with this, I was still more astonished to see the relics of a mammoth, lately dug out of a low piece of marsh ground in Poplar Swamp, a spot which must undoubtedly have been redeemed from the ocean. These bones were discovered within a few feet of the surface, in good preservation, but are now rapidly mouldering upon exposure to the atmosphere. One of the teeth weighs three and a quarter pounds, and the knee-joint according to my hasty measurement is two feet in circumference. It is probable that I shall pass the ensuing winter in Virginia. I feel it to be a duty to sacrifice my plans and inclinations to the acquisition of some hardihood of constitution. I congratulate you upon your enlargement from collegiate restraints, although I cannot hope that you have bettered your condition, if your college course has been as devoid of care and uneasiness as my own. Your feelings upon the occasion are natural, for the day of one's graduation is, so to speak, the day of initiation into the toils and mysteries of manhood. You speak as though your future pursuits were entirely undetermined. This is well; the danger in this age is of hurrying prematurely into the bustle and responsibility of public life. You appear to think of devoting a year or two to private study. If this is your plan let me exhort you to procure as many restraints and *stimuli* as you can; either by the superintendence of some literary friend, or by associating some companion in your studies. This I say upon the supposition that your character and feelings are like mine, and like most young men. It is difficult for one who feels himself entirely at leisure to exercise that decided resolution, and persevering self-denial without which it is impossible to make literary attainments. From experience which is now the subject of bitter regret, I know that the temptations to gratify imagination and taste and idle curiosity at the expense of mental discipline are almost irresistible.

I shall not ask forgiveness for suggesting, what has no doubt suggested itself to you, the importance of forming moral as well as intellectual character at this critical point of time. Religion, that bug-bear of the thoughtless and the voluptuary, and the laughing-stock of "the many" who know it only by name, is after all that can be said, the only safeguard to virtue, and the only source of real tranquillity of mind. Aside from the peace occasioned by the quelling of an angry conscience, and the release from fears of future evil, the positive joys of religion are truly unspeakable. The lofty and sublime contemplations, the solid and rational hopes, the intimacy with Him who ruleth over all, the remedy for every care which piety professes to afford, and which its votaries say it does afford, surely are sufficient recommendations to one who looks beyond the outskirts of this limited world.

PRINCETON, *September* 22, 1823.

The present week, of all weeks in the year, is a week of commotion and anxiety to me, as it is one of jovialness and satisfaction to thousands of my fellow Jerseymen. The noise, and bustle, and dust, and novelty which strike the senses on our commencement day, and even for several days before and after it, give my irritable fibres a most villanous agitation. You have witnessed one of our annual literary Saturnalia, if I remember rightly, and if so need not be told how this town appears more like the Amphyctionic council of all our American Bedlams, than of the lovers of science and letters. I am writing this letter, be it known, with the expectation of tearing it to pieces, as I hope to see you here at our holiday, and to be delivered from the necessity of addressing you in the imperfect language of ink and paper. However, as the second cord to my bow, I am delivering my mind of its present scum, which I have in mind to send in case we should not have the pleasure of seeing you here.

Tuesday, September 23.

I was prevented from concluding my letter yesterday, and have discovered from your classmate [T. L.] Janeway, that we shall not have the pleasure of a visit from you to-morrow. It was unwelcome intelligence. I was hoping to have had the pleasure of meeting you here at this season which presents more novelty and interesting speculation to a stranger than any other. I should have been glad of the opportunity of introducing you to the ancient and honorable fraternity of "American Whigs." Janeway has received a hereditary predilection for the Clios, and has (I think very properly) followed its dictates. My old college friends, and our family acquaintances, are already pouring in upon me. It is gratifying, as you will find hereafter, to meet after the lapse of two or three years, even those companions in study who were never intimates or confidants. Some of my co-bachelors have outstripped me in a variety of ways. Some (proh scelus!) have been guilty of matrimony. Some are on the verge of the same gulf. Some are licensed man-slayers. One or two have already begun to fill some space in the public eye as lawyers, in the south. The pleasure of our meeting has, however, received a damp from the recent intelligence of the death of Edward Thomas, captain's clerk on board the "John Adams."

He was graduated with me, and pursued legal studies for about two years. He was a young man of uncommon acuteness and vigour of intellect, and of promising abilities as an orator; and though singular and eccentric in some of his habits, was generally esteemed by his acquaintances. He is the sixth of the class of 1823 who have departed this life. A call so loud to me to be ready to depart also, has roused my sluggish mind to look around me for a moment; but alas the return to slumber is so much more natural to wicked man, that I am led to think that in most cases, the repetition of such alarms, unless effectual at first, seems only to deaden the feelings to all their influence. Death is not dreadful to me now; what new terrors may be disclosed by the dark and melancholy scenes of a sick chamber, and the more dark forebodings which are the harbingers of this imperial destroyer, I know not. My life and virtues and merits are so utterly destitute of having any value, intrinsic, or as purchasers of immortality, that, were my hopes based on them in any degree, I would be willing to take the shortest road out of this life. But I do daily see an increasing glory in that Saviour who was once to me an object, to say the least, of indifference, which declares him to be my ground of confidence, and my only source of joy. I confess that few, very few of my thoughts are fixed on him; I say few with reference to the degree in which I ought to fix my eye upon him, but joy, real and unequivocal joy, I never have, or expect or desire to have in any other.

Shall I leave this point? Perhaps the only effect on you is a revulsion of feeling such as I have myself experienced from a similar cause. I am far from wishing to obtrude my own notions or emotions upon any friend; and I know from experience, too well the impolicy and absurdity of recommending religion *pugnis et calcibus*, to cram my hortations down any man's throat. But I do wish to let our correspondence assume something more than the reserved Antarctic character of two shopkeepers. If there is any thing in religion which renders it unfit for communication, or repugnant to social confidence, or which like Free Masonry is not to be hinted at, or spoken about except in consecrated houses, away with it out of the earth! I would be the first to lift up both hands in execration of so icy and dissociating a principle. But I know it to be something far different. I know that there is not any exercise of those affections (which are ever seeking exercise somewhere) so truly social and endearing as the exercise of them upon the enlivening truths and realities of Jesus Christ's gospel. I know that there is an exquisite satisfaction in that kindly feeling which Christianity encourages and keeps alive. And I know that had this side of the picture met my eye some years ago, instead of the harsh lines which are sometimes foolishly exhibited, that I should not have so long like a condemned criminal shrunk and retreated with such mental imbecility from all that bore the stamp of religion. Godliness is profitable for *all things;* having the promise of this as well as the coming life.

Thursday.

This letter, you must begin to think, is long in finding a conclusion. I was turned out of my room, on the day before yesterday, to make space for a stranger; and, as this was done while I was abroad, this letter was shut up among my other effects until this afternoon. The dampness and coldness yesterday prevented such a multitude of persons from assembling as we are accustomed to see. Our village was consequently comparatively quiet. I have seen however several persons bearing sad marks of the frolicking last night. For any particulars relating to the exercises of the day, I refer you to Janeway, who, I believe, was a constant and attentive observer.

I am entirely run out of spirits by the continual excitement of the last two or three days. My Virginia bubble is exploded. I shall expect to spend the next year, Providence permitting, in my old course of seclusion. I am, upon the whole, glad of this disappointment. Although no one can be more fond of travelling than I, yet the pleasing retirement and warm attachments of our seminary have so enchained my affections that it was like tearing apart my heart's fibres to think of going away.

PRINCETON, *October* 23, 1823.

The openness and candour with which you have met my proposals of a new set of topics for our correspondence, have gratified me very much. I rejoice to find that the important interests of religion have gained so much of your attention, and would beg you not to suffer this attention to decrease or to remain without increase. To come more directly to the points of inquiry suggested by you. I entertain no shadow of a doubt that a patient and scriptural method of seeking God's favour was never yet fruitless. Indeed, while I profess to have faith in the word of God, no truth can be plainer; it rests on the immutable word of Jehovah. The pursuit may be a dark and tedious and discouraging one, and yet compared with the glory of that "$ἀμαράντινον τῆς δόξης στέφανον$," which is the prize held forth, how do all these labours dwindle to nothing. Among a host of Scripture passages, look at these: Ps. lxxxvi. 5. Joel. ii. 32. Rom. x. 12, 13. The search must be indeed most sincere. Compare the petitions which you have offered to God for this great favour with what you may conceive to be the cries of one pleading for his life, and then compare the temporal and the eternal life. Deut. iv. 29. Jer. xxix. 13. For encouragement, for truths calculated to awaken as well as to soothe the conscience, for advice and direction infinitely more infallible than that of a fellow worm, fly to the precious volume of God's word. There, be assured, a prayerful, indefatigable, daily search will open to you supplies suited to all your necessities. I would have you believe not one tittle of what, after diligent examination, you find not there. But then that holy book is to be approached without prejudice or prepossession. Let me use the words of Chalmers, " We must bring a free and unoccupied mind to the exercise. It must not be the pride or the obstinacy of self-formed opinions, or the haughty independence of him who thinks he has reached the manhood of his understanding. We must bring with us the docility of a child if we want to gain the kingdom of heaven. There must be no garbling of that which is entire, no darkening of that which is luminous, no softening down of that which is authoritative or severe. The Bible will allow of no compromise."—" If we could only abandon all our former conceptions, if we felt that our business was to submit to the oracles of God, and that we are not called upon to effect a reconciliation betwixt a revealed doctrine of the Bible and an assumed or encogitated principle of our own,—then we are satisfied that we should find the language of the New Testament to have as much clear, and precise, and didactive simplicity, as the language of any sage or philosopher which has come down to us." (Chalmers' Evidences, last chapter). Our reverence for the Bible is truly hypocritical when we are content to study it with less assiduity than a thousand things which we may know and eternally perish. I trust that I shall yet rejoice with you in the words of Is. xxv. 9.

I wish to discourage no one from the acquisition of any language. My remark to Janeway[1] was meant to have special reference to the το διδακτον of French works. I cordially concur with you and with the whole republic of letters, as to the inadequacy of a translation to convey the beauties of literature. I must still confess that after dabbling for six years in French literature, I find my ardour quite cooled as to the exquisite richness of that department of letters: and this has been the result with most of my acquaintances who have studied the language However, go on—no language is to be despised, especially one which opens the door to so vast a range of authors as the French.

[1] Supposed to be unfavourable to the study of the French language.

The exercise of mind too, which the study of language affords in comparing words and idioms, has a powerful influence in rendering our ideas precise and definite.

When you next happen to be in a book store please to price any small editions of Demosthenes and any of Xenophon's or Plato's works. I prefer German editions; and those which have the Greek text without notes or version.

PRINCETON, *December 8th,* 1823.

Your last letter has been lying unanswered for a month, and would probably lie a month longer, if I should wait until my mind is sufficiently free from occupation to leave me in a fit state to write a letter. I have indeed hours of release from study, but after a day of close confinement to metaphysical or ethical subjects, I confess that I feel less inclined to nothing than handling a pen. If you have ever spent three or four weeks in thinking

> "Of Providence, foreknowledge, will, and fate,
> Fix'd fate, free-will, foreknowledge absolute,
> And found no end in wandering mazes lost,"

you may conceive of the mental exhaustion which I now experience. Clarke and Leibnitz, Hume and Brown, have led me an enchanting, but dangerous flight through the clouds of speculation by day, and have danced before my brain in the phantasms of the night. It is my satisfaction to know after all the mortification consequent upon a view of the inscrutable nature of many questions in morals, that the path to heaven and perfect unalloyed enjoyment of the truth is open to the humblest and simplest child of Adam. The New Testament, while it inculcates a system unparalleled for its sublimity and consistency, is obscured by no sophistical refinements, and defies the attempts of philosophy to complete or systematize it more fully. The general impression left by an hour's humble reading of God's word is unlike the effect of any other work. It is a feeling of calm submissive tranquillity. I am inclined, therefore, to think that nothing tends so directly to the formation of a truly Christian character as the continual, prayerful, unquestioning perusal of the Scriptures. They do not present naked doctrines; they are addressed to the natural feelings, and they affect our hearts imperceptibly but powerfully. Let me pray you to be a diligent student of this holy book. He who takes delight in the Bible *must* imbibe its spirit; and its influence, I think, is all-powerful. After the learned prating of philosophers, the sweet and modest words of inspiration fall on my ear like melody.

Wednesday, 10th.

A goodly chasm in the epistle! and yet, I assure you, left without any possibility of remedy, by the variety of engagements which pull me hither and thither. Besides the recitations of this week, which force me to read about 600 octavo pages, I have to sit four hours in our Theological Society two nights in the week; and have now on hand, preparation for debating on next Monday night; item, an oration to be transcribed and committed for Tuesday, and one to be composed and committed for Monday. Except as it interferes with pleasant extra duties, I do not complain of this; it is infinitely preferable to an *ennuyeuse* vacation in which I begin and leave unfinished a thousand different things. Your situation in the city is truly enviable on one account,—the facilities afforded by it for the reasonable and convenient purchase of books. Many valuable works are knocked down at occasional auctions to persons who cannot at all appreciate them, and who get them for almost nothing. Our seminary is very full—our numbers more than 100. College rather thin. I dropped two sermons of Dr. Lindsly's into the office for you.[1] They would give more pleasure to one who discerned his characteristic manner, as we do, in every paragraph; I think they will please you, however, from the untamed vigour of the style. Our temporary teacher of Chemistry, Mr. Halsey, has come to hand, and is commencing operations.[2]

PRINCETON, *December 29, 1823.*

Your full letters are always welcome, and with the general principles of your last I am inclined to coincide. The venom and unhallowed fire which have sometimes characterized the controversies of Christians I can heartily agree with you in deprecating. The wisdom of the serpent is more sought after in this day by many than the mildness of the dove. I can also from the heart subscribe to the doctrine that "secret things belong to God," and that those only are to be set up as necessary tenets which God has revealed to us in his sacred oracles.[3] Polemics, I fear, will not abate in their virulence among the soi-distant lovers of truth,

---

[1] "Improvement of Time. Two Discourses delivered in the chapel of the College of New Jersey, December, 1822."

[2] Luther Halsey, D. D., Professor from 1824 to 1829.

[3] His correspondent had quoted Bishop Watson's sentence—"En codicem sacrum—here is the fountain of truth. Why do you follow the streams derived from it by the sophistry, or polluted by the error of men?"

> "Till warned, or by experience taught they learn
> That not to know at large of things remote,
> From use obscure and subtle, but to know
> That which before us lies in daily life
> Is the prime wisdom; what is more, is fume,
> Or emptiness, or fond impertinence:
> And renders us in things that most concern
> Unpractised, unprepared, and still to seek."
>
> *Paradise Lost*, B. 8.

While I would adhere to these opinions with all the powers of my soul, I would still desire to maintain a firm and unshaken zeal for the truth of the scriptures. It is not the " contending for the faith once delivered to the saints," which is reprehensible, but the manner of contending, so unholy and so repugnant to the spirit of the gospel. God forbid that I should conceive that one truth, even the least, of that system which he has revealed is unimportant, or undeserving of strenuous exertion for its maintenance. To our limited vision many doctrines may appear destitute of any practical bearing, as some parts of the animal fabric seem useless; and yet, so impious would it be to charge God with inculcating doctrines which might or might not be believed with equal security, that as to the symmetry of the Divine plan, I should say—

> "If from the chain a single link you strike,
> Tenth or ten thousandth breaks the chain alike."

The creed of professing Christians was originally brief and simple. All creeds are barriers erected against error, and of course must grow and change with the phases of heresy. The primitive confession of faith was one sentence, (Acts viii. 37.) The symbol called the Apostles' creed grew out of the necessity of the times, and was reared as a defence against those who denied the Godhead or the real passion of Christ. The Athanasian creed as it stands in the *English* Liturgy is still more complex, and our own formula being directed against a variety of opponents is quite a volume. Many of its clauses ought to be expunged, as referring to Catholic tenets, and peculiar errors, from which we are now sufficiently guarded. "The purest churches under heaven," says our Confession, "are subject both to mixture and error," and therefore I should not feel secure in adopting every sentiment of our church, while I consider the system called Calvinistic, as the only system founded on the obvious meaning of the Bible, the only system reconcileable to a sound philosophy, and the most consoling system to one who feels himself a lost sinner. I say this after having once risen against the doctrine of Rom. ix. 15, with all the enmity of a rebellious heart. I trust that God has convinced me that no "foreknowledge of my conduct" was his motive for rescuing me from the slavery of sin; (alas, had this been the case, my conduct would have secured me eternal wrath,) and that " not according to our works, but according to his own purpose and grace, which was given us in Christ Jesus before the world began." I wish to impose my private sentiments on no man; as I have already said, go to the Bible, and believe not one word which is not there written. But I entreat of you, let not metaphysical speculations, or prepossessions antecedent to inquiry, forestall your judgment.

Princeton, 26th January, 1824.

I know how to sympathize with you in your late disappointment, [a journey.] It is the twin to one which occasioned me some disquietude last autumn, and which I have not yet ceased to regret. Whether from the early associations produced by an ancient collection of travels, over which I used to pore in my first reading days, and which tinges with old remembrances my air-castles and my dreams to this day, or from some causes more latent, I do not profess to know, but there is in my character a restless, burning desire for peregrination, an anxious expectation of some opportunity to rove beyond seas and mountains. Such feelings, as wild and romantic, I have endeavoured to quell; and yet in all my studies the thought floats up, (and especially when I read or think of foreign countries,) that I am preparing to wander, at some day, far from home. Our wishes are not always proportioned or accommodated to our character and abilities, and perhaps the sooner this whim is crushed, the better. But all transmarine voyages apart, my wish to visit Virginia, the old dominion, the land of my fathers, my own natal soil,—to see the ruin (now a barn) in which my grandfather preached, the valley where I first saw the sun, the mountains where my father spent his boyhood, and where the Alexanders are "rife" even now; this wish I would not, and cannot repress. As to Greece, your second topic, it has all my heart. I have just been reading the report of Webster's noble speech, [on the Greek revolution.] It is apparent that he has laboured to keep under all undue enthusiasm, and that his sentiments instead of outrunning the popular feeling, have, as expressed, fallen far short of it. This man has commanded my highest admiration by what he has at times exhibited to the public.

The language of modern Greece, from what I can learn, has changed more as it regards idiom and construction, than in single words. The Romaic is modernized by the peculiar use of the auxiliaries and prepositions, and has lost that force which *declension* strictly so called, conferred on the old Greek. The most satisfactory piece I recollect on the subject, is in a No. of the *Quarterly*, some years back. *The Pilot* they are reading this moment down stairs. I have been in old times so whirled and crazed by novels, that I try to keep clear of the vortex, though I generally skim *this* class of books.

The *North American Review* is likely to keep up its reputation and merit. Mr. E., it is hinted, finds the sphere of clerical and even literary influence too small for his ambition. He is young, handsome, and fascinating, conscious of mental force, and well-informed as to his high character, and he intends, as is said, to make a launch into the political world. His studies for some years have had a leaning this way, and general policy has engrossed his pen, with a few exceptions.

Boston and Cambridge, which may be considered as, in an eminent degree, the seats of literature in America, are daily increasing their claim to this character. The men who enjoy the rich and sinecure professorships in the university find time and means abundant to woo the muses. Rational religion, in this sense of the term, lays too slight a hold upon the heart to excite great zeal for their tenets, and they appear before the world as literati, rather than as Christian ministers.

I do desire to see learning prosper, to be learned myself; I desire to be happy in the good things of this world, so far as consistent with virtue; I desire to commend Christianity to the world by all that charm which courtesy and cheerfulness can give to as rude a piece as I,—yet I could curse myself, (however unfaithful I may be now, or alas may be hereafter,) if I thought that I could ever consent to make merchandise of the cross, by bartering it for aught of earth. My wish is, in my humble measure, to make every effort tend to one point, the establishment of Christ's kingdom on earth, and in the hearts of men. And O that future devotedness might take the place of the worldly spirit that has, and does prey upon my peace. It would give me unfeigned joy, my dear friend, to see you brought to this noble stand which I wish we may both reach,—to renounce the joys, honours, cares of the present life, for the sake of living for God. Our only excuse, our only inability is our guilty, low, irrational love of the world and of self. God demands our hearts this moment. As a sovereign he thunders his requisition, as a father he whispers pardon, reconciliation, assistance. And what shall we mention to Him as the object of our preference to his service? Pleasure? gain? ease? glory? Life is a vapour, and we know it. Joy is fleeting. Let us determine, at least, to perish in search of God. I trust you suspect me of no wish to lead you to any system. Read God's word, without comment, without prepossession, without cavil.

PRINCETON, *February* 24, 1824.

Instead of being in the lecture room, my proper place at this hour, I am squandering away the time at home, and among other matters commencing to spin out something which may pass for a letter. I thank you for your last; for the length of it, and the information which you were so kind as to communicate. In addition to what I have already learnt from you, I should like to have this problem resolved, viz.: How could the " Allgemeine Litteratur Zeitung von Leipzig " be got at,—on what terms,— and with what hopes of regular transmission? You speak of having the small-pox near you, and among you;—we have had two cases in Princeton but its progress has, I think, been effectually stopped. One of our students has been very near death with the bilious colic, but has recovered. In the near prospect of death, he manifested great joy in the hope of soon meeting face to face the Saviour whom he had taken as his portion. Death, to him, seemed despoiled of all that is terrific. Bucknall, another of our students, is lying extremely ill with what appears a rapid consumption. Little hope is entertained of his recovery. So many friends, companions, and classmates have sunk around me, that I seem most loudly called on to be ready also, as being ignorant of the day or hour when my soul shall be demanded. Would to God that I might be excited to do what is remaining to be done with all my might,—to become more holy, and to strive not to be taken from the earth without having done any thing for the benefit of my fellow-men. My qualifications for the ministry are so slight and defective that I shudder at the thought of being in eighteen months invested with that sacred office. So much ignorance, inexperience, and immaturity, seem ill to befit the character of a teacher and pastor. The truth is, I feel too young; and could I dispose of my time profitably, I should be glad to intermit my regular theological course for a year or two. Dr. [J. P.] Wilson I have a great curiosity to hear, and if I should ever come to Philadelphia shall certainly make it a principal point in my memoranda to go to his church. Philadelphia would certainly lose a bright and shining light at his death. Apropos of preaching,—have you read [Edward] Irving? He has certainly been shamefully misrepresented by the tribe of angry critics; and yet with all his originality, and all his occasional strength and pathos, he makes me unspeakably splenetic with his nauseous affectation of obsolete words and manner, and his contempt for all logical method. Whoever compares him with Robert Hall, (the most eloquent and classical writer of the age, if my judgment is taken,) will see that mighty power, and a style rich and elegant, and matter original and weighty, are not inconsistent with the strictest observance of rhetorical rules, and the strictest conformity to the polite usage of language.

Mr. —— has thrown the gauntlet, as you have probably seen, into the peaceful camp of the Quakers, and challenged them with something of the old Cameronian spirit. Although I think that Quaker error ought to be opposed, and that the Quaker arguments do receive their answer in one and another part of his book, yet I see more wit than argument in his work, and more levity than becomes subjects so solemn, and a community so respectable. However, it will uncover the nakedness of Quakerism, I trust, to some of the rising generation, and make them ashamed of the mysticism which they have hitherto swallowed without knowing why or wherefore. I hope your progress in French is satisfactory. The pittance of knowledge which I once had is fast leaking out, as all knowledge that is neglected, must. I need some stimulus greater than any which I now enjoy to make me read French; I hardly open a French author once a month. To acquire a good knowledge of the language would be a strong inducement for me to spend some time in your city. My intimate friends in Philadelphia are very few at present. You are my only regular correspondent; and to knit, in my own name, all the old family acquaintances, is what I shall never attempt. Hutton of the Deaf and Dumb Asylum is a particular and inestimable friend, and with him I believe the list ends. Any thing favourable in the literary world?—in your city? You have probably read Sprague's ode for the Shakespeare jubilee. That production seems to me the best lyric that I have ever seen from an American pen. It breathes the spirit of Collins and Gray. I wish to see American literature take a start. I long for the time when our productions shall be truly *American*, not slavish copies of Transatlantic works, but impressed with the national character. Our forests, and mountains, and waters, surely furnish scenes second to none that European poets and romancers have hackneyed, and our mighty works of nature might, I should suppose, inspire a feeling as ethereal as ever prompted the Theban Pindar. On this score I can quarrel with Sprague.

New magazines, they tell me are afloat in both our great cities. I hope you will not let the New Yorker outdo you. I believe that, as far as enterprise is concerned, the New York magazine has its advantage in its proximity to the "land of notions."

The Lethean influence of Quakerism in your town is, I fear, almost as inimical to the Muses, as the commercial turmoil of New York; yet if Philadelphia cannot support a better monthly publication than either Blackwood's or Campbell's, [London *New Monthly*,] which, *me judice*, are the merest froth conceivable, then my notions of Philadelphia talent are amazingly out of the way. The great difficulty in America appears to be, that literary men must (from pecuniary motives) be professional men, and must needs give all their labour to their professions. In Europe there are literary men of leisure, by scores, who write for periodical works. The compensation made in England for compositions are sufficient to feed poor authors.

PRINCETON, *March* 17*th*, 1824.

You have begun the law. Success to you, and all your future clients. I am not one of those who suppose the profession of the law incompatible with the strictest integrity, although I think, what I believe no one denies, that its dangers and temptations are considerable. The general principles of politics and jurisprudence you will no doubt find agreeable; indeed, I should like very well to glance at the subject myself for a few months. We are fond of sketching fancy visions of future life. Where is it probable that you will turn your face after being admitted to practise? Do you expect to continue a Philadelphian, or do you banish all such queries? If you retort the question, as it would be natural to do, I must say, that my mind is in suspense. My constitution calls for a Northern climate. Lower Canada would suit me: my feelings and prepossessions would lead me southward, but slavery appals me: literary considerations make the Middle States alluring, though I can't say that this latitude fits my temperament. The wants of the church point out a large expanse of territory to the South and West, and I confess that (as the Quakers say) I *feel a drawing* to those three sister States north of the Ohio, where slavery has not set her foot. Is it probable that we shall ever appropinquate? Wherever I may go, I trust that duty and a desire of usefulness will sway me. If my life is spared, it is not improbable that I shall spend two or three years in itinerating. I feel daily my need of personal converse with the world which is to be the theatre and the subject of my future operations. The clown, the mere student, the bookworm, though vastly learned, is no more fit to produce a moral than a political revolution; yet this is what we aim at. I am happy to observe by the public prints, as well as by private information, that extemporary preaching is becoming more and more common, even in the frozen East and North, and that the opposition to the cold, unnatural, modern way of pleading with dying sinners, is increasing. Lawyers are not often heard to complain of an inability to extemporize, nor should a clergyman; and he who does is unfit for the pulpit. This change is peculiarly consolatory to me. I never expect to be able to read a sermon with any life; and as to committing to memory, I would rather write ten sermons than get one by heart. Upon this ground, I reckon our debating societies among the most interesting and important institutions about our Seminary.

Monday, 22d.

You may judge how little I am master of my own time by the abrupt manner in which I left what I had written; I shall now endeavour to finish. I observe that I spoke of *itinerating*, on the other page: my reference was to land-journeying, and I forgot to make any allusion to my dreams of transmarine peregrination, which event is always to be excepted in my calculations. Four years hence —— and where shall we be? what manner of persons? how employed? If the impenetrable curtain which screens the future could be drawn aside, we might see some astonishing and unexpected change. It may be that the grave may then contain my mortal part, or the depths of the sea; or care and affliction may have eaten out all hopes of terrestrial peace, or a thousand other results, now unthought of. All things here suffer change, all things created are fleeting, God only remains. My dear friend, shall we not attach ourselves to this only support which can sustain the final shock? Is it not desirable, is it not wise, to "lay hold on the strength of God"? Small as our experience is, it ought to have informed us that the joys of this world are sweet and fascinating only in the pursuit, and that supposing and granting that they were exquisite in possession, they fade away like the tints of morning clouds. This you have heard, no doubt, until, perhaps, you are weary of it. And yet if these things do not affect us *now*, when the heart is susceptible, when its fibres are not entwined so closely as they shall be around the world, when we have not become intoxicated with pleasure and glory, is it to be hoped that they will affect us when the storm and hurricane of life is maddening us? Pardon me for saying that I consider the present moment of your life a most critical moment, pregnant perhaps with eternal consequences. You have made election of a profession, and expect very soon to enter upon its active duties. Now I do not say that by becoming a lawyer you put yourself out of the reach of religious influence, or that the moral influence of your calling will be directly injurious to virtuous principles; but I say, with confidence, that in all probability, every successive step you now take will lead you further from a reasonable hope of salvation. I am speaking of human probabilities; we are not to take God's special dealings into our calculations. Do you find the love of honour leading you *now* from the consideration of the self-denying gospel? How will it be when ambition shall have received ten-fold strength from the continual fuel presented to it? Does multiplicity of business exclude prayer and devotion *now?* Look at the whirlpool of every lawyer's cases. Do you find your heart becoming more insensible to religious motives? Believe me, it is but the presage of more dreadful indifference. In this matter there is no stationary point. Hearts do not amend by indulgence, sin loses no power by having the reins given to it, the world becomes no less fascinating, God is not appeased by continued defiance. Refer to the situation of any lawyer, one, for instance, whose circumstances you could wish your own, and say candidly, does that situation afford advantages for the cultivation of piety, such advantages as you *now* enjoy. This very hour is the best possible season which remains for you. I press this motive because it is one which struck terror once to my soul, and opened my eyes to the dangers of my situation.

PRINCETON, *April* 13*th*, 1824.

Your long letters are always welcome, and I thank you for using that goodly sheet of foolscap; we are neither lovers nor courtiers, and may therefore venture to lay aside the gilt-edge now and then. The only complaint I intend to make with regard to your last is, that it is too much in the style of an apology. Did I say any thing in the way of expostulation or rebuke upon your commencing legal studies? Assuredly, however my pen may have slipped awry, nothing was further from my intention. I do most sincerely approve of your choice, and can say heartily "*Macte novâ virtute puer, sic itur ad astra.*" Were not my services most manifestly claimed in another field, I should make election of the same business. My views on the subject I cannot express more comprehensively than in the words of one of the first lawyers in New York. "It is hard," he lately said to a friend of mine when speaking of his son's becoming a lawyer— "It is hard for a lawyer to enter into the kingdom of heaven, and those who have tried, as I have, the vexation, and overwhelming pressure of an extensive practice, will confess that it is fraught with temptation and danger." But I leave this subject; above all, I shrink from disputing about it. You will pardon me for wishing to keep controversy, at least, out of our letters. Two years' continual sparring, in clubs, in debates, in the chamber, in the grove, at every corner, upon every knotty point in Divinity, have produced in me a satiety of argumentation. Private controversy has never resulted in my own change of opinion, and I am confident that I never convinced another. Pride is too strong to suffer candour to have its perfect work. You, no doubt, feel as I do, knowing that disputation must shoulder out all the other ingredients of our epistles. Somewhere I have read some saying of somebody's, that lovers are never tired of each other's conversation, because they are forever talking of themselves. I claim no experience in love matters, but I believe that the principle is correct. How naturally do we slide into discourse about ourselves, and our concerns! Grant me permission to talk of myself, and I will talk forever. After this confession you may understand, even if you cannot pardon my egregious egotism. And I ask no privilege which I am not willing to grant with interest, thinking with Horace, that

"Aequum est
Peccatis veniam poscentem reddere rursus."

You cannot gratify me more than by expatiating on your concerns, your habits, character, you may descend to the colour of your coat, or the tie of your neckcloth. According to my principles of letter-writing, a letter ought to be the mirror of its author; if he is a bad man, why let the epistle be so too; and let an egotist go on endlessly *de carissimo seipso*. I was gratified by the communication on Hume's death before I suspected you of being its author. Go on, I pray you, in this useful and delightful exercise of the pen. The friend who writes the "Student's notes," must be, truly, a valuable acquaintance. I had figured to myself a classical bachelor of some forty years as the writer of those pieces. There seemed to be evidences of maturity and sober judgment which pointed out the experienced author. As for me, though I defile many fair sheets, yet my abortions seldom satisfy me sufficiently to induce me to publish.[1] And indeed, to be praised without being known, seems so faint a stimulus that it would scarcely repay me for the transcription. When I can profit myself or others, I shall not be backward in plying the quill.

[1] But he, as well as the two other lads, had begun to amuse himself with writing for newspapers and magazines. I detect his hand in the "Christian Advocate," at least as early as February, 1824, in the article signed *Cyprian*, and he had hardly refrained so long from taking advantage of the literary columns of Mr. Walsh's "National Gazette." It was to that journal the series entitled "A Student's Notes" was contributed. They were ascribed to William B. Reed, then an under-graduate of the University of Pennsylvania.

This day is a day of penance to me, coming round once a month, being the day on which I have to commit a speech to memory; the most odious task in the whole circle of my duties. I never expect to commit a sermon, but must creep somewhere into the backwoods where unwritten discourses will be tolerated. Do you find me dull this morning? My sleep was unquiet last night, as it always is after an extraordinary excitement of the nervous system. I am often guilty of spending too many of my evening hours in "furious gossip," which produces a kind of mental inebriation, as delightful *pro tempore*, and as shocking in its effects as the hilarity of the wine-bibber. My circle of acquaintance in the Seminary is contracted, but I have somehow managed to glide into a cluster of congenial souls, the like of whom, for genuine, friendly, social feeling, and for mental elasticity and vigour, I have never seen before, and never expect to see. If you wish to see me in some of my happiest moments, picture me in imagination lolling in a cushioned elbow chair, surrounded by about six or seven whom I can name, pouring forth, or drinking in without the slightest reserve, the fresh and new-born thoughts, that such excitements may be supposed to generate. If I ever knew the pleasures of social life it has been here; if I ever heard eloquence, it has been here.

It is commonly said in Virginia, that the "Alexanders are a tonguey race." Let me have a long epistle, and let it be any thing that floats uppermost in the cerebellum. I fear I have given you the scum to-day. I have been much pleased with *Hodgson's* letters upon America; one candid and Christian traveller at least.

CHAPTER III.

LETTERS WHILE TUTOR IN COLLEGE.

1824—1825.

PRINCETON, *April* 21*st*, 1824.

It is my expectation to leave Trenton to-morrow at 6 A. M. in the steamboat, for your city. Without more ado I give you the state of the case. A week ago nothing was further from my intentions, but a few days since I was astounded by the information that the trustees of the College had elected me mathematical tutor. This was the more extraordinary as I have already twice, in the most peremptory manner, refused the office; and as the proper complement of officers is now in the faculty, the appointment is *extra*, and at an unusual time. When I heard it, last Wednesday, my feelings instantly revolted, and I said No with the most perfect determination and confidence. Upon weighing all circumstances, however, and finding upon consulting with my friends that they all, without exception, urged my acceptance, I have determined to enter upon the duties at the commencement of next session. As I have formerly said to you, my youth will permit me to spare two or three years from my theological course, with advantage: I feel, and my friends feel for me, that my mind needs maturing before taking upon me the character of a minister. It is, after all, an odious situation, and I expect it to be, by far, the most trying and mortifying that I have ever been placed in. Yet trials, and self-denial, and mortifications I must expect in almost every situation. I need to be buffeted about a little to call forth what little energy and firmness I may possess. As the session commences just as that of the Seminary closes, I must take my vacation now, or not at all: and my lank and sallow cheeks demand some speedy recreation. It has been long since we saw one another, and each of us has, probably, undergone much change. As for me I fancy that in the prominent traits both of the outer and the inner man, you will find me much the same boy as ever. I am no son of Anak, and have altered little in dimensions. There was indeed once some glow and bloom of health upon my face, which has departed. I confess, with the confidence of friendship, knowing that it is not exposing myself to ill-timed raillery, that melancholy has secretly and deeply preyed upon my spirits, more than my most intimate friends would judge from my demeanour. Often, the unnatural and excessive gaiety of my manner has been accompanied by bitter gnawings at the soul. From this I suffer less than formerly; nothing at present. My temperament is such that I am susceptible of the most deep emotions of pleasure as well as pain to a great degree, but the pleasure is generally succeeded by a proportionable depression.

PRINCETON, *May* 14, 1824.

Your communication by [James] Weatherby [of the Seminary] which I received this morning, admitted me to something very like a *tête-à-tête* with you. A letter, as the thought just now strikes me, should be as nearly as possible the transcript of one's common-talk; or perhaps a better description of a good, that is an acceptable letter, would be that it is a soliloquy in black and white, penned with the freedom of a private meditation, yet written for the eye of another, with whom the disclosures it contains, are just as safe as in their native bosom. It is for answering this description that I like your letters; and, by adhering to the same rule, I have occasionally disgorged to you some of my splenetic moanings. You must take me just as you find me; I don't ask you to pardon my failings; criticize them faithfully; but, prythee, bear with them. When I speak of melancholy to *you*, I speak of it seriously, and of melancholy in its truest and most appalling shape; not the puling, pensive, pleasing reveries of a moon-struck lover, or a young, novel-reading, boarding-school Miss; but that deep and horrible over-clouding of the soul, which none can understand but those who suffer it, which can be described only by faint and insufficient similitudes, which, until my nervous system received a violent shock, I never knew, and which I do sincerely wish you may always be able, as I never shall,—to laugh at. Nervous irritability (I am not *com-* but *ex*-plaining) I have got in a very fair way by right of primogeniture, and have increased by neglect of proper recreation and exercise.

You know how closely body and soul are united, and how mental and corporeal changes go hand in hand. But perhaps you do not know—and may you never—what it is to feel the *whole man* in a state of distressing disorder, without knowing whether the body has communicated the distemper to the mind, or the mind to the body; to feel the tremulous agitation of the whole material fabric of nerves, and the accompanying and more intolerable agitation of spirit, depression, blues, hypochondria, or what you will. Will you smile when I say that to shake off this state of soul—I call it so, for the suffering of body is trifling—is no less impossible than to shake off a fit of the stone? One is equally with the other a disease. Call it, if you please, a disorder of the imagination, and say that it is whim and folly. Granted; and yet it is no less dreadful, far more mortifying, equally beyond the influence of mere resolution. When a withered arm can stretch itself out for relief, then may a diseased mind heal itself. Could I once determine to be placid and cheerful, and so effect a change in the mental state, the cure would be already complete. Enough as to the physiology of the case— now for its reality in my own person. I am more easily excited to pleasure or pain than most persons. My joys are excessive; sometimes a little frantic. The same susceptibility makes me liable to depression from circumstances which would scarcely for a moment ruffle the feelings of some; and to depression, sometimes, which has no perceptible cause without. To compare levity and melancholy in a moral point of view, is comparing two sins equally repugnant to the mild placidity and cheerful calm which the truths of the gospel produce on a heart that is exercised aright. The latter afflicts *my* conscience least, because it is what I loathe, and what I would as joyfully shun as I would a delirium, and which it is just as much in my power to avoid. *Undue* mirth is a fault which brings with it, to me, its punishment, in the shape of the vapours which follow in its footsteps. Perhaps the words I may have used in a former letter convey to your mind an impression not exactly correct. Forebodings of future pain or misery are not often the subjects of my thoughts, but there comes over my soul, I can no otherwise describe it, a cloud, a blackness, a horror, which tinges every object without or within with a certain indefinable, vague, and terrific darkness; which absorbs the powers of the soul, and seems to concentrate all the faculties upon some hideous *something*, or *nothing*, and waste the mental energy in empty musing. I am sometimes months without such a visitation, and sometimes weeks with little else; and my condition has been somewhat this for a week past. But peace—let us rise into daylight.

I might write you a great deal of loose gossip, were it not for my pressing business, and my very, very kind acquaintances, who are too obliging to wait for any hint to come, and too dull to take any hint to go, and who never think of such a query as

"Is he at leisure?" I am indeed laid under the necessity of husbanding every hour. I have scarcely looked at mathematics for a year, and am expected to take the tuition of the Sophomore class, who have been at Algebra all the winter, as well as to induct them into geometry, and the Freshmen into Algebra. The preparation requisite is by no means slight. It is something more than what might enable one to undergo a strict examination upon the several subjects. The instructor must hold himself in continual readiness to detect every error, as soon as made, and to enter immediately into every variety in the mode of demonstration or solution. And, by the bye, the intensity of attention which this will require, in the recitation-room, will equal hours of study in the closet, as to exhaustion of spirits, as well as to improvement of the mind in fixed habits of thought.

The examination of the Theological Seminary is now going on. From this, I am now, as having no further connexion with the Seminary, exempt. Our printing press, though a little thing, is yet a mighty wonder here. The children, great and small, are turning up their eyes, and expanding their palms at the novel sight of "PRINCETON" at the foot of the title-page of a "Report" just printed.

My real troubles commence, unless Providence interpose in an unexpected manner, next Thursday. Then may you expect to hear of cracker-firing, of scraping (do you understand?) of funking, of door-bolting, of ducking, of rope-tripping, of window-breaking, of all the petty vengeance which unruly striplings wreak on their hapless instructors. My colleague in the tutorship, Mr. Samuel K. Talmage,[1] made a speech at the Bible So-

---

[1] Now President of Oglethorpe University, Georgia. In a public letter, written in August, 1859, Dr. Talmage says: "We were placed on terms of very intimate intercourse and communion as fellow-tutors during the year 1824. He had become pious since we had parted as students, and I now saw much of his inner life, as he disclosed it but to few. He had grown graver in manner, and somewhat prone to pensiveness of spirit. To the public eye he seemed retiring and apparently distant. But when with a friend in a retired walk, or in the *abandon* and intimacy of private personal intercourse, he was the most cheerful of companions, abounding in playful remark and discriminating observation. He had a keen relish for the humorous, and a nice appreciation of the virtues and defects of his fellowmen. He had a perfect horror of cant, pretension, bigotry, exclusiveness, and was himself remarkably free from all these failings, thus imparting an irresistible charm to his intercourse with friends.

"His piety was, even at that period, deep toned, and remarkably advanced for one of his age. He was at times overwhelmed with a sense of sinfulness, and has told me that often he could scarcely refrain from crying out in the college chapel from an awful sense of guilt before God, under the pungent appeals of the beloved Professors of the College and Theological Seminary, although he was sitting on the stage before the assembled students as one of the Faculty."

ciety anniversary in New York. How long shall it be before our turn comes?

What think you of the presidential squabble? Jackson brightens wonderfully. His recent letters—I mean his recently published letters, set the man's character in a noble light, and command my highest respect.

Saturday.

My boasting is generally fatal to my hopes, by throwing me off my guard. That cold, or a lineal descendant from it, has come upon me like a strong man armed. I have tried the valiant mode, of defying the cough, and going through thick and thin in spite of it, and the effect has been to fix it deeply in my lungs. I am now reduced to terms of submission, and am driven to the humble mode; i. e. sitting by the fire, keeping out of the wind, drinking teas and slops, and eating pectoral medicaments of various kinds. This regimen, together with an approach to starvation, promises to release me.

The title of an old Scotch song furnishes a key to many of my actions—"*For lack of gowd.*" My temptation to covet greater affluence is small, while I am at home; and even in your city, where baits are hung out everywhere, I presume that habit would soon make me able to withstand their influence. When I look around me at those who have silver and gold always *in promptu*, I cannot perceive that they are one whit happier than myself. Is ——, think you, more comfortable and easy, than when his only fortune was his tongue, his whiskers, and his front of brass? These thoughts you will doubtless be wonderfully surprised at, for their originality.

I would not call myself an admirer of the "Lake school of poetry," but I have seen passages in the works both of Coleridge and Wordsworth which have breathed the true spirit of poetry, and gone home—I know not and ask not why—to my inmost soul. If these lines[1] are not to be found in the "Sybilline Leaves," or perhaps in the "lines upon the vale of Chamouny," which I have not *ad unguem*, you will find there much that is cast in the same mould. It would be difficult to extract from the Lake-poets a longer passage than this without involving some of their "littlenesses," to use one of their own words, yet a good *delectus* might be culled out of them of such isolated morsels. If this little scrap, which, like the mutilated Torse, shows the hand of a master, is American, so much the better. Tell ——

---

[1] Referring to some twenty lines of an anonymous quotation on Niagara. They proved to be the American Brainerd's.

"The thoughts are strange which crowd into my brain," &c.

that Mr. [Moses C.] Searle [of the Seminary] is within nine inches of my elbow; has just played and sung the old favourite "O years are flown," &c., and "Suppliant" this moment. We have not heard his violoncello since Aunt —— left us, and George Potts [when in Seminary] used to make one in all our little concerts. The absence of the distant friends was more deeply felt than the presence of those at hand, and music has a power to bring back old recollections with a life peculiar to itself. The scene was not altogether to my liking. I am not fond of tears, and to me there is no "bliss" in them; they are at best a *quid pro quo*, a less evil for a greater, a price paid for getting rid of grief, or the swelling outrageousness of grief. Yet just now with my mother overwhelmed, my father to a considerable degree melted, Mr. Searle weeping, or something like it, and Bill looking amazingly comical between an attempted smile and an unaccountable quivering about the lower lip, premonitory, in some cases, of a "cry," I felt not a little incommoded, and read with might and main in an obsolete newspaper that happened to be within reach. "*Launce's*" dog in the Two Gentlemen of Verona was not more consummately hard-hearted.

Reed ["Student's Notes"] certainly is a fine writer. But do you not see a very close imitation of the mannerism of his favourite Gibbon? It is natural that he should glide into the same style, from continual intimacy, but there seems to me a studied copying of the gorgeous and protracted simile, the measured and rhythmical structure of sentences, and the elaborate circumlocutions of the great Heathen. He writes in a manly and eloquent manner, notwithstanding imperfections, which those who cannot equal him may discover.

My fears are not slight, that I shall, in these misanthropic walls, become "the mere student," and forget my duties to those without, as well as neglect to cultivate the society of the amiable and the tender. If I live until next Autumn, I shall, probably, be even more a clown than I now am, and need an evolution of six weeks among softening scenes to bend and mollify me.

Sunday, 11 *o'clock*.

I am left at home while the rest of the family have gone to church. My hours, in my present condition, are likely to hang heavily upon my hands, therefore a little serious talk with you will be both interesting and proper. My melancholy—I commence at the old point, for, you know, it is a physical impossibility to start from any other point than that in which the body is found at the moment when the motion commences;—my melancholy, if I may compare great things with small, and pretend even to the blemishes of a great man, is described to a tittle by Cowper, in one of his letters cited in the "May Advocate."[1] Like him, I find my bitterest ruminations so wrought up with fantastical thoughts and phantasies, that I am forced to laugh at my own creations, when I feel miserable enough to hang myself. That *tall fellow* whom he describes so happily, stands preëminent in my chamber of thought, and utters his eternal cry like the most pertinacious shad-woman.[2] Like him (P. S. you will see by reading the letter that I am wrong) I can be gloomy, yea wretched, without being sober, and the transition is oftener easier from hypochondria to levity, than to seriousness. Like him I find religion, and religious thoughts, not the causes or the concomitants of melancholy, but its surest remedy. When the promises of Scripture can be brought to bear, as I thank God they have sometimes been, upon my troubled mind, they have never, never failed to diffuse a calm and a sweet content which makes the Gospel more valuable, *as to this life*, to me, than it would be under different circumstances. Yet infatuated creatures that we are! that which we know, and have tasted to be the chief and only good, how ready are we to neglect and abandon! A hymn of Madame Guion, (whom the world calls fanatic,) translated by Cowper, impressed me deeply this morning. Among other lines, these:

> "Long plunged in sorrow, I resign
>   My soul to that dear hand of thine,
>   Without reserve or fear;
> That hand shall wipe my streaming eyes;
>   Or into smiles of glad surprise,
>   Transform the falling tear.
> My soul's possession is thy love;
>   In earth beneath, or heaven above,
>   I have no other store;
> And though with fervent suit I pray,
>   And importune thee night and day,
>   I ask thee nothing more."

Of sorrow she says:

> "It costs me no regret, that she,
>   Who followed Christ, should follow me;
>   And though, where'er she goes,
> Thorns spring spontaneous at her feet,
>   I love her—and extract a sweet
>   From all my bitter woes."

---

[1] The extracts in the "Advocate" were from the "Private Correspondence" of Cowper, first published by his kinsman, Dr. John Johnson, in 1824.

[2] "My thoughts are clad in a sober livery, for the most part as grave as that of a bishop's servant. They turn, too, upon spiritual subjects; but the tallest fellow and the loudest amongst them all, is he who is continually crying out with a loud voice, *actum est de te; periisti.*"—*Letter to Newton.*

Does it amuse you to hear *me* talk of *sorrows?* I confess that to complain would be a heinous ingratitude in me. I have had perhaps more external favours and forbearance at the hand of Providence than most persons, and I do desire to thank God; but still, there is a world within, a world that seems as vast and wonderful, and inexplicable as that without, to one who has the habit or the disease of poring inward upon it. And here, whether from imaginary fears (though these are not my great tormentors) or conflicts between inclination and duty, between a restless, ambitious, proud, and giddy soul, and a principle that strives to keep down its gigantic writhings, and labours to repress the upheavings and desperate agonies of effort, in the earthy spirit, which oftentimes gets the upper hand, and crowds under the poor weak element of piety, and triumphs in a mighty rage—here in the inner man, when the gale of hilarity, and the bustle and hurricane of business is blown over, and when religion, through sinful neglect, is not at work to make this ocean smooth,—" when," as Hurley[1] says, " I am brought to face at night, or in solitude, that phantom self, which all day long I have laboured to avoid; what can be conceived more horrible!" Enough, far, far too much am I drivelling to you of this. I grant you a truce. I was going to say, just when the unruly quill took the bit in his mouth and ran away with me, that no thought has within a day or two, struck me more forcibly than this—" why do we not live as we know most assuredly we ought to live?" Why do we not obey the imperative call of duty, of gratitude, which commands us to love God with all our soul, and reiterates the extent of this demand, with all our *strength*, &c.? Why despise the call of interest? Godliness, says Jehovah, who cannot lie, (and O my slight experience enables me to say Amen with exultation,) is profitable for *all things*, having the promise of the life which now is, and that which is to come. *I know* that the love of God in the heart does fill and satisfy it, partly by filling that void which, I know as surely, ambitious thoughts, or glorious success, or wealth, or pleasure can never fill; and partly by repressing and quenching a thousand vain desires which give us incessant and fruitless anxiety. I have been ambitious—What do I say? I am this moment, in spite of God's law, ambitious to a high degree. What has been its fruit? Am I happier? Do I not still, and will I not forever be gasping after something yet to come? something which never can come? Will fame gratify me? Will universal honour give me peace? Will a conquered world make *me* more content than my insane name-

[1] A Roman Catholic preacher whom he had heard in Philadelphia.

sake of Macedon? No! my experience, and universal testimony, and the word of Jehovah thunder, *No!* Did you ever read the life of Henry Martyn? If you have not, upon the strength of our friendship, I charge and entreat you to do so. My present perusal of it is about the sixth, which for me, who seldom read any book through, is strong proof of esteem. If there is on earth or on record a character which I love more than that of H. Martyn, I know it not. To meet *him* in heaven is a wish that burns intensely in my heart.

Upon taking the highest honours at Cambridge, an honour which ennobles a man in the eyes of the whole British nation, and gives him a name in the whole world of letters, and for which he had for four years laboriously toiled—he said: " I have grasped this bubble *honour*, and it vanishes in my hand,"—and thenceforward renounced the world and himself, and became a self-denied and honoured servant of God. Could I tread in his steps, I should feel no envy for the highest potentate, or the greatest scholar upon this footstool. And why cannot you and I, as well as Martyn, take up our cross and follow Christ? It is not that the gate is not thrown wide open. Every page of Scripture gives the lie to such a thought. It is solely because the way is so strait, that our worldly pleasures, our gods, our palpable enjoyments, (which lie close to us and are therefore appreciated,) our joys which are merely terrene cannot accompany us.

I have sometimes been inclined to murmur at the idea that we must *deny ourselves*, that we must give our *whole souls* to God, that it is impossible to " love the world " without being " the enemy of God,"—and to shrink from that yoke which, to my dim eye, seemed to bring no indemnity for the loss of good things; but the demands of the Scripture are inexorable, and it is not until we are willing to receive the whole truth and to obey it, that we can pretend to be willing to be saved. It is not because the gate of entrance is inaccessible, that I have felt my stubborn soul unwilling to strive to enter in. It is because it is too low for my pride, and too arduous for my indolence. " Believe," is a price too small, and " Work out your salvation with fear and trembling," a labour too great for unsanctified human nature. Is it instruction as to what we are to do that we need? He that has his Bible needs nothing else. Is it assistance in doing what we know is duty?

> " Were half the words thus vainly spent,
>   To heaven in supplication sent,
>   Our cheerful song would oftener be,
>   Hear what the Lord has done for me."
>   *Cowper.*

Monday, May 17th.

Dr. —— preached last night; the general impression left by his performance, was that his manner was by far too light for the pulpit. I think so too. He prayed that God would destroy and eradicate "*that cursed superstition*" (Popery) from South America. Such language I think not only unchristian, but upon his own principles, without foundation. The popish creed does contain, shrouded in great superstition, I confess—but still it does contain, the great fundamental saving doctrines of the Bible. Better far would it be to curse those doctrines which many in our communion hold, to wit, that every thought of man is an immediate effect of God's efficiency; that every blasphemous thought is, as much as every pious thought, caused by God's immediate agency. From my soul I could curse such blasphemy as this.

NASSAU HALL, No. 25, *May* 21, 1824.

This is my first letter since I came into this house. I have indeed, time for nothing but the incipient duties and preparations of my new situation. I can promise you but few such voluminous reports as my last epistle. So fully am I occupied with little arrangements relative to my own accommodation and the admission of students, that I have not been at our house since yesterday morning. It requires all the effrontery which I can assume to fill my gown with any kind of effect, to sit in the focal point of vision before a hundred carping young gentlemen, on the scaffold yclep'd the stage, to march through the congregation at the foot of the refectory steps with manifold tokens of respect, and then to march at their head, and sit in state at the upper end of the long college table, &c., &c. However, in all such matters, when a thing *must* be done, I am fond of putting the best face upon it, and—"neck or nothing" going forward. I have never gained any thing by shrinking, although few have oftener made experiment of it, and shrink I will not, though my head should be the price of daring. If you wish to view an original character, and gain a study for future sketches, come hither, and I will show you my *valet de place* James McCarrier, a true born Emeralder, whose delight is rendering services, and who knows no greater happiness than to be kept constantly running, and doing. The addition to college is small—6 or 7; it is seldom that a greater number is added at the commencement of the summer term. The examination of even this small band was tedious—an hour being consumed upon each. You will no doubt be pleased with the specimen of Princeton typography on the other side.[1]

---

[1] Proposals by Borrenstein for publishing a weekly paper under the title of "The Princeton Religious and Literary Gazette."

I foresee one thing with pleasure, that occupation is ousting melancholy thoughts and musings from my mind. I have so much *real* matter for anxiety, that the creations of fancy find little room. Love and regards to those who love and regard me.

NASSAU HALL, *May*, 1824.[1]

When I tell you that six hours and a half is the least portion of every day which I devote to Mathematics,—and I exclude the time of recitation,—you will be ready to pardon me for writing no more. My classes, the Freshman and Sophomore, have both made considerable progress in algebra, and the problems in Bonnycastle, especially in the last editions, are truly formidable. I am visited, too, by my hopeful youth from time to time, in order to be consulted respecting difficulties. These things require labour. Yet my motto shall ever be, *Perseverando*, or as my friend and servant Jemmy McCarrier would render it, "Wid patience and perseverance, a man may open an oyster, dear, wi' a rollin-pin." Add to these things such items as these. With us tutors, is left all the discretionary power for preserving order. No one can change his room without our permission,— or go to the tavern, or leave the bounds in study hours, or leave the refectory, or have a meal sent out to him, or take his seat after grace, or get a letter on Sunday, &c., &c., unless we give him leave. Besides going through the college thrice a day on a round of inspection, it is our rule to send for every student who fails to come voluntarily, and render an account of his absence from his chamber. This week, it becomes my duty to preside in the refectory, to conduct morning prayers in the chapel, and two prayer meetings connected with the college, as well as to have the more minute supervision of the students, and to take care that the edifice is never, for any time, left without one officer.

I should like if I had time to enter into a more free discourse with you upon Calvinism, than we have yet had. I think the matter may be talked over more satisfactorily, with less partiality and passion, and more probability of adhering to the subject, and attaining a conclusion, on paper, than *vivâ voce*; and therefore, I avoided all mention of the matter at our last interview. I rejoice that you seem little disposed to cavil, and sneer. Too many use invective instead of argument, especially against the doctrines of our church, which, somehow or other, like their propagator himself, are "despised and rejected of men." A dis-

---

[1] I insert the simple, incontrovertible statements that follow in this and other letters, for the benefit of such sciolists, young and old, as the boy to whom they were originally addressed.

torted view of Calvinism is often held up as a target, at which the Arminian discharges his arrows with great pomp and complacency, and marches off with his victorious laurels, won from those who hold no such doctrines as those which he opposes. With you, I find no such doctrine as that of *fate* in the New Testament, nor did any ever pretend to such a discovery, as far as my information extends. Yet like some whom you name, after reducing matters to certain ultimate principles, I am guilty of referring much that is inexplicable to the unsearchable ways of God; and I do it in common with Arminians themselves, who, unless their knowledge of human power be pitiably meagre, must yield up many points as beyond their ken; with Socinians themselves, who, professedly rejecting all mystery, are still saddled with doctrines which they cannot thoroughly explain, and from which an escape to professed infidelity cannot entirely save them. I am willing to say, with Cowper,

> "Deep in unfathomable mines
> Of never-failing skill,
> He treasures up his bright designs,
> And works his sovereign will.
> Blind unbelief is sure to err,
> And scan his work in vain:
> God is his own interpreter,
> And he will make it plain."

I know that doctrines in themselves true and important may be made instrumental in doing great evil; and if there are those concerning whom you speak, although I own that I know not whither to go in search of them, I doubt not that in their hands this doctrine must produce an ill effect. But if you mean to ask whether the belief of sovereign, unconditional election, leads, from its nature, to want of fervour in piety and preaching, I would not hesitate a second to say *no*, with full assurance of being able to sustain my negative by a host of examples. I would not propose this as a test of the truth of a doctrine, although if victory over an opponent were my aim, I would ask no better ground. Look around you, and answer to your own self, your own inquiry. Think you that the Arminian clergy are the most ardent men, or that they evince more zeal than our own preachers? Was Luther indifferent to the soul's interests of men when he thundered so nobly for God and truth? and yet he states the doctrine with a harshness which I dare not imitate. Was Martyn, was Newton, were Dr. Scott, Edwards, Davies, devoid of anxiety for the welfare of men? Was Whitefield, who traversed the earth in seeking the lost sheep; or Brainerd, whose labours in a solitary wilderness terminated his life, destitute of fervid benevolence? Yet all these men did assert most stoutly the hateful doctrine of election, even that "God hath chosen some, in Christ, unto everlasting life, out of his mere free grace and love, without any foresight of faith, or good works, or perseverance in either of them, or any thing in the creature, as conditions, or causes moving him thereunto, and all to the praise of his glorious grace." And what shall I say more, for time would fail me to tell of Eliot, and Buchanan, and Schwartz, and Ward, and Carey, and Marshman, and (as I should say if speaking to one of my own belief) of the great teacher and defender of the doctrine, the zealous and indefatigable apostle of the Gentiles. Indeed, if you inquire who they are that in every place are most zealous for the Lord of hosts, you will find them men who delight to dwell upon God's sovereignty, and man's guilt and impotence. The Methodists, to be consistent, ought to cleave to these doctrines, for they do hold, and contend for the sister truths of abounding grace; and the fervour of their zeal may be attributed to the influence of these doctrines. Upon *this* principle, I proceed in forming my own opinions. The Bible speaks the truth. The Bible teaches this, or that—ergo, This and that are true. The syllogism is reversed with many persons. Thus they argue: The Bible speaks nought but the truth. This or that doctrine is not the truth. Therefore, the Bible does not teach this or that doctrine. I speak logically for conciseness. The major of the first syllogism I have proved to my own satisfaction. If I had not, I would cease to give myself any trouble about religion. The minor is, to me, clear as day; and I have been forced into it by stress of absolute conviction. I ask for no further proof. Explanation I may require, but it would seem most philosophical, first to discover what the Bible does say, and then to ask why it does say so. Now all metaphysics apart,— although all metaphysics, as I have no doubt a brief study of the controversy would convince you, bears with full power in favour of Calvinism. *Read your Bible.* If you believe it firmly to be the word of God, you are fully prepared to commence the investigation. If you do not, without scruple, without the figment of a doubt, fully rest on it as a rule infallible, then cease, I pray you, to query with regard to doctrine. You cannot be satisfied as to the truth of a proposition, until you have a plenary reliance upon the testimony. Examine your reasons for believing the Bible to be God's word. What are they? Unless you can answer this satisfactorily to your own mind, pause, and investigate this base of all religious argumentation. Suppose that you should meet in the Bible this day, such a text as this, "He that sinneth *once*, shall forever be damned, and that without the possibility of atonement or rescue." How would it affect you? Would you believe it? If you continued to inspect the page, and still continued to find these words, and could find no escape or evasion, would you believe them? If not, then your confidence in the Bible is yet wavering. I hold myself ready to believe all and every the contents of the Bible. On reading such a text as that which I have made, I should, no doubt, be startled; I might doubt whether I understood it; I might suspect it to be an interpolation; but as soon as this doubt should be removed, so soon should I believe that proposition. The Unitarian, in such circumstances, says,—it is false, therefore God has not said it; therefore, though how it came there, I am unable to explain, yet believe it I will not. Evidently he is now tearing up the foundations of all his previous creed. He has proved, or he ought to have proved to his own mind, that the Scriptures are the word of God, and that all which they contain is true, or he ought to have some infallible touchstone by whose aid to discriminate between the true and the false. To make our own limited views and knowledge this touchstone, is obviously irrational; for thus the Hindoo who reads the Bible would reject the unity of the Godhead; the Mussulman would reject the spirituality of the Christian paradise; the lover of sin would denounce the doctrine of eternal punishment; and every carnal heart would answer against God, and say, " Why hast thou made me thus?" Our only firm footing is here.

A book comes to us purporting to be a revelation from God. Examine the proofs which it brings to substantiate this claim. If they are incontrovertible, believe the book, and believe every word in it. If they are insufficient, burn the volume. Now I think that the Bible tells me that there are three persons in the Godhead, and I believe it, as I believed my father when he told me that the earth moved round the sun, although my senses flatly contradicted it. And I think that God tells me in the Scriptures that " he hath chosen us in Christ before the foundation of the world,"—" *that* we should be (not *because* we should be) holy, and without blame before him in love." I cannot read Rom. viii. 30, and doubt whether sanctification be the cause of our election, or election of our sanctification. So 2 Tim. i. 9. We are " *created* in Christ,"—the expression is a notable one—" unto good works, which God hath ordained that we should walk in them." Can those works thus foreordained be the foundation of our election? Say so, and you embrace a difficulty liable to all the objections which can be urged against our doctrine. In the third chapter of the confession of faith you may find my creed on this subject. This is, what our church calls it, a high mystery, and yet not more so than a thousand other credible truths. And as to its repugnance to reason, I see it not. Does the certainty that an act will take place destroy the liberty of the agent? Yet this certainty is what God's decree secures, and it does nc more.

However, as I shall never cease to say—read your Bible; and if you read it candidly, I care not what else you read not. This simple means led Luther, and Calvin, and Melancthon, and Hamilton to the truth, from the corruptions of popery. This simple means brought the candid and pious Dr. Scott from Socinianism to Calvinism. And God's word has never failed to enlighten those who peruse it with sincerity.

June 1st.

The first of May I spent in your company, free from all cares, and all regular employment; this day finds me as closely chained to business as was ever a galley slave. Yet business is my balm, the *panacea* for all my ailings, and therefore I never can complain of the greatest amount of active useful labour, which it is possible for me to undergo.

I have been reading Irving's orations again; particularly the latter parts of his Argument, and my admiration for the man increases with every nearer view. If any living writer may be said to think for himself, Irving is that man: and even if he often draws hasty and incorrect conclusions, who would not pardon them, when the general character of the work is so manly and independent? His affection ceases, already, to appear so to me. His defence of eternal punishment is one of the most commanding arguments I ever read.

None of the casualties which you mention have yet befallen your tutor. Indeed, matters have proceeded, as yet, very swimmingly. There has been no act of the faculty this session calculated to excite the indignation of the young gentlemen, and until that takes place we may expect peace and safety. Open disrespect has never been shown to any of the present tutors during the eighteen months which they have spent here, and although, out of doors, and behind their backs, *I* have heard them reviled, and calumniated, and ridiculed, yet they tell me that they have never, even in the times of highest excitement, met with any thing short of external courtesy. I can certainly say this much for the manners of our students, that I never received more universal and continued deference from any persons whatever. I know, from my own recollections, that even when young men talk in the most braggadocio style, and vow eternal vengeance on their teachers, they are as meek as lambs in their presence. You would smile at the difference in the manner of a young man when he struts among his mates in the campus, and when he comes, with all possible humility, to ask leave to go into the town, or to be excused from recitation. Our laws are so well digested, and our discipline so exact, that, except in cases of general rebellion, no student dares to offer indignity to any officer. The faculty are always united in supporting their own authority, and the trustees in backing the faculty; and dismission or expulsion is what no young man, however depraved, will hazard for nothing. Their tricks are tricks of fear. They are done always under cover of darkness, and are generally such as it would disgrace them among their own comrades to avow. As to personal danger, I believe that a park of cannon would not keep me from what I think is my sworn duty. Strength of nerve I have not, but I am mistaken greatly if I dare not face any danger which these walls can ever harbour. Every student who falls under discipline, as many must, looks on the person who exercises it as his personal enemy; and hence, rancour and hatred I *do* expect. Every one who is guilty and suffers punishment, makes up the best story possible, to clear his character; and as the faculty make no official statements, these accounts from the culprits are those which gain currency. So that calumny and contempt I expect. Yet I know that the straightforward line of duty never led man wrong. I may suffer in a thousand ways, but if I am permitted to act conscientiously, then may I say, *Integer vitæ*, &c. I think—for I use the confidence of friendship—that without vain boasting, I can say, that my determination is to make the rule of duty my only rule in my new station. College popularity is a wind that is forever shifting, you know not why or wherefore, and it seldom long fans the faithful officer. For so changeable a thing, and a thing so worthless, let me never go a hair's breadth out of my way.

You speak with justice of the formality of ministers. It is a woeful truth, and it is with shuddering that I anticipate adding myself to the venerable corps which contains already so many drones. Yet there are those who, bating the inevitable imperfections of nature, are what their Saviour directed them to be; and perhaps the reason why they seem to be so few is, that they do not seek the glare and bustle of publicity, and pompous anniversaries. My own favourite Moravians do seem to have caught some of the apostolic spirit.

Your notions respecting the conduct of professors of religion, as far as you have clearly defined them, seem to contain a great deal that is true. Christians do, too much, connive at the levity and thoughtlessness of the world, although I think that, *cæteris paribus*, whatever is lawful and expedient for a non-professor, is lawful and proper for a professor of religion. It is every man's duty to love God, and therefore all the self-denial and obligations resulting from this love are the duty of every man. A *profession* of faith, is merely one of these resulting duties. God forbid that I should say aught in exculpation of our brotherhood; our guilt is rank; yet I sometimes think that the " world " who keep not *one* commandment, take an inconsistent pleasure in criminating the " church," who endeavour to obey in some. As for myself, I feel a daily compunction for my failings. There cannot, surely, be a human creature less satisfied with himself than I. In religion, in moral principle, in every branch of attainment and character, I see myself far, far below what I desire to be, and often can I enter into the spirit of the Apostle's remarks, Rom. vii. 14–25. I confess that I see very little in the selfish, secluded, torpid devotion of the monk, which savours of the glowing, expansive, ever *active* piety of the Apostles. I know too much of solitude to have very romantic ideas of the piety which is generated by it. Spleen and moroseness gain more rapid growth in the cell, than benevolence and humility.

Cicero comes next upon the docket. It requires no great independence of soul to think him a master in eloquence. This I do, and my conviction of his just claim to that character, increases with every new approach towards familiarity with his writings. I do not, it is true, rise into the raptures which some affect, and which a few may feel, and for this simple reason, I am not sufficiently versed in the Latin language. Every Frenchman who has been in America six months, knows more of English than I do of Latin; and yet who would set up such a man as a judge of the merits of Shakespeare? And believe me, the peculiar circumstances which render the latter writer obscure, exist in a threefold degree, with regard to the orator. Yet his invectives against Catiline, and especially the peroration " Pro Milone," I have felt, and felt in a manner that assured me how powerfully his words must have smitten the souls of those who listened.[1] Demosthenes I have never felt, and yet I dare not suspect a moment, that he was not a noble orator. I do not profess myself able to judge. I cannot feel the Greek language, and I can hardly feel the Latin. But the claims of these men do not rest on what may strike *us*, nor even on the universal suffrage of scholars, (I say universal, for with the exception of a few wrongheads, who would rather broach a new lie, than submit to

---

[1] In May of this year, he contributed to the National Gazette, ("from the portfolio of a solitary student,") an article on " Cicero de Amicitia;" and in July, another on " Middleton's Life, and Melmoth's Epistles of Cicero."

believe an old truth, I know none competent to judge who have dissented,) the effects, the unparalleled effects at the time, declare beyond all contradiction how eloquent, how superhuman were their powers.

Aikin's lines upon Melancholy, &c., have much reason in them. *I know*, as to my own case, that placidity of mind is the sole preventive and remedy. "Is not this like saying that ease of body is the best preventive of rheumatism?" Not exactly. Quiet of mind, equally removed from the intoxication of company and the intoxication of study; the medium between jollity and spleen, it is in the power of a man to whom belongs "mens sana in corpore sano" to preserve. This quiet is to be found, not in the bustle of life, not in the palæstra of literary ambition, not in mystic ravings, not in that most variable and tyrannous of all pursuits, authorship, but in a life of gentle, virtuous, regular business.

I have been confined to the house almost all this day, by the rain, so that I get more time than usual for writing. But when I do sit down to write, after the fatiguing, but pleasing studies of the day, my pen and my thoughts move heavily, and remind me of men whom I have seen walking home after gorging at a great dinner, hardly able to draw one foot before the other. For want of something better, I send you some lines which accompanied a bouquet, sent last summer to a little girl:

> Perhaps these flowers, so fragrant now, and fair,
> Culled from their native stalk with nicest care,
> Ere thy young hands have touched them, or thine eye
> Has hailed the promised gift, shall fade and die.
> Thus, ev'n in tasting, vanish all our joys,
> Frail as our clay-built frame, mere transitory toys.
> These various petals, bright as clouds of eve,
> From God's creative touch their hues receive;
> These tints so exquisite, this gorgeous frame
> So richly coloured, from his pencil came.
> Yet heaven-born as they are, and to the sight
> Of wond'ring eyes, too sweet to know a blight;
> Still must they fade, their season is a span
> Brief, gay, and brilliant, like the life of man,
> Seen, like a flash, through midnight clouds to quiver—
> A moment brightly seen—then gone forever.
> Use wisely then these flowrets, while they last,
> Quaff all their sweetness—or if thou canst cast
> Some charm about their evanescent bloom,
> That may prolong their day,—postpone their doom—
> Or perpetuity to odours give,
> Formed but a little season fresh to live,—
> This do—and kindly, from the withering breath
> Of blasting heat release these heirs of death.
> But shall no tender wish my gift attend?

> Yes, dearest ———, thy early, unchanged friend,
> Prays from his inmost soul, that every grace
> These emblem flowers can picture—in thy face,
> Thy form, thy manners, and thy opening mind,
> In sweetest harmony may be combined;
> And by some charm of richest heavenly dew
> Guarded from all that withering blasts can do.
> And when from Earth transplanted, may'st thou bloom
> In a new Paradise beyond the tomb.

Do you ever read Wordsworth? I should very much like to get a copy of his Lyrical Ballads. I wish the men who so belabour him in their critiques, would borrow from him a little of that rare originality and poetic fire which sometimes shine out among his quaint and childish thoughts. Have you ever skated? Then read this:

> "So through the darkness and the cold we flew,
> And not a voice was idle: with the din,
> Meanwhile the precipices rang aloud:
> The leafless trees and every icy crag
> Tinkled like iron: while the distant hills
> Into the tumult sent an alien sound
> Of melancholy, not unnoticed, while the stars
> Eastward were sparkling clear, and in the west
> The orange sky of evening died away."

O I feel it! I feel it! and it breathes into my soul all the soft recollections of just such a scene, a long, long time ago, when I was all sport and frolic. This accurate description, whether of objects of perception or consciousness, is, after all, what most enters into my heart. Here is a quotation that will bear studying, and I confess it moves me not a little. [Then followed the familiar lines, beginning:

> "Our birth is but a sleep and a forgetting."]

June 7th.

Had a cracker about two o'clock on the night before last; it was exploded at the prayer-hall door, which it burst open, about 25 yards from my head. I was not certain what it was that had awakened me, until my room was filled with powder-smoke, which came in through the glass ventilator above my door. No bones broken yet. Indeed the *physical* inconveniences of my station I do not regard one straw.

If you see a man in Philadelphia dressed in a Tartan plaid frock coat, with a cape,—note him. He is a captain in the regular service of the British. By his costume you may know him to be eccentric, but you must see him more closely to know all about him. He is a man of considerable property, living upon full pay, a bachelor, on an indefinite furlough, and yet is as economical as a miser, and as laborious, in teaching a school, as a pauper, and all from a purity and benignity of motive that I have hardly ever known in any other man. I know him to have given $2,000 in private charity during the last year. He lived thirteen years in India, is a thorough master of the Telinga, Hindoostanee, and Persian languages, and more than all, shows in the fervour of his conversation, and the beneficence and kindness of his life, that he is a sincere Christian. If you wish to see benevolence personified, see Capt. ——.

NASSAU HALL, *June* 19, 1824.

I think I shall throw up *gazetteering*. It is my desire, I confess, to leave something behind me that may testify, after my death, that I have not been altogether a useless stock in this world; but ten years will not be too much to spend in secret meditation before thinking of such a thing. If I die within that time, God's will be done. If I live, I shall be able to have matured my crude and now only germinating notions, and to judge what may, or may not, do good. Hear a short translation from *Herder*, a German philosopher : "With the greatest possible solicitude avoid authorship. Too early, or immoderately employed, it makes the head waste, and the heart empty, even were there no worse consequences. A person who reads only to print, in all probability reads amiss; and he who sends away through the pen and the press, every thought, the moment it occurs to him, will, in a short time, have sent all away, and will become a mere journeyman of the printing office, a *compositor*, " ein blosser Diener der Druckerey, ein Buchstabensetzer." This, from a fortunate author, has weight.

NASSAU HALL, *June* 21, 1824.

The one simple question with me is, " what says the Scripture ? " Unless we become as little children, we cannot enter into the kingdom of God, and in no point is the unquestioning humility of a child of God more put to the test, than in receiving doctrines which even in apostolic times, were rejected and opposed. Very few Pharisees ever came to Christ and those who did, were not wont to inquire of him how far his doctrine tallied with their preconceived opinions, but simply to believe. I beg you to remember, that I do not stake myself to answer for all, nor for any of the faults of Calvinists; I am not desirous in the slightest degree, of vindicating God's character against those who choose to accuse his doctrines of inconsistence with any doctrine whatever of free-will, or free-agency. " If any man will do his will, he shall know of the doctrine, whether it be of God," and I know not that he has anywhere promised to make plain, to a mind that is unwilling to obey his first commandment, those decrees which he has of his good pleasure chosen to reveal. "All the disputes between us and the Arminians may be reduced to these two questions: 1. Is God dependent upon man, or is man dependent upon God? 2. Is man a debtor to God, or is God a debtor to man?" Please to ponder upon them. According to Arminianism, as I have heard, grace has the name, but free-will has the game. But enough: and to use the words of the same minister whom I last quoted, "One moment's communion with God is worth all the controversial writings in the world"—and this communion I would fain have you to know.

[After mentioning what he considered his spiritual declension, for the last six months, the letter continues.] But I thank his name that he has caused the solitary reading and devotion of this my privacy to arouse me to some sense of the realities of religion. My determination now is this—and may God prevent my falling again by the hands of my adversary—henceforward to "seek the righteousness of God," "knowing that all other things shall be added unto me." "Henceforward let no man trouble me, for I bear in my body the marks of the Lord Jesus." I can enter with a sweetness which I never before experienced, into these words, Gal. iii. 8–19, and address them fervently to you. And, my dear friend, let me exhort you from a heart that knows no insincerity upon this subject, to seek, or rather *accept* that righteousness of God which he condescends to offer. "What am I to do?" say you? This is the work, saith Jesus, which he requireth of you, to believe on him whom he hath sent. If you wish to know what belief is, and what conversion is, I could not refer you to a better answer than that of one of the sailors on board the Thames to [Rev. C. S.] Stewart. See last Advocate.[1] Truly the wind bloweth where it listeth, and ye hear the sound thereof, but cannot tell whence it cometh or whither it goeth. So is every one who is born of the Spirit. You have turned over the Bible, and you have, I can say, without oracular insight into your heart, you have tried various ways of becoming pious; you have done this and that, and are perhaps wondering where that change so much spoken of is to be found. You have sought relief to your mind by endeavouring to shrink from those doctrines of God's sovereignty which you cannot but

---

[1] "It is not any thing you have done or can do. It is only believing and trusting to what Christ has done: it is having your sins pardoned and soul saved, because he died and shed his blood for sin, and it is nothing else."

see in the literal text of almost every book in the New Testament. Now answer to your own conscience; I do not assume the part of a questioner, or ask for an answer—Have you any free-will to be a Christian? If you have, why then, I am ready to cease inquiring of you; for this unanswerable question stares you in the face, Why am I not holy? If your heart is like mine, it is a sink of uncleanness, and so long as you endeavour to conceal this from yourself, you do but err. If you are able, from being dead in trespasses and sins, to raise yourself to life, (forgive the solecism; it lies in the absurd doctrine,) then why ask for assistance any longer? Arise and stand up in the perfection of Christian character. Look back on your past life, and tell me how many free acts you ever did. Did you ever do one thing, or take one step, which was not the effect of some preceding view or feeling? If you have, name it, and I will grant you the freedom of your will. Can you will to be everlastingly miserable? Sit down and try; and then say whether your will is free: if it is as much dependent on motives as the wheels of a watch on the spring, it is about as free. If it is not absolutely and literally *independent*, in all possible cases, to call it *free* is nugatory. The carnal mind, believe me, is enmity against God, and is not subject to his will, neither indeed can be. You must be born again. You may marvel, as did Nicodemus; and yet if I have told you earthly things, and you believe not, if the first doctrine of the Bible is beyond your comprehension, how shall you believe if I tell you of heavenly things? how shall the inscrutable and eternal things of God be clear to you?

Are you desirous of being converted to God, or does your pride cause you to reject the humbling terms of the Gospel? The gate of the kingdom is strait, and pride must crouch low before that little wicket gate can be entered. Now, answer conscience, and not me. Suppose God to judge of your desire to be converted by the means which you use, and the earnestness and importunity with which you use them, what do you suppose would be his estimate of the anxiety which you manifest? Answer to him, how many times you have earnestly sought in his word for the means of salvation. Ah! have you not oftener asked of man? or have you asked at all? I feel no hesitation in saying here as elsewhere, Go straight to the Scriptures. Sectarians may squabble as they please, yet I have no fear in directing any one to go to the fountain head, the Bible. You may say that you have. How many days did you ever devote to it? how many anxious nights? If the body, instead of the undying soul, was in peril, you would scarce think of aught beside. Remember the word is *strive* (αγωνιζετε) to enter, &c. And I predict that unless your eyes are opened by his Spirit that you will find no sweetness there; therefore pray, and that not in half-earnest, for that wisdom which he has promised to give to all who ask.

Nassau Hall, *July* 10, 1824.

I begin by informing you that I have finally been humbled by the *prostration* of my own will, which has been since birth free only to evil, to the point of entire submission to God. I have been a false and hypocritical professor, but God has in mercy brought me to a view of my utter impotence, of the justice of the law which would condemn me to eternal wrath, and of my being helpless in the hands of an Almighty Avenger. Henceforward, my single aim is, to submit myself to God as an instrument in his hands to be used for what he chooses. Death would be a release, should it come this instant; and except to do God's work, I desire not to breathe another moment. You talk of election, &c. Depend upon it you will ever sink into an abyss of perplexity and deeper and still deeper confusion, until you renounce a dependence upon your own powers of intellect. Spiritual vision or faith is as different from intellectual vision or mere belief (in a human sense) as their objects are diverse. The one is conversant with naked speculations which might forever play about the head and communicate no spark of heat. The other is the gift of God. If any man will do the will of God he shall know of the doctrine whether it be of God. Believe in the Lord Jesus Christ, and you shall be saved, and a part of this salvation is a knowledge of the truth. Christ is "made unto us knowledge," when you have received power to be the son of God through him, then shall you see in him all that it is necessary for you to know. Read 1 Cor. i. 18–31. It is the Spirit that teacheth. 1 Cor. ii. 6, 7, and 10 and 14. If you wish to understand these things let me direct you to the Scriptures. Quere. How many days did you ever devote exclusively to the prayerful reading of the Bible? And how great is the probability of your understanding it until you dig in it as for choice treasure? And how great is your anxiety on the subject, if you have never given even a week to the book? Are you not more fond of reading human discussions on the subject, than of going to the fountain-head? Do you not often dispute in your own mind certain propositions before you have had them fairly defined? Are you not a little afraid of finding certain doctrines in the Bible if you should search it too closely or candidly? If this doctrine should stand out prominently as a declaration of the word of God, "God will damn all men;" would you believe it? If God should thunder it in your ear would you believe it? If you would not, then you would be making God a liar; the very essence of that unbelief which keeps us from him. You wish to believe not as the word of God, but as the word of man; not because God says it, and you humbly credit whatever he says, but because it is demonstrated to you. At this rate you may become a grand skeptic, but never a Christian. If you do not come to the Scriptures with a mind equally willing to believe one thing as another, you come with a bias, you come without believing it to be the word of God, and you come in vain. Now observe, I assert nothing to be believed upon my *ipse dixit*, or that of any human creature. Please to read over in connexion, without stopping for any difficulties, or quarrelling about any doctrine, the gospel by John; read it three or four times; and if you do not see that the Scripture is clear and consistent, and plain, too, if we were not blinded by the God of this world, then I forfeit my character.

NASSAU HALL, *September* 20, 1824.

You have here another prospectus of another Princeton work which I trust will prove honourable to us, and useful to the cause.[1] The election of our next Professor of Languages is a matter of considerable interest to us at this time. I would hope that it might be Professor Patton, of Middlebury. He is a ripe scholar in modern as well as ancient languages, has made his researches upon the European continent, and in his private manners is said to be highly interesting.[2]

You suggest to me to write something on "Irving." The fact is just this, I should like to do it very well, but I feel no motion that way at present. I have not that enviable self-command which enables some men to decree that they will do this or that, and then sit down and effect it. I must take myself when I am in the notion of it. I must humour myself. Most of my scribbling is done at single sittings, and *currente calamo*. When I am full of a particular subject, and find that the ink will run, I usually drive the quill to its utmost, which is sometimes only ten lines. That I ever finished any thing, I dare not aver. I count those productions happy which have a beginning and an end, and of course are fit for the press. I would almost engage

---

[1] The hope has been abundantly realized, for the work referred to was the *Biblical Repertory*, the publication of which was begun in 1825, and is still continued, under the same editor, with the second title of "Princeton Review." The original proposals are "for the periodical publication of a collection of dissertations, principally in Biblical Literature. By Charles Hodge, Professor," &c.

[2] Mr. Robert B. Patton was elected.

to send you beginnings of essays enough to make your fortune, if you will only tack bodies to them. The enclosed tractate I did intend to purge and perfect, and perhaps make the first of a series, but for reasons like those above, I can't promise. If Walsh takes it, very well; if not, it may sleep among its brethren.

I pray you if you are going to write to me about La Fayette, that you will find out something new, or something that he is doing *himself*. I hear a great deal about what they are doing to him, taking him here and taking him there; but it might be the College shoe-black as for any life or character that there is in it. I am heartily sick of it, and make a point of skipping every column in the paper which has his name in it.

PRINCETON, *October* 2, 1824.

From amidst all the delightful confusion of vials, porringers, spoons, bowls, boxes, and the other paraphernalia of a sick room, with a head muddled with a week's debauch upon opium, and my whole person redolent with Castor oil and ipecacuanha, with griping, with retching, in short among all the little *agrémens* of a confinement with the dysentery, I am (by stealth) inditing you an epistle. On the day of La Fayette's transit, I was seized, after having had the honour, if honour it can be called, when conferred on all, of handling his fist, and gorging myself at what they were pleased to call a cold collation. I trust that I am getting well now, although I feel a lamentable feebleness in all my limbs, and a weakness in body and in brains. I scarcely know why it is, but so contrary is my disposition, that the occurrences of life operate upon me in a manner seemingly opposite to their natural tendencies. I am never less solemn than when on a sick bed; perhaps, in this case, because I have been drunk with opium all the time. I know that I ought to feel the solemnity of the occasion, but it is all the reverse. On the contrary, in the crowd, and in the *fête*, in the merry circle, I am most ready to have a long face, to feel a great vacuity, and to be deeply impressed with the emptiness of the world. Amongst other memorabilia of this siege, witness the following:

AD J. W. A. HEXAMETR. 5.

Crede mihi, juvenis docilis, me maxime tædet
Audire ægrotum esse virum, tam longe celebrem.
Pulveribus (quid tu Anglicè vocas?) te cumulârint,
Et medicus, veneranda materque, Aneliza, niger Ned.
Nunc spero finemque, quiem tibi sero dederunt.   J. A. A.

PRINCETON, *October* 27, 1824.

I am safely arrived at home, and find myself surrounded by all those peaceful enjoyments which one never relishes so much as after a short absence. I have little to communicate to you in the way of news or adventure. My passage in the steamboat was like most other steamboat passages, tedious and uninteresting; enlivened a little, however, by the company of two or three Spanish Americans, with one of whom, a young fellow from Cuba, I contrived to scrape an acquaintance. He was going to Mr. Brown's school at Lawrenceville. He informed me, probably erroneously, that it was the purpose of the Colombians to blockade Havana within three weeks. I have read "Redwood," and am much pleased with it. I think it may well rank with the Pilot and Pioneers. As a novel, it undoubtedly excels either, the style is chaste and beautiful, and the conversations as natural as any I have seen. Yet in description of scenery it is much inferior to Cooper's works. I still think that it scarcely merits the wonderful encomiums of the British Critics. I can assure you that Princeton is an exceedingly dull place in vacation, and I am forced to study with all my might as a refuge from ennui. I am looking between the covers of some Italian books, and intend to revise my German. It seems to me that Walsh's Gazette is very barren of any thing literary. I wish you would take up your pen. I know you will retort the request and therefore have my answer ready. I have thought of it repeatedly, and invoked the Muse, demon or what not, until I am despairing of ever again being in a writing mood. Surely there is nothing more thoroughly beyond the reach of a man's volitions (Dr. Johnson to the contrary notwithstanding) than the ability to write, not verses merely, but prose. I can think of no subject, and when I get a subject, I can engender no ideas.

NASSAU HALL, *November* 17, 1824.

I am now safely lodged in my cell in College, unmolested by the shrieks of children, or any form of domestic broils. And never did I feel so unspeakably listless, and insufferably lazy, as at this present time. Think yourself favoured if you get from me any thing like an intelligible or coherent letter. There is as yet no Freshman class, and I have but one class to instruct, and that upon a subject which I have attended to before, so that my labours are greatly diminished, and my diligence is inversely as my leisure. I have as yet done nothing like real and regular study. I have read Chaucer until I was tired, and then Jeremy Taylor, and then Brown's Philosophy, that poem under the guise of Metaphysics, and then taken a nap, or ruminated over the coals of a hickory fire, or scribbled somewhat of crude nonsense in my Book of Scraps, and thus pass my days. I must try to give you my notions of these several books. With Chaucer I have been highly gratified—excepting of course those grossly indelicate passages which should never have seen the light. There is a wonderful degree of natural incident, and simple, accurate description in his poems. Some of his tales are highly amusing, and some very tender and pathetic. The *Knightes tale* is an admirable Romaunt, full of delightful strokes of native feeling. The *Nonne's Preestes tale* is an admirable piece of humour, in which a cock and hen moralize in wondrous manner. The second *Nonne's tale* is a highly wrought Catholic legend, yet sweet and moving. *The Prioresse's tale*, has some passages of great beauty. The little Christian martyr, walking through the canton of the Jews, sings loudly:

> "As I have said, thurghout the Jewerie
> This litel child, as he came to and fro,
> Ful merily than wold he sing and crie
> *O Alma Redemptoris!* ever mo.
> The swetenesse hath his herte persed so
> Of Cristesmoder, that to her to pray
> He cannot stint of singing by the way."

As to the dialect, though perplexing at first, it soon becomes familiar. The Sermons of Bishop Taylor have been ranked among the finest prosaic specimens of imaginative writing. I never read any works which exhibit such an unrippled flow of easy, luxuriant thoughts, and rich illustration and similitude. There is nothing in modern writing like him. Irving reminds one of him. And by the way, I have had with me a friend just from Europe who heard both Chalmers and Irving. He gives the former greatly the preference. Brown's Philosophy you ought certainly to read forthwith, if it were only as a specimen of magnificent writing. He unites qualities which rarely meet in one individual; clearness of thought, and patience of analytic investigation, and strong unbiassed judgment, with the most rich imagination and the purest fund of eloquent and appropriate language. I do not envy the taste of the man who would lay down his work for any novel that ever was written. Pent up as I am within these walls, and chained still more closely by *ennui*, I seldom exert myself so much as to visit in the town. There is a club, consisting of all the literary gentlemen and clergymen of the place, which I have the privilege of attending, but this is not just the thing. The Round Table, too, has its weekly meetings, but the social circle I have not. There are many things which seem to conspire to make me an eremite. One of the principal temptations is the great facilities afforded to me for reading, as it regards leisure as well as books. Our libraries are abundant and always accessible. How it is with you I do not know; but I find it hard to prevent the dribbling away of much of my time upon periodical works and literary journals. We counted thirty journals the other day, taken by the individuals of the faculty. Our college library takes the four principal reviews, many scientific journals, &c. &c. I lounged away an hour this morning over the prize essays in the Cambridge Classical Journal, instead of studying Mathematics. It is a purpose (half-matured indeed) of mine to write a series of essays for Walsh, upon modern Latin poetry. The field is one comparatively novel, giving an opportunity for some research, some historical, biographical, and critical investigation, and one which to scholars I should suppose would prove interesting. What think you of it? I suppose you have read " Butler's Reminiscences." The book highly delighted me a year ago, and I see that you have had a very new edition of it in your city. The rules which he mentions as having guided his literary pursuits are admirable. I have had some addition made to my labours this afternoon by the arrival of a Freshman, which with a couple of private scholars in Mathematics will just about double my engagements.

NASSAU HALL, *December* 6, 1824.

I have not opened Blackstone since I saw you. The necessity of a unity in my pursuits has determined me to confine myself to theological reading—at least to the allied subjects.

I am glad that you have taken Brown in hand, the second volume I admire most, especially his remarks on, and indeed his whole theory of simple suggestion. His ideas upon virtue also pleased me very much. The lectures upon the emotions I thought less satisfactory than the rest of the work. After all, my ideas of the practical importance of metaphysics are very low. The only part of Brown which I should think absolutely useful, is the latter half of the third volume. I am, nevertheless, fond of the science; it is never dull to me. I have read no works on the subject which please me more than the articles Logic, Metaphysics, and Moral Philosophy, in the New Edinburgh Encyclopædia, written by Gordon of Edinburgh to whom Irving dedicates,—also a review of Stewart's Dissertations several years ago, in the Quarterly.—It was Brown's Cause and Effect which Fisher reviewed.[1] He promised a review of the

[1] Professor Fisher of Yale College, in the " Christian Spectator " of New Haven.

Lectures, but died before its completion. Brown's disquisitions upon touch are by no means satisfactory to me, although in the particular point of which you speak, I should think him correct. I have just concluded " Halyburton's rational inquiry into the principles of the Deists "; a heavy work, but one which displays in a masterly manner the nakedness of the Deistical creed. I am about to commence reading Edwards on the Will, a work of which some parts formerly had greatly pleased me, and which Calvinists always refer to as triumphantly decisive on their side. Chalmers, in one of his late works, mentions Edwards as the greatest of all metaphysicians; and Dugald Stewart is said to have declared that he was afraid to finish this work, lest he should become fatalist. Have you ever read Berkeley's Minute Philosopher? I recommend it as one of the most interesting books I ever read.

By the modern latin poets, I mean all such moderns as have written latin poetry, such as Vida, Casimir, Buchanan, Heinsius, Milton, &c., &c. This project I must of necessity abandon, as I have not the works of any of these excepting Buchanan. I am now almost ashamed to propose any thing more. I hope, however, ere long to transmit some sheets to you. My present monastic seclusion is truly delightful to me; uninterrupted leisure, and every facility for study, make it in all things such a situation as it would be criminal in me not to be satisfied with. Such, however, is the tendency of man to discontent, that I am continually looking forward to something in prospect; the ministry, settlement, actual labour, &c., &c., although I am firmly convinced, when I think seriously on the subject, that I shall never in this world have better means for happiness.

In French, I have lately read some of Voltaire's silly romances, *L'Ingenu* and *La Princesse de Babylon;* some of *Les Oraisons funèbres de Bossuet,* and *Sermons de Massillon.* The last of these are my favourite. I have read some of Bourdaloue and La Flechière, but they do not please me. I dare not promise myself the pleasure of a visit to Philadelphia within less time than four months. Handell's Messiah would be no slight inducement. Spring may have its charms, but winter is the season in which I delight. It is not merely because I always enjoy much better health, but because of the numerous domestic and social enjoyments of this comfortable season. And whether sitting among the lively circle at our fireside at home, or as I now do, by my own solitary but cheerful blaze, with my table spread, my candle lighted, my elbow chair adjusted, I feel nearer to contentment than in any other situation. When the nights are clear, I generally take a solitary walk about ten o'clock; this stirs up one's romantic feelings, braces the nerves, quickens the pulse, and prepares for a sweet sleep and pleasant dreams. As you may suppose, I am cast entirely upon my own resources for entertainment; my visits at home are necessarily flying calls, and my books and pen furnish most of my amusement. After hard study, Shakespeare or Horace or the Waverleys while away an hour.

NASSAU HALL, *December* 24, 1824.

We have had some serious disturbances in the college, originating in a rupture between the two societies, and which, we were apprehensive, would end in a battle-royal; we have however seen the conclusion of it, and are in peace. There is something wonderfully inflammable in the nature of young men, which is fostered and promoted by the manner of living together, here adopted. A feeling of resentment or indignation communicates itself like electricity, and what I most wonder at, is that we have not more riots. Mr. Hodge's new work will appear on the first of next month. I have been hard at work for some days, translating some German-latin for him. I am endeavouring as much as I can to concentrate my efforts towards a direct preparation for the active services of the pulpit and congregation, reading theology, and trying to write sermons. I tried my abilities at preaching the other night at the preaching society of the Seminary, in presence of most of the ladies of Princeton. It was the first regular sermon I ever wrote. I received a very sweet affectionate letter, not long ago from Mr. Summerfield; he is stationed at Baltimore for the winter. There is a Christian simplicity about all that this man says and does, which greatly charms me. Are Indian rubber shoes for ladies to be got in your city, and at what price?[1] My present course of reading is not of such a nature as would be likely to interest you in the recital. Edwards on the Will, I have concluded, with great admiration of the author's profundity and acuteness, and yet with the opinion that he is unguarded in his use of language, and that his book is liable to great misrepresentation.

I am now at the *Theses de Theologia Naturali*, by Alfonzo Turretine of Geneva, a successor of Calvin, but an Arminian, an elegant and learned writer.

NASSAU HALL, *January* 11, 1825.

To be busy, is to be happy; thus says my experience; and yet this forenoon is drawing to a close without my having done more than to "clear my decks for action," as the sailors say.

[1] I let this item stand for the sake of noting the date at which the article inquired for was still a novelty.

And herein I find the advantage of a strict methodical division of time, which precludes the tedious discussion of that most momentous of all questions, "What shall I do next?" Wesley's rule is a capital one: "Have a time for every thing, and do every thing at its time." Such have been my meditations upon the loss of this morning. And now, to your letter. Dugald Stewart's dissertations I have read with much satisfaction. You will find that the Quarterly abuses his work, as much as the Edinburgh praises it; in this, as in most cases, I think *veritas in medio jacet.* I have not read Playfair's dissertation, although my father estimates it much more highly than Stewart's. I suspect that the rumours respecting —— have their origin in his being what is called a Hopkinsian, *i. e.* a New England Calvinist. One of the main disputes among our clergy has reference to the question, "Whether Christ died for all men, or only for those who believe," and which in my opinion is a mere logomachy.

Did you read the representation made to Congress by Mr. Benton, respecting the inland trade with Mexico? It interested me very much, as all does which relates to our communication with Spanish America. I should have no objection to take an exploring tour upon that route. In looking forward upon my future course in life, I am often filled with great anxiety. There is more in our profession to give occasion to this than in others. Physicians and lawyers can generally make election of a situation for life; they need wait for no caucusing of old women, and no contested calls. They are not liable to be tossed from Dan to Beersheba without a settlement, or to submit to the indignity of setting up as candidates, and then being refused. For instance, I have not the most remote notion of my future settlement, whether I shall pitch my tent in a city or a desert, in New York or Missouri, in France or Paraguay. In truth, all that reliance upon Providence which we profess is thus brought to the test; and perhaps viewed in this light it is a useful discipline. You may think it both affected and fanatical, but I certainly see very little in this world worth living for, except to be public benefactors. This is not the result of any peculiar exercises, but arises from my daily experience of this fact, that earthly enjoyments excite, but cannot gratify; that I am daily pursuing some expected good, of which I am daily disappointed. The labours of the ministry excite most of my wishes and desires; and I confess, that to serve God in the Gospel of his Son, is the only desirable thing which I have in view. Yet I find myself daily entering with ardour upon the same pursuits which have already deluded me a thousand times. There is little new among us. An Atheneum is in projection, and will probably succeed. We have an anatomical lecture, in addition to our other literary exercises. The first number of Mr. Hodge's new work is issued, and has a fine appearance. I am also almost ashamed to tell you that we are brooding again upon the addled scheme of a Princeton newspaper; we have some hope that it may yet succeed. As to my reading, I have despatched Butler's Analogy, an immortal work for its power of argument and depth of original thought; also Dr. Hartley's Evidences of Christianity, decidedly the best work on the subject which I have seen, and contained in the 5th volume of Watson's tracts. Either of these books would make you a good Sunday's entertainment. I generally keep a volume of the British poets upon my table, to read "between meals." With all my attention, I am unable to see any thing in Dryden to raise him to the eminence which he has attained. His versification is undoubtedly fine, and he occasionally flashes out into exquisite elegance, but in general he is one of the dullest of poets. His prose, I think, cannot be too much extolled. He, as well as Milton, Cowper, and Cowley, give the lie to the saying "that no poet can write prose." Appearances seem to indicate that all our fears are to be realized with regard to the election of General Jackson. I suppose, in that case, we must try how loyally we can support his administration. Be it known to you that I have not yet relinquished that deplorable habit of smoking the weed. I have an idea that it suits my constitution very well; and under cover of such a notion as that, a man may do any thing.[1]

FROM MY CELL, NASSAU HALL, *February* 26, 1825.

The success of John Q. Adams has pleased me as much as it can have done you. As to William, when he could no longer disbelieve the report, he left his beard to grow to a lugubrious length in token of his chagrin. My only fear is that the tranquil and equitable administration of our President will be somewhat *ennuyante*. I am, like other scribblers, well enough pleased with the reception of my essay.[2] It is one of those things which attracts some attention among the good folks of Princeton, and it is amusing to hear their various conjectures as to the author.—*Byron* (to follow the items of your letter) is an author whose imagination and genius command my respect, and whose principles call forth my detestation. With all his powers, however, he is often pitiful and grovelling. Childe Harold, in my

---

[1] Notwithstanding this salvo, the habit proved seriously "deplorable," when his health compelled him to relinquish it.
[2] An article in the National Gazette.

view, stands far above the rest of his poems, and is the only one which will deserve the name of a classic. He seems to have been the victim of a scepticism which rather gave scope to his unhappy feelings and his perverted sensibility, than encouraged him in loose and merry libertinism. I have sometimes fancied that in his gayest passages I could discern the forced smile of a man whose sins were a heavy burden. There is no *talk* small or great in this corner of the world. Dr. Romeyn is dead—very suddenly. Dr. Milledoller is to succeed Dr. Livingston in the Theological chair at New Brunswick. Upon the 22d I had the pleasure of being fastened into my room at 2 A. M. and hearing the bell rung, horns blown, and the like noises for a season. I wish I had something interesting to send down to you, but there is an entire dearth. There is a court lately instituted among the students which affords them a good deal of talk and amusement. Addison acts as Clerk.

Have you ever read Madame de Staël's *Germany?* She has been well denominated *par excellence* the genius of her age. It is a work full of deep thoughts which, wonderful to tell, strike you as true and yet as new acquaintances. It is a most pleasing exercise to the mind to be engaged in the perusal of such a book. She wanders continually from her subject, but ever with her reader's full consent. I read her essay on the "influence of literature on society" with less pleasure. *Anatomy*—This has been my amusement for some time; with the assistance of some dry bones, and some elegant engravings by *Lizars* of Edinburgh, I have obtained a pretty good insight into Osteology. I should like the opportunity of attending a few dissections.

You talk about a sermon. What sermon? Well: let it be any sermon. Perhaps you mean one of my sermons; permit me to say that I am afraid it would do you very little good. My thoughts are so inefficient with regard to my own habits and practices, that I have very little hope that they will be more effectual when consigned to paper. Nothing to which I put my hand ever dissatisfies me so much as sermon writing. I am enough chagrined after every effort of this kind to throw the thing in the fire. Whatever complacency I may feel in any thing else, my sermons are truly mortifying to me. The ideas seem of the most unspeakably trite and shallow kind. As a *sermon*, you could not be pleased with one of mine. Let me recommend you to one Chalmers, or to good old Davies: as my composition you cannot need it, after having so full a specimen of all that I can do in that department. I could fall to work now and finish the sheet with an exhortation; and if I thought that I could induce you by it to come to the rational determination of seeking an interest in that salvation which you must *know* to be paramount in its claims to all other things, I would gladly do so; but after all the unanswerable arguments of Dr. Wilson, and all the pungent appeals of Mr. Skinner, what could I say? Why has religion crept out of our letters so entirely? Perhaps it is my fault. I am indeed glad that we have got clear of polemics, but I am by no means satisfied in conscience at letting the whole matter rest. You surely know me well enough to give me notice when my advances on this subject are unpleasant, and with this safeguard I wish you would let me know how far your resolutions have been matured by all the excellent instructions which you have from the pulpit. Like the other gifts of God, religion is put *mediately* in our power; and while the established means are neglected, we must stand self-convicted. Let me beg your devout attention to these things.

I received a letter the other day from an old friend, who is very calmly awaiting death with the consumption. In him, as in many others, I have an instance of the power of religion to despoil death of his terrors. It is perhaps foolish to express such unfounded anticipations, but I have long looked forward to an early death, and in truth I see no reason to deprecate it, unless it be, that I might act a more faithful part in future.

NASSAU HALL, *March* 22, 1825.

I preached another sermon last night, [a Seminary exercise,] with as little satisfaction to myself as ever I experienced. I do sincerely hope that I shall conjure up a little more life when I come to the real work. And now to say a little upon the very interesting topic which has often entered into our correspondence, I mean the matter of personal piety, permit me to say that you are mistaken if you suppose that I will under present circumstances exhort you to a mere use of means, however assiduous and sincere, as the mode of securing salvation. I will not say to you as a minister of your city once said, "Go on, persevere, be encouraged, I have known a woman seek Christ six and thirty years, and at last find him." No: this I consider at once unscriptural and cruel. I say, repent and believe. Do it now: delay not a moment; and instead of being encouraged, be alarmed at the awful truth, that every day you remain impenitent your burden of guilt, and your lot of wrath increases. Without *faith* it is *impossible* to please him; and whatever you do before repentance is odious in his sight. Though you should weep tears of blood, and macerate your body by prayer and fasting, nothing would rescue you from the curse until you submit to God. Compare this statement with Scripture, and "judge ye what is right." Do you say that you cannot pray aright, &c.? Let me quote from a work of the excellent Andrew Fuller a passage in point: "What shall we say then? Seeing he cannot repent, cannot find it in his heart to *endeavour* to repent, cannot pray sincerely for a heart to make such an endeavour;—shall we deny his assertions, (viz. of inability,) and tell him he is not so wicked as he makes himself? This might be more than we should be able to maintain. Or shall we allow them, and acquit him of obligation? Rather, ought we not to return to the place where we set out, admonishing him as the Scriptures do, to *repent and believe the gospel;* declaring to him that what he calls his inability is his sin and shame; and warning him against the idea of its availing him another day." I can fancy you rising in revolt against such doctrine: I remember when my heart was stoutly and bitterly set against it; and yet no sooner had I gained any knowledge of the truth and of my own heart, than I was convinced that nothing prevented my submitting to the righteousness of God, but a wilful, wicked, stubborn aversion to his most holy law, and to the humbling terms of salvation. I know that I can in no way evince the sincerity of my friendship more, than by dealing thus plainly with you. I do greatly fear that your present views will lead you to a kind of hardened indifference which naturally grows more and more hopeless, and is but the prelude to eternal death. The repentance I urge ($\mu\epsilon\tau\alpha\nu o\iota\alpha$, a change of mind) is a solemn and cordial determination of soul, to renounce sin as a thing odious, loathsome, and damning, and to embrace the service of God as infinitely excellent and desirable. I entreat you to make this most reasonable of all determinations. Make it this very day. What but a wilful enmity to God's holiness can induce you to delay? How can you venture, deliberately, to put off the solemn dedication of your heart to God even until to-morrow?

Nassau Hall, *April* 2, 1825.

You are right in your supposition that ministerial functions will suit me better than the tedious business of teaching. I say this with great pathos, as our semi-annual examination commences on Tuesday next.[1] Waiving the considerations of duty and religion, the active labours of preaching, &c., will be to me peculiarly interesting; and I trust that while I live, I shall be enabled to give myself "*wholly* to these things," according to the Apostolic injunction.

Law's "Call" is a book read by vast numbers of people. It

[1] He spent part of the vacation which followed, in a tour to Niagara.

is a *sine quâ non* among the Methodists; and while there is much in it to which I must except, I consider it a beautiful specimen of moderated asceticism. Gibbon says of the author, that he preached not a word more than he practised. Since you are dipping into practical works, let me recommend the following to be put on your catalogue, all of which are excellent, though far inferior to *Law* in style. Baxter's "Call to the Unconverted; Edwards' "Sermons," (Pres. Jonathan,) such as are addressed to the unconverted; Davies's *ibid.*; and "The Life of God in the Soul of Man," by Scougal, a book which was blessed to the conversion of Whitefield. Let me suggest, too, the propriety of allotting a certain portion of time for such reading, and adhering rigidly to your plan. We need every constraint to pin our minds down to a subject naturally unpleasant. Our [Princeton] paper, or, as it is pompously yclept, the "American Journal," *de omnibus rebus, et quibusdam aliis*, has commenced its course. To-morrow, if a cold the twin of that incubus I had last spring will permit me, I hope to sit down at the table of the Lord in commemoration of his death. We expect an addition of nine or ten new members. With proper sentiments and affections, such seasons cannot fail to be among the happiest and most sacred of a man's life. Such they have sometimes been to me, and oh that you would cast in your lot with us, and taste and see that the Lord is gracious. You are undoubtedly convinced that your defect is a defect of heart, and not of understanding; that you view divine truth in what Bacon calls "a dry light." Now to remedy this let me exhort you to force your mind to the solemn and daily contemplation of those subjects which seem most calculated to excite tender emotion, viz., your aggravated sins, the mercy and love of Christ, &c., &c. This contemplation is best of all attained in prayer, therefore cry mightily unto God for a "new heart" and a "right spirit"; bearing in mind all the while that your solemn and tremendous obligation to keep the whole law is no whit diminished, and that you do nothing satisfactory to God until you believe in Him who has kept the whole law for you.

NASSAU HALL, *May* 21, 1825.

I have just come from a room full of laughing girls, who had most of the accomplishments which make girls interesting—laughing, simpering, assenting, languishing, bridling, blushing, capering, &c., &c., to the end of the chapter *de laqueis femininis*: yet I return to my room with as deep a shade—not on my brow, (for there my bitterest thoughts seldom wear any wrinkles,) but over my mind. But why do I tell you this—except to indulge that strange egotism which talks of self, and seeks for sympathy where it is least deserved. The bloom of the opening summer has less charms than usual for me, and I am denied even the comfort of a fireside, and a friend, where to unveil my strange—and you will say—irrational gloom. I can easily imagine to myself the clusters of black coats, who clog your streets, [the General Assembly,] and the crowds with itching ears who run after a favourite preacher. To me, Philadelphia would be doubly dull at this crisis; I should choose to make my visits at a more quiet season; and if matters and things go on smoothly, I flatter myself with the expectation of spending some Sunday with you, during the ensuing summer.

I have exchanged mathematics for the classics, in which it has now become my duty to instruct. Horace has usurped the place of Euclid, and I have devolved the xs and ys to my friend Aikman.[1] As far as mere ease is concerned, it would have been much more agreeable to have stuck to the old track, which a year's toil had made familiar.

NASSAU HALL, *May* 28, 1825.

Niagara marks an epoch in my history. Its thunders will always rise in my recollection when sublimity is mentioned. I have said, and like to say little about it, because I find all words which *I* can use utterly inadequate to convey my ideas. I have seen many drawings, and read many descriptions of Niagara, but nothing produces any thing like the true impression, except a little *morceau* of poetry [by Brainard] you once sent me, and the description by Howison in a back volume of Blackwood.

You seem desperately *ennuyé*. Read Gibbon's autobiography again; it rouses me like a bugle: or Boswell's Johnson, or Butler's Reminiscences: or sit down to hard study. Add a few grains of mathematics, and a *quant. suff.* of Lee's Pills—and you are a sound man.

I keep myself alive by constant delving: four or five hours a day at languages; relieved by a little Biography, and a little Mineralogy, with which last study I have been amusing myself a little. Any thing which you can communicate upon the subject will be interesting. No scientific book has ever interested me more than the Geological Essay of Cuvier.

Did I mention to you the pleasing acquisition I have made of a new acquaintance in Lieut. David Hunter, U. S. A., of Fort Snelling, near the Falls of St. Anthony? He is the most agreeable soldier I know. We met at Gen. Porter's, Black Rock, and travelled in company. He has resided nearly three years, 700 miles from any permanent white settlement, among the Sioux

---

[1] The late Rev. Alexander Aikman.

Indians. From him I learnt more of that region than I have ever got elsewhere. I have a huge desire to cross the ocean, " but when, or where ? "—" Audax omnia perpeti, Gens humana ruit per vetitum."

NASSAU HALL, *Wednesday, June* 8, 1825.

For a month or two my mind has been in a state of painful vacillation between the wish to leave my present situation in autumn, and my desire to prolong my course of study, in compliance with the wishes of my father and friends. The peculiar circumstances of our profession render the future a gloomy void. In Canada or Missouri, in Maine or Florida, I *may* be found three years hence—but in which of these directions I shall go, no human soul can form any reasonable conjecture. For myself—as to situation, I am perfectly indifferent; always provided that I escape a large city. I am not averse to commencing with a Virginia Mission, though I have no idea of ever settling there. I should greatly prefer a high northern latitude; yet even there the summer (to me the trying season) might be intensely hot. I am too lazy ever to be a profound preacher; too desultory in my studies to secure rigid mental discipline; too whimsical to be contented; too cool and sleepy to be popular; too cautious to be efficient. With these rare qualifications, I can swim down the stream of life as well in one bark as another. To see me after dinner, gazing drowsily out of my window, with a book, mayhap upside down, or lounging among the silent walks of the vicinity, with my colleagues,—one would scarcely prognosticate much with regard to my future usefulness. I have so long acted on that delectable adage of Shakespeare's,—" No profit grows where is no pleasure taken,"—that I suffer my days and nights to flit away with scarce a memorial left in my memory or understanding. Writing is an unfailing amusement; but as to writing about Niagara, I should just as soon think of writing upon Milton's Paradise Lost. All my writing, too, goes now into our own journal. My principal rambles at Niagara were on the Canada side. Under the sheet of water at Table Rock, I was silly enough to go some distance with no increase of satisfaction. The Niagara River was high at the time, though probably not at its *maximum*. I have been informed, however, that an increase of water, by making the inequalities of the rock less, diminishes the sublimity of the cataract. Brock's Monument I thought a pitiful thing—by no means equal to your shot tower.

PRINCETON, *June* 21, 1825.

Let me, for want of something better, tell you what I have

been doing this morning. At a quarter before 5 o'clock, skipped out of bed with uncommon alacrity, and set out upon an exploring expedition in company with my good friend, Prof. Halsey, and Mr. Finch, member of the Brummagem Geological Society, a Henglishman, and a natural Istorian. Through lanes, and woods, and marshes, and meadows we made our way to a stream called Pretty Brook, alias Petty's Brook, which is the principal branch of Stony Brook. We traced this stream a mile or two, catching mussels, terrapins, bull-frogs, et hoc genus omne, picking weeds and flowers to which I found sesquipedalian names attached, examining the "red sandstone formation" (observe my proficiency) upon which Princeton is situated, and wading through puddles, and rivulets, until my feet were soaking. To variegate the scene, we went in to bathe in a mill-pond,—swam for about forty-five minutes, and taking up our baggage, reached the college at 9 o'clock. Sipped six cups of tea with the professor, looked very knowingly over a new invoice of minerals, and found myself at 10 in No. 25, where I now sit waiting every moment the three Freshmen. Having despatched a passage of the Anabasis, (I use the word in the double sense of finishing and murdering,) I proceed to answer your letter. As to inducements [to remain in Tutorship] they are many. I cannot ask more retirement, pleasanter company, greater literary and religious advantages, access to books, contiguity to the cities, competent support, good air—in fine, all externals that can make a man contented, than I have now, and have too, in the very bosom of our own family, and amid my most pleasing early recollections. As it respects the money matters, with my present $400, board, fuel, servants, library, &c., I am in a better situation than many ministers who have a wife and family to boot. In truth, nothing but a deep conviction of duty will take me from Princeton—my second birth-place—the birth-place of all within me that can distinguish me from a mere animal. The year just closed, has been the happiest, beyond comparison, in my life.

I have been turning my attention towards Mineralogy and Geology as a matter of amusement. I wish you would do the same; it would give us something to talk about, render travelling more interesting, and keep us alive in the warm months. You have great facilities, and the Schuylkill minerals are noted. We might accommodate one another by an exchange of specimens, though, by the by, I have none to barter. Some pieces of Talc and Mica from your vicinity would please me. Is there such a place as the Adelphi Mills—some such name, four miles from Philadelphia? I am told that there are fine specimens of graphic granite there, &c., &c. I have just read in addition to

Cuvier, Hayden's Geological Essays, am digging into Cleaveland, omitting for the present his Crystallography, and comparing the minerals here with his descriptions. I hate to be alone, and want your countenance. We have lately received for our Mineralogical cabinet a box of Italian specimens, presented by R. Lenox, Esq., of N. Y. They contain, besides volcanic productions, many beautiful petrifactions of fish, perfectly preserved, and of flowers so distinct, that you would think them artificial castings; also an extensive *hortus siccus* of Italian flowers. Mr. Halsey has already added about 250 articles to the cabinet, and is every day turning in something new. We expect to get Dr. Hosack's likeness to adorn the room where his donations are deposited. He is one of the few Alumni who remember Alma Mater.

Summerfield has indeed gone to his rest; for truly I never doubted less with regard to any man's salvation. He bore the insignia of a crucified Saviour too manifestly and constantly, to leave any doubt as to his union with him. I have two letters from him which I prize, as you may suppose, with a reverence and affection most peculiar. In my view of his character, his public performances, remarkable as they were, form a part far less prominent than his private manners, virtues, and Christian amiability. I never expect to see his like.

PRINCETON, *July* 4, 1825.

On this day of tumult and outrageous mirth, I am glad of an opportunity to escape, and have a little discourse with you, even on paper. I confess that I have not patriotism enough to get drunk on this joyful anniversary, or to take pleasure in seeing others so; or discernment enough to trace the connection between the exultation of freemen, and the squibs, cannons, and brutal sports of a mad populace. You have, however, a situation infinitely more favourable for speculations of this nature. The —— you mention cannot be from Kentucky—we never had such a man. If it is —— from ——, a lank, thin, limber-kneed man, with a face just like Voltaire, (in Lavater,) and a voice which, in prayer, preserves an unvaried monotone—I know the man; staunch in his orthodoxy, a born Polemic, yet, unless changed, as void of taste as of politeness; yet pious, zealous, harsh, imprudent, studious. I have never been so fully sensible of the beauty of Sir William Jones's style, as in a late perusal of his anniversary addresses to the Asiatic Society—a series of learned and interesting discourses, worthy of the character of that great man. An old Seminary friend, Theodore D. Woolsey, the profoundest classic I ever knew, is about to sail for Europe: he has been two years tutor in Yale, [afterwards President.] Waterbury is going on a Bible Society agency through New England. Christmas is married to Miss Jones of New York. Your humble servant is busy in preparing for an ordeal before the presbytery of New Brunswick at their August meeting. I hope, as I have already told you, I believe, to pay a visit this autumn to my native State, to climb the blue mountains upon which my eyes were turned almost as soon as they were opened upon any thing, to see friends at the head of families, who were infants when I was last among them, and to search for the graves of my ancestors, and the spots where their youthful days were passed.

My dreams of a transatlantic pilgrimage still float, almost daily, in my disordered imagination. My thoughts begin to rove, and before I know what I am doing, I find myself at London, Oxford, Göttingen, Florence, Constantinople, Alexandria, or Jerusalem. What is to be done with such a truant fancy? I fear that in a paroxysm I shall beg Southard [Secretary of the Navy] to give me a chaplaincy on some armed vessel—bah! what am I talking about? I shall be sufficiently schooled out of these vagaries by one year's labour in the backwoods.

Pray can you recommend any of the steel pens which are advertised? I shall want such a utensil in travelling. On Friday last 34 carriages (stage coaches and hacks) passed through Princeton on their way to New York. What mania possesses your citizens? Hogan, the Ex-Catholic, is building a mansion (*on dit*) near Trenton. He came on Sunday, a few weeks ago, to Chief Justice Ewing, and requested him to sign some instrument of writing which he brought. Mr. Ewing told him that it was not his custom to transact secular business on the Lord's day, and that it would be moreover invalid, and dismissed the pious Greek priest until a more convenient season.[1]

PRINCETON, *July* 16, 1825.

The *Guest* [Lafayette] spent last night in this place. A number of ladies were presented to him, and a supper, the best our village could afford, provided. He seemed much fatigued, and retired as soon as possible. This morning early he set out for Point Breeze to break his fast with M. le Comte de Survilliers. There is very little afloat in the way of literature which has much interested me. I have been reading "Townley's Illustrations of Biblical Literature," 3 vols., 8vo; a work which for solid entertainment I can most heartily recommend. I was led

---

[1] Hogan was a Roman Catholic priest in Philadelphia, who became notorious by his resistance to the authority of his bishop, which led to a public and bloody collision between the partisans of each.

from the title to expect nothing amusing, but have become almost an antiquary by reading it. Indeed, I have always been conscious of a propensity to look over old books, relics, and monuments. I was very much gratified in ransacking an obscure corner of our Library, to find two little manuscript common-place books of Dr. Witherspoon, containing various memoranda in his own handwriting, skeletons of sermons, &c.

My Grandfather, James Waddel, once preached in a little brick church in Orange county, Va.; his predecessor was one Mungo Marshall, whose tombstone was erected near the church. At this time, there is not one brick of the edifice upon another; and my mother brought me a fragment of the tomb, which the villanous wagoners have broken to pieces. This is very near the spot of my nativity.

PRINCETON, *August* 6, 1825.

I feel raised from the dead by the favourable change in the temperature; during the reign of that scorching heat, I could scarcely be said to live. After all possible stripping, ventilation, and refrigeration, I could only succeed in gasping and blowing over a book. A gentleman of your city who has spent the last year principally in the tropical parts of South America, told me this morning, that in lat. 4° 57′ North, he *suffered* nothing equal to the last attack of hot weather.

I see many notices of new works, but have seen and read none of them. Indeed, the nearer I approach the actual labours of the ministry, the more deeply am I impressed with the importance of giving myself *wholly* to its great concerns. Life is so short, my knowledge of subjects strictly belonging to my calling so slender, the work so great, and opposition so varied and strenuous, that I can scarcely forgive myself for wandering among a thousand things interesting, indeed, and instructive, but then irrelative to the grand scope of my ministrations. Putting *pastorum* for *vatum*, I may appropriate the lines of Horace,

> Denique sit quid vis simplex duntaxat et unum.
> Maxima pars vatum, (pater et juvenes patri digni,)
> Decipimur specie recti.

I am willing deliberately to sacrifice the character of a man of science, of taste, of varied and elegant accomplishments, with all its ease, honours, and emoluments, for that of a "man of God thoroughly furnished unto all good works"—a character which is to be sought in the study of the sacred volume. In the recesses of the mountains I shall probably be immured, where ardent piety and sound theology will be the qualifications most in request. The old copy-book adage contains volumes of meaning, *Time is short, but Art is long:* and the one department of Art, which under God I intend to devote myself to, is the art of fishing for men.

I was apprehended on Tuesday last by the Reverend Presbytery of New Brunswick, and kept under arrest four hours; during which time I was put to the question, regarding my knowledge of Ecclesiastical History, Theology, and Hebrew—and made to read two exercises upon passages of Scripture previously appointed.

On Monday, 8th instant, the examination of the Senior class [college] takes place, which continues a week—more or less. After that time six weeks of less anxiety ensue before the commencement.

I suppose entering upon the cares of this world, and departing from your relatives and home, is a thing which you put far away. No man need desire it. It begins to assume a serious aspect to me. Yet the cause in which I go forth is one which ensures me every encouragement. Never for a moment have I regretted that religion has been my choice, or that the ministry is to be my profession. My sole regret is that I have manifested so little devotion in the cause, and spent no more time and labour in forming a character suitable to the work. With regard to the whole matter, I can testify that the greatest happiness I have ever enjoyed has been in the exercise of religious feelings; and that all other sources of pleasure have in the end proved worse than nothing. I regret, therefore, that you have never made the serious and sincere resolution to renounce all worldly things—as a portion—and to devote yourself to God. I know, too, that difficulties must increase, and that five years hence, unless a callous and confirmed indifference shall preclude all such considerations, you will confess, if God has not renewed your heart, that you are tenfold more unable than now to obtain a proper spirit. I can say nothing new. But let me entreat you, as one not without some experience in these things, to have recourse to those means so often urged upon you; and above all, in view of your confessed alienation from God, to relinquish sin, and embrace the religion of the cross. You know that I speak what is reasonable; that your acts may be such, is my earnest prayer.

PRINCETON, *August* 21, 1825.

Since my examination I have found time to turn over the "History of the French Church" by Chas. Butler—a very entertaining collection of biographical and historical notices. For simple chasteness and perspicuity of style, perfect transparency,

I do not know his equal; and in sketches of character, I cannot but consider him a master. Perhaps his subjects prepossess me in his favour. Biography has always been my favourite reading: in this I include all such developments of manners and mind as one finds in correspondence, in anecdotes, as well as formed characters. No kind of study so excites my enthusiasm. One example is more to me than discourses innumerable. This I find in the Scriptures forcibly exemplified. The history of wars and revolutions, and discoveries, are eminently dull to me, except so far as I find in them individual traits of character portrayed. The history of opinion, and of mind, is all that takes much hold of my feelings. For this reason, I never could join in the enthusiastic admiration, common to most learned men, of Gibbon, and Hume, and Robertson; while the histories of Roscoe, and Middleton, and even the Biographical dictionary, are delightful. I am sure that no works have had so much influence upon my religious feelings, as those which give the lives of pious men. The memoirs of Martyn and Brainerd are my continual advisers. I have this month read with high satisfaction the Memoirs of Andrew Fuller, and Samuel Pearce, of the Baptist church. The latter of these had a soul of heavenly mould; and the man who can fail to love, when he reads his life, can have little sense of the beauty of holiness. Is there any thing in the Philadelphia library which would be of advantage in studying extensively the Ecclesiastical History of the Protestant Churches in Europe, during the eighteenth century? I should feel thankful for the names of a few books. What is there that will give one a tolerable idea of South America,—its present state,—geographical divisions,—the revolutions,—their rise, progress, and issue? I am always alive to this subject.

I should feign if I did not say, that I do earnestly desire to see you act with decision upon those religious truths which you profess to believe. Instruction, it would be very silly for me to attempt. You already anticipate all that I would say. You know the connexion between means and end. You know the power of truth. You believe the peculiar power of God's truth as revealed in the Bible. You know the efficiency of prayer and reflection. Now one word: If you fail through *any* defect, however small, in the use of these—all apology is shut out. Let me recommend the "Force of Truth," by Scott—and the life of Brainerd.

PRINCETON, *September* 12, 1825.

Nothing in our correspondence lately has given me more satisfaction than the resolution you express in your last, with respect to desultory reading. This bane of real study, (*haud inexpertus loquor*,) is opposed no less to the true enjoyment of letters, than to deep proficiency. There must be a stretch of mind to give the highest intellectual pleasure; and continuance at one department of study is necessary, if we would engender that happy enthusiasm which ensures success. None of my studies have afforded me more gratification than those which I have pursued with a strict method, and with an attention almost undivided to my peculiar branches. I have merely looked at Hopkinson's defence.[1] To confess the truth, I am unable to lash myself into any warmth of interest in these details: it would be quite as refreshing to me, to peruse the commodore's log-book. I rejoice, however, in his acquittal. My reading has of late been purely theological, if I except a little dipping into some of the unequalled descriptions of the "Faery Queene." "Horsley's Tracts against Priestly," I thought the most triumphant confutation I had ever read, until I fell upon "Magee on the Atonement," which I may safely declare gave me as much delight as any book I have ever seen, of a speculative kind. The nakedness of Unitarianism is there exposed with the most invincible argument, and the keenest satire. "Outram on Sacrifices," "Sermons de Durand and Bourdaloue," "Claude sur la Composition," &c., have taken up some of my time. I was at a friend's house the other day, where I heard a young lady from New York sing in exquisite style, "Like the gloom of night retiring;" you may be sure that my mind reverted to the *soirée* in —— Street. I soon go beyond the reach of music, among the mountain tops of Virginia, except such music as the north wind plays among the recesses of the hills. Look upon the map of Virginia at the smooth face of the counties Bath, Greenbrier, and Monroe, and you will see how I shall be cradled among the cliffs. Is there any fast, festival, or high day in any of your Popish places in the city, shortly? I have as you know a great hankering after such things: and I have been so lamentably disappointed in my various attempts to hear Harold preach, that I feel willing almost to travel forty miles if I had the certainty of so doing.[2] Apropos of Popery. My good friend and correspondent, Etienne Frontis, formerly of the Seminary, is now preaching in Monroe county, Michigan. He gave notice a few weeks ago that he would preach in French. The priests took the alarm, and threatened excommunication to any who should

---

[1] Of Commodore Stewart, then before a court-martial.
[2] Dr. Harold was for many years the most prominent Roman Catholic clergyman in Philadelphia; and not only as an orator, but as a polished gentleman.

go near the heretic. On Sunday morning the Priest, (Bellami,) who is just from France and knows not a word of English, preached on the subject; said the Protestants were divided into hundreds of sects, used a corrupt and false Bible, and that no good Catholic would go. Frontis made his discourse almost entirely from Scripture quotations, using the Catholic authorized version of *De Sacy*. Twenty of the Catholics heard him. The next Sunday Bellami said it was a pack of lies, that he was *un ministre de démon*, and the like gentle expressions, and excommunicated five persons. In the evening, at vespers, he looked round, and saw one of these men in his usual place; he threw off his vestments, and called on the people to turn out the heretic. "Turn him out yourself," said a loud voice from the crowd. Two men pulled off their coats to assist the priest, but the culprit, who had hitherto requested them not to interrupt his devotions, put himself into an attitude of carnal defence, and threatened to knock down the first who should touch him. None ventured on so stubborn a heretic. This excommunication was done by order of the Bishop *Richard*, who lives at Detroit, is a Jesuit, and a member of Congress from that territory.

I find it rather difficult to obey you with regard to disbelieving all reports of the yellow fever. We have some stories quite plausible of the existence of that malady in your city. However, I trust it will prove false. There have certainly been several cases in New Jersey, and at Bristol. It requires, I believe, some rare symptoms to indicate yellow fever to your Board of Health.

CHAPTER IV.

LETTERS WHILE A LICENTIATE.

1825—1827.

NEW BRUNSWICK, *October* 19, 1825.[1]

Where should I be but in New Brunswick? Here therefore I am, attending the meeting of the Synod of New Jersey, and enjoying the company of one or two friends. On returning home, I spent part of a day, and might spend many, in looking over the library of Professor Patton, which I had never before seen. In his own department, (languages,) his collection is superior to any thing I ever saw. He has the best editions, ancient and modern, of *all* the classics; and every book which can be named affording any facility in these studies. I found there also a uniform edition of the whole range of *Italian* literature; and all the German writers of eminence. Among other curiosities which his residence in Europe enabled him to pick up, he showed me a *Dante* of A. D. 1497, and an immense work containing views of all the ancient ruins of Rome. His collection of Atlases and Plates is noble indeed. I went to Freehold on Saturday and preached twice. The only business of importance which has presented itself as yet to the Synod, is the case of two complaints; one is from the congregation of Wall street, N. Y., against the Presbytery of Elizabethtown, who have refused to put their call into the hands of Dr. McDowell: another is the appeal of ——, who has been suspended from the ministry of the Gospel.

20th.—Mr. Hamilton, of Newark, preached a very long sermon last night upon Slavery.

[1] Mr. Alexander was licensed as a probationer for the ministry, October 4, 1825, by the Presbytery of New Brunswick in session at the village of Cranbury. His trial-sermon was on John iii. 3. The first discourse, under his license, was preached in the lecture-room of the Cedar Street church, New York, on the 8th October, from Jeremiah ii. 19. On the next day, which was Sunday, he repeated the sermon in one of the churches of Brooklyn, and preached in the Cedar Street church from Galatians ii. 16.

HOME, *November* 14, 1825.

I am so shortly to bid adieu to Princeton that I am more sensible than ever of the pleasures it has afforded me as a home. Since I saw you, I have been called to preach every Lord's day; and as this has always been out of Princeton, it has laid me under the necessity of riding up and down continually. Brunswick detained me a willing prisoner during the session of Synod; thence I went to Freehold—Trenton—Lawrenceville—Cranbury —and have just arrived here, after riding in the face of a cold November storm.

From your letter, you seem to be truly alive in Philadelphia. Surely you have no excuse for not being orators, when so much eloquence is sounding in your ears. I have been introduced to a Dr. Barber, an Englishman; but as he is of H. M. navy, it cannot be the lecturer [on elocution] of whom you tell. Griscom, you remember, speaks at some length of Thelwall and his system. I have no faith in these systems—being of the creed " *Orator nascitur* " &c. The Seminary has commenced with more than a hundred students; among the rest a coloured man from Schenectady—a very sensible, genteel personage. Our Legislature gave me amusement while I was in Trenton. The motion for an adjourned " *Setting* " (so the mover proposed it) was lost. I saw Seixas and his [deaf and dumb] pupils there, seeking patronage. Some of our Princeton folks have petitioned for a bank. What next? The proposed canal [Delaware and Raritan] will come, it is thought, within a mile and a half of Princeton. We are pleased with the thought of being able then to get Lehigh coal, with less expense of transportation.

My departure towards Virginia is fixed (Deo volente) at the 1st December. I feel not a little anxious with regard to my future course Yet two things support me: 1st. I have devoted myself to a good work, and am willing to be spent in it. 2d. I am under the care of a merciful Providence, by which all things will be conducted aright. Something of my own insufficiency I feel—deeply feel—and sometimes am conscious of an ardent desire to live only for the work of Christ: but alas! my ordinary tempers and manners savour little of the cross. Yet I know the excellence of what I try to preach, and am ready at all hazards to proclaim it, and recommend it to others.

BALTIMORE, *December* 5, 1825.

The introduction you were so good as to give me to Mr. Laussat[1] has proved a source of much satisfaction: his company

---

[1] Antony Laussat, then a student of law, and afterwards a member of

rendered agreeable the passage which would otherwise have been almost insufferable. To him I refer you for all the curiosities of our journey, viz., the circus riders, the odd and ludicrous disputes of the stage coach, the enlightened Senators, &c., &c., to the end of the chapter on steamboat adventures. On arriving here I went to Barnum's great establishment, which, extensive as it is, sinks to nothing in comparison with a new hotel which he is erecting, and which is larger than the New York City Hotel. After breakfast, I went to the house of the Rev. Mr. Nevins. He resides in a very large and handsome mansion in Belvidere street. No one could be more cordial and friendly than he has proved himself. On Sunday morning I heard Mr. Nevins preach, and there is no man living, whom, with my present knowledge of men, I should prefer to him as a preacher after my own heart. In the afternoon I filled his pulpit, and at night that of Dr. Glendy. At the latter place, I was pleased with discovering, after sermon, Mr. Laussat. Had I discovered him before, I should have felt less at ease. Last night I was inveigled into an address at the Monthly Concert of prayer.[1] Baltimore surpasses my highest expectations. I looked for much splendour in this great emporium and thoroughfare, but so much elegance, and neatness, and commercial bustle, and public improvement, I was not prepared to find. And the people whom I have as yet seen, are in manners and kind attention, superior to any *class* of persons I have ever known. There is something in the dialect of the Marylanders, especially as it flows from female lips, which is truly enchanting, being a golden mean between the curt and succinct enunciation (ut ita dicam) of the Yankee, and the full-mouthed rotundity and carelessness of the Virginian. It is worth your while to come to Baltimore, were it only to see the painting by *Paulin Guerin*, presented to the Cathedral here by Louis XVIII. Nothing in the arts ever so transfixed me. It is the taking down Jesus from the cross. The Cathedral itself I take to be the noblest piece of ecclesiastical architecture in the United States. It has a noble simplicity of design which enables you at a *coup d'œil* to apprehend its vast expression of sublimity. It is filled with paintings. The Unitarian synagogue which stands opposite is elegant. The Exchange contains a large hall or dome similar in its impression to the interior of your Bank. The Atheneum, Masonic Hall, Court House, Washington Mon-

---

the Philadelphia bar, but removed by death at an early period of what had already become a distinguished career. He died in 1833.

[1] On Wednesday of the same week he preached in the lecture-room of the First Church, and on the following Lord's day twice in the Second Church, (Dr. Glendy's,) and once at the Orphan Asylum.

ument, and Monument in honour of the battle, &c., are all, in their several details, truly interesting public works. I am in suspense with respect to my movements; shall probably go to Washington next Monday, and thence on through Fredericksburg to Petersburg. Mr. Laussat kindly called, but I was so unfortunate as to be absent. If you write within a week, please to direct here, to the care of the Rev. Mr. Nevins.

PETERSBURG, *December* 23, 1825.

When I came into Virginia, it was with little notion of the manner in which my time would be engrossed by necessary business, and constant avocations. Scarcely had I reached this place, before I found myself under commands to hold forth at the rate of five or six times in the week; and in addition, there is hardly a day in which nine or ten hours are not taken up in giving and receiving visits; and these not your short, formal city calls; but *bona fide* visitations, a houseful at a time, enlivened by the peculiarly abundant good cheer of this bountiful land, and the copious flowing of rum toddy, and the like refections. Could you see me galloping in the neighbourhood upon a high-blooded horse, in company with fellow equestrians, and a carriage load of beauty and vivacity, you would declare that all the Virginian in me had been at once resuscitated and matured. Corn bread and bacon, oysters and hominy, and toddy, dining out every day, and tongue wagging every hour, have kept my blood well in motion. But you wish to hear something of the country. Petersburg, as you know, is the county seat of Dinwiddie, situated upon the river Appomatox. It is an old settlement encircled by hills on almost every side. Population 8,000, and thickly built upon very uneven ground. In external appearance it would strike you, like most Southern towns, as squalid and slovenly: yet there are not a few very splendid mansions in this vicinity. The principal trade was once in tobacco; this has now been transferred to Richmond; and the markets here are chiefly stocked with cotton, which is becoming the staple article among planters here. As to society; I am free to declare, that I have never so enjoyed social and Christian intercourse in my life, as here. Without trying it, you can have no conception of what Southern hospitality means. After all my preparations and previous knowledge, I find myself daily surprised with the winning cordiality and kindness of the people. And this not merely in expression and words. Every house seems at once a home, and every individual devotes himself heartily and with manifest satisfaction to your service. If you look for splendour, you would be disappointed, except in the particulars of servants' attendance and diet. The tables of the seaboard Virginians are worthy of their fame. I am sometimes almost disconcerted with the multitude of servants waiting at table. Four of us were attended the other night by at least six genteel waiters. An old bachelor of great wealth, who is laid up with the gout, gives me the freedom of his spacious mansion, where I walk in and out at my pleasure. I should feel no hesitation at any time to take a horse and servant from his premises, and ride out ten miles to dinner; and such a liberty would evidently gratify him. There are in my uncle's [Dr. Benjamin H. Rice] congregation about twenty-five young men, who profess religion, and are more active in the cause than many ministers. From this you may judge what the people in general are; and you will not judge too favourably. Among these are rich merchants in the Liverpool trade, lawyers, and physicians. The number of agreeable and pious ladies is remarkable; and the easy access to everybody's [house] and heart, more free than I had ever expected in my fondest hopes. A man who comes here, must come with some equestrian skill, or expect to get his neck broken. I have to ride through narrow passes in the hills, going to make visits in the country, where you would suppose a horse could scarcely balance himself, and on steeds which seem to be trained to curvet and run away. Let me assure you that I have been more than once in "bodily fear." Labour is growing upon me. I am engaged to assist my uncle for a month, and have as much regular duty as though I were actually settled. This is well: it fills my thoughts, and directs my attention to the work of my vocation; and my daily experience is, that the world has fewest cares, and my heart purest peace, when I can in some measure live among earthly things without expecting my pleasures from them. Never shall I regret having made religion my choice, though it is every day my lamentation, that it has through my wilful inattention and unfaithfulness so little moderated my worldly affections, and lifted me above sublunary joys.

PETERSBURG, *January* 27, 1826.

You can have little idea of the manner in which I am pulled from post to pillar, or you would not wonder at my long silence. In Virginia, we pay longer visits, and more of them, than I have ever known anywhere else: and as much of my business consists of visiting among the people, especially the members of the church, I find my hours running away from me. Question. What news in Petersburg. Ans. None of any importance since the fire, which consumed about 50 houses. A number of attempts have been made within a few weeks to fire the town; which are traced to the negroes. One woman has confessed, and is in gaol. Item. The noted Wm. B. Giles, after having proposed himself as a candidate for the Senate and the House of Representatives, has been foiled in both attempts. Dr. Crump, of Cumberland, is elected to fill the place of John Randolph. *Quest.* 2d. What strikes you as being new or remarkable? *Ans.* The whole face of society exhibits an appearance very different from what one perceives in the North. Slavery of itself is enough to stamp a marked character upon the Southern population. The number of blacks which I met in the streets at first, struck me with surprise, but now every thing has become familiar. When I consider how much of the comfort, luxury, and style of Southern gentlemen would be retrenched by the removal of the slave population, I can no longer wonder at the tenacity with which they adhere to their pretended rights. The servants who wait upon genteel families, in consequence of having been bred among refined people all their lives, have often as great an air of gentility as their masters. The comfort of slaves in this country is greater, I am persuaded, than that of the free blacks, as a body, in any part of the United States. They are no doubt maltreated in many instances; so are children: but in general they are well clad, well fed, and kindly treated. Ignorance is their greatest curse, and this must ever follow in the train of slavery. The bad policy and destructive tendency of the system is increasingly felt: you hear daily complaints on the subject from those who have most servants. But what can they do? Slavery was not their choice. They cannot and ought not to turn them loose. They cannot afford to transport them; and generally the negroes would not consent to it. The probable result of this state of things is one which philanthropists scarcely dare contemplate. I cannot (to change the subject) say enough of the freedom and cordiality with which the social intercourse here is conducted. You must come and see for yourself. The money which in the North is spent upon the houses and furniture, is here laid out upon the table. I presume that no people in the world "live higher" than the Low Virginians, or Tuckahoes, and by these terms I mean all who live on this side of the Blue Ridge. There is a suavity and grace in the manners of gentlemen of the first rank in this State, and a peculiar fascination in their elocution, which you will understand better if you have ever seen Tazewell, Clay, or John Randolph. The ladies have a frankness which surprises a Northern man at first, and leads him to think that he is receiving special condescensions, when nothing more than common civility is intended.

The trade of Petersburg received a dreadful blow from the fire of 1815, in which five hundred houses were destroyed; and is daily suffering from the transfer of the tobacco trade to Richmond. The chief dependence now is upon cotton, the culture of which is becoming an object of attention here. About 30,000 bales of the new crop have already come into town. The number of commission merchants here is very large, in proportion to the population. I suppose half only of the heads of families here are Virginians. The trade is maintained by Yankees, Irishmen, and Scotchmen. I find my time taken up altogether by my duties as a preacher. There is no toleration here for reading sermons; so that my extemporary powers are called constantly into requisition. My business is one altogether delightful. In proportion to the zeal with which I devote myself to religion, I ever find my happiness increase; and I cannot but hope, that after having so long thought of religion theoretically, you will at length cast in your lot with us, and taste of the sweetness of piety, as a matter of experience and practice. I need not pretend to say with how much joy I would hail you as a Christian brother, if not a brother in the ministry of reconciliation. Will you not give [these] solemn claims a new hearing, and will you not seek [grace to] overcome those bonds which fasten you to the world. Of the guilt and danger of impenitence, it is needless for me to warn you; but let me say, Why will you not determine, immediately, and at all hazards, to beseech of God to grant you the influences of his Spirit?[1]

CHARLOTTE COUNTY, VA., *May* 19, 1826.

If you wish to know where Charlotte Co. lies, let me tell you that it is to be found in that rich plateau of Southern Virginia which has the fine Roanoke for its boundary on the south, just where that river is formed of the Staunton and the Dan. It is, moreover, the county of John Randolph, that greatest of oddities; for while I account him a great genius, an orator absolutely unrivalled in America, a ripe scholar, aye, and a *consistent* politician, I cannot help thinking him crazed. He arrived last night at his residence (Roanoke) in this neighbourhood, having travelled from Washington on horseback in two days, and after looking at his multitude of horses, he set out, about 8 o'clock, on his return to Washington. He has between three and four hundred negroes, who are treated with great kindness, and regard him with a feeling allied to adoration. This is a rich and fertile

---

[1] He remained in Petersburg until the middle of March. From the 19th of that month until the 9th of April, he was preaching in Richmond; on the 11th he preached in Petersburg, and on the 16th preached his first sermon in the church at Charlotte Court House, of which he was afterwards the pastor.

region, producing great quantities of prime tobacco, and, of course, growing wealthy. The manners of the people are plain, frank, hospitable, and independent; proud of their Virginianism, and all its peculiarities. I suppose that no set of people in the world live more at their ease, or indeed more luxuriously, so far as eating and drinking are concerned. No farmer would think of sitting down to dinner with less than four dishes of meat, or to breakfast without several different kinds of warm bread. It is, moreover, (I speak of this county,) a moral country; no gambling, no dissipation or frolicking. The spring, with all its freshness, has opened upon us, and the early fruits are pouring in abundantly. The face of the country exhibits no great variety; indeed, the forests of pine in many places obstruct the prospect altogether. All my moving from place to place is on horseback; and I ride from sixty to seventy miles in mere visits to the people whom I serve.

I wish you would pay a visit to this part of the world. It is a region through which no great road passes, and of course hardly any travellers; whoever visits it must come on horseback. I am about two days' ride from Richmond. Mr. Randolph is the Magnus Apollo of this county. Every one knows and fears him. His power of sarcasm and invective is such that no one pretends to contradict him. He has three several plantations in this county, all of them extensive. His horses (I mean those which are never used) are worth, I suppose, about $8,000. In conversation he is exactly what he is in the Senate; and from almost every one you will hear some of his repartees, or sarcasms. I think the Southern people begin to manifest some disposition to uphold Jackson in the next election. I have never yet met with a friend of Adams in this State. *Nota bene.* If you see my mother in Philadelphia shortly, I commission you to take her to some *good* miniature painter, and have her likeness. I want it small and portable, so as to be carried about my person. I leave the style to your taste. Remember, it is not to be framed for hanging up. Take notice, no " quaint device " of playthings in the hand; either bird, bible, or book, bodkin or barnacles, (I have seen them all.)[1]

RETIREMENT, CHARLOTTE Co., *January* 26, 1827.

I have been waiting with anxiety to hear from you, and have

[1] In June of this year, Mr. Alexander visited Baltimore and Petersburg, and returned to Charlotte before the end of the month. In July he preached frequently at Lynchburg, and in August at Lexington and other places in the county of Rockbridge. After this he was ill with bilious fever. He then made a visit to Princeton, and was in the Charlotte pulpit again November 26.

at last concluded either that I have made a mistake in our reckoning, or that you have never received my last letter. It is strongly impressed upon my mind that I wrote to you from Fredericksburg. I hope that you will bring about the usual equilibrium by a speedy reply to this letter. Were I to commence with the topic most current here, I should speak of Mr. Randolph. His recent defeat has filled this county with chagrin, and he will be returned for the lower House without competition. All the freeholders hereabouts treat the subject as if it were their own personal cause. How different just at this moment are our situations! You are enjoying all the recreations and delights of a great city, with such a multitude of attractions as to leave no excuse for ennui; I am almost a hermit, with no near neighbours, with no variety of scene. If I could for a little while drop into Carey & Lea's, [bookstore, in Philadelphia,] or even walk down Chestnut street, it would act as an elixir. I am ashamed that I have nothing to communicate to you; but this is the lamentable case. You must answer this letter in mere charity, and give me something to think about. I wish particularly to hear what Mr. Ridgely [a fellow-student in Seminary] is doing, where he preaches, &c.; also the state of your congregations, the ministerial squabbles, (horresco referens,) and such matters as you know I take an interest in. I should be glad to hear of any new books, or literary intelligence. You can scarcely imagine what a dearth of reading there is here. I am tempted to send on for a supply of books, but scarcely know what to order, and have not yet received any of my salary. I think that our friend John Q. [Adams] is gaining ground in Virginia, though not in this quarter. Everybody in these parts hates him, hates the Panama measures, hates Clay, hates roads and canals, hates internal improvement, and abominates the tariff. General Edward Carrington is the only man who dares to lift up his voice here in favour of the Administration: he speaks at almost every assemblage of people, though without support, and without converts. If you love shooting, come here; and without going off this plantation, you may bag your four dozen quails a day, with an occasional wild turkey. Pheasants and rabbits also abound. An acquaintance of mine has caught more than twenty foxes this winter, and is now following his hounds with great zeal. Who are to be the writers for this new ["American Quarterly"] Review? What European Magazines are republished in Philadelphia? Any new French books of interest? Remember me to all inquiring friends, and very affectionately to your own family, and believe me,

With sentiments of very distinguished considering, your most obedient servant.

RETIREMENT, CHARLOTTE CO., VA., *February* 16, 1827.

I have just returned from *Halifax*, the county which lies between Charlotte and North Carolina, and have little else to tell you than some of the varieties of the trip. My visit was principally to the family of Mr. Bruce, to which I beg leave to introduce you. His house is noted for its hospitality, and presents to the *bon vivant* as great temptations as can well be found in Virginia. At Mr. B.'s, we seldom sat down to table, during the week I spent there, with less than ten strangers. I also visited Gen. Edward C. Carrington, who has a seat upon Dan River, (which with the Staunton forms the Roanoke.) Gen. C. lay sick nine weeks in Princeton during the last war, having received a ball in his arm at Sackett's Harbour. He is a scholar and a gentleman, and has large possessions. The information which he has acquired in his travels in Europe, renders his conversation highly interesting. He is bold enough to advocate the cause of Adams and patriotism in the midst of this perverse and Jacksonian generation. Let me not forget to mention that Mr. Bruce proposed as a toast, at his table on Thursday last, the health of J. Q. A., which he, I, and about three more drank with right good will. You ask me what I am doing. It is a question soon answered: preaching, riding, visiting my charge, and studying, principally Hebrew. I have read a good deal of French lately, and also twelve books of the Iliad in Greek. I would try [to write] for the Quarterly, but I do not know what to review. Every thing becomes stale before it reaches me. The crocus and Persian iris are in bloom, and the frogs begin to sing, so that you may judge of the difference of climate. If nothing unforeseen occur to prevent, I shall be ordained on the 2d March. The solemnity of such an investiture is well calculated to excite some deep solicitude. Never did I feel more than at present my unfitness for the office. There is a frivolity and worldliness in my character, most remote from the sanctity of the Gospel. In my best moods, I feel great delight in its duties, and can with all my soul recommend its doctrines and spirit to all whom I love.

CHAPTER V.

LETTERS WHILE PASTOR IN VIRGINIA, AND UNTIL HE LEFT THE STATE.

1827—1829.

RETIREMENT, CHARLOTTE CO., VA., *March* 13, 1827.

We are now enjoying spring in all its sweetness. I am sitting with opened windows, into which the "sweet south" is breathing. Our gardens are redolent with vernal fragrance. The time of the singing of birds has come, and no country can boast of more charms in this respect than Virginia. The wood lark, and the mocking-bird are songsters of the first order. Read a graphic description of the latter in Wilson's Ornithology. They are sometimes taken to the North in cages, but in that case you seldom hear the rich gushing of their natural strains, as when they sit among the hawthorn bushes, and pour out melody for hours. The ploughs are all now in motion, and with this there arise many agreeable associations. This day I am twenty-three years old; and the recurrence of a birth-day when properly viewed gives occasion for many solemn reflections. How much of my life has passed fruitlessly! How little have I done in forming an elevated character! How many have been eminent public benefactors at this age! I feel as if my religious proficiency had been small indeed, compared with that of many whom I could name. Let me beg of you also, at this interesting period of your life, to ask seriously, what stand you intend to take with regard to the all-important matter of religion. In church matters I have some encouragements. My congregation, though small, is increasing, and I have reason to believe that the attachment which the people manifest is real. Mr. Randolph is daily expected at Roanoke. The citizens have determined to send him to Congress. I hope to hear him speak on the first

Monday in April. His silence has been remarkable during the last session.

I do not think it by any means incumbent upon me as an Adams man, or consistent as a preacher, to talk much about politics; but I am sorely vexed from day to day at the enormities of the opposition. My ears are forever ringing with the cant which has become so current on this subject. There is some show of reason, I must confess, in the arguments of the politicians here. The tariff forces them to pay more for many articles, and repays them with no advantage.

On the 3d inst. I was ordained to the work of the gospel ministry by the Hanover presbytery. A number of clergymen and a vast concourse of the laity were here present. More than thirty strangers lodged at this house on one night. It was a solemn service, one which I hope long to remember with feelings of awe as well as gratitude. Since that time I have been on a visit to Prince Edward [County] to assist a neighbouring preacher. I there saw such an instance of solitary life as I never before witnessed. Mrs. Spencer, a woman of nearly eighty years of age, has lived the life of a hermit for about thirty years. Her residence is a little log hut, at a distance from any other habitation, and she suffers no living being to remain with her during the night, or for any long period during the day. Her victuals are cooked about half a mile off, and sent to her once a day. She is crooked and withered; dresses always in white linen, and in the oldest fashion. Her whole time is spent in reading the Scriptures, singing, and prayer. Visitors sometimes have to remain nearly an hour at her door, before she concludes the prayer in which she may be engaged. She is the most unearthly being I ever beheld; her conversation is pleasant and rational; and her religion seems to be unfeigned and ardent. You may judge of the difference of climate, when I tell you that our fruit trees were in bloom, and many trees in leaf on the 10th instant. For about six weeks we have had weather of very mild temperature. Mr. [John C.] Calhoun passed through our county on the 11th inst. on his way home. On last Monday, when two or three thousand people were assembled at the court-house, we had several "stump speeches," as they are called. I think this mode of addressing the populace well calculated to advance popular eloquence; while it gives great room for the influence of demagogues. Two of the persons who spoke, were men of talents, and even eloquence. It is here that some of Mr. Randolph's most brilliant essays have been made, and his style of oratory has given a character to that of the people.

CHARLOTTE, *April* 10, 1827.

I do not remember in any "letters from the South," a description of a Virginia court day, and as I know of nothing which exhibits in more lively colours the distinctive traits of the State character, I will employ a little time in sketching a scene of this kind, which presented itself on Monday the 2d of April. The court of Charlotte Co. is regularly held upon the first Monday of every month, and there is usually a large concourse of people. This was an occasion of peculiar interest, as the elections for Congress and the State Legislature were then to take place. As the day was fine, I preferred walking, to the risk of having my horse alarmed, and driven away by the hurly-burly of such an assemblage. In making my way along the great road which leads from my lodgings to the place of public resort, I found it all alive with the cavalcades of planters and country-folk going to the raree show. A stranger would be forcibly struck with the perfect familiarity with which all ranks were mingling in conversation, as they moved along upon their fine pacing horses. Indeed, this sort of equality exists to a greater degree here than in any country with which I am acquainted. Here were young men, whose main object seemed to be the exhibition of their spirited horses, of the true race breed, and their equestrian skill. The great majority of persons were dressed in domestic, undyed cloth, partly from economy, and partly from a State pride, which leads many of our most wealthy men, in opposing the tariff, to reject all manufactures which are protected by the Government. A man would form a very incorrect estimate of the worldly circumstances of a Virginia planter who should measure his finances by the fineness of his coat. When I came near to the village, I observed hundreds of horses tied to the trees of a neighbouring grove, and further on could descry an immense and noisy multitude covering the space around the court-house. In one quarter, near to the taverns, were collected the mob, whose chief errand is to drink and quarrel. In another was exhibited a fair of all kinds of vendibles, stalls of mechanics and tradesmen, eatables and drinkables, with a long line of Yankee wagons, which are never wanting on these occasions. The loud cries of salesmen vending wares at public auction, were mingled with the vociferation of a stump orator, who in the midst of a countless crowd was advancing his claims as a candidate for the House of Delegates. I threaded my way into this living mass, for the purpose of hearing the oration. A grey-headed man was discoursing upon the necessity of amending the State constitution, and defending the propriety of calling a convention. His elocution was good, and his arguments very plausible, especially when he dwelt upon the very unequal representation in Virginia. This, however, happens to be the unpopular side of the question in our region, and the populace, while they respected the age and talents of the man, showed but faint signs of acquiescence. The candidate, upon retiring from the platform on which he had stood, was followed by a rival, who is well known as his standing opponent. The latter kept the people in a roar of laughter by a kind of dry humour which is peculiar to himself. Although far inferior to the other in abilities and learning, he excels him in all those qualities which go to form the character of a demagogue. He appealed to the interests of the planters and slave owners, he turned into ridicule all the arguments of the former speaker, and seemed to make his way to the hearts of the people. He was succeeded by the candidate for the Senate, Henry E. Watkins, of Prince Edward, a man of great address and suavity of manner; his speech was short but pungent and efficient, and although he lost his election, he left a most favourable impression upon the public mind. We had still another address from one of the late delegates, who proposed himself again as a candidate. Before commencing his oration, he announced to the people, that by a letter from Mr. Randolph, he was informed that we should not have the pleasure of seeing that gentleman, as he was confined to his bed by severe illness. This was a sore disappointment. It was generally expected that Mr. R. would have been present, and I had cherished the hope of hearing him once in my life. It would give you no satisfaction for me to recount to you the several topics of party politics upon which the several speakers dilated. We proceeded (or rather as many as *could* proceeded) to the court-house, where the polls were opened. The candidates, six in number, were ranged upon the Justices' bench, the clerks were seated below, and the election began, *viva voce*. The throng and confusion were great, and the result was that Mr. Randolph was unanimously elected for Congress, Col. Wyatt for the Senate, and the two former members to the Legislature of the State. After the election sundry petty squabbles took place among the persons who had been opposing one another in the contest. Towards night a scene of unspeakable riot took place; drinking and fighting drove away all thought of politics, and many a man was put to bed disabled by wounds and drunkenness. This part of Virginia has long been celebrated for its breed of horses. There is a scrupulous attention paid to the preservation of the immaculate English blood. Among the crowd on this day were snorting and rearing fourteen or fifteen stallions, some of which were indeed fine specimens of that noble creature. Among the rest, Mr. Randolph's celebrated English horse Roanoke, who is nine years old, and has never been "backed." That which principally contributes to this great collection of people on our court days, is the fact that all public business, and all private contracts, are settled at this time. All notes are made payable on these days, &c., &c. But you must be tired with Charlotte Court; I am sure that I am. I have succeeded in getting a reading room established in our little hamlet. We are just beginning; have subscribed for the American Quarterly, the North American, Edinburgh, Quarterly, Westminster, Blackwood's Magazine, United States Literary Gazette, Christian Observer, with a number of newspapers. This will superinduce the odours of literature upon our desert. If you will not come, I must proceed to give you a topographical description of this estate of Mrs. Le Grand's upon which I live.[1] If you will take the trouble of looking at the map of Virginia, you will see the village in which our court-house stands marked Marysville, and a little to the west of it a small river called Little Roanoke. Mrs. Le Grand's estate runs from the court-house southward about three miles, and in breadth is much less. On the north it reaches to the village. On the south and west it has little Roanoke for its boundary. On the west it is bounded by an estate of Mr. Randolph's called Bushy Forest. It is nearly level throughout, the few elevations being very inconsiderable. Most of the land is covered with thick forests, intersected by many roads. The most fertile portion is the flat land, through which the stream above mentioned runs. The central part is in the highest state of cultivation.

I must pause to tell you (what you certainly could never find out of yourself) that the birds are making melody this day in a manner more exquisite than usual. Be it known to you, as a matter of the utmost importance, that I am a most enthusiastic admirer of the singing of birds, and that I live in a region where I enjoy this sort of pleasure in perfection. I often stop for half

---

[1] In the "Life of Archibald Alexander, D. D.," Dr. J. W. Alexander, relating the first pastoral settlement of his father, says: "His residence was in the county of Charlotte, at the house of Major Edmund Read. And by a remarkable coincidence, one of his sons, the first settled in the ministry, dwelt in the same house thirty years afterwards, and enjoyed the hospitality of the same Christian lady, Paulina Le Grand, formerly Mrs. Read. Here, at the mansion still known as Retirement, about two miles from the Court House, Mr. [A.] Alexander resided three or four years." (Chap. viii.) The letter of April 10 contained a diagram of the dwelling and grounds of "Retirement." The coincidence of the father and son having their first pastorates over the same congregation, has been in a measure extended to the third generation—the eldest son of Dr. J. W. Alexander having been called to supply the same pulpit.

an hour to listen to that most capricious, sweet, jovial, fascinating musician, the *Mocking-bird*. Whatever may be the case with the European mimic, it is by no means true of ours, that he has no originality. I have never heard the song of any bird comparable to his, and I watch his habits very closely. He is to be found about sunrise upon the topmost twig of the highest tree, swelling and throbbing with the gush of melody, pouring out a stream of song, infinitely varied, of clear, liquid notes, trilled with inimitable rapidity, and wayward changes. No other bird ever excites my laughter; but his imitations are so exact, and so surprise the other birds, that I am often beguiled into a hearty laugh, in my solitary walks. And I have other favourites. The beautiful *Red-bird* I have never seen elsewhere. It is of a light, taper shape, of the deepest crimson, except a circle of black velvet on each side of the face. The melancholy *Whip-poor-will*, which begins its monotonous cry at twilight, though its note is not pleasing, has the power of making me listen often for a long time. And even the *Buzzard*, that foulest of fowls, has such a grace and majesty in his sailing among the clouds, that I almost forgive him his diet and his stench. If you were here *in propriâ personâ*, you would be ready to ask what I am doing, and what I am reading, and how I employ myself. I am sure I speak in moderation when I aver to you, that I have not enjoyed two days of uninterrupted study for the last two months. Riding, riding, riding—like a horse in a ferry-boat, an endless round. I am really losing all habits of study; and you may expect to see me coming on some of these days to the Assembly, with my elbows out, feathers in my hair, and the stupid look of a chimney-sweep.

I have been looking over Burke's works again, and especially his Reflections on the French Revolution. Surely he is the prince of English writers. His description of Marie Antoinette is the most delicious morsel in our language. And then the profundity of his reasoning, the political sagacity of his views, the rich contexture of his language, all render him the most fascinating and commanding of writers on Government. And now let me wind up this overgrown affair, by telling you how sincerely I am thine.

CHARLOTTE, *May* 13, 1827.

The General Assembly I suppose is now in session. Mr. Maxwell[1] is a member of it, he who attracted so much notice last year by his Bible Society speech. I hope he will make himself heard among you. He is, in my judgment, the very best

---

[1] The late Wm. Maxwell, Esq.

orator I know anywhere. I have never heard Tazewell, with whom he maintains a successful competition at the bar. Mr. Maxwell is a man of wealth and influence, and he casts both with great effect into the scale of Christianity. He is, though a native Virginian, the faithful and fearless champion of the oppressed Africans. For a publication of his on this subject, the Norfolk people menaced him with an application of tar and feathers. When he avowed himself the author of the paper, which was published anonymously, his opposers shrunk away before a character so universally revered. He is a bachelor, lives in good style, has an elegant library, is a most agreeable companion, and a finished scholar. I had the pleasure of meeting him recently at Petersburg, and afterwards of accompanying him to Norfolk, and there spending a short time at his house. I am sorry that you did not visit Norfolk. The situation of that town is inferior to that of none in America, as a seaport. The bay and roads afford a roadstead of the safest and most beautiful kind. The town, however, is in a low condition. Richmond has intercepted the trade in the staple commodity, the yellow fever has depopulated it, a recent fire has left it in a state of dilapidation, and the loss of the Colonial trade has almost completed its ruin. They still hope for better times. The Dismal Swamp canal, which is in progress, will open to it all the rivers which fall into Albemarle Sound. It must then become the great cotton market of Virginia and North Carolina. Their navy yard, already extensive, is to be greatly increased. I saw there two seventy-fours, a frigate, and a sloop of war. A naval hospital is commenced upon a large scale. It was with feelings of reverence that I passed the ruins of old Jamestown. The remnant of the old church tower is still visible, overgrown with ivy. Large trees are growing within the church walls. There is but one habitable dwelling at the place, and I saw ploughs moving among the tombs. This is certainly the most venerable spot in our country. I thought of Raleigh and Smith, and more than all of the generous Pocahontas. By the by, I have met with many persons who trace their origin to this squaw. Much as I admire my own name, I think that the noble James River should still be called the Powhatan. I have seen its formation in the mountains, its impetuous torrent among the rocks of the Blue Ridge, its turbulent passage among the cliffs above Richmond, its broad majestic flow beyond, and its sublime expansion between the Capes, and at each successive view have felt new admiration at the mighty flood which welcomed the first adventurers of the 17th century.

I have just received a letter from Mr. [Professor] Hodge, who is at the University of Hallé. He spent the winter in Paris, and gives a most glowing account of the literary advantages of that city. Sixty or seventy professors lecture gratuitously, and a library of 700,000 volumes is open to every one. At Hallé there are professors enough to fill a pamphlet, and about eleven hundred students.

CHARLOTTE COUNTY, *June* 2, 1827.

I have looked for no book with more avidity of expectation than the life of Napoleon, and I do not join in the lamentation of those who regret that Sir Walter has given so large a share of his labour to the incipient measures of the Revolution. Never has such a spectacle been set before the world, as in the convulsive efforts of the French nation to put an end to tyranny. Never has there been exhibited such a union of physical and intellectual greatness, with the lowest and most debasing passion. The leaders of the Revolution fascinate us into admiration at their energy and daring, while their atrocity fills us with contempt and abhorrence. Danton, Mirabeau, Marat, Robespierre, Hebert, Clootz; such were the comets which first astonished, and then consumed the nation. The *Liberty* whom they adored, would have her emblem in a gigantic goddess, whose brow and glance are fired with the enthusiasm of genius, while the lower visage is that of the brute, the satyr, the fiend.

STATE OF VIRGINIA, COUNTY OF CHARLOTTE,
PARISH OF CORNWALL, *July* 3, 1827.

Alack! when shall my ears cease to be molested with endless harangues upon tobacco? I declare it to be the most fertile subject known among men. The glossary of the planters would compose a volume, and their discourse is stark naught without an interpreter. What would you understand by such slang as this? "Have you *primed* your *crap*, Col. Gouge?" (Every man is on the army list.) "No, sir, I had to *clod* in May, and my 'bacco in the low grounds is *fired*." "I sent my last *crap* to Farmville; they made a *break*, and said it was *funked, too lean*, and *fired* too much. It was *struck* too soon, and was in *nice order*." "Well, I've got through *priseing*, the weather was so *givvy*, that the tobacco was in *high order* to *come and go*," &c. *What have you been reading?* A. I have been reading the 2d No. of the American Quarterly, also *Mad. de Stael's* French Revolution; a work of great originality and force, yet unjust to Bonaparte, idolatrous to Necker, and full of Anglomanie. No American can read without delight her eulogy of the good La Fayette: also *George Buchanan's* Latin poems, of which the great Scaliger said "Buchananus unus est in tota Europâ, omnes post se relinquens in Latina poesi." His version of the Psalms is probably the most elegant that ever was made in any language. But in his other poems the real character of his mind shines forth. His satire is at once bitter and ludicrous, and in his attacks upon the Franciscans, I discern the boldness of his countryman and acquaintance John Knox, united with Virgilian elegance, and a power of invective all his own. It has been said of the three Roman satirists, "Horatius ridet, Juvenalis verberat, Persius jugulat." Now, Buchanan does all three in regular succession; he taunts, he scourges, he annihilates. I had no idea of the enormous and unutterable vices attributed to the monks, until I read his poems. As a specimen of the dialect used by the instructor of James I. take the following sentence. A. D. 1570: "Thair is a certane kynd of Beist callit Chamœlion, engenderit in six cowntreis as the Sone hes mair strenth in than in this Yle of Brettane, the quhilk albeit it be small of corporance, noghttheless it is of ane strange nature," &c. He was the friend and correspondent of Roger Ascham, Tycho Brahe, Beza, Grotius, &c. I have also read again such of Cicero's works as I own; greatly longing to possess them all, and in good truth might I tell thee my desire, I would fain have all the Roman writers, so rich are they in goodly matter, and adorned after so shining a manner with every device of wit and similitude. What is called the *Regent's edition* would suit me very well. I have also read some of the works of Rapin, Pascal, De la Houssaye, in French; of Owen, Baxter and Boston, Bates and Cecil, in English; Mastricht, Mark, Witsius, in modern Latin, and Calvin, Dwight, and McDowell, in modern English. Item, Peter's Letters, [by Lockhart,] and a course of Mathematics. *Ques.* 2. *What have you written?* 1. Letters. 2. A few pieces for Rice's Magazine,[1] signed Atlanticus, Quis, M. R———n, and one anonymous intituled "The Minister of Christ." I have *not* written a single sermon since I have been in Charlotte, though I have composed more than a hundred. *Ques.* 3. *How do you spend your time?* Here is my *plan* for days which I spend at home, not always adhered to. Rise at 4; shower-bath; dress; shave; a walk or exercise in the garden; family prayers at 6; breakfast ¼ before 7; read Scriptures; a lesson in Hebrew; Greek Testament in course with commentaries; Old Testament with commentaries; cursory reading of Greek Testament; English Bible; preparation for sermons; theology; German; I have luncheon at 11, dinner at 2½; after dinner I expatiate, read

---

[1] "The Virginia Literary and Evangelical Magazine," edited by the Rev. Dr. John H. Rice, from 1817 to 1829.

every thing, ride, walk, lie on the grass, &c.; tea at 7; family worship at 8; bed at 9.

On June 16th we had a visit from Mr. Tucker, Professor of Moral Philosophy, &c., in the University of Virginia. He is a native of Bermuda, and has been on a visit to a brother who lives at Charlotte Court House. They have at the university some 170 students. Blatterman's school is most frequented. Poor old Williamsburg has about 15 students; Hampden Sydney about 80, and Washington college about 40. I take a lively interest in the improvements of our country, notwithstanding my being hemmed in with political heretics.

"Faithful among the faithless only found."
Milton (aside).

I take no trouble to conceal my sentiments, although I enter into no disputes. Although I hear incessant eulogies of General Jackson, yet I am utterly at a loss to discover among the wagonloads of chaff which they pour forth about him, one grain of real qualification for the Presidency. The temperature is canicular, tropical. I remember not any suffering from heat so great as I now experience. The direct rays of the sun are far more oppressive than any thing I have felt in the Middle States, or even on the other side of the Blue Ridge. Accept my congratulations upon your entrance into the practical arena of litigation. May you prove false the assertion of Burke, who while he acknowledges that legal science strengthens the mind, says, "but it is not apt, except in persons very happily born, to liberalize the mind exactly in the same proportion." Or rather, will I say may you prove that you are one thus happily born.

CHARLOTTE COURT HOUSE, *August* 25, 1827.

I have only strength enough to write a mere note. My mind and body are racked with the lingering distresses of a bilious fever, shorter (as yet) but more violent in its immediate symptoms, than that of last summer. Through the mercy of God, I am spared again (I hope) to praise him more sincerely, and serve him more faithfully. Death has been viewed by me as a precious entrance into eternal bliss. My dear and early friend, I have only strength enough to say, devote your heart, your life, your all to the blessed Jesus.

The physician thinks me altogether free from *disease*, nothing now but *resuscitation* is needed. I think I am well, unless imprudence bring on a relapse.

29th, Tuesday.

Very much improved. Fever gone, and only weakness and irritation of bowels remaining. An inundation almost unexampled has just swept away half the river crops of tobacco. Some $50,000 loss to our planters.

I shall, Deo volente, write soon again. You may say confidently that I am better.[1]

PRINCETON, *March* 19, 1828.

The 6th No. of the Philadelphia Monthly [Magazine] reached us yesterday. It frowned such dullness upon the title-page that I did not dare to read it. *Me judice*, these *general* discursive essays about science and literature are insufferable. Why do not some of you pounce down upon some of the elegancies of either department, and afford some leaven to the stupid mass? But hold, I am incompetent to judge, and far too splenetic to censure with candour. Pray inform me how you and the practice agree. Does the magnificence and awful grandeur of the divine science of law, as developed and exhibited within the walls of your courts, stupefy you with amazement? Or have you wrought yourself into the belief that a cross-examination is the purest occasion of attic wit, and a feverish court room the arena for eloquence? Alack! The world looks barren to me. I am unable to face its calculating and censorious actors. I am too inert to be useful: too greedy of knowledge to digest any for use. Unworthy of the holy calling which has separated me nominally from the world, I have too much of worldly attachment to be bold and decided in my Master's cause. I am such a one as needs a task master through life: left to myself I am a mere butterfly, sipping at every flower. Divine mercy has again and again spared me; and I still wonder for what end, so useless do I appear to myself.

PRINCETON, *April* 4, 1828.

It is a pleasant thing to me to look back and see how long and uninterrupted has been the correspondence instituted between us in boyhood; and equally delightful to have a friend with whom I can make a happy and welcome exchange of many thoughts which burden the mind when retained, and which cannot be revealed to all the world. I count upon your known forbearance when I undertake another letter in my present exile from the busy world. These old scenes encourage no inquiry: they reward it not when made. Were I able to walk through our dull street, I should see a few well-known faces which predict a total barrenness of all intelligence, a few college lads, newly initiated into the mysteries of academic strut and arro-

---

[1] After this apparent recovery a relapse took place in the latter part of September; but he was able to reach Princeton on the 9th October, and there he passed several months under a severe continuance of the same disease.

gance, and a few dames whose catechetical and commiserating visages hold out no sign of enjoyment to one, who for six months has endured the visitation of "How do you feel? Pain in your side? Pale! Bloated! Put out your tongue. La! how moping," &c., &c. Were I to corner myself with some of the old ladies, I might indeed learn some of the antiquities, as that Gen. Washington had his hair clubbed at the battle of Princeton, &c., &c.

The news of Princeton is as follows: A mineral spring has been discovered; that is, as in similar cases, a hole in the mud has been discovered which possesses rather more nastiness than the common water, which tastes like a gunwashing, like a blacksmith's tub, like a what not. I have no fondness for these terrene slops; it will afford many walks, however, for the boys and girls.

I have read "Sketches of Persia," and have been much amused, but Morier's several works on that interesting country are incomparably more entertaining and instructive. I long to read Bishop Heber's books. [Travels in India.] Of American literature, I observe nothing which attracts me. We certainly have no poet, and I tremble for fear that W. Irving has not made Horace's inquiry as to his Life of Columbus " *Quid ferre recusent, quid valeant humeri.*" Dr. Miller is writing a book upon ruling Elders, in opposition I suppose to Dr. Wilson, who has been publishing for several years on the same subject in the Christian Spectator of New Haven.

We hear occasionally from Mr. Hodge, who is at Berlin. He talks of the low state of religion, and the abounding prevalence of fantastic systems of metaphysics. I long to visit Europe, but have no prospect of ever going thither. It is a boyish wish, which perhaps will die away if I should ever have a family.

Addison has just completed the Koran in Arabic, [he completed his nineteenth year this month,] a work which few have attempted in America. He has added Spanish and Italian to his list of languages.

I should relish highly a visit to Philadelphia: but my coat of rusticity has now as many folds as the shield of Ajax. I am surprised to find upon enumeration how few actual acquaintances I have in your city. Still there is no place where I would rather live, while I know my utter incompetency to fulfil the duties of a city pastor. It is my happiness as a son to see my dear parents, and their family enjoying health and happiness. These are favours which demand new recognitions of God's holy and beneficent care. May you also long enjoy such blessings, with the richer satisfaction of pure confidence in our blessed Redeemer.

PRINCETON, *May* 6, 1828.

After taking so sudden a departure from the hospitalities of Philadelphia, it seems right that I should hasten to make reply to your last letter; and have only to complain that the mail is about to depart, leaving me but short space to frame an epistle. To-morrow I expect to go to New York, in company with Mr. Kirk, and thence probably to New Haven and Boston.[1] The country is as lovely as the sweet and genial breath of spring can make it. From the window where I sit, I look upon fields covered with a rich and sudden verdure, and upon orchards in their fullest bloom. Something, however, has so chilled my nature, that I have none of those delightful emotions which I used to experience, when I carried Thomson's Seasons on my long walks, and found a pastoral scene in every grove.

PRINCETON, *July* 18, 1828.

In consequence of delay in answering your last letter, I found myself cut off from the opportunity of doing it at all, as I was afraid to direct to Petersburg, lest you should have left that place, and as you did not communicate to me the intended length of your visit. Like yourself I am about to excurse, but in a different direction, and set out to-morrow for Long Branch. My situation is superlatively *ennuyante*. Without a charge, without regular labour, or the stimulus of definite prospects, I suffer much from the increase of indolent and melancholy musings. As soon as summer is fairly over, I expect to revisit Virginia, with the view of winding up my concerns there, and then looking around me for some situation suitable to my talents and inclinations. It gives me pain to look about me, and see how little there is which could interest you in the repetition. Princeton knows few changes, except changes of weather and of servants. Mr. Gibson is building a house and a barn; Mr. Voorhees, a store; Mr. Joline's Cato has come back; we have got a new cow. These are the principal articles of news. In politics there is a slight change among some of the old Federalists, whose eyes are opened to see the treachery of John Q. A., and who are endeavouring to make his preference of the Democrats, and his old renunciation of Federalism, a ground for their changing sides, and espousing the cause of Jackson. This attempt to revive ancient feuds is too late, and the influence of such men as Jos. Hopkinson, &c., will weigh with the Federalists of New Jersey. The cause of Mr. Adams is sustained, as I fully believe, by the great mass of enlightened and sober men. As for myself, I

[1] The trip extended to Andover, Albany, and the Catskill Mountains.

admire the man for that simple dignity which has marked all his proceedings. How pitiful are the Southern recalcitrations against the tariff! They remind one of the pet of a child who will not eat his dinner, because he is forbidden the use of certain articles. I have only just finished Scott's Life of Napoleon. It is a fine history, but evidently a most hurried production. I admire the candour of Sir Walter, who, as an Englishman and a Tory, might have been expected to have great prejudices against Napoleon. I have also read the "Fair Maid of Perth." The court scenes, and the Highland part of the story, I think very dull, but Henry Gow and his neighbours are equal to any thing he has yet written. Especially after those pitiful stories in the first of the Canongates, we have reason to be agreeably disappointed. Have just finished Pollok's Course of Time. Without making him equal to Milton, as some of the English reviewers have done, I admire his work exceedingly. There is much grandeur of thought, great simplicity of language, and at times the discovery of a satiric vein, which place the author in a high rank among contemporary poets.

I have sent a piece to Littell for his projected "Remember me," [an "Annual":] it is hard to say whether I should be most mortified by seeing it in print, or by having it rejected. It is a sort of Tale: scene, Athens: date about A. D. 100–112.

Addison has finished Ariosto, and is now at Boccacio. He has read about half of Corneille, which I have also read. In Spanish, Addison began with Don Quixote and has read it over and over.

PRINCETON, *August* 28, 1828.

The peregrinations in which we have both been engaged, have made sad infractions upon the ordinary regularity of our correspondence. This I the rather regret, as you are at present my only regular correspondent. I am obliged to you for your letter from Utica, and I should have answered it, had I not supposed that your journey would have been more rapid than it has proved. You will have heard that I have visited your city since you last saw me. My pleasure was greatly abridged in consequence of your absence, as I was without a Cicerone, and involved in a very different sphere from the agreeable little circle of friends with whom I commonly hold intercourse in Philadelphia. My time at present hangs rather heavily upon my hands. Being in that amphibious state between actual labour and total idleness, without a settlement, and yet subject to the constant demands of persons who need preaching, I feel myself very much impaired in mind and spirits. Surely I am losing all that romantic sentimentalism which used to sweeten even my ordinary walks, and create a fairy world in moments of idleness. In the month of October I expect to revisit Virginia, to close my connexion with an affectionate and beloved people, and shall, with leave of Providence, return about the first of the year, with the hope of finding a resting place nearer home. I already feel that it is deeply injurious to a young man to be so long in forming permanent connexions. The habits acquired in this changeable sort of life are peculiarly adverse to mental improvement and maturity of character. I have read nothing very interesting of late. Vivian Grey is an amusing, but most incoherent and extravagant book. If his pictures of Germany are correct, it is certainly the most crazy country upon the globe. The German language has been an object of my attention, at intervals, for some time. I am still very far from being able to read it with any comfort: yet I am encouraged by the report of its rich literary stores to persevere in my application to it. As to politics, the Jackson men around us are nearly frantic. Meeting upon meeting, where the demagogues disgorge the *crambe recocta* of " Coalition, Tergiversation," &c. The attempt to draw off the Federalists from the Administration has had some effect: yet my hopes are still strong that Adams will be re-elected.

A new society connected with the college has been formed, called the Philological Society, to which Prof. Patton has given the use of his choice and extensive Library. We heard to-day from Mr. Hodge—date 28th July, London. He expected to sail on the first of August, so that we expect him almost daily. He has transmitted a large collection of books for the Seminary, principally works in German upon Theology and Criticism. The heat and the drought take away all the vigour of my system, and have influenced this letter by their torrifying powers. Excuse my dullness, if you cannot sympathize with it, and believe me, as heretofore—Thine.

PRINCETON, *October* 4, 1828.

As to my future course in life, I am able to speak only negatively; I shall never seek a settlement south of the Potomac unless driven to it by necessity. As to Trenton, the place has no charms for me; yet in my present circumstances I must do something, and the unanimity and cordiality of the call to that place, in the absence of all other " openings," cause me to look with some favour upon the situation. It would be no small satisfaction to me to be placed within a few hours' sail of Philadelphia, and I might expect to be a more frequent visitor to your city. I am weary of the sickly sympathy manifested for that miscreant Shelley. Surely the just indignation of the public towards a hireling Atheist and seducer, deserves a better name than persecution. His unintelligible poems can never redeem a character such as his. I am glad to see some signs of an interest in German literature, manifested in the article [in Philadelphia Magazine] on Schiller; I should be still more pleased to meet with some of his works. I have recently read some of them with great satisfaction. The other members of the Weimar quaternion would be fit subjects for as many articles, viz.: Goethe, Herder, and Wieland. The articles which appear from time to time in the American Quarterly upon German literature, certainly manifest a familiarity with the subject; but they are too vague and superficial. Instead of being reviews of the celebrated works, or sketches of character, they are such loose table talk upon the subject in general, as might be taken down in short hand from the conversation of any German scholar.

I have just read the whole of Molière's Comedies. Those which are in prose would all be considered farces among us. They are certainly as amusing as any thing I have ever read. My reading at present is principally theological, which, though interesting to me, does not afford the same subjects for conversation or correspondence as some lighter studies. I have been toiling through some recent specimens of German Infidelity, which Mr. Hodge has brought over, and am also reading a more evangelical work, Neander's Ecclesiastical History.

I suppose Archibald in the plenitude of his Jacksonianism has informed you that Princeton is ornamented with a Hickory pole, in the most conspicuous part of the village. It is strange to see with what phrenetic zeal the Hickories are traversing all the country. Invasion or civil war could scarcely produce a greater fermentation among the populace. My fear is that New Jersey will give her vote for the Chieftain; and indeed, further, that he will be our President. Among the novelties of New Jersey there is an attempt to institute a school, in which some hours of every day are to be spent in agriculture, or other manual labour. This is somewhat upon the plan of Fellenbergh, and seems to be well adapted to the wants of our country. The principal agent in this scheme is Mr. Monteith, late Professor of Languages in Hamilton College. We have had a rumour here that a Brazilian squadron had been in Long Island Sound apparently with hostile intent, and that the Hudson and other vessels were despatched upon this business; but as the papers contain nothing on the subject, it is probably a false report. I have tried to respect the South American Governments, but in vain. Their bravery is a sort of animal courage, and their independence mere lawlessness. Greece seems destined to be divided among the beasts of prey which have been so long sitting in judgment upon her fate. But you are not likely to feel great interest in my political speculations. I have been reading Milton's prose works with great delight, and I specially recommend to you his speech for unlicensed printing, if you have never read it. My time passes on in a very dull manner. I have had to preach every Sunday, without stimulus enough to lead me to the preparation which is my duty. I rise about seven, and spend most of my time in studying German; walk a little in the woods, and along the brooks, visit none, and have no company, no correspondent except yourself. My health is generally pretty good, and I have as yet escaped the bilious attack which I have had some reason to dread.

RETIREMENT, CHARLOTTE Co., VA., *November* 16, 1828.

What I shall ever find to fill this portentous sheet, is yet to be determined, and I hope you will judge of its merits by measurement, and send me an equivalent. On my return to Virginia, I found the whole population in a ferment upon the subject of the Presidential election. Jackson is carrying it with a high hand, and there seems little doubt among the politicians here as to his election. Mr. Randolph attended the assemblage here, dressed in a coat of Virginia homespun, and leather breeches, whipped his servant in the public court-yard, and uttered some oracular predictions. It was the 5th of November, and he said, "This is the anniversary of the gunpowder plot, and I hope we are doing that which will blow the 'school-master' sky-high." The pecuniary embarrassments are very great in this region,—five failures within a few months in this county. A rise in some articles, as wheat and whisky, promises something for the valley and the mountains. There is no longer any doubt that a convention will be called in Virginia, which will establish universal suffrage, and probably remove the seat of government to Staunton or Charlottesville. My sentimental journey to Virginia might interest you, if I had not given you the same details more than once before. I found some agreeable young ladies on board the Norfolk boat, who had spent some time in Scotland, and was introduced to a sensible young Englishman, who gave me much entertainment and information. The dirty, gloomy, ugly town of Petersburg presents the same appearance as it did three years ago, when I entered it for the first time. I now perceived that I was in Virginia by the gangs of negroes, some with burdens on their heads, others driving wagons of cotton and tobacco, women arrayed in men's hats, and children with scarcely any raiment at all. I preached five times in Petersburg, and came "up the country," by the mail route, in company with Mrs.

Taylor of Petersburg, sister of Judge Marshall, a lady of genius and information. I expect never to see so many persons so rejoiced to meet with me, as appeared at the little church last Sunday. It is painful indeed to leave friends so cordial and sincere, but I believe I am pursuing the path of duty. I enjoy here a delightful retreat from the world, and suitable opportunities for study, if I had such books as I desire. For my solitary walks, I have a boundless range, affording many varieties of rural prospect, and I indulge myself in many woodland rambles. In such a retirement, however, I feel the need of some extrinsic excitement which might urge to continued exertion: the total absence of this, and the stagnation of mind consequent upon this want, convince me that I shall not lose by going forward a few steps nearer to the busy world. I hope to be able to indulge my writing propensities, as I shall be nearer to the vehicles of thought and literature, and may perhaps stumble upon some department of knowledge, in which I may be useful. If I can sufficiently lash up my indolent powers, I will prepare a review for Walsh, and if the Monthly still survives, perhaps communicate some morceaux to its columns. If you have any pamphlets or papers of any sort, pray send them hitherward, where there is a perfect destitution of such provender. Saxe Weimar's travels proved dull enough. It is plain that a man may be a duke and yet have very little nobility in his thoughts: he is too much like Miss Wright,—not a spark of genius or life, nor even amusing German mysticism. I am very sure I could make more reputable travels in Germany, and would actually do it, if his Highness or anybody else would pay my bills. The "Remember Me" will have been quite obsolete before I get a glance at my famous production. In case the man gives any quid pro quo, I shall try my luck for another number. Having been lately engaged in reading a Life of Erasmus, it has struck me that I might spend some months profitably upon the biography of some eminent man, but cannot make any selection from the rolls of fame. Melancthon, Sir Walter Raleigh, and Grotius have danced before my imagination without leading me to any decision. I have also projected a translation of Milton's Latin Correspondence, which has never yet appeared in an English dress.[1] I have in readiness for the Christian Advocate a small essay upon "Christian Old Age."[2] The noted Mr. Nettleton spent most of the last summer in an adjoining county, (Prince Edward,) and

[1] This last project was taken up by his correspondent, and the translation was published by Mr. Littell, in April, 1829.
[2] Printed in the April number of 1829. In the August number he gave a "Sketch of the Life of Cyprian."

was made the instrument of a wonderful reformation. Multitudes of irreligious persons have been brought into the church, and among the rest some of the most respectable professional men in this region of country. In the church next to mine, 118 have professed religion during the last few months. This revival still continues, and is extending itself in the counties of Lunenburg, Cumberland, and Buckingham. The Theological Seminary at Hampden Sidney is about to have a new professor [Biblical Literature] in Mr. Goodrich, who was educated at Princeton, and who has been acting as teacher for a year or two in Prince Edward. They have about 120 students in the University [of Virginia.] Dr. [R. M.] Patterson [of Philadelphia] was received with much cordiality [as Professor.] I have just heard of the death of Noel Robertson, a young preacher who was with me in the Seminary. He left North Carolina for the sake of his health, but has been cut off when he supposed that he had found a salubrious climate. How affecting a monition to myself! I see clearly that those men are the happiest who are most entirely devoted to a religious life, and who not only profess religion as I do, but exemplify it in their daily conduct.

CHARLOTTE, *December* 9, 1828.

Since I wrote I remember that Butler has published a life of Grotius, and just now I am so taken up with preaching and visits T.T.L., that I can scarcely find time to put pen to paper. If spared to reach Trenton, I may hope to have most of my mornings in my study, and this will be to me a sort of Paradise. When I preach in the week, it steals away a whole day, and a single visit is sometimes nearly as bad. Most cheerfully will I relinquish to you the Latin Letters of Milton; I feel almost certain that they have never been translated, and you will find it, I think, a pleasant and a popular enterprise. They are certainly difficult, and often obscure from the frequency of recondite classical allusions, but it is the same obscurity which pervades all his compositions. Of the history of his correspondents, I fear little can be known. From the various biographical dictionaries within your reach, and from attentive perusals of his memoirs and the history of his times, something may be gleaned. I take higher ground in favour of translations than you seem willing to assume. Good translators are among the greatest benefactors of the age. The great Mosheim gave the impulse to German literature, by translating the Essayists of England, and the immense work of Cudworth; and if I live to learn German, I intend to set about the business in good sober earnest. We may translate works truly great, useful, and popular; we can write originally little above mediocrity. Wieland and Schlegel have both translated Shakspeare; Bishop Marsh has translated Michaelis, and a great work of Eichhorn remains unknown to most of us because no one has been bold enough to turn it into English. I had just been reading [Rev. John] Newton when your letter came, and was pleased to find your opinion coincident with my own. The constant correspondent of Cowper could not be an ordinary man. His letters, though numerous, I think his best productions. If you wish to be delighted, get Hayley's Edition of all Cowper's Letters in five or six 8vo vols. : probably in your library. I have been reading the original Letters of Abelard and Heloise, which have set the characters of these great and unfortunate people in a better light than Pope's amorous and fiery epistles. I am indeed strongly tempted to think that the poor ―――― became a true penitent. If you wish to read a beautiful, lucid, and unanswerable piece of reasoning, read Paley's Horæ Paulinæ. In the October number of the Biblical Repertory, you may see a translation of mine from Rosenmüller. Mr. Hodge has applied to me to review the life of Erasmus, which he put into my hands, for his work, [April, 1829.] This will prevent my undertaking it for the Am. Quarterly. Yesterday I saw a family of blacks who were suing for their freedom in the superior court of this county. It was delightful to see the joy and exultation of the poor creatures when they succeeded. They seemed to think that nothing now remained for them but to eat, drink, and do nothing for the remnant of their days. I have been reading Miss Hannah More's works. There is an unaccountable prejudice against that good and useful woman. I esteem her to be the best of female writers, and had she written on a subject more consonant with popular taste, than those she has chosen, I have no doubt she would have attained as great celebrity as Madame de Staël. The latter is truly great, but the evident straining after point so common to French writers is peculiarly displeasing in her works. Mrs. More's best work in my judgment is her "Hints towards Forming the Character of a Young Princess;" a book which convinces me that she was well qualified to treat that difficult and interesting science,—the philosophy and ethics of history. I must confess that she is sometimes deficient in vivacity, and always in brilliancy, but her thoughts are always reasonable and profound, and her aim towards practical good. The question *Cui bono?* is one appropriate to all our literary toils. Especially in composition I think it should be more my endeavour than it has heretofore been, to do something which may be profitable. The thought of benefiting our contemporaries is one which ought to excite the most sacred ambition, if such an expression may be tolerated. "For what am I living?" ought indeed to open our eyes to those practical duties which arise out of our social relations. This is undoubtedly very new to you, and perfectly original. I venture the thought because it has recently dwelt much upon my own mind.

The die is indeed cast, and Adams must trudge. I am determined now to suspend my judgment, until I can see what measures the General will introduce. Can you guess who will form the cabinet? I have thought of Van Buren, Benton, Hayne, and McLean. I hope to be able to look in for a short time upon the great people at Washington. Perhaps you may desire a trip about the same time, and meet me there. I cannot tell you how much I admire your city life. If, for instance, I had the command of the "Library" which you have, I should think it worth $500 a year. No subject and scarcely a book to which you may not have immediate access. But my duty as well as interest is to learn contentment with the exact situation in which I am likely to be placed. To be near you, so as to correspond not by letter merely, but by personal interview, will be a peculiar pleasure. I am young, but the friends of my childhood are strangely scattered. With the exception of Kirk, you are the only one that adheres. *Our* friendship has been made more secure in my opinion by its eminent sobriety; it has been free from romance and sentimentality. I know that you would be much overpowered if on meeting you I should give you an embrace, and tell you how greatly I loved you: yet such is the friendship of many. Some have thus caressed me, who do not at this moment care one straw for me, or my interests. I rejoice in any thing which promises your return to your Latin classics: though you have probably become rusty, yet you may be assured that six months occasional reading will renew your ability to read them with pleasure. Try the experiment with Cicero's Offices, and I ensure you that you will find the task a delightful one. What I have learned of Latin has been preserved not by classical reading, but the perusal of Latin works on Theology. The classics are more in your line than mine, and I hope you will pursue the study. Strange as the idea may at first appear, I believe that a series of essays upon some of the less familiar classics, as Seneca, Lucan, Plautus, or Pliny, would be a work quite *new* and interesting to the *Scavans* of our country. Let your ink take some such channel. I expect to leave Charlotte upon the 17th inst.[1]

---

[1] He preached his farewell sermon at the Charlotte church, December 28, from John xvi. 23.

CHAPTER VI.

LETTERS WHILE PASTOR IN TRENTON.

1829—1832.

TRENTON, NEW JERSEY, GREENE STREET, NEAR
HANOVER STREET, *January* 16, 1829.[1]

What chiragra has disabled that faithful hand of yours which so seldom gives just cause for complaint? Now mark it well—if you should have written to me, before this shall have been received, you must consider this gratuitous epistle as an answer to the said writing. My first business in my new lodgings is to write this epistle. I am peaceably inducted into my very pleasant little study facing a retired street, within five minutes' walk of my church, and convenient to the tavern, barber's shop, and post office. I have no shelves, desks, or any array of literary appointments as yet; and as to my ill-fated books, where are they? The Delaware has broken up to-day with prodigious violence, and some damage to property. Our little town is improving in manufactures. M. Sartori has brought over from France a complete apparatus for calico printing, together with experienced artificers. A dam across the river is talked of, and the Canal bill is before the Assembly. Upon next Tuesday an important suit in chancery is to be called up, brought by the manufacturing company of Paterson against the Morris Canal Company; the former charging the latter with withdrawing the waters of the Rockaway River from their manufactories.

In fulfilling my office as pastor, I am called every day to visit a young girl of seventeen in the last stage of consumption.

---

[1] Mr. Alexander was elected pastor of the congregation at Trenton in the autumn of 1828. He accepted the call, and preached his first sermon Saturday, January 10, 1829, preparatory to the Lord's Supper on the following day. The Presbytery did not meet for his installation until February 11. On that occasion his father presided, Dr. Miller delivered a discourse, the Rev. Mr. Cooley gave the charge to the pastor, and the Rev. Mr. Perkins, of Allentown, the charge to the congregation.

You know the flush of uncommon beauty, and the brilliancy of eye which sometimes characterize the countenances of those who are the victims of this hopeless disorder. These are in an eminent manner exemplified in this interesting creature. She was a belle, and one of the most thoughtless, and it was her sin and folly to defer preparation for death until the last hours of her life. In consequence of this she had suffered unspeakable pangs of remorse and apprehension, and my sympathies have been awakened by the appeals of this lovely yet dying penitent to me a feeble instrument, for some ground of hope. After many struggles, I cannot but hope that she has found secure rest in an unconditional surrender of herself to the mercies of God in Christ. No less than four young ladies within my limits are apparently dying with pulmonary complaints.

I have a notion of undertaking a history of New Jersey. Such a work is in great demand, and I am at the very fountain-head of information on the subject. I can have free access to all the old State papers. I have not got myself at all fixed yet, but am *progressing*, (see Webster in loco.) Pray did you know that *bridegroom* ought to be spelt *bridegoom?* See Webster's Dictionary again. If you ever get sight of a Dutch grammar please to buy it for me.

TRENTON, *January* 24, 1829.

It is difficult for me just at this time to enjoy as much leisure as I wish, as I have many visits to make, and have set out with the determination of writing at least part of my discourses. My father was here upon the 22d, and preached a sermon upon Intemperance. The legislature adjourned to attend, but not more than a dozen of them were present, much as they needed it. I mentioned to you in my last, the case of an interesting girl who seemed to be dying. She has now departed with great increase of hope in her last hours. I preached a discourse over her remains. Such scenes as these make me sometimes feel the vanity of all things below, and the importance of being more wholly devoted to preparation for eternity; but alas! the impression is too often momentary. My church numbers about two hundred and fifty communicants, but I think this is rather more than the number really attending with us. The Chief Justice (Ewing) of the State, is one of my main supporters, and Mr. Southard will soon be a hearer. Under the new circumstances I feel a greater stimulus to what may be called the external or literary part of preparation, than I ever experienced among my simple flock in Virginia. If you have never read Dunlop's History of Roman Literature, make it your business to peruse it immediately. It is at once learned and entertaining, enthusiastic and profound. At this time a company of Indians are the lions of Trenton, on their way to your city. As you have probably ventured very little into the palpable obscure of the German metaphysics, let me give you a single paragraph from a work which I have been reading; it refers to Fichte, one of the most popular of the followers of Kant. " The philosophy of Fichte speaks thus : I do not assume as a postulate that I am immortal, but I know it immediately, or intuitively, and I act as an immortal being, as an absolute and practical *Ich* (I), I am myself immortal; I have eternal life in myself, and God is in me, and united to me, while the absolute *I am myself* and God as an absolute *self*, can be nothing else than the absolute practical *Ich*, which is the object of thought. According to Fichte I am at every moment of my practical existence *God within;* for God is nothing else but what I am. Kant *believes* that there is a God: Fichte is intuitively certain of it, because his God is nothing else than the idea of his *Ich*." What think you of this? Surely the hospital would be the proper place for such philosophers, and yet all Germany is enamoured of such notions. Since I commenced this farraginous letter, my books have arrived, to my inexpressible joy. No husband ever greeted his wife more gladly after a six months' absence. My books are indeed my treasure, and limited as their number is, they are dear to me, as being the source of my greatest enjoyment. My study is my Paradise; and when evening has closed in upon me, and I find myself seated by a sparkling fire, with no threatening of interruption, and with a mind at ease, I envy not the autocrat of all the Russias.

TRENTON, *February* 17, 1829

I have been reading German until my head tingles with the echoes of harsh and sesquipedalian words, yet I leave the study with regret, because I find it more and more an interesting language, opening to me immense stores in every department of literature. The history of human opinion is one of the most agreeable of all subjects, and I have been reading an excellent history of Theological Science, by Professor Stäudlin of Göttingen. I have often given you a schedule of my daily employments; take the following for the present: it is my plan, but I need not say that I vary more or less every day, in practice. Rise at 7; breakfast at 8; study Original Scriptures, Theology, and Sermons until dinner at 1; afternoon spent in visiting; tea at 6; and then meetings, visits, reading, writing, &c., &c., until 11 or 12, when I creep into my cold bed. So far as I can learn any thing of my people, they seem disposed to treat me well, and are very much such a flock as I like to serve. There is intelligence enough to afford me some stimulus, and as I generally observe a regular theological method in the succession of my morning discourses, I am enabled to make my reading in divinity a preparation for the pulpit.

I am desirous of investigating what is commonly called the "Revival of Letters," especially in its relations to the Reformation. You may render me great assistance by referring me to books, and answering occasional queries on the subject. Be so good as to keep a quire of paper for such notes. For instance, What book is written expressly upon this subject? When did the revival of literature begin to take place? by whose means? What names are most distinguished in this great revolution? What books refer to it? Are any of the Latin works of Petrarca in your (Philadelphia) library? any ancient life of Petrarca? What can you find about Peter D'Ailly, (1425,) his works and influence, (in Latin Petrus de Alliacus?) John Gerson, Nic. v. Clemange. Laurentius Valla. Marsilius Ficinus. Ludovicus Vives. Any facts, or references, or books, will be gratefully received. I am in no great hurry, and as you read you may find some important items. In Noah's "Enquirer" of the 18th inst., I see a notice of the Anniversary of Tom Paine's birth-day, on the 29th ult., by the Society of Free Inquirers. It is a horrible outrage upon the moral and religious public. It would seem, however, to be punishment enough to be pilloried as they are by name, in their own account of their orgies. The Canal bill in this State, I apprehend, will either fail, or be encumbered with conditions never to be fulfilled. Our lower House of Legislature have just adopted a new school-system, similar in its leading features to that of New York. So far as attendance upon public worship, &c., is concerned, I am encouraged more and more every week; and am peculiarly comfortable and happy in my private circumstances.

If there is such an old-fashioned thing in any of your stores as an hour-glass, or a half-hour glass, (I prefer the latter,) oblige me by buying it for me, as I have a penchant for such a piece of furniture. I am just reading Irving's Columbus for the first time, with much pleasure. I esteem it the first of American classics, and can never be affected enough to join in the clamour against his crystal flow of purest English. The moral solemnity of Columbus's character, never before struck me; his perseverance, his noble confidence in truth, his stubborn resistance of every opposition. Our unfortunate Bombastes, Joel Barlow, showed some judgment in the choice of a subject, but he puffed it up like a bladder, and painted it like a butterfly, and even

American vanity could not keep up the bubble. I cannot express to you how much I loathe French poetry. Amazing! that a nation of taste should persevere in writing epics to the tune of—

" 'Tis the voice of the sluggard, I heard him complain
You have waked me too soon, I must slumber again."
E. g. " Quel besoin si pressant avez-vous de rimer?
Et qui diantre vous pousse à vous faire imprimer? "

John Wesley says, in one of his journals, that you might as well undertake to play an oration upon the jews-harp, as to write a heroic poem in French. Have you access to the following works? viz.: "Joh. Hen. Maii Vita Reuchlini." Humphry Hody's " De Græcis illustribus literarum Græcarum in Italia instauratoribus." "Museum Helveticum," (vol. iv., p. 163;) also any good history of the invention of printing, and its effects? You see my eye is fixed upon my great work, [see p. 122.] It shall not exceed three 4tos, wire-wove, hot-pressed paper, russia gilt. J. Murray, Albemarle st., price six guineas to subscribers, dedicated to the hon. John Hall, sen., Chief Justice of the United States.

TRENTON, *March* 2, 1829.

Mr. Walsh[1] seems much delighted to find a divine so truly wedded to his own system of Christian benevolence as Dr. Onderdonk shows himself to be. I cannot but consider the address of the Rt. Rev. gentleman one of the weakest defences even of that groundless scheme. Will he pretend to say that our country is not as well supplied with the means of grace as Palestine was when Paul went to the Gentiles? We *have* begun at Jerusalem, we still maintain our great force at home. The missionaries to the heathen are not one in a thousand of the teachers of religion. At what point shall we begin to send the truth abroad? when all at home are truly converted? Upon this principle the heathen will never be brought to God without a miracle. It is not true that we rob the cause of home missions by maintaining foreign missions; nor are the supporters of the latter indifferent to the former, for generally speaking, the money for sustaining both comes out of the same pockets. As to that truly Walshian sentence about " the proclivity of our country to the centrifugal and romantic," it is a proclivity which finds its precedent in the Christianity of the apostles. The school system lately adopted by our legislature, promises more for the good of New Jersey than any thing which has been known for a long time in our State. It owes its passage to the zeal and labour of a single man,

[1] In his opposition to foreign missionaries, on the ground that home duties were neglected.

Rev. Robert Baird, who has been keeping the subject before the minds of the people, in newspaper essays, for some months. If we aspire to *usefulness*, I know no way in which we can promise ourselves so much real success, though without noise or eclat. I have been advised to write a Commentary for the use of Sabbath school teachers, and I have the subject under consideration. It must soon be decided, or I shall be anticipated by some more rapid genius. I lecture to the teachers every Thursday evening, and bestow more preparatory labour upon this, than upon any of my services; it is by far the most delightful of my employments.

The Delaware is closed with ice, and the weather still savours more of winter than of spring. The suffering poor among us have excited some commiseration, and subscriptions are now in circulation for their relief. I have been reading Hare's Chemistry, and am greatly attracted by his wonderful mechanical ingenuity. Since leaving college, this is the only book which I have read upon the subject. Surely it would be profitable for us to review those studies, which we profess to think so important in the education of others.

TRENTON, *March* 26, 1829.

I have abandoned my literary projects, and have determined to set about a brief commentary upon the historical parts of the New Testament for the use of Sunday school teachers. The importance of such a work must be at once obvious. It need not be mentioned. If no one anticipates me I hope to be thus in some degree useful. I write in a straggling and tremulous manner, for I had a chill last night, and after sitting up until one, at your review,[1] and eating no breakfast, I am totally unfit to put pen to paper. I have read the documents upon the Panama mission so far as they have been published, and cannot perceive that they add much to Mr. Adams's reputation for wisdom. They set that scheme more in the light of a chimera than any thing I have before seen. From the review of Irving's new work, ["Conquest of Granada,"] I am not disposed to expect much from it. Mere battles are interesting to me only in real history, and not often there. I have no doubt that the reading which has been rendered necessary by your late undertaking, has impressed upon your mind the truth that biography is one of the most fascinating studies, and that the lives of the most eminent men have generally been written in a very slovenly manner. Let me recommend to you to set about the life of some eminent literary

[1] Of the translation of Milton's letters for the American Quarterly Review, June, 1829.

character. You may be sure of readers, if you make a proper selection. Amidst all the changes of public taste, biographies have been popular in every age. The life of Sir Walter Raleigh is so nearly connected with our own country's history, that it might be made a very attractive work. Gibbon once undertook the job, if I remember right.

TRENTON, *April* 4, 1829.

Those same letters of Milton are, in my opinion, as frothy a set of articles as I ever read. Suppose we publish *our* familiar letters; I am sure that the correspondence will be much more entertaining. I am truly ashamed of the stuff I have written as a Review, but do not see how I can amend it; it is quite short, and has little reference to the work, which indeed scarcely admits of extracts. I spent last evening at the house of Dr. Belleville, a French physician, who has been fifty years in this country. He is a devoted follower of Voltaire, but otherwise a venerable and estimable man. He is intimate with Survilliers, and supposes that he will publish an extended narrative of the events of the revolution and empire, in which he took any part. He represents the ex-king as a truly amiable man, of a literary turn, spending much of his time in his splendid library of French and Italian works. The Doctor showed me two very exquisite French prints of Joseph's daughters, presented by themselves. I have just been to a meeting held by Mr. Case, a Methodist missionary from Upper Canada, with some Indian converts. Mr. C. is a man without pretension, but is an honest-hearted and pious missionary, and I was sincerely gratified. Judge [Bushrod] Washington and his lady are here. There has been nothing very interesting in the Circuit Court.

TRENTON, *April* 8, 1829.

I have been reading John Adams's Defence of the American Constitution, and have found it a very interesting work. I am especially pleased with his abstract of the history of the Italian republic, which I have never found so clearly given in any other book. It has almost set me upon studying Italian, and reading Machiavel, Guicciardini, Malavolti, &c., in the original. A general survey of all history, with reference to the principles of our constitution, would be a great and useful work. It seems to me that our Colleges ought to have lectures upon that very subject. The simple principles assumed as fundamental by Adams, have really cast a new light upon all the history I have read. The annals of all nations seem to be a commentary upon the doctrine that the three primary forms of government must be so tempered and balanced in every government, as to check the extravagance of each. My translation from Rosenmüller, and Review of Scholz, have appeared in the Biblical Repertory.

TRENTON, *May* 4, 1829.

I entertain lively anticipations with regard to the results of your introduction to the modern Johnson, [Mr. Walsh.] There are few men in our country whose acquaintance would be a greater prize. May you have many profitable and pleasant hours in his conversazioni. I hope that you will come forth from the den of lions, unscathed as Daniel. I have some curiosity to know how many letters I have written to you.[1] I have the most of yours, but among my various peregrinations some of them have been lost. I am unable to accept your invitation to dinner on the 5th, yet I will drink to the continuance of our correspondence in *water*, the only beverage to which I have access. Judge Gould's letter is in my view one of the most just and most severe castigations that Mr. Adams has received. Not that I love J. Q. A. less, but that I love Federalism more. I have been reading Terence lately with much pleasure. He is the only Latin poet in whose writings I have ever found simple pathos. I might except some of Virgil's sad descriptions, but in the case of Virgil, the pomp of the verse, and the artificial epithets, detract from the effect. In the Andria and Hecyra of Terence, there are some of the most charming touches of deep feeling. Erasmus knew Terence and Horace by heart. Who ever could say as much for Milton or Pope? I have seen a man who could repeat four books of Paradise Lost.

I am fully persuaded that there is no department in which a man may be so sure of arriving at eminence as in the modern languages. All my study of this kind has been for amusement, and yet I am surprised at my own progress, and convinced that one who would devote himself to the subject, might in five years have the choice of authors in German, French, Spanish, Italian, Dutch, and Portuguese. A scholar in modern languages may take what department he chooses, read always what is entertaining, and yet have the reputation of a great linguist or critic.

If I had the access which you have to libraries of French and Italian works, I should make these languages a main object; but where one must buy every book, at an exorbitant price, the private student labours under great disadvantages. Will you oblige me by purchasing "A selection from Italian prose-writers, with translations according to the Hamiltonian system"? My

---

[1] This was the ninety-ninth.

reasons for wishing this is, that my greatest difficulty in languages arises from the particles, and little words, especially auxiliary verbs, and oblique cases of pronouns, as well as adverbs and conjunctions which have various meanings. These may all be learned in a week's time from a living teacher, or a very literal translation. I find no books so well adapted to take away the darkness of a new language as travels and biography. I wish to get Goldoni's life by himself, if it can be procured separately. Is the life of Boccacio at a moderate price? Quere. How should we exist if so separated as to have our correspondence by letter broken up? After ten years' use it has become with me almost a necessary of life. I have just read Carter's travels, [in Europe,] and like it well, with two exceptions. 1. He is forever foisting in the classics, reading Catullus on the grass; Horace in the diligence; Virgil passim: while he betrays wonderful ignorance in some simple points of antiquity, does not know what a Hermes is, which Kennet might have taught him, and denies the well-known tradition of Luke's having been a painter. 2. He compares every thing with New York, and makes out the latter to be the greatest city in the world.

TRENTON, *May* 11, 1829.

With this, my hundredth letter, accept my warmest congratulations and wishes for the continuance of our correspondence. A catalogue of our many topics would be quite extensive. I am often amused when I call to mind the freaks of fancy which used to enliven our early letters. By the bye, did I ever tell you that I remember having seen your first attempt at epistolary writing? It was a letter to your aunt, now deceased, who received it while she was on a visit to my mother.

When I have another inspiration I will patch up something for the [National] Gazette. I will translate some classical excerpts, to be incorporated among his own, if he will accept them; likewise a brief memoir of the celebrated Buchanan. In your library hours, look me out a few hints, particularly opinions of scholars as to his latinity and poetry. I have Johnson's works, but cannot turn to the compliment which I remember he pays to Buchanan. Mayhap it is in Bozzy. Have you seen any book upon Italian literature, which takes the same view of it which Dunlop does of Roman? Prof. Ticknor, of Harvard, has furnished the Spanish student with a useful manual of this kind. I have been reading over the last twelve books of the Iliad, Terence's Eunuchus, and have got half through Plautus. Spring has some hard struggles with the winter, which seems disposed to adhere to the throne, being made arrogant, I suppose, by so long a reign. There is a good deal of verdure about Trenton; yet I sigh for the open country, and remember with regret the tracts over which I could expatiate in Virginia, the forests, the streams,

"The mossed oaks
Which have outlived the eagle."

Yet I should be loth to have you suppose that I am discontented. In no place I think, except Princeton, could I be more at ease. There is no sort of liberty more precious in my eyes than the liberty of visiting only when and where you please. Now this is what a Pastor cannot enjoy. He must visit all his people; and if he does this faithfully, he is cut off from almost every other out of door's work. In Princeton I scarcely ever went anywhere oftener than necessity drove me. You may conceive how little qualified I am for indiscriminate visits. I am averse to making new acquaintances, and fond of sitting at home, while I have an exquisite relish for the society of one or two whose pursuits are congenial, and with whom I can live without any mask of ceremony or dignity.

Mr. Southard is very much broken; stoops like a man of seventy, and seems melancholy. If he recovers, he will probably be our next Governor. My old room-mate Waterbury has removed to Portsmouth, N. H. Kirk has abundant encouragement at Albany; great increase of numbers in his church.

TRENTON, *May* 15, 1829.

Dull—headache last-night—exceedingly Mondayish. Read Schiller's Don Carlos on Saturday, and do not hesitate to pronounce it the finest tragedy I ever perused. Am reading Wallenstein, which is considered his chef-d'œuvre. Also the Decamerone of Boccacio. The Biblical Repertory is likely to become a more important work; a number of clergymen have determined to establish it as a theological review.

Lafayette's hogshead of dirt[1] is, I think, unworthy of the good sense he has always manifested; it is in genuine French taste, however. As a testimony of his affection for America, we cannot but receive it respectfully. He might have requested to be interred at Mount Vernon, which would have been more truly honourable.

May 26.

Rain, rain, rain. I had intended to rise very early and take a walk upon the banks of our delightful river, but am weather

---

[1] He sent for a quantity of the soil of the United States for his private cemetery.

bound. Leigh Hunt's book is exceedingly amusing. I have half a notion to write my own life. Coleridge's Biographia Literaria is a book that will amply remunerate you for any hours you may spend over it. I do not know whether I mentioned to you that Attorney-General Berrien will deliver the annual oration before the Societies at Princeton. You will inform me of what is to be seen in the Academy of Arts, and as soon as possible any very interesting business before the [General] Assembly. I have finished "Wallenstein," which is in three parts; it is a drama of intense interest. Schiller approaches in style to the highest flights of Shakspeare, and produces much of the same deep and personal interest in the fortunes of his heroes, that is experienced in reading Scott's most commanding works. I have tried to admire Corneille, but I need no force to fill me with wonder at the powers of the great German poet. Mr. [Rev. I. V.] Brown's High School [at Lawrenceville] has opened with thirty-six scholars, his buildings are in rapid progress. His "French gentleman" is Mr. Louis Hargous, the best Frenchman I have ever seen, and one who is a most accurate and well-read English scholar; his "Native of Germany," is C. J. Haldemann, a lawyer and P. D. of Heidelberg, a pupil of the celebrated Dr. Paulus. His principal teachers are Rev. L. Leake, of N. J., and his son George Brown. It will be a good school.

TRENTON, *June* 27, 1829.

Presuming that you will be able to redeem time enough from your review of the "Egarements" and your musical refections to perstringe a sheet of foolscap, I take my pen to inform you that I am not in good health, and hoping that these lines will find you not in the same. Bile, bile, bile! thou chief of mysteries! The old women tell of the stomach's being full of bile, and how it gets into the blood and eyes, and makes the face yellow. The doctors talk of secretions and excretions, of structural and functional derangement of the liver. I shall probably be forced to go to the springs before long. If you are disposed to go in company, it would add much to my satisfaction; yet my jaunt would probably be simply to Saratoga and Ballston, without many divergent steps. I have really no time nor spirit at present for writing for Walsh. This laborious commentary takes up as much time as an extensive and critical work would do; for while the results are very simple and concise, I am under the necessity of collating a number of works, and am forced "depromere magno acervo." Have you read Cadwallader Colden's letter on Masonry? It is the most conclusive argument which I have seen on the subject, and the more weighty as coming from a mason of high standing.

I visited Mr. Brown's school, and am much pleased with his arrangements, while I cannot but think there is something visionary in the new-fangled gymnastics. Boys, if kept at it as a part of their work, will soon be glad to exchange climbing a mast, and vaulting over a wooden horse, for climbing cherry-trees and playing at ball. The suffrage of all ages is in favour of some of our traditionary games, and if I mistake not, even in Greece and Rome, to the example of which we constantly defer, children were left to the freedom of their own will, with regard to their sports. Military exercises, if they could be introduced without the military spirit, would be a happy improvement in physical education, and riding, fencing, (to which you will add dancing,) and the ordinary athletics, have stood the test of centuries. The most important change in the new German system is the increase of teachers, as connected with separate rooms for the various classes. This ought to ensure competent instruction in every branch, and give a variety to the daily course which is highly desirable. The modern languages I hope to see taught in every respectable academy, to which I would certainly add *facilities* for music and drawing. This discourse is doubtless edifying, and is occasioned partly by my desire to fill the sheet, and partly by the interest which I happen to be taking at this time in the subject. [Pause—during which I have lectured upon John v. 17–30.] There is in Schiller a memoir of the Marechal de Vielleville, who made a great figure in France during the reigns of Francis I. and Henry II. It is one of the most stirring pieces of old chivalric history which I have ever read. In a different line it excites the same sort of interest with the life of Cellini, and is quite a romance in itself. If there were any way of publishing it, I would translate it; but it is too long for a magazine, and too short to be put by itself. It is 147 pp. very small duodecimo.

TRENTON, *July* 6, 1829.

I preached a 4th of July sermon yesterday from Deut. viii. 10-20; read the passage. The 2d company of State Fencibles [of Philadelphia] was present; they came up to celebrate the 4th, which they did by trudging about in the mire, and ducking themselves thoroughly. I went directly on to Princeton on Tuesday, and there remained until Friday. My health is quite comfortable, and I still hope to get through the summer without any serious attack of my annual complaint. Cold work at Saratoga, I guess. It would be delightful now to make an excursion to Quebec. I am half resolved to undertake it. Our friends have a charming week before them, without fear of being roasted or suffocated. Wordsworth, among many silly affectations, has a number of splendid passages. He makes one love nature, and directs the attention to a thousand neglected objects of every day's occurrence; while there is a purity and a benevolence in all his thoughts which are rare and charming.

My feeling of good-for-nothing-ness is such that I would gladly spend my whole time for some weeks in riding about the country. It is an excuse for doing nothing, while it occupies the mind, and dissipates ennui. William delivered, or was to deliver, an oration at Harlingen (a Dutch village in the hills north of Princeton) on Saturday last. There was no celebration in this place; indeed, this town is evidently in its dotage. The houses totter, and even our church-steeple has a paralytic tremour, whenever the bell is rung. The very river loses its animation as soon as it reaches Trenton, and in some lanes the grass contends with the pavement. Heigh-ho! I sigh for the greenness and variety of Princeton. Perhaps the change is solely in myself, age creeping on, animal vigour decaying. Some gray hairs variegate my head, and I have a monitory decay of the teeth, and trembling of the hand. I beg leave to say that you have no business to be remaining in Philadelphia during the summer. You ought to strike out some untrodden path, where no tourists have ever roamed. Make a classical tour through Maryland. Go to the west end of Lake Erie. Spend a week at Cape Henlopen. Take ship with me for Newfoundland. Niagara is as common as a Navarino hat, and Saratoga is no better than a beer-stall. I have a great desire to go to Cuba, not just at this season however. Have you obtained for me the chaplaincy at the Navy Yard?

Mr. Randolph reminds Mr. Walsh (29th ult.) of "the beautiful birds of the Spice Islands, they must fly against the wind." How aptly might Mr. R. retort that there are certain birds that always fly *with* the wind, "from what quarter soever it may blow." In Mr. W.'s tirades against the enlarged charities of the day, and his exclusive plea for our own poor, he reminds me of an occurrence recorded in John xii. 4, 5, not that I would insinuate that the cases are parallel. It is the glory of Christian benevolence that it is discursive, and makes itself felt beyond the little circle of home. After all I acknowledge that there may be, and perhaps are, too many divergent channels of charity.

A clear day—how nature seems to rejoice! The humming birds are already at the creeper which runs over my window, and I hear songs on every side; quaker women walk about " in glory and in joy; " horses are taken to bathe in the river; carts of hay crowd into the streets; babies paddle about in the mud-puddles; these are the rural sights and sounds which I now perceive. O for a breeze from the kennels of Water street, [Philadelphia,] or a glimpse of lowly Willing's alley, or the proclamation of raspberries; or any thing to make me think I was in the midst of a bustling city. Among the attendant benefits of war, it ought to be mentioned that it burns up dismal old towns, and makes room for new ones.

You will consider this as an answer to the letter which you have written to-day. It and its precursor are so long, that you must confess yourself in debt, though they contain nothing.

TRENTON, *July* 15, 1829.

You might keep up an interesting series of translations of the notices of American literature in the "Révue Encyclopédique." Mr. Walsh would furnish you the Révue, and, I suppose, be glad of the articles. If I were a cit I should do it myself. In the [German] Conversations-lexicon, I am informed that Joseph Bonaparte occupies the late seat of Gen. Moreau in Pennsylvania, that the two great national works of the U. S. are Marshall's Washington, and Wirt's P. Henry. I have just read Goethe's Goetz von Berlichingen, with vast delight. It has all the excellences of Ivanhoe, in dramatic form. You can get an idea of the subject from Scott's synonymous abortion. Goethe was an idolater of Byron, though he justly charged the latter with stealing largely from him. Among Americanisms insert the following: "*Slatted over.*" Illustration: At last Middlesex court, a woman giving evidence against her husband, testified that he "slatted her over;" this she repeated many times. The daughter also testified that he had several times when angry "slatted her over;" and all the witnesses concurred in declaring that he frequently "slatted her over." Bench and bar were non-plussed. No light could be thrown on the mystery. At last W. C. A. asked one of the grand jury whether this was a provincialism of South Amboy. He said it was partially so, being confined in its use to the "Devil's half-acre," where it meant "push her." I imagine that Webster's dictionary will never be current. The plan of citing *names*, instead of *passages*, is unsatisfactory and unfair.

CAPE ISLAND, [CAPE MAY,] *August* 4, 1829.

After a beautiful sunrise, we have now a heavy storm of rain, brought up with a S. b. W. wind. This gives me an hour of leisure for writing, whereas I should otherwise have been at sea about this time. A party of us had made arrangements to take a pilot-boat for Cape Henlopen, but were afraid of a storm. We had between forty and fifty passengers on our way down, and although we encountered a squall, all things went off pleasantly enough. On landing I found that we were to be under conduct of the renowned Aaron Skellinger, who figures in the various characters of wagon-driver, boat-builder, superintendent of sunday school, precentor and leader of fishing parties. We took lodging at the smallest and least fashionable house, and I have had no reason to repent my choice. The company is quiet, the attendance good, and the fare even sumptuous. Mrs. Bennett, our hostess, is the mother of Hughes who keeps the "Big House." We have here Judge Hallowell of your city. I have never spent so many pleasant hours at any place of summer resort. The beach is delightful, and the company very agreeable. Mr. Duncan of Baltimore, Dr. Collins of Washington, Mr. Latimer of Philadelphia, and several Baltimore ladies, are those with whom I chiefly consort. The usual walks and rides are taken, the ordinary quantity of fish, oysters, crabs, terrapins, lobsters, and game is consumed, and I take the surf twice every day, viz.: at $4\frac{1}{2}$ A. M., and 6 P. M. Occasionally I have tried it at noon. Preached last Sunday at the Cold Spring Church, where a good portion of the strangers attended.

A great majority of the men about here are pilots. Upon the two capes they reckon eighty. It interests me very much to talk with them about their adventures. It was but a few minutes ago that I saw two of them pass through a raging surf to reach a boat which lay beyond the breakers. The face of the country gives me an agreeable surprise, as well as the people, who have that happy mediocrity and thrift which are so conspicuous in New England, whence the settlers of Cape May migrated. A number of very remarkable cures have been wrought by the salt water this season, especially in cases of rheumatism. A gentleman from Kentucky who came here upon crutches, gave them to his landlord at his departure. This place is in my estimation incomparably above Long Branch, and I have scarcely experienced a single moment of ennui or disappointment since my arrival. I have, however, regretted every day that you did not accompany us. To-morrow, if the day is fair, we propose going over to Cape Henlopen and Lewistown, and on Saturday, with leave of Providence, I shall meet you in the "gude town."

From the freshness of the air, and the frequency of sea breezes, I have been exempt from all suffering from heat; during the noon-tide, however, I read; have made out to finish Goethe's Wilhelm Meister, an untranslatable and fascinating romance. It reminds me of the characteristic excellences of Tristram Shandy and Gil Blas, and abounds in a delicate naïveté and in luscious descriptions. I am now groaning over the Sorrows of Werter, an unprincipled book, but one which has been barbarously caricatured in the English version. I have also read a number of Luther's Letters, some of which are gross to a degree.

TRENTON, *August* 24, 1829.

Quid rei? that is to say, What is the matter? Are you absent, or sick, or has some calamity really befallen you? N. B. I have just read Capt. [Basil] Hall's Travels, and have had many hearty laughs over it. I am not disposed altogether to condemn the work, as Mr. Walsh and Stone [Commercial Advertiser] do. He gives us rough handling, it is true, but then it seems to be the expression of honest John Bullism. If our eyes were but open, we might learn some important lessons from his strictures. Inter nos, I accede to many of his political doctrines, and join in his abomination of absolute democracy. He certainly deserves our praise for his suppression of all names, except when he speaks in commendation. My Commentary is done up, that is, supplanted by a work nearly complete, of the same kind, by Rev. Albert Barnes, of Morristown.

TRENTON, *September* 14, 1829.

I have been rather dilatory in consequence of a press of business which has entirely prevented that quiet state of mind in which one desires to write a letter. Our opinions of Capt. Hall just crossed one another, and I am pleased to find that we do not altogether differ about his merits. If you abstract all that he has said concerning our government, what remains will be rather commendatory. Addison has consigned to me his papers and notes upon Sacred Geography, and I have been engaged in finishing the book, [for Am. Sunday School Union,] so that we shall have it between us. The labour has been very irksome. I spent twelve hours last week verifying the texts of Scripture referred to, by looking for all of them. The mere geographical part is interesting, although it is discouraging to find how little is really known of the site of many ancient places. I was invited to preach at the Tenth Church [Philadelphia, then without a pastor] on the 12th. " Qui bene latuit bene vixit." Had a very pleasant interview of three or four hours with Skinner and Christmas. The death of Mr. [Rev. Matthias] Bruen, is a severe stroke to the church and to his aged father. He was eminently useful as a member of the public religious associations of New York. I am told that his library is one of the most splendid in America. There is a Miss —— from —— here, who is one of the most intelligent young ladies I know. Approaching a little to the *bas-bleu*, she has gayety and wit enough to throw a little charm around the formidableness of her learning. It is really a treat to be with her.

O si sic omnia! (viz. feminæ.) There is a peculiar force in what Dr. Johnson said of Mrs. Thrale, if I remember aright: "Thrale is a good creature to sit by; she understands what you say." I have been trying for some time to pay a visit to your city, but have been sometimes unwell, sometimes day and night at Geography, sometimes necessarily at Princeton, and at present without a decent pair of pantaloons. I will send you a couple of pieces by Addison and myself for Walsh. [Gazette.] We propose to continue writing in Co. [under signature of *Didymus*.] Addison pretends that he is completing his review. [J. A. A. reviewed Mohammedan History in the American Quarterly Review, March, 1830, and the Gulistan of Sadi, and Anthon's Horace, in September, 1830.]

Pray do you know any thing of Vertot's History of the Knights of Malta? I have lately seen it very highly extolled, especially in a piece of Schiller's. Item. Does your library contain "The Travels of Theodore Ducas, by Mills"? Again, for what price can Mitford's History of Greece be obtained? N. B. Gibbon's Rome may be imported from Germany in 12mo, 12 vols., good paper and print, for 6 Rix dollars, ($4.20.) I have seen a specimen. Dr. Livingston's Life was taken by *A. Gunn*, (as appears from the advertisement.) I want the book, having a great veneration for the character of the good old Dr. He was to the Ref. Dutch church what Bishop White is to the Episcopal, except that he had incomparably more learning and eloquence. I shall ever remember him as the best specimen of the ancient school of clerical manners.

TRENTON, *September* 23, 1829.

Mr. Walsh has got an honourable advantage of the scurrilous writer in the National Journal. That paper is taking too much the ground which the Telegraph occupied while it was in the opposition. Mr. W. certainly deserves the credit of being dignified and courteous, whether right or wrong. I am in no respect, however, more pleased with the present powers. Read the new Post-Office decrees, as an illustration of the grammatical rule touching the use of "shall" and "will." Mr. ——— has been some days in Trenton. He spent several hours with me last evening. I should imagine from his language that the New Haven school approximates more towards German liberality, or rather indifference to doctrine, than any community of Theologians out of Massachusetts. He said, for instance, that he viewed the verbal coincidences of the first three gospels, as arising from the copying an original oral gospel, which long passed from person to person; that we must admit that the Bible contains a Mythology, as well as a Theology. You are aware that the latter hypothesis is that by means of which the German Neologists explain away all the miracles. I beg that you will come on to commencement, at least to hear Berrien's speech. Our trustees seem to have no power to supply the two vacancies in the faculty of the college. I propose that we apply for the appointments: I will teach language, and you chemistry. I have always thought—to speak seriously—that a situation as Editor would suit your tastes and talents remarkably well. But how or where? If Mr. Walsh wanted a partner, and you could turn your coat, that would undoubtedly be the place, but of either of these contingencies I have no expectation. A weekly journal, purely literary and scientific, ought to find patronage in your city; something which should have the excellences of Museum, the weekly Reviews of England, and the literary part of Walsh. Is there no publisher who would enterprise such a thing, and assume the pecuniary responsibility? This might perhaps be out of the line in which you wish to move; if so, you must either become author, or Jackson man. By opening your mouth foully for the Administration, you may be made consul at Martinique, by the time that ———— has been done over by the climate.

This is one of those gloomy days which makes a man willing to keep close within doors. At such times, I find myself less disposed either to converse or make any special exertion, than when the sun enlivens all nature. I have no reason to complain of low spirits, a malady of which I scarcely know any thing at present; but there is often a sort of pettishness and ill-humour, which is produced in equal degrees by a long beard, a dirty shirt, or nasty weather. I have been reading Schiller's History of the Thirty Years' War in Germany, in which Gustavus Adolphus, Oxenstiern, and Wallenstein were so much celebrated. It is a masterpiece of history, and abounds especially in distinct and striking portraits of great characters. His Lectures on Universal History are also very fine; though they abound in infidel sentiments. When I can get a copy to suit me I intend to read the Odyssey; and am about going over Terence, which I have already studied at long intervals. If I had access to a complete library, I should attempt the ancient historians, in translations. To toil through the original would be to me a mere waste of time. The article on Cromwell [Christian Spectator] by [W. T.] Dwight is very boldly and ably written, but perhaps goes too far, as it is intended to show that he was a genuine patriot, and a sincerely pious Christian. Still I believe that the general opinions of Cromwell are far too dark, being drawn from the suspicious representations of royalists. As if unwilling to judge him by his deeds, some of which are bad enough, they attribute even his good actions to hypocrisy.

TRENTON, *October* 14, 1829.

You have seen the appointments made by the trustees for Princeton college. In Mr. Vethake [Natural Philosophy] they have a great acquisition. Every day or two I have been hoping to visit Philadelphia, but obstacles have continually risen up. Just now, the sudden death of one of my people, and the apparently mortal disease of another, must detain me. Mr. Berrien's discourse exceeded all expectations. It was not profound, and contained few indications of comprehensive grasp of mind, or creative genius, yet from its exquisite polish it will appear well in print. Mr. B.'s manner is the most perfect specimen of artificial oratory I have ever witnessed.

How is it that Texas has just been discovered to be so remarkably fertile and valuable? In Darby's Gazetteer I find it represented as a barren waste, almost entirely destitute of spring water, and destined forever to be a wilderness. This, I suppose, is to be the Panama question of the Jackson cabinet. I understand that Gov. Giles is publishing an opinion that a separation of the Northern from the Southern States would be highly advantageous to the latter. In such an event, which is no longer improbable, it is to be wished that you and I may not have migrated south of the Potomac; Faxit Deus! By way of a Hindoo idol, in the last Philadelphian, we had an exact copy of the Ephesian Diana; see Calmet's Dictionary.

You ask me my opinion about preachers. I think that of the 17th century, John Howe and Barrow are the first; and of the 19th Robert Hall, whom I prefer to any sermonizer I have ever read. His sermon entitled "Modern Infidelity Considered," is unequalled. For deep pathos, Samuel Davies is surpassed by none, but he often sins against good taste. I am reading Gough's History of the Quakers, and am more and more convinced that George Fox was the true progenitor of the Hicksites.

PRINCETON, *October* 24, 1829.

It is probable that a letter from you lies unopened in the post-office at Trenton, as I have been absent a week at Synod, which met at the delightful town of Newark, and from which I returned last night, much exhausted with late and early sessions. On Monday's afternoon boat I expect to take passage for Philadelphia expecting to leave it upon the succeeding day for Richmond. I may spend a few hours with you. A partial engagement has been entered into by the directing committee of the

Biblical Repertory *and Theological Review* [its additional title] to make me editor, (I still residing in Trenton.)

TRENTON, *December* 4, 1829.

Yea: it is not to be dissembled that I feel a very lively satisfaction in finding myself in my own den, by my own fire, dipping into the accustomed inkstand, and listening (as I do this moment) to the clock of my own church. This pleasure is enhanced by finding a welcome, where I expected a scolding,[1] and by renewed assurances of regard from my people; a regard which I reciprocate more cordially every day. In hours of discontent, I sometimes wish myself a thousand leagues away, and fancy that no one has so many perplexities; but the difficulties which afflict me arise, I am sure, from my own culpable indisposition to be faithful, and whither could I fly, where a slothful and evil heart would not make me unhappy? Once I have had experience of the wretchedness of leaving an affectionate people, and the experiment is one of which I crave no repetition. Unless, like ———, I could depart, without notice to quit, or any premonitory grumblings, I should scarcely sustain the mortification of declaring such an intention. At the house of Chief Justice Ewing, I saw to-day, in a frame, the original letter of acknowledgment sent by Gen. Washington to the ladies of Trenton, after his triumphal entry. It hangs very appropriately under a print from Sully's " Passage of the Delaware." The worshipful Legislature of our State have adjourned until January 1st. A bare probability that the Canal Bill will pass. About half of this town has just changed hands, by the recent sale of the real estate of the late Abraham Hunt. The manufactures of the place are in the " sear and yellow leaf." Sartori's calico factory has expired. Page's cotton factory has finally stopped. The Wells's, proprietors of the only remaining and principal manufacturing establishment, have gone to Pottsville. The prospect is lamentable. Unless the canal should be made, and should be profitable, the place is gone at once, and the final blow will be struck by the removal of State business.

I have turned over in my mind many times, since I saw you, the case of Doddridge, as exhibited in his Correspondence,[2] and have been much puzzled to come to any conclusion as to the bearing which these new revelations have upon his religious character. Perhaps he was not a pious man at all, when he wrote that letter, and flamed out in such exorbitant affection. Perhaps

---

[1] He had spent the month of November in a visit to Charlotte Court House, Virginia.

[2] Diary and Correspondence, then lately published by his great-grandson.

a grain of wheat might have existed amidst the bushel of worldly chaff, and these may be the worst specimens of his whole life. Perhaps he was just such a frivolous, inconsistent, volatile clergyman, as one you wot of, who sometimes fears that his religion is a mere name, and whose conversation and life are a daily source of mortification and compunction. It gives me pain to be forced to look at the nakedness of a Father in Israel, as it does to read that vile calumny of the infidel ——, upon the Father of his Country. May we not gather from these and other such testimonials the truth, that we over-rate the greatness of our predecessors, and that the sages and Christians of former days were fallible and human, like ourselves? (See Ecclesiastes vii., 10.)

Suffer me to give you a French pun which I had from Mr. Hargous. A celebrated café of Paris, much frequented by the provincials during the revolution, had the sign of John the Baptist, under which was "*Au grand Saint Jean Baptiste.*" The authorities informed the publican that saints were now abolished, and that the sign must come down. He replied that it would ruin him, as everybody knew it by that name; but after some study changed the face into that of a monkey, and the inscription so as to have the same sound, "*Au grand Singe, en Baptiste.*"

I observe that Martin, whose illustrations of Milton have attracted our attention, is mentioned as the greatest master of design in England: he was brought into notice by West. If you should see offered in the shops any single engraving from his paintings, I should like to hear of it. Delightful wintry weather, and proposals for a snow. If the sleighing should be good, you will do well to come up before Christmas. Next Thursday is Thanksgiving Day, by order of the Governor, a sort of movable feast which comes in place of saints' days. I recommend the foregoing epistle as a specimen of connected and systematic thought, natural arrangement, and artful transition.

TRENTON, *December* 25, 1829.

You have expressed my sentiments precisely with regard to Summerfield's Life [by Holland.] Not one description of his manner of preaching! not a word which conveys the slightest idea of that which we all remember as the most striking thing about him; if we except a few newspaper squibs. If it were not for what the book contains of his own, I would not harbour it. The two letters which I have, are after all as good as any there.

There is a young man by the name of Winchester, from Baltimore, in the Princeton Seminary, who is one of the best speakers I have heard there. In case of a want in your city, it might be advisable to give him a trial. The Spruce streeters will show much ignorance of such matters if they continue to search after old men, or antiquated young ones.[1] Addison is much pleased with his new employments, [with Prof. Patton in his lately established school.] The school promises to succeed beyond expectation.

Whatever the advantages of early rising may be, there is one gratification which it affords, viz., the delight of sitting in your chair, with fixed and staring eyes, perfectly content to indulge in meditation, as comatose as a cat, and even at times purring for very pleasure; in a word, asleep with your eyes open.

TRENTON, *December* 26, 1829.

In your newspaper scheme, as in all that concerns your welfare, I feel sincerely and deeply interested; and let me say in the gross, all that you have asked, I will do—so far as my ability reaches. But do not expect too much: remember that I am pulled hither and thither, that I now have much anxiety about the Repertory, and make allowances for the moments of lassitude, ennui, and good-for-nothing-ness which are occurring from time to time. As to the name I concur, ["Morning Journal."] It is simple and significant. A hyper-critic might perhaps see some tautology in it, but it is good. As to literature, you are certainly right in not making it prominent at the *first*. I shall keep a sheet always ready for scraps, and contributions to your Balaam-box. I have recently heard a gentleman of intelligence say that during the wars of Napoleon, Duane [of the "Aurora"] was distinguished above all his contemporary editors for the extent and accuracy of his geographical information, and so arranged his foreign extracts, and his comments, as to give his readers a clear view of every great movement of the campaigns. Generally speaking, the foreign news is so huddled together, that it is almost impossible to arrange it into a whole, even with much study. This evil is much diminished where an editor will take the pains to give, in a sentence or two, by way of coup d'œil, the result of his readings. Nothing from abroad is more interesting than views taken by foreigners of American manners, men, and measures. I am always pleased, also, to have in addition to the mere facts, extracts from the Editorial treatises which so much abound in London papers. Bow-street trials are not to be despised, and indeed I suppose you are already convinced that you must be very unfastidious, so as to please "the many-headed monster." There are even artifices which an editor may and must use, however undignified he might consider them under

---

[1] The Rev. Samuel G. Winchester was called to the Spruce Street congregation shortly after the date of this letter, and was installed May 4, 1830.

other circumstances. He may frame a paragraph so as to introduce a quotation, and he may find Ayscough's Index no despicable auxiliary.

There is no literary labour which brings a man so much before the heterogeneous mass of human society as the editing a newspaper. Other writings may be said to pertain to one class of judges, but you write for the democracy at large. In this your views must be somewhat like those of ancient Greeks, who read their productions to the populace. I am far from thinking, however, that there needs to be any sacrifice of independence or integrity in an editor. A sop may here and there be thrown to the barking Cerberus, but even this monster may be appeased by the " golden branch " which Eneas carried.

If you are short of " horrid murders " and " shocking accidents " and " awful dispensations ! ! ! " I can furnish them by the gross, as I have been reading Schiller lately, and have my imagination sufficiently wrought up.

I suppose you begin with the new year; and I wish you a happy year of it. You may, if you are going to take party ground, make a very good article upon Branch's message, [Secretary of Navy,] showing that all his recommendations which are of any value were made before by his predecessor. The New York Commercial is in my view a very good model. Mr. Walsh is always dignified and able, but always in buckram.[1]

TRENTON, *February* 17, 1830.

A bill legalizing horse-racing has gone through second reading in the House. Lobby members very brisk, some for railroads, some for canal, some for oysters, some for race course, or as one of our members endorsed it on his bill *rase corss*. Apropos of spelling, I saw an endorsement on a file of bills : " An act to abbollish prisoners for debt, in certin cases. Posponded." I certainly approve of the wisdom of the house in *posponding* any bill so cruel in its purposes. If you alight in any way upon any papers relating to Institutions for the *Blind* or the *Deaf and Dumb*, let me have sight of them, as I am engaged in collecting upon these subjects. I have been applied to, to write an article upon " Prison Discipline " for Dr. Lieber's Encyclopædia [Americana.] An odd subject surely for me.

I am in some difficulty about the Hebrew accents, those I mean which are used as musical notes. Stuart refers to the following books. Will you inform me whether they are in any of

---

[1] During the six months that the daily newspaper referred to in this letter was under the editorial direction of his friend, Mr. Alexander was a frequent contributor to its columns.

your libraries, and whether any musical notes are given? *Jablonskii Præf. ad Bib. Heb.* § 24, and *Bartoloccii Bibliotheca Rabbinica*, Tom. iv., p. 431.

I am very much discouraged as to my ever being of much use in the world, from a mortifying conviction of my very great fickleness of purpose, or rather perhaps I ought in justice to myself to say, variableness of feeling. A subject or an enterprise deeply interests and engages me for a month, and then before I am able to do any thing practically, I have come under the influence of a new passion which urges me in another direction. It is humbling to say so, but I really believe myself to be a visionary. Just at this moment, I am very much impressed with a sentiment which I cannot express otherwise than thus: "It is the duty of some men to devote their attention to the relief of the temporal miseries of mankind." Let me explain. I do not exclude spiritual beneficence; I do not mean that a man should become a knight errant; but I verily think that Christians are not touched as they should be with human suffering, bodily suffering, privation, &c., &c. Now, if a few men would concentrate their thoughts upon this, write upon it, paragraph upon it, influence the press, talk upon it, in a word Clarksonize, I believe great things must be done. In reading the N. T. I have recently been much struck with the fact that *all* the miracles of our Saviour were acts of benevolence, and usually in *relief of human bodily distresses.* Now, the thought has powerfully come over me, Am I, and are Christians, acting in any degree like their master? I have recently preached upon the subject from Heb. xiii., 3. I have an idea that the amount of effort now put forth in Christendom would produce a hundred times as much real good, if it were systematized and properly directed. Perhaps this crude thought will not be lost upon you. It may serve to gender cogitations of your own and to direct your scissors.

TRENTON, *June* 7, 1830.

I feel, I am sure, more tenderly than ever, the obligations of that friendship which has so long and so happily subsisted between us. My regret is, that your loss is such, that condolence and counsel are the most that the kindest friend can offer. Believing, as we both do, that all human affairs are under a most wise and holy ordering, our *judgment* may rest in firm assurance that all is right; we may be convinced that it ought not to be otherwise. To school the heart is more difficult, but I believe it to be possible through the application of the same truths. Let me earnestly beg of you, then, to seek by prayer and the reading of the Scriptures, that acquiescence in the will of God, which you will find nowhere else. And let me suggest that you strive to obtain, not merely the mitigation of natural sorrow, but that instruction which God so plainly means to convey by this dispensation. After all, "the heart knoweth its own bitterness," and to every adviser, you may perhaps be forced to say with Job, "miserable comforters are ye all." For this reason, then, it is the dictate of wisdom to cease from man, and go directly to the fountain of all grace and consolation. There are many topics of worldly condolence which will occur to you—as the contrast with the heavier woes of others, the deliverance of your beloved partner from all sorrow and languishment—but the aching void will still remain, until you apply to the great origin of all good, and have the love of God shed abroad in your heart. O let your strongest efforts be put forth, at this seasonable time, to obtain the gift of God, and eternal life. Your mind labours under conviction of human inability, without a due apprehension of the correlative truth, that the grace of God is ready to supply your defect of power. In the January number of the Biblical Repertory, p. 113, you will find an article on the means of repentance, which I think would tend to remove some of your difficulties. When your mind will bear such exertion, give it a perusal. It is, I believe, usually found that when any person sets about this work, with a real desire to be reconciled to God, he does attain the object of his endeavours. This is what you need to make you happy under the adversities which you have so early begun to suffer. Now it is with you (strange as the expression may seem) a favoured time, and I do think that the door stands open through which you may enter to eternal joy. My dear friend, give yourself to these thoughts, bring your mind to dwell upon the presence of Jehovah, the selfishness and evils of your heart, the necessity of regeneration, and the mercy of God in Jesus Christ. Only seek this as earnestly as we seek worldly satisfaction, and you shall assuredly find.

By a coincidence surely unsought by me, I am just preparing to go on to Virginia to be married.[1]

TRENTON, *July* 13, 1830.

You will be disposed to excuse my delay in answering your last, if you will consider the great burden of calls and ceremonies which lies on me at this time. My mind often reverts to you and your bereavement. While I do not pretend to understand the bitterness of the cup which you are called to drink, I

---

[1] Mr. Alexander was married at the residence of Mrs. Le Grand, near Charlotte Court House, on the 18th June, to Miss Elizabeth C. Cabell, daughter of George Cabell, M. D.

believe I can much more understandingly than before, speak of the endearments of the marriage state. With a dear friend by my side who can sympathize with me in all the varied feelings which I experience, I can form a better conception than formerly of what your loss is. Yet again I say, "the heart knoweth its own bitterness." It is not to renew your grief that I touch on this topic, for I would gladly, if I could, divert your mind from the remembrance of those painful scenes, but there is a profit in affliction, which is to be obtained only by consideration of the cause of sorrow. My hope is that in this valley of humiliation, you will be instructed and led to surrender yourself to God. It would give my wife and me very great pleasure to see you in Trenton. We are living in the very humblest manner; some of my friends think too much so for my station, but it is absolutely necessary.

Mr. Southard has been making a speech at Newark, which was attended by a vast audience, is greatly admired, and will be printed. I should like to introduce you to him. He is one of the most agreeable companions I have ever found, and pays us far more attention than we could ever demand of him. His popularity in this State is rapidly rising to its former acme.

The cause of Temperance has received a great impulse in our town: our Governor, Chief-Justice, Attorney-General, Senator, and many leading members of the bar, are decided advocates of the new measures. Addison is about to buy the whole 1001 Nights, in the original Arabic. He has completed for Patton a revision of Donegan's Greek Lexicon, comparing every word with Schneider's ditto.

Under my present circumstances, it would be strange if I were unhappy; it will still be gratifying to you to know that I enjoy a degree of satisfaction far above my fondest expectations. Let me not forget, however, that all human joys are fleeting, and that before another year I may mourn under a sad reverse, by loss of health, or a thousand possible occurrences. This is a truth which I am sure is deeply impressed upon your mind. May you not only find out the inadequacy of the "broken cisterns," but come to "the fountain of living water."

Trenton, *July* 27, 1830, 2½ P. M.,
97° Fahrenheit in shade.

I went on Tuesday to New Brunswick to hear Mr. Wirt's oration.[1] The air was ovenish, the assembly large and highly respectable, the speech two hours long, apparently extemporary,

---
[1] At the commencement of Rutgers College.

and a noble specimen of polished, patriotic, eloquent speaking. The subject might be thus stated: "The mental and moral discipline demanded of American youth by the peculiar character of the age and country, with principal reference to patrotic manliness, integrity, and decision of character." There was a strong touch at the times. I came back quite sick, and spent one or two days in bed. Such a continuance of torrid weather I have never felt. Let me beg of you, if you have not already done so, to fly from the city for a few weeks. I have never felt so entirely good for nothing as I do at this time; I am desiccated and toasted to that degree that I feel like a dried animal, and almost look for my skin to crack.

I am projecting, under my father's guidance, a large work, say two vols. thick 8vo, title undetermined, but something like this, a "Biographical and Bibliographical Dictionary of Theology," or "Theological Biography and Bibliography," intended to furnish, in alphabetical order, a sketch (brief) of the life, and a list of the books, (with some estimate of their value,) of all writers on Theology. The thing is new, plainly a desideratum. What say you to a partnership? You may, by aid of Library, &c., assist thus: Look through all the Biographical Dictionaries within reach, note *names* of authors, book where their history may be found, and digest the same into an index. Also furnish the short articles, without reference to order in the first draught. It may be expected to occupy several years of smart labour.[1]

Trenton is remarkably healthy thus far. Should our hopes in this respect be realized, this may be recommended as the pleasantest summer retreat upon the Delaware. Bristol and Burlington are pretty pictures from the water, but the dullest and most intolerable places on earth. Trenton is homely, but well situated, and affords a greater variety of pleasant drives in its vicinity than *any* place I know. House rent is just nothing here, and it is almost as near (by steamboat) to the city, as Bristol or Burlington. The movements of the Jacobin party calling themselves (often *lucus a non* &c.) the "Working Men," give me unfeigned alarm, more than any threats of disunion, or violence of mere party rage. If we love our country, something must be done. It will not do to despise so formidable an array. They are indeed, with us, not the *dregs*, but in the exercise of their elective franchise, the *primum mobile* of this nation. The Godwinism, Owenism, *sans culottism*, (aut quocunque gaudent nomine,) which possesses them, may ruin us. Could not a series

---

[1] This project was not executed. I do not know what progress was made in it.

of "Letters to Working Men" be put in some popular Journal, commending honest labour, asserting the rights of mechanics, &c., but unveiling the naked deformity of this levelling system? Could not you serve your country, by doing something of the sort? It would be arduous, but by so doing, you would deserve well of posterity. No better work, I truly think, could just now engage any honest patriot. If I could, I would try, but I cannot.[1]

I am well and happy, and I desire to be thankful; the only source of disquietude at present is my apparent want of usefulness among my people. Nemo ab omni parte beatus; and when I compare my lot with that of many others, I am ashamed of my ingratitude. May we learn, my dear friend, to look for peace and comfort in something higher than even the innocent joys of life. This is the lesson which it is so easy to inculcate, but so impossible, I had almost said, to practise. In suffering my affections to cling to earthly objects, as I lament that they do, I feel that I am laying up for myself future miseries. God alone can reveal himself, so as to "call us away from earth and sense."

TRENTON, *August* 23, 1830.

I consider the manifesto of the Cherokees as a very moving paper. After all, iniquitous as the proceedings have been with regard to this injured people, yet considering the manner in which their tribes always pine away from contiguity to the whites, I am strongly inclined to think that their separate existence will be prolonged by their translation beyond the Mississippi. I have been reading Voltaire's correspondence with the King of Prussia, but I shall read no more. Never have I seen such horrid blasphemies in print; chiefly, however, in the letters of Frederick. Voltaire is more cunning and reserved, and says just enough to draw out the sentiments of that incarnate fiend, who glories in Atheism, and justifies —— *ex professo*. Three young Spaniards called on me to-day, asking for alms; they had a statement drawn up in very good Latin, which I found was written by one of them, who passed for a doctor of medicine. They were modest, well-looking fellows. The *generous* Joseph Bonaparte lately had a poor fellow apprehended, tried, convicted, and cast into prison, for having stolen from him *six silver spoons!*

---

[1] This plan was at length executed by himself in a series of articles furnished to the *Newark Daily Advertiser*, under the signature of *Charles Quill*. The first series, of forty-six papers, was collected in a volume entitled "The American Mechanic," and published by Perkins, of Philadelphia, in 1838: the second, of forty-five papers, was issued by the same publisher in 1839, under the title of "The Working Man."

he who gained his wealth by abstracting the treasures of Spain, and rifling the churches which fell in his way. He proposes to remove, as the railroad will pass directly through his estate.

TRENTON, *September* 7, 1830.

The Scotch mist which prevails is highly promotive of cerebral development, as I judge by the effusion at the nostrils this morning. Which end of the newspapers must a man begin at to get the order of events in the new revolution? I have read so many accounts, in such varied arrangement, that the jumble is inextricable. Is such a thing as a map of Paris attainable? It is like to be interesting at this time. Is there not a striking coincidence between the history of French and English liberty? thus:

Charles I.	Louis XVI.
Civil war.	Revolution.
Cromwell.	Napoleon.
Charles II.	Louis XVIII.
James II.	Charles X.
Constitution.	— ? —

My sanguine hope is—using these lights of history, and the parallel strikes me even in its *details*—that the French will settle down upon a limited monarchy, with a liberal charter, annual parliaments, just representation, and universal liberty of conscience. France would then be a glorious land. So mote it be! I have just been inditing a pompous piece of fustian upon the new French Revolution, to be spoken by a lad on the night before commencement, bearing in mind the direction once given to my brother, by a similar applicant, on a like occasion. "What sort of a speech shall I write you?" "Oh! a real *bombastic* one, just like your own." Mr. Frelinghuysen is here at this time, full of the subject of Temperance. He is a singular instance of a man zealously devoted to every good enterprise, without the slightest eccentricity. I am told that the state of frenzy at Charleston between the nullifiers and their opponents is truly alarming; so much so, that Judge Grimke has resigned his seat on the bench, that he may go to the State Legislature. I hope Mr. Walsh's word of exhortation appended to his remarks on the Revolution in France may not be lost upon them. I wish you could give us another call, during the pleasant season of autumn. I cannot (as we read in story books) ask you to come into the country for fruits of the earth, for you have the richest supply in your city. Give me leave to say, nevertheless, that there is some enjoyment in partaking of them nearer to the place of their production. I am reading Broussais' Physiology at this time. The medical men make such a noise about his 'revelations," that I wish to find out what he has revealed, and whether any light is thrown upon the "glorious uncertainty" of medicine. I came up in the boat with Vethake, who is just from France. He says that in all the shops and cafes where only one paper was taken, it was anti-ministerial; hopes much from the improved notions of the French respecting liberty; thinks the present movement got up neither by Jacobins nor Bonapartists; that the latter are very few; the Duc d'Orleans a universal favourite (of V.'s, perhaps because he was professor of mathematics in Switzerland.)

TRENTON, *October* 1, 1830.

Notwithstanding the criminal apathy of my heart in the concerns of immortal souls, I experience a lively pleasure in the comfortable assurance afforded by your last letter, that you have joined yourself to the Lord in an everlasting covenant. It is not enough, according to the Scriptures, "to believe with the heart," unless also we "confess with the mouth the Lord Jesus." May the Lord ever be with you, enriching your soul with the graces and consolations of the Holy Spirit. I am convinced that many of us suffer exceedingly from having very low views of the heights of religious joy which are attainable in this life. I have been this morning to see my neighbour ———, who has just been raised up from the jaws of death. I had scarcely supposed it possible for one so uniformly pious and exemplary to receive so great an accession of spiritual life and peace. His views of the Saviour's glory, the excellence of divine truth, ministerial responsibility and his personal vileness, seemed to be really unutterable. As a contrast to this, I called to see a man who cannot live, as we think, more than a day or two, who is almost in despair, on account of his long-neglect of religion. The changes in the faculty [of College] are important, viz. : Dr. Torrey, of New York, Professor of Chemistry ; Dr. Samuel B. Howell, of Anatomy and Physiology ; Vethake, of Natural Philosophy ; Hargous, of Modern Languages ; and Addison [Alexander], Adjunct Professor of Ancient Languages and Literature, with the duties of tutor. My father sets out this week for Boston, where he has not been since 1799. Addison goes the same way next week.

The commencement went off with the usual hubbub, the valedictory was truly excellent and eloquent ; a "defence of pulpit eloquence," spoken by a young man of your State, named Hart.[1] I have never seen so many tears shed in that house.

I spent four days of last week in New York. The signs of

---

[1] John S Hart; afterwards adjunct Professor of Languages.

increasing infidelity and atheism greatly alarmed me. Just opposite the Bible House, is a "liberal book-store," the most daring and demoniacal opposer of every thing good. At the door I saw, among many other MS. "Bulletins," as they are called, a ribald and blasphemous travestie of the Litany, around which was gathered a group of men and boys.

TRENTON, *October* 15, 1830.

I scarcely know what to say to you about the *extent* of the Atonement, so much has my mind been tossed and perplexed on the subject. The point, however, to which I have to cling as the very foundation of all my dearest personal hopes is, that the death of Christ was a proper sacrifice, vicarious, implying substitution and the enduring a penalty. Let me beg of you to read Magie on the Atonement. The key to the *nature* of the Atonement is to be sought, I think, in the ancient sacrifices. Now the difficulty is here, in my mind: If I admit that the Atonement is general, I can no longer hold that Christ atoned for *persons*, but for sin in general. It becomes a mere indication of his displeasure at sin considered abstractly, and I become lost in the vagueness of such a scheme. The limitation of the Atonement, arises in my view, simply from the purpose of Jehovah in it. Now, it does appear to me that every argument against this, lies against the decree of election itself, and is, therefore, inconsistent in any Calvinist. Suppose I say that the Atonement is general, still the great objection lies: "How can God sincerely offer this Atonement to those whom He has decreed not to furnish with the will to accept of it?" When I view the Atonement as *sufficient* for all, I do so only because from the very nature of it, as rendered by a Divine Saviour, it has infinite merit. As to its *intention*, even Hopkinsians hold a virtual limitation. I do not profess to have the clear view which some have on this point. I offer Christ to *all*, because this is plainly and undeniably in the ministerial commission. I maintain substitution and imputation, because I think without them there is no sacrifice, no meaning in ancient types. In the October No. of the "Methodist Magazine and Quarterly Review of N. Y.," there is a very able defence of Arminianism against the Pelagianism of New Haven, with which last Mr. Barnes's opponents suppose him to coincide. If there is any thing in ecclesiastical authority, I think it might be amply proved that the ancient fathers, the Church of Rome, the Church of England, the Remonstrants or Arminians, the Lutherans, and the Methodists held the substitution of Christ in the Atonement, and that it was left for Socinians and the divines of New England to deny it. At the same time the churches of Rome, Eng land, and the Methodists, and Lutherans, do all maintain a universal Atonement. May the Lord direct us into his truth!

My father is, or has been, in Boston, attending the meeting of the A. Board of C. for For. Miss. The Christian Spectator is exceedingly bitter against Dr. Woods, and all New England is likely to be in a ferment. When such disputes get among the laity, especially women, they become dreadful. I have heard horrid extremes of fatalism, under the notion of Calvinistic doctrine.

If you should meet with Mr. Rezeau Brown, late tutor in Nassau Hall, in your city, you will, I think, be pleased with him. He is a gentlemanly, somewhat accomplished, and exemplary young man; and has long been my particular friend.[1]

TRENTON, *November* 8, 1830.

I returned this morning from Allentown, where I preached yesterday, Mr. Hodge supplying my pulpit in the mean time. It is an uninteresting inland town, out of the way both of commerce and information. Yet I found some worthy Christian people there, and enjoyed much satisfaction in discoursing to, and with them. I am charmed with Leighton, and recommend to you immediately to read his Commentary on 1st Peter. All his writings are practical, and abound in the most lively and beautiful imagery. Doddridge appears, from his editorial preface, to rank him higher than any of his contemporaries. Owen on the Spirit, I have read with much pleasure, and I hope profit. The fourth book "on the necessity of holiness," seems to me eminently calculated to quicken the diligence of Christians; the third chapter is golden. No works have ever given me happier impulses in my religious course than those of the English non-conformists of the 17th century. On the next Lord's day, I have to preach a sermon at the request of the Temperance Society. I shall confine myself, not to the cause, symptoms, and remedy, but to the defence of total abstinence and of the association for promoting it. Joseph Bonaparte sent up, last Saturday, an invitation to both Houses of Legislature, to go and dine with him, (or at least visit his place.) Most of them went. He is said to be much exasperated at the railroad-men for taking their route directly through his park, and it is supposed that this "gineral inwite," as the messenger called it, is a sort of genteel ———. He says that his improvements are this moment equal to any which Europe affords, and that he has expended $300,000 on

---

[1] This most estimable man died in 1833, at the age of 25. He was son of the Rev. Dr. I. V. Brown, and was licensed as a probationer for the ministry in 1831. A memoir of him was written by Mr. Alexander, and published in the Biblical Repertory, October, 1834.

them. Please drop into the letter-box of the Philadelphian, the following note: "A few weeks since you honoured with an insertion, my humble attempt at a metrical version of Gerhard's hymn: '*O Haupt voll Blut und Wunden.*'[1] Two entire lines of the second stanza are omitted, and the sense thereby destroyed. It should read thus, (as well as I can remember—)

> 'How art thou pale with anguish,
> With bitter grief and scorn;
> How doth the visage languish
> That once was bright as morn.'

"Respectfully, DIDYMUS."

Addison is just entering upon a course of life which will be very trying, but I hope useful. [Patton's school.] He will study theology with my father.

In the last sermon of the National Preacher, the following text is quoted as Scripture: "He rolleth sin like a sweet morsel under the tongue." This is the third time I have heard this same false citation.[2]

TRENTON, *November* 27, 1830.

The passage in Matt. i., from Isaiah vii., is very difficult, but I tremble at the thought of giving up the prophecy, not so much on account of this particular text, as because Socinians and Neologists have made this very principle of "accommodation," the great engine against all our arguments from the quotations in the New Testament. I believe most fully that it is a strict prediction of Jesus, in one of the most remarkable designations of his peculiar character. For 1. It cannot refer to either of the sons of Isaiah, (vii. 3, and viii. 3), for one was already of some age, the other neither named Immanuel, nor born of a virgin. 2. Nor to any other common child, for the emphasis of the verse points to something extraordinary — "a sign." 3. Nor to Hezekiah, for, by computation, he was now a youth, and was nine years old when his father was made king. In the 17th verse, there is an evident transition to the child of Isaiah, comp. viii. 4. 4. We read of no child called Immanuel. 5. This is a part of that connected prophecy which ends c. x. 4, and includes the

---

[1] This was one of his earliest exercises in his favourite employment on German hymnology. His first translation of Gerhard's Passion hymn was incomplete; he rewrote it, besides making versions of several other hymns, for Dr. Schaff's monthly *Kirchenfreund*. A collection of those translations, together with two of Latin hymns, was published in the *Mercersburg Review* for 1859. Mr. Alexander contributed an article on the general subject of German hymns to the Biblical Repertory in 1850. His version of Gerhard has been greatly mutilated by copyists. Professor Park's "Sabbath Hymn Book" gives but four of the ten stanzas, (hymn 293,) "O sacred head, now wounded!"

[2] The true text is: "Though wickedness be sweet in his mouth, though he hide it under his tongue."—*Job* xx. 12.

prediction, "Unto us a child is born," &c., which I suppose no Christian would desire to set aside. Kennicott says: "The text contains two distinct prophecies; each literal, and each to be understood in one sense only, the first relating to Christ, the second to Isaiah's son, the first in verses 13–15, the second in verse 16." He also thus reads v. 16, "But before *this* child (pointing to his own son) shall know to refuse the evil," &c. See Lowth's Isaiah, in loco. 6. The ancient Jews applied this passage to the Messiah. 7. It may be made to have a probable connexion with the context. The promise to Ahaz is for encouragement: how? In no way that I can see if a "young woman" (as some say) should bear, &c. This is no sign; but thus—the perpetuity of David's kingdom is thus promised anew, "God remembers his promise to David, and most miraculously shall it be accomplished, a virgin," &c. 8. Because if it is not to be taken as prophetical, the Hebrew word is not to be rendered *virgin*, which meaning even the Jewish LXX. give, and which is the common meaning. 9. But I take my stand upon the formula $\iota\nu\alpha\ \pi\lambda\eta\rho\omega\vartheta\eta$ &c. If this does not express that a prediction was fulfilled, how could it have been expressed? The "accommodation" system is that which leaves our minds in most painful vacillation, upon every occurrence of a citation. The Bible is written for plain men, and the whole Christian church has rejoiced in this passage as a prediction and a promise, until within a few years. Many other acknowledged predictions are just as much perplexed in the original context, and my mind finds no rest, if I am left to find out for myself, when the formula "it is fulfilled" means fulfilment, and when it means something else. Why may not that God, who through all ages was looking forward to the Advent, interpose among irrelative matters a prediction, which besides its proximate application, referred forward to Christ? especially when men were to be *inspired* to expound and apply the prediction. I fear that in the end, all the types in which the church has hitherto found so much of the Saviour, and most of the prophecies concerning him shall be discarded. The Jews apply Isa. ix. 6, to Hezekiah; and why not? if the context is to decide. So far my comments upon this *locus vexatissimus*. It is very lately that I learned that any Christian writer doubted about this verse, though I know how the principle, upon which this evidence is set aside, has been used by all the German neologists.

The other subject is, to my mind, far more difficult, and a complete reconciliation of the genealogies in the Old Testament, in Matthew and in Luke, is scarcely to be expected at the present day. The great object was to satisfy the minds of Jews at that day; and this, we know, was accomplished. The tables of pedigree were probably copied from public documents existing at the time, and acknowledged to be the best. We are very much in the dark with regard to the laws (often arbitrary) by which genealogical tables were constructed. We know, however, of some anomalies; as for instance, that, among the Hebrews, a man was often said to be the *son* of his grandfather, or even of a more remote progenitor; and again, that in defect of male issue, when the list ended in a woman, her husband was named as the *son* of *her* father. The omission of several names in the line of succession cannot now be fully accounted for. It is evident, however, that it did not vitiate the pedigree, for Matthew surely knew as well as we can, the exact line of kings, &c., and the great object was to have a list brought down from some ancient progenitor. It is doubtful why the generations are divided into three periods of fourteen each. It could not be with a view of fixing the exact number of the whole line, for then none would have been omitted; besides, to make out the number fourteen in each of these periods, the person who ends the first must begin the next, and the person who closes the second, must stand at the head of the last, and Jesus must not be included in the last. Thus: 1. Abraham—David; 2. David—Josias; 3. Josias—Joseph, each fourteen.

This division into fourteens, I take to have been a mnemonical contrivance, which may explain some of the omissions. Each period commences with some important epoch, and as they were nearly equal, the names were so arranged as to make them perfectly so. From Abraham to David, you will observe that all three lists coincide. It is plain also that Matthew does not confine himself to the *natural* descent, but gives the legal, as where he calls Salathiel the son of Jechonias; while Luke, from Eli upwards, gives the natural line. Strange to say, I have found most satisfaction on this difficult subject in Dr. Adam Clarke's Commentary, which I beg you will look at. He gives a full analysis of the learned Dr. Barret's investigations of the whole matter. As an instance of five or six generations omitted in a genealogical table, see Ezra vii. his own pedigree—[then follows a citation from Lightfoot on v. 16.]

As you are upon the subject of Natural History, let me say, that by far the best account which I have seen of the Camel and the Lion, is contained in the first vol. of the Library of Entertaining Knowledge. The authorities there cited, are recent and highly respectable.—I congratulate you upon the reappearance of the sun, after so long a succession of clouds and rains. I take it for granted that this English weather has contributed greatly to the emolument of Dr. H., the antidyspeptic bookseller.—In looking over the late numbers of the Library of Useful Knowledge, I am surprised to find a History of the American Revolution, and still more to discover, upon perusal, that it is thoroughly American in its tone. Even in the matter of Major André, there is not a word of reproach. This sufficiently indicates the Whiggism of the Society.—My enthusiasm about the French Revolution has come down to zero. We may well fear a repetition of former enormities in Paris.—There is to be, on the second Tuesday of next month, in Milford, Hunterdon county, New Jersey, a public disputation between one Lane, a member and teacher of the *Christ-ian* sect, and the Rev. William L. McCalla, upon the divinity of Christ and kindred subjects. There has been great excitement in these parts, produced by the irruption of these heretics. I should very much like to be present at the conflict, but the weather is so precarious at this season, that I must probably content myself with a distant rumour. If W. L. Mc. C must fight, I wish it might always be with those who are without

I saw an Album the other day, in which the great Mr. Webster had inserted the following gem; I give it verbatim:

> "Some to this Album may give fame,
> And some may get fame from it;
> Among the last my place I claim,
> And write my name upon it.
>   D. WEBSTER."

TRENTON, *December* 20, 1830.

I can with great sincerity plead the abundance of my indispensable labours in excuse of my delay in answering your long and acceptable letter. Sickness among my people, absence from home, and a number of supernumerary engagements have filled up every available niche of time. I regret that in the Barnes controversy so much acrimony and personal rancour have prevailed. My mind has been much harassed by the invitation of the A. S. S. Union.[1] I gave their first offer a refusal, but received soon after a pressing letter from Mr. A. Henry, and an "ambassage" consisting of Messrs. Porter and Vinton, who held a colloquy with me of some hours. After all my meditations, I have pretty much determined to stay where I am. Upon making the trial, my feelings will not suffer me at present to give up the proper work of the ministry. This, however, should not be rumoured, until I have formally notified the gentlemen of the Board. You know that I would rather live in Philadelphia than anywhere else, and that I have peculiar difficulties in parochial duties, yet after seeeking divine direction, and communing with my conscience,

[1] To enter its service as a secretary.

I cannot see my path clearly marked out in that direction, and I dare not follow an impulse of mere inclination. A year hence, circumstances might so change in my congregation as to alter my views, but at present I feel justified in declining; especially as I am conscious of no peculiar fitness for this special office. Dr. Thomas Y. How, once so famous for his pulpit eloquence, and his controversy with Dr. Miller, is here delivering lectures on Political and Moral subjects, with a voluntary collection at the close. I have not heard him, as his first lecture only has been delivered, and that on Sunday evening. I have at last fallen in with *Howe's* works, and find myself possessed of a rich mine of truth and piety. He is profound, and (for the age) elegant, and his spiritual flights are the most sublime and sustained I have ever read. The latter part of his " Living Temple,' is among the most original, striking, and impulsive works I have ever seen. Above all, I wonder at his singularly Catholic spirit, in an age when the " mint, anise, and cummin " were deemed so weighty.

We have had a horrid case of death from *Mania a potu;* the victim was one of the most violent opponents of our Temperance Society, a few weeks ago. Another drunkard is now vomiting blood, and like to die. Yet I suppose not one drunkard will take warning. The man who told me these circumstances, I saw in liquor half an hour afterwards. Every day I am more impressed with the importance of being zealous in the Temperance Reformation. I am reading Robert Hall's works with much *gout;* but am astonished at his political venom. Yet I own some of the acts of our administration go far to make me likeminded. I have got no credit from having taken part with the miserable Indians in a sermon on Thanksgiving day.

You must pardon my unusual brevity; I am absolutely worn out with writing all day. You cannot write too soon, or too long. " Ros cœli sit super habitaculum tuum ! "

TRENTON, *January* 8, 1831.

As to the Barnes controversy I may say that I should feel very badly if it should ever become necessary for me to give a vote upon it. Viewing it in gross, I am clear that the measures of the Orthodox party were uncalled for, and inconsistent with their toleration of such men as * * * * * *. Their spirit has been bitter and unfraternal, yet that of the Moderate men has not been altogether dove-like. With respect to what I consider the fundamental principle of Mr. B.'s friends, viz.: that it is unconstitutional to condemn a book, without arraigning its author, and that Presbytery is incompetent to examine into the orthodoxy or heterodoxy of a member, without a regular accusation, I am fully with the present majority. The cases of Davis, Craighead, &c., are precedents which establish the principle; and I should feel free at any time, as a member of any judicature, to call up and censure any book, of any sect, by which the purity of the church might be endangered. As to the probable result in the General Assembly, I do not see how any thing can come up before that body, except the mere question of order, as to the right of examining the book. At the time when the complainants appealed to the higher court, there had been no definitive sentence passed upon Mr. Barnes or his sermon. I see no way, therefore, in which their final decision can be adduced in the General Assembly, in any orderly manner. That body will, therefore, I hope, throw the matter out of doors, after deciding the point of order; as to which, we may presume, there cannot be much debate, unless it is taken up as a mere party question. My impressions upon reading Mr. Barnes' defence are twofold. I am gratified to perceive that he is so much nearer the truth than I had supposed. I am pained at the want of candour in many parts of that production. In illustration let me refer you to the paragraph in which he justifies his assertion, that it is easier for an unregenerate man to love God, than to hate him. His reply does not touch the objection, and involves a violent perversion of common language. Not one reader in ten thousand would have alighted upon the construction which he gives the phrases. In common candour, he ought to have taken back, or qualified those unhappy expressions. The defence of his statements on Imputation, is plainly an after thought, and the ground taken very diverse from that of the sermon. His allegations concerning the old Calvinists, are, I think, triumphantly answered in the article on Imputation in the Repertory.

Can you tell me under whose auspices my father's Evidences have been published in England, or any thing about the edition? We shall have a terrible attack upon Hopkinson's Sunday Mail Review, in the forthcoming Repertory. I suppose that Walsh will be full of ire or contempt. You have, no doubt, read some of the speeches of Sir Henry Parnell, who seemed to have a principal hand in oversetting the Wellington administration. Mr. Hodge gave me some anecdotes concerning his eldest son and heir, which I think will interest you. When Hodge was in Paris, he lodged at the house of Oberlin, (nephew of the celebrated,) and had for a chamber-fellow this John Parnell, whom he describes as the most eminently devoted and pious young man he ever knew. His father offered him preferment, with the certainty of a Bishopric in the established church, which he declined. He then procured him a commission in the Duke of Gloucester's

Cold-stream regiment, which he resigned while at Paris. He lived in the plainest style, and gave away every little saving in charity. He used to rise at three every morning for devotion, and was at heart a Dissenter and a Calvinist. Mr. Hodge read me this week, a letter which he had just got from him at Marseilles. He was on his way to Persia as a missionary at Bagdad, and was supporting (as H. supposes) the large company with whom he goes. The worst is that none of them are ordained. They go as missionaries of Irving's "true Apostolical School." I am alarmed at the progress of the ultra-temperance doctrine; I mean that of Stuart's tract, that total abstinence ought to be made a term of church communion. It will undoubtedly produce great divisions in our church, if it receive any countenance. Think of it, and put something in the Advocate, if you agree with me. I have just been forestalled in a little work for which I have been preparing a Bible Gazetteer. The A. S. S. U. have applied to Rezeau Brown, the author of Franke's life, to do it. The average majority of the Clay Congressional ticket in New Jersey, is 1094. The whole ticket has gone in. It turned principally on the Indian question. Pollok's Course of Time is even more popular in Germany than in England and America. It is translated by one of the most popular preachers, William Hey, Hofprediger (court preacher) at Gotha. Find out for me some Catholic work, which may do for a Review in the Repertory, and lead me to study that controversy carefully.

TRENTON, *February* 8, 1831.

Do you see the magnificent relinquishment of $300,000 by John Watts, of New York, in favour of an Orphan House? May the blessings of heaven rest on him and his seed! I think I see every day new signs of increasing beneficence in the Christian work. The late "Missionary Reporter" contains several cheering notices. I preached last Lord's day evening from Psalm lxxii.; a precious passage. Read it once more. Our Presbytery will probably determine to support one missionary in the foreign field, under the A. B. C. F. M. How pleasant it would be if every Presbytery would begin to do its duty by adopting this measure. Edward Kirk's church, in Albany, which is composed chiefly of poor persons, sends regularly, once a month, $50 to the Board at Boston. If our Presbyteries would take this in hand, several objects would be attained: 1. The churches would feel more interest; 2. The money would be more easily collected; 3. The fears of the orthodox lest unsound men should be sent, might be precluded; 4. And piety at home would undoubtedly revive. The kingdom of our Lord Jesus Christ will come, and we are bound not only to pray, but to expect its arrival. My thoughts have been led into this channel, with much delight, by reading "Hengstenberg's Christologie," a German work, in which the prophecies of the Old Testament concerning the Messiah are taken up in order, criticised, defended against rationalists, and expounded. Having thus been led to examine them in connexion, I am smitten with their glory.[1] I wish you would read his remarks on Isaiah vii. 14. Hengstenberg is Professor of Theology in the University of Berlin, and one of the first Arabic and Hebrew scholars in Germany. He is about twenty-eight years old, and exemplarily pious. Religion is not advancing among us, and I have never seen less hope concerning my people than just now. Yet taking our Presbytery at large, there are pleasing indications. Since I have known New Brunswick Presbytery, we have never had any bickering or strife, any hard speeches or alienations; and our last meeting was one of melting affection and humiliation.

TRENTON, *Feb.* 24, 1831.

Some there may be, who grieve to see so soon
The feud commenc'd twixt Jackson and Calhoun:
Still one poor satirist may join the while,
And twist his muscles to sardonic smile.
Folly and vice conjoined and set on high,
Tempt e'en the sage to sneer, where he might sigh.
For who but feels the quick, indignant thrill
Of kindling rage, when arbitrary will
Drives from its last retreat the wasted tribe,
And Justice winks upon the golden bribe?
But why should reason, justice, pity, aim
To cope with fury in its boist'rous claim?
Breathe but a wish, the sleek and well-fed pack,
Bred to such clamours, open at your back.
Fly from the field, and Billingsgate let loose
Shall drench your head with slander and abuse.
'Twas once the rule—those better days are fled—
For those who lived upon the people's bread
To task their strength by every sage device,
To prop the state, and frown on reigning vice:
And he who held the purse-strings of the state
Scorned to descend to wars of party hate:
Spent not his nights, nor wore away his eyes
In darkly forging periodic lies.
O'er sheets of grave finance he felt too pure
To frame *Black Lists*, a purpose to secure.
Alas! how changed, the verse need scarcely tell,
The Press (our glory) spreads the truth too well.

---

[1] In the April (1831) Repertory, Mr. Alexander published a translation, by himself, of Hengstenberg's interpretation of the first promise of the Messiah. To the same number he contributed a paper on the works of John Howe.

From distant fields the "heaven-born man" returns,
To whom the incense of the million burns:
See from th' Augean toils of stern reform
The classic ——— rise to guide the storm;
Rake from the muck-heap of confuted lies
Each putrid forgery, a golden prize.
With quill in hand, he sallies to the press
And *telegraphs* the mingled bitterness.
What though in days when inexpert and raw,
He praised the patriot who gave him law—
Raised from the Clay he leaned on through the storm,
He soars in loftier tracts of new reform;
Smiles at the simple innocence of youth,
And takes a last embrace of awkward truth.
  Now, master of all work, he keeps accounts,
And proves by "rule of faults" the vast amounts
Of past default, embezzlement, and bribe:
Then lo! from cypherer, he rises scribe,
Displays the treasures of tra-montane wit,
And prompts the Chieftain in his drowsy fit.
For 'tis not always that the best of men
Can wield with equal skill the sword and pen,
Hand new commissions from the privy drawer,
And pen a message at his *escritoir*.
And should not *spelling* always be so pat,
Noster Homerus sometimes *dormitat.*
Three pairs of spectacles cannot suffice
To make a head, too long neglected, wise;
And barbecues around a forest pole
Promote the "flow" of every thing but "soul."
How useful then, in framing exposés
To number such among his choice relays;
And should the piebald message sometimes soar,
And sometimes plunge in deep and heavy lore,
Muse not to find it bathic and yet stilted,
By many hands the article was quilted * * * * *.
    Hiatus valde deflendus!

I have received a second intimation from Lexington, Ky., that I was to be called to succeed John C. Young, who is now President of Danville College. I have sent them word that I cannot entertain their overtures. Dr. McLeod, the veteran seceder of New York, and a man of undoubted talents and extensive learning, is about to edit a magazine to be "intituled" The Christian Expositor; to be the vehicle for publishing his own works. He is a native of the Isle of Skye, and has a brother in the Royal army in India. Dr. Rowan of New York, who has hitherto looked with much distrust upon the special measures for promoting revivals, expressed to me on Tuesday evening, his strong conviction that the meetings in New York had been greatly blessed, and that the work was manifestly of God. Some of the most sturdy, old-fashioned Dutch and Scotch Presbyterians have been conciliated and gained over. I know how to understand the suspicious feelings of many of your old people. It is the reigning sentiment among the more influential persons of my church. The foreign news by the *Sully* up to the 19th ult., looks more and more like war. I cannot help feeling a deep interest in the efforts of the Poles; but how is it possible for them to avoid the impending tempest? How unfortunate it is that they have not revolutionized their language! Czartoryski, Czarnocki, Astrawsky, Wladislas-Ostrowsky, Barzykowsky: "a book was writ of late called Tetrachordon"—see Milton's sonnet. The first article in the next Repertory [April, 1831] is from my father, containing the substance of his lecture on predestination, which some of his students esteem one of his best attempts at Theologizing.

TRENTON, *March* 10, 1831.

I am not able to take "the Presbyterian," though I am pleased with the numbers which they sent me. It is devoutly to be wished, that in "contending for the faith" which is enjoined, they may not "strive," which is forbidden. A large number of persons will be suspicious of the paper from their dread of contention. The Misadelphia[1] Presbytery has not gained much credit in the view of those who hear the bruit, without understanding the matter in debate. I fear that the Sunday School Journal will become flat from the introduction of so many journals, which will give it the intolerable sameness of the [Missionary] Reporter. This I should greatly regret, for I know of no religious paper more likely to be extensively useful. The accounts from New York are truly cheering. In some of the little neighbourhoods near Princeton, in which the Seminary students labour, there are pleasing signs of religious awakening; as also in Queeenston, or Jugtown, the N. E. extremity of the village, several conversions. I have spent some truly delightful hours with Mr. Nasmith,[2] the City Mission man. Both my people and myself have, I trust, been refreshed and awakened by meeting with him. Seldom have I met with so much zeal with so little roughness. It is true my opportunities of judging were slender, yet I cannot but rank him among the best men of the age. He was the intimate friend of John Urquhart, of whose writing he

---

[1] Altering the prefix of the city's Greek name, to denote the prevailing polemics.

[2] David Nasmith, from Scotland, was instrumental in promoting various organizations for the temporal and spiritual benefit of the poor in the United States, as well as in Great Britain. He died in 1839.

showed me a specimen; also a letter of Legh Richmond to himself, just after the death of his son Wilberforce; autograph letters and documents of Joseph Wolff, Mr. Judson, Earl Rawdon, Dr. Greville Ewing, Dr. Patterson of Russia, Wardlaw, and the author of the (Glasgow) Protestant, David Brown, and Dr. Morrison of China, and Marshman of Serampore, &c., &c. He is a remarkable young man for energy, and I may add talents, and I hope you will find him an agreeable and profitable friend. If he has not letters to Mr. Barnes, I wish you would use means to have them brought into contact. Some good will come of it. I am not sure that Mr. Nasmith's plan of City Missions may not require important modifications to adapt it to America, but it is a noble enterprise. If carried out, it is a powerful organization of our churches as missionary bodies. New York has determined to have forty of these agents or missionaries in that city, Charleston eight. We are resolved to make a trial here. In the Seminary at Princeton, the number of young men who have devoted themselves to foreign missions, is greater than the whole number of those who have actually gone into the field in time past. This is a good indication; but are there not wonderful signs of the times, in every direction to which we can turn our eyes? May the Lord enable us, my dear friend, to live in the enjoyment of a spirit consonant with these things! I have been sadly thinking this morning of my own stupidity and insufficiency. I am a barren tree, long spared, in infinite mercy; but when will it be otherwise? If I could live *one year* as I ought to live, even as some *do* live, how gladly would I give up all that there is in life. I speak my genuine sentiments when I say I know not what to do; I feel that I am a babe. On one hand is dependence on myself; it has cast me down a thousand times, so that I fear to make a resolution; on the other hand is listlessness and inaction; through the influence of which I wait, and wait, and wait—and do nothing. Let us pray for one another, as I still have a hope that we know how to pray. I have some comfort in that precious word, 1 John ii. 1–3.

TRENTON, *March* 29, 1831.

The Presbyterian pleases me very much, and is thus far a very instructive paper. Pray who is the author of the "Experiences"? They go to my very heart, and seem to me to give the hint for the right kind of religious diary. I requested the printer to hand you such proofs of this No. [of Repertory] as contain Greek and Hebrew. Remember that my omission of the accents is intentional, and a measure to which I am driven by desperation of their ever putting them right. I insert only the spiritus asper. I cannot read a number of the names in your list, and many words in your letters I discover only by circumstantial evidence. Still you are better than Mr. ———. An article of his was sent to the Committee, and after being attempted by three, was thrown aside in despair; it was absolutely illegible. His other piece was well copied, and is much approved. You have perhaps heard of the awakening around Princeton. It ought not to have been mentioned in the papers. In Princeton proper, there is little or no revival, except in college. They have had a four-days' meeting there; with what results I know not. I should have attended, had I not been kept here by a concurrence of duties. My own people are in a lamentable condition, yet I have in my own feelings more encouragement than ever since I have been here, and have been enabled for some time past, to give myself almost wholly to pastoral labours; so that my breast is quite sore with the unintermitted exertion of lungs in singing, and prayer, and talking. The members of the church are evidently more awake, giving more attention to the signs of the times, and joining cordially in little family circles for conference, religious intelligence, and prayer; but the body of the people and many in the church are dead. For the last six evenings I have attended meetings in different precincts, each of which was more encouraging than the preceding. Last Sunday afternoon I preached to the convicts in the State's prison. A more attentive audience I never had. Every eye was fixed; no averted look, no smiles, no shuffling, and at least a dozen were in tears. I spoke from the parable of the prodigal, and they seemed to sing with peculiar life—

> "Take off his clothes of sin and shame,
> The father gives command," &c.

I think I never felt more the unspeakable privilege of preaching the "unsearchable riches of Christ." Last week I conversed with those who are in the cells; one of whom was once an attendant (four times only) on our Sunday School; and another (24 years old) a convicted robber. The latter is as mild and comely a youth as you could well select; yet he has twice knocked down his keepers, and nearly killed a turnkey. Both of these men heard me with attention and tenderness. Let me recommend to you, if you have not attempted it, to try the delightful experiment of taking the gospel into the cells of your prisons, and to keep notes of cases and conversations. I have made some fruitless attempts to have a Bible class among the blacks; they are strangely averse to white interference. Since I lived in Virginia, I feel a peculiar yearning over these poor creatures, and sometimes feel as if I could joyfully devote myself to labouring among them. The heavy rain keeps me from a row of visits which I had intended to make at this hour, and such is my guilty disinclination to this duty, that I am almost glad of the excuse. This and other kindred feelings convince me that I lack that love of souls which is the only permanent spur to ministerial faithfulness. Yet I sometimes feel a persuasion that the Lord will accept, for Christ's sake, a duty performed against the current of natural feelings, faithfully and tremblingly, even if it is not so much a free-will offering as a self-denial. Though I have not the experience I desire, yet I think I long for it more than for any earthly happiness. Were it not for the Repertory, I should try to spend a week in New York.

By all means put in practice your project of turning to Greek and Hebrew. Let me, however, forewarn you, that if you use Stuart's Hebrew Grammar, you will become a Hebraist, not *by* it, but in spite of it.

TRENTON, *April* 14, 1831.

Since I last wrote, it has pleased God to make me the father of a boy; for which, and the comfortable state in which my wife is, I desire to be deeply thankful. This event, which is an epoch in our poor little lives, took place on the morning of the 8th inst. The child is called "Archibald George," as simple Archibald is no designation in our family. When I consider how great the sufferings of the female sex are, I scarcely know how to explain the matter, or assign the final cause, unless it be that God in great mercy chooses to apply suffering, as a means of grace, to those who are intended to be useful in forming the infant mind and giving early impressions. Since last Sabbath (our communion then occurred) we perceive something like a more awakened state of feeling amongst us. Several, I believe, to be deeply anxious, and several converted, and a number more in that peculiar state of susceptibility and attention, which is neither conviction, nor yet indifference, but a mean betwixt the two. Could I divide myself into a dozen, I might find ample employment. Some men perform this operation by means of their zealous members; but we are not sufficiently awake for my congregation to aid much. Still it is my hope that the spirit of grace and supplications which seems to be poured out, is but the beginning of a more extensive and gracious effusion. Fifteen were admitted to our communion on last Lord's day, ten of whom were from the Pennsylvania side of the Delaware. I am solicitous to know what are the safest and best methods of instituting and conducting inquiry meetings. Let me know even to particulars what are the results of your observation during the increased attention to religion in Philadelphia.

There are dangers attendant upon revivals of religion, which escape the notice of those who are most active in promoting them, while they are obvious to sharp-sighted men, who suspect the whole affair of revivals. "Fas est a hoste doceri." It is unwise for some of our brethren to repel, as they do, all inquiry as to the prudence of their measures. A great and lamentable evil, into which weak but sometimes pious men fall, is the indiscriminate application of special means to all circumstances and cases, without regarding the principle upon which such and such measures have been instituted with success. Thus the imitators of Mr. Nettleton make sad work by doing what they have seen him do, without possessing that almost superhuman sagacity which enables him to avoid failure, by addressing his efforts to certain principles of human nature. This is, no doubt, religious empiricism; and I constantly feel myself hampered by its existence among the more zealous part of my flock. It is like a good quack-ess of my neighbourhood, who is always saying: "take this," and "take that." It is the same error under a different form with that of the old formal, respectable, anti-revival Presbyterians. These say: "Our fathers did so and so, and we will do so too." The others say: "Mr. Finney does so and so, and you must do so." I freely confess that I have had much doubt respecting "anxious meetings," as they are commonly called, especially as I have sometimes seen them conducted. There is a certain stage of an awakening when they are indispensable; *i. e.* where the number of seeking souls is great; but many of my brethren use them as a *means of awakening.* How far is this correct? An individual is tender and somewhat alarmed; comes with a vague impression to the inquiry-meeting; is conversed with; is visibly set apart as an inquirer; is thus self-committed; must do something, or seem to do something; is there not room for fear of evil? of hypocrisy? And from the perfunctory manner in which discourse is conducted, is there not sometimes much daubing with untempered mortar? I want the aid of your eyes and judgment in this matter, and I believe I propose my doubts in the spirit of candour. I *may* have a meeting of the kind before a week is over my head. If you will accept of a translation I made a year ago of Gesenius' Elementarbuch, extending as far as through the vowel system, you shall have it.

Tell Packard without delay to print a set of texts on the *verse system,* for at least two months. Thousands would adopt it at once. We can do nothing till we have this indispensable basis of union.

My dear friend, is your heart attaining more and more to a felt communion with the Lord Jesus Christ as your head, and source of all vital influence? Here, alas! I err most. "Looking unto Jesus," is a motto suited to every hour. Duties performed, as I perform so many, with a legal spirit, are heavy to the soul and scarcely acceptable to God. In word or in deed to do all in the name of the Lord Jesus, *giving thanks*, rejoicing, relying on Him; this I find in the New Testament, in Whitefield, in the Tennents, in Newton, in some living men; but not in all who are zealous and bustling around me. "To know Him, and the power of his resurrection, and the fellowship of His sufferings," &c., Paul, the active Paul, seemed to think the great mark at which he might ever aim. Here I am conscious of a daily and habitual short-coming. The Christian paradox is, When most active, most dependent. The two ideas are beautifully comprised in the words: "I can do all things through Christ which strengtheneth me." When we are most abundant in labours, we feel most our dependence on God; and if we would stimulate ourselves to Christian activity, we can take no better way than to dwell in meditation and prayer on the truth that it is "God who worketh in us," &c., and that "He giveth more grace." By the bye, Mr. ―― preached us last evening a plain, pungent, sound, effective discourse. If Cecil is right, that "eloquence is vehement simplicity," then is ―― eloquent, with all his hemming and grossiêreté. I hope I have learned something from his earnest, humble, and solemn manner in private. I am ashamed of being so timorous in a cause which might make a coward bold, and have never appreciated the full weight of the command, "preach to *every creature*," as some appear to do. ――, I should think, (having only your fragmentary extract to judge from,) is endeavouring to persuade himself that he is converted, upon insufficient grounds. "Edwards on the Affections," abridged by Ellerby, would admirably apply to his case. Ah! perhaps, I sometimes have thought, this same error is my own. Natural conscience and intellectual light may go very far; but to be *born again*, to have "all things become new," to have "crucified the flesh with the affections and lusts," to have the leading of the Spirit, the mind of the Spirit, the walk of the Spirit, the seal of the Spirit, the inhabitation of the Spirit; this is that which I long after, but do not often ascertain to my satisfaction.

TRENTON, *April* 23, 1831.

Our letters appear to me to assume a more useful character since we have entered more into sober discourse upon the realities of religion; and they may become means of mutual instruction and correction, if we should do no more than occasionally start a question for future elimination. What you say of me and mine, gives me that peculiar satisfaction which the sincere expression of amicable feelings always does; " he that is a friend, must *shew* himself friendly." And now let me say in reply: "The Lord hear thee," &c., Ps. xx. 1–4.

Payson deeply affects me, but not as Brainerd does; in one case you have the *man* always before your mind in alto-relievo; in the other, you are directed away from him to the work of the Spirit in him. Edwards' concluding remarks to the Life of Brainerd, are wonderfully searching and appropriate at the present religious crisis. There seems more reason than ever to hope that the Barnes' question in the General Assembly, will be discussed and issued in a holy manner; and may set at rest a great class of questions. What you say of extraordinary and doubtful measures for exciting religious feeling, tallies exactly with what I hear from ———'s anxious-meetings, and from other quarters. I dare not attempt such things, though if I should, I am persuaded I could next week say in the Evangelist that we have forty inquirers. I feel that this is a question of awful responsibility; and oh how strongly do I wish to be led aright, and to avoid cowardice and formality; but then, human souls and the cause of Christ are not surely fit subjects for these perilous psychological experiments.

Have you ever read "Francke's Guide to the Study of the Holy Scriptures, Philad., D. Hogan, 1823"? If not, read it. The translation is horrid, and obscure beyond any thing of the kind, but the book is truly golden. You will profit by his advice as to Hebrew. You know he was an eminent Hebraist. The Princeton scholars, after Stuart, pronounce the Kametz like *aw* in *awl*, or *a* in *tall, fall*. This the Jews do not, nor does Lee, nor Gesenius, nor Frey, nor any cognate dialect except Persian, as Addison has clearly shown me. The true sound is the German, French, Italian, Spanish, Arabic, Syriac A, as *a* in *father*. Gesenius and Lee say it is a great abuse to pronounce ר like *dh*, (that is *th* in *that*,) as some do. Beware of Portuguese Jews. I have heard several of them read ת like *s* in *sing, this*; and Kametz like *o* in *pole*. Read from the very start with the tone or accent on the proper syllable; this the former Princeton students all neglected; *e. g.* they said kătáltem for kătăltém. When two ways are equally easy, the right is best and shortest. You may in a half hour, learn this without knowing any thing of the accentual system; which is a fanfaronade. Read Lee's Grammar, that is, *dip* into it for your amusement. I have found, after toiling through many grammars, no rules so practical and useful as those at the end of *Bythner's* " Lyra Prophetica." Following a hint of Henry Martyn, (v. Life,) I have arranged all the Hebrew verbs according to the *last* radical, the *last but one*, &c. A moment's thought will show you the use of this; as so many words differ only in the *last* radical, and as irregular inflections affect chiefly the ultimate and penultimate. Addison's plan is to go doggedly to work and commit roots. This is the universal method of the Pundits in teaching Sanscrit. I fear I shall have to take a jaunt soon. I am very lean and nervous, and worn down by constant pacing—pacing—pacing. Yesterday without seeking it, I discovered three cases of hopeful conversion; all isolated; all young; all in silence; one of them very striking and remarkable. They attribute nothing to human means, yet I have a satisfaction in knowing that I have recently spoken pointedly to two of them more than once. I have just returned from the funeral of Ebenezer Rose, late an elder in the Trenton First Church, [now Ewing township,] he would have been eighty-seven years old this day; his disease, cancer of the mouth. He was a saint indeed, and to his dying day enjoyed those rapturous exercises which we are too much accustomed to think belong to young converts only. A church-full of people were present, and much tenderness of feeling prevailed.

I find the little " Help to the Gospels " [a Sunday School book] very useful in my private reading and meditations. It seems to me better suited for adult Christians in solitude, than for schools. Even the tautological questions serve to fix the minutiæ of the passage in my mind. As far as I am able to learn, Mr. Nettleton does none of those objectionable things which many less experienced labourers in revivals lay so much stress on. In Virginia I had a good opportunity of learning his methods, and so far as I am informed, every thing was conducted with remarkable decorum and solemnity. We need something like " Class-meetings " to prevent the frequent collapses after revivals. True they are susceptible of abuse, but not more than anxious-meetings; I think far less. The plan is, at any rate, a masterpiece of religious policy. 1 have read eight out of the ten volumes of Wesley's works, and esteem him one of the greatest and best men that ever lived. My father has just arrived, to preach for me to-morrow.

TRENTON, *May* 30, 1831.

If you have any intention of meeting me at Burlington, I do you to wit that by a change of the measures I' am to minister there on *Friday*, not Thursday evening. Should you get there before me, leave a card or note in Bessonett's tap-room. I left my wife on Friday, and have heard nothing since from her; you will be pleased to learn that she was then convalescent, though still very, very weak, and much emaciated. You know, my dear friend, far better than I, how severe are those pangs which reach us through a beloved one: pardon this seeming tearing open of a wound. How hard to the flesh is the lesson 1 Cor. vii. 29–31. I lately preached on it; but only the Spirit can write it on our hearts. Have you read Matthew Henry's life? (by Williams, Bost. 1830.) I have never read a more truly instructive, or cheering biography. Read it, for the sake of bleeding orthodoxy. Apropos let me give you some facts. My authority is unexceptionable; but you may rebate for hyperboles in the transmission. P——, the Cambridge Unitarian professor, was at the examination in Princeton. He told a judicious and veracious man, and the latter told me, that he considered —— and his school as approximating very nearly to their (the Unitarian) views, in all that is essentially distinctive, and as travelling the road which the Boston liberals had pursued; and added: "they will soon stand on our ground." He said also, that —— (late Editor Unitarian Miscellany, and a low humanitarian and Priestleyite) brought him the Review of ——, with great glee, as indicating a going over to their sentiments in the main questions. *On dit*, likewise, that —— has advised the Boston Orthodox ministers to revert to the old plan of exchanging with the Unitarians in preaching, as the best method of bringing them round. Do not charge me with slandering; if these are true statements, they ought to be pondered; and they, at least, *excuse* the apparent illiberality of some ancient and tried friends of our church, who tremble at the introduction of a liberality so wide as to take in latitudinarians. My own conviction is this: that the Newhavenites, while they confess the divinity of Christ, and the agency of the Holy Spirit, do (in their *system*) deny all that makes these doctrines indispensable. Prof. ——, who has talked much with ——, says that the latter avows his belief that the only reason why he adds the agency of the Spirit to his system is that he finds it in the Scriptures, not that there is any place in his scheme, which can be filled by this doctrine only.

PRINCETON, *June* 14, 1831.

For some eight or nine days I have been here in dry dock, enjoying the otium without the dignitate, and the several refraichissemens of milk diet, blue pill, and cathartic extract. If I had known exactly where to find you, I should probably before this have fallen upon your neck in quocunque loco, for I have greatly desiderated a compagnon de voyage, and am now seriously meditating a jaunt to Saratoga. Professor Vethake may do me the kindness of sharing my ennui, but of this I dubitate. The atrabilious temperament is favourable to polemics, and I have accordingly made a tilt against the wine-sacks of Pelagius Taylor et id genus omne, having been delving very doggedly at the controversial divinity of the 17th century. Truly I am astounded at the acumen and learning of the Reformed theologians; I mean those of whom a specimen appears at the Synod of Dort, A. D. 1618–'19. The scholastic studies of the age, while they perhaps confined the mind to a narrow channel, increased the vigorous impetuosity of the torrent. I perceive no important point in the controversy *actuellement* agitated in America, which was not apprehended and brought out in full proportion and relief by these ancients. You will observe that at this famous Synod, all the articles of high-Calvinism were signed by Carleton, Bp. of Llandaff, by Bp. Hall, by Davenant, and Ward, master of Sydney College, Cambridge. I descend now to the earth, to say that it is moistened with a precious shower, and that the country is better than the town; and this I say, after having received another importunate though informal solicitation to the American Sunday School Union. I am holding myself in suspense: of this, not a whisper. Princeton is certainly the pleasantest summer retreat in the world. So judgeth a semi-native. I have been reading the second book of Cicero de Oratore, with very much delight. I then tried the Orations, but ennuyated so furiously that I surrendered. Also a file of " Archives du Christianisme," 1831, in which are noticeable the following: The persecution of "dissidentes" in Neufchatel continues. Sunday School spirit rising in France, in connexion with the noted " Methode Jacotot." Adolphe Monod, a young evangelical, is the greatest pulpit orator in France. The Protestants have great hopes of the revival of piety. N. B. The orthodoxy of the reviving Church of France, is that of the Reformers. Pray take a voyage, and write me letters from the other side. Seriously I recommend it to you, and I believe that you might thereby fit yourself for new usefulness in this country. Great Britain at least would fill up a pleasant and profitable year. However, the great query with all of us should be, where and how can we fit ourselves best for the Lord's work. The mere romance, even of religious effort, which tinges our views, is doubtless to be rejected. When I left you in Philadelphia, I intended to return before the mob [General Assembly] dispersed, but being indisposed and nervous, I took better counsel and remained procul a negotiis. And furthermore, lest I should be like the Irishman in "modern Chivalry," who cast himself from his coach into a row, crying "heaven direct me to the right side," I determined to study the matters in debate a little more impartially and deliberately. Perhaps I could point to clergymen who have committed themselves as partisans, much in advance of their own convictions. Such things may do in paltry politics where the dispute is "de lanâ caprina," but in matters affecting the plan of salvation, they are perilous. I am hourly admonished of my danger of judging before having evidence.

The great danger as to the upshot of the Barnes' controversy, seems to be this: The case which is held up to public view, and which excites to a kind of phrenzy men and even babes and women is: *Must Mr. B. be sustained?* Now, though this involves the doctrinal question, yet independently of the latter, it is decided, pro or con., upon general and worldly principles, often those of mere feeling; and this decision once made in either direction, there is a prepossession formed which militates for a lifetime with candid search after the truth. I suspect that scores of spinsters in your city have become far more "liberal" theologians than ever Mr. B. will be. Our Princeton men are considered by certain soi-disant standards as "sneaking," "on the fence," &c. There certainly is such a thing as righteous moderation, and those who have practised it have, as far as I know, in every age stood between two fires, incurring the wrath of both sides. It requires perhaps more solidity than some of these juvenile seignors have imagined, to keep this position where two seas meet. A crowd is a very convenient support to men of weak spines. But lest I degenerate into personalities and nosmetipsisms,—you will remember that I desire your company upon a jaunt. I don't pledge myself to go, but write instanter.

PRINCETON, *June* 17, 1831.

I write somewhat hastily to advise you that I expect, with Divine permission, to go to-morrow to New York, on my way to Saratoga. So much are our ailments antipodal to one another, that from your letter I perceive that we cannot at present pursue health in partnership. Mine is the yellow, bilious, liverish, dyspeptical, summer complaint—the beginning of those diseases which have already so often brought me down. And if you have (as I hope you will find not to be the case) any pulmonary lesion, or tendency to phthisic, I suppose you are right in avoiding both Saratoga and the seashore. There are some of the Virginia springs which I have more confidence in than any thing I know of on earth, (I speak of the disorder you fear,) except a prompt exile to low southern latitudes. I have in recollection, several cases of entire cure from the latter. Most, however, wait until the lungs have become actually affected with tubercles, which come to abscesses when it is too late to travel; and many content themselves with a resting-place too far north. St. Augustine is the spot I should aim at in such a case. I think you will have the offer of the Sunday School Union secretaryship, which I have just told Mr. Baird I could not accept. I have no belief that my health could endure the labour which, to an indefinite extent, would be heaped upon a secretary whose work is so little circumscribed by determinate limits. I propose to remain a few days at Saratoga, or Ballston; perhaps as long as the waters may suit me. I go purely for health, and expect to suffer a good deal from intercourse with frivolous and uncongenial people. I shall be pleased to fall in with some who may instruct me in methods of usefulness, or in any truth of which I am ignorant, and shall aim at interviews with ministers and pious laymen. My child has never been well, having had strong symptoms of hydrocephalus since his birth. He is small and always sick, and cannot use milk in any form or measure. The Lord do with him what shall be for His glory! thus we try to feel, yet my heart cries aloud: " O that Ishmael might live before thee." Never have I much cheerful hope except when I study to resign myself and mine, totally and unreservedly, to a merciful Saviour and King. I am myself a bruised reed, always crushed when set to sustain the right kind of work, yet through infinite grace not yet broken.

TRENTON, *July* 16, 1831.

I am pleased to hear that you are so agreeably situated at Germantown, [near Philadelphia,] and have no doubt that if you can avoid *ennui,* your health will be speedily re-established. The scenes you daily survey are faintly present to my recollections, from having been visited by our family for several successive summers. As it regards air and rural peculiarities, I consider Trenton as altogether a country-place. In three minutes I can, from our door, bury myself in thick forests, or "babble of green fields" in as pleasant meadows as I know, or hearken to the murmur of the Delaware rapids; and since I have lived here, we have had no epidemic. I was absent six weeks, and during that period my services were needed at only one funeral. I visited New York, Albany, (where I endured the 4th,) Troy, Lansingburgh, Waterford, Ballston, Saratoga, and Hudson. The rains rendered my sojourn at the springs uncomfortable, but at the same time refreshed nature so as to make the North River scenery indescribably charming. I found great benefit from the Congress water; the other springs were, to me, mere poison. In hepatic affections of every kind, I look upon the Congress spring as approaching the nature of a specific. I was driven away too soon, by the insufferable plague of listlessness, attached to all watering-places, and by a raging tooth-ache. " Causâ sublata, tollitur effectus." I have the stubborn root in my pocket. I have just negatived an invitation to preach Sunday after next at Baltimore, second church, with a view to my being called to supply Mr. Breckinridge's place. And, in truth, having in my jaunt seen a number of congregations, and many ministers, (all lamenting hinderances and grievances,) I should be unwilling to exchange Trenton for any *pastoral charge* which I have ever seen, excepting only Charlotte C. H. Va., which it would be sheer madness for me to undertake with my atrabilious temperament. Last Lord's day we were favoured with the addition of eleven persons to our church, four of whom are active men. This is a good addition in a place where we have to draw upon the same congregation at all times, for we have no floating population or rival churches to select from. There are, I suppose, fifteen or twenty inquiring souls among us, and for four months the standard of piety has been quietly and steadily rising. Could this continue, it is just what I desire. I say so after having been in the furnace of new measures in the Troy Presbytery. I hope, however, that I am learning to be forbearing. I am perhaps as thin and feeble as you ever saw me, though relieved within a few weeks from my violent head-aches and bilious symptoms. Every hour I am made to think of death, and feel how slight is my tenure upon all that unduly engages my attention. May we so enter into the great realities of another world, as to be prepared to depart joyfully whenever the summons may come.

PRINCETON, *August* 6, 1831.

It was but a few minutes ago that I had the first hint of your having been seriously indisposed, and I cannot forbear writing without delay. Your silence was indeed long, but as your letters for some time past have made no mention of any thing further than the debility of the summer, I had no suspicion that your health was impaired. And even now, I hear only vaguely that your constitution seems to be threatened. While I endeavour to cherish every hope, I am very anxious to know how you are, and wherein I can contribute to your comfort. I should not thus coldly maintain a distant conversation, if it were practicable for me to pay you a visit; but this is providentially precluded by a lameness from a sprain, which, with my other ailments has kept me to my chamber for nearly three weeks. I have been very weak and thin for months past; and though the symptoms of disease have nearly vanished, I am so much unnerved as to be next to useless. I know of nothing so well adapted to satisfy the mind under trials of this kind, as the simple truth, that we and all our concerns are ruled and disposed of by a Sovereign Mediator, whose, I humbly trust, we are, and whom we serve, for " they also *serve* who only stand and wait," as Milton beautifully and consolingly expresses it. I wish I were able to speak of deeper and richer experience of the truth that it is good to be afflicted. So often have I been chastised with personal suffering, that I am at times alarmed to think that this trying visitation has so little purified and elevated my soul. Yet there have been seasons of affliction, especially of sickness, in which I have known more of the power and of the joy of religion, than ever in my life, and in which I have understood how glorious is that grace of the gospel which can " give songs in the night " of pain and weariness. An ordinary concomitant of bodily weakness is depression of spirits, and morbid susceptibility of impressions which alarm or grieve the mind. Under these, the most resolute and the best men have sometimes bowed, and it becomes important to learn how we may be relieved from an influence so deleterious to the spiritual exercises of the heart. And here, I really believe, we too often undervalue the treasures of the Word of God, and especially the unspeakable gift—the crowning mercy—our Lord Jesus Christ. In times of peril and sickness, I have remarkably felt that I had made too little of access to the Saviour himself. Joy is more certainly diffused through our souls, by a simple, filial approach to the cross, than by any means which I have any idea of. This is remarkably characteristic of the apostolic and primitive experience. The triumphant hope and glorying of the apostle Paul, exhibited in the first part of the 2d Epistle to the Corinthians, seems to have flowed from such childlike faith : " We had the sentence of death in ourselves, that we should not trust in ourselves, but in God which raiseth the dead : who delivered us from so great a death, and doth deliver : in whom we trust that he will yet deliver us : ye also helping together by prayer," &c. ; " As the sufferings of Christ abound in us, so our consolation aboundeth *by Christ.*" The 4th and 5th chapters have revived my soul in some degree, within a few weeks past, when I have had very melancholy prospects as to my future health and usefulness.

Do we not restrict our faith in prayer too much to *spiritual* blessings? I know these are infinitely the more important, and that our petitions for earthly good are to be under submission to the Divine will; but then how plain it is, that when Christ was on earth, he listened to the requests of the sick and mourning, that he never chided any one who asked healing and deliverance, as asking amiss, and that he invariably heard the prayer of all such. How plain, but how much forgotten, that he is the same Saviour now, with just the same views of poor, suffering, and sinning men. How explicit the promise, James v. 14. But however tried, it is still undeniable, that if we believe, all things shall work together for our good, and with this assurance we may pray with absolute certainty that our prayers shall be answered in kind, or in a higher and nobler measure and way than we intend.

Let me assure you that I shall endeavour to offer my feeble petitions for your temporal and spiritual welfare. My belief of the prevalence of the prayers which we make in behalf of individuals is strong. Dr. Rice remarked, in a letter of his which I lately read, that he had often, he thought, been prayed back to life from the jaws of death. He is now slowly rising from a long illness, which baffled all the means used, and all the hopes of his friends. After all, however, our prospect would be dark indeed, if we had only this world to which we might cling. Blessed be God, our anchor is *within* the vail, and our hope is of an inheritance incorruptible. To see Jesus, and with him to see all saints· who have gone before, is a glory which we may expect; and the belief of this, independent of all other things, is support under the greatest trials. All these things occur to you daily; yet they may not be without some force when coming from the pen of a sincere friend.

PRINCETON, *August* 17, 1831.

In strictness of epistolary exchange, I ought to wait for a letter from you, but as I suppose you are more of an invalid just now than myself, I shall wave the rule and give you such things as I have. Since I have been unwell, I have read a book by J. G. Pike, containing some eighty or a hundred death-bed accounts of pious men. Although clumsily compiled, it is rich in refreshing matter. Apropos of Martyn's life; the London Christian Observer (somewhere about 1814–17) has many private letters of his, which are better than any thing in his published "Life." I was struck with the remarks on the truth "that we must die *alone*," especially as so singularly and beyond his meaning verified in the circumstances of his own decease. Middleton's Evangelical Biography, 4 vols., Lond., is a fine work. I am particularly pleased with the dying triumphs, under poignant sufferings, of the celebrated *Andrew Rivet*. Very deeply do I sympathize with some of your feelings, respecting the lowness of piety in many professors—above all in myself—the want of πληροφορια, and the idolatry of this world. Still I find it more to my comfort, certainly more to my profit, to acknowledge the grace of God in those manifestations of piety which *do* exist—manifestations which none but God can produce, and which are intended to show forth his glory, and therefore to be recognised by us. All the religion of Bible examples, so far as they are given in detail, is mixed and alloyed, saving only that of our blessed Saviour; and "weak faith" is a necessary term of relation and comparison, unless all faith is the same *in degree*, which would preclude the growth of our graces, and render the comparison of the "grain of mustard" nugatory. No doubt hypocrites will pervert this to their own destruction, and our reason might tempt us to elevate a standard which should make no allowance for defect, but such is not the scriptural account. The fear of death is a natural sentiment, which often exists by association in hearts which have more unquestionable marks of piety than the most ardent desire of death could be. Whatever explanation we may give of it, it cannot be denied that men, of whose piety we are assured by inspiration, have prayed to be delivered from death—Psalm vi.; especially Hezekiah—Isaiah chap. xxxvii.—and God was pleased to grant this as a blessing, and holy men have rendered thanksgiving for the deliverance as a mercy—Psalm cxvi. Epaphroditus "was sick, nigh unto death, but God *had mercy on* him." The soul ought unconditionally to submit to God, willing to live or die; but I am ready to think that more has been made of willingness to die, as an evidence of piety, than the Scriptures make of it. Long life is even promised as a blessing; I suppose for two principal reasons—1st, that we may do more for saving souls, (a work confined, for all that we know, to this life;) and 2dly, that we may attain greater piety, and thus have a greater capacity for heaven, and greater reward there. This is perfectly consistent with Paul's estimate of heaven as "far better," for the *rest* is at any moment better than the *labour ;* still, the latter may be lawfully desired, in order to an increased enjoyment of the former. It is right to wish to see in all the faith of Abraham; but we see only one Abraham in the Bible, and many imperfect Davids, Jobs, and Peters. Moreover, I doubt not the same kind of faith is in exercise as often now. Understand me now, not as suggesting that we should be *content* with lower measures; by no means; but as dissenting from the doubt which you say you have of the *reality* of your own faith and that of the Christian community generally. This doubt is not, I think, encouraged by the tenor of Scripture, and tends, not to piety, but to the rejection of it. For surely the heart-rending conclusion that *all* are wrong, saps the foundation of Christianity itself. So, also, there is a sinful complaint under affliction, so sinful as to vitiate all a man's title; and a complaint (such as the hundreds of David) which is compatible with the actual vigour of entire submission. "If it be possible let this cup pass." We may say this in *faith*, and to say this is not to rebel. Chastisement would be nothing, were it not felt to be afflictive; and no affliction is joyous; *afterward* it yieldeth the peaceable fruits of righteousness. The feelings you express have given me pain, for I have had them all, and I would pray all who value the sweetness, and serenity, and joy of piety, to war against them as morbid. On this subject I have recently read some of Newton's letters with profit. This is a day of solemnity in the Seminary. Six young men are just about to depart on foreign missions, and the professors and students are observing a day of fasting and prayer with them. They are beloved youth—all of them manifesting a primitive zeal and love. The Lord go with them and bless them. We have great, glorious tidings of wonderful awakenings in Virginia—in my old region, and also at Lexington, where many of my relations are hopefully converted. My heart sinks at the thought that now, when I am laid aside, I can look back on so little good done. I hope the Lord has service for you in his church, and will speedily restore you. My friends Christmas, Aikman, and Wilson are gone! May God have mercy not on you only but on me also, lest I should have sorrow upon sorrow; yet let us, as frail and dying creatures, live in view of death.

"O for an overcoming faith
To cheer my dying hours."

My health is in statu quo; my lameness better, my child convalescent, and my wife well. The Lord be praised for his mercies. My mind reposes with rather more than usual peace on the divine promise $ου$ $μη$ $σε$ $ανω$, $ου$ $δ'$ $ου$ $μη$ $σε$ $εγκαταλιπω$.[1]

TRENTON, *October* 11, 1831.

Without descending to the use of superlatives, I am pleased to know that you have returned so much better, and that our correspondence has recommenced. For your two letters I am thankful, though at this time I have not wherewithal to pay you in kind. At this moment I am jaded by writing almost all day for the Repertory, for which I generally have to provide thirty or forty pages of balaam. I am pretty much determined to dissolve my connexion with it [as editor] after this number. To come at once to the most important matter now pending between us, viz., your intentions with regard to the ministry; you know already that I rejoice at your views, and desire that your wishes may be

---

[1] The five negatives of this text (Heb. xiii. 5) are thus rendered in Doddridge's Expositor: "I will not, I will not leave thee, I will never, never, never forsake thee."

realized. The commonplaces (however momentous) on the responsibility, &c., I shall omit, as being as open to your view as to mine. I seriously wish you could come to Princeton; and this, I think, apart from any personal predilections. Every day I regret that I did not take the full course there, (having been tutor, as you remember.) Now, as a private student, you would have about the same advantages that I have now, and I assure you that they can in no degree supply the want of the facilities of the Seminary. I am far from considering the mere lectures of the Professors as the most important part. I hold the benefits, arising from the relation which the students have to one another, as incalculably great, and that particular kind of life as affording an admirable discipline.

I wrote thus far on the 11th, and now, after having been absent at Synod, and some other things, proceed upon the 23d October. The meeting of our Synod was interesting; no judicial or party business, no heat—not enough even to warm the debate. Revivals have visited about half our churches, and what is strange, principally those of the ultra [old school] of Newton Presbytery. In one church (Mansfield) a great revival is in progress without any new measures, not even an inquiry meeting. I lay no stress upon this, but mention it as repelling the invidious charge of our opposing brethren that revivals are the seals of new doctrine and new measures only. For my own part, I believe that revivals depend not so much, as is thought, upon phases of doctrine, or petty arrangements, as upon the ardent piety and zealous labours of humble Christianity, apart from all these things. You are aware that the Princeton men are in very ill odour with the *extrême droite* of the Philadelphia Presbytery. The Repertory is considered as a craven publication, because it did not take sides at once on the Barnes controversy. Now all this is exceedingly impolitic in the Philadelphia gentlemen. By excluding as "fence-men" all who have not fully participated in their panic, they run the risk of reducing their party to a mere handful. The truth is, the Princetonians are as thoroughly old-school in their theology as Dr. Green himself, but they are unable to see that it is the path of duty to denounce every dissentient individual, more particularly as it requires no sagacity to observe that the policy of Wm. L. McCalla, &c., can never result in the adoption of their measures by the church at large.

Among my people there is nothing very encouraging. The absence of a pastor has always a disorganizing effect upon a congregation. Some among us profess to desire a revival, but I plainly discern the prevalence of a common error among our professors; they wish to shift from themselves the responsibility of a great and united effort towards a revival, and to put all their hopes in a four days' meeting. I preached last Sunday in defence of revivals and against this error.

TRENTON, *November* 21, 1831.

I thought, and still think, that my last contained every thing with reference to your proposed course of study which I am able to communicate, except in the matter of books, which I now take up as being the most important item of your inquiries. And first, I must altogether decline attempting a precise, exact enumeration of the works which must be read. Nemo dat quod non habet. If I had such a list, three-fourths of my daily reading might be spared. Such a list must vary with the peculiar character of every individual's studies, and the rather in your case, as you propose a course not altogether regular. I could not venture to name such books on my own responsibility. When at Princeton, the Professors used to name, at the end of each lecture, the best authors for consultation on those topics; and a list digested in this manner, might be made without difficulty, though it would fill a quire of paper. To do as well as I can, however, as you have laid out of the inquiry works on the "Evidences," and as I suppose you to know as well as myself what books are standard in Ecclesiastical History and Hermeneutics, I shall confine myself to Theology.

1. *Works Introductory, or showing how to study.* Taylor's Scheme of SS. Div., (in Watson's Tracts, vol. 1;) Leighton's Lectures; Franke's Guide.

2. *Systems.* Turretine or Pictet, (French,) for the Reformed; Stackhouse for the Arminians of England; Richard Watson for the Wesleyans; Ridgely; Dwight.

3. *Character of God.* Clarke's Sermons; Witherspoon, vol. 4; Saurin, vol. 1; Paley; Charnock on Div. Att.; Tillotson, vol. 1; Hopkins, vol. 1; Edwards on God's Last End; Emmons.

4. *Trinity.* Horsley; J. Pye Smith; Woods; Stuart; Ware; Norton; Channing; Morus Epit. Theol. Christ.; Sherlock's Vind. of Trin.; Priestley; Belsham's Essays; Jamieson's Vindication; Bates' Works; Abaddie on Div. of Christ; Nares' Remarks on the Improved Version; Bulli Defens. Fid. Nicen; Pearson on the Creed; a chapter of Hooker's Ecc. Polity; Owen on the Person of Christ; Wardlaw; Wynpersee; Clarke on the Trinity; Allix's Judgment of Ancient Jewish Church; Mordecai's Analogy; Socinus; Select parts of Barrow; Calvin; Döderlein and Flatt.

5. *Decrees, &c.* Calvin; 5 Edwards, 351–500; 1 Turretine; 1 Hopkins, c. 4; Arminii Op. pp. 98, 458, 634; Twisse (supra-

lapsarian) de Scientia Med.; Zanchii de Predest.; 4 Witherspoon, 75; Fuller's Gos. Worthy, &c.; Baxter's Cath. Theol., part 1; Witsii Econ. Fœd. B. iij. c. 4; Dickinson on the 5 points; Whitby on the same; Cole on Sovereignty of God; Scott and Tomline; Oeuvres de Claude, vol. 4; Edwards on Will; West's Moral Agency; Priestley, Lib. and Necessity; Leibnitz cont. with Clarke, (usually bound together, in Lat. and French;) Collins on Necessity; Warburton's Div. Leg., p. 1, p. 46; 1 Hopkins; King's Origin Evil; Williams' Vindication.

6. *Original Sin and Depravity.* Taylor on Or. Sin; Edwards do.; 1 Smalley's Sermons; 1 Turretine; Whitby on O. S.; 1 Emmons; Stapfer, (who treats the whole range of polemics;) Witsii Ec. Fœd., vol. 1; Boston's Fourfold State; 4 Witherspoon; Scott and Tomline; Wesley's Sermons; Strong's Sermons; 1 Bellamy; Burgess on O. S.; Spring's Disquisition; Fletcher's Appeal.

7. *Atonement.* Daubeny on Atone.; Magie; Griffin; Beman; Owen's Vind. Evang.; Outram de Sacrificiis; Calvin, Turretine, &c; Selections on the At.; West on At.; Taylor and Hampton; Wardlaw on Extended At.; Bates; Murdock's, Stuart's, and Dana's Sermons; Fuller's and Scott's Essays; Edwards, (select;) 1 Bellamy, 390; Burge on At.; Barrow's Sermons on Univ. Redemp.; Grotii de Satisfac., (a noble work on the "forensic" question;) Owen's Salus Electorum; Van Maestricht, De Moor, and Marckius on all Calvinistic points; Veysie's Bampton Lectures.

8. *Regeneration.* Besides above: Owen on Spirit, (large;) Bellamy, Scott, Witherspoon, Doddridge; Witsius; 2 Charnock; Noesselti de interno test. Spir. Sanct.; Backus on Reg.; Edwards; Park St. Lectures; Dwight; Hopkins on Holiness; Fiddes' Treat. on Morals; Edwards' Affections.

9. *Justification.* Oeuvres de Claude; Owen on Just.; Witherspoon; Taylor's Key to Romans; Edwards on Just.; 2 Barrow, 41; 2 Tillotson, 346; Bulli Opera, Harmon. Apost.; Tuckney's Prælect. I. p. 26.

10. *Perseverance.* Dickinson; Whitby; 1 Wesley's Serm.; Zanchii Miscell. de Persev. Sanct.; De Moor; 5 Toplady; 2 Gill, 313; 1 Newton, 162; 2 Hornbeck's Compend. B. 1, c. 4.

11. *Future State—Heaven and Hell—Universalism, &c.* 1 Belsham's Essays; 1 Priestley on Matthew and Sp.; 2 Hopkins, 213; Warburton; Tillotson, Ser. X.; 2 Barrow, 343; Bates and Howe *in loco.* Edwards agt. Chauncey; Ballou; Huntington's Calv. Improved; Strong's Benevolence and Misery; Purves' Humble Attempt; 2 Döderlein, 173; Burge on Atone. Appx.; Spaulding's Univ. destroys itself; 1 Ham-

mond's W. 709; Foster's Nat. Religion, c. 9; Simpson's Essays, p. 1; Godwin on Punishment of Sin.

12. *Sacraments.* Clinton on Bap.; Worcester, do.; P. Edwards; Baldwin, do.; Wall on do.; Waterland; Gale agt. Wall; Addington's Reasons; Judson and Pond; Gill; Tenney's Summ. View; 2 Tillotson, Serm. 25; Grove on L. Supp.; Doolittle, do.; Hall and Mason on Com.

I must here pause; I have drawn the above from lists which I have, and from general recollection, and am after all persuaded that it will be of no manner of use to you; yet your request laid me under an obligation to try, and I have really done what I could. Your wants, as they rise, will direct to inquiries which can be better answered in detail. Your course of study cannot but be profitable. I suggest one objection to your " paraphrase"—perhaps it has no weight; will not the method of paraphrasing every passage tempt you to run ahead of your light, to define what is undefined, and supply what is unsupplied in your own mind, and thus to commit yourself prematurely? Many a hiatus will occur; for some passages can only be understood after a survey of the whole ground. However, judge of this yourself. I wish I could tell you of any thing specially encouraging in my congregation; there is nothing, and as usual I can trace the great fault and deficiency to my own door. Nothing of moment in church or state has reached my ears. I am sick of imbecile revolutions in Europe, and unchristian squabbles at home. O for a corner where Theological warfare is unknown!

TRENTON, *December* 26, 1831.

Have you ever read any of Abp. Leighton? If not, I conjure you to take the book up in some calm moment, and read some ten pages by way of specimen. It is nearest to the beloved disciple John of any thing human I have ever read. I recommend this author, from sweet experience of his preciousness; particularly his commentary on 1 Peter, which I am now concluding for the second time. He was a hater of polemics, and shared the usual fate of all moderate men. I have filial weakness enough to think my father has some traits in common with him. I think you are pursuing the best possible method in learning Hebrew. It would give me unspeakable satisfaction to have Mr. Leeser's[1] instructions. Make the most of them. If I

---

[1] The learned Isaac Leeser, now minister of the Franklin Street Synagogue in Philadelphia. I cannot forbear quoting the following sentence of a note received from Mr. Leeser when this page was in the printer's hands: "If I had known that the funeral would have taken place on the day it did, I should have made it my duty to be at the grave which now encloses him;

had him here, I would give a large piece of my salary to spend an hour with him every day. I read Hebrew several hours *per diem*, going though the Psalms once a month, and reading from four to ten chapters besides, in regular course, analysing a certain number of verses. The most I can say is, that my eyes are opened to the exuberant treasures of a boundless mine, while my instruments are still too awkwardly handled to make much of them my own. Let me recommend to you to spend as much time as you can conscientiously upon this study, as you know that in language, more than in any thing else, long intervals occasion the loss of much that is learned. The exegetical method of studying theology is certainly the right one. The simple view in which *systems* seem to me valuable, are as indexes to the subjects of Scripture. *Turretine* is in theology *instar omnium;* that is, so far forth as Blackstone is in law. I would not have you concur in all his scholastic distinctions; but the whole ground is traversed, every question mooted, and even where hairs are split, the mental energy and logical adroitness with which the feat is achieved present one with an exercise of reasoning equal to any thing in Chillingworth. I conscientiously believe I should say all this of him, if he were a Socinian. That he is not, but rather an ultra-Calvinist, I am pleased, for I find in him, among many that are untenable, triumphant arguments for all our doctrines. Making due allowance for the difference of age, Watson the Methodist is the only systematizer within my knowledge, who approaches the same eminence; of whom I may use Addison's words: "He reasons like Paley, and descants like Hall." How painful to think of Edward Irving's hallucinations! [the gift of tongues, &c.] Devoutly would I say: "Lord, what is man!" These are among Satan's most cunning devices—and oh, how deep-rooted is that structure of truth, which has lived through a thousand such concussions, from without and from within! I have been reading the huge folio Journal of George Fox, the proto-quaker. I find in him more of unadulterated enthusiasm than I remember to have ever found exemplified; intolerable vanity, and spiritual pride; no acknowledgment of sin all his life long; no trace of penitence; great bitterness of spirit, exceedingly little talent, ludicrous ignorance of the doctrines he opposes, *perhaps* evidence of piety. A vast difference between him and

and if it had not appeared strange, I would have spoken parting words after the beloved. In Germany and France, at the interment of a man like Alexander, Jews and Christians mingle their regret by free speech and loud sympathy." Mr. Alexander's high personal respect for his Jewish friend and correspondent, did not prevent him from expressing his opinion of " Modern Judaism " in his review of Leeser's translation of Johlson; Repertory, January, 1831.

the editor of the book, William Penn. How I should like to join you in Hebrew with Mr. Leeser! We have not a Jew in Trenton, nor any Hebrew scholar, and it is hard to pursue a study altogether uncountenanced and alone. My health, though improved, is far from good, and I suffer considerably from bilious or dyspeptic symptoms. I am truly sorry to hear of Mr. Wirt's illness; even though he should never be high in office, he may exert a happy influence on many who are. Do you not think in looking around the country, that, within a few years, many more of our "great men" have pledged themselves in favour of true Christianity, than at any former period? This is encouraging.

TRENTON, *January* 17, 1832.

I have been a good deal interested in the great Quaker trial, which has been before our Chancery Court. As you are not likely to have any published report of the argument, I shall give you some of the positions taken. Wood and Williamson (our late Governor) for the Orthodox; Wall and Southard for the Hicksites. The decision is likely to affect all the property in New Jersey. The evidence is printed, and fills two large volumes. The Orthodox take this ground: the property belongs *to the Society of Friends*. There are two ways of determining who are the real Simon Pures: 1. By their adhesion to the genuine Yearly Meeting of Philadelphia; 2. By their adherence to the true Quaker faith. The Hicksites are separatists—voluntary seceders from the Yearly Meeting, for in 1827 they formed another, not a reorganization of the old, but a new one, on new principles, of their own party. The true Yearly Meeting still remains, has done nothing to destroy itself, and is the lineal descendant of all precedent Yearly Meetings. 3. The Hicksites are seceders from the Quaker faith; their Yearly Meetings recognised E. Hicks as a preacher of the truth; and their leading preachers and writers are Unitarian. The society, though it has no *creeds*, qua tales, has received, established, characteristic *principles*, easily learned from the current of their writings. Friends have often "dealt with" ministers for preaching unsound doctrine, thus establishing that there is some doctrinal test. They are, as a body, Trinitarian, and they have "disowned" the Hicksites, who are thereby, as by their voluntary secession, ipso facto disinherited as Quakers. The Hicksites rejoin: 1. Friends are not called by men's names; they are not Hicksites; the Yearly Meeting of 1827 ceased to be the Yearly Meeting when, in opposition to a vast majority, they elected Samuel Bettle their clerk, and did other things which they were not competent to do. The majority then reorganized the true Yearly Meeting, which they have continued.

They have never separated from the Society of Friends; they are the majority, and the society is a pure democracy, in which majorities govern. The division is not on doctrinal, but on disciplinary grounds. Their Yearly Meeting is independent of all others, though not recognised by those of England, New England, and the Southern States.

2. Quakers have no *creeds;* this is characteristic of them. The Spirit is their bond; they have always repudiated doctrinal tests. The Scriptures are their creed. They may believe what they choose, and they, as a republican majority, are at liberty to say what is sound Quakerism. They believe the doctrines of ancient Friends; further than this no court has a right to exact a profession: they stand upon their rights of conscience, and will assert or deny no doctrines. This is no question of doctrine. Elias Hicks was a good, great, and holy man; slandered and persecuted. He did not deny Christ's divinity, atonement, inspiration, a future state. He believed with ancient Friends. But, granting that he was in error, they are not affected by it. They refuse the name of Hicksites, are not identified with him, have not taken his writings as their creed, will not stand or fall with him, will not say what they believe, except that they believe the Scriptures, and are in unity with ancient Friends. The argument began on the 3d inst., and lasted more than a week. Wood and Williamson are equal to any men, in argument, I have ever heard, and they have displayed a wonderful research. Southard is the main dependence of the other party, and he dealt too much in declamation. It is hard to say how it will go.[1] We have had a number of Philadelphia Orthodox Quakers here, the most distinguished of whom is Thomas Evans, whom the Orthodox hold up as their great Theologian and champion. His pamphlets, testimony, and conversation, evince him to be an extraordinary—I think, a pious man.

Many look for a general *split* of the two sides [Presbyterian church] next spring. Let us pray for something better. I mean, that the pious, humble, moderate, and (moderately) orthodox should come out from the ultras of both sides, and cohere as the Presbyterian church. Dr. Dickey's paper is good, and many men, I think, are beginning to feel that we are tempting the Spirit of God to leave us by our biting and devouring one another. O how could we breathe out our souls in death, after the rancour exhibited in several of last week's publications! The greatest heresy is want of love. Dr. Rice used to urge on his students the motto *Love is power.* On this text I think I could preach a good sermon; I would that I better knew how to act

---

[1] The judgment was for the Orthodox side.

upon it. A few days more, and we shall see these things in a different light. Some truths I hold to be fundamental. These I would enforce, *on our own*, by discipline; in others, let us be forbearing. As to the devotional aid for your friend, I can think of no book exactly the thing. If she is a young Christian, Doddridge's Rise and Progress is the best I know of, especially on the subject of daily self-examination. Yet I have derived more benefit from Bickersteth on Prayer, than from any similar work. *Sacra Privata*, by Wilson, Bp. of "Sodor and Man," is a book of heavenly devotion, arranged according to the days of the week; but it savours a little of Arminianism, on the subject of human merit. Jay's Exercises for the Closet is a capital book; on the whole, however, I should be inclined to recommend Bickersteth. Among your plans for doing good, invent some one by which pastors may gain pastoral access to servants, apprentices, &c. These one cannot see in pastoral visitation, and they shun the respectable bible classes; yet they often are the most hopeful members of a congregation.

TRENTON, *March* 5, 1832.

I have kept yours, of the 9th ult., two days longer than you kept my last, but not from any exactitude in calculation; the press of Repertory and other writing kept me busy last week; and I have, besides, been a good deal indisposed. Little trials sometimes come upon me, which, though not important enough to call for human condolence, drive me to the throne of grace, with an earnestness which I do not experience in times of sunshine. How it is with others, I cannot tell; but it seems to me, that I need a constant series of inward or outward conflicts, to make me value divine comforts. Never can I so truly appropriate the divine promises, as when dark clouds overhang my worldly prospects. The benefit of afflictions is one of those things, concerning which I cannot entertain a momentary doubt.

We have here two aged Indians, one 61, the other 71 years of age, Delawares from Green Bay, both pious. The elder, Bartholomew Calvin, was born in this vicinity, at Crossweeksung, and was sent to Princeton College while a boy, by John Brainerd. The outbreaking of the revolution arrested his studies. I have had some pleasant hours with them. They have claims on government for their old lands. Do not suffer yourself to fall into extremes as to ardour in pulpit delivery. Dr. Wilson is the single instance among ten thousand failures in the a-pathetic school; a noble instance, I grant, but rather an exception than a precedent. Perhaps the best rule is to abominate the expression of a feeling which one does not experience, but not to repress feeling where the subject is adapted to excite it. I do not call to mind any English sentence, in which the phrase "protracted" is used in a good sense; yet we say "protracted meeting"—why not "continued meeting"?

Among my pastoral trials, is the conviction (as a thief of the worst and most inveterate stamp) of a man, who has been 20 years an apparently devout member of my church. I never missed him from his pew, nor ever observed him inattentive. It gave occasion to one or two sermons on "offences," "hypocrisy," and "self-deception," which I trust may be useful; but it affords great glorying to the aliens. I took occasion to press this idea, which I think valuable, that, granting that there is such a thing in the world as a *hypocrite,* the very place where we must reasonably expect to find him, is in the Church of Christ: hence no reproach ought to be cast on the latter. You may have been told that I was invited (with the prospect of a call) to preach in Baltimore; I have declined it. If I am to be a pastor, and nothing but necessity could make me willing to be any thing else, I believe I have more openings to serve Christ here, than in any more laborious charge. I have counted up about fifty persons, with whom I have had religious conversation, and who are more or less tender. A great excitement would bring these to the anxious seat, and probably into the church; but without this, *I* have an access to them which no other person could have, for a long time; and which I should not have to the same number elsewhere. The same kind of argument applies to a number of other topics. Still, I feel my constitution to be inadequate to the labours. I usually carry an aching head to a pillow of restlessness every Sunday, Wednesday, and Thursday night; and am truly incompetent for pastoral visitation. Yet, the life of a minister has great satisfactions and rewards, which I trust you may experience in a far higher degree than your unfaithful friend. Some of my most delightful hours have been spent in sick-rooms, by dying-beds, or among poor, unlettered believers, or especially in rejoicing with them that do rejoice for the first time in Christ. A singular case of hallucination has just come to my knowledge; a sweet, pious, and otherwise intelligent young girl, of my flock, thinks she has had a supernatural monition from a dying friend that *she* is soon to die also. I shall not be surprised if the impression on her mind should verify the prediction. We are in a fair way to have Trenton made an island, by the canal, feeder, water-power-race, (now "being" digged,) creek, and river, which surround us on every hand. Thousands of Irish Catholics are here. Bishop Kenrick preached, confirmed, anointed, spat, curtseyed, besprinkled, and mumbled, in our chapel yesterday. Read Cramp's Text-book of Popery; it is highly instructive, and gives good authority.

TRENTON, *March* 27, 1832.

The family [Mrs. Rice] which has entertained me for more than three years has just moved, and me with them, so that I am in a great bustle, and scarcely self-possessed enough to write a letter: you must be content with something brief. The past winter has been one of more ailments to me than common, and I am coming out of it almost as much debilitated as after a summer's sweat. Yet I have to be thankful that since October I have not lost a Sabbath by indisposition. Perhaps you knew Rev. Robert Roy, who has recently died in Monmouth county, New Jersey. He was a man of as much Christian faith, and uninterrupted joy, as I have ever known. He preached until his voice was absolutely inaudible, from pulmonary decay. Some acquaintances of mine use a curious argument in favour of Mr. Finney, namely, that as soon as Mr. Nettleton opposed him, the latter ceased to have revivals. The argument goes upon a false fact, to my knowledge. We have an eccentric Methodist in Trenton, who declares that certain of their ministers have committed the unpardonable sin, by refusing to countenance all his measures. This is quite an improvement upon some of our denunciatory proceedings. I wish all parties would read what Edwards says hereupon, in his work on Revivals. I dare not condemn a multitude of things, which I would as little dare to do. There is, it seems to me, an inordinate stress laid by both parties upon mere *measures*, as unreasonable as argument about mere ceremonies. On one hand a truly superstitious reliance is placed on certain methods of conducting meetings, &c.; on the other, certain measures are denounced as if they were absolutely anti-christian. One man has anxious meetings, another anxious seats, a third calls them out in the aisle, a fourth invites them to his study, a fifth visits them at home. Here are diversities of methods, but no ground, I think, for violent controversy. Various methods have been blessed, to my knowledge, in various revivals, and new ones are yet to be invented. On this subject, I think our old men are too tenacious. Nothing is worse in my estimation, *because* it is new, unless indeed it be doctrine. It is hard to determine in all cases what measures are the best, but almost any are better than total listlessness.

TRENTON, *May* 23, 1832.

Your sentiments about "systems" are, as far as I can see, just my own, although you seem to think otherwise.[1] Please

---

[1] The allusions here are to an article by Alexander in the Repertory for April, "On the use and abuse of Systematic Theology."

observe I compared, not the *system*, but *exegesis* to the *telescope;* also that I have reiterated your sentiment three or four times about " not asking a man to believe, &c., on the authority of Copernicus;" also that I have not insinuated that there was any bona fide opposition to systems in new-school men, inasmuch as they are systematizing as fast as they can; *e. g.* Duffield on Regeneration; also that I have denounced the setting systems on a parity with the Bible. What then, you will say, is left? Only the practical question, "Is this system, as such, so un-useful or injurious, as to deserve utter banishment?" It is difficult to speak of one's own practice without egotism, but I find it the shortest way here of expressing my sincere convictions, and you must bear with the fault. I have never read through any system of theology;* I read as much in Wesley and Watson as in Turretine. My days are almost entirely spent in studies purely exegetical, in which it has been my principle for a long time, not to approach a commentary until, if possible, I had arrived at some rational exposition of the passage. Yet I wrote the article in question sincerely, and in opposition to the cant of multitudes, especially in our seminaries, who are far from going to hermeneutics in their flight from dogmatics, but pick up their objections, and their doctrines too, from the last influential patron with whom they have studied. And I have not fabricated one objection, but have had them all urged upon me in repeated conversations; some of them having been noted down in Princeton, long ago. I shall not say another word, however, upon this question, for I hate even the appearance of controversy, in letters as in conversation, and rejoice that, with many more real differences of opinion, we have scarcely ever had one wordy war in the course of some dozen years. What a noble book " Saturday Evening " [by Isaac Taylor]'is. I have to lay it down, at every few pages, and muse. It has made me hope more for the church, and desire more to be in heaven. Before such a genius—let critics say what they will—I stand in awe; and whether he is a New-Schoolite, a Methodist, or (as I conclude) a Churchman, I give him the homage due from a little and cold to a great and flaming spirit.

Just at this time I am floundering in that perilous channel, the vii. c. Romans. I am at the Greek and the versions, without commentaries, and am hoping to steer clear of radical error. The noblest help in New Testament study is the Greek Concordance, which is better than any dictionary. Some of our lexicons are nothing short of Commentaries; though you have no

---

* I since remember Calvin's Institutes.

doubt observed this, just read Schleusner or Wahl upon such a word as πνευματικὸς. The concordance, on the contrary, makes the Spirit of God the commentator. A—— has just committed to memory the Epistle to the Hebrews in Greek and English, and about twenty of the Psalms in Hebrew. At his instance I have attempted a little in this way, and find it a great advantage; for I can speculate upon the meaning of a passage while I lie awake in bed, as I very often do of late.

As to the Assembly, I really know not what to think or to say, or even to wish. What would I have? Certainly peace; if possible unity of doctrine; then unity of organization; if we cannot be το αυτο φρονοῦντες, we may at least be την αυτην αγαπην εχοντες, (Philip. ii.;) and the way to attain this seems to be αλληλους ἡγουμενοι ὑπερεχοντας ἑαυτῶν. Alas! who does this? certainly not I; for which I desire to humble myself, and to seek greater measures of self-renunciation and self-neglect. My sentiments are changed since last Assembly; not so much as to men or measures, as spirit. I do not recognize in Mr. ——'s denunciations the spirit of Jesus; nay, nor even of the ardent Paul. Mr. —— and Mr. ——, I try to bless God for it, do not preach "another gospel," and I hope to meet them in heaven, where we shall wonder and smile (with new light) when we look back to see the time we have lost from a glorious work in comparing the trowels, and quarrelling over the hods and mortar of the spiritual temple. "Christ *is* preached, and I therein rejoice, yea and will rejoice," even though, as to the manner, some may preach him of "envy," "strife," or "ill-will."

By adopting the practice of going out very early in the morning, often before sunrise, I think I have become a little more vigorous. External nature, especially at this season, produces a remarkable and happy modification of my religious feelings; and after a glorious sunrise, I feel better all day. David no doubt felt the force of such influences: witness in particular the 104th Psalm, which I have often read while looking upon the very pictures delineated in the latter part of it. From my little study window, I catch a glimpse of green fields (about three panes full) and eastern clouds, and this helps me in the morning. I always esteemed it a great blessing, at my father's house, to be able to look out eastward upon a thousand acres of meadow land, and a hundred and sixty degrees of hill and mountain on the horizon. I hold this to be not romance but reason. My health is very poor; far more so than I usually express; my breast has been in a peculiarly weak condition for some weeks.

TRENTON, *June* 6, 1832.

I cannot undertake Newton's Life, [for Sunday School Union;] my hands are more than full of writing. I am "gleaning" in Biblical Antiquities for the Sunday School Journal, which fills up my "horæ subcesivæ;" have from a third to a half of every Repertory to write; am in the trying season of the year, and also (I think) a little alive to the importance of renewed exertion for the revival of religion among my people.

I am apprehensive that most readers pass over my Gleanings as a mere compilation from the little abridged Jahn, which issued from the Andover press. On the contrary, they are carefully compiled from his Biblische Archäologie in 5 vols. 8vo, which has never been translated. Most of them were delivered as Lectures to my S. S. Teachers, which accounts for the style. When I get through the "old store" I shall be able to simplify more. The "Drunkard's Progress" is admirable: pray, improve on that hint—for the cuts may be cut out and pasted in cottages, to great benefit of many. Let us have the "Bad boy's progress," &c.

I rejoice in the comparative harmony of our Assembly, as reported by my father. Surely we have enemies enough without. You and I cannot expect to live long here; let us stir one another up to new and redoubled efforts.

Excuse haste, for I have now to write a Sunday School Sermon, to revive, if I can, our drooping schools.[1]

TRENTON, *June* 19, 1832.

In self-vindication, I deny your calumnious charge about my writing so many sermons. No sir, I do not write three sermons in five months. What if I write Life of Elijah? Am I forestalled? Give me a list of eminent men whose lives you have not. Gardiner? Spencer? Urquhart? Bunyan? You may count on me for any thing small. In plain sincerity I should be sorry to see my hitherto published "Gleanings" [in the Sunday School Journal] collected into a stack. The sheaves are bound up too loosely. If my life is spared, and our heavenly Father smile on the enterprise, I will some day produce a Gazetteer for the Bible which shall deserve in some degree the character of completeness. Scripture Geography is (among English scholars) "the earth without form, and void, and darkness upon the face of the deep." I have many plates in Jahn which might be copied. Help me to find cuts for my Gleanings. Hereafter I shall treat the subject so as by no possibility to tread on Nevin's toes, [" Bib-

---

[1] This sermon was printed in four numbers of the Sunday School Journal, (July and August, 1832,) under the head of "Plain Suggestions."

lical Antiquities," published by S. S. Union,] unless where he is wrong. In spiritual tendency his is the best extant.

The embarrassments which make me cry "no time," you appear not yet to understand. This instant I am called down by a man, who probably will sit an hour and leave me to guess why he called.—Better than I thought, for he gave me five dollars, missionary money, but kept me an hour, which I could not refuse, for I believe he received benefit, and was quickened by my suggestions. Yet I scarcely have two hours solid, except before breakfast, for spiritual nourishment. In a sickly season, I have not two waking hours in which I can sit down to read, much less to write. Once a fortnight I am knocked up by headache. Yet I love my work. O that I were more faithful!

TRENTON, *June* 20, 1832.

I am unable to speak from knowledge of Townsend's arrangement of the Old Testament; the New Testament I have pretty carefully examined, and am disposed to recommend it; though the merit of such a work is suspended almost wholly on the accuracy of the chronological theory adopted by its author; and this, you know, is a knotty, and, perhaps, inexplicable subject. You have read "Bickersteth's Scripture Help"? also his own abridgment of it? Both these works, if they have not been, should without delay be published by the Union. For my own use, I know no better work so far forth as the writer means it to extend. Introductions to the Scripture of a plain kind are very needful, and one to the New Testament, I think, I will endeavour to provide.[1] I have a work by Rosenmüller, called "Views in Palestine," containing 25 views of landscapes, localities, cities, ruins, 'paysages,' &c., in Palestine, with letterpress descriptive. They are well done; size somewhere about 12 × 18 inches. Could not a *miniature* of this, with more letterpress (original) be made a very fine book for the Union?[2]

I perceive plainly that the report of Cholera from Quebec, Montreal, and White Hall, has alarmed our population. God grant that I may be enabled to use the opportunity for inculcating truth. Surely we are all called upon to do something extraordinary, earnest, and without the delay of a moment. On consultation with my session, I have determined to have a day of special fasting, without waiting for proclamation. Gen. Jackson, perhaps you are aware, has refused to accede to the proposal of

---

[1] This he accomplished for both Testaments in "The Scripture Guide; a familiar introduction to the Study of the Bible," published by the Union in 1838. Pp. 263.

[2] He assisted in realizing this.

the New York Clergy, to have a national fast, though Madison proclaimed one about the time of the War. C. McIlvaine [now Bishop] said, that he and his Church would prostrate themselves before God, if no other one in America did so. You will of course, by this time, be up and doing in Philadelphia. Pray put this thought into shape, and publish it in daily papers, viz. : " the affectation of courage or indifference, or fool-hardiness, on the approach of such a pestilence, is a contempt of God ; a Pharaoh-like hardening of the heart : like Nineveh, we should all be in sackcloth. The question is not between evangelical and rational Christians, nor even between Christians and infidels, but between Theists and Atheists ; for if there is a God and a controlling power, then it is wise to humble ourselves before him." The alarming probability is, that Rev. xvi. 9 will be in many fulfilled : on the outpouring of the vial, " men were scorched with great heat, and blasphemed the name of God, *which hath power over these plagues :* and they *repented not* to give him glory : " and again, under the 5th vial, " they gnawed their tongues for pain, and blasphemed the God of heaven." I confess that I am very deeply impressed with the conviction that we ought to be awake as we have never been before, in calling aloud upon sinners to save themselves from this untoward generation of practical atheism. To neglect the call is emphatically to *harden the heart.* " *To-day* (let us say) if ye will hear his voice, harden not your heart." Such are our sinners, and such the exigency of the time, that we should " save them with fear, pulling them out of the fire." Whether we have Cholera or not, we have no time to lose : should the panic produce only a conviction of this in ministers and believers, it will be a messenger of judgment and also of mercy. The public press may take happy advantage of the fears of men, to lead them to conviction : though I am persuaded that the natural tendency of the bruit made about the subject, and the incessant conversations on it in familiar style, is baneful to the soul. When the Lord's judgments are abroad, O that the inhabitants might learn righteousness. Now is the time, I think, for a tract to be written called *Blood on the Door Post*, (with reference to the sprinkled paschal blood in Egypt,) and left at every door.[1] Now is the time for us to forget our petty squabbles about which leg we shall put foremost in our *measures* to convert men to God, and for earnest effort in the cause of the Redeemer. Just look at New York, how the city authorities and people are on the alert in endeavouring to bar

---

[1] In a few weeks after this he prepared a tract under this title, which was published by the Sunday School Union. It was also inserted in the Sunday School Journal, August 29, 1832.

out the plague. And what are Christians doing, in any kind of proportion to the emergency? It does seem to me to be a pitiful and vile desertion of the cause of human souls, for us to be engaged deeply in any thing else, especially just now, than efforts to save them—to save them from spiritual plagues—to save them *now!* Suggest to me, if you can, any and every hint which may be useful in availing myself of the general 'sensation' for the advantage of souls: any methods happily struck out among your clergymen and active Christians. I find my own soul somewhat sweetened by the precious, precious thought of a presiding, guiding, governing, almighty Saviour, Lord, and elder brother. I am sorry (Dr. or) Mr. Cox brings undue zeal to bear upon the Papists; I would not have "railing accusation" brought against them any more than against "the devil;" yet I am not disposed to make concessions to a church, of which the very assumption of infallibility precludes any apology for ancient tenets. These tenets I will take from their Councils (especially Trent) and nowhere else. I have one———, a Romish priest near me, running about to every corner of my church, and taking no repulse even from people that have no toleration for his presence. Such a specimen of vexatious and pragmatical zeal I never saw. Until I see in him or some other papist of the thousand whom we have here, some stray symptom of grace, I shall not be disposed to come down to any more liberal or charitable ground than that of the universal Protestant Church; viz., that Popery is a delusion greatly destructive to souls. The evidence of this I see almost every hour passing my window. If these thousand Papists were to die next week with Cholera, I have every reason to think that not one of them would have a conception of any preparation beyond the opus operatum of ceremonies. This is my conclusion from personal conversation, and various reports of credible members of my church. O that the Bible and the accompanying Spirit of God might rid the world of blindness and impenitence!

PRINCETON,[1] *July* 18, 1832.

The Jacotot method of instruction has made, and is making great noise in France and Belgium. It is not a theory, but a practice; admits of a singular adaptation to *our* system. I will (D. V.) give you a little series on it for the S. S. Journal.[2] The

---

[1] Mr. Alexander was for some weeks with his family at Princeton, on account of the illness of his eldest child, but continued to perform his pastoral duties in Trenton.

[2] His correspondent had lately become the editor of the large weekly "Journal" published by the Sunday School Union. To this paper Mr.

"Library of Useful Knowledge" is too abstruse [for use of Journal]. "The Library of Entertaining Knowledge" is just the thing for your purpose. The "Plain why and because" is a mere salmagundi; an aggregation, not a selection, still less a digest, and therefore a catch-penny. "Wonders of Nature and Art," by J. Taylor, London, 12mo, many plates; very good.

My notion is that the whole field of *Juvenile Education* comes within your scope. You may make the S. S. Journal easily the best journal of Education extant. For this purpose—1, you ought to have correspondents in Europe, and the Missions, such as Ceylon and Hawaii, &c.; 2, you ought to take a French and a German Journal on Education, and have a man to read and extract from each. You ought, 3, to have always before you this great idea, that the Bible is the central instrument in universal Education; that beginning with this, the whole Encyclopedia may be traversed; that to this hive every thing should be carried. You ought, (need I say it?) 4, to endeavour to make every number save souls. May God help you in this responsible undertaking!

PRINCETON, *Aug.* 4, 1832.

By this time perhaps you have seen in the New York papers, that Cholera rages in Princeton. Through Divine Mercy this is not true. There have indeed been three deaths of Irishmen in the town, and nearly twenty on the neighbouring canal. Great uproar has been occasioned by some cits who are rusticated here, and who condemned the little Health-Board for having a hospital within the borough. William has been with a large proportion of those who have died; some he has watched and rubbed all night; some he has picked up and carried in his arms to their dying beds. He almost got out of bed himself to do this, and has turned night into day. Some of the theological students have deserved nobly of our neighbourhood, by their devotion in nursing, &c. This morning, I learn that a highly respectable contractor on the canal—7 miles hence—Mr. Spencer, died last night. The disease is at Scudder's mills, 3 miles; and Kingston, 3 miles; all cases Irish Catholics. Princeton is nevertheless uncommonly healthy. The Institutions have not been formally dismissed, but whoever will, goes. I am much

Alexander had already been a large contributor; but from June, 1832, to June, 1841, there are few numbers that did not contain something from his pen. His articles were not confined to the subject of education, but embraced a large miscellany, in verse as well as prose, translations, compilations, extracts, as well as original.

flattered by your consideration of my garden dialogue, and pleased, of course, with your arrangements. [One of his works for children—" the Flower Book."]

In estimating this letter, please remember that I write within full hearing of my little boy's cries. Oh! I have new understanding, since I became a father, of that expression "As a father *pitieth* his children," &c. I will send you a number of the Princeton " Courier ; " the article " to the Fearful," was written for you, but the state of things here made me print it without delay.

N. B. I am filling a small 4to blank book with scraps for you. Among others one book called the *Monkey*, which perhaps you may think too quizzical; n'importe, do as you please with all I send. It contains also some Luther-ana, written long ago without reference to Sunday Schools, but a few of them may suit you: also a translation of *Jacotot's* method of teaching.

Take a copy book, lay it by you, and write down in it, at the time the idea sprouts, what you have to say to me; send this, when full, with dates noted, by a private hand: I will attempt the same. I propose to write a " book of the Stars ; " will Jacob Green account it piracy for me to borrow from his Astronomical Recreations ? Prayer is not made often enough, explicitly enough, or fervently enough for physicians, nurses, and persons exposed to the plague ; nor for the souls of those who are just dying.

PRINCETON, *Aug.* 6, 1832.

I returned to Princeton last night from the funeral of my principal supporter and friend in Trenton, Chief Justice Ewing. He gave a decided testimony to the power of faith. He died at $3\frac{1}{2}$ A. M. on Sunday morning, after an illness of 23 hours; decidedly Cholera. He was not only one of the most temperate, and equable, and regular, but one of the halest men in America. You may imagine the consternation. May our covenant God protect us and all we love. O for grace to use up all our talent!

PRINCETON, *Aug.* 28, 1832.

Family trials and personal indisposition have prevented my remittances to the Journal, as regularly as could be desired. You must not rely on me in any such way, for any thing, as to make a disappointment injurious. My little boy still lives, but in great weakness and great suffering. I shall not undertake to describe our anxieties. It is better for me to say—what I believe we can both say truly—we do in a sense "take pleasure in infirmities, in distresses," &c.

As I have a very strong desire that you should be useful in your present sphere, and that you should continue in it, I will be frank enough to say a few words upon the subject. I perceive a change within no long period, from comparative transparency of style, to what may be called constrained, stilted, and, in some cases, even affected. Whether this arises from the influence of any author you have lately read, or a diffidence as to the value of your thoughts when simply expressed, or (as I have detected this in my own case) from mere haste—I pray you have an eye to it. Above every thing else let us be plain and clear. I have very seldom exercised the censorial function—you will bear me witness—but I am sincerely of opinion that you are on a track which may lead you out of the simple path of greatest usefulness. And I am daily trying to contend against a temptation of the same kind, to write in German text (so to speak) what is better written in plain Script. I would not for a thousand guineas write in the style of "Saturday Evening," though I admire it above most people. I make no doubt that you will understand my object, without my throwing in any apologies. Be assured you are in no danger, if you can only resist the alluring spoil of a classic word, a Latin termination, or a recondite turn, and then pursue the rule, "think with the wise and speak with the vulgar."

I have a little book ready for you, which will make from 50—75 pp. of a child's book. Has any one written Spencer's life? If my life is spared, and my pieces succeed, I will (D. V.) devote much of my time to babes' books. My health scarcely admits more. No Cholera here, blessed be God: none in Trenton.

PRINCETON, *September 6,* 1832.

If I can, I will herewith send a piece called *Harvest.* Do what you choose with it. Give it, and any thing else from me, what title you please. Tell me what you think of the plan of the said *Harvest,* and criticize my child's books unmercifully, for I have a great desire to do my best in that line. The Cholera Hospital of the Canal is in the lot behind our garden here. Two persons have just been carried to it; one hopeless. We had thought the disease gone.

I am unable to say much about my little boy. We feel it to be a great trial: yet sometimes I taste some sweetness in the cup. O there is nothing but Christianity that enables one to *face* an affliction.

PRINCETON, *Sept.* 14, 1832.

The circulation of the S. S. Journal is less than I thought. This seems to be an evil incident to all papers which profess to advocate a single cause. As a general religious newspaper, it is the best I know. The ——— becomes more secular every week. His English correspondent should be made usher in some of your girls' boarding-schools. He gets into raptures at all the dear, sweet, pretty, charming things he sees. Faugh! These sentimental literary ——— make one retch. I do not feel any particular competency to write brief tracts of the kind you mention: it is a gift by itself. Put a few evangelical hymns on some of your supernumerary fragments. Or, say a moral ballad out of the cheap repository. Coming to Philadelphia often crosses my mind: and I am in a very desponding condition as to this affair. If I could leave my people in any good hands I might do so, for I am afraid I do little good among them. The mere correspondence of any society, however, would not satisfy my conscience. I must preach, or lecture, or teach. If I had 300 or 400 persons whom I might instruct, in a colloquial popular way in the Bible, its Geography, Antiquities, &c., &c., it would seem to suit my poor wandering mind. My aim is to do something before I die to reach the millions of youth in our land. I have made up my mind to go for the nursery practice. Let others take the fathers and grandfathers, if I can only make an impression on the children. This I wish to do by writing; and I am not sure (though you may think it paradoxical) that I will not do more in this way, as a pastor, than if I were to set about it ex professo.

As to the "chapters and verses;" all I meant to correct was the statement that the *Bible* was not divided into verses until Stephens' time. This is true only of the New Testament. The *numbering* of the verses was introduced by Athias, (see 2 Horne 155;) but the division itself, the *Soph-Passuk* (:), was coeval with the accentuation, which indeed is governed by it, *e. g. Silluk*.

Our little boy varies so little, except from one painful symptom to another, that I do not say much of him. We find the trial severe; more so by far than the ordinary death of a child. But we are wonderfully helped. Even now we find that "He who tempers the wind to the shorn lamb," makes our way smoother than one could suppose. We need the prayers of our friends.

Need I warn you not to think of the Ministry as free from temptations? The very habit of constantly dealing with Divine truth *for the use of others* is a great cause of dreadful formality;

it obtunds the moral sensibility, impairs the tenderness of conscience, and dissociates the actions of the head and heart, to an alarming degree. In preparation and preaching I have often found that subjects which warmed and melted me in the closet, have flowed from my lips in the desk with some animation of manner, but with almost no emotion. Then the *trials* of the ministry to a man who has a conscience, are unspeakable. Who can ever say "I have done all I ought for these souls?"[1]

[1] Soon after the date of this letter Mr. Alexander received two invitations to engage in other employments—one from the American Sunday School Union, the other from the proprietors of "The Presbyterian"—both in Philadelphia. The state of his health made him willing to entertain a proposal to intermit his labours as a pastor, but he was greatly perplexed by the choice presented to him. In a letter of October 1 he wrote: "I have made up my mind (Deo volente) to leave Trenton. I am no longer able to impose myself on a kind people as their pastor. I believe, under God, I might do something for truth, order, and moderation, by editing the Presbyterian." On the 15th he inquires for details of the services expected by the Union. "Should the labour require any thing like the assiduous sitting of an ordinary club, I could not endure it. If matters are to depend very much upon my head, as to planning, ordering, allotting, &c., you know as well as I can tell you, that I have no ability that way. I have always said and felt that I can make a good second or associate, but a most wretched principal. The main objections urged against my accepting your offer, among my acquaintances, are such as these: that all the employments which I should have, as your Secretary, would not be of a kind to improve my mind, or carry forward those pursuits in which I have hitherto been employed; whereas the editorial duties would be the reverse. That all the influence which I might exert specially in harmonizing our distracted church, would be thrown into a different channel. That however high the objects of the Sunday School, the details of the proposed office would be essentially *secular*. That I am, more than most persons, ill adapted for a station requiring scheming, management, practical judgment, knowledge of men, enlarged views, &c. This is especially urged by ———, and I am the less able to resolve this scruple, inasmuch as no man can safely judge of his own character and talents."

Again, on the first of November (from Trenton): "I cannot describe to you the painful uncertainty in which my mind is placed respecting the two situations offered to me. This uncertainty is by no means relieved by the visit I made to the city; for while I feel more deeply the claims of both, the labours of both are more fully before my eyes. Such is my state of doubt, that were I *instanter* to decide for either, I believe no subsequent light or disappointment could make me feel as if I had done morally wrong. I feel a total want of that sort of business tact which this great enterprise demands. I am indebted to the Board for being willing to make so hazardous an experiment; but I am not the less fearful lest it should result in an entire failure. I never could do any thing in the way of begging money; and the kind of service which Mr. Baird has rendered, is as foreign to my whole taste, education, talents, and habits, as banking would be. On the other hand, feeling all the unpleasantnesses of the editorial office, there is certainly a definiteness about the service to be rendered which permits me at least to say, this is a thing which I could do."

He finally chose the editorial position, and entered upon its duties in January, 1833. His connection with the Trenton congregation terminated formally on the last day of October, 1832;. but his family still continuing there, he supplied the pulpit many of the Sabbaths of that winter. In the year 1859 the editor of these letters published a "History of the Presbyterian Church in Trenton," and at my request, my friend and predecessor had given me some recollections of his pastorate, in the form of a letter, which appears in that volume. It is so characteristic, and makes such a suitable close to this chapter of the correspondence, that I do not hesitate to reproduce it here:

"NEW YORK, *February* 10, 1859.

"MY DEAR FRIEND :—The retrospect of my ministerial life brings to view so many defects, and such unfruitfulness, that I have never been able to take pleasure in numbering up sermons preached, visits made, and members added; nor have I any anniversary or autobiographical discourses to which I could refer. At your request, however, I cannot refuse to give you a few reminiscences of my connexion with the church of which you are the pastor.

"A great intimacy subsisted between my father and our predecessor, the Rev. JAMES F. ARMSTRONG, and the friendship between their respective descendants continues to this day. Mr. Armstrong had been the friend of Witherspoon, Smith, and Kollock. He was laid aside from preaching, by a disabling and distressing rheumatism, before I ever entered his delightful and hospitable house—rich in good books, good talk, and good cheer—where old and young were alike made welcome and happy. But this brought me acquainted with Trenton, with that family, and especially with Chief Justice EWING, by whose means and influence, more than any other, I was afterwards led to settlement among them. The family of Mr., afterwards Judge, Ewing, was the home of my childhood and youth; which led that distinguished and excellent man to look upon my early performances in the pulpit with undue partiality. By him, and by the late General SAMUEL R. HAMILTON, who was a Princeton man, my name was brought before the congregation, and I was installed as their pastor, by a committee of Presbytery, on the eleventh day of February, 1829. I had, however, begun my labours with them on the tenth of January, when I preached from 1 Cor. xi. 28. My strictly pastoral labours ended on the last day of October, 1832, when I preached from Ezekiel xvi. 61, 62; though I continued to supply the pulpit until the end of the year. My term of settlement may therefore be called four years. The records of the Church-session will show the number of accessions to the communion of the church; these were few. There was nothing like a revival of religion during my continuance with them, and it was cause of painful thought to me that my labours were so little owned to the awakening of sinners. Neither am I aware that there was any remarkable addition to the number of hearers. But the people were forbearing and affectionate towards their young and inexperienced minister, who for most of the time was feeble in health, and was subjected, as you know, to some unusual afflictions in regard to his early children.

In those days we worshipped in the old church, which was sufficiently capacious, with one of the old-time high pulpits. The congregation had been trained to habits of remarkable punctuality and attention. Notwithstanding some inroads of new measures during the previous period, under the labours of a so-called Evangelist, the church was as sound and staid a Presbyterian body as I have ever seen. It comprised some excellent and experienced Christians, and among these the valued elders whose names you have recorded. Good Mr. McNeely was slow but sure; an upright man, of more kindness than appeared at first; of little vivacity, and no leaning towards risks or innovation. Mr. Voorhees and Mr. Samuel Brearley came later into the session; both, in my judgment, judicious and godly men. Mrs. ARMSTRONG, the venerable relict of the pastor first named, does not belong particularly to my part of the narrative, except that she chose to treat me with the regard of a mother for a son. She was then in health and strength, and lived to exhibit a dignified, serene, and beautiful old age. Having come of a distinguished family, the Livingstons of New York, she never ceased to gather around her fireside some of the most elegant and cultivated society. Her conversation, though quiet, was instructive, turning often upon the heroes of the Revolution. She was, I think, at Princeton during the battle; indeed, she was a native of that town. From that excellent family I received support and encouragement of the most useful and delicate kind, during a time of manifold trials. My term of service was marked by no striking external events, no great enlargement, excitement, or disaster. The long-suffering of God was great towards a timid and often disheartened servant, who remembers the period with mingled thankfulness and humiliation.

"At this time the Trenton church contained some excellent specimens of solid, instructed, old school Presbyterianism. I shall never forget the lessons which it was my privilege to receive from aged and experienced Christians, who must often have looked with wonder and pity on the young minister who undertook the responsible task of guiding them. The dying scenes which a pastor beholds in his early years make a deep impression; and I recall some which were very edifying, and which attested the power of the doctrines which had been inculcated. Among my most valued parishioners was a man in humble life, who has lately gone to his rest, I mean JAMES POLLOCK. At a later day he was most wisely made an elder. At that time he lived in a small house on Mill Hill, and worked as a dyer in one of the woollen factories on the Assanpink. His figure was somewhat bent, and his hands were always blue, from the colours used in his trade. But his eye was piercing and eloquent; his countenance would shine like a lantern from the light within; and the flame of his strong and impassioned thought made his discourse as interesting as I ever heard from any man. He had the texts of Scripture, as many Scotchmen have, at his finger-ends, and could adduce and apply passages in a most unexpected manner. The great Scottish writers were familiar to him. I think his favorite uninspired volume was Rutherford's "Christ's Dying and Drawing Sinners to Himself." I lent him Calvin's Institutes, which he returned with expressions of high admiration for *Mr. Caulvin*. His acquaintance with the reformation history of his native land, in both its great periods, was remarkable, being such as would have done credit to any learned clergyman. Unlike many who resemble him in attainment, Mr. Pollock was inwardly and deeply affected by the truths which he knew. His speech was always seasoned with salt, and I deemed it a means to grace to listen to his ardent and continuous discourse. He was certainly a great talker, but without assumption or any wearying of competent hearers. His dialect was broad, west-country Scotch, for he was from Beith, in Ayrshire; and while I was resident his sense of the peculiarity kept him from praying in the meetings, though none could otherwise have been more acceptable. Having from my childhood been used to Scotch Presbyterians, and knowing how some of the narrower among them will stickle for every pin of the covenanted tabernacle, and every shred and token, as if ordained in the decalogue, I was both surprised and delighted to observe how large-minded Mr. Pollock was, in respect to every improvement, however different from the ways of his youth. I have witnessed his faith during grievous illnesses, and I rejoice to know that he was enabled to give a clear dying testimony for the Redeemer whom he loved. Such are the men who are the glory of our Presbyterian churches.

"During the term of my incumbency it is remarkable that the two persons who had most influence in congregational affairs were not communicants, though they were closely connected with all that occurred in the church; these were Chief Justice EWING and Mr. SOUTHARD, afterwards Secretary of the Navy. It deserves to be noted, among the traits of a Presbyterianism which is passing away, that Judge Ewing, as a baptized member of the church, always pleaded his rights, and once in a public meeting declared himself amenable to the discipline of church courts. (Discipline, chap. i. § 6, page 456.) There is good reason to believe that he was a subject of renewing grace long before his last illness in 1832. During this brief period of suffering he made a distinct and touching avowal of his faith in Christ.

"Judge Ewing is justly reckoned among the greatest ornaments of the New Jersey bar. His acquaintance with his own department of knowledge was both extensive and profound, closely resembling that of the English black-letter lawyers, who at this moment have as many imitators at the New Jersey bar as anywhere in America. He was eminently conservative in Church and State; punctual in adherence to rule and precedent, incapable of being led into any vagaries, sound in judgment, tenacious of opinion, indefatigable in labour, and incorruptibly honest and honourable, so as to be proverbially cited all over the State. In a very remarkable degree he kept himself abreast of the general literature of the day, and was even lavish in regard to the purchase of books. He was a truly elegant gentleman, of the old school; an instructive and agreeable companion, and a hospitable entertainer. He deserves to be named in any record of the church, for I am persuaded that there was no human being to whom its interests were more dear. As the warm and condescending friend of my boyhood in youth, he has a grateful tribute from my revering affection.

"In one particular the people of Trenton were more observant of our Form of Government (see chap. xxi.) than is common. When from any cause there was no one to preach, the service was nevertheless carried on by the elders, according to the book, and a sermon was read. The reader on these occasions was always Mr. Ewing, and the discourse which he selected was always one of Witherspoon's; the choice in both cases being significant. I have often been led to consider how much better this is, for instance in country congregations, than the rambling away to hear some ignorant haranguer, perhaps of an erroneous sect, or the listening to a frothy exhortation from some zealous and forward brother, without gifts and without authority.

"The name of Dr. FRANCIS A. EWING, son of the Chief Justice, naturally occurs to our thoughts here. Space is not allowed for that extended notice which might elsewhere be proper, for the Doctor's was a character well deserving close study. Though a professional man by title, he was in fact and of choice much more a man of letters and a recluse student of science. His attainments were large and accurate, though made in an irregular way, and though he never seemed to others to be studying at all. In the classical languages, in French, in the natural sciences, and in all that concerns elegant literature and the fine arts, he was singularly full and accurate. In matters of taste he was cultivated, correct, and almost fastidious. Music was his delight, and he was equally versed in the science and the art. It was after the term of my pastorship that he developed his skill as an organist, but at a much earlier day he devoted himself for years to the gratuitous instruction of the choir; and though I have heard many noted precentors, I can remember none who had greater power of adaptation and expression. Though his own voice was slender and uninviting, he long made his influence felt in rendering all that was musical subservient to the spirit of worship.

"Dr. Ewing professed his faith in Christ during my years of ministry. His early religious exercises were very deep and searching, and the change of his affections and purposes was marked. He had peculiarities of temper and habit which kept him much aloof from general society, and thus abridged his influence. His likes and dislikes were strong, and if he had more readily believed the good will of others towards himself, he would have been more useful and more happy. I should sin against truth if I did not say that towards me he was for forty years a warm, forbearing, tender, and at times most efficient friend. I have been with him at junctures when it was impossible not to detect, through all his extraordinary reserve, the workings of a heart agitated and swayed by gracious principle.

"SAMUEL L. SOUTHARD was also a member of the congregation, and a friend of all that promised its good. More sprightly and versatile than Mr. Ewing, he resembled a tropical tree of rapid growth. Few men ever attained earlier celebrity in New Jersey. This perhaps tended to produce a certain character which showed itself in good-natured egotism. Mr. Southard was a man of genius and eloquence, who made great impressions on a first interview, or by a single argument. He loved society, and shone in company. His entertainments will be long remembered by the associates of his youth. It is not my province to speak of his great efforts at the bar; he was always named after Stockton, Johnson, and Ewing, and with Frelinghuysen, Williamson, Wood, and their coëvals. Having been bred under the discipline of Dr. Finley, at Baskingridge, he was thoroughly versed in Presbyterian doctrine and ways; loving and preferring this branch of the Church to the day of his death. Defection from its ranks gave him sincere grief, as I am ready more largely to attest, if need be. In those days of his prime, Mr. Southard was greatly under the salutary influence of the Chief Justice, who was his Mentor; I think he felt the loss of this great man in some important points. So earnestly and even tenderly did he yield himself to divine impressions, that his friends confidently expected that he would become a communicant. During this period he was an ardent advocate of the Temperance Society, then in its early stage. I remember attending a meeting at Lawrenceville, in company with my learned friend, the present Chief Justice, where Mr. Southard, following Mr. Frelinghuysen, made an impassioned address in favor of abstinence and the pledge. In regard to religious things, the change to Washington did not tend to increase solemnity or zeal. I have been informed that Mr. Southard felt the deep impression of divine truth at the close of his days. As a young minister, I received from him the affectionate forbearance of an elder brother, and I shall always cherish his memory with love.

"Before closing this hurried letter of reminiscences, let me note that the ruling elders during my day were Robert McNeely, Nathaniel Burrowes, John Voorhees, and Samuel Brearley, all good and believing men, and all gone to the other world. The trustees were Messrs. Rose, Chambers, Ewing, Burroughs, and Fish; of whom likewise all are gone, except my esteemed friends, Messrs. Burroughs and Fish.

"Before taking my pen from the paper, let it be permitted to me to give expression to a feeling of personal regard to the late Mrs. Rice and her family, under whose roof my years of early ministry in Trenton were passed. She was a woman of a meek and quiet spirit, and was honoured and beloved, during a long life, for the benignity of her temper, and the kindliness of her words. Juliette Rice, her daughter, was a person who in some circumstances would have become distinguished. To sincere piety, she added more than usual cultivation, delicacy of taste, refinement of manners, and a balance of good qualities which elevated her to a place among the most accomplished and even the exclusive. Under the disadvantage of a deafness almost total, and a pulmonary disease which slowly wasted her away, she manifested a sweet, uncomplaining disposition, and a steady faith in Christ. Amidst the kindness of these good people I spent the first months of my married life, and welcomed the tender mercies of God in our first-born son, long since taken to be with the Lord.

"Thus I end my rambling letter, (which, by-the-by, is only the last article of an epistolary series extending through forty years,) and am, as always,

"Your faithful friend, JAMES W. ALEXANDER.

" The Rev. Dr. HALL."

CHAPTER VII.

LETTERS WHILE EDITOR OF THE PRESBYTERIAN.[1]

1833.

TRENTON, *January* 8, 1833.

AFTER weather of May, one is hardly prepared for the rigours of such a day as this. I am myself fond of cold weather, but have been more indisposed this winter than usual. This has been the sole cause of my avoiding the city for a time. You intimate that you are going to draw in from the Journal, and give yourself more to book-making. I a little regret this; though, by experiment, I know that you will write books better and more of them, in consequence of having the paper as a stated employment, than if you totally gave yourself up to authorship. Next to preaching, there is no employment I should relish more, than writing books for the Union. I think you have peculiar tact as an editor, of which I feel myself more devoid than I had thought.

To you, I need not say any thing of the unspeakable and increasing joys of Christian wedlock; joys which become purer and more exquisite as they lose the adventitious glare of early romance; joys which are increased by affliction, and raised by religion to the very summit of terrestrial blessings. You will not refuse the counsel, though it may be very familiar, when I urge on you to begin, as soon as possible, with the freest, confidential, mutual, unbosoming on the subject of personal experience. I hear many husbands and wives complaining of a shyness here.

For the last three or four months, there has been a wonder-

---

[1] During the year of his employment as editor, he spent so much time in Philadelphia, that our frequent personal intercourse precluded the usual frequency of correspondence. In the course of this year he preached thirteen times in Trenton, sixteen times in Philadelphia, and fifteen times in Princeton and its neighbourhood.

ful work of grace (so I must call it, notwithstanding blemishes) in the Methodist Church here. I think 150 have been supposedly converted. It goes on uniformly, and some of the changes are surprising. While our other churches suffer, I am persuaded the cause of Christ gains. Such zeal I never saw. They seem disposed to attempt the conversion of every soul in Trenton. God grant them success. I cannot but say that God is with them of a truth, though we have lost a number of hearers. It is not the minister, but the private members who have been instrumental in this.

TRENTON, *January* 17, 1833.

You will have seen in the Presbyterian, No. 1 of Dr. Miller's letters; and, I doubt not, you approve its spirit. It is a sincere attempt at pacification; and, like all such attempts, will displease the extremes. I have nearly finished the Life of *Nicholas Ferrar*, a wonderful man of the reigns of James and Charles 1.[1] There is one scruple which your committee may have about it: his piety, which was eminent, exhibits itself very much in attachment to his king, his church, fasts, feasts, liturgies, &c. I preached last night, with much comfort, from Psalm lxxvii. 7, "Will the Lord cast off forever?"—Answer 1. No. His *attributes* forbid the thought. 2. No. His *gift of Christ* forbids: "He that spared not his own Son," &c. 3. No. His dealings towards the *church* forbid. 4. No. His dealings in time past to *us* forbid. 5. No. His special promises forbid. Application: 1. To *have* this safety we must have interest in Christ. 2. To enjoy the comfort of this, we must have a good persuasion of our interest. 3. To be raised in triumph above all despondency, we must have the full assurance of hope. May such blessings be ours! I am reading a file of the London Gazette, 1682–7.

TRENTON, *February* 1, 1833.

I *had* commenced the Life of Elijah, and made some considerable mental preparation, and written some twenty pages; but I hereby decline it, as the author in whose hands it is, is immeasurably above me in this style. I say this ex animo. I will, Deo volente, go to work upon Bunyan. I have Southey's life of him, but want some other. Ferrar is done, and awaits an opportunity. I am not sanguine about it, and shall be neither surprised nor mortified if it is rejected. It has these grand faults: It is meager in dates and consecutiveness; it is too much padded out with remark, and it is too ascetic for the age.

[1] This work was published by a bookseller of Philadelphia.

Yet it is a little morsel of history, entirely unique; and would be read with much interest. A French gentleman lately told me it was considered a vulgarism to write as capitals the *L* and *D*, in such names as *l'Enfant, d'Arvieux*, &c.; unless at the beginning of a sentence. Perhaps I shall begin my "Mother's Book," before Bunyan. Scripture biography I am conscious of no talent for; my life of Elijah would have been an experiment. I am at a Jane-Scott-"ische"[1] book about the Bible. I do not at all satisfy myself in it. I have a favourite plan which I wish to execute, whether the Union should patronize it or not—*Conversations on the Life of Christ.* This I shall begin without delay.[2]

I shall be glad to publish your remarks on catechisms, reserving to myself the usual right of stricture. Your argument goes to prove that catechising is not conducted in the right manner. The piece in the Repertory does not give due credit to the Union questions, and appears to assume that " the present system " is identical with the old parrot-system. You ought to correct this impression. Yet I think, Gall's plan is the right one. I even find great benefit to myself from reading the New Testament with his dissecting Helps. I wish I had access to his publications; I have seen only those republished here. I think I could concoct out of them something useful.

I find no employment so delightful to me, as writing little books. I am determined not to put my name on them, and I even doubt whether I shall ever agree to say " by the author of so and so." You will perceive that Mr. Ferrar established a bona fide Sunday School in 1626. I have no doubt that Paul had one at Corinth and Ephesus.

PRINCETON, *August* 7, 1833.

Princeton has never been freer from disease than for two months. I found the air restorative on the first draught of it, and the society still more so. I have recently seen some astonishing experiments, original with Prof. Henry, in further proof of the identity of magnetism and galvanism. He has made the strongest magnet ever seen, and has one nearly complete which will sustain 5,000 lbs. when charged from a voltaic battery.

I have tried to *glean* [" Biblical antiquities "] but cannot promise you any thing regular, as I dare not apply myself, and yet have a mass of matter constantly demanded by the two daughters of the horse-leech, the Presbyterian and Repertory. You must let me off with occasional contributions in no regular series.

[1] " Jane Scott," on prayer, was one of his own Sunday School books. ' The Only Son " was another of his writings about this time, (224 pages.)
[2] His series under this head appeared in the Journal.

I am endeavouring to find out the *precise and complete* history of the Missionary Concert, [Monthly Prayer;] have you any references on that subject, which can be useful to me? This village still increases; some half-dozen handsome houses are building, besides the new College, the Seminary Chapel, and the Episcopal Church. Bishop —— is, in my poor judgment, a puerile and namby-pamby writer. See his published discourse over the corner-stone of the Church here.

I am really pained at heart about my late poor charge. They are dividing, dwindling, and scattering; cannot agree in any one; and though the place is rapidly growing, and soon to grow yet more, the congregation decays. Their appeals to *me* produce an effect which you can never know, until you have have broken the peculiar cords which unite a pastor and flock.[1] There was *one* case of undeniable Cholera Maligna here, but it was like a bolt of lightning, without precursor or consequent.

Aug. 14.—As I have at this present 20 grains of calomel in my carcase, you will not expect me to be very hilarious. I had been much better, but am suffering almost all the time with a severe rheumatism in my game leg. Dr. Miller's son [Samuel] took part of the first honour yesterday. I forgot to say that —— called on Lee at Cambridge, and was taken by him to the library, and saw the celebrated Beza MS., and Beza's autograph letter; also Burckhardt's Arabic MSS. at Edinburgh, (which he glorifies amazingly.) He bought a book at *Blackwood's*, and took his last cup of coffee at *Ambrose's*.

I am, in extreme haste, your nauseous friend.

PRINCETON, *November* 4, 1833.

You perhaps know that I am not in favour of a separate Sunday School Society. But I am not sure but that to *prevent* such an organization, it will be needful to concede a separate Society, for *printing* our sectarian characteristics. Further than this, I am not willing to advocate any thing. I do not understand you as complaining of my inserting "Consistency"; but if any one should complain, I can only say, that the question is becoming common, is discussed in our judicatories, and that we ought to have a fair understanding about it. Moreover, I sincerely wish some Presbyterian friend of the A. S. U. would come out in the Presbyterian. I assure you of a fair hearing, for any reasonable time and space.

You, no doubt, have heard more than I, of the synodical pro-

---

[1] His successor, the Rev. John W. Yeomans, was installed October 7, 1834, on which occasion Mr. Alexander preached.

ceeding touching your Presbytery. Non nostri tantas componere lites! Of the technical and ecclesiastical correctness of what the synod has done, I entertain no doubt, and of the anti-presbyterial tendency of the affinity system, I have as little; but I greatly question the wisdom of this new measure. One thing is plain enough. Two who are so little agreed as the old and new side, cannot long walk together. I look for a rupture with much certainty, and rebus sic stantibus, could not mourn over it, if it were possible to divide upon the principles of our book. New students are coming into the Seminary and College; two young men have *walked* from Tennessee, carrying all their clothes in their packs. Such men are worth helping; such men do the work of the Church. I mean to help you about the Journal, but must wait till I get a stove in my study ; for, be it known to you, that I write these presents in a room, where my wife, two children, and a nurse, are all discoursing.[1]

[1] Mr. Alexander's connexion with "The Presbyterian" continued from November, 1832, until the close of the volume for 1833. Before the end of the year, however, he accepted the appointment of Professor of Rhetoric and Belles-Lettres in the College of New Jersey, and entered upon its duties.

CHAPTER VIII.

LETTERS WHILE PROFESSOR IN THE COLLEGE OF NEW JERSEY.

1833—1844.

PRINCETON, *December* 12, 1833.

In answer to yours of the 29th ult., I have very little to say in the way of news; it is *you* who are now in the centre, while I am far off from the " stir and smoke of this dim spot, which men call earth;" not, however, in my affections and habits, as I should desire to be. What you say, and what I have elsewhere heard, concerning the Catholic disputation, is mortifying and humiliating. There was a time, before the rise of periodical literature, when oral disputes were necessary and useful; but I am inclined to think that, in the present state of society, the press is the proper engine, the most favourable to dispassionate investigation and fair conclusion. Dr. Ewing's [1] Natural History will be a work of much labour, concisely and judiciously prepared. If I ever can run a little ahead of my proximate employments, I do really mean to journalize some more for you. What think you of my giving *you*, what I had projected for my own paper, a series of *Letters to a Younger Brother?* One appeared in the Presbyterian. It might be made into a book. But then I should insist on not confining myself to religious topics. The heads which I had drafted were: 1. *Religion,* under which, The Great Concern, Bible Reading, Prayer, Divine Worship, Benevolence is Piety, Filial Duty, Regard for Teachers, &c. 2. *Studies;* Memory, Languages, Books Recommended, Study for God. 3. *Manners and Habits;* Habits in General, Good Manners, Early Rising, Temperance, Recreations, Company, &c. 4. *General Instruction.* 5. *Mis-*

---

[1] Dr. Francis A. Ewing, commemorated in the letter on page 201. The Natural History was published in 1835, and reviewed by Mr. Alexander in the Repertory of October of that year.

cellaneous.[1] I am getting into my routine. Though my engagements are by no means numerous, yet having to deal with a number of acute fellows, I cannot avoid a considerable tension of mind. I attend the Seniors four times a week, on one of which occasions I spend about an hour in lecturing; the subject is Rhetoric and Composition. The Latin of the two higher classes is also consigned to me. At present, I have the Juniors five times a week on Tully's Orator. I occasionally lecture to them. Attend prayers every evening, preach in my turn in the chapel, and every Lord's day afternoon at Queenston. Every fortnight a literary club meets, viz.: Drs. Alexander, Miller, Carnahan, Howell, Maclean, and [B. H.] Rice; Professors Dod, Maclean, Henry, Jaeger, Alexander; Tutors S. Alexander, Hart, and Wilson. It is truly a delightful soirée. On alternate weeks a strictly *Clerical* association meets. On Monday, we have a stated faculty meeting, and in the evening a faculty prayer-meeting. On Tuesday evening a College prayer-meeting. On Thursday evening Dr. Rice preaches. My College employments, with the Repertory and Presbyterian, make me a busy man, and I am far from being the less happy on this account. While I used to have your *Cut-Book* to give me texts, I used to be much more fertile in Sunday School scraps. Now it has occurred to me, that if I were to buy up several hundreds of the little French cuts, which they have for scrap-tables, and for transferring, and which they call *Croquis*, &c., I should have abundance of hints. I might paste these little pictures into my MSS., and your wood-engraver could copy them. This may strike you as whimsical; but, seriously, I can do little or nothing without suggestions of this kind.

December 16.—My letter still unfinished. But I do not know that a letter derives its chief value from being done at one lick. Do you know that John Proudfit is appointed Professor of Greek in the New York University? I have just been reading a narrative by Robert Baxter, who was Irving's chief prophet, and who has recanted of the horrible delusions of the "Tongues," &c. I formerly thought there was more fraud than fanaticism, but this has convinced me that they are nearly crazy. Notwithstanding his recantation, Baxter is still regarded by Irving as having been truly inspired, but as having grieved the Spirit.

PRINCETON, *January* 23, 1834.

I have been making a little book out of the remnant of cuts

---

[1] He began his series of letters in the Sunday School Journal, January, 1834, and continued them to twenty numbers, when they were collected in a volume.

for the Gleanings. It will be done in a day or two. I have a *leetle* book also, in the style of "Amelia Finley," an attempt at the Socratic method. But the new labours of my station, especially writing lectures, must, for a time, stay my hand very much. Some of my chief pleasures are in writing for and talking with children.

PRINCETON, *March* 6, 1834.

We are all going on here much as usual. Indeed, there is a happy dearth of all news, except the sickening, dull, stale, and unprofitable reverberation of the monetary question. The burning of the Penn is awful indeed.[1] Mitchelmore I knew well; he was a plain, honest Israelite, without guile, without pride, without one fiery or one bitter ingredient. He was an Englishman, and had been in Britain a Methodist exhorter. I doubt not he has been caught up to the Lord God of Elijah. Of the following particulars you may make such use as you choose: Mr. Wirt[2] was long incog. as the author of the "British Spy;" and I do not know that the secret would have transpired, except from this circumstance: Wirt had caught from Dr. Waddel an enthusiastic admiration of Robert Boyle, as one of the first who had practically carried out the inductive principles of Bacon, and as eminently a Christian philosopher. In the "Spy" he made allusions to Boyle, whose works were then little read, and it was found that these works were scarcely ever taken out of the public library at Richmond except by Mr. Wirt. Nothing in the "Spy" attracted more attention than the account of Dr. Waddel. In June, 1830, I took advantage of a private interview, to ask Mr. Wirt how far the account might be taken as authentic history. He replied that there was no fiction, except in the grouping. He had thrown into one scene circumstances and discourses, which had in point of fact been scattered through various interviews. Yet he had heard all the sentiments from his lips; and on the retrospect he still considered Dr. W. as inferior to no man he had ever heard, in eloquence. For his day, Dr. W. was an eminently learned man. The contents of his library evince an acquaintance with all the learned languages, and the best works in science and literature which were then and there accessible. A few years ago I fell upon a MS. copy of the Minutes of the Old Hanover Presbytery, from which I made the following gleanings: Dr. Waddel was licensed to

---

[1] The steamboat William Penn was burnt on the Delaware March 4. The Rev. John Mitchelmore threw himself from the flames into the river, and was drowned.

[2] The death of Mr. Wirt had lately taken place.

preach, April 2, 1761, at Tinkling Spring, Virginia. His sermons were from Philip. ii. 9, 10, and John v. 40, and his probationary lecture from Isa. lxi. 1–3. At the meeting of Presbytery, at the same place, October 7, 1761, there is the following minute, which needs no comment: "The following calls were put in to Presbytery for Mr. Waddel, viz., one from Upper Falling and the Peaks of Otter; one from Nutbush and Grapy Creek; one from Brown's Meeting House and Jennings' Gap; one from the Fork of James River in Augusta; and one from Halifax: none of which he thought fit to take under consideration." Also a further minute, October 7, 1762: "Mr. Waddel accepts a call from Lancaster and Northumberland." He was ordained at Prince Edward, June 16, 1762. On April 3d, 1774, he was called to Opaken and Cedar Creek. May 1st, 1776, he was called to Tinkling Spring. His decease was reported to Presbytery October 4, 1805. He departed this life September 17, 1805.

Much love to all yours, from me and mine. Excuse my brevity, as I am not at ease.

PRINCETON, *April* 10, 1834.

I owe you an apology for disappointing you twice, in the communications to the paper. The truth is, I have been pressed above measure. First, I have a very oppressive catarrh; then our semi-annual examination lasted 8 days, 7 hours a day, accompanied with other winding-up business; then I am labouring spasmodically to get something instanter for the Repertory; besides an engagement under which I lie to furnish something at once for Rev. John Breckinridge's [Education] annual; and, finally, the New Jersey Lyceum has been meeting here and devolved a good deal of extra work on me.

Mr. and Mrs. Graves (of and for Bombay) have been spending a day with us. Mr. G. is a specimen of meek and affectionate Christianity, such as it does one good to see. The flame of missionary zeal rises considerably in the Seminary after every interview with such a man. The report here is, that the elections in New York have been accompanied with outrages; but we have no particulars. Let me know when any of my S. S. books are accepted. I have several small affairs on the anvil. After one session's trial, I find my present situation more agreeable to the flesh, and, as yet, less incident to trials, than any in which I have previously been. My indisposition this week prevents my fulfilling a purpose of attending a protracted meeting in Queenston, where I preach every Lord's day. The Seminary has just received a set of good old Mr. Simeon's works (21 vols.) from the author; altogether the most splendid London books, paper, binding, &c., I ever saw. You will do me a favour by mentioning to me, from time to time, such Hebrew books as you may see offered for sale; as I am particularly desirous to furnish myself with the best editions of Bibles and Lexicons. I am obliged to you for an occasional English paper; a repetition of the favour will renew my obligation; and so of any other papers, as I no longer pasture upon that sort of clover. Some of these days I mean to have a paper here; but nothing can be done till the Assembly has decided a question or two.

PRINCETON, *June* 3, 1834.

You must excuse me about the motto; like lapidary inscriptions, it requires a Parr to adjust it; and the delicate "nuances" of sententious, elliptical latinity are beyond my reach. In a delicate matter of the kind, I would apply to such a man as Schipper, but to no American. A new memoir of Calvin is published in Berlin, by Henry, Pastor of the French Church there. Calvin on the New Testament has gone through an immense 2d edition, under Tholuck's auspices. ——— was told by Prof. Rheinwald of Bonn, that while almost every system of opinion had been deduced from the Bible by the speculations of modern Germans, no one had been wild enough to dream of diocesan episcopacy, which (he said) had not one adherent in Protestant Germany, as being destitute of a vestige of authority. Our College is growing; we have now 185 students, and still some are coming. Of these about 60 are religious professors. On looking into Guericke, I am unable to find any thing but the following note, Guericke Kirchengeschicte, p. 1013: "Indeed, somewhat earlier than this, (that is than Gustavus Vasa's mission to the Laplanders, in 1559, which he notes in the text as the first Protestant mission,) Calvin and the Church of Geneva had sent missionaries for Christians and heathen to Brasil; which undertaking, however, was soon relinquished." It is a serious fact, that the Hegel-ians (the reigning philosophical sect in Germany) hold as their two fundamental axioms, that, (1) Esse et non-esse idem sunt; (2) Omnis veritas sui contradictionem continet!!! Fichte's leading truth was "*Ich bin Ich*"!! There is no writer more execrated among the pious Germans than John Locke.

Dr. ——— was much laughed at in London, for pronouncing *Quay* as it is written: all the élite pronounce *route* as French, see Walker. A "fine man" is unintelligible in England; a *fine woman* is a handsome one. Every one says *fortnīte*, see Walker. *Chateaubríand* is the Parisian style. Of course you will thank me for these dicta. I find *progress* [the verb] in Shakspeare, B. Jonson, and Quarles, but accented on penultimate.

In correcting sheets, be sure to resolve all the diphthongs in Latin: the old way æ and œ is going out of use in Europe. You use *realize* in an unauthorized sense, though I own the word is absolutely needed.

PRINCETON, *June* 23, 1834.

Amice amicissime,

I am pleased to see you quoting from the "Penny Magazine," which happens to be my great hobby at this time. It is certainly the cheapest book in the world, and is full of entertainment without a line of trash. My father is quite enthusiastic about it. Nevertheless, it is lamentable that (negatively) it is so irreligious. You might extract something from every number. You will have Dr. Rauch and all the Germans on the back of you, for that irreverent article about Fichte and Hegel; "experto crede Jacobo." The review of —— is very paltry; with such a subject, a dunce might have been severe. And what asinine abortion of a critic (see the "Decline of Poetry" in ——) has discovered that Wordsworth is dull and unpoetical, and Darwin, (oh! oh! oh!) a model!!! If ——'s review is dead, Walsh's is mortified in some of its members.

PRINCETON, *July* 14, 1834.

I have passed the happiest summer thus far that I have known for years; let me record it as the gift of Providence. The greenness, the airiness, the fragrance, the healthfulness, the over—over—overflowing of fruits, and the otherwise varied delightfulness of Princeton, have made up for the loss or want of many urbane luxuries. I am looking towards Long Branch for next week. I am endeavouring to get all the books I can, relating to the English Language and Literature—Anglo-Saxon, History of our Tongue, History of Literature in England, History of Poetry, including specimens of old English books. Now, do, I beg you, bear this in mind; memorandum such as you see or hear of; even buy, at my risk, when you see a rare bargain. My boys are in statu quo, save that the younger has acquired the English language, and amuses us by his sage discourse.

It is common in our papers to talk of Neander as a minister; he is a layman. I am reading old Fuller's Church History of Britain with great delight; though the more prelatical he grows, the more do I grow puritanical. I regret that the British Church Establishment is going to fall down. The consequence, I fear, will be not increased piety, but the rampancy of fanat icism, latitudinarianism, and popery. Though I hold in derision the barefaced logical impositions of the prelatical argument, and hate the tyranny of the English Church, I reverence the antique sublimity of the structure. I feel [the awkwardness] of being a dissenter in England, but more the ridiculosity of wearing the cast-off clothes of British Churchism in America. I admire the past history of the Anglican Church, but in England as well as here, quantum mutatus ab illo! In theology and all clerical science and literature how shallow, how superficial!

Mr. ―― and Mr. ―― told me that the only organ of their sort of Dissenters was the "Congregational Magazine;" that the "Evangelical" was a granny; that the "Eclectic" has played false to their cause; that the "Christian Advocate" was discountenanced by all sober disssenters as wickedly and roughly radical and jacobinical; and that they encouraged a weekly paper, called "The Patriot," of London, which they believed to be able, and sound to their cause.

Lately I have made friends with Coleridge, at least for a time, and am reading his "Aids" again with a peculiar sort of mystical pleasure.

―― has just left Princeton, having spent here some twenty hours. He scrupled to eat with us, but gave us much of his company, which was very agreeable. I was deeply affected at the naïveté with which this poor, childlike, Christless Jew, described the state of mind in which he is, and must needs be so long as he denies the Messiah; on the threshold, but with a vail over his heart which hides the way, the truth, and the life. Let us pray for his illumination; and I entreat you, without an approach to controversy, to encourage in him the development of those feelings of want, which may lead him to see Christianity to be the necessary complement of Judaism.

Price for me an instruction-book for the violoncello. Music is my main medicament just now.

PRINCETON, *September* 12, 1834.

You must not ask me who is the best sermon writer. If suddenly cornered, I should say *Baxter*. On second thought, Robert Hall. Then a mixture of Baxter, Barrow, and Taylor. I have Sherlock, but never become interested. Indeed, I scarcely read sermons.

I will go so far, as with more than ordinary earnestness, to recommend to you to get, *own*, put on your table, and study, a book with this title, "Letters Practical and Consolatory, designed to illustrate the nature and tendency of the Gospel, by David Russell, Minister of the Gospel, Dundee, 4th Ed., Edinburgh, 1830, 2 vols., 12mo." Who this Russell is I know not, probably a Scotch Dissenter; but I have read no human production which comes nearer my views of Calvinism: it is theology without one shred of scholasticism; orthodoxy without one film of mystification; purity without one note of ecclesiastical harshness. I have so far reconsidered my former resolution, as to determine (as you have already let the cat out of the bag) to put on my Sunday School volumes hereafter, (by leave of Providence sparing and enabling me to write any more,) "By the author of Jane Scott, Hebrew Customs, Harvest, &c." The Father's Magazine has some good things in it; but why have a department and a pigeon-hole, and a magazine for every thing? Next we may look for an Old Maid's Magazine—Barbers' Department —Society for the illumination of back-cellars, with a travelling agent. Soberly, do not the Scriptures indicate a less cumbrous, more simple mode of propagating Christianity? Perhaps I judge ill because I am not in active life.

In immense haste (before breakfast!) thine.

PRINCETON, *Sept.* 17, 1834.

A very interesting letter has been received from Mrs. Missionary Thomson, formerly schoolmistress Hanna of this place. Suppose the American S. S. Union should send her, and the other missionaries in Palestine, each a copy of your chart of Jerusalem, and Geography maps, furnished with blank leaves, that from year to year they may correct the topography on the spot. After you and I are dead, the good work might still be going on.

On looking over my little works, I am brought back to my original judgment, that the best way is to write *for the cuts*, and not cut for the writing. Therefore let me have proofs of such cuts as you are willing to repeat in this way. I am afraid the Greek and English New Testament [in parallel columns] will be misunderstood, and so scouted by Dr. ———, if there is no further explanation. He may take it into his noddle that some dunce has wished to help lazy or ignorant ministers; whereas it is meant for the most learned—a mechanical help, one page instead of two distinct books. Say a word in the right ear, to this point.

With reference to English preachers, the best article I ever saw is in the first volume of the Edinburgh Presbyterian Review. The great defect in the Churchmen, even of their golden era, the 17th century, is Energy, including in that term both pungency and pathos. I can just now think of none but Barrow, who is powerful. Taylor is rich, and often pathetic, always brilliant and poetical, but never commanding. Those whom we (upon

English tradition) celebrate, while they are argumentative, instructive, sensible, and terse, are, to my feelings, tame. A mixture of Edwards and Davies, who are all our own, would be a phœnix. Strange as it would seem to one who had not made the comparison, the French preachers have more addresses to the conscience, heart, and will, than any I ever saw in print. Bourdaloue is full of holy unction, Bossuet is Demosthenes in canonicals, and Massillon is the fusion of all great qualities into so perfect a mass that his powers are scarcely appreciated. The same thing leads, I think, to the undervaluing of R. Hall. This extreme elegance makes one suspect there is no strength, because there is no ruggedness. I have Sherlock, and know some fine places in him, but as a whole he does not take possession of me. Paley's plain sermons are striking for their " good roundabout sense; " look at them for half an hour. Some of the late C. Wolfe's sermons (" Not a Drum was heard, nor a Funeral Note ") surpass any modern English preachments for heart-rending appeals—even of terror. Our American Episcopalians seem to me mere milk and water, even compared with the Christian Observer-school; which latter class, I verily believe, contains the very best men in England. Except on church-order, you never hear from our churchmen a sermon of square-hewn thought. Their best evangelical discourses which I have heard, arise no higher than John Newton's or Mr. Jay's. I ought to have named Cecil, who, if he had *written* sermons, would have been (what my father considers him) the most commanding sermonizer of his connexion, at that day. Of all styles of sermonizing, however, the most sneakingly mean, in my humble judgment, is that of which the ———— [a periodical made up of sermons] is the representative: I speak of course of the majority of specimens. No exposition of Scripture in its scope and connexion, apart from which insulated verses may mean any thing, and are at best single rays of the spectrum, and not light : few even of these insulated texts; in default of the latter, not even any profound series of doctrinal statements ;. but mere paragraphs, about equal to the " Improvement " of an old sermon ; false sententiousness; shallow illustration of what was before plain as day ; every thing sacrificed to supposed pungency, and baseless notation. Who, from all the volumes of the ————, would get a solid structure of Scripture truth ? And is not this what preaching should convey ? And after all, this modern New England preaching is less moving, less reaching, less awakening, than that of the preceding age. Ca-ira ! So much for your asking any thing *ex cathedra.*

PRINCETON, *September* 30, 1834.

I heartily regret that you have had [in Philadelphia] 25 deaths by cholera-morbus and cholera; Avertat Deus! The consecration of Trinity Church here was an uncommon effort; it lasted some four hours. Bishops White, Ives, and Doane present, and altogether twenty clergymen. Bishop W. preached an hour. The good old patriarch remained to commencement. On commencement evening, I drank tea with the three Bishops at [Professor A. B.] Dod's, and have seldom had a pleasanter soirée. It was like being transported to a purer age, to talk with the primate, and I value the interview as unique; he was inimitably paternal and really instructive. As to ——, he is an insufferable mix of upstart Yankeeism, froth, affectation, and ludicrous vanity. Bishop McIlvaine's charge is a lovely paper. O si sic omnia! Read it for your own heart's good. [J. S.] Hart and [Stephen] Alexander are made adjunct professors in our college. You can now come hither in the canal from Bordentown. Did I tell you that Dr. Hodge was writing a popular commentary on the Romans?

PRINCETON, *October* 31, 1834.

So Coleridge is gone!—the last of the Platonists. I both dislike and love his beautiful, dreamy philosophizings; and cannot hear him either blamed or lauded. His poetry I never read, (*i. e.* Byronicè *redde*.)

Tell Mr. Packard I can only promise to *think* about the Life of Jacob.[1] Also say, that the prints, though exceedingly beautiful, are so much of a marine character, that I fear I shall have to return them to him, with my sincere thanks.

Let me beg you to take it as a prominent, perpetual object of selections, &c., for your Journal, to hold up the great truth, that *the Bible is the book to educate the age*. Why not have it the *chief* thing in the family, in the school, in the academy, in the university? The day is coming; and if you and I can introduce the minutest corner of this wedge, we shall be benefactors of the race. I can *amuse* a child about the Bible; I can teach logic, rhetoric, ethics, and salvation from the Bible. May we not have a *Bible School?* Sow the seed, my dear friend, meekly, prayerfully; it must grow! A series of Lectures on Archæology, including Geography, with a full apparatus of transparent maps, figures, landscapes, specimens of trees, fruits, stones, dresses, &c., &c., &c., might help on the great wheel several revolutions in our cities. Hold a protracted meeting of a

---

[1] His "Life of Jacob and his son Joseph" was published by the Union in 1836, pp. 191.

week, and have two or three sermons or lectures a day, (prepared long before,) on different points of Education, Bible exposition, Illustration, Juvenile training, Sunday Schools, &c., then print it.

I want to write a volume, somewhat secular, after the fashion of "Uncle Philip," [by Rev. Dr. Hawks,] teaching some physical principles, but interweaving religion. In a word, the book is to be one of excitement rather than instruction; intended to awaken a thirst for knowledge of all kinds.

PRINCETON, *Nov* 19, 1834.

What you say about —— is distressing to me, though not wholly unexpected. I trust you are by this time relieved; if not, you know to whom we have given our dear children. It is a sweet Christian exercise for parents to give away their offspring daily, and daily to receive them as a fresh gift. Of a truth, I know something of like affliction; a daily burden, but tempered with hourly-dropping balm. I do not wish a hair's weight of the past to have been taken off. Mr. —— I have not seen, for he does not come till next month. I am prepared to love him, always provided that he does not obtrude dispute about the apostolical succession. If he does, I am off. My life is too short to be spent on these "endless genealogies." Politics have left me in the rear: where ignorance is bliss, 'tis folly to be wise. I believe we are tolerably well governed. By all means write "The Beloved Disciple." Lardner will give you all you want, and reference to everybody else: you ought also to read St. John's life in Butler's "Lives of the Saints," not the copy in 3 *vols.*, but in 12 *vols.*, 8vo. I concealed my name to my lullabies, for the very reason which leads the Moravian to exclude all adults, when he preaches to children. Mrs. Sigourney's are poetic, but not baby-like, mine are baby-like, but not poetical. They are "Cherries are ripe," also the tune; "Father and Mother 'tis time to arise;" "The A B C;" "Up in the Morning." The A B C tune I adapted from a Ranz-des-Vaches. We have admitted fifty less or more to college, and an uncommonly large accession to the seminary. Professor Stephen Alexander has gone to Ebenezer, Ga., with a splendid telescope (made by Ultzschneider and Fraunhofer at Munich) to observe the central solar eclipse on the 30th inst. This eclipse is quite an American affair, and the European savans will look to us for the elements of astronomical correction, &c. Alexander is equal to Payne himself as an observer. The results will be given to your Philosophical Society. There will not be such another eclipse till 1869. Qu. Does this justify a *Sabbath* observation?

With much whimsy, there are some eximious things in Simpson on Popular Education. I was already a full convert to the doctrine that babes ought to be taught, not books but things. Precocity is plainly a brain-disease. I am filled with enthusiasm about having the Bible more taught. Instead of a mere *reading-book* in schools, it must be taught, after the Sunday School fashion; geography, archæology and all. All our girls must read the Greek Testament. I mean to teach a few on the plan of Locke. By an interlinear version any merchant's clerk may learn Hebrew. Don't tell this to the old-school grammarians. The Bible—the Bible—it is this which must save America. It is this which must save the church; not by spasmodic transitory attempts, on emergencies, but by being a perennial wellhead of divine truth. I talk of writing an introduction to the New Testament for you. I have finished about a dozen of the penny books ordered by Mr. Packard; having no suitable cuts, I have to *describe* what the cut should be. If I had a hundred little cuts, I could write two dozen in a twinkling. As it is, I fear some difficulty, and the works themselves will probably not suit Mr. P.'s *ideal*.[1]

PRINCETON, *November* 23, 1834.

I have finished the baby-books; they wait for a bearer. Henry Clay left us to-day, but I could not intrust him with so great a charge. I saw him for some hour or so. I hope you will have a good touch of the rheumatism, so that you may never laugh at me again. Apropos, this strange influenza comes on with singular pains, and even temporary paralysis.

I am printing in the Trenton Emporium some letters to Gov. Vroom, on Education. I read a letter of [Rev. Mr. Nevins on the death of his wife] which for pathos, naïveté, and unaffectedness, supasses any thing of the sort I ever saw. In one quality Nevins exceeds all men I know; he is frank and childlike without an effort, and without knowing it.

PRINCETON, *December* 9, 1834.

I am, late at night, and in the sick room of my George, who has been dangerously ill, writing you a scrawl, as I have an opportunity to-morrow. Let me say a word now about some notions of —— about scriptural books, which impress me as true and good, and are a little exemplified in his book. He talks thus to me: Don't try to vary the Bible language too much; say what you will, it is most intelligible to children. Don't try too

---

[1] The result was "The Infant's Library," consisting of twenty-four of the smallest size in which any thing in the shape of a book can be printed, and in the smallest language. It may be amusing to know that in "The Sabbath Breaker," "James" and "Edward" represent himself and Mr. Kirk, in an incident of their boyhood.

much to improve upon the Bible; let what you add be exegetical and brief. He says moreover, (and I own I never thought of it before, though it is specious,) that a thousand books may yet be woven out of the raw Bible material, with very little alteration of the text. Thus one may take all that relates to the archæology of Hebrew *houses*, and make a book of it; and that, mark me, not by casting the Scripture parts into the pigeonholes of formal artificial arrangement, but *following the exact order* of the Scripture story. Take one subject, and chase it through the whole canon. Doesn't this merit a thought? I am engaged (meaning to work slowly, and scrap-wise) at a life of Christ—blessed theme! O that we may daily ponder on it! You will readily see how my thoughts course one another in the channel, which, but for Sunday Schools, would never have existed for me. I am a little wild on the subject of making the Bible the grand organ of mental and spiritual development. Suppose one knows the Bible, and from it as a centre radiates into the thousand subsidiary knowledges, will he not know all he needs? Will not you and I make this the rule for bringing up our children? Why may not our female friends be made to read the Greek Testament? I will engage to teach any of the poor things that lose their time on French, to read the New Testament in less time. Why does not Dr. Ely take the beautiful scriptural motto for his Philadelphian—ἡ φιλαδελφια μενετο![1] I am deep in Mrs. [Hannah] More's life; a lovely book, from which I augur great things for evangelical religion. I preach every Sunday to a dear little flock of poor people, in Queenston, where I think the Spirit of the Lord is not altogether absent. Yesterday, alas! I witnessed, in a Magdalen, (if the name is not a libel on Christ's friend,) something very like death-bed despair.

I ought to be a very thankful man, for, with "manifold temptations," I am as happy in my present site, as a miserable sinner ought to expect. I am very sure that some of us do not discipline the flesh enough in our prosperity, by voluntary abstinence from many things which are lawful but inexpedient. Paul talks (in Greek terms of force) of bringing under and subjecting the body. Might we not sometimes fast? Might we not curtail expenses and retrench style? Might we not risk a little worldly sneer for being nearer the primitive model? May we not hope for more uncommon manifestations, when we make more uncommon sacrifices to walk in Christ's steps? Austin says sweetly, *Nudus nudum sequor Christum*. I more and more sicken at human dilutions of the Word, and love the taste of the fresh fountain. Good night.

[1] "Let brotherly love (Philadelphia) continue."

PRINCETON, *December* 10, 1834.

I hope your map and manual will mark an epoch—you know every thing nowadays marks an epoch—and will open many eyes to the wants of the world.[1] I own, though I have often studied the map gospel-wise, I never had so impressive a view. Every one who sees it is so struck. Apropos, I find it good to use a small atlas as a prayer-book; it defines, systematizes, and condenses one's desires. I have read large portions of —— with great care. I am surprised that he should *stereotype* such a work; it seems to shut the door against all future retractation, which, if I understand him, is inconsistent with his views of theological perfectibility. I am horrified with meeting in his remarks the self-same rationalistic canon of interpretation which has dethroned Christ in German divinity; I mean what is involved in the concession that David's imprecations *may* be *wicked* imprecations. Then, *ex æquali*, as the Germans argue, Paul's deductions *may* be *foolish* deductions. This I regard as far worse than specific aberrations even into heretical doctrines; for it unsettles the base of all doctrines. I doubt not this evil seed will soon germinate. The caricature of *imputation* is disingenuous. Pray by whom has the old doctrine, as he states it, been held? The reader will understand him, "by old Calvinists." It has been in terms disavowed by every successive theologian of eminence. Edwards has never been regarded as an interpreter of our doctrines. The view given in the Repertory for 1830, p. 425, I pledge myself to substantiate, if it were proper, from Turretin, Witsius, Owen, Dr. Mason, and our Princeton lectures; and these may be assumed as saying what Calvinism is, whether it be in itself right or wrong. The nonsense which —— pretends to refute, is not imputation, but its exact reverse. After many years suffering torments of doubt about Romans 5th, I left all commentaries and confined myself to the Greek text, with a lexicon, (I do not mean a New Testament lexicon, which is merely a comment arranged alphabetically,) and my opinion of that glorious passage I regard as a key to the whole Pauline system.

Your "Harvey Boys" I think excellent for the end in view. The plural of *wharf*, however, in spite of Philadelphians, is *wharfs* not *wharves*. I hereby give notice to your committee, that I have in good progress a book of dialogues, intended, 1, to make the Bible an object of interest; 2, to explain its form, divisions, books, chapters, verses, &c.; 3, to show how to study

[1] A map, designating by colours and marks the state of the world as to the progress of Christianity, with a manual of missionary doctrine and statistics.

it;—in a word, an *Introduction to the Bible.* The continued affliction of your little girl excites our sympathy. When God sees that the trial has done its work, he will remove it; until then let patience have its perfect work. I think I rejoice that the Lord reigneth, and that the angels of these little ones do behold the face of our Father who is in heaven. I hope no changes in your employments will take you away from the service of these little ones. Many who are in it are incompetent or unfaithful. Let us seek to be made wise and directed.

Monday, Dec. 12.—The lowest degree of cold here, by Professor Henry's standard thermometer, was—11°. In Albany, you see it was 32°! Surely one had better go to Pekin than to New Orleans. I should regard [Rev. Joel] Parker as more of a martyr than any of our missionaries.[1] Your [Missionary] chart hangs in full view of my bed, and I hope many of my nightly and morning thoughts will take their direction from it. No publication of the year so permanently affects me. "Thy kingdom come!" Brewer of Smyrna is a noble fellow; he seems to me to lead the van in the Levant.

Read the 56th Psalm, with reference to Parker and the Orleans folk. The people of Nineveh shall rise up in the judgment with this generation, and condemn it, for they repented at the preaching of Jonas. I have a fearful belief, that the open rejection of God in his ministers, will call down temporal and marked judgments. Greatly as I differ from Joel Parker, I feel called upon to pray for him with affection. The Christians of Germany, *i. e.* the *real* Christians, are all (except Neander and his school) legitimatists, who regard the king as God's earthly image, and hold the twofold command, Fear God *and* honor the king, as indivisible. They cannot abstract democracy from infidelity. This loyalty, in some of them, is very lovely. There is a family of *Gerlachs,* one high in office (Louis) at Halle, a privy-counsellor; one a professor and pastor (Otto) at Berlin; one a Major, and aid of the king. The first two are geniuses, men of profound learning, and —— regards Louis as the *greatest* man he met in Germany. I read much of their writing in

---

[1] Mr. (now Dr.) Parker, in soliciting aid at the North for the erection of the church in New Orleans of which he was pastor, was reported to have spoken disparagingly of that city, and was threatened with violence if he should return to it. After sending proofs of the falseness of the allegation, Mr. Parker sailed for New Orleans; but such were the apprehensions of the captain and passengers, that he and his family were put on shore before reaching the city. A public meeting was assembled for the purpose of expelling the minister: Mr. Parker addressed the multitude in person; his friends rallied; the church on Lafayette Square was erected, and he retained his position with new efficiency.

Hengstenberg's paper; and Dr. H. had lately a charming letter from Otto, who is at a commentary for the plebs. I laid down the "Zeitung" of April 23, to pen this, in which Louis v. Gerlach undertakes the maintenance of this thesis: "That Liberalism and Absolutism, though seeming opposites, may be traced to a common trunk, viz., the severance of the State from God." Not so bad. "God (says he) is the sole source of all liberty. He is the sole, legitimate, supreme Sovereign. Therefore a prince who does not consider his lordship as God's loan, who does not limit it by God's law, and who places the highest source and principle of his rights, not in the divine will, but in some earthly end of state, (Staatszweck,) or who does not accord to his subjects the sacred rights given them of God, is a true *Revolutionist*. And a popular association, however democratically constituted, which makes their own will, or the will of the sovereign multitude, the highest state-law, is truly *despotic*." Now for a truly German sentence, from *Ringseis*, a Catholic, General-medical-Counsellor of the king of Bavaria; the allusion is to the reigning philosophy of Hegel, who denies any personal God: "As in Philosophy and Theology, there has been substituted for one God in three persons, an impersonal Supreme Being, a moral world-government, or world-order; so in politics, there has been substituted for a personal lord of the country, uniting in himself all powers—the ghost of an abstract, *hateless, loveless* STATE!!"

I feel indignant at the piece by N. N. in the Boston Recorder, on Presbyterianism. If our church were to fall to pieces, Presbytery would not be touched; nay, nor if we were resolved into our separate presbyteries: even in this last case, we should be infinitely above the no-organization of Congregationalism. How indelicate such Yankee meddling! If we chose to turn the tables, how easy to twit them with the Unitarian defection; yet the latter are all Congregationalists. "Presbyterianism a failure!" Marry come up! We have existed a century under our present organization; and then look at the masses of Dutch and Scotch Presbyterians. It is as if the Hottentots who live in isolated sheds should sneer at the Tremont House, because mayhap its united chambers occasion some dirt or some inconvenience. What we *have* suffered, has been by the Congregationalism with which we are inoculated. Either system may stand by itself, but a mixture is pork and molasses, or cider and coffee.

PRINCETON, *December* 15, 1834.

More to disburden a throbbing and full heart, than to communicate much good, I write to you. I know you will feel a pang, when I tell you that this afternoon, at 3 o'clock, God was pleased to take away my little Archibald—our Benjamin, the son of our hopes. Blessed be God for all his mercies! Last evening he was as well as a child could be, to appearance. About 7 he began to show symptoms of croup, which gradually advanced, in spite of the most vigorous practice of our physician, who was with us almost from first to last, until he died in our arms. His last moments were sweet; he simply fell asleep, no pang, no distortion; he lies like a lovely smiling marble. He was two years four months old. Twenty hours' illness! A little before his death he clasped his hands and said, "I want to say my prayers." Judge what we feel. My dear friend, the tears I poured in torrents over his dying form were tears of joy—blessed be God for it! Never had I such faith of immortality. My wife and I yield with a composure, for which we can never be thankful enough, to the resumption of the precious gift. We have been in the practice of deliberately giving up our children to God, every day. O how I rejoiced in this, as I felt his last pulses, and found his precious hand turning to clay in mine.

We have too much caressed and prized this dear boy. Disappointed in our first, whom we held by a spider's thread, we counted much upon Archibald. He was lovely, and precocious. In a moment we are blasted! But why do I repeat these things? Join us in giving thanks to God for the wonderful (I will not say resignation, but) comfort we have. Join us in praising Him who can make us glory in tribulations also. Join us in prayer that we may be *kept* in faith. "Hold thou me up and I shall be safe."

I wish to learn the lesson of this dispensation. I wish to be more entirely consecrated to the work of God. If God write us *childless* (an awful word now—once it seemed a trifle) I will try to find children in the Sunday School. O my friend! I have a dear child in heaven! Only a few hours in heaven! Is not this an honour—a joy—a triumph? let me then determine to lead a heavenly life here. When shall we " use this world as not abusing it "? When shall we who have wives, live as though we had none? A little while and all these shadows will fly away, and we shall find ourselves amidst the realities of eternity. For some time previous to this dispensation, I have found myself under a leading to thoughts more serious than common; greater desires to cut off superfluous pursuits, to take up unaccustomed crosses, and to cultivate humble love. Alas! how little have I succeeded in doing so.

I cannot well say much on other topics. Remember me and mine at the throne of grace.

PRINCETON, *February* 17, 1835.

Tell Mr. Packard I and the rest of us think very highly of "Ann Conover" [a book for female domestics]: one great excellence it hath, the talk is "real talk" without provincialism.

Among the thousand and one things I have in my plans, is the *Apprentice,* a book for ditto. I endeavour to have as many plans as I can: thereby I find work for all moods of mind. Mr. P. sent me a book which Dr. Julius left with him. It is a sensible and pious book, but purely German, and not suited to our meridian. There are gross passages about the vices of boys, and that which relates to intellectual and moral culture is only a moiety. The spirit of the work is good, and there are beautiful passages; it might be very useful among the German population; but I do not find a single chapter which would merit translation as it is. I have selected 20 texts for baby sermons, to publish with my name. I wish my first 'onymous work to be one which shall have nought to do with literary ambition. O how much better I love my nursery-work, than my rhetoric! I feel pleased to think that the truth we are throwing so widely among the nation of children, cannot all die. While many things are against us, God's truth will not perish.

Feb. 19.—I am still in the house with my throat and palate; which I turn to some little account in the way of Sunday School writing. The absorbing power of composition makes it a great solace when one is unwell. I doubt whether Baxter or Hannah More would have scribbled so much if they had not been valetudinarians. ☞ Put a paragraph into your paper, recommending to some writer a book expressly intended for *Factory Children,* There are many thousands of these in the United States, and they are cut off from instruction and home influence, and exposed to numberless corruptions. I witnessed this in Trenton, but it must be immensely worse in Lowell, Paterson, &c., &c. The person who does this should be intimately acquainted with the factory system. But for want of this knowledge, I would set about it myself. I agree with you fully about ———. At times I am almost converted to the extreme doctrine of "no controversy." We are too anxious lest God should not maintain his own truth. I know no cause why we may not devote ourselves to other work. In my sorrows I think I could make a useful little pocket volume for bereaved parents, but I am held back by the belief that nobody will publish for me but the S. S. Union, and your committee would not adopt a book so exclusively for adults.

VOL. I.—10*

Princeton, *March* 21, 1835.

I saw in one of the Catholic Journals that the highest honours of the *De Propaganda Fide* were awarded to a young Kentuckian named Martin J. Spalding;[1] and shortly after, that he had come home as a priest. He is at Bardstown, and I lately saw a letter from him to an old schoolmate in this place, which is one of the finest, adroitest, and most learned defences of popery I ever read. If, instead of reviling the Catholics, we would surpass them in schools, in personal charities, in persevering missions, and in the preparation of our ministers, I believe we should make more head against them. Every day I live I become more sick of controversy; I cannot persuade myself that the Church was meant to be kept always in hot water. As to our own church a split seems to be inevitable. I honour the men who seem to be labouring *directly* for the conversion of souls. In closing our long session at College, it is matter of gratitude that with nearly two hundred students, we have had no occasion for rigorous discipline, no suspensions, and no disorders beyond the merest boyish pranks. I sigh, however, when I think how far we are from the state of revival which is said to exist in Jefferson and Dartmouth. Nothing short of this can effect what I should desire.

Princeton, *April* 17, 1835.

A hurt finger makes me write with some deliberation, so you must not mistake my calligraphy for that of another. This letter begins without object, but perhaps may amuse you as well as if it were divided into heads. To-morrow, Deo volente, I go with my little family to Trenton. I appreciate the kindness of your invitation, but our journeying is attended necessarily with so many arrangements, and so much sickroom apparatus, that Trenton is our ultima Thule. I may run down and see you. Among many reasons for gratitude, one is the service of a good servant. We have a young girl for child's-nurse, who for more than a year has been with us constantly, and in whom we have never discovered any faults at all. She is a plant of the Sunday School, and is in my opinion quite a prodigy, for parts and acquisitions. Our boys have become wonderful zoologists. We had two raccoons domesticated during the winter. One eloped after a few days, the second stayed six months, and then fled also. A hare lived in the cellar a week or two, and then forsook civilization in disgust. An opossum died under our hands; and, last of all, a most dignified owl broke gaol and escaped within a week past. I shall miss Walsh very much if he goes abroad, for his pithy paragraphs have become a necessary condiment. * * * But what mercy is there in the Fanaticism of the

[1] Bishop of the diocese of Louisville since September, 1848.

Symbol? O for a cycle of peace! O for a breathing spell from these unnatural contentions! I feel as if I could join with any who would humbly unite in direct and kind efforts to save sinners and relieve human misery. Cannot a poor believer go along in his pilgrimage heavenward, without being always on military duty? At judgment I heartily believe that some heresies of heart and temper will be charged as worse than heavy doctrinal errors. To you I may say this, because you understand me as holding, not merely that the tenets of our church are true, but that they are very important. But I see how easy it is to "hold the truth" in rancour, and hate, which is the grand error of depraved human nature; yea, and of diabolism itself. I regret to see that Mr. ——, in his Lectures, betrays throughout a polemical attitude, and evidently is fuller of animosity against the foes of revival-measures, than of direct zeal for the saving of souls. Is this not a common error? ——'s day is probably over, as Nettleton's was, and for the same cause; thus Moses could not enter the land; but where are our Joshuas? Sometimes there seems to me to be an opening just now for a united attempt to awaken religious feeling in the churches, without the shibboleths of measures. Surely too much has been made of these measures, both pro and contra. But my preachment is already too long, as my practice is so defective. Nevertheless, I believe my happiest hours are spent on Sunday afternoons in labouring among my little charge [the congregation of colored persons]. I am humbled when I think how little effect results from my discourses. I write at a table with three chattering girls, and my thoughts ramble.

PRINCETON, *June* 3, 1835.

I should have concluded that you were still at the Pittsburg furnace, had not —— incidentally mentioned your return. The vacation slipped away strangely without my seeing you, and when I heard you were gone westward, I thought it not worth while to make my visit to the city. For some weeks I have two recitations a day, and the only absence I can expect is a trip to New York, which I make to-morrow, to preach for Dr. Spring's people. We have 215 in college, and consequently have divided several of the classes, thus exactly doubling our labours. Look at two articles of Professor Henry's, in the late number of the Transactions of the American Philosophical Society. He and Faraday of London seem to have hit on the same discovery simultaneously.

My little boy is better than we have seen him for a year or two. Though he is on his back all the time, he is, through Divine mercy, exquisitely happy. I was not pleased with the spirit of the Colonization meetings in New York. I am tending towards a middle ground which neither party will allow: *i. e.* I abhor slavery, and think the public mind should be enlightened, and every lawful means immediately taken for an eventual and speedy abolition; but I also approve of the plan of Colonization, on grounds altogether distinct from the question of slavery. Thus I open my mind to the full, legitimate impressions of all the anti-slavery arguments. I have seldom heard a man so powerfully eloquent as G. Thompson, though he is hot-headed, arrogant, and imprudent in excess.

PRINCETON, *July* 2, 1835.

I am in my room, and have been in my bed, with a quite severe attack of fever. After being blooded profusely, both in arm and jugular, physicked and dieted; and after having a hammering in my head as if the Cyclops had transferred their anvil to my brain-pan, I am now free from symptoms of disease, though haggard, weak, and thin. Perhaps I may exhibit my anatomy at No. 119 South 8th street before many days. I scarcely know why I am spared, unless in infinite mercy, that I may make my calling and election sure. What you say of —— scarcely surprises me; I had somehow got the notion that he was (to use a word of my quondam sexton) "a notionable man." —— made great misstatements in his speech about the duties of the professors here. They have no day without a lecture, and they are employed almost every evening; besides, they do *not* constantly repeat the old lectures. I know not a busier man in the world than my old father. And half of every day is spent in talking with students privately. True, he does not chase them from room to room, or run through the roll, but he never chains up his gate, or pleads any business to exclude any one, at any hour.

Much that you say of ministers and their ways is, no doubt, true. I dissent, however, from one of your statements of *fact*. I do not believe that ministers herd too much together; if they were more together, it would be better. In such a place as Princeton, where we are aggregated in a literary capacity, it may be the case, yet how is the fact even here? Dr. Rice probably talks ten times with lay-people for once that he talks with a preacher. In Trenton I consorted five hundred times with laics, for every once with a clerk. And in Charlotte, the ratio was, I doubt not, 1000 to 1.

PRINCETON, *August* 11, 1835.

Not only do busiest men do the most, but our busiest times are those in which we work most *extra*. So it has been. At

Saratoga, of all places in the world, I could not find time to write to you; and to-day, in the busiest week of the year, viz., that of our final examination, lo! I am inditing a missive. I was nineteen days at the Springs. All the time comfortable; health bettered, spirits prime, flesh not increased, beauty ditto, face nigrified three shades, nose germinal, ruddy, &c., &c. N. B. I plucked up courage to take a shower-bath, and with more decided good than I ever had from any remedial process. I saw "all the world and his mother" at the Springs. Inter alios et alias; Rev. Dr. Lyell, Rev. Hugh Smith, Van Buren, Cambreleng, Gov. Wolf, Gov. Marcy, Dr. Proudfit, Prof. Alonzo Potter, Sir Wm. Barnaby, Governor of Bermuda, General Nelson of Trinidad, Roberts Vaux, Perdicaris, Miomotsky, Pres. Wayland, Mr. Pierpoint, Major Jack Downing of New York, Mrs. Bradstreet, (the female lawyer,) Dr. Cox of England, T. P. H——, (Temperance agent, *fou* on the wine question: N. B. Temperance Ship spoken at Albany, high and dry on the Wine-bank; crew drunk or crazy; mutiny below hatches, headed by one Delavan; pilots afraid to venture out, as the vessel has careened and threatens to go down under a heavy sea from Stuart's cove,) S. V. S. Wilder, Lane, (one of the founders of the Seminary of that ilk,) Signore Fabi and Garenghi of the Opera, pictures of Adam and Eve, which ———, in my hearing, solemnly recommended in a sermon.

Here are a few ——— ana. He is vehemently against the present Temperance-society freaks: "When men grow wiser than the Bible, I am off. I go the whole figure: if Christ did not so foresee the present as to make a sufficient rule for our times, I shut the lids of my Bible; it is henceforth no Bible for me." Of Coleridge: "I do not understand him; bright fogs; some few rays of truth beyond the vulgar seem to have impinged on his mind, but after several reflections, so as to be seen in a wrong place. We want a metaphysic which shall *settle things*. Among us all opinion is in flux; nothing arrived at; settled truth is our object. What I long to see accomplished is, that we should come to *conclusions* about something, and hold them fast; to leave out of view what Germans or what Britons think of this or that, and march up in manly sort to some points of truth. *That* is the intellect for me which *settles things;* makes dark things clear, and undefined things definite: so does not Coleridge. I judge of teaching by *fruits*. The fruits of Coleridgeism, where I have seen it, are extravagancies. If there is a Metaphysic, it *must be* very clear: the true system must of necessity be a plain one. What point has Coleridge cleared?" I hope you are not suffering with the heat. Come up, come up, and breathe a little vapor from good mother earth, whom you have interred under a world of flaming bricks in your great Babel. Love to Mrs., misses, and master.

COLLEGE OF NEW JERSEY, *August* 28, 1835.

The "Life of Kilpin," by the American Tract Society, is one of the loveliest Sunday School books I have ever read. It will furnish you some grand excerpts for the Journal; especially are his sermons to children grand, according to my notion. And the appended memoir of his son, is one of the most wonderful juvenile biographies. Read it incontinently.

When you next propose an excursion anywhither, do me the honour to ask me to go along. I can never do such things of my own motion, greatly as I need travelling, and I am so liable to sudden attacks of severe disorder, that I am scarcely fit to travel alone. Todd's "Student's Manual" is a good book; I wish every College student had one.

I have myself, in reading Owen, marked some sixty passages, repudiating the objectionable imputation [as charged against strict Calvinists] in every form of diction which he could use. This is only important to defend us from the charge of not agreeing with our standards, *i. e.* simply a point of doctrine-history, (Dogmengeschichte.) It strikes me as remarkable that neither W—— nor B——, has the slightest metaphysical acumen; F—— has less, if there can be a negative quantity; and B—— less still!! I think none the less of them, except that they do not stick to their last. M——, E——, and L——, are the true hair-splitting metaphysicians; and all three do more harm than good. Jenkyn (on atonement) seems to make conscience of forming his system without any reference to exegesis, the only basis of a true theology. I cannot but view his atonement as none at all. He says the "Eden experiment has failed, the Sinai experiment has failed"—quere: what becomes of you and me, if the *Calvary experiment* fail?

August 25.—A box from Germany; beautiful editions of Calvin on New Testament; Vulgate, by Van Ess; Neander's history, as far as Charlemagne; another massive volume of the arch-geographer Ritter; I have Tholuck's University sermons, etc. Apropos of geography, Neander has supervised and had engraved a capital map of all places mentioned in the New Testament and the early fathers. You will see it at the end of his history of the "Planting of Christianity." On Sunday night, died, at Englishtown, in the sweet peace of the gospel, Ira Condict Gulick, a promising, gifted, and exemplary member of the Sophomore class. It was his dying request that a discourse should be delivered by President Carnahan, from Ecc. xii. 1: "Remember now thy Creator," &c. His funeral was attended by the members of the Sophomore class, in number sixty-five. Mr. G. was a younger brother of the Rev. Peter J. Gulick of the Sandwich mission. Onderdonk's theory, *i. e.* that the New Testament contains plain notices of a regular, successive, threefold ordination of the apostles, outrages my common sense more than Stuart's wine theory. In each case a desperate preconception is taken to the Bible to find support there, per fas et nefas. The spread of my little books is pleasing to my mind, as it flatters my hope of not dying without leaving some few souls the better for my having been born. Rejoice, my friend, in the station you hold; never let the truth grow stale in your estimation, that what we do for infants, we do for the best interests of man, in the most hopeful way. I go, God willing, to New York, on the 29th to preach at the Brick Church. I have been reading Tholuck's Sermons; they have some passages equal in eloquence, unction, and pungency, to any thing I know.

PRINCETON, *September* 4, 1835.

I was in New York about the bursting of the Lunar bubble.[1] Thousands were taken in, even savans; notwithstanding the internal evidence against it. For it seems very plain that no light, however intense, cast upon the spectrum or image of the telescope, can *add* any clearness to this image; inasmuch as such light, however intense, comes not from the moon, (therefore can tell us nothing new about her,) but from the hydro-oxygen flame, and the canvas. It is like throwing a flood of light on a shadow, in order to see the substance. Night before last, I looked at the moon through our Fraunhofer, and I saw the annular mountains as clearly as you see these marks ——— ——— but no griffins, gorgons, or chimaeras. I dined at an eating house, on the next chair to ———; he looks wan and eye-sunken. Not for an instant do I doubt either his piety or his ignorance. The new regions of New York city are lordly, and I have seen nothing approaching them. I spent a grand evening with [Chancellor] Kent. Ask me about it, when we meet. On Sunday, I hope to preach to the children of a rural district, and to parents; also catechize. I chatted a little with Joshua Leavitt; he groweth fat. The late fire burnt round the three Dutch parsonages, and almost took the Bible House, which was on fire several times. Fanshaw, next day, gave $500 to Mariners'

---

[1] A long and grave report in one of the newspapers of pretended telescopic discoveries.

Church, which he had offered as premium of insurance, just before wind changed, and saved his furniture. Same day, Phelps, Starr, (Bible-binder,) and A. Tappan, gave each a thousand to same object. Fanatic or not, New York religion is the *go-ahead* system. O for a good 8vo on *Money*, the God of Americans; its use, its abuse, how far right to make haste to be rich, whether we can get *too much* honestly, about giving, about luxury, surplusage, legacies, &c.,—a noble theme, and a layman must do it.

PRINCETON, *September* 23, 1835.

My present belief is, that it will be my duty not to go to Virginia, as I had intended. The case is thus: my good father and mother, after so long a time, and doubtless for the last time together, are going to see the land of their nativity, their youth, their marriage. They will take ———, and so my wife will become prima donna here. My father is quite full of a plan for hawking your books about the country; he even talks of buying a complete set for himself. I wish you would be liberal enough to give me a fine selection of your [S. S. Union] works to send to Rev. Prof. Otto von Gerlach of Berlin; it would insert the wedge in Prussia. Do you know that my grand difficulty in making baby books has been that of getting few enough words in a page? Well, ——— has invented the method of ruling his page like a multiplication-table, with just squares enough for the complement. This is measured prose with a witness! I have been wearing myself down with the examination this afternoon, and am almost broken-winded. Happily it is my last duty of the pedagogical sort for the academical year. We have a student in the Seminary, who is the son of Lord Brougham's half sister, and the grandson of Lord Rothsay. How pleasing it would be, if we could be all the time engaged in labours for the conversion of souls, and the exaltation of the Bible! When we talk of the scriptural plan of missions to the heathen, ought we not to look especially at the plan of Paul, the *Apostle of the Gentiles?* You will discern my hand in the New York Observer; pray, do not be jealous, as I do not mean to forsake you. I am almost a convert to the German notion of a Spirit of the Age, independent of communication, breaking forth in simultaneous manifestation. Look at the reigning *mobs;* convent-burnings in Spain, and commotions even in quiet Berlin. I am taking hold again of my book of introduction to the Scripture, which has lain by several months; I hope to do something at my 10th chapter this week. The researches are laborious and long, though the results will seem very small and simple. Quere: may we not receive a hallowing impression, though vague and unrepresentable in words, from portions of Scripture which we do not understand, such as Ezekiel, Canticles, or Revelation? and may not this be a part of their intention? This struck me mightily last night, while reading some picturesque passages in the original Apocalypse. Here is a sentence from a sermon of Tholuck: " Not only to *us* is that unseen One nigh, who rules these lips while I speak to you, but over all existences doth he reign and influence; as well the comet in its orbit, as the small worm that crawls in dust, hath he folded in the broad shadow of his mantle. ' Do I not fill heaven and earth?' saith the Lord in our text. ' If I ascend into heaven thou art there, if I make my bed in hell, behold thou art there.' " Again: " A voice rings in thine ears, My child, why hast thou not sought me? Yea, from infancy up, first when thou wast sitting in thy mother's embrace, while she told thee the story of the dear Redeemer, and then in thy boyhood, when in starry nights thou gazedst on the grandeur of thy heavenly Father's mansions, and thine eyes shed drops of thankfulness, that among all his million worlds he forgot not thee, poor child; and then in thy youth, when sin conflicted sorely with thee, and thou learnedst the truth, ' he that trusteth in his own heart is a fool;' everywhere and all the way, has thy Father's voice cried to thee: ' Wherefore seekest thou me not, for I am still thy Father.' "—How Madame de Staël depicts Lucian in one word, " il est le *Voltaire* de l'antiquité." We are making ready for our feast of tabernacles [commencement]. A German rationalist, resident formerly, perhaps now, in Illinois, has vilified your Union books, in a book of travels, at Hamburg. The worst he can say is that they are too evangelical.

As you have a little touch of Anglomania, let me recommend to you to buy Tanner's second map of England separately, and have a linen back pasted on it. It is a delightful companion to one's English reading. I have seen nothing like it.

PRINCETON, *November* 3, 1835.

I have just come from the funeral of Dr. Howell, the best physician and one of the best friends I ever knew; and never has there been so sincere a mourning general in our village. The Church was verily a Bochim. The Dr. was signally a gentleman and a man of science. His integrity, his generosity, his public spirit, his delicacy, and his sensibility, were uncommon. He was a model of uncalculating liberality and chivalrous honour; and all his failings were the running over at the brim of these virtues. Though bred a hickory quaker, he was growing in religious knowledge, and has given, to my mind, unequivocal evidence of faith in Christ during his late trials. His son William preceded him a few weeks; his eldest daughter lies ill now; his second daughter is slowly recovering; his wife has had the early symptoms [typhus fever], as has his eldest son. Such a house of grief I never saw, and it has fallen chiefly on me to minister to these minds diseased. Out of this one house I know of no cases of the complaint in the place. We hear from my parents that they are well and prosperous in their way through Virginia. You have seen the Life of Dr. Rice? It interests me, of course, but I lament the publicity given to many foibles of men still alive. I rejoice that Wordsworth is publishing in Philadelphia; heartily and religiously do I believe that our money-loving and gain-reckoning generation would be profited by the leaven of the Coleridge and Wordsworth philosophical poesy, even though this has its whimsies. Newark is a wonderful place now; pop. 20,000, exported manufactures this year $8,000,000. Of young men between 15 and 25, four to five thousand. I never had such an audience as there, on the 25th; I preached at the invitation of the Young Men's Society. The Churches there are all alive, and the place is a little, sublimated New York. I called on Col. Stone [editor of "Commercial Advertiser"] in New York, in his den, and found him courtly and facete. In the progress of mobs, I see every thing portentous; worse this, by far, than abolition. And though I conceive the anti-slavers to be rash and pragmatical, yet I think the arrogance of the South is palpably their worst policy. This wedge is in, and drives deeper year by year. And I rejoice that you and I are not laden with negro souls and bodies. Amazingly orthodox as I am, I own I should relish a little breathing spell; at least a trial, whether some of the sheep could not be fed to a certain degree, even though the shepherds did not play at quarterstaff over their heads. However, my head is not wise on these great points. Let me hear about any apostolic blows and knocks that you wot of. Bush is making a lexicon. Who is Nehemiah ——? I suppose he comes of the family of the Peleg Pecks, and Chenaniah Coffins, and Remembrance Reids, whose names, in the ——— Review, show forth the glory of the anti-anonymous system. Adieu. Thine particularly.

PRINCETON, *November* 27, 1835.

Horace Binney's eulogy [on Chief Justice Tilghman] is Attic. The introduction and a few sentences here and there are too antithetical, so as to be both stiff and obscure; otherwise it looks to me like a piece of severe rhetoric worthy of Athens. I have wanted to ask you, for some time, this question : Though you publish many Scripture biographies, and though they are taken out of the libraries, as is every thing else, yet are they really perused, sought after, delighted in ? In this I feel interested. As an antiquary (N. B. Johnson uses the noun " antiquarian " in Pref. to Dict.) I have a grand treat just now. ———— brought me from Virginia a load of MSS., letters of old Dr. Waddel, pieces of sermons, numerous skeletons, and letters *to* him. He ordered all his papers to be burned before his death; these escaped casually. Also a MS. Diary of Col. James Gordon, my mother's maternal grandfather, the first of the line in Virginia. The family was Scotch, but he came from Ireland to Lancaster Co., Virginia. Look at the singularly fine commercial site of that county. He was a merchant in direct trade with England, and I read of ships arriving every day. He was a Presbyterian among hundreds of Episcopalians, and in constant feuds with the fox-hunting parsons. Every few pages, I read of Whitefield, Davies, Todd, and Waddel. Date 1759–'65. Some historical dates may be fixed by this.

I breed so many plans which cannot be accomplished in one brief lifetime, especially of books, that I have sometimes half a mind to send you a half dozen or so of skeletons, that you may get them fitted up with flesh and skin. One of the best classical scholars I know was never at school till he entered College, but was taught wholly by his grandmother !

PRINCETON, *December* 17, 1835.

I think it my duty to decline the invitation so kindly given me by (you say not whom else) you, to preach to the teachers, &c. ; on the sole ground, that I cannot take the time or strength to make a discourse.[1] I am particularly full of writing ; I have been a full month kept from any other writing by preparing for the Repertory. I have lectures to write, and preach at least every Sunday, besides preparing four chapters for Bible classes each week, and conducting two private classes in belles-lettres in addition to my official task, and my constant private instruction of two boys in my study. I have just done a most lengthy investigation of the Servetus affair, in which I have wearied through some thousand of pages.[2] The collateral information I have thus got of Calvin's character, is very delightful. You

---

[1] He afterwards consented to perform the service, but was stopped by a snow-storm on the journey to Philadelphia.

[2] He gave an article on the life of Servetus in the Repertory for January, 1836.

would be greatly pleased with the 3d vol. of Scott's Continuation of Milner; read an English copy by all manner of means.

PRINCETON, *February* 2, 1836.

I bless God for that part of my imperfect education which resides in *good systems*, and wish every student could read ten where our young men now read one. I should somewhat doubt the expediency of a Sunday School Memoir of Zinzendorf. On the whole, I think he was a good man, but his character is very ticklish. He passed through very evil report, and probably, from his being so often and so unfavourably mentioned in Wesley's Journals, lies under a traditionary prejudice among Methodists. He came near the brink of very gross Arminianism, and his early hymns were so carnal in their expression, that they have been left out. Aaron Burr has been dying some months, and his grave bespoken here, but he hangs on. He has given our College a portrait of his father, the President, by J. S. Copley, the father of Lord Lyndhurst. The latter part of the last Report of the A. B. C. F. Missions is capitally written. Don't take these for words of course, but read the few last pages. I have never been so filled with the reality of increase in missionary zeal, as in comparing several successive reports. Try this experiment. Take the reports of the Board, and compare the "reading part," the plans, the appeals to the church, from the first to the last. What an amazing difference! What an increase of light, of courage, of large plan, of *hope!* How much higher the standard of duty, as it regards the Church and individuals! I have never been able to rid my mind of an impression, that matters will not come right, in the work of evangelism, till we see men setting out "on their own hook" (as to destination and support) in the missionary enterprise; staking all, relying on God, and penetrating deserts or hostile kingdoms, after the apostolical manner. Perhaps this is fanatical. If we are as much on the alert in a French war, as we seem to have been with regard to the Seminoles, shall we not be in a fine posture of defence? Suppose, as has been said, the fleet of King Philippe should pounce on Pensacola, how much of the South might be ravaged by him, and the savages, before our redoubtable army could be created! I am against war, in any and every one of the contingencies mentioned. "Will honour set a leg?" Yet I am far from being a Quaker on the general question; for I would fight the Seminoles, tooth and nail. My palate has, for a year or two, been growing so (perhaps under some mistaken idea of increasing my taste) that I begin to think of having it docked.

PRINCETON, *March* 10, 1836.

We learn by tradition, that the crust of our earth was once of the nature of soil, but from all appearances snow is the real substance at present. Since my futile attempt to get to you, I have taken one or two voluntary sleigh-rides, with which I am abundantly satisfied for the winter. Through great favour of Providence, our large family, including myself, have enjoyed a remarkable exemption from disease during the rigours of the season. My wife and children in particular have been very well, and we are the more able to value the blessing, from having had so much experience the other way. I learn there is a great revival in Yale College, which began on the day of prayer, as several revivals there have done. There are very pleasing indications in my late charge in Trenton. Do you observe that the new Master of the Rolls is brother of good Edward Bickersteth, and the new Lord Chancellor son of H. More's witty old correspondent, Sir W. W. Pepys? This looks well. It looks as if Providence was not forsaking a country, when the seed of the righteous are exalted. The legal decision of Chief Justice Savage about the Trades Unions, strikes me as important. Every thing nowadays seems to betoken the triumph, at least for a season, of ignorance, violence, agrarianism, and the canaille; and the worst is, that when a country comes out of this fit, it usually falls into that of despotism. The excesses of the Temperance advocates have brought me to a serious question, whether the whole pledge system is not wrong.

PRINCETON, *April* 14, 1836.

I have read the address of Mr. Barnes's congregation. The only important item is the statement of doctrinal questions. If this has any meaning, it plainly is, that the doctrines which Mr. Barnes is required to hold, which Synod holds, and for not holding which Mr. B. is suspended, are, inter alia: 1. That God made a *formal and express* covenant, &c. 2. That Adam's sin is my *personal* sin. 3. That Christ's sufferings are the *precise* sufferings. 4. That Christ's righteousness becomes my *personal* righteousness. 5. That man is involuntary in (actual) sin. You know I dissent from the decision of the Synod, but the above representation shocks me. For, 1. Mr. Barnes was never required to maintain any such doctrine. 2. These are not the points alleged. 3. I never heard of a member of Synod who held any one of them. 4. I pledge my character, that no man in America can be found who pretends to hold any two of them. We have a lovely day after yesterday's storm. Our session is now closed, and I am only waiting for a little fixment in order to set out on my

Virginia trip, which I expect to do on Tuesday next. Our trustees have made Jaeger professor of French, in place of Hargous, resigned. I have read " Good's Better Covenant," published by Hooker, with high interest, and I hope profit. The book justifies all [Bishop] McIlvaine's laudation; a lovely work. Hug's Introduction to the New Testament is translated at Andover; if well done, it will be worth possessing, being the best book on the subject, by a very learned Roman Catholic. Our little bookseller here will send a few copies of my " Gift" [to the Afflicted]. I have been writing a series of six articles on " Civic and Rural Decoration," in a Newark paper, of which I send you the only number I have. By the Christian Observer I perceive that the Churchmen of England are again agitating the question about an emendation of the Liturgy, much as in the reign of William III. To this they seem to be driven by fear of the radicals. Among a new importation from London, I see a new life of Watts, by one Milner. The first volume of the Church of Scotland Magazine is mainly occupied in defending establishments, and abusing Colton and America. Maria Monk [a professed convert from Popery] is again dragged out in all her feculence and purulence in the newly risen " Protestant Vindicator," which I hoped had gone to its own place. You probably see by the papers what a hoax there has been about Miss Frederica Misca, who turns out, instead of a German baroness, to be a Pennsylvania huckster.

PRINCETON, *May* 30, 1836.

For six weeks, nearly, I have laboured under a terrible cough, giving me sore trouble at night, and from its continuance quite threatening. The doctors have repeatedly told me that I must expect to suffer in this way, as long as my uvula or pendulous palate dragged on my tongue, as it has done for eighteen months past. Yesterday I had the tip end nipped off; but this seeming insufficient, I have to-day submitted to the excision of an additional lump of some size. After having thus lost my palate, I am, as you may readily suppose, disqualified for lecturing on *Taste*, and am snugly confined to my room, until such time as I may be relieved. My father is in Baltimore, and has been in Washington, where he saw Jackson and Van Buren. He speaks of the disorder in the House of Representatives as exceeding any thing he ever witnessed. I saw something of the same, and could not but call to mind the charges made against our General Assembly, by ignorant or peevish persons, as being more unruly than secular bodies of equal size. I always considered it as false in fact, and it is to be also considered that the Assembly has but a fortnight in which to bring into order men of every section, some of whom have never before been in any deliberative body. So ——— has covered his retreat by a book, in which, I dare say, deserter-like, he abuses those he has left. This has become the mode; indeed, is it not in human nature? I am reminded of a sentence of Parr's: " Proselytes, after a few misgivings, soon glow with the real or pretended fervor of zealots. In order to obtain protection against the indignation of the persons whom they have deserted, they adopt every prejudice, inflame every passion, and minister indiscriminately to every good and every bad purpose of the party to whom they have delivered over their interests and their honour."

Our college has opened with a larger accession than is common at the season. The eastern storm has been so long and close since my return, that I can hardly tell how our northern country looks. It seems to me, in looking over the history of the church, that the real progress of religion has been in a very small degree dependent on the spread or permanency of any external form of polity. The external form has shot out great branches, and taken root, while at the same time the spirit of religion has become almost extinct; witness the Romish church, the Anglican church under Queen Anne, and in Virginia. The external form has, on the other hand, been violated and trampled on, while the spirit of religion, taking a large view, has made immense progress; witness the *early* Reformation; the Moravian offset from Lutheranism, and the Wesleyan Reformation in England. This thought runs beautifully through the whole of Neander's Church History. He looks for the unity of the church in something internal. Hurlbut of your city has furnished an admirable selection of Cicero's letters, with notes. In all classical antiquity, so far as I have any glimpses, there is no better reading for youth, as I am sure in all pagan history there is no better character. This I say the more readily after a careful perusal of his familiar epistles. Democracy and I are less and less friends every day I live. Yet nothing else would do for a country like ours. It must be several ages yet before we have a noblesse, or a literary caste; and until we have, nominal aristocracy would be as ridiculous as the " Duc de Limonade," &c., of St. Domingo.

PRINCETON, *June* 13, 1836.

Having been doctored for a time under misprision of whooping or chin-cough, I am at length duly convicted, having caught it of Mr. Carrington's children, and conveyed it to my own. During the intervals I feel quite well, but at the paroxysms I have the feeling of being choked to death, and that sometimes for a minute. I shall always have a sincere pity for children under this visitation. As to the operation on my palate, it is so plain a one that if I could have seen and reached the spot, I should not have scrupled to do it for myself. It is now well. Reperusing the life of Hannah More; with more admiration and instruction than before. Truly the circle in which she moved was brilliant and great, beyond compare; but look ye, when you or I talk of emigrating to England, let us never forget that *we* could never gain access to that aristocratic class. The caste would forever exclude us, and our Americanism would be semi-barbarism. And therefore I should prefer the upper circle here, to the English middlings, who cringe and truckle with a servility which no American could endure. I have looked over ———'s sermon on sects, which seems to me to contain an infinite deal of nothing. I have in vain tried to deduce from it any one practical canon, which is not already acted on. The best reply to it would be an article I once read in the Vermont "Chronicle," entitled "Hypostasization," or some such hard word, showing that when we broke all the sectarian vessels, we spilled all the Christian liquor at the same time. Romish unity I can understand, but the unity which is to arise from the compromise and suppression of every thing peculiar, I cannot understand; and if there were a society on the principle that no sectarian proclivities of doctrine should be preached, which ——— suggests to be a good principle for preaching, I should abhor it little less than I do the Pope's church. Indeed, it is only the liberty of declaring within each separate pale the supposed truths of the gospel, in their length and breadth, which for a moment reconciles me to the compromise of the Sunday School Union, or the Tract Society. The stars in their courses seem to fight against the Marion [college, &c., in Missouri] humbug; indictment, inundation, murder, flogging, lynching. I ween some of the stockholders begin to be reminded of the South Sea bubble.

It occurs to me that a tract might be written in the dialogue form, after the model of H. More's Village Politics, against the Trades Unions; but how could it be circulated? *Females* and *ladies* have ousted the noble old word *woman*. Fanny Kemble laughs at old Riker for having called her a *female*. N. B. All negro wenches are ladies. "I met two *males* with white hats;" how does that sound? I wish this new dictionary of Richardson's could be held up as a shield against the barbarous missiles of Noah Webster. ——— writes from London that his health is greatly amended, and that for a guinea a day he has worse fare than his mother's upper servants. In one respect I am glad he has gone; he is an American who will not sink or mask any one peculiarity out of fear of John Bull, and who will beard our impertinent English critics even in Exeter Hall. He has moreover strength of mind and vigorous eloquence. When I was in Washington I saw some moulds for statues by a pupil of Thorwaldsen, from Rome, and also busts by him of Clay, Jackson, Southard, &c. They were very striking. East wind and raw weather again. Farmers say we shall have no small grain. Happy land is ours where famine has never come!

PRINCETON, *July* 10, 1836.

Princeton is now in a state of Anglican viridity, enough to cure half the people " in populous city pent." I have a shuddering, I hope not superstitious, about Girard College. Its cornerstone lies on the credit of Christ's ministers, and thus (Luke x. 16) on the honour of Christ.[1] Institutions, having no immortal souls, are punished in this life, and therefore I do confidently forebode some signal frown of Providence on that institution. Yet I speak hesitatingly, for *e contra*—shall we leave it to be the prey and organ of the devil and his angels? We are all too apt, however, to give an undue weight to selfish considerations in making our election of our lot, and our satisfaction of mind is therefore all the greater when we can feel that we choose the humbler and thornier path for Christ's sake. Having been repeatedly called to this anxious sort of inquiry, I have come to this result: that when we pray for guidance, we *receive* it, but do not always know, even when we take the decisive step, that it is just the right thing; we leap, so to speak, in the dark, or in the best light we have, and then find ourselves on solid ground, and are ultimately convinced that what we did was " of the Lord."

PRINCETON, *Aug.* 23, 1836.

Your absence from the city detracted somewhat from my usual satisfactions, and during the only secular hour which I had to bestow on the Union, both the worshipful secretaries were absent. I saw Mr. Packard in perspective at the 10th church [from the pulpit] but had no " speech of him."

I had never heard, until your last, of any opposition to your Union from the Boston Recorder. It may be observed, however, that the eastern folk are great friends of all national societies which centre at Boston. Some years ago —— and —— had a controversy, as to whether the Massachusetts Missionary Society should be swallowed up by the American Home Missionary Society. It cannot be long before the Episcopalians will have

[1] The will of Girard excluded clergymen from the College, even as transient visiters.

to desist from their taunts at non-prelatical sects for their discord. In Bishop White they have lost a great balance-wheel. They may look for troubles at home. Witness the lamentable feud between their Goliath, Dr. C—— and Bp. S——, the quarrel between McC—— and his late vestry, the erratic proceedings of C——, and the despotism of D——.

You will perhaps smile when I tell you that I have been taking some lessons in drawing. This I have done with special reference to making pictures for some of my projected books. Having had to supply Prof. Maclean's place in part, during his absence, I do scarcely any thing else in my study but pore over Greek tragedy; an employment which I find irksome, except that I am enlivened by the hope of gaining a more accurate knowledge of New Testament grammar.

If you will look into Walker, you will discover that half our good speakers mispronounce the following words: "access, recess, exhaust, transient, transition, relaxation, exhortation, isolate, enthusiasm, ecclesiastical." I have read no traveller's account more graphic or satisfactory than R. J. Breckinridge's letters from England in his Baltimore magazine. On the 20th inst. a young Irish maid, being phrenetic, precipitated herself from the garret window to the ground, and was not seriously injured, though she continues crazy. I have seen a recent letter from Tholuck, in which that good man writes despondingly about the state of evangelical religion in Germany. We are expecting every day a large importation of new German books. The old king of Prussia is crazy. The heir apparent is a pious man, and vehemently opposed to the Neologists. I hope we shall have no more stupid *Hobys* from England to act as spies on their return. Suppose we should pursue a similar course with regard to their treatment of the wild Irish; or that B—— should wage a crusade against their marine-impressment, or their tithe-laws.

I believe you are an honorary member of the Am. Whig Society of our college. Among our improvements here, we propose to erect two separate edifices for the accommodation of the two literary societies. A subscription to this end is going about among our graduates. You may mention it publicly or privately upon any suitable occasion. It is a fine idea of Vitringa's that Isaiah, in the passage, "doves to their windows," alludes to merchant vessels returning with outspread sails to their ports. I have this day finished the critical study of the Phoenissæ of Euripides, and am disposed to accord to that great poet the praise which is commonly given for his ingenuity, correctness, and tragic pathos. Take some occasion to brush up your French by reading the letters of Archbishop Fenelon. Surely there have lived few more holy men upon our globe. It is pleasing under the worst forms of church opinion to discover the undeniable operations of the Holy Spirit.

PRINCETON, *Aug.* 26, 1836.

I agree to every word you say about *memoirs*.¹ In the case of ———, for instance, a dear and honored friend of mine, I can see no demand for a biography. Diaries are often mere diarrhœas or defecations of a man's most troubled and worst thoughts. I have been so fully employed as to be unable to lay a finger to any Sunday School job for several months. There are some archæological pictures which I will endeavour to copy for you as soon as may be. It is also in my earnest intention to give you somewhat for the "Youth's Friend," [a monthly magazine.] My present attitude about Temperance is this: I regard the teetotalers as the only consistent society, but have some slight scruples about the whole principle, when I look at its abuses and corollaries. Do you ever see a foot-stove in a church nowadays? I remember when they were almost as indispensable in winter, as fans are in summer.

If the principle of infinite series can be exemplified in practice, it will be in the case of the ———'s French correspondent. Arminius's motto was *Bona conscientia paradisus;* Calvin's, *Promptè et sincerè;* Erasmus's, *Cedo nulli.* I expect to preach to the children at Kingston, at their Sunday School Anniversary next Sunday.

PRINCETON, *Sept.* 24, 1836.

I am sorry that you are so confirmed a cockney as to be unfit for travel. My case differs from yours; for a week before I set out anywhither, I am in a perfect tremor and feeze, but after about forty miles I become entirely nonchalant, and feel as if I could journey a year. You alarm me about your water-drinking propensity. Blessed sir! have you not read Dr. ———'s hydrophobic stricture, thereanent? See "Permanent Documents," appendix, p. 25. Are you ignorant that "water dilutes the gastric juice," and is a species of intemperance? Little as I meddle in politics, or believe in panics, I am alarmed at the unexampled audacity of the 19 Van Buren electors of Maryland. It seems to have come to this, that when the wagon of state goes in a road unpleasant to a minority of passengers, they may be allowed to

---

¹ His correspondent had remarked, that it seemed to be understood in the religious world, that every one who had kept a diary or written letters, must have his biography written.

remove all the linch-pins and cut the traces. Take this in connexion with Dallas's doctrine that conventions may annul compacts, and we have the spectre of anarchy and civil war before us. I fear things must be worse before they are better. Yet how natural is Hezekiah's selfishness, "There shall be peace and truth in *my* days." I join you in lamentation on the desert state of our religious field. Perhaps the remedy is to be sought in striving to build up individual piety, with less confidence in the omnipotence of associations, unions, and polity. The more we talk and plan, the more we seem to differ. Fenelon has some truth in his advice: " Parlez a Dieu pour la paix de l'eglise, et ne parlez point aux hommes." At [Aaron] Burr's burial, we had as pall-bearers, Judge Edwards, General Swartwout, sen., who was Burr's second in the duel, and ———, who has also killed his man. Dr. ———, in rallying Dr. Rice about assisting at the rites, said a good text would have been "By this time he stinketh." I have been this morning to see the eldest son of our late physician [Dr. Howell] dying, as I believe. I trust he is departing in faith. His little sister lies only not as ill as he. My little private scholar ——— is also very sick; all in the same house. Offer one hearty prayer for these afflicted people. I never knew such a case. All the cases I know of are in this one house, yet it is new, high, ventilated, sweet and clean. Entre nous—I have been sounded to discover whether I would be president of South Hanover College ; now if you will be a good boy, and sign the Act and Testimony, and return to the ways of your father's father, I will make you vice-president. You will not need webbed-feet, like the Marionites. I certify that the college is above high-water mark. I attended a pleasing Sunday School Anniversary last Sunday at Cranbury ; a church full of children. Henry is a true man to the cause.

PRINCETON, *October*, 1836.

Your favour of last week I found on my return from Newark, where I had been spending a week very delightfully. While there I fell into conversation with one of the leading politicians of New Jersey, a professor of religion, who took the following ground against Sunday Schools, a ground quite new to me : He holds that it is the duty of the Christian public to institute as fast as possible a system of schools all over the land, which shall teach religion as well as learning. Every thing which delays this, or which is short of this, he deprecates. He therefore regards the energies of the church as wasted upon the 'endeavour to teach a portion of the children a mere thirtieth of their time. The effort which carries forward the Sunday School enterprise would almost accomplish the other. The man is sincere and enthusiastic, and I give you his views in all their strength.

We are to have two of Dr. King's Greeks in college. They are intelligent fellows; one of them a noble specimen. They read the Attic Greek works with scarcely any difficulty. I wish you would visit Newark on your Sunday School business. I know no such place out of New England. Within the last month they have raised in the Presbyterian churches there a little less than $12,000, for public objects. Among the rest $3,500 for a new African church, of which not a cent was given by Abolitionists.

PRINCETON, *Nov.* 13, 1836.

I am sensibly affected by the peril and the escape of ———, and unite with you in giving thanks. No doubt, you already feel the lesson to be better than many volumes, and many sermons. You will probably never lose the benefit of these softening and humanizing scenes. "By these things men live, and in all these things is the life of the spirit." And do not charge me with meaning to take an ungenerous advantage of you in an argument, when I say with earnest conviction, that such experiences better fit a man for feeding Christ's sheep, than even the ascetic *devotions* of a bachelor. If I have ever made any "proof" of my "ministry," it has been in the house of mourning, and by means of knowledge learned in the same. The thought has occurred to me, that the angels, although perfect in holiness, cannot have *that* perfection of holiness which saints have, inasmuch as they have never known the discipline of tears. They cannot know what it is to bleed with a wife or a child. And analogously, how much is contained in that character of our highpriest, that he was "tempted in all points like as we are." My thoughts run more naturally in this strain, because we have two sick children.

PRINCETON, *Nov.* 29, 1836.

I will try to write the questions on Hebrews; but have you considered how large a book it will make? Among perverted texts, none suffer more than 2 Cor. v. 11. "Knowing therefore the *terror of the Lord* we persuade men." Very pretty theories are spun out of it. But look at the Greek, τὸν φόβον τοῦ κυρίου—it is the unvarying expression for the *fear of the Lord*, or true religion, everywhere else so translated; and why not here also, as well as in Acts ix. 31? Outof many instances in the LXX., take these at random: Job xxviii. 28. Psalm xxxiv. 11. Isa. xi. 3. Proverbs xxiii. 17; i. 7; ij. 5; viii. 13. Our college is full; we have admitted 62. The junior class has 86. If you ever see a paper called the Newark Daily Advertiser, you will recognize two old friends—*C. S. A.* every day; and your humble servant every two or three days, under the title *Literary Trifles*. Mr. Walsh had one gross error in his English, which I am sorry to see his successor imitates. It is saying "I doubt *that*" for "I doubt *whether*." Not only is the latter the authorized phrase, but it has a different meaning. In old English, *I doubt that he will fail* means, I fear, or suspect that he will fail. The adverb "whether" is exactly suited to express the libration of the mind between alternatives which *doubt* imports.

PRINCETON, *Dec.* 27, 1836.

Last night, after returning from Brunswick, where I had been for three days, I received the paper you sent me, containing the news of your bereavement. May the Lord make it an abundantly useful dispensation! I might dwell on the fact that the increasing afflictions of your child made it desirable that she might be transplanted to a more genial climate, if I did not know how little this consideration has to do with our affections, or if I had not learned by experience that the feeblest is always the darling of the parent's heart. A better rest for your mind will be found in considerations purely evangelical, and connected with the covenant of grace. This stroke is a part of the gospel compact. It has been, I doubt not, sent, and sent at this time, with a specialty of purpose, as to your sanctification and salvation. In the belief of this, I am less disposed to suggest topics for your consideration, than to direct you to listen to that voice of the Spirit which accompanies the stroke. If you carefully observe what great truths of Christianity are at this time most weighty on your soul, or most precious, you will find it good to note these, and treasure them up for future contemplation and practice. In these seasons of night we are permitted to discern those stars which are hidden by the glare of day. Such sins also as now weigh upon your conscience may be those which the dispensation is intended to cut away. After all, it is safest to put the word of God into your hands, and to leave you to imbibe those truths for which your heart shall manifest the greatest affinity. "I will hear what God the Lord will speak."

Such are my pressing engagements, viz.: 14 hours of lecture and recitation a week, besides Bible-class, preaching, and Repertory, that I scarcely foresee a time when I can really fall to work upon the Questions.

Did I say to you that we have here a very interesting Italian gentleman named Borsieri? He was 15 years imprisoned in the fortress of Spielberg, in Moravia, for conspiracy against the Austrian domination over Lombardy. He is several times mentioned in the celebrated Memoirs of Silvio Pellico, as an intimate friend of the latter. He is a man of great accomplishment, speaking Latin, French, and German, but he has very little English.

TRENTON, *January* 7, 1837.

My father is strongly inclined to the opinion, that your Union should have an agent at Calcutta, for the purpose of circulating your books and plans throughout British India.[1]

[After speaking of the perils of ministers under the temptations of money.] Truly and unaffectedly I am alarmed at these things, and most of all alarmed at what I discern in myself, of desires for more ease, style, and luxury than is compatible with the sincere preaching of self-denial. It is in vain for us to cry out against the luxury of Popish priests, in the face of such things. I believe, that the majority of Popish priests are poor and live low. It is also vain for us to prate about the self-denials of the ministry.

I am more and more pleased with Mr. [John W.] Williams's *redaction* of the [Philadelphia] National Gazette. Sometimes he is prolix and not enough *degagé*, but always sober and generally elegant. As a litterateur he must certainly take the highest rank.[2] I purpose to send a piece from the Italian to his paper, if I can get a breathing-spell. Since I wrote my ["Jacob and"] "Joseph," I have met with a good suggestion in Josephus. Why did Joseph demand Benjamin to be brought down to Egypt? It is a question not easily answered. Josephus supposes it was because from his own experience of their cruelty, Joseph feared they had made way with Benjamin, as they had wished to do with himself. And also that he put the cup into Benjamin's sack in order to make trial of his brethren, whether they would stand by Benjamin, when he should be accused of stealing the cup, or whether they would abandon him to his fate.

---

[1] Large supplies of the publications of the Society had already been sent to India upon the orders of British and American missionaries. Mr. C. E. Trevelyan, in the civil service of the Government at Calcutta, was specially zealous in this work, and several of the original books of the Union were translated into Hindoostanee.

[2] Mr. Williams also succeeded Mr. Walsh in sharing the editorial charge of the American Quarterly Review; but his promising career was cut off by his death at an early age, in August, 1837.

PRINCETON, *March* 10, 1837.

From the inconvenience of having two habitats, [College and dwelling,] your last favour is not within my reach, and I must rather ask than answer. Serious and numerous engagements have so fractured my days that I could not feel free to bestow any of my horæ subcesivæ on the luxury of letter-writing. I have been at Trenton assisting at the sessions of our law-makers, and witnessing their squabbles on the surplus revenue [of the United States] which is producing the same sort of scramble and fight that ensues upon a largess of coppers among a group of sweeps. The worser side has the best of the battle, and the principal, not the mere interest, is to be distributed, like the body of a ——— you wot of, [Judges xix. 29,] and with about as much chance of being ever reintegrated. Trenton will probably double its trade and population next year. ——— is the most elegant builder of a sermon, quà talis, within my knowledge. I found great satisfaction in going to see some of my old parishioners in their affliction. One of these is James Pollock,[1] a Scotchman from Ayrshire, a poor dyer, and a broken-down invalid, but rich in faith and intellectual resources. For nine weeks he had suffered anguish from calculi, having spasms which, as he said, would certainly have killed him if they had followed one another on successive days; he was under salivation when I saw him, though he was dressed and sitting in his chair. I wish I could give you some idea of this man's manner and discourse. His face was illuminated by a fire of Christian animation beyond any thing I ever saw, and he poured forth, in the very broadest Scotch dialect, the strongest Calvinism of Paul, every point of which seemed in his soul to be turned into rich experience. Pollock is the best theologian, and the best master of church history, I know, out of the clerical profession; nor *in it* do I know five whom I consider his superiors. He declared to me that under agonies of bodily pain his views of Christ and of the sovereign, distinguishing grace of the plan of salvation, had wholly neutralized his sense of suffering. This man's stern and holy enthusiasm is felt with amazing influence in the factory to which he is attached. Though very poor, he overawes and prevents the profaneness, drinking, and scoffing, which are always ready to break out in such places. My tears are not easily come at, but I was childishly overcome in listening to his Chalmerian discourse. If I ever saw a native genius, or a glorius Covenanter, it is in the person of James Pollock. A second visit I paid to a widow

---

[1] Mr. Pollock is mentioned before on page 199. He died December, 1856, at the age of 73.

in her 81st year, who declared to me that she had seen no moment since I last met with her, in which she did not joyfully await the summons of Christ. And when I asked her how she viewed her own doings, she absolutely burst into tears, as she disclaimed all righteousness of her own. I declare to you my satisfaction and strengthening of faith from these two cases. Let the infidel solve the problem: How, at an age, and amidst pains and sicknesses, which naturally cause despondency, and subdue hope, the fear of the direst of human ills is swallowed up in Christian expectation?

I have not for weeks done any thing at the questions on Hebrews, and see no chance of resuming them for a month or two. It is, for years, my canon, to do no writing or serious study by night; and you may imagine my days from the following schedule: 9. A.M., at my study, with two boys, Livy and Mair, correct exercises, and overlook their Algebra; meantime preparing for class, and writing for Repertory. 11. A.M. Lecture or Recitation. 12—1½ exercise and college business; 2, at study as above. Hear Xenophon. Class at 3¼. Prayers at 5. All days alike. I have not yet told you that the Assembly's Board of Education and Missions, have nominated me their speaker at certain palavers to be holden in May, at Natchez, Louisville, Pittsburg, &c. If the Lord will, I shall set out soon after April 10th. The Natchez meeting, which comes first, falls in the first week in May. Rev. W. Chester goes along. He intimated that your Board wished a representative, but however much I should love to serve you, I think it would hurt all three to have an individual acting for the Co. Charles Matthews, I believe, used to enact some fourteen characters in one night, but poor I shall scarcely have vim enough for one. Now, if *you* will but accompany, we may hope for a happy, useful journey; and perhaps we may never again have the chance of seeing the mighty lap of this Occidental virgin world.

No conviction of my soul gains more strength than that our great study should be *The Bible*. I reproach my butterfly mind every night, for her idle excursions. Yet one consolation I certainly find: though I am much away from my Bible, as I am much away from my wife and boys, yet when I *do* get back, I feel that I love them mightily. O how! how! how shall we check the waste of mind upon the ever-increasing frivolities of literature! Literature needs a Deluge. We are antediluvians in this regard. Is God about to banish our impertinent rivalry of *his* book, by sweeping our books away? by war, discord, or other calamity? I hope not. Let me begin reform at home. I am ashamed of piddling all my days among periodical scraps, and short-lived nothings, while whole tracts of Scripture remain unexplored. Query. What would John, Paul, or Peter, if arisen in our day, do in the premises? I am sick at heart of a book-and-paper surfeit. I wish I could get some remedy.

PRINCETON, *April* 3, 1837.

On Saturday, 25th ult., I went to New York to preach for [Rev. George] Potts. It was my intention to stay some days, in order to purchase a little furniture for housekeeping, which we are about to attempt: (Apropos of which we cordially join in tendering to you and yours such things as we have, now, henceforth, and forever. Make my best speech in the premises to ———;) but a grievous assault of [pain] disconcerted me, and I was fain to come home. My employers have so fixed the anniversaries at the West (at Louisville on the 24th and Pittsburg a week later) that the trip seems hardly worth making; and if I do not get better, I shall not dare to go at all. In that event, I shall hope to spend a little time in my old Philadelphian haunts. I heard ——— and ——— [two celebrated "revivalists"] in New York. The former has taken all the wind out of the latter's sails, as to revivals. The Broadway Tabernacle is the noblest house for a great auditory that ever I saw. Perhaps 2,500 filled the seats on Sunday week at night. ——— is on the cool, metaphysical tack; but the mad bull will butt and bellow sometimes. The sermon was an odious caricature of old Hopkinsian divinity, such as ferments in the head of an ill-trained but vigorous mind, and throws up a scum of crudities. "Government," "Government," "Government," nothing but government—till I began to feel as if the Creator was but a secondary administrator, put to hard shifts to save appearances. It was a sermon well adapted to make ———, *e. g.* "I suppose all the united malice of all the devils in hell would not keep a poor sinner in hell *to all eternity.* O no. None but *God* can have firmness enough to do that, &c." These were his words so far as I remember.

As to ———, the account of him in the ———, is far below the reality. His manner is drunken, he adores his person, and perpetually protrudes "Mr. ———," as he suburbanically calls himself. His ordinary compellation of the hearer is *"Mister!"* He is profane to an extreme in foisting in the divine names merely to point a phrase, as "the vilest infidel under God's heaven;" the "greatest mind God Almighty ever made;" and all this in the tone of a Yankee bar-keeper. I heard no false doctrine from him. You see the Literary and Theological Review goes beyond us [Repertory] on Voluntary Associations.

M——— is in a feud with his S. S. Superintendent, an abolitionist, who refuses to be amenable to M. and turns the S. S. into an anti-slavery association. All the pastors complain of a tendency to such jarring. If such should really be the tendency of the present arrangements, the sooner we alter them the better; for I am high-church enough to abandon any thing which disturbs our divinely constituted relations of ruler and ruled. I wish you could see your way clear to have some of your [Union] books translated into Italian, for the Levant, where the language is extensively used. If you could, we have here a highly accomplished Italian, for many years fellow-prisoner of Silvio Pellico, and of Comte Confalonieri, who could do such work under my inspection. He is a Milanese, named *Pietro Borsieri.*

Princeton, *April* 29, 1837.

During my vacation, I have been absent, first for a week at Newark; for a day or two, then, at Trenton; and lastly for a day or two at Bound Brook, Somerset, where our Presbytery met. This, with the accumulated cares of raking together a little furniture, has kept me from much study-work or correspondence. We have not yet got into our house, partly from want of things, but chiefly from the delay of a servante whom we have engaged. I am living in the back-parlor, however, which I have to take as a study, or else have no room for my friends, which is after all the great charm of one's own house. Mrs. Samuel Bayard died last week in Westmoreland, Va., at the late residence of Mrs. Washington; who, by-the-bye, died a year or two ago, here, at the residence of Mr. Bayard. ——— stopped for a few days. I was here only part of the time. He gave many interesting accounts. Thinks it likely that the High Church tories of the Church and the Kirk, finding that the Catholic adhesion to the liberal side must ruin the conservative interest, will consent to give Ireland a *Catholic* establishment; in consequence of which, the *three* established churches can trample down the Whigs, &c. He says there is more piety in proportion to the population in the Canton de Vaud, than in any part of the world. There is English preaching at seven places in Paris. At our Presbytery we appointed Dr. Alexander and Mr. Yeomans as commissioners, [to General Assembly;] and Messrs. [I. V.] Brown and Shafer with two elders as delegates to the Convention, [preliminary to Assembly.] I see but one plan, and that I have often stated to you: *Reduce the Church to its constituent Presbyteries.* These are all that are essential to the notion of a Presbyterian Church. These may coalesce as they see fit.

PRINCETON, *May* 23, 1837.

You are enough acquainted with my penchant for "laid" or other non-porous writing paper to be able to buy me a parcel. I prefer the old-fashioned and old drab, or white, to the blue, and abominate the machine paper, which looks mottled when held up to the light.

But I write expressly to demand of you the reason why you have not sent me, as in duty bound, a *Daily Bulletin* of the Sanhedrin: yea a *daily* letter, full of facts, number of votes, and pungencies, &c. Prithee begin, and honour at sight this bill for one epistle per diem while the General Assembly is sitting. I suppose you have divided the Church, and excommunicated New England, while I have been sowing my beet seed, and blistering my puny fingers with spade and hoe. Know ye, however, that we gardeners of Jersey contemn all the prettinesses of your civic parterres and flower beds, and go for massy hills of corn, unsightly ridges of potatoes, and stupendous poles of nodding hop-vines. Come up and behold a second Cato the Censor, another Cincinnatus, a great experimenter in the union of leeks and letters; come and taste of my rhubarb pies, (the only esculent I yet boast,) my embryo radishes, my beans just up, my parsley and sage not up at all, and my nasturtions not pickled nor planted.

College has opened. Prospects better than we feared. My daily duties forbid my going to the Assembly.

I passed some days at New Brunswick, where there is a great revival in three several places, viz., the Baptist Church, the Presbyterian Church, and the Free Church.

PRINCETON, *June* 14, 1837.

I could not get down to the city, because when I was not teaching, I felt constrained to be in New Brunswick, to aid Bro. [Jos. H.] Jones, one of my most intimate brethren, for whom I have within ten days preached six sermons, and attended as many meetings more. That ultra old school town is shaken by a great awakening, still in blessed progress. In the Baptist Church 109 have been baptized; others inquiring. In the Dutch Church (Dr. S. B. How's) 35 have been admitted; perhaps as many more awakened. In Jones's Church, some 70 entertain the Christian hope, and about 30 are awakened.[1] In Rutgers College, out of 80 youths, 68 are thought to have believed in Christ.

---

[1] According to the "Outline of a Work of Grace," published by Dr. Jones in 1839, the whole number received into the communion of the Presbyterian Church was 149; the aggregate of admission into all the churches about 600.

David Abeel, the missionary, lives there; labouring beyond his strength, for he has come back from St. Croix, I fear, to die with his aged parents.[1] After so many years of preaching with comparatively little visible effect, it was a gratifying and unspeakably gracious favour conferred on me, to allow me to witness some remarkable instances of apparent fruits. And still more, the whole tenour of this revival has been very pleasing to me, as confirming that high Calvinistic view of the gratuity of salvation, and the efficacy of the "gospel," as contradistinguished from "obligation," in which I grow day by day more exclusively rooted. I dare say my creed, if written out in full, would be condemned by many an Arminian, and many a New England Calvinist, or Antinomian, but it meets me unavoidably in every page of Paul. David Abeel is, I suppose, quite as good a man as Henry Martyn; indeed, so heavenly is his temper, that I feel a presentiment while in his company, that he is "ready to be offered." I could wish and pray otherwise. The effect his labours have had on the Dutch Church, are such (in missionary matters) as I have never seen from the labours of one individual. Twice he has been ready to re-embark for China, and both times brought to death's door. If he have a reprieve, he will make another attempt before long.

We have about 220 on our College roll. Dr. Nesbit's library is secured for the Seminary, so long as they teach orthodoxy.

NEW BRUNSWICK, *July* 13, 1837.

Last week I was at Bound Brook, on the Raritan, at a special meeting. The revival of religion has extended thither, to the flock of the Rev. Mr. Rodgers. About a hundred are inquiring. On Monday I took a drive of 46 miles, from Princeton to Somerville, thence down the Raritan to this city, and so home. The county of Somerset, in the parts through which I passed, is wholly settled by the Dutch; you know their neatness, thrift, and morality are proverbial. I never saw the country look so enchanting. The dense masses of herbage and forest are luxuriant in consequence of the rains, and every sort of crop promising beyond all previous supposition. The grass, oats, rye, flax, and wheat are excellent, and the corn better thereabouts than in any other region within my knowledge. Those who are accustomed to pass through the sands of lower Jersey have no conception of the beauty, fertility, and picturesqueness of the middle and upper counties. The Dutch farms realize the ideal of rural

[1] Dr. Abeel returned to China in October, 1838, but was driven home by his declining health in January 1845, and died at Albany, September 4, 1846.

comfort. It is "a land of hills and valleys, and drinketh water of the rain of heaven."

Yesterday I came hither; my third visit to this revived church. The work of the Lord is still advancing here, though the phase of divine influence is somewhat varied. As might be expected, the number of awakenings is smaller; but some of the most remarkable conversions have occurred within a day or two; including several professional men, and other persons of great influence. The Baptists have immersed a hundred and fifty. The Dutch number some 50—70 converts; the Presbyterians 130—150. The Methodists have a great excitement. All the students of Rutgers College but five or six are now hopefully pious. I perceive no one thing in the Presbyterian church which is undesirable, nor any flagging in the prayers or efforts of pastor or people. In the Sunday School the state of feeling is more full of promise than it has been at any time. All day, and much of the night, Mr. Jones is engaged with inquirers. Over the river, in Piscataway, and Metutchen, also in Plainfield, and (somewhat) in Rahway, there is revival. These influences, except in the case of Bound Brook, have been most extensive among the Baptists. There has been here no veiling or modifying of high Calvinistic tenets, in order to keep the sinner under the yoke of obligation, or to precipitate the resolved efforts of his own soul, as abstracted from Divine power. The doctrines which have been blessed are the "primer doctrines," taught in the old way, and in old phraseology. Indeed I may say of the preaching, what Brainerd says of that which was used to awaken his Indians: "It has been from first to last a strain of gospel invitation."

COLLEGE, *August* 10, 1837.

What you say about a good penny paper, is most true, and has often occurred to me; only for *weekly*, I should certainly read *daily*. Some capital is needed to set such a thing on foot, but I am sure no book or magazine which could be issued from the press would have so wide an influence. The pious laymen of Philadelphia ought not to rest until the thing is done. So William IV. is dead, and a virgin once more on the chief throne of the world. If poets were not extinct, here would be a tempting subject. I hope I shall never so far undervalue charity as not to lament the false fire kindled in church controversies; but I comfort myself with the thoughts, that what we love we always contend for; that the most flourishing seasons for piety have been those of the most active debates: witness the days of Augustin, of Luther, of the English Nonconformists; that the conservative principle of Protestantism is discussion of all points; and that the friction of debate is temporary, while the gain on the side of truth is permanent. I am sure there has been no age in which controvertists have been more polite towards one another than the present. My —— is so little of a Philadelphia lady, that I believe in my heart she has as few thoughts about old and new school, as about the Sunnites and Shiites of the Mohammedan "persuasion." Abeel is coming to spend some days with me; his health is slowly failing.

The life of Scott [Lockhart's life of Sir Walter] is a capital book indeed. One sees how much may be accomplished by assiduity. Another good lesson is the danger of involving one's self in pecuniary connexions with "the trade." The last days of July I passed in Trenton with my little family. I must say that all my recollections of that homely town are soft and pleasant; and when we go there, we are made welcome by a circle of hearty friends. A book ought to be written with this title: "The Aged Christian's Book: printed in large type for the convenience of old persons." It should be in the largest character attainable. Such topics as these: The Trials of Old Age; The Temptations of Old Age; The Duties of Old Age; The Consolations of Old Age, &c., &c. It should be a large book, with little matter in it. Why has no Tract Society thought of such a thing? My little introduction to the Bible can soon be finished, as I find I shall have to exclude a large amount of matter, hinting in the preface that the same may be wrought into a second volume, or work. It will not greatly exceed in matter, if at all, one volume of Nevin's Antiquities. Hereafter I must confine myself to my former description of books—I mean those which can be written currente calamo, requiring no consultation and research; for unless I can make my Sunday School labours a sort of recreation, it is impossible for me to persevere in them. By this time you will have seen what we have been doing in the Repertory. Some of our theologians consider the metaphysical argument of the paper on Beecher [Dr. Lyman Beecher's "Views in Theology"] as unsurpassed for acumen, philosophical lore, and rigid ratiocination, by any thing which has appeared in our cycle. The writer is certainly a man of extraordinary versatility; as much at home among the poets and the schoolmen as the mathematicians. There are occasions on which I feel a distrust for all books but the Bible, as feeling that the best communications of men come to me modified by the discipline of a sect or the idiosyncrasy of an individual. The liquor has the tang of the cask. This I feel most as it regards books of experimental religion; sometimes turning over successively the stirring or tender productions of Catholics, Methodists, Moravians, and Presbyterians, and then resorting at last to the infallible source of all. I am more and more persuaded that the practice of preaching on a single text has greatly impaired the influence of the pulpit. The diabolical Voltaire spoke truth for once when he said : " En effet, parler long-temps sur une citation d'une ligne ou deux, se fatiguer à compasser tout son discours sur cette ligne, un tel travail parait un jeu peu digne de la gravité de ce ministère. Le texte devient une espèce de devise, ou plutôt d'énigme, que le discours développe. . . . . C'est dans la décadence des lettres qu'il commença, et le temps l'a consacré." (Louis XIV., t. iii., c. 32.)

The one great rule for Bible-study appears to me to be this : Read the text—the text—the text. Read it over and over, over and over. Read continually and largely. Thus while particulars become impressed by repetition, we do not lose the general connexion. No men ever lived, me judice, who knew the tenth part as much of the contents of the Bible as the Puritans, and thus it was they read it. They were never without their little Bibles. Among them I regard Charnock as far the most wonderful in this regard, and Flavel next. To my taste Flavel is the most uniformly interesting, engaging, and refreshing writer on religion, ancient or modern. I always feel that I am talking with a Christian, fresh and ruddy, in perfect health and spirits, with no cloud or megrim, and with every power available at the moment.

Mr. Poinsett has offered Prof. Dod the West Point professorship of Ethics, with the Chaplaincy. I do not suppose he will very seriously entertain the proposition. Our final Examination is drawing towards a close ; it is a work *plenum sudoris* in this weather. The library of old Dr. Nesbit has come to the Seminary. It is chiefly of books in the modern languages.

PRINCETON, *Sept.* 21, 1837.

Since I last corresponded with you, I have had a return of illness, something between cholera morbus and dysentery, which confined me to my bed. I am convalescent, though still in my room. I have just made up into a parcel my MS. of the Juvenile Introduction to the Bible, which I have had on hand for the last three years. It contains about 59,000 words ; from which a calculation may be made. Look over the table of contents, and read a chapter, so as to get some idea of the plan. There is nothing in it to offend any sect of Protestant Christians, except that the Quakers may take exception to my calling the Scriptures (as they do themselves) the Word of God. I flatter myself that it contains much information, which will be new to many who are neither children nor youth; and I pray that it may recommend the most delightful and blessed of all books to many a new reader. We had six lectures from Mr. Wolff, [Rev. Joseph Wolff, a Christian Jew,] of which I heard three. He was very interesting in private. What amazes me is, how a man, purblind and simple as a babe, who can scarcely take care of himself for two squares, should have traversed so much of the earth.

I have been considering the smallness of the benefit which we are content to derive from our ordinary afflictions. For instance: you and I have been sick lately; what good has it done our souls? Are we more heavenly-minded, and better fitted for communion with God? "Yes, yes," we are ready to reply, "but these are small afflictions, to which I scarcely look for any advantage." Thus we seem to render great trials necessary; whereas, I suppose, every disquietude we meet ought to be received as a message from God.

Our commencement is in danger of being frustrated, in some measure. The Whig members of the graduating class have all refused to speak, in consequence of a supposition that the faculty had slighted their Society in the award of honours; especially the Valedictory. There is a mighty storm in our teapot.

What do you think of a Sunday School Book called the Farmer's Boy, or some such title, of some length, intended to be a manual for young fellows in the country, connecting all agricultural operations with the corresponding Biblical facts, and giving a spiritual, but natural turn, to the works and changes of the husbandman? I meditate something of this sort. The church in this village is at length sufficiently finished to admit of worship in it. The Tract Society have issued a tract, called "The Child a Hundred Years old!" Some of the old commentators did indeed give this ultra-spiritual and ultra-natural turn to Isaiah lxv. 20; but the passage, as half a glance reveals, is a promise of longevity in the New Jerusalem; the "new heavens and new earth." Our version does not keep up the parallelism of the original, which is thus: "The child, a hundred years old, shall die; the sinner, a hundred years old, shall be accursed," *i. e.* as I take it, "Such shall be the longevity, that he who dies at 100, shall be regarded as a mere child, nay, as being cut off prematurely for his sins, accursed." Read the context. N. B. I am pretty much convinced by Dr. Burnet's work, that the final conflagration will destroy our world, only as the deluge did. Peter intimates that the present earth is a "new earth," in relation to what he calls the "world that then was." If he says of the present world that it shall be "burnt up," he also says of the antediluvian world, that it "perished." And he adds "Nevertheless we look for new heavens and a new earth." (2 Peter iii. 13.) Read Chalmers's Sermon on the New Heavens and New Earth. I am also inclined to think the common notions of the Millennium as inconsistent with the Scriptures, which always represent the Judgment as bursting suddenly on the world; pressing this with a moral bearing, to alarm our fears; which can have no effect, when we believe in an interval before the Judgment, of full a thousand years. Do not regard me as demented, but look at these two subjects in the light of mere Scripture, and candidly sit down without book, and write down your answer to the following question: On what clear scriptural grounds do I entertain the common notion, that things will ripen into a glorious period of just a thousand years?

COLLEGE N. J., *November* 17, 1837.

Vide several of my rhyming experiments in the Newark Daily, under the signature of Cleon.[1] I am afraid you could not get the stereotype classics [197 volumes, Leipsic] at the low

---

[1] I insert one specimen.

THE ARM-CHAIR.

Now let the curtain drop; the day
With mixing cares has passed away:
The grate is brilliant, and the light
From shaded lamps shows softly bright.
Wheel round the table, and prepare
The spacious, slumber-tempting chair.
But yield not yet to slumber's power;
Sacred to wisdom be the hour.
Here, in the genial warmth reclining,
Rest and activity combining,
The wearied frame may seek repose
While the rapt soul with pleasure glows.
Spread forth the books, a well-kept store,
Select, though few; I ask no more
Than these, to guide my flight sublime,
The master-pieces of all time.
Through these while musing I descry
The forms of sage philosophy;
Great ancients come in shadowy mien
To people the ideal scene.
I soar with Plato; or I fight
The battles of the Stagirite.
With Xenophon serene I flow,
Or cull from each, with Cicero.
Or if blest Poesy invite
To mingle in her mystic rite,

terms at which they are furnished to us. Neither would I recommend to you to get the whole set; there are many of them which you would never want. The course which I have pursued has been to buy about seventy volumes, including the chief books in Greek, and in Latin prose, and then I have the whole of the Latin poets in one volume, which cost me five dollars. Old Tauchnitz, the great Leipsic publisher, was an enemy of evangelical religion, and disinherited his son Karl, for being a pietist. The latter became a Baptist preacher and missionary; but within a very short time the old man died intestate, and the whole of his vast resources and establishment has fallen to his son, who is sincerely bent upon the promotion of true piety.

> I hear the hoary blind man sing
> Till Troy-plains with the war-clang ring;
> Or quaff the chaste exuberance
> Of tragic Greeks in choral dance.
> Then Maro, silver bard, beguiles,
> Or love-sick Ovid spreads his wiles,
> Or Flaccus through the thyrsus smiles.
>
>   Nor, pedant, would I all despise
> What moderns have of great or wise;
> Dante, tremendous in his dreams;
> Or Ariosto's wayward streams;
> Or Tasso's tale of knightly fire,
> Or Petrarch weeping o'er the lyre.
> Thy page, Cervantes, shall dispel
> The vapours from their haunted cell;
> And keen Le Sage and gay Molière
> The mask from every passion tear.
>
>   But who shall venture to rehearse
> The mighty band, in prose or verse,
> Of mother Britain, and fair France,
> Whose genius might the soul entrance?
> A taste of these might well beguile
> The speeding hours, till daylight smile.
> But limbs grow dull, and eyes grow dim,
> A respite now for eye and limb:
> Stir up the fire, the volume close,
> A moment this for choice repose.
> Safe from the blast of rough November,
> Silent I many a friend remember,
> Whose presence might the midnight brighten,
> When, hark!—the moment's load to lighten,
> A well-known knock—wide flies the door—
> Of musing and of books no more;
> The friend of many a year drops in,
> And converse grave, or jocund din
> Completes the joy, and quells the care,
> Till, satiate e'en with richest fare,
> I nod upon the elbow chair.

Hengstenberg, in reviewing ———, ridicules his determining the acceptation of a word in a certain place, by counting up the passages where it occurs in that sense; but says, this may answer very well in a country where they can enumerate to a fraction the converted and the half converted. In the Christian Observer for Feb. 1830, p. 97, is a piece of Mr. Wolff's, wherein he saith, "the Son of Man will come again in the clouds of heaven, in the year 1847, and govern in person as man and God in the literal city of Jerusalem. . . . I, Joseph Wolff, shall see with my own eyes, Abraham, Isaac, and Jacob, in their glorified bodies," &c. I think it a happy interpretation of Wolff's, where he makes the word γενεα, "generation," mean the Jewish race: "this *race* shall not pass away" (*i. e.* be merged in other nations) until all these things be accomplished. Matt. xxiv. 34. He wishes to be captured by the Indians. Professor Henry has returned. In England he was caressed like a brother, everywhere, and by all the savans. The British Association passed a special vote of thanks to him, and three other foreigners. Our college was never so full. We have already admitted about 70. Among these are two room-mates named "Cake" and "Pitcher." Your mention of Neshamony reminds me of the tasteful change of that euphonious Indian name to "Hartsville Crossroads." So, in our own presbytery, what was whilom Assampink is now "Dutch Neck." We have a new and handsome church edifice. While it was building the negroes worshipped apart, in a little place of their own. The majority of the pew-holders wish them to remain as a separate congregation. By-the-bye, we are said to have a larger proportion of blacks in our population, than any town in the free States. If they come back, they will take up about half the gallery. There are about 80 black communicants. I am clear that in a church of Jesus Christ, there is neither black nor white; and that we have no right to consider the accident of colour in any degree. Yet I think the blacks very unwise in insisting on such a privilege now. Some years ago there would not have been the slightest difficulty in admitting them, but in consequence of the abolition movements the prejudice of the lower classes of whites against the blacks has become exorbitant and inhuman. We have a copy of the celebrated "Oxford (semi-papal) Tracts." One of them is on the excellencies of the Romish Breviary; which, by the way, *i. e.* the Breviary, I am now, for the first time, reading. It contains some delightful prayers and hymns, in a mass of putrid martyrology and idolatry. There is something graceful and melodious in the following collect, in the Christmas service: "Concede, quaesumus, omnipotens Deus, ut nos Unigeniti tui nova per carnem nativitas liberet, quos sub peccati jugo vetusta servitus tenet. Per eundem Dominum. Amen." There is scarcely an Orthodox Quaker in our region who has not joined either our church or the Episcopalian; mostly the latter. I heard Daniel Webster make a great speech, *sub dio*, in Newark. The gaoler of our State's Prison is a pious Methodist, and every Sabbath enters every cell and talks on religion with each prisoner. Cottle says that for a very long time Coleridge used a pint of laudanum a day, and sometimes even a quart.

PRINCETON, *January* 9, 1838.

I wish you and yours a most happy new year, in the enjoyment of every blessing of Providence and grace. The weather is such as might tempt one to suspect that we need another rectification of our calendar, like the Julian and Gregorian. The trial of —— —— is an ecclesiastico-juridical curiosity. Never before were the shades of guilt, criminality, and guilt "without criminality" so nicely appreciated. I would suggest the use of decimal fractions, in the next award of the kind. Or rather some negative algebraical quantities must have been employed to render the amount of such verdicts $=$ an entire acquittal.

No one groans more than I under the abuses of extempore prayer. How much time is lost, how much weariness produced, by periphrastic introductions, diffuse dilutions, and vain repetitions. Many pulpit prayers are largely made up of passages evidently meant to impress truth on the auditor. Whole strains of this sort: "O Lord, may sinners feel that time is short; that this is the only season for repentance; and that unless they believe, &c., &c." A man might thus tell his Maker what to make sinners feel through the whole extent of the catechism: "May we feel that our chief end is to glorify God and to enjoy him forever."[1] I nauseate all such perversions. Still I never could submit to one stereotype form for every day of my life. I should be pleased to have a few forms, varying, we may say through a month, expressing those things which we are to pray for always, with license to use a short extemporaneous prayer

---

[1] In another letter he had made the following criticism on a prayer in a Sunday-school book: "The prayer at the end labours under a fault very common—the abuse of the auxiliary 'may.' Compare this form with similar petitions in the Psalms. In some public prayers I hear the petition turned into a veritable interrogation by the awkward use of 'may' with a negative; thus 'May we not find this an unprofitable meeting! (?)' Direct petition, in the supplicatory imperative is best: thus 'create within me a clean heart.' It has sometimes occurred to me that the length of prayers is greatly increased by the pleonasms of mere form, as '*Do thou* grant,' '*Do thou* bless,' 'We beseech,' (fifty times.)"

besides: this is exactly the Lutheran method.[1] I fear we shall get into trouble with John Bull about this rascally Canada affair; especially since the steamboat business, [burning of the Caroline.] We have for years been too self-satisfied with our peaceful security. —— has been here; he is very full of information about the *adyta* of the English Universities. He says their professors, as a general rule, do nothing at all, unless they have churches; nor are they expected to do any thing, except in the way of book-making and general influence; nor do they receive any salaries, except a mere pittance. He visited most of the great chartered schools. By-the-bye, he is the most erudite classical scholar within my acquaintance, though not possessing an *ingenium vegetum*, or very great energy. If you see, some time hence in the Newark paper, a rhyming squib, intituled "American Titles of Honour," and signed with my finals, you may know where it comes from.[2] I find much comfort thus far

---

[1] Every one who has heard the prayers of the letter-writer will be thankful that he did not avail himself of a privilege which is not denied to the conductors of the public worship of our Church.

[2] [For the Newark Daily Advertiser.]

AMERICAN TITLES OF HONOUR.

The lust of greatness is a sturdy stock,
Which springs indigenous in every soil;
Though every twig and spreading branch you dock,
The trunk puts forth new shoots to mock your toil:
So when our sires, with democratic zeal,
Plucked off each garter, and put out each star,
And, mad to equalize the common weal,
On quartered shields and coronets made war,
'Twas but the lopping of the hydra's head,
And rage for honours was asleep, not dead.

Roam where you please our plain republic o'er,
A host of titled worthies you shall meet:
Judges and Presidents beset your door,
And Squires and Governors walk every street.
The mode spreads bravely: we may hope, ere long,
To leave rude "Mister" to raw lads at school,
Till every yeoman of the civic throng
Shall have his trade for title by fair rule:
Then Stage-man Stokes shall call on Lawyer Lee,
And Barber Boggs ask Butcher Brown to tea.

Captains, once known in harness on the field,
Now swarm in steamboats, oyster-craft, and inns,
While city troops their bloodless laurels yield
To scores of Generals, all plumes and grins.
The civic crown, too, hath its grave possessors,
Doctors in Physick, Law, Divinity;

in preaching to my Africans. The house is crowded by decorous and attentive people, and it seems a little like being a missionary. Then one can enjoy a total " abandon," and use every mode of address or illustration, without the dread of blundering. Strange as it may seem, I have already met with some insult, as the preacher to the blacks, in returning from their place of worship : it was from some of the lowest of the white canaille. One case of very powerful awakening has occurred under my unworthy labours. Every new perusal of the prophecies brings me more and more to the conclusion, that commentators have undertaken to explain too much as already past. Thus the 39th and 40th of Ezekiel, about Gog and Magog, seem to me to contain expressions far too sublime to have their accomplishment in the invasions of Antiochus, &c. I look somewhat confidently for a real restoration of Israel to their own land. Considering the part that our Continent occupies in the unfolding history of the church and the world, might not one judge *a priori* that it would have some place in the book of prophecy ? Yet I do not know that any discovery of this kind has been made. The grand fault of ———'s style I cannot otherwise express than by saying it is the exact antipodes of *quaintness*. It is in its ultimatum in Dr. J. P. Wilson and Bishop White. It arises, I suppose, from a dread of antithesis and conceited balance in period, and the result is a certain approach to lameness in the gait, and listlessness in the air, of his periods.

The little Swedish translation of my whisky book gives me great joy and encouragement.[1]

PRINCETON, *March ult.* 1838.

We have had spring and winter since I saw you. The last spell of cold has been especially biting. The 6th No. of [Sir

> Bishops and Deacons, Provosts and Professors,
> No more forego their title than their fee.
> A powdered Count is teaching us to dance,
> While Marquises are plain " Monsieurs," in France.
>
> Peace reigns on every hand, yet warlike signs
> Hang out in half the names of half the nation ;
> For scarce a loafer on his bulk reclines
> Who boasts not of some martial appellation.
> Militia Ensigns keep your Cash and Journal,
> And gay lieutenants kindly cart your coal ;
> Your next-door tailor is a whiskered Colonel,
> And Majors count your ballots at the poll.
> Till oft perplexed by doubting claims you stare,
> Nor well can choose 'twixt Adjutant and Mayor.
> S. L. R.

[1] " The Glass of Whisky," one of the series of " The Infant's Library."

Walter] Scott's Life surpasses all in interest—to my feelings—chiefly because it has so much of his diary, and relates so much about his afflictions. I lament that drinking and cursing are henceforward to be associated, in the minds of the young, with such a genius and such a gentleman; and that amid all his sorrows he seems to have received not one ray of divine light. His diary contains some grand hints about modes of composition. We have a most promising young man now a tutor here, for whom I wish I could find a good place. His name is Moffat; once a shepherd's boy in Glencree, [Scotland.] His linguistical attainments are extraordinary, in languages both ancient and modern. He is B. A. of our college.[1] Good Joseph W——f, it appears, has got back to England. The wonder is how a man so little endowed with worldly wisdom can make his way at all. When he came here, he went first to ——'s, where he lodged. That evening he was to preach. He had on a shirt which was absolutely japanned with dirt. —— said to him, "Mr. W., as you expect to appear in public to-night, perhaps you would like to make some change in your dress?" Mr. W. looked down, surveying his filthy raiment, and answered, "O no, I believe I shall need nothing of that kind." After a suitable delay, —— said again, "Mr. W., it will put us to no trouble; your room is ready, your valise there; you will find water, &c." W—— looked hastily in the glass, and said, "I thank you, I think I shall do as I am." —— became alarmed at his unseemliness, and at length said, "Mr. W., your mind is so occupied with greater things, that you are naturally indifferent about, &c., &c.; let me suggest the propriety of your changing, &c., &c." Mr. W. went up stairs, stayed some time, and came down precisely in statu quo! ——, almost baffled, said "It seems to me, Mr. W., that you have not succeeded in changing your apparel." "O yes, yes," said W., "have I not? let me see; perhaps I forgot to do it. Yes, sure enough, I was thinking of something else." Up he goes again, and finally endues a white coloured shirt. On coming down he said to Mrs. ——, "Madam, will you have the goodness to go up, and pack up my portmanteau? it is a thing I never could do in my life." He next borrowed a white handkerchief of ——, with which shortly after he dried the ink of a very blotted sheet which he had written, saying, "This I learned in India—this I learned in India!" If you think this a very foolish story, remember that you read it

---

[1] The catalogue of "our College" shows that places have been found for the accomplished tutor. After filling classical professorships in Lafayette College and Miami University, the Rev. Dr. Moffat has had in the College of New Jersey, since 1852, the chair of Greek, or Latin, with History.

on All-Fools' Day. There is a Dutch adage which likeneth March to a lion, and says, "he shaketh his tail;" from atmospheric appearances he is minded to give us a few wags more before he goes out. Eleven days more will complete our long term: I can't say that I am very fond of vacations; I have not money to travel, and I love home perhaps too much. I am afraid Dr. Ewing's tune will not enrich him; yet it is very good, and we ought to encourage every issue of religious music, especially from the music stores. In point of harmony it is exact and technically classical. The melody is scarcely popular enough.

TRENTON, *May* 11, 1838.

I came hither with hen and chicks, on Tuesday; but getting wet and cold on the way, I have been in a quasi colic for some days. Unless I run down to see you on Monday, I shall expect to be here until the 17th.

With regard to ———'s dubitations about the Girard College, I am not as clear as 1 could desire. The two grand points strike me as being these : 1. Is connexion with such an establishment right? 2. Is it likely to be permanent? Formerly I was inclined to say *No*, to the first; at present, I am undecided. There is very great force in the suggestion that we ought not to leave this engine in the devil's hands, no not for an hour; and that ——— may retire, if disappointed. I incline to say to him, Accept the offer. It is a wonderful providence that a machine contrived against religion should thus be put within the direction of Christian men: the counsel of Ahithophel is seemingly turned into foolishness. You can tell, better than I, whether the power is like to abide in the same hands, and whether there is a probability of ———'s holding the place for a number of years.

Our Jersey folks have a custom of uniting in clubs for the purchase of clams, a load at a time, thus getting them at wholesale prices: these are called *clam-classes*. The time appears to have come, when the spirit of the age demands a special effort, for the formation of a great national universal clam-class; and a convention for that purpose will be holden on the 31st of June, at Little Egg Harbor. The Hon. Mr. Buckingham (M. P.) has kindly consented to appear on that occasion, when odes will be sung composed for the occasion by Mrs. ——— and ———. It is proposed to issue a paper called the American Clam Reporter.

PRINCETON, *July* 5, 1838.

Just look what a blot that is! But this is nothing "inter amicos," and as Corporal Nym saith, "things must be as they may." So two New Yorkers (both whilom Philadelphians) have gone over sea: S—— and P——. The latter promised me not to chew tobacco in "the presence." Are there ten men in Philadelphia, barring schoolmasters, who know that the penult [of the name of the city] is long? A friend in the Sandwich Islands writes, that forty feet square will support a native all the year round. I gained some clearer conceptions from his saying, "Each of the islands is the top of a submarine mountain." The same writer (a man of sense and veracity) adds, "there is probably no country, small or great, in which there is less visible immorality, in proportion to the population."

I am reading Prescott's Ferdinand and Isabella. There is no American work of which, as it regards fame of letters, I would rather be the author. So far as I have gone, he gives the Papishes their own. See, in the May Blackwood, a most funny thing, "Father Tom and the Pope." Dr. [John] Breckinridge has determined to accept his appointment as general agent of the Presbyterian Board of Foreign Missions. I think I have never suffered so little from heat as this summer; yet I feel that the last two days have been particularly hot. It is now 9 A.M. and in my study the mercury stands at 81°; yesterday, in a hotter place, but shady, it was at noon 96°. The country has, however, been in beautiful foliage and refreshed with many little rains. "The 9th Bridgewater Treatise" by C. Babbage, is a fragment of wonderful genius. By recourse to the "Newark Daily" you will see some able papers, by a great political economist, on Trades Unions, [Charles Quill.] I am persuaded that it is our duty as Christian patriots, to encourage husbandry, and discourage overgrown manufactures. God has spread a wide country before us, yet thousands are herding in our factory towns, under influences ruinous to body and soul. These bloated establishments invite and receive some of the grandest villains of the old country. All our manufacturing towns are in an abnormal state. The policy engendered in these communities is necessarily agrarian; and the human race deteriorates, physically. I feel it to be incumbent on myself to say all I can for emigration to the West; and for the same reason I have come to look on a high protective Tariff as a great sin.

PRINCETON, *July* 30, 1838.

There is some difference between being moved, and being fixed, or I should say we were established in our new place.[1] I believe you know its whereabout. Every object is painfully commemorative of its late beautiful owner: we even have her

---

[1] The house which had been occupied by the Rev. Dr. John Breckinridge.

flowers; and the magnolia which stands near our back-door, it was almost the last of her worldly deeds to have planted. The house is far too large for my family or furniture; but the terms were such as I felt no right to decline, especially as by acceding to them, I should be doing all I could for ———, and at the same time introduce my own children to better air, ampler space, and goodlier prospects. The walk to College, in the hot season, is dreadful even to my imagination; how I shall endure it, I know not: but I am somewhat satisfied that I have come hither without self-seeking—and the Lord will provide.

And now let me proceed to say, my dear friend, how much happiness you will give us, if you will come and rusticate with us. If you will become uncivic for a while, so far as to forego Schuylkill water, butter, baths, trottoir, and omnibi, and commute the same for sunrises, sunsets, dirt, dust, chickens, corn, tomatoes, prospects, breezes, sweat and disorder—you may find yourself all the better. I give you my first invitation, as you are my earliest friend, (how good a one, let our biographers determine:) and ——— entertains towards you precisely analogous tempers.

Our final examination begins August 6th, during which I shall be much occupied, for about ten days. We have been two days in our present residence, and are thus far well-pleased, except with the amazing increase of housewifeship. It is something of a job to keep out of mischief three cats, one dog, forty fowls, and mice ad libitum; the latter having declared independence during the late troubles and vacancy. My books I have not yet moved; but I have Wilberforce's Life, (5 vols.,) "John Murray, Albemarle Street," to read on the back-piazza, which looks to the sunsetting.[1] The drought is such just here, (for around our village showers have been frequent,) that the pastures are like a sheaf of dry straw; hence, milk, in which I expected much delectation, is scanty. My corn is tall, but likely to bear little; potatoes will fail utterly, unless it rain; tomato-vines crisp as macaroons; yet, blessed be God, we have plenty of water as yet. Some recent mortification and trials of pride have, I think, done me good, and led me to meditate on my undue care about the opinion of fellow-worms. O if we could more crucify that old man, and vivify that new!

A call from yourself and boy, would be àpropos at any moment; when you bring the rest, you had better come after our examination, which (to all intents) ends August 15th. In both these statements I use absolute frankness, meaning you and yours to take my invitation in the rustic and old-time sense,

---

[1] He reviewed this work in the Repertory, October, 1838.

without discount. Many thanks for English papers. They are always treats. I suffer from Anglomanie.

PRINCETON, *July* 30, 1838.

Hortation seems to me to be the pulpit-error of the age, which has emasculated the church.[1]

Of Charles Quill as followeth : I never arranged the topics for publication, and so far as I remember, never dreamed of such a thing until it was suggested by some one. I am indifferent about it now. I will give anybody the right of a first edition for fifty copies, provided that it be printed under typographical inspection of yourself, J. A. A., or myself. No book of mine, with my consent, shall be clad in the dirty shirt of [Noah] Websterism. Wilberforce's Diary, from the extracts given, must have been honest indeed. It is new to have the private exercises of a great statesman, (bosom friend of the greatest minister England ever had,) while in the very heat of parliamentary debate. I think him from this reading (of two volumes) a greater and a better man than I supposed, but how narrow a churchman, how ignorant an anti-Calvinist ! Perhaps he gets better. I regard the last volume of the ——— as a religious imposture : ——— has crammed the garbage of craniology down our throats under cover of Paul and Peter's milk and meat. We are disgraced by the special pleading of [the Presbyterian Church case in the Supreme Court of Pennsylvania.] I am sure we are right, but I am afraid God means to strip us of our worldly goods.

In this matter of preaching, with which I began, I feel quite earnest, as believing that most of my earlier sermons were constructed on a wrong principle. I would be plain, but O, I wish I had *fed* my hearers with more truth, and given them less harangue.

Addison and I are taking lessons in barking, howling, and ventriloquism from an elocutionist named Bronson, and who with much stuff has also certain discoveries on which I thought I myself had hit—see last Repertory[2]—but which he carries out so

---

[1] In a postscript to this sentence, dated August 4, he adds : "Yesterday I heard my father preach to our students on Eccl. xii. 1, a text which I had handled a few weeks previous before the same hearers. I was never more humbled, nor more struck with my own past fault in this line. *My* discourse was all appeal ; *his* was all argument, even bare and quite dialectic in places. My sermon was like a flash in the pan, and his like a ball *lodged*, lodged where to work afterwards."

[2] He refers to his own review of Gardiner's "Music of Nature," in the July Repertory.

as to convince me that the Laryngitis (erroneously called Bronchitis) is preventable.

CHARLOTTE CO., VA., *October* 13, 1838.

By the blessing of God we had a very prosperous journey hither, escaping all bad weather and mishaps. Unless a letter miscarry, you will read something from me in Kinney's paper.[1] The associations of this region make me full ten years younger, especially as I have to be several hours of every day on horseback, which has always had a very exhilarating effect on me. The two contiguous plantations of Carrington and Mrs. Legrand contain about 6,000 acres, and afford abundant rides and walks without entering a public road. The little village has greatly improved, having new Baptist and Presbyterian churches, since my day; also a large girls' school and a respectable boys' ditto. The drought in this country almost destroyed many of the crops, especially the most indispensable, viz., corn. Late profuse rains have made the country very green, but are too late. The tobacco crop, though short, will be answerably high priced. —— will make 200 dollars' worth of that article on one little island of less than two acres. I write this before breakfast, having had a happy stroll, this lovely frosty morning, over a most picturesque portion of the estate. Flocks of sheep on an almost boundless green, unenclosed, have a patriarchal look; and at this hour I can scarcely go abroad without hearing the mocking-bird. I do not remember, in my former residences here to have observed that this fowl sang in the autumn. Such, however, is the undeniable fact. I think I find the intelligence and refinement of this land altogether against Van Buren; and even on the Abolition Question, there prevails a moderation much in advance of the temper I witnessed less than three years ago. In the Holy War, there is active skirmishing hereabout. Those party lines which, with us, have been drawn for years, are now only in the process of demarcation here. The consequence is feud on feud, "bellum plusquam civile;" house against house, mother against daughter, &c., &c. The Old School are about four to one. But vide Papers.

CHARLOTTE COURT HOUSE, VIRGINIA, *October* 19, 1838.

This is a mighty rainy day. More rain here in two weeks of October, than during all the summer. The promising prices of wheat set our planters at sowing. Mr. Carrington is just

[1] He sent several travelling letters to the "Newark Advertiser" during his absence.

putting 100 acres in wheat. The mulberry mania is rife. Serious talk of exchanging tobacco for silk cultivation. The lithograph of Childs, from a painting by Harding, is said to give the best idea of Randolph. R. affected to be a Cato in his frugality. Though he laid out thousands on his sixty horses, his stud being often worth perhaps $30,000, and had all his personal apparel from London, he lived in a mean house and never would allow a carpet to be on his floors. The will last established by the Court of Appeals emancipates the negroes, but by a law of Virginia, repealed however last year, any one, not privy to the proceedings in the court of probate, may, within ten years, bring a suit in Chancery, to try the issue "devisavit vel non devisavit." ―――― has availed himself of this, and hung up more than 300 negroes in a distant Chancery. Yesterday ――――, a lawyer of great eminence, and, next to Judge Lee, Randolph's most confidential actuary, told me, that in every will and every important codicil, Randolph evinced the great concern he had for his servants. They adored him as almost above the human standard, and preferred being his slaves to being free. It is perhaps (after all our abstractions) better for these negroes, as a set, that they are not freed. I say this seriously, founding my judgment on the following striking fact: Richard and John Randolph were brothers, and divided between them the estate of their father. Each took a moiety of the slaves. Richard set his free: John retained his on the estates. Col. Madison published the history of the former moiety and their offspring. They have almost become extinct; those who remain are wandering and drunken thieves, degraded below the level of humanity, and beyond the reach of Gospel means. The slaves of Roanoke are the descendants of the other moiety. They are nearly four hundred, and though not free, are sleek, fat, healthy, happy, and many of them to all appearance ripe for heaven. These I know to be facts, and they are worth more to me than a volume of dissertations on the right to freedom. At the same time, everybody here considers it highly inequitable that these people are kept from the benefits intended by their master.

You know [the late William] Maxwell, and that he is made President of Hampden Sidney College. Father Comfort [of Kingston] is here at present with his son David.

I am somewhat disposed to reconsider the expressions of my last letter touching the temper of the Church controversy here. Since I have seen ministers, and heard from Synod, I think there is prospect of pacification. The new school are about 1 to 5, or at most 1 to 4. They are scattered, divided, in some cases differing from us by the merest shade, and disheartened. They are moreover, generally, mistaken good men. On the other hand, the Old Schoolmen are more and more for moderation, the oscillatory pendulum is making shorter and shorter arcs. I augur good for Virginia. There is really no ground for dissension apart from the quarrel of churches afar off.

Yours of Oct. 11 (postmark 12) got here on the 16th. I am obliged to you for your concern for the goosequills; but I am not sure that I know what you mean. I have said, in one place and another, something fitted to direct the mechanic in his reading, and I have purposely avoided being more explicit, lest I should do more harm than good, by discouraging beginners, &c. Away from home, I cannot enterprise the thing now; but if there be time when I get to Philadelphia I will consult about it. There has been no publication of the evidence in Randolph's case. Every thing came out on the trials; a necessary consequence of the intricate suits, in which each expectant was by turn induced to prove J. R. insane.

The manners and customs here are not the best for an invalid. A visit of relations, some 20 in number, horses, coaches, retinue, &c., lasts, at least, one day, sometimes a week. Where one comes 17 miles, as ——— did, to see us, it is out of the question to make a morning call. And when, in turn, we go to see some of our kin, the solemnities of an old-time ceremonious dinner are any thing but reviving to a queasy stomach. It is more of a paradise to Henry, [his son.] He has the run of miles, if he so pleases, with ample attendance. Every half hour "Henry and his Bearer" appear with peaches, or figs, or chinquepins, or 'simmons, or sweet potatoes "roast with fire;" or he is in chase of a peacock, or picking cotton out of the pod, or learning to talk "nigger." One of Mrs. Le Grand's black girls, æt. 14, said more than once to my wife, with a face of great importunity—"Miss Betsy, do pray ax missus to gi' me to ye." There seems to be a vague impression (grossly incorrect by-the-bye) on the minds of these creatures, that they shall be happier and have less care by removal northward.

I have, as a general plan, conversed particularly and pointedly about religion, with every negro whom I could get alone, in walks, rides, &c. I have been tenderly affected in so doing. Many seem to me to be genuine saints. Many show that they have been seekers for years on years, but have never been directed, privately, by any competent person. In every case they are as perfectly accessible as my Henry. Even where they are wicked, they listen, and their conscience is prompt. The ——— Antinomianism is the rock on which thousands are wrecked. The scene we saw in Locust street [a religious excitement] is acted at every meeting. Yet even among these, I am sure, Christ hath his sheep. A hundred lay missionaries might now go into this field and convert thousands. They ought to be Southern men, and the South ought to furnish them forthwith. I am so filled with this, that I try to introduce the theme in every circle. Mrs. Le Grand lodges and boards a good Episcopalian (a Connecticut man, but twenty years in Va.) awaiting orders, for this business among her slaves. He has this moment returned, on foot and through a smart rain, from the overseer's house two miles off, where he instructed a group of fifteen last night. Now it is my deliberate belief, that more of these slaves are likely to go to heaven, than of an equal number of servants of pious people in our Middle States; and such being the hopefulness of the work, how earnestly ought Christians to engage in it! Thousands might be got to attend public preaching, as hundreds now do. The law (thanks to the meddling of anti-slavery societies) forbids schools, and public teaching to read; it was not so when I lived here: but I hold it to be our business to *save their souls;* and however criminal slavery may be, I see with my eyes that God has so overruled it, as that the slaves are more open to Gospel truth than any human beings on the globe. They are, I know, under temptations to hypocrisy: but grant they are pretending more than they feel, one has nevertheless the chance to lodge truth in their minds. The instances of this are affecting. In one short walk yesterday, I had talks with two men. One was loading his wagon with billets of wood, in a clearing of the forest. As he hung over the side of the wagon, his face beamed with the expression of sincere and intense emotion. He declared he had "long, long, yes for many years, desired to have true religion. Yes," said he, "master, true religion—that sort of religion which will do when I lie on my death-bed." I read over and over to him Matt. v. 6, commenting, &c. This occurs daily, and this is easy work, and work which anybody may perform. This is, moreover, the best preparative for freedom. I find your journal highly prized here; occasionally have something which may do to read aloud to slaves. The Episcopalians (who have never caught the itch of abolition) are doing something in this line. I preached twice last Sunday, and twice the Sunday before, and have attended two prayer meetings. There is an extraordinary supineness here as to the doing of good. The most that I see going on is in the Sunday School. The Episcopal clergy hereabouts are all evangelical and hard-working men. John Clark, who preaches nearest here, cannot, I suppose, make the circuit of his preaching-places without riding sixty miles.

PRINCETON, *November* 26, 1838.

Well—here we are, but in a mighty cold house. We have not yet broken in our stoves, &c., to any sort of availableness. My little affairs went on well during my absence, and my little garden crops exceeded expectation. College is very full, and becoming fuller. Look about you, and tell me whether you see a good English edition of all Cowper's works: also has Sparks issued Franklin's? Since you spoke to me about Wilberforce, I have been told that ——— has talked about doing an abridgment. This will prevent my moving in it.[1]

I wait to see the fate of my Quills, before I attempt a similar series for City Clerks, &c. Any and every hint you can memorandum about this topic, will be of great value to me. You are in the midst of such youth—know their haunts, tastes, temptations, &c. I have a book opened for materials, and will enter every thing as it comes to hand. Any scraps from your scissors will be in place. Henry James has re-gone to England. He and H. Walsh, and Platt, all once together in the Seminary, have become Sandemanians, and joined the Scotch Baptists, in New York, a little sect, headed by Buchanan, H. B. M. Consul. They have no preaching, but assemble on Sundays, when the "elders" and others expound and pray. James has issued a tract which I will try to keep for you, intituled "The Gospel Good News to Sinners," and Walsh another, "The True Grace of God." These are in many points quite good, and their chief mistake is that they have found out something. All they say about the *object* of faith is just what Russell says, and just what I say myself.[2] But they add other things.

I spent an hour this morning with good old Mr. [Samuel] Bayard. He showed me letters from W. Pitt, Lord Erskine, Lord Lansdowne, and Sir John Sinclair: the latter being a stringent request for the recipe for cornbread and buckwheat cakes. Also several letters from Wilberforce. From one of these, lying before me, (Beckenham Kent, 11 Jan. 1826,) I copy what follows: keep the extract for use some day: "I wish you had added some particulars both of your own personal and family circumstances, and of any of the religious and benevolent institutions, or any other particulars in your Country, in the concerns of which I take a warm interest. The growing connexion between our two Countries that is formed by your common pro-

---

[1] An abridgment of Wilberforce's biography was made by Caspar Morris, M. D., of Philadelphia, and published in 1839.

[2] Russell's "Letters," see a previous page. In a subsequent letter he writes: "What Russell says on faith is just what my labouring soul long ago rested on as the ark on Ararat."

secution of beneficent undertakings, is a subject of solid enjoyment to my mind; and I cannot but persuade myself that the mutual Esteem and Regard which will arise out of this connexion, will tend to destroy the effect of those malignant endeavours, which in both Countries, I fear, are still made, to alienate from each other the affections of their respective members. Surely it would be littleness of mind as well as a want of true principle that could render the inhabitants of Great Britain and the United States disposed to feel otherwise towards each other, than as brethren, descended from one common stock, bound together by a common language, and by Institutions of at least a congenial spirit. I will even indulge the hope, that in this instance, the hostilities that have been carried on, by confirming in each a respect for the other, may produce the effect which is sometimes seen to result from temporary differences in private life, of providing for the solid maintenance of future friendship. Let it be the endeavour of all good men to confirm and augment these kind dispositions. Such, I am sure, is the spirit with which I am actuated, and I doubt not it is felt by the correspondent whom I am now addressing."

PRINCETON, *November* 30, 1838.

An old Baptist preacher used to visit Mrs. ———, during her last husband's life, and pray for "the head and head*ess*" of the family. The preface to Bush's Genesis, which I have read in proof, contains some very remarkable facts concerning the text of the English Version. Altogether, it is a comprehensive and valuable performance. I have before me a beautiful English MS. on vellum: a religious treatise, chiefly on the Creed. I have not read it fully, so as to make up my mind, but it cannot be later than A.D. 1400. It has *sodeyn—clepid—goostli* (spiritual)—*ben* (are)—*clerkis—honde—scullen* (should)—*thilke* (those)—*pepil—covetise*, &c. I am deep in grubbing among German metaphysics, to write an article for the Repertory, against the attempts to introduce their poison among us.[1]
——— is doing his little all to bring in Cousin, which will bring in Schelling, which will bring in Atheism, which will bring in the devil. It is affecting to see that 10—20 Turks have, without a preacher, been awakened by Goodell's version of the

---

[1] This became the paper (65 pages) on *Transcendentalism* in the number for January, 1839. One part of the argument (reviewing Cousin) was prepared by the late Professor A. B. Dod. The entire paper, with parts of the article on "The Latest form of Infidelity," by another hand, in the Repertory of 1840, was, upon request, permitted to be reprinted in a pamphlet at Boston.

"Dairyman's Daughter." The more I read of human philosophy, the more I prize the childlike spirit; the more I love the book of books. Like Goliath's sword, "there is none like it." Why are we not more devoted to the study of it? Can we do a better work than to get people to read it?

PRINCETON, *December* 25, 1838.

I wish you a merry Christmas, though merry or unmerry it is now nearly over. Melvill's Sermons have been a great treat to me; read some of them by all means. [Dr.] Skinner's book[1] is very fine. I am astonished at the crystalline purity of his diction; he lacks nothing but tenderness. Another volume of [Paul] Henry's Life of Calvin [in German]: he has raked together 1,200 autograph letters of Calvin.[2]

[After some comments on the sin of what he calls the "Demas-ism" of ministers.] This matter in a kind and affectionate way ought to be agitated among all who think aright upon it until some nucleus of amended opinion be formed. Get Dr. [David] Magie's late tract on Support of Ministry.[3] How honourable to his Presbytery that not one of their twenty-two ministers does any thing but preach; no schools; no farms. O si sic omnes! Really, I know no topic more momentous. Just imagine our thousand preachers all devoted, all labouring, even as *some* of them do! My conscience is much exercised about this matter, as a personal case. [—— an ex-missionary] has been

---

[1] The "Religion of the Bible," and "Aids to Preaching and Hearing," by Dr. Skinner, both appeared in 1839, and were reviewed in the Repertory, January, 1841.

[2] Mr. Alexander wrote the full abstract of the successive volumes, which appeared in the Repertory for January, 1837, and July, 1839. Another writer furnished the conclusion in April, 1848.

[3] "An Address of the Presbytery of Elizabethtown to the Churches under its care," on the "claims of the Gospel Ministry to an adequate support." This tract was the text of a standard treatise on the whole subject in the Repertory of April, 1839, which bears the marks of Mr. Alexander's style of opinions, although, as in numerous other instances, I cannot positively identify it. In that article the sentiments of the letter as to the secular employments of some ministers are duly qualified: ex. gr. "It cannot be denied that throughout our land an alarming portion of the clergy are withdrawn from their appropriate duties by the necessity of providing for their own support. Who are to blame for this? Those who create this necessity, or those who submit to it? The remedy of this evil, perhaps the greatest which now afflicts our Church, can only be provided by the people. If they force their pastors to choose between working or starving, they must expect them to work, to engage in the business of the world, and more or less, alas! to imbibe its spirit; for the ministers, at least,

"The world's infectious; few bring back at eve,
Immaculate, the manners of the morn."

vilely used by ———, who took a spite at the missionaries, as most visitors do, who consort with Sanballat, Tobiah, and the other foreign residents. Quere. If the late change of opinion among 7,000 savages, in those isles, [Sandwich,] were any but a religious change, would not the world ring with it?

Among many commentators whom I have to consult, I find none like Calvin—he oftenest beards the real difficulty, and oftenest knocks it down, and drags it out. Look at Nordheimer's Grammatical Analysis, for a specimen of unmatchable American printing. Respects and affections.

PRINCETON, *January* 23, 1839.

If you have not read "Lane's Modern Egypt," in the series of "Entertaining Knowledge," you have a great treat before you. No book, not even Burckhardt's, has given me so minute an acquaintance with Islam, &c. I mean to concoct some of the biblical memoranda for your S. S. Journal.[1] When you seem to attribute some of the evil reports concerning ministers to their worldliness, or rather hint that by living holier lives they will have more chance of escape, I must dissent; however pure men may be, Satan will cause his children to "say all manner of evil against" them.

I am unfeignedly friendly to the American Board, [Foreign Missions,] but I never felt that in giving one mite, I bound myself to give a second; and now that we have a board of our own, I do not expect to give another penny to the former while I live. I have no feeling of duty towards this excellent body; while to our own church-boards I feel bound, as likely to draw out the contributions of thousands who would not otherwise contribute. The new measures you propose, for filling the ——— Church, are certainly innocent and I believe politic. Why might not the *elders* of a church sign a card of invitation to the canaille, to come in? Methinks no work of the age is more important than the getting the mob of our cities in contact with Gospel-truth.

I write at a hand-gallop. I have preached five times in eight days, lectured four times, examined a class, made a Tract speech, and heard seven recitations. I am therefore pushed hard.[2]

PRINCETON, *March* 21, 1839.

I have felt anxious for a week or more about your family, and not the less so, since your note by my father. I sincerely

---

[1] This was done in a series of articles entitled "The Bible Illustrated from Egypt."

[2] It may be mentioned here that during the term of his Professorship, Mr. Alexander preached, on an average, sixty times each year.

hope you may be carried through this trial without a bereavement; but if not—I have nothing I can say but to recommend to you absolute and filial submission: I hope you know its necessity and its virtue; and I doubt not a moment the trial is meant to go a certain length towards slaying the body of sin in you and ———. In the ordinary course of gracious discipline nothing seems to kill sin in us so surely as these stripes. May they be few and light!

PRINCETON, *April* 9, 1839.

I have not for some days written to you, being doubtful in what strain I should address you, as I could hear nothing about your child, and it is only this hour that I have learned that it has pleased God to take her away from you. Let me assure you, that my wife and I sorrow with you, as knowing in some measure the heart of bereaved parents. In such times one can only say "It is the Lord." Here is our stay in every affliction. "The Lord reigneth." "It is well." It has fallen to your lot to have a number of family afflictions, and no doubt they have been, whether you know it or not, among your greatest blessings. No one can rejoice in such strokes, in themselves considered; but when viewing them in connexion with great grace vouchsafed along with them, we may "glory in tribulation also." The stroke must be heaviest, as it is most unwonted, to the afflicted mother. Here, if anywhere, "the heart knoweth its own bitterness;" and I would not intermeddle; but even here grace does often so soothe the agonized heart, as to bring joy out of the midst of grief. Our dear children are not lost, but sent before. They await our coming, and perhaps rejoice, not merely as redeemed creatures, but as *ours;* as bone of our bone, and flesh of our flesh. Probably they know more of us, than we of them. Certainly they know more of Christ. You are familiar with the expressions of Jeremy Taylor and Leighton, concerning the loss of children: they are both touching, but Taylor's the most so; for he had many children, and all his sons died before him, while Leighton was a bachelor. "No man can tell" (says Taylor) "but he that loves his children, how many delicious accents make a man's heart dance in the pretty conversation of those dear pledges—their childishness, their stammering, their little angers, their innocence, their imperfections, their necessities, are so many little emanations of joy and comfort, to him that delights in their person and society." I trust that Mrs. Hall and yourself will be enabled to receive just that measure and kind of benefit which it seems to be the Master's will to communicate.

PRINCETON, *April* 25, 1839.

Of course there has been very great concern about the church case.[1] In a spiritual point of view I cannot see that the Old School have lost much. At the same time it is undeniably a grievous chastisement; and the difficulty of knowing what to do is extreme. Some, I hear, are strongly in favour of going back, rescinding the exscinding acts, &c., and taking the chance of ruling in the joint body. I cannot see this to be proper, as it would establish a portentous precedent touching religious liberty and ecclesiastical independence. It would concede to the civil power the authority to determine, not only what relates to our corporate privileges, in which I grant them absolute sway, but what is purely ecclesiastical; viz., to say that A B and C (whom we, by regular church acts, have put out of the church) are a part of the church. This point I cannot yield. We do not seriously believe that the New School men have been anxious to get the property; especially we believe they would, if they could, leave Princeton property, &c., in its former hands. There would be an odium attached to any sudden change. Princeton funds cannot be employed anywhere but here—and here the New School do not want a Seminary. It can cost them little therefore to be generous; but how to effect this is the question. They cannot make us a title; nor can we comfortably sit down in their possessions, as incumbents by mere sufferance. Some have supposed that the New School might consent to an amicable separation, even now, and unite with us in applying to the Legislature to have the succession continued in two branches.

PRINCETON, *May* 1, 1839.

I went to our Presbytery last week at Lambertville. J. A. A. was ordained. I came home viâ Trenton. There I attended for several days the Methodist Annual Conference for this State: about 120 ministers. A highly respectable body. Bishops Waugh and Hedding presided by turns. I was much pleased with almost every thing they did, and with their business ways; great promptness and affection; nothing carping or disputatious. Nothing surprised or amused me more than the rigid scrutiny to which each minister's character is subjected annually. The whole list is gone through regularly, each name called, and testimony taken as to the faithfulness, competency, and even health of every man. They had a great gun from Illinois, called Cav-

---

[1] The verdict of the jury in Pennsylvania, in favour of the New School section of the Church, afterwards reversed, on the points of law, by the Supreme Court.

anagh. [Rev. J. P.] Durbin and [N.] Bangs are there. They sit more than a week. Mr. Yeomans lays the corner stone of his new church to-morrow; 100 feet by 62. I was introduced to [J. J.] Gurney the other day, and was charmed with his *personel*. Dr. [John] Breckinridge arrived here yesterday, being, to a day, the time fixed months ago. He says he has never failed to meet his most distant appointments, except when he has been thrown out by the rest of the Sabbath. He averaged 50 miles a day for nine months. My father is writing a history of African Colonization. I never saw the country look more beautiful than it does after the late showers. By reference to my book I find the season two weeks, at least, earlier than the last. The *Clericus multicaulis*[1] increases in this State. H. P. Goodrich is to be President of Marion College, vice W. S. Potts, restored to St. Louis.

May 14.—A chasm of nearly two weeks. I have in the meanwhile been overrun with our spring visiters, examinations, gardening operations, and incommoded by a very painful affection of the throat, which still continues: it is a muscular or spasmodic something about the door of the stomach, very choking and uncomfortable. College opens on the 16th. I think we shall number 250. An old Church of England missionary from Ceylon is here.

Mr. Perkins says nothing to me about a 3d ed. of *Quill*. I have feared that his expectations were disappointed about the 2d. If so, he may be somewhat brightened by the following extract of a letter to me from Prof. Bush of New York: "I met to-day one of our most intelligent, most wealthy, and most useful citizens (a mechanic) with a bundle of books under his arm, (here I omit sundry bits of blarney,) and which were a part of near a hundred copies that he had purchased for gratuitous distribution among the different classes of operatives in the city"—" had no doubt that thousands of them might be sold every year in this city among the class for whom they are designed." Pye Smith seems to outstrip even his great co-eval ——— in the race towards neology. They say [Rev. E. N.] Kirk has quite repristinated the old Spa Fields (Lady Huntingdon's) Chapel in London; I see one of his sermons in the "Pulpit." The people from America who go over to help the French Protestants are guilty of one unpardonable error, in my judgment. Instead of aiming to quicken and raise the old Protestant Church, which still exists, and has government patronage, they attempt little independent, or secession bodies, which not unnaturally excite

---

[1] Speculations in the mulberry-tree for raising silkworms.

the suspicion as well of the government as of the other Protestants. The creed of the Reformed Church of France is as sound as ever, and as a proof of what we might hope, by going to work patiently and judiciously, the government have placed at Montauban Seminary two orthodox professors, viz., de Félice and Adolphe Monod. Several thousand U. S. troops are to be in camp at Trenton, during the summer.[1]

Princeton, June 10, 1839.

A more lovely season I have not known. Our fields, groves, and gardens are one tissue of green; and for a day or two past the air has been fraught with the richest odours. Some of our little copses near the brook are paradisiacal in their look, smell, and coolness. In my garden I have found great benefit to my health, and many fascinations. With the little interval for prayers and breakfast I usually work in it from $5\frac{1}{2}$ to $8\frac{1}{2}$ o'clock. From a space as big as your front parlour, we have picked 42 quarts of strawberries, chiefly hautboys, and the season is not half done. Of these 15 quarts in one day. For some reason they are exceeding sour. I wish you were here to partake of them, for we have to disperse the greater part among our neighbours. Other garden truck, with me, is rather backward. I little expected that *you* would ever have occasion to conflict with ———. He is so rabid a man, that, except where one's conscience should make pertinacity a duty, I should use all lawful means to avoid encountering him. His strategy is that of Indian warfare. I have looked over ———'s book; prettily got up, and neat in style, but very much what a "smart young lady" would have produced on the same topic. It has some places absolutely puling. There are three things totally wanting: 1st. Exposition of Scripture. 2d. Theological discussion of any thing about his subject which lies under the mere surface. 3d. Evangelical unction or spirituality. And I fear some parts are (what Gilbert Stuart said of Sir J. Reynolds's Lectures on Painting) "a beautiful apology for bad practice." Gurney has been here. I heard him twice, and twice companied with him. I think him a good and even a great man. Very affable, instructive, and orthodox. One of his sermons was a poetico-mystical

---

[1] Soon after the date of this letter, its writer's first-born child died, after years of suffering with congenital hydrocephalus. "To *you*" (wrote his father) "I may say, with hope of being credited, it is a loss to part with even so distressed a child. His little bird-like voice was the first morning sound we used to hear. The Lord has done well and mercifully to us, and especially to him." To the Sunday School Journal of this year he gave two numbers on "Scriptural Account of Suffering Parents."

rhapsody of the most exquisite kind; it was really quite Platonic. I sigh to be a pastor, instead of a professor: *Qui fit Mæcenas*, etc.

PRINCETON, *June* 28, 1839.

I do not think a more favourable opening for Christian effort is anywhere offered at this time than at the encampment near Trenton: and my sole object is to get you to exert yourself a little in Philadelphia on this behalf. I am told there are some pious men among the officers, but who they are I know not. There are about a thousand souls there perpetually in camp; the number will be doubled in a few days. Many of these, I suppose, have not had the gospel for years; and, after the dissolution of the Camp of Instruction, many of them will go away to die in the remotest parts of our frontier. In walking through the camp on Tuesday, I was shocked with the unaccountable prevalence of cursing and swearing. If the Swearer's Prayer, and similar papers, could be distributed among them, the happiest effects might ensue. There is a good deal of time for reading; and some plan for a weekly distribution of Tracts would be truly promising. A large portion of these ought to be in German, as there are several Germans in every company. In this, and every other method, the approach ought to be made very carefully through the officers, who seem to be gentlemen of the highest breeding. No man can fail to be struck with the bearing of such officers as General Eustis, Col. Fanning, (who lost an arm at Chippewa,) Major Ringgold, &c., &c.

The Quartermaster General has erected a pulpit, and the way is open for public services on Sunday; but as there is no regular official provision for this, there is danger that persons will occupy it who are not the most likely to do good: I do not here refer to sect, or theological opinion, but to pulpit talent. I do not think an impressive extempore speaker could find a better audience.

To prevent sectarian alarm, I wish you could enlist in this one or two evangelical Episcopalians; and get a few dollars' worth of German tracts put into the hands of some person who would see that they are distributed. Especially, if you could in any way gain access to some of the officers, much might with the blessing of God be accomplished. We fear to be too prominent in this matter in Princeton, but various means have been taken to let the officers know that we would furnish any amount of preaching. Mr. Starr, the Episcopal minister of Trenton, would be an excellent *point d'appui* for any endeavours. Cannot you find some layman of zeal and address and knowledge of men, who could spend a day a week in Trenton for such a cause?

I attended the funeral of a dragoon in the camp. Music, procession, flags, horse led as mourner, but not one word of service, nor any intimation that the thing they were burying had a soul; all the nonchalance of a drill. Such a book as "Narrative of a Soldier," edited by Dr. Wardlaw, and once reprinted in this country, would be likely to make impression. I have seldom felt more moved in behalf of any set of men; and as I cannot do much, if any thing, in proper person, I trust I shall not fail to get your strenuous aid. Take a friend and run up for a few hours to the camp. The selection is admirable; the beau-ideal of a summer encampment: a most extensive plain, skirted by a young forest, in which the tents are arranged with much taste. The cleanliness, regularity, and silence are exemplary. It is favourable for religious effort, that intemperance is rigidly excluded. I believe there is not a drop of intoxicating liquor. It occurs to me that a serious Methodist might accomplish great things there. When I look at these men, and remember how much was done among soldiers by Wesley, Whitefield, and others, I am convinced that he who should be blessed so far as to institute successful measures for labouring among them, would save souls, hide multitudes of sins, and furnish delightful recollections for life.

PRINCETON, *July* 3, 1839.

It is impossible for either ——— or myself to undertake what you propose, in the present state of our engagements. Indeed, I consider the week-day work in camp almost as important as the preaching. I regret that we have no one to nominate. The person ought to be one of the "workers," who could go in and out of tent or hospital as ——— would do; not however that I recommend him. This facility of talk with rank and file, I should reckon a main matter. Some active, zealous, affectionate Episcopalian, of whatever kind otherwise, would encounter least prejudice, yet great talent or eloquence would not be thrown away. The work is so important that even a settled clergyman might lay his account with taking this for a summer retreat; and a lovelier one it would be hard to find. I should feel an emotion of more than common joy, if I could hear that Dr. Tyng, Mr. Suddards, and a few such men, had made an arrangement to give sermons.

Just look at it: for the first time in our day—perhaps for the last—the United States Army is present (at least representatively) at one place, quite accessible, in a favourable season, hard by hundreds of ministers, and thousands of Christians. The conversion of two or three officers might give a direction to the future history of our military men. I was pleased to see a Bible openly laid out in the tent of a captain.

It is a question with me whether the safest way is to move the Secretary at War to make a regular appointment. Such a motion might frustrate our plan. We know not what influences may be working in high places. The incumbent might be a Pharisee, a Catholic, a Socinian, or a *petit-maitre* in black, like ———, who lately sent us a dancing-master with a letter of introduction. Besides, there might be some show of resistance from the staff. But if the officers could once hear such a man as Dr. Tyng, Mr. Boardman, Mr. Suddards, or Dr. Breckinridge, they would be anxious for more. But in whatever way the thing is accomplished, it ought to be done speedily. I am told there are more than fifty on the sick list, and there will be both sickness and death before the end of August. Even while the other matter is in suspense, there should be a real working, stirring layman sent up with Bibles and Tracts, both German and English. A few German hymn books might be well. If I seem to press unduly in this matter, let me plead that the king's business requireth haste; and my conviction that if you or I could get this ball fairly rolling, it would be worth more than any six months' preaching we are likely to do. May the weak effort have Divine guidance and success!

PRINCETON, *August* 15, 1839.

I should like to advise with you a little about the sequel to the American Mechanic, which I have been preparing, ["the Working Man."] The plan is just the same, but I have pitched the tone of it two or three degrees higher, as to style, allusion, &c. Still I wish it to be a book for the working classes.[1] I feel encouraged to bestow such little labours as I may be able to put forth, more and more on the working classes, the rather because they are the great object of the infidels, socialists, agrarians. Owenites, Wrightites, and diabolians generally.

If you want to read a splendid piece of dialectical wit, take hold of the review of Gladstone in the last Edinburgh Review; it cuts up apostolical succession irretrievably. Wonderful news from Bengal. I can't find the places on my maps. It is worth notice, that the only very great success of the word, just now, is in that very field which sundry decry; viz., Foreign Missions. Grant that seven-tenths of the baptized, there and in the Sandwich isles, are deceivers or deceived, the case is still as good as

---

[1] Three editions of the American Mechanic, in book-form, had appeared. "The Working Man" was not, like its predecessor, first published in a newspaper.

that of most of the *nations* which were converted to Christianity under the later empire: yet these nations are now nominally Christian. It is an infinite blessing to abolish idolatry. I still have it in purpose to write "The Apprentice" for the Union, and have the plan already laid out.

PRINCETON, *October* 3, 1839.

Our meeting of Presbytery at Cranbury was the fullest one in 17 years—27 bishops and 17 elders; a truly pleasant and edifying meeting. I hope we all received benefit. All our churches, except six, have either built fine new edifices, or wholly re-modelled the old ones; and one of the six is about to do the same. In some of our congregations the use of intoxicating drink is almost at an end. One pastor said that almost all his youth had committed the Gospel of John. I found at Presbytery that among our pastors the current is setting very strong against the use of Question Books. Nicholas Biddle was at our Commencement, and showed much interest. Our Museum room with post-chambers, &c., is one of the handsomest college rooms I have ever seen. The alligator, now in it, has not eaten any thing for six months, and is nevertheless quite lively, though by no means amiable. I have been "sounded" about the presidentship of the Newark (Del.) College. "Ancient Manuscript," signed A. in New York Observer is from your humble servant. Dr. Green said in his address to the Seminary Students, "As to mustaches and all whiskers, let us leave them to the goats and the dandies;" and then he called on ———, who was "bearded like a pard," to make the concluding prayer. On Saturday, I saw the closing service of the U. S. troops at Camp Washington, [Trenton,] by Gens. Scott and Poinsett. As a "sight" it surpassed any thing I have seen. The evolutions and firing of the light artillery were wonderful; cannons flying about at a gallop. The large body of dragoons were so black and stalwart, with their long-bayoneted carbines, that when in solid column they might be taken for knights of the middle ages. I have come to the conclusion that Baxter's style, which is not at all obsolete now, is the best extant, in respect to clearness, Saxon purity, vivacity, directness, strength, and pungency; it is not always elegant, or concise, or tender, or melodious. His "Dying Thoughts" is a great book: I mean, as he wrote it, vide vol. 18 of his works. Dr. John Breckinridge is in Kentucky. It occurs to me to say of him, that I never saw him idle or lounging a moment, nor ever diverted to minor matters or levity; I never saw in him the slightest tendency to worldliness; I never saw him in any company, even of the most fashionable political grandee, where he did not take a high religious stand, and avow high Christian opinions, with an air of conscious superiority; and I never detected him in any sort of self-pleasing or shrinking from sacrifices or hard duty. I know no minister whose private intercourse is so purely and zealously religious. I think this way of reading verse about at [family] prayers is a shocking abuse. To my ear also it destroys the *sense*. I have no notion of turning family worship into a Madam's school.

November 27, 1839.

You see a man may come to the degradation of writing on ruled paper, for lack of better. I have such a dislike to doing things "on compulsion," that I have half a mind to write betwixt the lines; but I content myself with merely entering my protest, and reserving all the rights of irregularity. A dozen at least of our small mechanics have burnt their fingers with the mulberry-speculation; some to the tune of thousands: another proof of the folly of making haste to be rich out of one's proper calling. Trees bought at 20 to 30 cents are selling (if sold at all) at 2 mills apiece. This day I have seen a handbill advertisement of a great vendue of stock, &c., on the farm of a licentiate of our Presbytery; a thousand-dollar bull, *Sambo*, pedigree vaunted, references to the "Herd Book," &c., also 60 odd calves. A few weeks ago I saw in the common papers attestations to the worth of an English bull, by an eminent bishop of ——— Presbytery. Perpend the following remarkable passage of the Apocrypha, viz., Ecclesiasticus xxxviii. 25: "How can he get wisdom that holdeth the plough, and that glorieth in the goad, that driveth oxen, and is occupied in their labours, and whose talk is of bullocks?" Read the whole. By-the-bye, the said Ecclesiasticus might be often quoted, as we quote other uninspired productions. Read some sublime passages in chapter 50. Qu. Might not you surprise some readers of the Journal by quotations from this book, as from an old Jewish work? The accession to the Seminary (near 50) is greater than on any occasion, but two, since its foundation. This is very cheering, considering the division of church, and the nearness of the New York Seminary. You will see I am aboard of the Apprentices again in the Newark Daily. Some of the views expressed are favorite ones with me, and have been produced in some measure by a number of facts of a nature which I cannot make public.

O how I should rejoice to see a paper set up in Philadelphia, on the following principles: [1.] *Size*: A little bigger than the Sunday School Journal. [2.] *Time*: Weekly. [3.] *Looks*: Beautiful type, with as little variety as to type or leads as possible. [4.] *Church Connexion:* none. [5.] *Doctrine:* Evangelical, but not committed to anything; yet admitting all we believe. [6.] *Disputes:* = 0. [7.] *Worldly News:* = 0, but not bound to exclude items. [8.] *Contents:* 1. News of Christ's kingdom; a resumé and coup d'œil of the field of missions; seldom giving long journals, but sketches of the real good done by all sects; revivals. 2. Experimental and Practical Religion, not excluding Biblical Interpretation and Saving Doctrine; chiefly, however, the former.

Is not this a good notion? Or perhaps you would rather say 16 pp. 8vo, so as to bind. I solemnly believe such a paper would honour Christ more than any publication known to me in the world.

I was called the other day to see a dying man several miles out in the country. It was a wretched hovel of a place, reminding me of some of Crabbe's inimitable descriptions. Neither the sick man nor any of his household could read, and they were as ignorant as heathen. The front door of the house was unhinged, and merely lying up against the posts. We need such a districting of all our neighbourhoods as should infallibly bring every such place under inspection. This work has been tolerably well done around here, but this man has been almost always drunk until he was seized with consumption. I wish in my soul that all the alcohol could be annihilated. Every day exposes to view more and more its horrific, soul-destroying power. I am ready to go "full-chisel" for the 15-gallon law. These coal-stoves will let out the gas (or *gaz*, as you elegantly call it in the city, and nowhere else, I suppose, on earth) in certain states of weather, so that I am almost inclined to revert to wood fires. I had a piece of genuine Irish peat lately presented to me.

PRINCETON, *December* 9, 1839.

We have a Sciot (or Chian) here a-lecturing. He wears a red cap and a capote, and is a smart fellow: name, Castanis. Apropos de Journaux, the worst thing your Board ever did for S. S. J., was to destroy its weekly character, [making it semi-monthly.] The interval at which it now appears is next to the cycle of the moon, and is representable only by the equation $T = \pi + \sqrt{\left\{\pi + B\left(\dfrac{-4}{\sqrt{x-a}}\right)A\right\}}$ Its arrival is always unexpected, a mere windfall. A sheet, by a given mail, however small it be, is looked for. Again—say what we will, the title hurts it, except with Sunday School folk. I never read a number of it, without perceiving its value, yet I don't find myself looking out for it. I therefore believe that just such a sheet, weekly, without reference to any association or enterprise, would go down nicely. Only the leading character should be NEWS; but news of the Kingdom. The Seminary has 112, and additions every week; among these additions only one is from a New England College. By a prolepsis of a week, I preached the semi-centurial sermon at Freehold.[1] What an ugly thing State policy is, when it leads such a power as England to prop such a power as Turkey. I believe it to be all in vain, and that the book of Prophecy has doomed that empire to a curse. Eli Smith gave me new views of the exhaustion of the empire, and Lamartine lately said Turkey was perishing for want of Turks. Think of a million Russians going over to the Greek Church from the Romish, and Nicholas backing his father-in-law of Prussia about the mixed marriages. In lately reading the epistles to the Thessalonians, without note or comment, I have been driven almost irresistibly into the opinion, which I long rejected, that the Papal Power in some way is the *Man of Sin;* I say " in some way" because I know not yet whether it is the Pope as an individual, or the abstract Pope, or the collective Church. The Jewish letters of those Scotchmen [in the London " Record "] are very interesting; they quote Scripture after a different fashion from our Yankees—always excepting Goodell. Our old friend Mr. [Samuel] Bayard, now in his 73d year, is one of the most pleasing specimens of religious serenity and hope that I have seen. He is tottering over the grave, but his inward man is renewed day by day.[2]

I have heard, and have observed, that almost all the New England ministers have a trick of often sinking, or bending the knees, while preaching, the body being erect. This " squat," whether taught in the course of Sacred Rhetoric or not, arises, I think, from the necessity of bringing the eye near to the MS., at times, and the desire to do this without leaning over; make the experiment yourself, and observe it strikingly set forth in ———— and ————. It is plain from 1 Cor. xiv. 35, that any *man* might ask questions in the church; indeed, that chapter shows their assemblies to have been much less starched than ours. Do you know what *Usher* is derived from ? From *Huissier* French, and that from *Ostiarius.* Take a leisurely course

---

[1] The General Assembly appointed December 8, 1839, for the commemoration of the fiftieth anniversary of the organization of that body: Mr. Alexander's text was Ezekiel xxxvi. 37, 38.

[2] Mr. Bayard was an elder in the Princeton church, and the author of " Letters on the Sacrament of the Lord's Supper," a new edition of which was made the text of an article on the subject, by Mr. Alexander, in the Repertory of January, 1840.

through Plutarch, and you will find some unmatchable picking for the Journal. I find this odious verse-about way of reading at prayers growing into use among our ministers. At —————— I was between a booby with a cold in his head, who shouted like a clam-man, and snuffled like a distempered horse, and a Miss, whose words were scarce audible. I hold it to be essential to the due performance of that duty that the Scriptures should be *well* read, as well as possible, and therefore by one person. In the other case, the brats are all the while counting on ahead to see what verse will come to them, or losing the place and reading the wrong one, while mamma is finding the place for Tom, and Sally and Joe are fighting for the bigger share of the book they are daubing and dog-earing between them. I set a higher value every day on this ordinance, and in a plain familiar way have expounded the New Testament regularly (only in the mornings) as far as 2 Cor. v., always studying the passage as laboriously as I can, and sometimes some hours. And I believe there is no portion of the Scriptures with which I am so well acquainted, and no preparation for preaching that is so useful to me. I have a notion to re-read my five volumes of Luther's Letters, and to translate such short letters and extracts, chronologicè, as would suit the Journal.[1]

PRINCETON, *December* 21, 1839.

What tragedies we have in our banks—failures, peculation, robbery, suicide! For some years I have had the fact forced on my observation, that a large proportion of felones-de-se are made desperate by pecuniary embarrassment. It is horrible to contemplate the temptations to fraud, held out by banks to those without and within them. *Borrowing*, which should be, and in a healthful state is a dernier resort, is now a substantive part of worldly business. Endorsing, in nine cases out of ten, is a deliberate promise to pay that which one knows he cannot pay: the contingency, in my view, does not alter the morality of the transaction. When we say of our extensive Credit System, that it is necessary to our great operations, we should first show that our operations are not *too great*. A ruinous amount of steam is necessary to speed of 100 miles an hour; but this speed is too great. I do not see that the overtrading of the mass is less culpable than the overtrading of an individual. Is it not plain, that the aggregate of liabilities (that is, of obligation to pay) in our country, nay in the commercial world, is greater than the aggregate ability of the promisors? The moral influence of the

[1] This was done for several successive months in 1839–'40.

Credit System strikes me as one of the most malign influences to which our country is subjected. I have near me a (black) parishioner, not long for this world, a young woman, whose case will, I think, some day, make an interesting article for the S. S. Journal, or for a book, as showing the value of Sunday School texts and especially hymns, on a dying bed.[1] We, who pretend to be refined folks, greatly undervalue hymns and psalms. Now I have often observed, that, from the natural fondness of the common mind, and the infant mind, for metre and rhyme, the great body of theology and experience in the lower classes is preserved in the shape of hymns. They read the psalm-book, they repeat and sing the verses, &c. Hence we should not neglect sacred song, I mean the plain sort, with our children and scholars.

My present feeling is that I will write no more irreligious books. Life is short. The great work is to save souls. All our economical, political, and literary reformations are mere adjusting of the outer twig; religion changes the sap of root and trunk. This I never felt more than now. I see that when a people become godly, all the rest follows. In the same connexion I see the value of preaching. Let me earnestly exhort you, on the strength of my own sad experience, not to allow yourself to trust to a flow of extempore thought and expression in the pulpit, but to labour *every* sermon, however obscure or ignorant the auditory may be. Drs. Skinner and Spring have proved what can be done by devoting all one's soul to the simple work of sermon making. I wish I had done something of the kind. —— has made a few days' visit here. He says the Taylorites have had a number of successive meetings of Associations to censure the East Windsor and Pastoral Union folks, but they "blessed them altogether." Num. xxiii. 2. I am reading the Oxford Tracts, and am struck—1, with the exquisite simplicity of the English style; 2, the strange absence of logical power; 3, the dangerous fascination of the monkish piety. The two most fashionable American tailors in Paris, partners, are named *Cutter* & *Tryon*. We have in College *Cattell* & *Colt*, (contiguous on the roll,) *Burnet* & *Cook-us*, (ditto,) *Cake* & *Pitcher*, (room-mates,) *Nabb* & *Tabb*, (room-mates,) *Nixon* & *Dixon*, *Sturgeon* and three *Whaleys*. Could not your Pennsylvania Secretary Mr. *Skunk* send us a son? For the pronunciation of my name, take the following couplets from Crabbe, a sound authority in my view:

---

[1] His "Notices of a Coloured Sunday Scholar lately deceased," appeared in the Journal July 1, 1840.

> "The plan was specious, for the mind of *James*,
> Accorded duly with his uncle's *schemes*."

> "For now no crazed fanatic's frantic *dreams*,
> Seemed vile as James's conduct, or as *James*."

PRINCETON, *January* 18, 1840.

If you want an exquisite morsel for a column of the Journal, see a piece of Jean Paul (Richter)'s, admirably translated in "Christian Observer" for 1835, April. It is a gem. And while you have the volume in hand, cull a child's hymn from p. 502. I do not know a book from which there is more to be sifted for a periodical than the back volumes of the "Christian Observer." I think Dr. Bache's Report on Education in Europe, a noble work. Spend an hour in digesting some of his statements about religion, viz. : In what countries does it form a part of education ? is it regarded as a substantive, integral part of the course ? how taught ? how much time ? with what relation to the Bible ? &c. Being a teacher, and a dilletante-one, I was really kept awake by the book one night. It will do immense good, I believe, collaterally. I am hard at work upon another story-book for the Union, if it do not grow too big. It is not *about* children, or in the Childese language, for I am getting skeptical about that. I find my babes more interested about GOLIATH, than about the tiniest infant in monosyllables. I'll not tell you the title, for fear you steal it, as some swindler has done Mr. P——'s. Tell the said P. that I'm not the first man who hung back from the penitentiary ; and that I agree that he's twice as much at home there as I could be. So I must wait a while to qualify myself [to discuss the solitary system.] On the 17th, at 7 P. M., the mercury here was —8°. Dr. Demmé [of the German Lutheran Church, Philadelphia] has kindly sent me a copy of his Sermon before the Synod. It is really an excellent and even eloquent production, so as to surprise me very much. We have really few men among us who can preach as effective a discourse in English. It is faithful and warm, and has some original turns of Scripture quotation. I can't say how well the production may look in a version, especially by the author himself, as his German style is very racy and idiomatic. The following statement came to me, as from ————— : The German atheism (pantheism or Emersonism or Carlyle-ism) makes fearful progress in Boston, so that there are not a few who are willing to say (I pray that I may not sin in writing it) that Deus est "a great ——— ;" This is a deceiver and anti-Christ. Such is the career and tendency of Unitarianism. Read 1 John ii. 23. Query : why may not *Job* be one of the books which Noah had in his little library in the ark ?

There is no notice of any thing postdiluvian? The expressions in i. 6 sound *ante*-diluvian. Behemoth and Leviathan are with difficulty brought under any of the Linnean mammalia. The length of the speeches, of the mourning, of the feasts, and the increase of Job's family at the close, are very much like the incidents of a sexcentenarian life. Faber or Bush would give $50 for the patent right to so beautiful a hypothesis. The poor man (in the house where none could read) is no more; I hope well for him. ——— (on dit) is a great admirer of Carlyle! I confess I like not these changes from what ——— and Mines, &c., *once* were, (*i. e.*) revival-men, however rash, to the decorous, lady-like, semi-high-churchism and semi-Oxonianism which converts souls in silk gloves. The fancy-lecturers I don't like at all; this saves no souls. Time is short. I don't, moreover, like this perpetual reproduction of the old controversy. I don't like ———'s doctrine (v. N. Y. Evang.) that enemies are never to be forgiven (till they repent, *i. e.*) while they are such. I don't like "fine" preaching, or preachers; and (lest you should think I like any thing) let me add, I don't like myself, or my past or present ways, especially my having made so much of *preparing* as scarcely to have begun to work; my having laboured so much *indirectly* when I might have done the same *directly*; my having set the soul's salvation too far off. O if we could live one real year of effective gospel service, we might be willing to depart. Preaching Christ is the best, hardest, sweetest work, on this side of beholding him. I trust we shall do both. Blessings on your family, and may they see the "salvation of Israel." Comp. Ps. lix. 35, 36, and liii. 6.

AEOLIC CASTLE, PRINCETON, *Feb.* 11, 1840.

As to ———, (the man hanged at St. Louis,) I remember him well; but how little can we rely on even dying confessions! how hard to get the truth of a Popish martyrdom in China, when a murderer's execution in Missouri cannot be given correctly. ——— was indeed a Sunday School scholar; but—1, his father was one of the vilest drunkards in our place, and died such; 2, his younger brother (said to be crazed of grief) is crazy *a potu*; 3, his uncle has been, to my knowledge, a wretched sot for twenty years; and 4, his "godly mother" has, I am told, been tipsy (as often before) since her son was hanged. The paper does not state that his repentings were all poured into the auricle of a Romish priest.

Mr. ———'s complaints are sickly. I should be glad to see him very often, but he must come to me, as life is too short for us busy folks to make calls. Out of at least twenty similarly situated men here, I never visit one without business. And he who will count up the sheets I write in a week, not to mention College and even pastoral cares, will not wonder. I shall nevertheless take means to show him that he will be welcome at all times. I rejoice to meet Christian friends and never grudge the time, but the man who wants to see me must take the trouble to come in. I see there is a bill before the ―――― legislature to discharter ―――― [a Seminary where young men and women were received as scholars.] I wonder the grand inquest has let them alone. Such mingling of boys and girls is giving a bribe to Belial. I could state cases enough of the evil of such propinquity.

FRIDAY, *Feb.* 14, 1840.

In regard to what I proposed respecting pieces on "Committing Verses to Memory," (pray why don't some of the word-mongers make a simple verb to express this daily-used idea? *memorize* is awful, yet almost necessary,) I am not so fit as you think; because, to say truth, I am not so whole-hearted in my attachment to the present mode of question-teaching, as I might be; and he who takes up the cudgel for you ought to be so. I am ready enough to write something on the getting-by-heart portion of the subject. After next Monday, however, I have a new class, on a new and difficult book, (Juvenal,) and shall have no time except "nights,"—therefore don't look for much from me. I have an interesting book about Iceland, from which I may perhaps get you something for Journal. Bush concluded his lectures here last evening; they have not been as full of matter as they ought to have been. His phraseology comes next to ――――'s. He prayed about the "unconsuming naphtha which lighted the war-fires on a thousand mountains;" and said on one occasion, "we are now ready to make our inquisitorial entrée into the chambers of the Apocalypse." In all this, however, he displays a power of diction and harmony of phrase which is totally absent in ――――. I wish I was a Quaker! I mean I wish I could carry off things with the equanimity which they seem to enjoy. Tell Mr. P―――― that he certainly errs in thinking I have any special hints touching the objects of his embassy, [a visit to Great Britain.] Every thing which I could say has doubtless occurred to him a hundred times. Of proper *Sunday* school teaching, I have a notion that they have very little to teach us in Britain. But much may be picked up, especially in the "Guid Town," as to the operation of Gall's and of Wood's plans, and the methods of scriptural instruction adopted in the common schools. If the Am. S. S. Union had the means, and saw the thing in its true light, they would lose no time in having an agent to do what Dr. Bache has done; I mean in reference to religious instruction. Bache's book has suggested many inquiries to me, especially about the "simultaneous" system. By-the-bye, no book which I have read for ten years has given me so much food for thought, or suggested so many plans, as that same report to the Girard College: it is to Victor Cousin's, what the *elevation* of an edifice is to the *plan*, or what the bill of fare is to the dinner. Tell Mr. P——, that by *topographical* cuts I mean views of places, scenery, plans, maps, &c.; by *archæological*, every depiction of biblical or Oriental houses, men, animals, modes of life, every thing, in short, which could interest a reader of a book of Antiquities; cuts, in short, *generically* like those in the Bible Dictionary. I won't tell you what I mean by the *emblematical*. Antiquities can be taught only by pictures. With a good supply of such we might go on with small numbers, which at length would grow into quite a volume. I feel a strong leaning towards a work of the kind myself. Wouldn't it be good for us if we had a fair and full answer to the following queries, from every country in Europe? "What class of books is at this moment most decidedly popular and effective with the common mind—fiction, prose, or poetry? in what form—style? with what embellishment? how brought within their reach?" Of course we ought to feel the world's pulse with all the fingers we can lay on its wrist. (!) There's a figure for ye!

We are all of us in danger of undervaluing the importance of our posts, and our means of usefulness. I make this remark in order to introduce another, viz., that I should "deeply" regret any change of an ordinary kind, which should remove you from the S. S. U. You know very well that the publishing crank is turned by yourself and P——; in a sort, therefore, you have control of the juvenile literature of increasing thousands. You know the delicacy of the post, you know how slight a straw laid over your rails would (hear! hear!) turn the locomotive off the track. (Cheers.) Again, I can conceive of no situation in which you could possibly set so much truth a-running over our wicked nation as this. Lastly, I don't know what I should do with my superabundant material, and superfluity of wisdom, if I did not shower it over the infant mind through the watering-pot of your publications. Next to lastly; I sincerely hope that by conciliating measures on the part of the Union, it may act a mediatory part between several conflicting parties, and connect together the peaceable men of all. Did you ever get fully possessed with the notion that it was Saturday on a Friday? such is my condition now, and it is like nothing so much as getting one's head turned on board a vessel.

Yesterday I examined Betsey Stockton's[1] school; I wish I knew of a white school where religion was so faithfully inculcated. Perhaps the great revivals in the Sandwich Isles are meant to prepare the way for persecutions: if so, we may expect to see a new stature of Christians. I wish you would in some shape or other call the attention of some Low Churchman to Daillé's celebrated work *de Usu Patrum*. Look at Bayle, art. *Daillé*. I never read such a piece of annihilating argument. I can't imagine an impartial mind to feel the Oxford Tracts as weighing a grain after such a book. The author's original was in French, entitled *du Vrai usage des Pères*. It exists in Latin also. The English version, though excellent, is rather antiquated, having appeared in 1675. As nobody, nowadays, could *write* the book, so nobody can answer it. I am amazed that it has not been mentioned on the Low Church side: but indeed, from the nature of the issue, the patristical erudition (how I hate the Latin part of our language, but what can a man do?) is chiefly on the Oxford side. That is a noble letter of blessed old Bp. White, in the Episcopal Recorder, a man worthier of saintship than half the saints, even of the "first four Councils:" a few like that would drive the nail. As it is, I confidently expect the Oxford Tracts to split the Church, and that by a vast majority on the wrong side. N. B. To preserve the point of a metallic pen (which I can't use to any advantage) a good way is to have a little vessel of very fine *shot* by your inkstand into which to stick the pen after wiping; it prevents both rust and warping. I lately mentioned to you the case of a black girl who seemed to be dying. She is convalescent, but is in a very strange condition, for she *won't get well*; that is literally the state of the case. She insists upon dying—wants to go to heaven—yet is free from disease, eats mince-pie, gains some flesh, &c. She will lie all day in one posture, and will not sit up. She evidently thinks the *desire of death* good *per se*. My visits to her are now offensive I think. Dod is ill in bed with a fever; he has carried your plan of going without an overcoat to the extreme; he always looked as if he was trying not to shiver. The hot room he has, to be sure, been guilty of: so have not I. Lest you should mistake my meaning about the book I have on the anvil for you, observe what follows. The subject is, *The Best Way of Doing Good*. The form, a grave story; just enough to support the dialogue. There is a young Christian of wealth and education introduced, as trying to do good in a certain neighbourhood, and his experience is divided into three stages, in which he attempts

---

[1] A coloured woman, who had accompanied the Rev. C. S. Stewart's family to the Sandwich Islands mission.

I. *Doing good to men's bodies,*—by giving money, helping poor, feeding beggars, &c., &c. II. *Doing good to men's minds,*—which he undertakes from a belief, derived from the foregoing experiment, that popular ignorance is the grand source of evil. III. *Doing good to men's souls,*—the best way of accomplishing the other two, illustrated by the effects of true piety in a bad neighbourhood.[1]

PRINCETON, *Feb.* 26, 1840.

The following is verbatim from a letter of Oct. 26, from Peter Harris, the African Prince, who is now at Monrovia, to a negro here. It describes a native dinner. You will admit that the " sir"ring is ultra-American : " They had great dinner that day, sir. Well, sir, they had two washbowl full of rice, and the other bowl full of chicken soup, head and all in the bowl, sir. The way them Missionaries eat that rice and the soup—it was the sin ! They set on the ground, sir, with country-mat spread on the ground : they did not set on the chair, sir; they set on the ground. They did not have any knifes or forks when they was eating that rice, sir, and they only had three spoon. The way them five men eat that rice with three spoon, I tell you, the first man take his spoonfull of rice in his mouth, then he hand the spoon to next man ; so on till it get round."

I send herewith, if possible, ———'s penultimate publication. I hope you will carefully read it. He has been here, and is as strongly fixed in his opinions as if he were inspired. Sandeman is not now his leader, but the late John Walker of Ireland, formerly a church clergyman and fellow of Trinity College, Dublin. I have been reading this Walker, who is a reasoner of singular power. The sect in Ireland is called " Separatists." They hold that Faith is Belief; that the corrupt nature is never less corrupt in this world; that baptism is to be administered only to proselytes; that Christians are to hold no fellowship in any religious exercise with any but themselves; and that they are the only true believers. [After mentioning some instances of false preaching of which he had heard, the letter proceeds.] Such a gospel as this is very unlike the New Testament. Indeed, I am getting to "test" systems a good deal by the way I feel in going right from them to the pure word of God. More and more am I afraid of the *best* human compositions on religion : some are nearer, and some further; but all the streams have an

---

[1] This work appeared in 1844, under the title of " Good, Better, Best; or, The Three Ways of making a Happy World." Pp. 321. It was republished in London, in 1856, with an Introduction by the Rev. Dr. Candlish, of Edinburgh.

earthly taste from the soil they run through. In connexion with what you say about the Eucharist, I have some notions about the other sacraments, (as we call them.) Do we not, in our squabbles about the amount of water, &c., lose sight of one great intent of the ordinance? viz., *the public avowal of any person as a leader, or as worthy of being accredited.* In this sense *proselytes* were baptized long before Christ. And I believe the word is often used chiefly in this sense, just as we use *subscription.* Thus Christ was himself baptized: *i. e.* he acknowledged John's mission. So Mark xvi. 16, He that believeth, *and is baptized,* &c. Compare Rom. vi. 3, "baptized," εις Χριστον Ιησουν; 1 Cor. i. 13, "were ye baptized," εις τὸ ὄνομα Παυλοῦ; 1 Cor. i. 15, 1 Cor. x. 2, "baptized," εις τον Μωυσην. Not that I doubt the symbolical meaning, but I see great force in such passages when viewed in immediate connexion with the idea of "*yielding oneself* a *disciple.*" The Oxford notions on these subjects have never made one sore place in my whole surface: most errors do, until I am armed afresh by the study of the questions. The attempt of the Tracts to throw a venerable mystic halo about the pedigree of their Nag's Head Succession is really farcical.

PRINCETON, *March* 21, 1840.

[After declining an appointment to preach the annual sermon for the American Sunday School Union, in May.] It is with much pain that I bring myself to say the aforesaid. But I am sincere in it. I am conscious of no special ability on set occasions; I suffer distresses, which to many would be inconceivable, while such an engagement is pending. The season also is one when I wish not to lade myself with labour. Next week I have to preach the ordination sermon of a foreign missionary [Wm. H. McAuley, at Kingston, March 25.] The week after is our examination. Then the vacation, in which I ought to go to Virginia. I see by the New Orleans papers that [Rev. John] Breckinridge is abused as making many converts, producing excitement, thinning theatres, &c. Good sign. Rose (the black girl) died last night in great peace and holy joy. Though there is not much to quote, I never attended a more satisfactory deathbed, (I take in two or three months.) There are here two young men, not long in their majority, the sole relics of a respectable Quaker family. They are farmers, and educated, and both tottering over the grave with consumption. The best is, they are lovely Christians, full of heavenly hope; now members of Mr. Hare's church, but bred Quakers. A grand book might be made (for the English market) out of a full and fair account of the New Harmony (Owenite) Institute in the West. Say and

McCulloch, and some other men, could tell some good stories of Socialism. It would sell in England and do much to cripple Owen. I am and we are thine and yourn, J. W. A. & Co.

PRINCETON, *March* 31, 1840.

Have you arrived at that stage of ministerial experience at which one receives anonymous letters, telling him to preach this, or preach that? I got one to-day; I suppose from a woman, as every other word was underscored. After the acquittal of Wood, [for murder of daughter on plea of insanity,] I suppose insane murderers will increase in Pennsylvania. Such things, no doubt, go into the account of national sins. I hope there is a change working among the Africans of this vicinity, and they are very numerous, in regard to the Colonization Society. Their prejudices have been mighty, but since Peter Harris writes to them about Africa, they have to admit some things which they once denied. Two of the best educated among them are going to take the African Repository, and one of these is willing to go out and see for himself. My father, who has this more at heart than any thing in the world, is writing a series in the Newark paper. He has had a large history of Colonization ready for the press more than a year. He regards the experiment as tried, and the foundation as firmly laid, and thinks repression (as to emigration) is more necessary than stimulation. I perceive Buxton founds his last hope on the colonizing plan, and you may see by the "Record" that a new paper is set up in London, called "The African Colonizer." Do you know that we have a whole family of pure Malays living here? They were brought here by Van Polanen, a Dutch gentleman, who was governor of Batavia. The children are all grown. Let me say something to you about *Facts*. One authentic fact is a great thing. There is a life and power in fact, which is not in fiction. They are more striking than fiction. In reading a book, you find yourself suddenly arrested by certain statements, just as in hearing the noises of children you are perhaps little moved till the sounds form themselves into a tune. These passages we often find to be *facts*. The best characters in Scott's Novels and Crabbe's Poems, are from real life. In religious things, no genuine record of a soul's history, or of any segment of it, is unimportant. God's way of working is always marked and self-consistent. In a real history, I care not of what, the parts hang together in a definite relation like the limbs in a human body, or the features in a face; the connexion in a fiction is often forced and sometimes impossible. *Corollary.* 1. We ought to keep an eye open perpetually for religious facts. 2. We ought to record them. 3. We ought to record them with great care, in cases where the enormity of the transaction, or some delicacy of circumstance, absolutely forbids their publication *at present*. These are the very facts which are often most striking and valuable. Lay them by, and a year or two hence, they may be brought out with much force. 4. Ministers ought to keep a record of "cases" in their pastoral practice. That they do not, either mentally or verbally, argues a certain skepticism as to the reality or moment of the exercises. These thoughts have come on me with increased impression within a short time; and as I have lost some fifteen years' use of them, I give them over to you. I think more of [Dr. E. D.] Griffin's sermons than I expected. They have that sort of power which arises from the extirpation of superfluous words, in a very remarkable degree. In most cases I like the doctrine; always bearing in mind that they are avowedly *awakening* sermons. We have two Cherokees in College. One of them I taught eight weeks, without knowing that he had any thing of the red-man about him. As you are not near enough to me to give me your old coats, you may give me old notions instead; as an encouragement, here are some of mine: *The Power of Christian Love* is a great subject. "Love is Power," was Dr. J. H. Rice's motto. "Light and Love" is Justin Edwards's. In managing my children, in rebuking my servants, in quelling refractory boys, in every thing great and small, I find that want of love causes failure. Often, for the moment, every thing seems against this; but events always bring me back to it. I hope I have more disposition to yield and give up even rights, for love's sake; but we are dreadfully infested in the church with a sort of feudal honour, which raises itself by the side of Christian principle. For example: I am insulted. Christianity says *Suffer it;* Chivalry says *Resent it;* at least *shew that you feel it.* How common in fashionable (??!) Christian intercourse, and among ministers in ecclesiastical bodies. After an hour or two in such scenes, how like springs in the Zahara is it to read a chapter or two of the Life of Christ! As I grow older as a parent, my views are changing fast as to the degree of conformity to the world which we should allow in our children. I am horror-struck to count up the profligate children of pious persons and even ministers. The door at which those influences enter, which countervail parental instruction and example, I am persuaded, is *yielding to the ways of good society.* By dress, books, and amusements, an atmosphere is formed which is not that of Christianity. More than ever do I feel that our families must stand in a kind but determined opposition to the fashions of the world, breasting the waves, like the

Eddystone Light House. And I have found nothing yet which requires more courage and independence than to rise even a tittle, but decidedly, above the *par* of the religious world around us. Surely the way in which we commonly go on is not that way of self-denial and sacrifice and cross-bearing which the New Testament talks of: "then is the offence of the Cross ceased." Our slender influence on the circle of our friends is often to be traced to our leaving so little difference between us. I plead guilty to every count. I am at a great loss what to do about the Temperance Question. My sole difficulty is *Pledge or no Pledge*. As to the Wine Question, it has long seemed to me frivolous to stand over the corpses of a thousand drunkards asking whether their brandy had water or wine in it. I am made up in mind and conscience to avoid the means of drunkenness in my family. On this I have acted some months. We have dozens of young men in and about Princeton who are drunk every little while, and always on wine. Our students commonly begin on malt-liquors. But I am not so clear as to the Pledge. I do not see my way plain as to taking the high ground respecting morals, which some do. And I abhor as hell the doctrine that our blessed and omniscient Saviour can be conceived to have made wine *ignorantly*. That the wine he made was intoxicating, I believe as fully as I do that he made it. Our students need an example. I am really at a loss. We need divine direction at every step, and for want of seeking it, and waiting for His counsel, (Ps. cvi. 13,) we so often rush into errors.

PRINCETON, MONDAY AFTER PALM SUNDAY, AND FEAST OF ST. HERMENGILD MARTYR, 10th OF NISAN, 5600.

My edition of Luther's Letters contains 2324, and has no Index of names; I may therefore err in some slight degree. I find 14 letters to Jerome Weller, and have looked through them. In no one do I find any thing resembling the advice about concubinage. The other matters are, no doubt, those which occur in the letter of Nov. 6, 1530, in number 1322. Luther is advising Weller about a dreadful hypochondria and despair, which is the subject of several letters. His words are as follows: " Et quoties istis cogitationibus te vexaverit Diabolus, illice quære confabulationem hominum, aut largius bibe, aut jocare, nugare aut aliquid hilarius facito. Est nonnunquam largius bibendum, atque adeo peccatum aliquod faciendum in odium et contemtum diaboli, ne quid loci relinquamus illi, ut conscientiam nobis faciat de rebus levissimis, alioqui vincimur, si nimis anxie curaverimus ne quid peccemus. Proinde, si quando dicet Diabolus, noli bibere, tu sic fac illi respondeas: atqui ab eam causam maxime bibam, quod tu prohibes, atque adeo largius in nomine Jesu Christi bibam. Sic semper contraria facienda sunt eorum, quæ Satan vetat. Quid causæ aliud esse censes, quod ego sic meracius bibam, liberius confabuler, commesser sæpius, quam ut ludam Diabolum ac vexem, qui me vexare et ludere paraverat. Utinam possem aliquid insigne peccati designare modo ad eludendum Diabolum, ut intelligeret, me nullum peccatum agnoscere ac me nullius peccati mihi esse conscium. Omnino totus decalogus amovendus est nobis ex oculis et animo, nobis, inquam quos sic petit ac vescat Diabolus." [Dr. Martin Luther's Briefe, u. s. w., ed. De Wette, Berlin, 1827, vol. iv., p. 188.] I ought to say that I have found nothing approaching to the ignorant rashness of this in any other part of his correspondence.

While we are upon casuistry, I wish to make a stricture on your canon, that "a man ought not to write and publish aught which he would not say *ore tenus*." I think I once before said, and I still think, that the rule is unsound. It should read thus: "which he *might not lawfully* say *ore tenus*." Our duty, it strikes me, is in no degree dependent on our *willingness* to do this or that. One man may be uncharitable in boldly saying one thing, and another man may be uncharitable in timidly withholding another thing. —————— would say many a thing which neither you nor I would utter. Many a man would say to another's face, what he would not print. I have known the grossest calumnies justified by people's adding, "I say nothing behind his back which I would not say before his face;" it was so, but it only proved that effrontery was added to injustice. The true question should be, I think, "Is it a duty to the public to say so and so? is it true? can it be said charitably?" In point of fact, no doubt most of the hard things said are uncharitable.

I think exactly as you do about [Rev. John] Newton's Letters and Conversation; his other works seem to me of little value in comparison. We have had a very interesting visit from the Rev. Dr. Lang of the "Kirk," from Sydney, New South Wales. Very heavy in the pulpit, but amazingly interesting in private. He has had an Odyssey of voyages for that colony, and its religious interests. I am struck and fired with the greatness of the field. I wish you may talk with him. What an opening for Sunday School Books! Free colonists are pouring in, from the better class of Scotch and Irish Presbyterians. Last year 15,000 went out. Sydney has 30,000 inhabitants, and is a very beautiful city. He thinks New Zealand will certainly be colonized by England, and be a great Austral Britain. See how analogous to Great Britain it is on the globe, antipodal, insular, &c. My mind expands when I look at the mighty conquests of our language. If we could only pour in the gospel with this tide of conquest and colonization! Since, in our day, God so signally blesses colonies for the spread of civilization, ought we not to follow the lead of Providence, and strike in as much as possible with the divine plan? The hope of great effects is more reasonable from such efforts than from insulated assaults on the mass of heathenism. It is the difference between firing a ball against a walled town, and entering a great breach with a victorous army. *Fact* 34. An alligator lived more than six months in our Museum with nothing but cold water; mention to the Temp. Society, before Lent is out. *Fact* 35. We have had several sorts of common snakes, domiciliated for days together, in our yard, and I and my child have handled them freely without being hurt. We dedicated our [Presbyterian] new African meeting-house yesterday. A pleasant "season," and really delightful singing. Eli Smith is here; he strikes me, as on former occasions, as a man of the first class of minds, always direct, clear, and decided in what he utters.

PRINCETON, *May* 4, 1840.

I have been endeavouring to attend to a little direct ministerial duty this vacation, at Cranbury, Freehold, and Trenton, whence I am this day returned. At Cranbury they now have two new church buildings. At Freehold I found a very pleasant state of things. —— declares to me that he does not know of a man, or woman, or child, (of suitable age,) whom he has not recently talked to in the most direct manner on the state of his or her soul; generally with prayer, and, in some instances, repeatedly. About 40 are hopeful converts, and the place is small. There is also a revival in Mr. Webster's church, Middletown Point, another feeble church, but greatly strengthened by the awakening of the leading men in the town. Also a struggling little congregation at Upper Freehold [Betts's] has had a similar ingathering. And the old [Tennent] Church of Freehold, has added perhaps 40—50. In all these places the work is going on in as healthful a way as I have ever yet seen, though not without some things which make me indulge painful scruples as to the plan of perpetual meetings. Mr. Yeomans has done wonders in Trenton, as to temporalities. I do not suppose $20,000 were ever laid out more for the adorning of a city, than in the New Presbyterian church there. Internally it is certainly the pleasantest place of worship I ever was in. A new organ has just been installed, and Dr. Ewing is the organist. It is worthy of note that within two years the following churches in our Presbytery have erected new and convenient churches, viz., Trenton, New Brunswick, Cranbury (2), Freehold, Princeton, Dutch Neck, Nottingham; Bound Brook a little before this period built anew, and Ewing, Pennington, and Allentown, have turned their old edifices inside out. Our meeting of Presbytery was a very pleasing one, and excited good hopes. The Mormons, however, are making serious progress within our bounds. At Thom's River they have about 40 converts, quite substantial people. They profess to speak with tongues, and to work miracles, believe in baptismal regeneration and immersion—are high-church, as thinking none salvable but themselves—hold to the divine legation of Joe Smith, who has been in Monmouth. They make much use of singing. It is a dangerous feature of their system, that they talk almost always *in secret* with one another, about their peculiarities, and not to the uninitiated. Their chief man at present is named *Rigdon*. Their chief book is the "Book of Mormon," which I have seen. They also have "The Warning Voice," by one Winchester, who has been in Philadelphia. Some of their books they are said to conceal very carefully. They always dip at night. I dined at a house where I met an old lady named Cubberly, who had been with me to a long service, in a heavy rain, at the age of 91. Her descendants, she said, are 170. The Seminary examination begins to-day. I am (on dit) unanimously called to the pastoral care of the Hanover [or College Church] Prince Edward County, Virginia. I think as you do of Davies. The completest life I know of, is in Dr. J. H. Rice's Lit. and Evang. Magazine. With a little pruning, I think his sermons are perhaps the best extant; and even the exuberance would scarcely be felt in an impassioned speaker such as he was. Everywhere in Virginia he has left his track in the conversion of leading men and women, whose children and grandchildren remain. Read the Life of Rev. Devereux Jarratt, an Episcopal minister; it contains much interesting about Davies. See also *Gillies's Collections*, a book which, somewhat abridged, the Board [of Publication] ought to publish.

———— has no family-talent, [as a pastor,] which, after all, I am repentant enough to think at least half the matter. What he attempts he carries through, but he attempts nothing warm. I think a large portion of our churches are in a good state of preparation for awakening measures, especially in the county of Monmouth; which, by marl, is becoming the richest, after having been the poorest county in New Jersey. Our county of Mercer has just erected a court-house in South-Trenton; which, I suppose, is equalled by no similar county building (out of great cities) in America. It is a beautiful Ionic building, and costs $50,000.

PRINCETON, *May* 5, 1840.

It is, perhaps, unnecessary for me to say that I have, as yet, no official and incontestable evidence of the call I mentioned, to Prince Edward. It is a good living, and in the choice part of Virginia. The College and Seminary always form part of the congregation. I am in pain to know what is my duty. I have always sat in my present chair with a feeling that it was right only as a refuge during ill-health. At present, through great mercy, I am perhaps only for a short interval, in the enjoyment of the best health I have had since I left College. I think I can say, *ex animo*, I wish to go where I may most fully exhaust my talents, quantulacunque sint, in the service of Christ. It may seem strange to you, that no invitation has shaken me more.[1]

Meekness seems in many minds to be confounded with imbecility, indecision, or fear; and I own that, in point of fact, it too seldom escapes some measure of pusillanimity; but if we could have the magnanimous love of Christ, or of Paul, or of John—how it would attract, and govern!

I am inclined to hope that the Assembly will be conservative. Such seems to me the natural tendency of things. As no great church-crisis exists, many Presbyteries will feel free to send moderate men, whom they have respected all along, but whom they durst not send during the conflict.

The cold of this day threatens to bring on a frost, which will perhaps destroy our fruit, and nip my bunch-beans. I have begun to take my usual pleasures in the garden, an enjoyment discovered by me too late, but one which grows in my esteem.

———'s daughter, aged 5 years, reads every book which a girl of 16 would do, tales and novels included. She is quite forward in French. I am drivelling this stuff out after 10 at night: I had better prepare my head and heart for the pillow, so "manum de tabula." Good night.

PRINCETON, *June* 4, 1840.

I think I would rather write Baxter's English, than any I know, though I would not wish to write always what he has done. He well describes his own style: "May I speak pertinently, plainly, piercingly, and somewhat properly, I have enough." (Premonition to Saints' Rest.) He was not afraid of *idioms*, the real strength and glory of a language, and espe-

---

[1] The call was declined.

cially of ours. The quality of plain, straightforward, market-English is rare in books. It is somewhat dangerous for us cis-atlantics to attempt, for in becoming idiomatic we become provincial, witness *Finney*. But read Bunyan, Fuller, Swift, Cobbet, Hare, ["Sermons to a Country Congregation," 1838,] and you will see what I mean. This was, after all, what was meant by *Attic* Greek as distinguished from the κοινη διαλεκτος: and *Attic salt* was the very sort of wit which circulated among Athenian hucksters, and which we find in Fuller and Charles Lamb. There was great wisdom in making the speech of the people the standard of good Greek, and great advantage in being so small a State. If you have never done it, don't fail to read the "Rest," the "Call," and the "Gildas Salvianus," as he wrote them, and free from the emasculations of Methodist abridgers, and do it in Duncan's impression, London, 23 vols., 1830. It would be a good notion to excerpt and reprint some of the noble passages of the "Saints' Rest" which have been omitted in the abridgment. With all my admiration of Baxter's parenetic writings, I must say that he seems to me never to get upon a *doctrinal* point without doing mischief. Except in the schoolmen, (whom he greatly studied,) I have never seen such subtilty of distinctions. For a good specimen (as I suppose) of his pulpit prayers, see his "Dying Thoughts," vol. 18, p. 413 and seq. As you seem to have acquired a little interest in Samuel Davies, (whose name was always pronounced *Davis*,) I will add these items: I was told by Mrs. Dr. J. Woodhull, daughter of Gilbert Tennent, that he was very attentive to his dress, so as to excite much observation, and always had a ring on his finger, and a gold-headed cane. I was told the same thing by an aunt of my father's. My mother has heard it said in her father's house, that Mr. Davies used to say that he wore this ring to remind him of eternity—without beginning and without end. I have a MS. journal of Col. James Gordon, of Lancaster co., Va., who married Gen. [and President] Harrison's aunt, and whose daughter Dr. Waddel married. The names of Davies, Whitefield, and Waddel, often occur on the same page, and the places, and times, and texts of all their preachings are given. The amount of labours performed by Va. ministers in that day was amazing. You remember the affecting remarks of Davies about his little ones; several of them lived ungodly. In his manuscript journal he complains of great harshness and jealousy on the part of Gilbert Tennent, while they were in England. Do not fail to get hold of the life of Devereux Jarratt. It will give you a lively idea of those times. I know very well a daughter of Mr. Jarratt's, and my father knew the man himself. He was "a speckled bird" among the Churchmen of that day.

PRINCETON, *June* 10, 1840.

The religious prospects of the University of Virginia are really encouraging. It seems as if Providence was throwing contempt on old Jefferson's ashes. I have lately visited Mrs. ———, who is on her death-bed with consumption; I could scarcely keep from envying her. When I see a Christian die I lose my fears. It is grand impolicy in ——— to print any of his sermons. "It is as easy to paint fire (says old Gurnall) with the heat, as with pen and ink to commit that to paper which occurs in preaching. There is as much difference between a sermon in the pulpit, and printed in a book, as between milk in the warm breast, and in a sucking-bottle." It may not be so with such preachers as ——— or ———, whose discourses have sometimes been preached in the pulpit, then delivered at a commencement, then published in the ———, and then issued as the Preface to a work. In my notion a sermon is a sermon, and nothing else; if you make it with any thing ulterior in view, you destroy it as a sermon. It is death to a good sermon, as to a good love-letter, to publish it. It is dead beer, sour champagne, cold coffee, an effete cigar, a daguerrotype portrait.

I have lately re-read Southey's Thalaba; it is certainly a wonderful poem, though the freshness and simplicity of the first two cantos are not sustained.

I beg to be presented to ——— and your amiable babes, and am, with all the et ceteras,

Yours and theirs.

PRINCETON, *June* 22, 1840.

I have many independent sources of evidence showing that evangelical religion is greatly advancing in Virginia under the labours of Episcopalians. Most of their clergy are good and hard-working men. The Alexandria Seminary has been a great blessing to them. As to *God forbid*[1] I know of no case such as you ask about; it is, however, hazardous to assert a negative. I have looked at the Hebrew of all the places mentioned by Cruden, and the word is uniformly חָלִילָה literally *ad profana*, "*i. e.* (says Gesenius) *absit*, vox detestantis." Respecting the New Testament phrase by all means read what Dr. Hodge says on Romans iii. 4. "The Scriptures," says he, "do not authorize such a use of the name of God," &c. An expurgated

---

[1] The translation of μη γενοιτο in our version.

edition of Jeremy Taylor's Holy Living and Dying would be one of the loveliest books in the language. I mean such expurgation as Howard Malcom has effected in Law's Serious Call. We cannot set too many such books afloat. Some of the Psalms of David might be rendered into blank verse, with better effect than in rhyme. Such a one is the 18th. De Wette's German translation of them makes many passages more clear by exchanging future tenses for present or past. Anagram by ———; *Old Tippecanoe=People can do it.* Every year I am more and more surprised, in tracing the course of our College Alumni, to see how many thoughtless, wild, and even wicked young men, (especially of the South,) who have left us without any sign of good, become true Christians in the course of a few years at home. Even of cases which I know, I think I could enumerate thirty or forty. This is really encouraging, and ought to be mentioned as an offset to the real and imaginary dangers and evils of a public education. I seriously think, after some inquiry, that where one piously-bred boy is corrupted, five neglected receive the seeds of divine truth. If we were faithful, how many such instances would there be! What an amount of rhetorical passion ——— infuses into his speeches: I don't know any of our orators who ventures upon so much, nor any of our agents who has kept alive his enthusiasm so long for one cause. It is pleasing to observe how hired agents become devoted to a single charity heart and soul, and then equally devoted to another. I am not at all pleased with ———'s Critique. It is full of the slang of the pseudo-German school, even to such words as *Stand-point,* (Standpunkt:) why not call a glove a *Hand-shoe,* (Hand-schuh,) as the Germans do? I am more and more convinced that no man need regret the extremest ignorance of every German metaphysician that has written.

I have just opened the Record of May 13, which contains Packard's speech. He seems to have been well received, with the exception of the usual blackguardism of the next speaker about slavery. If I should ever speak on British Boards, I think that I would forestall that by blazing away beforehand against the British for having introduced slavery among us, and kept up the slave-trade so many years. It is plain that the report of the "worthy gentleman's" speech is defective in the extreme. The bones of old Boney [in Paris] will be as really *adored* as ever any relics were. The *simiotigre,* as Alfieri called the French, will make a wonderful work over them. I doubt whether France contains in it as honest a man as Wellington; but I confess to a violent antipathy to the great nation. Except from necessity, they seem to me to be the same people they were during the

Revolution. What a blessing it is to belong to the Teutonic race! The more I see of the black-eyed races of the South of Europe, the less I respect them. Next to Britain I would live in Prussia. Last year we had 90 quarts of strawberries; this year not nine, the season being just done. The last article of the Edinburgh Review for April on the "State of Parties" is fine reading—no doubt by "Tom" Macaulay. It is very unjust, however, in many particulars. I see the General Assembly of Scotland have gone very strongly against Lord Aberdeen's Bill; no doubt rightly, but, I apprehend, to the ruin of their establishment. I am much struck with the tone of piety which pervades Dr. Chalmers's writings on the subject. I am not without reasons for thinking that the last sermon I preached to the blacks was the means of awakening the only white person present. Strange are the ways of Providence! I think it is too much our way to rank modern philosophers who reject the Gospel, with ancient sages who did not know it. But if Plato is in hell—how far nearer absence of pain must he be than Gibbon! the former having almost guessed at truth without revelation, the latter, after a perfect education in it, having rejected it! The grand error of free-thinkers, and that which, I think, should be pressed home upon them, is their obstinate persistency in going blindfold when a light from heaven is offered to them. Suppose a man should profess to doubt all the acknowledged principles of chemistry and blow himself up, by going into a foul mine, when a thousand safety-lamps had been offered to him. Our minds are too often disposed to regard that as venial, which God regards as heinous. Perhaps the very rejection of such a book as the Bible, even without a word of external evidence, is proof positive of enmity to God. Pride of understanding ruins learned men by hundreds and thousands; it is destroying, I fear, all the philosophers of Germany. To become as little children is a great attainment. May it be ours! It evidently means a great deal. Especially it means *faith:* what is *credulity* in our babe, towards us, is *faith* in us, towards God. After this page of homily, I allow you to have a recess for a few minutes. Look at that hard place, 2 Sam. xxiii. 5. De Wette translates, and as I think in exact accordance with the Hebrew: "Yea, and is not my house so, before God?" &c., &c., &c. "Yea, all my salvation and all my desire, will he not make it grow?" In verse 17 of the same chap., and in 1 Chr. xi. 19, the phrase is not equivalent to our "God-forbid," but rather (1) "Be it far from me, Jehovah!" (2) "Be it far from me, from God." Some little chronological tables might with advantage be dispersed over a Bible; some light from the following neglected relationships: viz.:

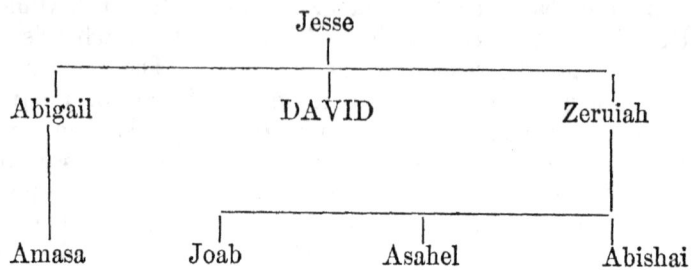

A few self-made charts of this kind tracing out the relations mentioned in Scripture, would, by degrees, enlarge and distinct-ify (we need a word) a man's historical knowledge of Scripture. Half the readers do not know whether Zeruiah was male or female.

PRINCETON, *July* 1, 1840.

Bishop Chase (in the "Record") talks of moneys "*rising of*" so many dollars! Show me an English authority for "*over* ten thousand dollars!" Yet Walter Scott says, "I have done a *monstrous sight* of work," (Diary, July 13, 1826;) this I thought a Philadelphianism. "*Leave* me alone," I never heard but in your town; it is a German idiom exact; "*Lassen mich allein.*" We have had a visit from ———, who is zealous about a prize tract just from England, which demonstrates that the Scripture wine was not intoxicating. He says Louis Philippe told him he would gladly sign the teetotal pledge, but that he feared his subjects would say he was a fool. *That* is the thing they will never say of him, even if they shed his blood on Napoleon's ashes. I do not much expect to be at Trenton; we expect to have a Colonization effort here on that day. The iron is now hot, and the Buxton influence should be driven forwards with all power while it lasts. My mind has run very much lately on Colonization (in general) as God's means of civilizing and Christianizing the world, and on the part which the Anglo-Saxon race is taking. From ———'s letters, as from the British papers, I see how far worse, after all, the spirit of party is in England than here. How it is embittered by politics, by the Establishment, by the feeling of rank, and by the admitted heats and outbreaks of the platform! Would it be possible for *any* American Committee or Board to treat *any* accredited British agent as *every* American ditto is treated there, by some or other of them? I trow not.

Give my kindest regards to ——— and the rest of your *white* family, as they say in Virginia, to distinguish from a man's *black* ditto, which is sometimes quite patriarchal.

I am, was, have been, had been, shall be, &c., through all the tenses, Yours.

PRINCETON, *July* 22, 1840.

I enclose with this the MS. of *Lame John*.[1] It was begun under the title of *Lame Jack*, which I greatly prefer, but the resemblance to Miss Edgeworth's *Lame Jervas*, and Capt. Marryat's *Poor Jack*, made me fear to add a third great work of the sort.

No book of mine has less plot or less fiction. Almost every page is a copy of scenes and incidents under my eye at the time of writing, or remembered by me. If I do not err, this copying of real life will interest young readers.

Believe me very respectfully, Yours and Theirs, (sc. the unknown Committee, which is not unlike the *Chambre Introuvable* of the French Revolution,) and am, et cetera,

JAMES ALAXANDREW,
as my carpenter spells the name.

PRINCETON, *July*, 1840.

Bishops abound. Last Sunday we had Samuel Michigan, yestreen Levi North Carolina, next week we are to have Charles Ohio. The fourth passed without any thing very remarkable, except a Colonization meeting at which Capt. Stockton spoke and Langdon Cheves attended. The Captain is admirable in elocution and gesture. A knifegrinder from Worcestershire, speaking to me yesterday of the sects in this country, said *literatim*: "you seem to have a great many of the Prispeterians, and also of the Priscotarians." Our blackberry woman has come to an estate in France; name Ancillon: we have eaten her dewberries within the week. A girl applied to us as child's nurse a week or two ago; last week she fell out of a tree and was killed. Tell me, if you know, who the Mr. Peter is, who translated Schiller's William Tell, lately published by Perkins.[2]

So far as I know there is no book in defence of Christianity extant in French, of a kind to meet French infidels, and be circulated in France where the need is greatest. My father has had an urgent demand this week for any thing of the sort in French or Spanish, in a letter from a native Spaniard, nephew

---

[1] "Lame John; or, the Charitable Poor Man." Published 1840. Pp. 137.
[2] He was the British Consul in Philadelphia.

of a Romish priest. Can we neglect this without sin? My father has received innumerable letters from persons converted as well as convinced by his "Evidences;" one last week from an Episcopal clergyman.

PRINCETON, *August*, 1840.

Read a grand article on *Style* in the July Blackwood. Do your children get a chance to fly kites? it is a very graceful and interesting pastime. Among the Tract Society's volumes is the Life of ———. I must in candour say it is a worthless book. It is such prima facie, but doubly so to us who intimately knew the subject of the memoir for years. He was a very warm-hearted Christian, but as great a mixture of weakness, imprudence, and pomposity as I ever saw in my life. Some of those who loved him most were most surprised and ashamed when they saw him made a lion of. Harris's Mammon and Abbott's Young Christian seem to me very objectionable. Most of their [Tract Society's] other permanent volumes I think good. I stand astonished at the extent of their circulation. What an engine! We are (our house) about equidistant from three most sage musicians—an owl which perches and screeches every evening in Dr. Hodge's trees, and two of Elliot's "animals" [asses] at Capt. Stockton's. I never knew fully before what braying meant. Come out before the season is over. Signora Upupa is engaged for a few nights only, and one of the *Asinelle* is lately confined. How is a man ever to be sure how another man's name is spelt? Shakspeare's is three different ways in his autograph will. In preparing an article, I had scruples about "Sydney Smith;" found it with *y* in the Record, *i* in Lockhart's Scott, and both *i* and *y* in John Murray's Byron, and got it wrong at last. I have heard ———, and, I think, ———, say Byron: the noble Lord himself rhymes it with *iron* and *siren*.

Do you ever read the Spectator? Read it, by extracts, with or to your daughter. It is crystal water after gutter ditto. Some of Steele's are more racy English than Addison's. What pomp of American verbosity could express what follows, about Westminster Abbey: "When I look upon the tombs of the great every emotion of envy dies in me."

"The better vulgar "—a fine phrase of Warburton's.

I would subscribe two prices for a bona fide old-time Walshian gazette. I owe something to that man:

> "But why then publish? Granville the polite
> And *Knowing Walsh* would tell me I could write."
> *Pope.*

It is some weeks since I was enabled to close the canon of

the New Testament, having, in my small way, expounded the whole in course, at morning prayers. And I am sure I love the book more for having so done. I have begun again.

Some of our wretched wags in College had a strolling painter in the gallery, last Sunday, busy taking ———'s likeness, while he preached!

This evening is very cool; enough so, I guess, for a blanket. A neighbour's child, 18 months old, has swallowed 15 percussion caps, (invented, you know, by Forsyth, a Scotch clergyman.)

In *private* I have found forms of prayer very valuable. They suggest *what* to pray for, which we may forget. I have thought it would be good to make for one's self a *liturgy of subjects;* we are so apt to forget. Have a book; put a general topic at top of page; leave space to add particulars. Romaine used to have a list of friends, and prayed it over every Friday afternoon.

Sam [now Rev. S. D. Alexander] is going on Tuesday to Sullivan co., N. Y., on the Erie railroad, as a Surveyor. He is a moral boy, but very careless. God grant him a new heart!

Some papistical books on Christian morals are, exceptis excipiendis, among the best I ever read. To-day I have been reading the "Spiritual Combat," a famous book among them, from which I think I have derived real benefit. It is one of the most original productions I ever perused. Read any chapter of it, and you will see what I mean. It is anonymous.

We have a very wide horizon where we now live, and surely nothing of pyrotechny can equal the lightnings of this evening. Last night—moon shining—I stood by a fence, coming from Dod's, and speculated a colt, as I thought it, grazing in a pasture: it came right up to me, and lo it was an ass! Really now, it was quite a noble creature of the kind.

I sometimes find my evenings quite light and hilarious after a very tort day. This morning I attended a funeral, sat at Dod's *examen*, heard a long recitation, and, after a bite, examined 76 fellows in Latin, came home exanimatus, drank three cups of strong tea, played half an hour on a flute, and feel better this moment than I did when I got up. What wonderful machines these are! Sometimes the grasshopper is a burden to me. I have been reading O. A. Brownson's *Charles Ellwood*, which purports to be his own experience. No American book is better written—the style, in places, is exquisite; but it is the deadliest assault on religion; and though he does not quote a German word, it is Kant-ism applied to American infidel politics. The system is the more dangerous because it is alive; in this having an unspeakable advantage over the Unitarianism of ——— and Co., which is corpse-like, and has never moved among the *people.*

Tell ——— that I beseech him to write an off-hand article for the Repertory, on the subject he once touched in some letters; viz., the danger and folly of an un-religious Education for the country. Let him fill it with his British recollections, &c. He is precisely the man to do it. The call is imperative, and this is the nick of time. I wish I could make him know how earnestly I desire this.[1] Both your Union and the Tract Society would profit by it; and if he does it as he can, it may do more good than a thousand sermons. Don't wait for method or references; let him strike it off hot, and it will burn in the deeper. If this is not our vocation just now, I know not what is. I am afraid the devil is getting hold of the common-school crank.

It is plain that the [London] Record has several writers of its editorials. The man who writes on the Scotch church is truly a powerful fellow. When I read what he says (and he has confuted my foregoing conclusions on sundry points) I feel as if I was in the gripe of a Cornish wrestler.

Lord Byron, in a paper of Strictures, written at Ravenna, in 1821, takes Campbell to task for misquoting Shakspeare, and says: "*A great poet quoting another should be correct.*" In the very same article he designates Bacon as the "greatest—wisest—meanest of mankind." The allusion is obvious, but the distich of Pope runs thus:

> "If parts allure thee, think how Bacon shined
> The wisest, brightest, meanest of mankind."

I wish you would attend one of our Final Examinations; indeed, I wish they were public. Nothing could do so much justice to our methods of teaching. It lasts from 8 to 10 days; hours $8\frac{1}{2}$—12, and 2—5. Most of the subjects (about 16) are, on the English-University plan, from papers, embodying the chief points of the whole subject; the same paper to each; not seen before the moment; no book, reference, or communication allowed. Some of the best scholars answer every question in full, writing 3 or $3\frac{1}{2}$ hours at a stretch, and filling several sheets. There is perfect silence, and it is a fine moral spectacle to see 70 odd young men so intensely employed. Of course there are many who do little or nothing; but the examination is absolutely fair, and the comparison between man and man exact. I doubt not that our whole course of study will be more faithful, under the urgency of this motive. I will try to enclose such of our papers as are printed, for a few are exhibited on a blackboard. The paper is always a fresh one, and such as no chance

---

[1] It was done in an article of fifty-three pages in the Repertory of July, 1841.

can enable any one to answer who has not some knowledge of every portion, and exact knowledge of certain parts proposed.

I have received 78 answers to my examination-paper. I will send you a copy of the paper, and perhaps one of the answers. The following question from Dod's examination paper of Juniors is sent for Tom's use:

"Find the length of an arc of the Tractory, its differential equation being $\frac{dy}{dx} = \frac{y}{\sqrt{a^2 - y^2}}$ Correct the integral on the supposition that the arc commences at the origin, where $y = a$."

A Simeon (Charles) here might be a great blessing: he ought, however, to be disconnected with the college police. *Our advices are like those of the Newgate ordinary.* ☞ Talk fully with P—— about the religious-education-literature, (as above,) for I think it *the* question of our age and land. If we could leave that matter on its right foot, we might die. If I were a raging, athletic, outdoor man, I would stake every thing upon it. New England will do her own work, well or ill; but who will do it for the non-New-England States?

I think you are too severe upon the absconding clergy. The thing is no doubt an abuse, as it now exists, but there is after all, at the bottom, a real necessity for some recreation and change of scene. Only it ought to be under some well-understood arrangement, so as to prevent this summer complaint of the people. Why must all clergymen need winding up at the same month? Why need there be so much stiffness about not preaching in another's pulpit? Why not agree together and have a rotation of Hejiras? This I don't understand. The source of the evil in some of the best pastors, I suppose, is undue night-work during the working season.

John F. Caruthers of Lexington is dead. Our large connexion in Rockbridge could not have met with a single loss so serious. He was a man of extraordinary talent for business, and of prudence unsurpassed, an elder, and a conscientious Christian. I believe, long a Sunday School Superintendent. Old Dr. Hillyer is dead also, a truly good old man. How beautiful is goodness! Fierce orthodoxy burns as well as warms, but Christlike gentleness sheds life all around it.

CHARLOTTE COURT HOUSE, VA., *Oct.* 27, 1840.

It is with great difficulty that I snatch an interval from excessive company to write you a letter, and I shall probably be stopped before I get done. My wife, two boys, and nurse stopped at the University, [Charlottesville.] Though they all were somewhat better, they were not in a state to brave a land-journey over mountains. Mr. ——'s carriage had been sent for us; leaving, therefore, my family with Dr. [Prof. J. L.] Cabell, I reached this place in four days. We had to lie by for heavy storms. We got here last Thursday. We shall, if the Lord will, meet at Judge Cabell's about the 6th prox. There has been a great religous excitement here; about 105 converts of different sects. Twenty of these have joined the Presbyterians. The feeling extends on every side to neighbouring congregations. The new measures are rife, but connected with old doctrine, except in the case of the Methodists.

I have met with B. W. Leigh, W. C. Rives, Alexander Rives, Governor Barbour, and a few more of that class. I heard Rives in Albemarle. He spoke three hours, and was very eloquent. The Harrison cause is triumphant here. It is supported with a high and dignified zeal, which I like better than the Tippecanoe fury of our canaille in the cities. B. W. Leigh is an honest statesman. I heard him pronounce a most cordial, discriminating, and copious eulogy on the people of Massachusetts. The most painful thing, in visiting this old slave-holding country, is to see, after fifteen years' acquaintance, none of those municipal and domestic improvements which strike one in the north. The University is more of a place than I thought. Their professors do more, especially in the way of lecture, than any I know. Bonnycastle is a wonderful man for genius and learning. Tucker is a man of elegant *English* gentlemanhood; just like Walsh in the cast of his mind, and his talk. Each professor is bound, under penalty, to deliver 132 lectures in the year. Library, 17,000 volumes. Annual appropriation from State $15,000. After as good counsel as I can get, I am under the necessity of declining the invitation of the Sunday School Union.

PRINCETON, *November* 18, 1840.

We all got home well, and found our house swept and garnished, and fires made, but no servants. We are little better off now, in the last particular. Mr. Crane went to drive a cow out of his yard, and fell down dead. I am anxious to make out a statement, with reference to all our public charities, boards, &c., in answer to these questions: 1. What is the amount of receipts, yearly? 2. What part of this goes for *expenses?* i. e. is not laid out on the direct object. 3. What part of this sum goes to *Agents*, as salary or compensation? You have access to more reports than I, and if you could amuse yourself on a rainy day, by a few figures, you would please me. We have matriculated 63 new students, being more than we have ever received, so far as I know, at so early a day. The Seminary has admitted 34, also a large number. Addison is this year lecturing on the whole of the passages quoted from the Old Testament in the New. I learn that —— and others came forth strongly against the A. S. S. Union, and some of them even against the Bible Society, at the Synodical meeting at Wilkesbarre. I learn also that very large minorities in the two westernmost synods of New York refuse to join the New School Assembly. Perfectionism and Oberlinism are making stealthy but wide advances in that great country. I find all my binding O. K. This symbol may be variously rendered, viz., " O qu'est!" or, " Au quai." Prof. —— says the English laugh very much at the American and Walkerian pronunciation of *buoy;* and that no Englishman ever gives it any sound but that of *boy,* as the sailors do. I hear a sleigh-bell, while I write, after dark; the mercury has been below 32° all day. One of our students, Frederick William Mark, died during the vacation at New York. He was a Bavarian Jew.

PRINCETON, *November* 24, 1840.

The death of Mr. Davis at the Virginia University is a horrible comment on the Southern, I may almost say American, practice of using deadly weapons.[1] I parted with Davis at the junction of the two railways, (he accompanied us from Richmond,) on the Wednesday before the Friday on which he was shot. He was, I have every reason to think, a truly pious man, of the Episcopal church. As a professor he was one of their best—a black-letter lawyer of great reading, and a good lecturer. I think he married a grand-niece of Jefferson's.

PRINCETON, *December* 1, 1840.

I guess that will be versification enough for one sheet.[2] Mr. John Wray of the Seminary is to call some day this week for a coat for me. Any message, cartel, paper, or what not, might by said Wray be privily inserted into pocket of said coat, and then will be conveyed to me, even though Mr. Wray meant only to take raiment. Tell Tom that Henry had a dead owl yesterday, and started a live hare (rabbit) in the garden to-day. The severe cold drives animals near to their natural enemies. My brother Sam is hard at work in Orange co. Prof. Henry gets all his winter butter at 16 cts. the pound, which is a clever thing in him. Numbers of the " air-tight stoves" coming into use here,

---

[1] John A. G. Davis, Professor of Law, was shot by a student, as the Professor was approaching him for the purpose of detecting him in disorderly conduct.

[2] " A Christian Lyric," and " Lord, hear the Seaman's Cry," for the Sunday School Journal.

(not I,) Dr. R., Dr. H., Prof. H., Prof. D., Dr. M.: wood needn't be touched for half a day together—three-fourths of a cord of wood take you through winter. Introductor of the same, Dr. John N. Campbell, of Albany. I consider Longfellow's "Village Blacksmith" the best American fugitive poem I ever read, and if I had a daughter of competency to get any thing by heart, I would make her rehearse it to me while shaving, (*i. e.* while I was shaving.) I have a Scotch boy named Kenneth MacKenzie, which means Kenneth the son of Kenzie; but he is the son of Allan McKenzie, who gardens for me. When I was in Buckingham, Va., I saw a stuffed pine snake, more than seven feet long, and as thick at the thickest as my leg. It had been killed on the estate where I saw it: on the same place I saw a rattlesnake, which was showed to me by the lady who had killed it. I saw a good many gold mines, but most of them are "being" given up. The gold occurs in hard quartz, and the thing is to get it out. The grinding is a terrible process, and no flux has been found yet. A poor Jew named Levon lectured (!) here Sunday evening [oh! oh!] a layman—highly recommended by —— &c., &c. Pray, if Leeser is in town, decoy him off till said Levon has exhibited. I gave him a coin, which twenty Christians within half a mile deserve as much, and need more. Hurrah for beggars! Vive la begatelle!

Dec. 2, 1840.—I left off at the bottom of page 6, late last night, for I can't do night-work; notwithstanding the excellent rule of Miss Taylor, "Let each day's work be done *by night.*" V. Original Hymns for Sunday Schools. I have never seen any decent hymns for children, but Watts's. I have heard say that —— was desirous to enter on regular pastoral duty, and that he would entertain kindly any vocation from Philadelphia; whether in the place of such clergy as are pumped dry, or to found a new church by abstracting the best elders and Diveses from two or three churches. Part of this, it now occurs to me, I did not *hear*, but I as good as heard it—in a Masonic sense I might swear I heard it. As there is the greatest anxiety everywhere to know who nominated Harrison first, &c., &c., I beg you to bear in mind, that I claim the honour of naming Chang and Eng, Esqs., of Siam, the one for President, the other for Vice President. Their claims are manifest, &c., &c. When next you pass Frederick Brown's druggery, please ask how they sell pyroligneous acid, such as is used for meat. I mean to prepare my winter's bacon with it, at the suggestion of the Professors at the Va. University, who have the best bacon I ever ate, without the ordinary plague and delay of smoking. As to "boughten" hams, to use a Jersey phrase, I would not put a morsel in my head, save from necessity.

PRINCETON, *December* 8, 1840.

Just thus far had I got in writing, when Dick brought your letter of the 6th. Allow me to open it. . . . I thank you for your care about the Kisterbock [stove] : the word has now become a noun-common. Our country is covered with snow, which will keep me for some time from the basin. A sleigh just called for me to call on Mrs. ——. There is something in bridal-dress which always reminds me of a corpse: white *silk* is a very ghastly thing. The December No. of the Missionary Herald is very interesting, especially in that part which concerns the Nestorian mission. But why should these Yankees be so rank to introduce extempore prayer among the poor Nestorians, when they acknowledge that their liturgy is sound enough? I have been reading some more of Luther's, and the Elector of Saxony's letters, &c., about the time of the Diet at Ratisbon, 1540, and the more I read, the more am I filled with unfeigned admiration and love for those two heroic men. They are like the strong characters of the Bible—great lights—great shades—but gigantic mind and heart—accomplishing a thousandfold more for Christ in one lifetime than hundreds of us correct, cautious, temperate creatures.[1] There is something very chaste and

[1] It may not be an inappropriate note upon this sentiment to insert the following lines written by Mr. Alexander near this time :

The power of grace has tempered into one
The strongest contraries beneath the sun ;
Nor is there aught of work divine more great
Than the new creature in its altered state ;
When by heaven's pencil on the soul are traced
The self-same lines by which the Lord is graced.
If all were softness, where were Christian might ?
If all affection, where the reason's light ?
If bold contention for the truth were all,
How could the spirit into meekness fall ?
While trust and penitence together move,
Zeal dwells with quiet, action blends with love ;
Nor contemplation though foretasting bliss,
In viewing that world fails to work in this.
The mingling opposites, like rainbow hues,
Blend in one beam, and all discordance lose.
'Tis God's own work, and every several grace,
Like gems in Aaron's breastplate, hath its place ;
Each unto each reflects a lustrous hue,
Unlike yet joined, well-known yet ever new.
Each priceless when alone, but when thus set,
With mutual radiance fairer, costlier yet ;
And all combining in a concord just,
To show divinity set forth in dust ;
A thousand charms in one redeemed face,
All to the praise of glory and of grace.
Lord spread such harmony within this breast,
And draw thy lines till all be there exprest.

charming in the cold brilliancy of these snowy moonlight nights. Venus had a brilliancy greater than I remember. This morning I observed a hawk of the largest kind making circles over our lot, as if stress of weather had tamed him.

If "Lame John" be well received by the gracious Public, I will probably follow it up with a story of which the hero will be the lad Mark Lee [a character in "Lame John"] elevated to a youthful country school-master. It will give occasion to show ways of usefulness in that capacity, and especially to convey many scriptural and other proper lessons to school-boys. The thought occurred to me while writing the chapter about the school. I have several bits of rhyme for your paper, but I refrain from troubling you with a commodity of which there is a glut in the market.

The last chapter of "Ten-Thousand-a-Year," about the Rev. Morphine Velvet, is capital. I wish it might be marked, and inwardly digested by all the clergy who are gaped after by the self-supposed aristocracy. Warren, if it is he, is certainly a very powerful writer. Dr. Nettleton took tea with us, and talked in his usual strong but somewhat tedious manner. Mr. Suydam, of New Brunswick, has been missing for some days. [He had been murdered.] I learn he was President of the Bank, and a member of the Dutch church, and of unblemished reputation. He disappeared on Thanksgiving Day, Dec. 3, left his house saying he was going to the bank, and would be back to accompany his wife to church—did not even take his overcoat. The canal has been dragged without success; and his family have not the slightest clew. I doubt not the "root of all evil" is somehow or other the root of this. You are Dutch enough, I suppose, to know the pronunciation of this common name—Sid-dám. The true Dutch pronunciation is Soī-dám. Prof. H. says the statistics of health show that the use of coal, or heated air from furnaces, is very deleterious; that the gases which sometimes escape are noxious, especially some which come off last, and without smell. I can't but think of poor "Accum," who found every table strewed with "culinary poisons." We cannot make ourselves immortal; and it would be well if we could look more at what is beyond. Capt. David Hunter and wife are here—he is a Princetonian—mentioned in Murray's (the Englishman's) travels. His wife—a fine woman—is noted for having, in the Far West, accompanied her husband 700 miles on horseback. They now live at Chicago. Present me truly to your wife and young ones, and to your mother and family, and am, yours, &c., J. W. A.

PRINCETON, *December* 16, 1840.

I don't think I can do any longer without a *scrap-book:* so many things do I lose which I have cut from the papers; valuable authorities, &c. Will you look me out one? I hope there is nothing poisonous about the proofs you sent me of ———, they have a scent that is pharmaceutical in a high degree. Please send me "The Practical Spelling Book, with Reading Lessons," by Gallaudet and Hooker, published at Hartford. No news yet of the Kisterbock, at the basin; but they are horribly neglectful there, as all country officials are about every thing. Comfort yourself, among some crosses, that when you want any thing got, or any thing done, you can have it in less than three weeks. A joiner has been a month making me a small box, and a shoemaker two weeks making a pair of shoes. I regard myself as well used [as to his publications] from beginning to end, except by the engraver. Qu. Did he ever see a real tree? do walk him out of that attic some Saturday afternoon as far as the State House yard: show him the trunk of a tree, and give him a lesson. More and more do I trace disease, especially of the young, headaches, &c., to *bad ventilation.* Air may be very bad even if it don't stink. Mr. H—— has had the most astonishing relief from nausea, vertigo, &c., since he opened all the sashes of his lecture room at hours when the class is out. Inquire about this at schools. We take great care about a little wet feet, yet we drink air that is the excrement of hundreds of foul lungs. I don't file —— [a periodical] though I should like to rasp him. I'll send one or two. I know of five or six men who are silently wearing out life in most devoted labour among the slaves. Slavery must and will end; I hope peaceably; but, anyhow, we ought to save the souls of this generation. There are 1,700 black Baptist communicants in Richmond. Of these as many are elect souls, I believe, as of any 1,700 of white Baptists, taken at random. Two infants (one a brother of a boy that lives with us) have been badly scalded by pulling, the one a tea-pot, the other a coffee-pot, over them. The former one has entirely lost its eyes: a singular coincidence in the same place and week. Nothing but a special Divine guardianship keeps our little ones from daily dangers.

PRINCETON, *December* 22, 1840.

Have you seen "Christian Ballads?" (!) Such is the produce of a ritual religion. There is indeed (though much poetry) no trace of religion, except the religion of a babe or a bell-ringer, a sceneshifter or a verger. I counted more than fifty several places about "bells," "chimes," and the like: *e. g.:*

> "The sun is up betimes,
>   And the dappled East is blushing,
>   And the bonny matin chimes,
>   They are gushing—Christians—gushing."
>
> P. 66.

He is surplice-smitten. It is on every few pages. Though he affects old English, he is ignorant that *enow* is the old plural of *enough*. In all my reading I never met with so sickening a comment on a system. Give me the roughest old Scotch Irish seceder that ever croaked Rouse's psalms, rather than such foppish, puling, mawkish, water-gruel, ascetic church-dandies.

These reverses of the British in Scinde and Beloochistan were very distinctly predicted in the last Blackwood before the news came.

"Fencing the tables" is carried, in my opinion, to an unscriptural height. I am also persuaded that our church is running into a great error, in disallowing the membership of baptized persons who are not communicants. Our book, and the practice of all the Reformed Churches, (New England excepted,) is plain enough.

O how much more is the presumption in favour of Catholic Christianity than of those who cry with every breath "the temple of the Lord, the temple of the Lord are *we*," whether Papists, Oxonians, Baptists, or Separatists! How much more exercise of Christian tempers with the former than the latter! I can get along with a Quaker, but not with a bigot.

PRINCETON, *January* 1, 1841.

A Methodist preacher called on my father on Christmas, and informed him that he was unconverted, exhorted him, &c. If you had been much among the Baptist Antinomians of Virginia, you would have been less amazed at the case of the woman and son.[1] I used to ride, every week, by the house of a desperate drunkard, often in almost death-throes from this, yet always in a state of assurance. Such men have come down among us by thousands from the Antinomians of the commonwealth: hear Baxter, Works, v. 23, p. 39:

"I labour with my utmost skill, to convince common drunk-

---

[1] His correspondent had been greatly moved at the anxiety evinced by a mother for her dying son, whom she was exhorting and entreating in the most pathetic manner to give her some hope of his being in peace, reminding him that she had faithfully instructed him in the Scriptures all his life. The next day he found the son in his dying agonies, and the mother intoxicated, and discovered that it was the habitual vice of both.

ards, swearers, worldlings, &c., of their misery, and I cannot do it for my life; and this false faith is the main reason. They tell me, I know I am a sinner, and so are you, and all, as well as I. But if any man sin 'we have an Advocate with the Father, Jesus Christ the righteous;' I put my whole trust in him, and cast my salvation on him; for ' He that believeth on him, shall not perish, but have everlasting life.' If I tell them of the nature of true faith, and the necessity of obedience, they answer me that they know their own hearts better than I, and are sure they do really rest on Christ, and trust him with their souls. And for obedience, they will mend as well as they can, and as God will give them grace; and, in the mean time, they will not boast as the Pharisee, but cry 'Lord be merciful to me a sinner.'"

It appears from "Ten-Thousand-a-Year," (perhaps as good authority touching neckcloths (hemp apart) as Lang,) that "haberdashers' shopboys" at Tagrag's wore *white neckcloths*. Lang is logical in stickling for all three—gown, hat, and white cravat; no doubt, in his heart, he missed that "holy tone" of which he is such a master, and which he will propagate among his "transported" hearers in sæcula. I have been filing my letters for 1840, and find at least half a dozen of yours without date; just think what confusion this will produce when your "Remains" are published. The earliest letter of yours which I have *in retentis* is Sept. 25, 1822. Mr. Connell of the Seminary is spending New Year's Day in town, and may be used as a courier.[1] I mourn that —— should have spoken so unadvisedly with his lips; sorry should I be to utter such a dictum. It would have come well from a raving Jacobin in Robespierrian days. Is France better for the going up of atheism, and the going down of papism? Calvin says (bene) on Coloss. i. that the way to make all other things vanish, is to keep Christ in full view; and that the way to drive out error, is to proclaim Christ.

January 19, 1841.

I have long been of the opinion that our ideas about geography are often twisted for life, in consequence of our learning from maps, in the first instance, instead of globes. Be kind enough, in your walks, to cheapen a pair of globes for me. Read Nichols' Architecture of the heavens, by all means. It has been mangled by Dick, in his "Celestial Scenery;" who is a

---

[1] The Rev. J. Martin Connell. This estimable man, whom the editor remembers as a Sunday-school pupil of his in Philadelphia, died from the effects of injuries received in the dreadful collision of railway cars near Burlington, N. J., in August, 1855.

mere bookmaker; and the New York editor and publisher has disgraced himself and the country by his notes and glossary. He talks about the "elder Sir John Herschell," meaning Sir William; and says of Tycho Brahe, "He first asserted the principle that the earth remains fixed, and that the sun moves around it, *which was disproved by Copernicus*," (p. 145.) N. B. Copernicus died 1543, and Brahe was born 1546. This is a mere sample. I have a religious attachment to the books I read when a child. You once got me (at Judge Peters's sale) the Christian Magazine; can you do the like for me in regard to the "World Displayed," 8 vols. 8vo; it is a book of travels and voyages. The 3d will be remembered as the "cold Sunday." I had a fair trial of it, as I went in an open sleigh, facing the wind, to attend the funeral of an insane girl, three miles off, on the top of Rocky Hill. I have seldom known such a change of temperature. On Monday, 4th, my thermometer was at $-1°$; on the 7th at $+54°$. Bethune is very severe on our country colleges in his Philomathean address. The evils he speaks of (though exaggerated by him) are real; so would be the evils of sending country youth to town; the effects of which are beautifully set forth in the case of the medical students. What will the French do, now that they have interred old Bonaparte's bony parts? I am making some little researches, from year to year, in the Anglo-Saxon: name any books you see in that line. The National Intelligencer is now one of our best papers. Walsh has a piece in almost every number, and I like him as much as ever. I never see any thing rancorous or unfair in the Intelligencer. Is it not probable that Great Britain will get possession of all the West African coast? they seem to be looking that way; and it would no doubt hasten the civilization of the world.

———, who has been seven times to Canton, and stayed eight years the last visit, said to me on Saturday, that he had no doubt the British would meet exactly the same reception at every place all the way to Pekin, as at Chu-san. He tells me Gutzlaff has been in mere secular employments for some time past. I am really afraid the Amistad blackies will be sent to Cuba: if so, I don't believe the British will let them be hanged; and the Spanish are pretty much under Palmerston's palm just now. I see ——— re-iterates ———'s speech about the Catholics, [that the case of an infidel is better than that of a Papist.] Put the case thus: I am to choose between

1	&	2
A man who *worships* Christ, (whatever else he may do, or not do.)		A man who *blasphemes* Christ, (whatever else he may do, or not do.)

For observe, both say a "Deist of the school of *Voltaire*," whose watchword was "Écrasez l'Infame!" Rotteck's Universal History ought to be marked as an infidel book.

PRINCETON, *February* 12, 1841.

What bitter weather! you would say so if, like me, you had come from Cranbury this morning, in the teeth of a northwester. The mercury was at 3° this morning. I went, by appointment, to preach a Temperance sermon. In the sufferings of my children I experience a feminine distress, which makes me enter tenderly into that passage: "as a father *pitieth* his children," &c. The cold is such that I have not been drawn out this evening, even to hear Dr. Parker, and see his Chinaman. I hope his Mandarin-ship will take no offence thereanent. A copy of Mrs. Hooker's works has been sent to the "Editor" of the Princeton Review, which, though not the editor, I have appropriated, with the intention of writing something about it.[1] Mrs. Hooker was a writer after my heart, and her prose is immeasurably above that of Mrs. ———, who travels on very high stilts. The following remark of Dr. Johnson is so good that you ought to put it into your Journal. It respects the question what children should be taught first: "Sir, it is no matter what you teach them first, any more than what leg you shall put into your breeches first. Sir, you may stand disputing which is best to put in first, but in the mean time your breech is bare. Sir, while you are considering which of two things you should teach your child first, another boy has learnt them both." I have in a manner read ——— on ———. Its facts are strong; but don't you always feel a sinking of respect, when you find a treatise made up of scissors-scraps? I grow in my conviction, that in our day, when men have a thousand things to read, and won't read long at any thing, the books which reach the mass and colour its opinions, are not books of research, but books of feeling, of point, even of eccentricity; books written with a gush, currente calamo. I have a treat before me, in the Correspondence of Zuingle, which has just come over from Germany; he is one of the prime saints and martyrs in my calendar.[2] Major Downing's "there's nothin' cuts like the plaguy truth," is a good version of the French proverb: "il n'y-a que la verité qui blesse." There are no hymns, for unction, like the German. I read them liturgically. They are pure outgoings of gospel feeling. The best I

---

[1] This he did in the short notices in the April Repertory. Mrs. Hooker was the writer of the Lives of David, Elijah, Elisha, and Daniel, for the Sunday School Union.

[2] He reviewed the works in the April Repertory.

know are old Paul Gerhardt's. I never saw the works of John Huss till this week. They fill a very large folio volume. Does a mechanic who becomes literary become thereby a happier man? query, how happy might ———— now be as a farrier? Juvenal discusses the question, and says of Demosthenes:

> Dis ille adversis genitus, fatoque sinistro,
> Quem pater ardentis massæ fuligine lippus
> *A carbone, et forcipibus,* gladiosque parante
> *Incude,* et luteo Vulcano ad rhetora misit.
> Sat. x.

If you should ever want to quote the vulgar proverb, "It takes all kinds of people to make a world," you may give it in the terms of John Locke: "The world has people of all sorts." I love to hunt out a *proverb;* which Lord John Russell well describes as "One man's wit, all men's wisdom." I count it a signal exemption, for which to be thankful, that, after years of throat-affection, I have not had any symptom this winter, even for a moment. I know not whether there is any connexion, but I have, in washing, used a sponge, and made a more thorough application of the cold water to my neck and throat. We have now had [Feb. 15] five days of very severe weather, and from our bleak and exposed situation here, we suffer far more than any difference of the thermometer would indicate. I saw a traveller very snugly seated in a wagon like a house, drawn by one horse, and a smoking stove-pipe sticking out above. I find by reading Zuingle's letters, that he was a polished scholar, as much so as Erasmus or Melancthon, intimately acquainted with all the ancient classics, holding correspondence in Greek, and employing a latinity which is as nervous and elegant as that of Calvin. He had a heroic courage, and remarkable prudence. The edition I am reading gives the letters *to* as well as *from* him, so that I am quite transported to Reformation times.[1] This is what I like. No novel can awaken an interest like these realities. We now have the correspondence of Melancthon, (to and from,) Luther, Calvin, Erasmus, and Zuingle, whose name is spelt a dozen ways.

PRINCETON, *March* 5, 1841.[2]

I see by the Presbyterian, that Dr. Doane has made an assault on Bishop Boardman. Methinks the Doctor's blank verse

---

[1] Mr. Alexander reviewed D'Aubigné's Reformation in the Repertory, January, 1842; and McCrie's Reformation in Spain, July, 1850.

[2] About this time Mr. Alexander received a unanimous election to the Presidency of Lafayette College, Easton, Pennsylvania. which he declined.

will not run well in controversy. The article in the London Quarterly on American orators is worth reading. What he says about convicts is more true than some folks would like to be remembered. I happen to know three or four high families who are so descended, and a number more who sprang from "redemptioners." It was customary in Virginia for white men to indenture themselves to the captain, for four years. My grandfather used to go to Baltimore and buy such. Two of my father's early schoolmasters were well educated Englishmen of this class. The Hebrew of Exodus ii. 6, is more expressive than the English: "behold a weeping child." Nordheimer's 2d volume [Hebrew Grammar] is beautiful, especially the Hebrew, which is exquisite. He has been here; told me every page of copy was written four times, and every signature read ten times, the first proof occupying him twelve hours, as he collated every reference in the proof. Gesenius has spoken well of it. I have seen the beautiful species of currency which your banks are emitting. I am not versed in bankology, but am inclined to think the whole system akin to συινδλινγ.[1] We know as little how the matters are conducted, as in the old lottery systems. I wish they would make Walsh minister to France, Clay to England, and ——— to Guinea. I find the following good verses in an old play of 1610:

> "Our life is but a sailing to our death
> Through the world's ocean; it makes no matter then,
> Whether we put into the world's vast sea
> Shipped in a pinnace, or an argosy."

Frost fish or smelts are now in season. They are a great delicacy, and last only a few days. They are taken, so far as I know, nowhere in these parts but on the Raritan. Being always caught as they ascend the river, on its opening, they are full of roe. We buy them at 18 cents the quart. I feel less respect for Milner [Church History] than I did, since I have examined the truth of what he says about Zuingle, whom he disparages very unjustly in comparing him with Luther. How much we lose in reading the Bible, by not having that fresh feeling of novelty and interest which they had in the apostolic age, and even at the reformation; we come to the book already acquainted with its contents, in its most important parts.[2] Perhaps the best way

---

[1] The allusion is probably to a device resorted to by some banks to evade the penalty of not redeeming their *notes* with coin, by issuing their currency in the form of *checks*.

[2] In one of his posthumous "Sacramental Discourses" he says: "Sometimes we are ready to wish it were possible to travel backward on our line

to gain something of this vividness is to read large portions without any human comment, and in as complete forgetfulness as we can attain of our own age. Latterly I have more frequently thought than I used to do, that we make too little of the Holy Spirit's agency with the Scriptures as indispensable, perpetual, immediate. Do we not in fact read the Bible as if our unaided powers would secure us from error? Few texts have been oftener in my mind than 1 John ii. 26, 27; especially in reference to the diversity of opinions which men profess to derive from the Bible. The "Word *and* the Spirit" conveys the true doctrine.

Harrison is now President, so I suppose the hens will lay ready-roasted eggs, and money drop out of the clouds. The speeches in parliament, 1641, which I have been reading, are much more pious than any I have ever heard in General Assembly. Our legislature can't get a suitable man to be judge, vice Dayton resigned. If they had the magnanimity of a hen-partridge, they would at once give it to ———; but Whigs are as party-bound as other folks. I fear *pretension* is getting to be our national character. We get the Paris "Sémeur," of which the principle seems to be to exclude news; the very opposite of what I think the ideal of a religious journal. Dry reviews, continued from week to week. As room is allowed me, I hope you will permit me to take this method, however unusual, of defining my position with regard to you, by declaring, in terms of the utmost frankness, how truly I am, dear Sir, Your most obedient servant.

Princeton, *March* 12, 1841.

Vide "Gift for the Holidays," pp. 125, 126, "neither he nor Charles *were* considerate." Is it possible that I wrote this? if so, it ought to have been made grammar. I have frequently had a misgiving as if the worshipful committee altered my English; but as I write in haste, I bring no impeachments. So again, p. 70, "the girl who spoke *friendly* to him," is a form which I never use in my waking hours. At the same time, I think it quite as likely that the blunders are mine, as not. The Newark Daily advertises a series of "protracted sermons;" not such a rarity. Walsh's admissions about the Sabbath (in the former of his two communications this week, in National Intelli-

of experience, to that point in childhood when gospel grace first came to our cognizance; or else to stand in the position of some serious inquiring heathen who opens his ear and heart to the news of a redeeming God; that by either of these ways we might get rid of the dulness and indifference which our worn and jaded souls derive from long hardening of custom" gencer) are invaluable, and ought to be made prominent in every religious paper in the country; but alas! our religious editors copy only from one another. I received your paper with obituary of Dr. Rauch since I began this. The *Daub* who was his "spiritual father," was, I think, one of the worst of the modern pantheists. The main proposition of all semi-Germans, is that no matter how gross or atheistical any *philosophy* may be, it may still be held in connexion with Christianity. Let me give you a few items from Sandwich Islands, which you will not see in the [Missionary] Herald. The king is very immoral, and is a mere tool. The islands will pass before long into the hands of some foreign power. The missionaries went out Congregationalists. It is a sufficient confutation of that theory, that it cannot be set up among the heathen. They had, by resolution, in 1830, to deny the right of "government" to their new converts. In 1831, they were forced to appoint *Elders*. In 1835, they adopted our rules of discipline. In 1839, they found themselves necessitated to unite as a presbytery, having acted as one before. They are now regularly organized in four presbyteries, (not a word of this in the Herald,) none voting against, but four or five non-liquets. Exactly thus, I doubt not, Presbytery grew out of the mother-church at Jerusalem. "It is no small matter," says one, "that the missionary of the A. B. C. must surrender his right to personal liberty, his right to acquire property, and the liberty of the press." One of the leading missionaries thinks that the present method of doing the missionary work by *one* method, and through boards and committees, checks the fruitfulness of the church in methods of converting the world.

PRINCETON, *March* 24, 1841.

Robinson's trial [for murder of Suydam] is going on in Brunswick. Graham, of New York, is his principal counsel; and he is every thing that such a case could demand. Though one might expect the jury to agree in a verdict of Guilty without leaving the box, some suppose he may yet be cleared. And, further, if this should be the case, I have heard fears expressed of a Porteus mob, and summary execution. The rainbow and sunset yesterday were surpassing. The new series of the Penny Magazine is a beautiful book. I am pleased to observe in it a little spice of religion now and then, not very decided, it is true, but enough to show that they feel the necessity of deferring to the Christian opinion of the age. ——— is a better preacher than nine-tenths of those I hear. He has that "holy-tone," which, after all, carries great weight with the multitude.

You will not forget that to-morrow (25) is LADY DAY. † ⸸ †
The adjustment of the difference [in the Senate] between King
[of Alabama] and Clay [of Kentucky] is certainly a matter for
national thanksgiving. Perhaps I mentioned to you that Stacy
G. Potts, Esq., of Trenton, (an elder of the church,) and his
brother, the Rev. Wm. S. Potts, of St. Louis, are going abroad,
shortly. Their first visit is, I believe, to the Continent, and they
will be gone about eight months. Dr. Carnahan says Henry
Kollock [of Savannah] was the most eloquent and impassioned
preacher he ever heard.[1] The congregation at Norfolk, Va., is
vacant, and will be a delightful place for some one. They have
a new church, and will probably give 1,300 to 1,500 dollars.
Right on the sea, incomparable "water privileges," easy run to
Richmond and Baltimore, healthy place, good society: fish,
oysters, soft-crabs, &c., on the direct railway line to the South,
a climate resembling the remote South in winter, and much tempered by the breezes in summer. I have passed some delightful
days there. Peter Harris (African Prince) writes to my father,
ending thus,

"Your remaining friend   Peter Harris."

PRINCETON, *April* 9, 1841.

A longer period than common has passed since I wrote to
you. I have been in a state of bodily and mental uneasiness,
with the details of which I do not mean to plague you, but which
has made me somewhat unfit for letter-writing, in which I never
can engage but with an easy mind. To record troublesome
thoughts always seemed to me to increase them. Apropos of
which, Cicero seems to have had different notions of the matter,
if one may judge from his 4th book of ep. *ad Atticum;* by all
odds, the fullest revelation of humiliating, unmanly sorrow I
ever read; but exceedingly interesting and instructive. The
Tristia of Ovid come next, but that is poetry. I confess I like
Ovid far better than it is fashionable among critics to do: his
flow of versification is so easy and unrippled. Seneca is another
contraband author whom I love to read. (N. B. Here I change
one bad pen for another.) I finished my part of the semi-annual examination this morning. Our session ends next Thurssay. This day week Peter Robinson is to be hanged, nominally
in private, really in public. They might as well not hang a
man at all as hang him in secret. I have to-night been reading
a book I never saw or heard of before; the *younger* Lord Lyt-

---

[1] Dr. Carnahan's opinion is given at length in the memoir of Dr. Kollock in vol. iv. of Dr. Sprague's "Annals of the Pulpit."

telton's letters.[1] He was a great genius and profligate, a Byron of his day, an elegant epistolist; they are well worth an hour's attention, and contain first rate anecdotes about Chatham, Burke, Mansfield, Fox, &c. The death of our President [Harrison] ought to be loked upon by every one of us as a visitation of God, a great national rebuke, a lesson to ambition. How easily, by a single death, God can discomfit all the plans of a party! I am not without fears of a war with England; and, if it come, it will, as Wellington has said several times, not be a *small* war. I have been reading Bickersteth on the prophecies. Independently of his hypothesis, the spirit of the book is delightfully devout, humble, and tender. The question of the Millennium has occupied my attention a good deal for a year or two. I have abandoned my old traditionary views, without having settled on new ones. From the Scriptures alone I have been led to some *negative* results with a good degree of firmness. For example, I cannot dare apply the warnings about Christ's *coming*, to the hour of death; nor can I say one word about a millennium *before* Christ's coming. It is now more than a year since I wrote down a number of conclusions on this point, derived chiefly from Rev. xx. studied without note or comment. I conjecture that some of my old friends in Trenton may be unwise enough to vex me with solicitations to return to them; this I shall discourage in every way, if it should happen. Nothing would bring me to such a course, but a conviction, such as I have not, that I am doing wrong in keeping my present post. The natural and proper way [for a congregation in view of a new pastor] is to invite him to supply them a few Sabbaths. From this nothing should make him shrink. I am convinced, that in the sight of God, my declining to preach as a candidate has often been a sinful tribute to my own pride. We ought to be as willing to seek a place of labour for Christ, as the people to seek our services. This is my serious opinion, after having long acted on the other and the worldly plan. True, a man's reputation is a talent, and should not be jeoparded by his making himself cheap.

Our trials vary, but we all have them, and we all (Christians) profit by them. The Lord provides and will provide. Our path is wonderful, but he describes the whole line.

TRENTON, *April* 27, 1841.

We came here on Saturday, and I suppose met you in the carriage from the depot. I am sorry I could not see you, and

[1] They proved to be not genuine, but were fabricated by Alexander Combe.

am more disquieted than comforted by being here. Indeed I slept very little last night; for, altogether against my expectation or desire, certain of the people have been at me about a return to them.[1] No one (but some of the most trifling street prattlers) had breathed a word to me about their looking to me-ward; and I confess your letter made little impression on my belief, at the time I received it. I have stayed within (regretting that I happened to choose this time for my visit) and have heard nothing from any leading member of the congregation; but from what transpires from some of the lighter sort I am led to think that a considerable portion of the people are bent upon subjecting me once more to the painful decision of a question of conscience. I have great difficulty in expressing to you the exact state of my mind, because I scarcely know what it is myself. I would gladly do so if I durst. I could not come here without a great pecuniary loss, and the resumption of burdens from which my spirit is yet sore. Nevertheless, as I have never dreamed that I should ever be settled here again, and as, notwithstanding, some of the people mean to force me into a determination, I must lie still for a week or two, and "hear what God the Lord will speak." I feel in regard to it exactly as I would in regard to a call to go to China. I hope I shall be directed; nay, I believe I shall be.

TRENTON, *May* 3, 1841.

I remain here to-day, to further the plan I have, in regard to this business, which becomes more and more painful to me every moment. I have sent the following to Dr. Ewing.

"This communication respects a matter which I have not mentioned to you, but one in which I have a very painful interest. It is, I am told, intended to make out a call for me this afternoon. It is my earnest wish that this should not be done. The only reason why I do not arrest the matter by a positive refusal beforehand, is a scruple of conscience lest I should be running in the face of Providence. But the most delightful news I could have, would be that you had called ———. The longer I meditate on it, the greater seems to me the probability that I shall not feel myself competent to a pastoral charge. My presence here (altogether unconcerted) has awakened some expectation. I now wish to say with earnestness that I should be inexpressibly relieved, if the Congregation would drop all further consideration of me. I am, &c., &c."

I do not here say to Ewing all that this means. To you I

---

[1] The pastor, Dr. Yeomans, having accepted the Presidency of Lafayette College, Pennsylvania.

explain thus:—if they should fail to call ——, divide, or otherwise seem likely to go to ruin, I might after all be driven to accept a future call.[1]

My prevalent feeling is that even if they should be so rash as to call me, I shall not come. The conflict of my feelings is great, and I never was more sensible of my weakness. I came home from you in a wet, cold, and somewhat open car, and took a bad cold, with rheumatism.

I do not regard this as a confidential letter. I have said the same thing to everybody here.

TRENTON, *May* 7, 1841.

I have been detained from Philadelphia by sickness, having had another wetting since I was there, and a severe catarrh with sore throat. The first official notice I had of the congregational doings was last night, though I was sufficiently acquainted with what occurred at the meeting; what that was, as to manner and feeling, I had rather leave you to learn from others.

I felt it to be my duty to go to Princeton, for consultation. I did not talk with my colleagues. Results of advisement thus far, thus: Dr. Hodge is vehemently against my leaving Princeton. Reasons, these: 1. "You are as useful in Princeton as you would be in Trenton." 2. "I grant you ought to be a pastor, but not in Trenton," innuendo that I might be settled in Philadelphia or New York. 3. "The Trenton people cannot support you." 4. " —— would make them as good a pastor, and in some respects a better one." This is the only argument of his which weighs with me, and I assent to it, without affectation. My father says, "The pulpit is your proper place. You have health enough at present, and have no right to count on future contingencies; but the people cannot support you, and you ought not to stir a step, without explicit arrangements on this head." The *feelings* of my relations are in favour of my being in Trenton. My Princeton friends have not made a point of my health, as I expected, and this, more than any thing else, disturbs all my provisional calculations.

I wish I could tell you what I am likely to do. I shall probably decide late in next week. Alas! I am all out at sea. I try to place myself in thought before the judgment-seat, and to ask "From which of the two places would you choose to be summoned?" If I leave Princeton, I leave a great array of worldly comforts, air, verdure, house, ice-house, garden, literary circles, libraries, periodicals, leisure, and ease pecuniary; and

[1] He was unanimously re-elected pastor May 3, 1841.

assume responsibilities, care, labour, vexations, and straits. What to do I know not. If the finger of God should distinctly point either way, I should not have a moment of disappointment. If they do not give me more salary, the thing is at an end; it is an obstacle *in limine,* and precludes the necessity of vexing myself about the other considerations.

If I were put on my oath, and asked which way the balance of probability now librates, I could not answer.

Write to me freely, and (I hope the phrase is not outworn by hypocritical abuse) give me your prayers. Pray leave nothing unsaid which may do me good. I am harassed beyond expression.[1]

PRINCETON, *May* 25, 1841.

I know not that I ever enjoyed mere *weather* so much as the last three days. There is such a burst of vegetation, such a concurrence of plants and birds which are usually separate, that the green and fragrant earth seems almost paradisiacal. A sparrow has "laid her young" at our very door, and I suppose we have twenty nests on our premises. A bob-o'-lincoln sings his bravuras back of our garden from morn till night; I know no note so rich as some of his; indeed his strain, taken singly, is incomparable; but the mocking-bird has a thousand, and even the robin a good many. I am full of College-work thus far, mingled with a pleasing interspersion of *proves* as the διαβολοι always call them. I have engaged to supply Father Comfort's pulpit [the Kingston Church] for three months, not however necessarily in person. He goes to Illinois—pretty well for threescore and fifteen. I have read, since I came home, a stout slice of Chillingworth, some of Mrs. Hawkes, (excellent,) two plays of Plautus, two satires of Juvenal, one book of Wordsworth's Excursion, one book of Cicero's Letters, one book of Ovid's Tristia, a few pages of Lucretius, and about a third of Herbert's Poems; there's a task for you. I have, of course, doffed my leathern jerkin, and have begun my summer washings in the mornings, my lettuce-eatings at noon, and my star-gazing at night. I have preached once, had two head-aches, and palpitation of the heart to a remarkable degree. There is something wrong, I am sure, about my arterial system. What think you of Nagle's pictures? I am told they are exhibited. We have a full College, more admitted than last year, about 100 new ones since last commencement, in all 200+. What a series of designs Retzch might make out of the history of Joseph! It is an incomparable story.

[1] Soon after this, the offer of the call was positively declined.

PRINCETON, *June* 3, 1841.

I write with a very sore eye, therefore stenographically. You know, no doubt, that you were called unanimously, on Monday. You will, of course, go. Four or five persons were for hearing others, but they came in very heartily. I see no way for you to refuse such a call as that to Trenton; I trust it is from above.

PRINCETON, *June* 6, 1843.

I gather from your letters, that your mind is pretty much made up to accept the Trenton call, and the belief of this gives me unfeigned satisfaction. In your success there, I feel a more than ordinary interest, and I have a confidence that these hopes will not be disappointed. The call is, I am sure, a cordial one, and I think the sooner you pitch your tent among the people, the better. In a letter of ⸺⸺, there is a suggestion which I cannot convey to you better than in his own words: "Pray tell Mr. Hall, if you can, to let on steam in his preaching. He certainly can do it, to such extent at least as to remove all appearance of deficiency." I accord in this, and it is the only point respecting which I have heard any misgiving expressed; and I would not mention it if I were not assured that it is perfectly within your power to remove the difficulty at once. You utter voice enough, I am persuaded, but there is a want of sharpness and percussion in your utterance, which causes the stream of words to flow indolently and somewhat indistinctly, and this is seriously the case in the cadence of every period. Perhaps every thing will be accomplished, if you give yourself up with a greater *abandon* in delivery; as there is no possibility of your laying yourself open to the charge of being theatrical, affected, or extravagant. The only other point is one in which you cannot be too much interested. The Trenton people lack frequent pastoral visits. They need this, and they look for it. I have told them that in my opinion you would not be backward in this class of duties; and my private judgment is, that you have advantages in this particular. Such is the character of the people, that they would be satisfied with inferior pulpit performances, if these were accompanied with a free and easy social intercourse.

I think our Presbytery meets in August at Middletown-Point; but if you are ready, I should advise you to cause the elders to have a meeting called *pro re nata*. The sooner the thing is over, the easier you will feel.

I told Mr. Stryker that I would see them supplied till you began to preach. You may relieve me very much therefore, by assuming this office as speedy as possible; and I hope, in your next, you will say something on this point, as I am engaged to supply Mr. Comfort's church for three months, besides a sermon every Lord's-day to my blacks.

PRINCETON, *June* 14, 1841.

Addison told me you meant to be in Trenton yesterday, and as I had made no engagement to supply except till you should come, and none whatever for yesterday in particular, I felt myself at ease; till Dr. Miller called on me and told me Mr. Stryker wished me to know that they relied on me. I therefore sent down Mr. Dixon. I consider all the care of supply, henceforward, as devolved off me and on you. I am glad you are coming, and coming at once. It is right, seemly, and promising good. As to your elocution, *Question* 1. "Is it to throw my arms about more?" *Answer.* No. *Question* 2. "To vary my tones?" *Answer.* No. Your arms and tones are well enough. It is to make yourself fully heard, without an effort on the part of the hearer. Though familiar with your voice, it was with the greatest difficulty that your last words of sentences were heard by me. The "indolence" I mean is consistent with too great rapidity, being a want of distinctness in the syllabication, rather than a too small volume of voice. After all, the only thing which you ought to carry on your mind when you go to the pulpit is to speak as loudly and distinctly as you possibly can.

The last accounts from Dr. [John] Breckinridge were rather unfavourable again.[1] I saw sitting together, at College-prayers, the sons of three men very generally known in America, Eli Whitney, Francis Blair, and N. Biddle. I shall have less of Philadelphia news, now that you are about to be a Trentonian, unless you get a free-ticket on the railroad, and go to the city every week. My hopes about strawberries are very much disappointed; we have had but two messes.

With best regards for ―――― and the youth, I am, was, have been, shall be, may or can be, might, could, would, or should be, shall or will have been, &c.

PRINCETON, *July* 6, 1841.

Your note-ling of yesterday informed me of your settlement in your new habitation. I hope you will find it, and all your being and doing in it, useful and happy. A son of Bishop Hobart and three classmates (of the New York Seminary) are

---

[1] Dr. Breckinridge died August 4, 1841.

going to Wisconsin to found a mission on the primitive plan—take a central point, live as cænobites, radiate a hundred miles each way, found a school, which is to be a College, which is to be a Theological Seminary.

We had a quiet Independence-day. The storm at night both shamed and extinguished the students' fireworks. My series of domiciliary pupils has been—1, W. C. Carrington; 2, Samuel D. Alexander; 3, Henry M. Alexander; 4, S. Harrison Howell; 5, Samuel M. Breckinridge; 6, R. F. Stockton. More persons in this neighbourhood seem to be seriously inquiring than usual; I mean within a few miles. A son of the Rev. Howard Malcom, in the Seminary, has been very active. N. B. The hack or stage-coach which comes from Trenton hither every evening is a delightful conveyance at this season. The sunset, the verdure, the tout-ensemble, are charming. Pusey comes out, in defence of Newman's No. 90, in a vol. of pp. 217.

PRINCETON, *July* 10, 1841.

I have Stephens [Central America] in hand. My interest in the musty ruins is nothing to what I feel in the country and people. The book is as interesting as a tragedy or an epic. But for simplicity and graphic-ness of description, I have had nothing since Crusoe, equal to Dana's "Two Years before the Mast." I wish our people would read such books in place of novels. Many females whom I know, almost confine their reading to the latter, taking whatever comes. Give them a side-blow at this in Trenton. I have No. 90; quibble on quibble.

Give our love to ———, and tell her we assuredly expect her to come up and pay a farthing in the pound of the visits I have been making her for something less than 40 years.

PRINCETON, *August* 19, 1841.

We had a great deal of wine-bibbing and some brawling among our students on the day of the Seniors' dismissal. I am now rapidly verging towards T-totality.

Dr. ——— professes himself hugely delighted with the review of ———. For myself, while I regard it as a true and just unmasking of a charlatan, I do not think the public well enough acquainted with the facts respecting that bad man to make them appreciate the critique. I shall not go to Grande Ligne with Kirk, being detained by various things. Father Comfort has returned. There are 40—60 persons awakened in his church. Dr. Rice is holding a four-nights-meeting in Queenston. We have got a cook! [put the foregoing in small caps.] How do you feel without the editorial kettle tied to your tail?

As you sometimes go to the city, and I never, volens,—I want you to get me a pen (I mean a dozen of pens) of a kind which I once got at your instance. They were very large in the barrel, indeed much the largest metal-pens I have seen, and the tube of the quill was complete. I think they were Gillott's; though he makes a smaller sort. Alward, our Seminary and College alumnus, is dead of the African fever—a dreadful blow after the loss of David White. Chaplain Grier has brought from Attica a pot of honey of Hymettus, as a present to my mother. It is thought to taste of roses. Bennett [N. Y. Herald] has done us a service, by making fun of a late ball here, so that at a later one the females were all afraid to go. Old Mr. ———'s description of life at a watering-place is: "to eat in a crowd, and sleep in a closet." ——— thinks of preaching altogether expoundingly; he has long done so, all but the morning-sermon. Tholuck is married again, after long viduity. Baird passed through yesterday from Washington. He says the Cabinet will abide, and that a Bank of Exchanges will pass. I should like that. I am no Bank-man.

Unless you could see the Rev. Mr. ———, the following anecdote will be lost on you. He is 6+ feet high, red hair and every thing, and bows to the earth; in other things a Dominie Samson. Mr. S., an eminent lawyer of Baltimore, told me to-day that he once fell in with ———, whom he had known in Princeton; S. invited him to dinner, and set before him some of the choicest wine the country could furnish. ——— drank a glass, and then asked with indescribable naïveté: "Is it *domestic*, sir?" A decided Calvinistic woman in this town lives in the house of a Methodist. She lately said of him, "He is as kind to me as a son, but I hate him, he is such an Arminian." My father preached five times last week, and already four times this week.

PRINCETON, *Aug.* 30, 1841.

I have had a good deal of preaching labour lately, as all around us, in the country, there is a state of great awakening. In Mr. Comfort's congregation, I dare say, there are seventy or eighty inquirers, and perhaps thirty who have believed. It is thus far remarkably free from any the least new doctrine, new measures, noise, enthusiasm, and opposition. In Mapleton, a neighbourhood between us and Kingston, on the Canal, it is believed that every person above ten years of age, is seriously concerned. Here the awakening commenced; and in some degree through the labours of a half-witted bound boy, who would not rest till he got meetings established in a certain schoolhouse. In the Rocky Hill district north of this, and at Centreville north-west of us, each about four miles off, there is a like appearance of good. In the former place, I knew of four blind persons in one house converted. The seriousness is extending itself into the Blawenburg Dutch Church, (Mr. Talmage's.) Some of the very worst and most hopeless men in our country-side have been brought to Christ. I spent Thursday night at ——, where five children (all he has) are seemingly renewed. In Princeton-proper, I know of but three or four persons inquiring; but I think more of the communicants are stirred up, than I have observed for ten years. Dr. Rice has been much aided by the Rev. Samuel J. Cassels, of Georgia, some years pastor at Macon, who has come to the North to make up some deficiencies in his theological education.[1] Though an ugly, little, swarthy man, he is one of the very best preachers I ever heard, both for instruction and pathos. I wish you may find him out. The addition to the Seminary is not as great as last year, perhaps in consequence of the change of time in opening the year; this, it is hoped, will be temporary. It was a happy providence, that Dr. Robinson's book [on Palestine] should embody the labours of four such men as Eli Smith, Robinson, Ritter, and Catherwood. Dr. Green is still here. You may still look out for a Presidentship, as the Marshall throne is not filled. This is said by the "oldest inhabitant" to have been the rainiest August that ever was.

PRINCETON, *September* 10, 1841.

You have, no doubt, heard of the awakening in Bucks Co., near you. There are some new cases of awakening, occurring slowly, in our congregation. Mr. Cassels, a truly Christian man, leaves us on Monday for Norfolk.

Poor [Rev. Samuel G.] Winchester's death is a sad blow, and great warning. He was found stiff and cold in bed, though he had been sick some time before. Young Sawyer left us yesterday, to take Alward's place in Africa. C. C. Jones, of S. C., preaches to the slaves three times on Sunday, and every evening in the week. Yet this is the man whom the young Andoverians would not let preach in their chapel. Sit anima mea cum Jonesio!

PRINCETON, *September* 18, 1841.

Why do ministers regard it as necessary to sit in the pulpit, when no service falls to them? It is a poor seat; the superero gatory head distracts the audience; and the presence of a man

---

[1] Mr. Cassels died 1853–'4.

behind is no help to him that preaches. Mr. Cassels has left us for Norfolk, carrying with him great respect and affection. I discern in him no newschoolism, no new ways of doing things to make people stare and ask why, no harshness or consciousness, and no vanity. He preached at the rate of seven sermons a week all the time he was here. About twenty persons here, or more, profess to be inquirers. Two or three cases of awakening in College. Scott, of Stockholm, has been here; a pleasant, unaffected, good, sensible man, and as mellifluous a Wesleyan as ever I listened to. His statements about the Swedish Churches were very startling, and I would record some of them, but that I have a notion that you have met with him. There is some encouragement among my blacks. I am very dubious about inquiry-meetings, and my doubts are always greatest while they are going on. If admitted, I am clear that no one but the pastor should ever talk with the inquirer; especially, that ignorant or foolish helpers should not bring their trowels and daub. The natural, the scriptural, and the safe way, is for the pastor to see them at his house or theirs. But then this great means of excitement must be foregone, and this is really the reason why ministers cling to it. As it regards instruction, the worst place in the world for it, is a crowded room, where there is buz-buz-buz. I am (perhaps culpably) lukewarm about Tyler, Ewing & Co. I did not vote for Tip or Ty. I thought and think Clay our greatest statesman. Yet I have no zeal for the all-absorbing monetary question. With us Money is Politics. The fear of War with England much more occupies me, as a man and as a Christian. A man may dispute whether he will carry his money in a purse or a pocket-book, while an enemy is levelling a musket at his heart; and if he cocks his hat and brags, *more Kentuckico*, the case is not bettered. What think you of a weekly lecture on the *Life of Christ*, without texts, but taking up the history, harmonizing it, and applying?[1] The weekly converse of the preacher's own soul with such an object would be worth something. Sixteen Southern Presbyterian ministers have died in thirteen months. Some of these are very important, Baxter, Breckinridge, Winchester, Phelps, Cunningham, and Sloss. I am seriously convinced that more harm is done by newspaper-reading, than by novel-reading. I know men who spend 2—6 hours daily over newspapers. There is no other production so heterogeneous and incoherent; there is none in

---

[1] He had begun such a course, and given sixteen lectures, at the close of his ministry in Duane street, (October 31, 1848, to May 29, 1849.) He began it anew with the Fifth Avenue congregation January 27, 1852, and continued it at the Tuesday meetings until February 27, 1855.

which we read so much that is not even interesting. Probably each of us spends a hundred hours of morning-time per annum, on 1, Repeated matter; 2, Accidents; 3, Crimes; 4, Idle narrative; 5, Unintelligible or useless statements; 6, Error and Falsehood; 7, Advertisements and proper names. What better recipe for making a weak mind addle? We take the tone of our company. Suppose a man's bosom-friend to talk an hour a day, exactly like his newspaper. I am told Dr. Wilson used to read only a small weekly sheet; and I have heard that Mr. Wirt, during his most active forensic labours, spent three years without reading a newspaper. But this is fine talk from one Ex-editor to another.

PRINCETON, *September* 29, 1841.

I the rather missed you [at Commencement] because of the visit of "General J. [Josiah] Harlan, Aide-de-Camp of Dost Mahomed, Ameer of Cabool;" certes the most distingué of our numerous visiters. He spoke kindly of you, and expected to meet you. He is a noble, gentlemanly, and soldierly man in his port, and endlessly rich in sorts of knowledge which are perfectly new to us. —— has a high opinion of him, and says the Russian government would do any thing to get him on their side against the Anglo-Indian operations. His moustache, gold-spurs, and signet-ring 2,000 years old, are great distinctions. I should very much prize further communication with him. You doubtless remember Joseph Wolff's account of him in his "Researches," p. 180, Phil. 1837.[1] Peter McCall [of Philadelphia] delivered a polished oration yesterday. Our services to-day were as long and exhausting as usual. I lament their probable influence on the minds of our young men, among whom there has been a spirit of religious inquiry. Fifteen or more have been recently awakened, almost all of whom are among our best scholars; I trust several of these are converted. But they all go to their homes at this time. Three Scotch clergymen, Johnston, Ferriar, and Allison, have arrived in New York, men of polish, and good preachers, intending to settle among us. The cause of their emigration is painful, viz., the ruin of their congregations by the

---

[1] From Mr. Wolff's book I collect the following sketch of my old friend, now living on his farm in Pennsylvania. Mr. Wolff met Harlan at Goozerat in June, 1832, and describes him as then "the Governor of the place and province." He was born of a Quaker family in Philadelphia, 1799: engaged at first in Commercial business; then became surgeon in the Government hospital in Calcutta; resigned the British service and entered that of the native prince of Cabool. He had returned to the United States not long before the Commencement above referred to, after an absence of nearly twenty years. In 1842 Mr. Harlan published "A Memoir of India and Avghanistaun."

inroads of Chartism. They are all, however, of the secession. Adams, whom Colt murdered, [in New York,] was the printer of our Missionary Chronicle, and a pious man. If you are fond of sweet-potatoes in winter, let me recommend to you to put up a few bushels in sand. The sand should be perfectly dried in an oven, after the bread has been removed. This is the proper time to do it. As many as eleven of my Africans are under serious impressions. In College we have had no excitement, and not even an inquiry-meeting, but a wide-spread seriousness, daily short prayer-meetings, and much private conversation. Mr. Cassels will probably be settled at Norfolk. The air-tight stove is adopted by Prof. Henry, Dod, Hodge, Miller, and Dr. Rice. Its two great advantages are (1) absolute cleanliness, and (2) perfect manageability, so that a fire may be kept 24 hours so low that you can scarcely feel it, and yet may be raised high in three minutes. It *may* be abused so as to be a mere common sheet iron stove, but this is not the intention. The great art is repressing the fury of the little creature. Mine kept about flesh-warm all last night, and on sliding up the door this morning, I had it roaring in two minutes. Then I shut all up except a minute crevice, and so it has been some hours. It is meant for a room of which the door is kept shut. You will learn the whole trick in two days. Wood dry as possible, charge say 4—6 billets. I would begin with hickory, but sound maple is as good, when you know the article. Blood has gone to Ireland; it was time that he should be extravasated.

PRINCETON, *Nov.* 13 and 14, 1841.

Our journey to Virginia, and my return, were accomplished with much less trouble, danger, and fatigue, than I had feared. The kindness of Providence was signal towards us, in regard to weather, conveyances, and the like. I trust my little flock is safely folded in Charlotte. I do not desire soon to have a trip of the same solicitude; yet I feel it to be a sacred duty to record the loving-kindness of the Lord in every part of it. My situation here is lonely enough, and I feel it more than if I were alone in another house. I am, moreover, somewhat confined by a cold and rheumatism in all one side.

I was greatly encouraged by the sight of the Virginia Synod, [at Richmond.] The number of highly respectable and faithful ministers in the prime of life, is very large. Making allowances for the idiosyncrasies of some, the following list is remarkable: McFarland, the Browns (5 brothers, sons of a minister, not all in Va.,) Leyburn, Stevenson, Skinner, Love, Stewart, White, Cassels, Graham, Armistead, Alkinson, Peyton, Harrison, Benj.

Smith, Foote, Stanton, Whary, McPhail, Dutton, Sparrow, Plumer. Every one of these is a man of pulpit talents and influence. They think the interest of Presbyterianism advancing. The Synod proper had adjourned, but they all remained over Sunday and communed together—a delightful solemnity. Plumer's large church was crowded with communicants, many of whom had come several days' journey. I am sure I spoke with a hundred acquaintances not residing in Richmond. I preached on Monday to a most awakened audience.

I wished to see Greenough's statue of Washington; but, though erected, it was not uncovered. The patent-office at Washington is a great show; the largest room, it is said, in America. If you ever go to Washington, do not go to Brown's hotel. The Exchange House in Richmond is beyond comparison the finest hotel I ever saw, not excepting the Tremont at Boston, by the late landlord of which it is kept. It lacks nothing but gas. For attendance of servants it is ten times better than the Tremont. This is a great change, in the view of one who remembers the former dens of Richmond.

The addition to College cannot be fully stated yet. We have matriculated about fifty, thus far. It looks as if Van Buren would be next President; and I see much less to choose, than I once did, between the parties. That we are victims of Banking, I see too plainly. McLean, of Monmouth, expects to have his organ up next week.

I take breakfast and tea entirely alone. You can't tell how I miss the children. What a doleful place is a childless house. Let me assure you that to have a sick wife 400 miles off, is no small trial; I hope it may do me good.

PRINCETON, *December* 8, 1841.

I have not for a long time seen a book, so well adapted to awaken the heart and conscience of a minister, or so well deserving to lie on his table, as the Life and Death of Joseph Alleine, written by Baxter and others, and lately printed by Carter. Your Pole [a beggar] came here, and in excellent Latin swindled us all out of sundry " vetera vestimenta," and money likewise. I love Banks less and less. They tempt men to borrow—make money nominally plenty—and then, when trouble comes, are the first creditors to exact, and the last to have mercy. All ———'s other creditors here would have waited—yet the Bank, after having handled $60,000 of his money, beat up his quarters near midnight for $2,100. I know they have the right—to the pound of flesh. Ask your Catharina if she is familiar with the following passage, in the " Taming of the Shrew :"

> "You lie in faith; for you are called plain Kate,
> And bonny Kate, and sometimes Kate the cross;
> But Kate, the prettiest Kate in Christendom,
> Kate of *Kate-Hall*, my superdainty Kate,
> For dainties are all cates."

What follows is an exact copy of an epitaph in Cranbury Church Yard, on a stone set up within the year:

> "Her blooming cheeks was no defence
> Against the scarlet fever,
> In five days' time she was cut down
> To be with Christ forever." [1]

A very pungent little book by one Ford, of England, is issued by Carter, intituled *Decapolis;* proper to circulate among believing Christians, to make them seek the conversion of the ungodly. I am using my copy in college, or I would send it to you. I think its circulation worth several sermons. —— has a letter from Geneva, saying that a friar of a Dominican convent, in Italy, has lately renounced popery, in consequence of his reading Calvin's Institutes, to which he was directed by the Index Expurgatorius. I rejoice that the Board are about to publish Daille on the Use of the Fathers; I do not know any thing to pat against Oxfordism. Don't fail to get the Board's little Life of Philip Henry; librum vere aureum. My father abridged it. Love to Madame, Mesdemoiselles, et les petits bons hommes. I am deeply yours.

PRINCETON, *ult.*, 1841.

A happy New Year, in all the senses, especially the best, to you and you-ess and the youths! Your letter of the 25th was of a more Christian length than your late foregoing ones. Pray, don't let press of business tend to curtail a correspondence which has lasted some half a century, or less. If I send you ——'s sermon, it is not as a sample of rhetoric purity; the metaphors are mixed as much as communion-wines. Dr. Torrey has hired the Bayard House: he deposits in our library his herbarium, equal in bulk to 500 folio volumes, and containing, as I remember, 50,000 species; the number of existing species, by estimate, is 100,000.

More than once I remember to have expressed to you my sense of the importance of writing down things *on the spot*—con-

---

[1] His correspondent was able to return an inscription copied from a stone in a Trenton marble (not church) yard.

> "The boiling coffee did on me fall,
> And by it I was slain;
> But Christ has bought my liberty,
> And in him I'll rise again."

versations of an interesting kind—death-bed facts—striking retributions—successful cures of soul-sickness—results of experience as to matters of duty, or policy—cases in one's own family, children, &c. Such records are valuable when one is gone. " I agree," says H. Walpole, " with Mr. Gray, 'that any man living may make a book worth reading, if he will but set down with truth what he has seen or heard, no matter whether the book is well written or not.'" I wish the practice were commoner of introducing the text by the introduction, and not the introduction by the text.

How nicely one might see the river from your window, if it were not for Mr. Potts's house. In 1780 a Mr. Shirley built a house on the Thames, on purpose to intercept a view of the river from his opposite neighbour; the people gave it the name of Spite-*hall*. My good old father, after spying out for threescore years, strongly maintains, that there is less and less appearance of amalgamation among Protestant sects; that is, so far as their admitting one another's ordinances goes; *e. g.* the Episcopals and the Baptists are more exclusive than formerly. The newspapers are intolerably dull; what more unprofitable and really nauseous than legislative debates, murders, bankruptcies, &c.? There ought to be an epitome for scholars and busy men. One of the few things I can read is Walsh's Letters [from Paris] to the National Intelligencer. Will it be worth your reception for me to mail one to you now and then? We have a tutor descended from Jonathan Edwards, and two students, grandsons of Drs. McWhorter and Richards. We have a half-hour prayer meeting every evening. This term, already, we have heard of the conversion of five of our late " students," some of whom were great rowdies. In 1 Cor. ix. ult., I don't believe that ἀδόκιμος means " castaway," in the usual acceptation. It is a word of the palæstra; the apostle says, " I keep under my body, lest I become *unfit* for service—for contention." I know of an excellent place for a young lady, as governess, in Goochland co., Va. $300 a-year and found—pious old-school family: piano-teaching required. Dod has the advowson of the benefice.

The Costa Rica earthquake is awful indeed; read about it in your newspaper: if it had extended a few minutes northwarder, —— would no doubt have a sermon on it.

—— is a truly good man, and a man of strong mind and strong delivery, but he has made the grand mistake of spending his strength chiefly in rebuke. I do not mean that he is too minatory; this I should not easily think one, if this were all, but he aims at showing faults, and constantly " plies the conscience," as he would call it. I do not think such preaching, alone, ever fails to be deadening. It does little good to awaken mere conscience, without reaching the heart. We know better what we ought to do, than we feel motives to do otherwise. I think this the great difference between New England, and the best Old England preachers of the best time. It is wonderful how different is the strain of address to Christians in the New Testament epistles.

I see Kirk is like to be settled in Boston, over a new church. His manner of preaching has attracted many stragglers from the Unitarian ranks. I hope he will be useful there.

The notice of Yeomans' inaugural in the Repertory is by Dr. Miller, as are sundry of the short notices. The Doctor is in another dispute with some layman in the Episcopal Recorder, who has really treated the old gentleman most dishonestly, attributing an odious phrase to him, which he protests he never used. If [Dr. E.] Robinson's maps can be got apart from the book, one ought to have them. O, it is grand to have such a feeling of reality in reading about the "holy places;" Ramah, Shiloh, Nob, Mizpeh, &c. They are engraved at Berlin, and printed at London.

PRINCETON, *January* 15, 1842.

Don't you think, on the whole, we have had quite a mild winter? The roads have been very dreadful. I learn with pain, that poor —— has probably lost another child with scarlet fever. My father had a letter from him on Friday, and he was despairing of it then. O how deep such rebukes pierce! For a season life is a cup which has lost its zest. What is there but God and Heaven that can do any thing for a man in such a case? Our Congress is really blackguard, and more so every year. Just listen to the fish-market talk of —— &c. Don't think I read 'em; enough runs over from ——, who, I suppose, has not failed to read, mark, learn, and inwardly digest, every speech, bill, report, nay word, of every session of Congress, as reported by his own-side papers, for fifteen years. His memory of every thing, but especially of what he has witnessed, is unparalleled by any thing I ever met with. There appears to be no *distance* in his retrospects, no dimness. Every day he brings things to my recollection, which I, as older, ought to remember better than he, and that with such a particularity as few men could show in regard to the last week. Dr. Phillips's people wish to move up town. Yet it seems to me, even if the congregation go up, the edifice ought to be left. There are many churches in the very bowels of London. There must be every Sunday thousands of strangers in New York, and in that part of it, not to speak of clerks, &c., who lodge in the upper stories of places of business. Why would not it be a good plan for some to keep the house, pay a minister, reserve pews for themselves and numerous retainers, but throw open the body of the pews to the poor and strangers? To the poor the gospel is *not* preached in our crack Presbyterian churches. Mr. Olmsted of Flemington admitted nineteen on the 9th. Dr. Rice preached six times for him. [Professor] Dod has given your steeple a reprieve until Lecture 2d. Our steeple here (viz., of the Seminary) is said to be of the BREWER order. As for expositions of the text Gen. iii. 15, you need not look far. I believe the common, and, as I think, (to one who has an inkling of a Messiah,) the obvious meaning has been defended by all interpreters from the Christian era. There is, perhaps, no interpretation more catholic; whence this prediction alone has received a specific technical designation, πρωτευαγγελιον. Even Adam Clarke, and Turner of New York, who generally give the lowest sense, plead for its Messianic application. No other fulfilment seems to me at all satisfactory, or even true. But if you wish a full examination of the question, read Hengstenberg's Christology, vol. 1, on the *Protevangelium ;* or, see Melvill's sermon on the text; it seems an argumentative discourse. The original Hebrew, compared with Gal. iii. 16, weighs very much with me; though I confess I never could make it a doubtful matter. I have written a sermon to-day on "Our polity is in heaven." Observe how much more point the Greek has in Col. iii. 1 and 2. ζητεῖτε. / φρονεῖτε. The English is feeble in comparison, and the antithesis is entirely lost. I have been studying the Colossians lately with a good deal of attention. There is a fund of motives to holiness in chap. iii. Mede thinks the Jews will all be converted simultaneously, and that Paul's conversion was a type of it.

PRINCETON, *January* 18, 1842.

"Hic murus aëneus esto,
Nil conscire sibi, nullâ pallescere culpâ.
Roscia, dic sodes, melior lex, an puerorum est
Nænia, quæ regnum rectè facientibus offert,
Et maribus Curiis et decantata Camillis?
Isne tibi meliùs suadet, *qui rem facias ; rem,
Si possis, rectè ; si non, quocunque modo rem.*"
Horat. Ep. 1, *lib.* 1.

There are some quotable verses in the same epistle, on avarice, and it is really wonderful how often Horace lashes this particular vice:

Vilius argentum est auro, virtutibus aurum.
—O cives, cives, quærenda pecunia primum est,
Virtus post nummos.

Perhaps you will remember that Pope has an imitation of the Epistle above cited, and he gives the critical lines thus, which I write as prose: "Who counsels best? who whispers, 'Be but great, With praise or infamy, leave that to fate; Get place and wealth, if possible with grace; If not, by any means get wealth and place.'" I was much struck with a saying of Addison, that we make too great a gap between some books of Scripture, and that Joshua evidently just kept up the journal after Moses' death. This would explain several difficulties. The beans you pretended you were going to give me have not arrived; having been left at Snowden's inn, and no doubt devoured by the legislature. If this letter, which goes by the same hand, should fail to reach you, please let me know in your answer. Mr. Cassels reports a revival at Norfolk. I expect, with leave of Providence, to go to Virginia about the middle of February. I found the following passage to-night in a letter of Bussy-Rabutin, (1675,) "Si vous n'en pouvez trouver d'autre [encre] que celle dont vous vous servites l'année passée, souvenez-vous de m'écrire sur papier noir, car enfin, je veux lire ce que vous m'ecrivez." Not so bad. We have four of the Scriptural unclean beasts now in Princeton, "the camel, the cony, the hare, and the hog." Hogg and Colt stall together in college. The distinction of meats has now given place to the distinction of drinks. If you have not a Greek Lexicon of the critical kind, I would nominate Rose's Parkhurst, which I have used a number of years. —— has obtained two bottles of the unfermented wine. It is merely a light syrup, like poor molasses, with no vinous taste to my palate, and when diluted, as ordered, not unlike vapid raspberry-vinegar. Nothing but an insane love of a hypothesis could bring one to believe, that such was the "fruit of the vine," used at the Passover. They are agitating this question among our old-school churches in Kentucky; Grundy leading the treacle-ites, and W. L. Breckinridge the wine-ites.

PRINCETON, *January* 25–6, 1842.

Walter Lowrie, who has waited three months for a vessel to go for Canton, has got off at last. He made all his Seminary preparations with a view to Africa, and very reluctantly gave up the latter destination. A couple of young Germans, one of them Israelitish, have been canvassing our town as spectacle-mongers. I am told they have had a shop in Trenton. The Jew read Hebrew for me very well; he is, moreover, a musician. I got a penknife from him cheaper than they are found in the shops. ——, alack! is coming here to brawl against Pop-pery. Have you ever read Wiseman's Lectures on the Connexion of Science and Religion? It is worth reading; and the earlier lectures, tracing the pedigree of languages, give what the great Germans have discovered in this field, which is, so far as I know, the only English account of the same. It is an economy of time to read such books. I have seen nothing in your Trenton papers in laudation of Dod's lecture; doubtless in consequence of your practices with the editors, on behalf of your steeplehouse. Resuming the subject of Wiseman, as above, I add, that if Stephens had read this book, he would not have evinced himself to be so " hideously unprovided" of antiquarian preparation for his Southern Researches. It throws great light on the history of our Indians. Of the beans I have as yet seen nothing, and " de" not " apparentibus," and not " existentibus "—I hope you have a recollection of your law-maxims. According to the proverb, " bis dat qui cito dat," you have given me only half the amount, and I am told the parcel has been broken, and some bestowed on Dr. Miller! The confusion of the dramatis personæ in Canticles does not exist in Hebrew, where the *verbs* have gender, and you know at each moment whether it is the sponsus or the sponsor who is addressed. Our lack of gender is felt also in Ecc. xii. 3, " the grinders cease because they are few, and those that look out of the windows be darkened:" the original gives, " the female-grinders keep holiday, &c., and the female-lookers-out-of-windows, &c." I dare say many hearers think the grinders are the " dentes molares." The tee-totallers are making great conquests in Kentucky, under the command of two distinguished Ebriates, as reformed *i*nebriates may be called. Why so tender about naming them drunkards?

I have just been reading over, at one sitting, the epistle to the Colossians. I have done so many times within a month, both in Greek and in all the translations I have, which are more than ten. This way of frequent reperusal, continuously, I learned of my father, many years ago. It is well to intermix it with critical study of the same portion. I like to confine myself to one book for a time, and as it were, *live in it*, till I feel very familiar. I usually find great satisfaction during such a period, in preaching from such a book, thus studied. We greatly need a book of " Introduction to the New Testament." Horne is useful, but has no mark of unity produced by an original conception; it is a scissors-book. Hug is all the reverse; you are sensible of the charm of a genius on every page: by all means, mean to get it, when you have the means; but the pun is too mean. A book might be made containing only such matters as are in Horne's 2d and 4th volumes; leaving out of view a great deal about Interpretation, which, after all, must be left to common sense. Notwithstanding what I have said of Horne, I would, seriously, rather be the author of it than of any book in our language. Strange, that living, as he does, in one of the greatest libraries of the world, he should have written nothing else. I find laymen of intelligence greatly awakened and benefited by the book. It was so with Mr. Wirt; and [Rev. Mr.] Hare lately made the same remark to me. To return to Hug, I have found his Life of Paul, and account of his character and writings, more instructive than any thing I have ever read on the subject. Before you publish that you are going to lecture on "Phee-Phaw-Phum," you ought to remember that many read an advertisement who do not go to hear a lecture, and that with such, your taste, dignity, and judgment will suffer; as they will not hear the really wise remarks you utter. I fear our friend, the Shah-Bulkh-Bidden-B'hoo —— will be in "King Cambyses' vein." A temperance society was formed last night here; on the "Washingtonian" plan, I guess. I expect, to-morrow, to go to the Birchine visitation at Brunswick. Mr. Hare is to lecture at our Mechanics' Institute on Edom.

CHARLOTTE COURT HOUSE, VA., *February* 23, 1842.

From the appearance of this ink, I am seriously afraid the paper will be blank when it reaches you. I arrived here on the 18th. My journey was more exposed than common. I had to travel all one cold night, in a stage, alone, over such roads as I never saw, and then all the next day. The James River at Carterville could not be crossed, by reason of the tempestuous current, thermometer at 19.° I slept on the Goochland side, in the lock-keeper's house," three in a bed," in an unfinished house. I find my wife better than when I heard from her. As to personal comfort, I can conceive of nothing, as to external circumstances, family, servants, and the like, more favourable than what she enjoys at Ingleside, [five miles from Charlotte Court House.] My children have undergone the most extraordinary transformation as to health. Henry has, through mercy, escaped every ailment this winter. My friends think he bears every exposure quite as well as country children; he is out all day, and has his feet wet for hours. But then he is excited by his traps, birds, squirrel, and horses. Jemmy is almost as sturdy as your Caldwell. Since I saw him he has learnt to *converse*, and some of his remarks are odd enough. He informed me, as a fact in zoology, that " the little lambs suck the big lambs." Quite enough this, however, of a subject which seldom fails to disgust any but the speaker. I try to be thankful for this alleviation of my trials. I have preached seven times since I reached Virginia; sometimes with more enlargement than is my wont. Mrs. Le Grand's house is still full, from day to day. There is not a small mechanic or labouring family in all the village or vicinage who does not freely come to her for aid, or as freely enter her doors. I sincerely think I have never seen the human being who lives so much for others. Mere sacrifice of money is little: in her case, it is sacrifice of health, time, privacy, convenience, ease, and (virtually) of life. She is about 78, and is ill enough any day to keep her bed, which she never kept except when in severe pain or extreme languor. Her cough is deadly and her attenuation extreme. You must write frequently, and remember I hear little of what the world is doing. The remoteness and quietude of the situation strikes me exceedingly. I roam over the plantations, as little obnoxious to observation or criticism as if I were in the Pacific regions. Our weather is wintry. Crocuses were blown in Richmond, but we have since had it very cold. I calculated that a fire such as is kept in my wife's room, of hickory, would cost me about $200 a year in Princeton. I know no luxury greater than a constantly glowing fire of wood, replenished *ad libitum.* Mr. C—— averages three cords of wood a day on his estate. The slaves use it without measurement, all going to a common pile. I have not yet heard from the North. I saw Lord Morpeth in Richmond. Judge Cabell dined with him at the lieutenant-governor's, Rutherford's, and was much pleased with his mild and unpretending manners. Bishop Meade seems to be doing much for Evangelical piety in this State. There has been a great stir in Petersburg, involving the Episcopal church; ninety-three were confirmed in Mr. Cobbs's church. It is not known whether a coadjutor will be appointed to Meade. Johns has been spoken of. The Methodists have made great inroads here. There were formerly none; they are now building a respectable house. Their gain has been greater, by reason of the yielding of Presbyterians to their Thomsonian practice. In Hampden Sydney College there are about thirty students, and about as many in the Seminary. There are five schools in this village. Among these is Michael Osborne's lately erected girls' school, which has twenty-six already. I find much entertainment from the company of Dr. Brown, nephew of the Edinburgh metaphysician. He is a brother-in-law of Hart, the pastor. He was educated at Edinburgh and Paris, and is a bachelor and a genius. He is a great opposer of total abstinence, though, I believe, a temperate man, and declares that the cases of bronchitis which he has known among sedentary people all arise from that state of body which would be prevented by a moderate stimulus, such as the clergy used to admit of. I have battled with him at great disadvantage, as his stores of medical authority overwhelm me, and he denies point-blank the testimonies of the physicians who are relied on by Tee-totalers. Being out as much by night as day, and frequently riding on horseback thirty miles a night, and even swimming rivers, he says that nothing disarms these exposures, but fire or diffusive stimulus of some sort; of which alcohol is the only one which can be given often safely. He denies that it is ineffectual to keep off cold. He was a Temperance-man five years ago. The abstinence folk are making great advances in this State. At Lynchburg they have more than a thousand signatures. They have adopted the phrases, " revival," " awakening," " conviction," and " conversion." —— says he thinks these excitements highly deleterious to the cause of religion. Public opinion is made to bear upon those who dissent, and abstinence is like to be made a term of communion by many. In the country hereabouts, the body of the people have always been temperate, and Total Abstinence has few adherents.

INGLESIDE, CHARLOTTE CO., VA., *March* 10, 1842.

I have one of yours. The date I do not record, as I am away from my file. If you should have written in answer to my last, before this reaches you, please to write again: I shall await your reply to this. The weather is mild but pluvious. There have been great freshes here, perhaps thirty during the season. Peas are quite high; peach and plum trees in blossom some days. Birds are pairing, and their number, on this estate, is remarkable.* Mr. Carrington saw four wild turkey-cocks on his grounds a day or two ago. You will have seen, by the papers, that J. R. of Roanoke's will freeing the slaves has been established. I happen to know that this is false. The clerks here are busy copying the voluminous testimony. There is no decision of the last suit. Meanwhile, the proceeds of the immense estate go to the Tuckers and Coalters and Bryan. The evidence in the case is very extraordinary. The following is a true copy, literatim et punctatim, of a letter, most reluctantly produced by my quondam elder ——, as a part of his testimony. —— is above 70. "To Henry A. Watkins, Come and see me if you can—I mean if you are able I beseech you—If you cannot come pray for me—for the effectual fervent *prayer of a righteous man* AVAILETH MUCH. ¶ *Friday* 10—but in fact 11 of April, un-

---

* While I close this, a mocking-bird is making matchless music near me.

blotted—I am in extremis on the word of a Christian. I write with a blotting pen upon greasy paper, unclean all offensive in the eye of God—because I am under the powerful influence of the Prince of Darkness who tempts me with a —— and champagne."

I have been preaching a good deal to the negroes, a delightful work, promising, I think, as much good as any labour a man can engage in. Within a year or two much more attention is paid to this, especially by some of the Methodists. A preacher, named Skidmore, himself a slaveholder, has some thirty plantations under his charge, at one of which he preaches *every evening*. He enrolls the names, and conducts every meeting of the slaves on the plan of a Class-meeting. I am much affected by the negro singing. There is a softness in their voices, which penetrates me, and in these meetings they all sing, down to the infants. Mrs. ——'s cook (emerita) Patty, she says, is " as pious a woman, and a lady of as delicate sensibilities as I ever saw ; she is one of the very best friends I have in the world." And Mrs. —— is second to no woman I ever saw in judgment, taste, and education. The negro dialects of English are a curious study. *E. g.* The slaves on this plantation are part from Mr. C.'s, part from Mrs. C.'s estate. There are some pronunciations and phrases which never pass from one set to the other. Thus the Carrington negroes all say " Gi we súm-hin-núrra fúh we bekfuss," *i. e.* " Give us something or other for our breakfast." But the Monte-Video negroes (whom Judge Cabell once owned, on James River) and none other, so far as Mrs. C. knows, pronounce e long where it ought to be short, thus: *báde* for *bed*; *Hālen* for *Helen*; also *Constāntia* for *Constantia*. My children, having nurses of the latter, have adopted this elegancy. There is no way of accounting for this phenomenon, but by supposing that the progenitors of these respective sets came from different African tribes. For several days we have had as visiters Mr. John Henry, son of Patrick, his wife, my wife's cousin, and two little daughters. Mr. H. cut a walking-stick, cherry, from the head of his father's grave, as a present for Gen. Harrison, who received it a few days before his last illness. He tells me that his mother was told by the mother of Patrick, that the latter always used to drive her in a gig to hear Mr. Davies preach ; æt. about 14 : place Hanover Co. Patrick Henry was a great violinist for that day ; so is his son. I have always considered this region of Virginia more favourable to the highest popular eloquence than any other. There are twenty men in this county, whose elocution is enviable. The " cleverest " man since Randolph is Wood Bouldin, son of T. T. Bouldin, who succeeded J.

R. in the House of Representatives, and who died there of a fit. The Venables are an extraordinary family. I have often heard my father say that Col. Sam. Venable was the wisest man he ever saw. He married a Carrington, half-sister of my good host. He had twelve children. His wife lived to see them all married, and all converted. Dr. Paul Venable counted up to me 142 descendants of these his parents, all now living. Each of these families is rich, and they are all democrats, and all Old School Presbyterians. Of the father of H. C. (old Judge Carrington) the descendants are about 400. Such things are important elements of the state of society. I am more and more convinced of the injustice we do the slaveholders. Of their feelings towards their negroes I can form a better notion than formerly, by examining my own towards the slaves who wait on my wife and mind my children. It is a feeling most like that we have to near relations. Nanette is a mild but active brown woman, with whom I would trust any interest we have. She is an invalid, however, and in the North would long since have died in an alms-house. As it is, she will be well housed, well fed, protected, and happy, if she lives to be 100. There are two blind women (80—90) on this estate, who have done nothing for years. It is touching to see them walking out, arm in arm, to bask in the sun.

INGLESIDE, C. CY., VA., *March* 21, 1842.

Your letter, though not quite as full as usual, was very acceptable in these ends of the earth. You can have no idea how far one feels here from all the foci of news. Yesterday was July. I attended two full services, right on the back of one another: the last one was a funeral sermon of a black. I had a large collection, and preached from " Thou fool, this night, &c." Great attention, and hysterics in at least seven. The singing was transporting; positively I never enjoyed any thing more at the Musical Fund. I have preached eighteen times in Virginia. I have met here an original. —— is a Yale man, about as deaf as ——. Has an office built in the yard, lined with glazed cases, wherein 2,000 volumes. As much of a *litterateur* as I ever saw. Was a member of the Virginia Convention in 1830. Thorough scholar in Greek, Latin, and French. Perfect health and athletic vigour. A boxer, in all the forms. As to diet and bathing, almost a Cornaro. Has not eaten warm bread for ten years. Shaves in his shirt in a cold room in winter. A pedestrian: has walked all over Canada, and several times over New England. The last day of his return from Canada to Norfolk, he walked fifty-five miles, and then was at office business, on his feet, till ten at night. For this journey he *trained*, on Capt. Barclay's scheme;

two meals a day, of rare beef and Madeira, and stale bread; this for three weeks. He has every sort of gymnastical contrivance. Always stands at study, with legs wide apart, and no support. His chest is like the keel of a boat. He is an intimate friend of Upshur, Judge B. Tucker, and other ultra States-Right men, to which party he belongs. I have met with nothing like him for knowledge of history, biography, heraldry, and the like. He is an eloquent talker. His father-in-law ——, entered the army at 19, and was desperately wounded at the battle of Eutaw, in 1781, being shot through the thigh and bayoneted in the breast. Though he was years getting well, he is now, at 80, ruddy, erect on his horse, in good flesh, and has lost only one tooth! There are many such men here. This is owing to exercise, and simple habits. Patrick Henry was a fiddle player, and that by note, and scientific too, for that day. My grandfather Waddel also played fiddle, as Mrs. Hoge told me, who has heard him. So do John and Winston Henry, sons of Patrick. Patrick, late in life, turned in to enriching himself, and died immensely wealthy. His power over men was his great implement. I expect to visit his grave at Mr. J. Henry's, Red Hill. All fruit trees are going out of blossom here. Peas are a foot high. This part of Virginia produced capital light-horse-men in the old war, and will do so again. The boys are Centaurs, and I wonder daily at the coolness with which Mrs. C., a very cautious mother, sees her son, 9 years old, galloping like the wind, through woods and over fences and ditches, on a colt or a mule or any thing that has legs. Pray at what epoch did you begin to aspirate the *h* in *humble*, and to write *a humble?* and when will you begin to say *a honest man*, or as —— does, *a herb?* I have heard cockneys say *a hour*. Nothing so much engages my thoughts as the spiritual case of the negroes. I seize every chance to preach to them. Of no people, I think, is a larger portion regenerate. They are unspeakably superior to our Northern free blacks, retaining a thousand African traits of kindliness and hilarity, from being together in masses. I may say with Abram ——, " I love a nigger, they are better than we." So they are: grateful, devoted, self-sacrificing for their masters. I do believe that there are a dozen on this estate who would risk their lives in an instant for my wife. They are, under ordinary masters, a happy people. Their chief suffering is from cold weather. In summer they are always well, plump, and joyous. The only thing I am anxious about *for them*, is their illumination. Several wait on my wife, who are as well-bred and (in heart) refined as ladies.

When you or I depart this life, the letters of the survivor, (free as they have been about persons who may then be alive) might prove very mischievous to the surviving party. I think, therefore, we both ought to provide for the return of the letters to the writers or the family of the writers : I beg you will not fail to append a conspicuous advertisement in respect to this, to any parcels retained by you; I will do the like. I was 38 on the 13th. The thought overwhelmed me. It was communion day. In regard to *new measures*, I wish I had always observed this rule, viz.: " Never vent any *general principle* about them ; speak to the individual case ; nor then but when forced."

Mrs. Le Grand's, Charlotte C. H., *March* 25, 1842.

Your news of the progress of religion is good. In Virginia there are a few revivals. To-morrow Plumer [Richmond] will receive ∓ fifty. My mind has been, and is, filled with the negroes. What I say on this point I say with, I do believe, as much love for the race as any man feels ; and with an extent of observation perhaps as large as I can pretend to on any subject, having seen the worst as well as the best of their condition. And the result of all, increasingly, is, what you I am sure would agree to if you were on the spot, that the *average physical evils* of their case are not greater than of sailors, soldiers, shoeblacks, or low operatives ; while their *moral evils* are unspeakably great. My point is this, then : The soul of the negro is precious and must be saved. Aim at this, at this first, at this directly, at this independently of their bondage, and the other desirable ends will be promoted even more surely than if the latter were made the great object. A gradual emancipation is that to which the interior economy of the North-Southern States was tending, is tending, and will reach ; it is desirable ; in my view it is inevitable ; it is craved by thousands here ; but an emancipation even gradual may arrive in such sort as to leave a host of blacks to be damned, who, by the other means, may be Christianized, while their eventual freedom is not less certain. It is the salvation of the slave, which is infinitely the most important, which moreover Southern Christians *can* be led to seek, and of which the very seeking directly tends to emancipation. I say this, on the obvious principle, that when the owner by seeking the salvation of his slave, gets (as he must) to love him, he will not rest (I speak of the mass) without trying to make him a freeman. I cannot describe the pleasure I have had in preaching and talking to the slaves : if I have ever done any good, this is the way. I have just been in Mrs. Le Grand's garden, which is a faery-land. There are blooming and perfuming at this moment, and by wholesale, yellow-jasmines, double-peach, hyacinths, Siberian-crab, tulip, violets, pansies, jonquils, &c. The forests are very imperfectly leafing. After several freshes, the plows are going for corn, oats having been sown. N. B.—As to the anomaly of the plural nominative with singular verb, in our version, it is as certain a usage in old English, as in Greek, though I confess not so common. I have had my attention drawn to it, some years ago, and in other English books. Pres. Maxwell [of Hampden Sidney] and Mr. [Rev. Patrick J.] Sparrow were here yesterday, on the way to Presbytery, in Halifax Co. They are expected to stop as they return. Maxwell has good spirits, on such small provocation. Lexington has become a flourishing literary place for Virginia. The military school has rather helped the college; for, as Gen. Carrington said to me, "Among soldiers the *point d'honneur* is *obedience*." They are meaning to have a monthly magazine at Union Seminary, which is as flourishing as it has ever been. Since I came to Virginia I have preached nineteen sermons. Since I came to Ingleside, there has been one house-burning and one death. A little [negro] girl æt. 12, daughter of Mr. C.'s miller " Henry;" peripneumony; just before dying said, "I see a beautiful dress." Bystanders said, "She is out of her head." Child answered, "No, I a'nt out o' my head, I am dyin' "—and caused " Christian Moses " (Mr. C.'s head-man, so called to distinguish him from " Long Moses ") to be sent for, to sing for her a certain hymn. Poor souls, their hearts go forth almost always in hymns. The other night, after preaching to an unmixed negro flock, we sang " When I can read my title clear," &c., and the feeling I caught was almost that of enthusiasm. Every voice joining, all loud, and all true enough in tone to have satisfied Haydn. Abram Venable is licensed by Presbytery to preach to them. I lately counted up the living descendants of Col. Sam. Venable (my father's Mentor) and his wife (half-sister of Henry Carrington) = 140 odd. Of the original *Woodsons*, (*i. e.* the first English emigrants,) the descendants, by a rough calculation, are 20,000. The contiguous settlement of many among these, and their unmixed English-hood conditions very much the state of *old*-Virginia society.

CHARLOTTE C. H., *April* 26, 1842.

Your acceptable favour, 18th inst. is accepted. We have resolved on realizing what has all along been our plan, viz., to seize the first possibility of setting off. This we propose to attempt on the 2d of May; meaning to go viâ P. Edward, Cartersville, Canal, Richmond, Norfolk, &c.; in every step consulting ease of motion. Our good friends here have prevented us in one important item—the getting to the canal, 60 or 70 miles from here. I was in expectation of hackney-travel from Prince Edward, and had written to engage the same, as Mr. C.'s carriage-pair have become disabled; and though he has about a dozen horses, none of them would be both safe and able. But Mrs. Le Grand has come in to relieve us in this strait. The plan is this: to take her carriage and horses and coachman Billy, (who was at my grandfather's as a lad when my father was a boy;) to have a light wagon with a horse of Mr. Carrington's, and his man Fontaine, for change, and for the trunks; with our affectionate nurse Nanette in the carriage, and a saddle-horse, (Margery Daw, so called from her easy amble; the nag I have uniformly bestridden in my last two visits.) When I remonstrated against so overwhelming a favour, Mr. C. (whom may God ever bless!) said: "Say no more, sir, it costs me nothing. I have no money to give you, but I can give you service: and remember what Jack Randolph used to say was a Virginian estate, 'plenty of serfs, plenty of horses, but not a shilling.'" We may be a fortnight and more in getting to Philadelphia, where I hope to stay a day or two. If there is any thing which could make it, in the least, burdensome to your mother, for us to pass these days under her long-tried roof, do be frank enough to say so in a line to Richmond. She gave me the kindest invitation, but I am ignorant of their family-movements just now. It is summer here; 83° at 5 *p. m.* yesterday in shade. Henry picked ripe strawberries in the field. Your Trenton and church news is just the thing; I prize your particularity; and joy in your success, almost with a personal gratification. You have bragged twice in a heathenish or lenten manner of your shad; know ye, that the Roanoke shad has been in season for weeks past, and was on the table the day your letter came; though I seldom eat the animal. Cherries are red. In Mecklenburg I picked ripe strawberries nearly two weeks ago. I there saw eglantine and coral-honeysuckles, wild, and as "plenty as blackberries." The calycanthus scents whole swamps oppressively. In Abram Venable's garden of three acres, I counted 66 beds of tulips in bloom, and in an average bed I counted 144 tulips; = 9,504 actually blooming; every shade and contour. He is equally curious in roses. His house is in full view of Prestwould, seat of the late Sir Peyton Skipwith, now occupied by Humberstone Skipwith, the 2d son. Sir Grey lives abroad. There is nothing on Virginia tables which I should care to transport, but cornbread (plain) and bacon; and I have no hope of ever seeing either elsewhere. Peas are ripe. My Henry, in chasing a hare with a dog, came across a venomous moccasin-snake; the dog killed both hare and snake. Two other children were in company, not a hundred yards from the house.

PRINCETON, *June* 3, 1842.

I expected to find you in the city, when I heard that you had gone thither; but you passed us on the river, and not being civil enough to salute us, left me under the impression that you were not in the Flamingo, or whatsoever name you may have given your craft. My children, though perfect rustics, are well; an unspeakable blessing just now, [their mother an invalid in Philadelphia.] Say what is necessary to the Rices and other Tridentine friends. Give my love to them, and to Mrs. ——, and all and sundry misses and masters. I heard Krebs [in General Assembly] open the defence of the [wife's sister marriage.] He spoke all Wednesday afternoon, and much of yesterday morning. Then arose Colin McIvor and declared that he could say his say in four hours. I fled. It is now several years since I was, even as a hearer, in the Assembly: I have no lust for going again.

PRINCETON, *June* 30, 1842.

Yesterday was exactly eight months since I took my wife away. That she should, at last, have got home, even as well as she is, should mark the day *albo lapillo* of thankfulness. The events and anxieties of the last twelvemonth have given me deep thoughts about myself, and about life. I rejoice that as I grow grayer, I do not feel, as —— lately told me he felt, a growing distrust in my kind. On the contrary, I have so lived upon kindnesses, in time of need, and often from strangers, that I can only attribute the whole to that system of inexplicable divine favour, which follows and overwhelms us, despite our manifold sins and provocations. And feeling, I do think, a firmer purpose to spend my remnant of life in service, and a stronger hatred to the unslain body of death within me, I cling more to the freest views of the Divine salvation; and more and more seek to behold the gift of Christ as the gift of every thing: 1 Cor iii. 22, 23. Surely there must have been somewhere, in the teaching of the Reformers, a wonderful spring, to act so powerfully and rapidly and widely. I think I find this, when I read in their works, especially those of Luther, certain declarations which are less frequent, earnest, and prominent, in later reformed writers, even those who adhered to the same confession; especially *free justification;* change of *state*, as distinct from change of moral character; which latter was as much insisted on by good Romanists. It was the same thing when Whitefield and Wesley preached; and in this they agreed; and there was the same effect. And I am convinced, that just so far as we seek to save God's free grace in justifying from abuse, by any condition in the sinner, except simple reception of Christ, which is only a condition-sine-qua-non, the more we produce practical Antinomianism. No communities have ever been so *thoroughly* moral as those who were most evangelical—I mean the least legal: *e. g.* the Scotch, in their best days; when everybody was externally Christian. The universal offer of a present, free salvation, to every son and daughter of Adam, for Christ's sake, is what I hold for *Gospel;* it is the good news which made the Reformation, which makes every true revival, and which makes us work, if we ever work what is right. It is the favourite topic of the old Calvinistic preachers of the 17th century; and of Boston, &c. Some of these thoughts have been suggested to me, by reading McCrie's life by his son.

PRINCETON, *July* 13, 1842.

I exclaimed at the improvement of your hand, before I perceived that it was all along of the ruled paper. Dr. A. goes toward Niagara, on Friday, to be away for two Sundays at least. J. W. A. cannot leave home by reason of college engagements, especially one on Monday morning. J. A. A. has a very severe and disabling catarrh, and an engagement elsewhere, to boot. Dr. R. consents to be with you—I taking his two services. Lord Congleton, who slew himself last month, is succeeded by his son John Parnell, an intimate friend, abroad, of Dr. Hodge, [see page 156;] he went out, as missionary, on his own hook, with Mr. Groves, to Bagdad, India, &c. In three years, the number of camels destroyed in the Affghanistaun war = 50,000. I believe the *domestic* use of mercury worse than ditto of alcohol. I am no longer a member of any Temperance Society of any sort, except that which is 1,800 years old. I look on the present seat of war in the Affghaun region as one of the most interesting spots on earth, physically, historically, prospectively, Christianly. Think of Cabul being 6,000 feet above the sea. Think of the Indus, no river such a barrier; of the Khyber-pass, impassable in general, but just passed by Pollock; it is the gut of the river which runs by Cabul to the Indus. Think of the edging of English toward Russian power. I hope we shall live to see a Presbyterian mission on that sublime plateau. All I hear of the Congregational missions makes me more in favour of our own. You see they had to make two presbyteries, even in Sandwich-aiai. Independency can't begin, of itself, as somebody said somewhere. Try to imagine it beginning among heathen. A parochial episcopacy and then a bench of presbyters is the only thing conceivable; and this is presbytery. The Churchman may well sneer at Goode's book, ["Divine Rule of Faith and Practice:"] it is a demolishing book to them. My garden is in a poor state, in consequence of my absence at seed-time. I have neither peas nor early beans, but abundance of the "wind-compelling" roots, called radishes. Girls' schools are humbugs; *i. e.* in the long run. Yet Prof. —— has just got back from an examination of Rutgers Institute, New York city: 400 pupils. He says the attainments in mathematics surpass any thing he has ever seen among lads; and I know no better judge. And therefore, I am, with every complimental respect and regard, &c.

PRINCETON, *September* 2, 1842.

Yours of yesterday informed me, to my sincere satisfaction, that you were home and well again. I hope you may always get along with the same punctuality of pastoral presence: but do not fail, while strong, to bear the infirmities of the weak. I am delivered from my cough, but much feebler than while I had it; having been so tied at home as to be unable to fly even for a week from my sources of care. Do you see that, at the Dartmouth Commencement, Dr. —— has been disparaging the reformation, and glorifying the Dark Ages? At the same place, President Lord preached a most eloquent sermon against all the boastful Philosophies; maintaining Scripture to be the only safe, and the sufficient guide, and snubbing the metaphysicians in the very style of superiority which they assume. The whole argument that there is more nearness of kin between a woman and her husband's brother, than between a woman and her sister's husband, may be thus conveniently expressed in symbols: "A = a, but a is not equal to A." Capt. Stockton has been trying his big gun; it tears every thing to flinders. Dallas Bache was here last week. He is elected *vice* Emmett, of the University of Virginia.

PHILADELPHIA, *October* 12, 1842.

It is reversing matters, with a witness, for me to write from Philadelphia to you in Trenton. We came here on the 1st, by the Doctor's prescription, and my wife has amended very much, so that she walked a mile with me this morning. We have a room at No. 163 South 9th, Mrs. Bowers's. We see some of your mother's family every day. Harlan is lionizing in New York. Humphrey of London, James's quondam fellow-prentice, is here; they say he is one of the first artists in his line, [engraving.] Mr. J. L. Wilson is here; arrived from Guinea on the 9th. Surely you ought to be here. I miss you very much, especially as —— has been manœuvring in Massachusetts ever since I came, and ——, who is rather an unexhilarating companion, at best, foams away most of every day in the Burlington steamboat. The Board of Publication bestowed on me an eleemosynary ten dollars' worth of books this morning. Very smiling likeness of Dr. Parker in the shops. I have to preach for [J. H.] Jones, on "Sabbath first." The Presbytery is now largely British-Irish, *e. g.* Tudehope, Macklin, Hoge, Loughridge, and Stuart. I heard McCalla make a speech, of which part follows: "I beg leave to state, that my connexion with this body is precisely that which the apostle Paul had with the soldier to whom he was attached in prison; namely a *chain*."—" I have been for twenty years a sufferer for conscience' sake; the hostility between me and you, has been altogether towards myself." His speech, though ——, was first-rate, for diction and delivery. I have preached as often as I was able; perhaps more. Anna and I went on Sunday evening to the "Mariners' Church," where was an immense throng. The mariners discoursed; each had his psalm, his doctrine, his tongue, (for one was a Seminole, whose conversion was miraculous,) his revelation. The singing was grandly methodistic. The handsome Indian boy I mentioned, has really a powerful natural eloquence, notwithstanding a stutter and broken English. I was convinced that good is doing at that church, though by means as Finneyitish as could well be. A semi-genteel seaman, with forehead as per margin, [there was a profile here,] acted as a sort of Valentine to the "Orson," [the Mariners' Chaplain was the late Rev. Orson Douglas,] and descanted on the following text, which he stated to be in the Bible, "There is no repentance in the grave, whither thou goest." Election is over: you know the result. I saw a furniture cart, full of placards and a band of music, on which the painted letters made with a placard the following cross-reading "To hire— Whigs of Middle Ward;" solemn fact. Mention it over the way. There was no fighting and less drunkenness than common.

—— sits next to me at table, and is an ultra Philadelphia punster already. He is as mercurial and jovial as —— is saturnine, or his father martial or —— (at present furloughed) terrestrial; I don't like the other adjective, or I should get all the old planets into my period.

I hope to spend part of Monday and Tuesday in Trenton. Till then account of me as truly yours.

PRINCETON, *December* 19, 1842.

Do not omit to read the ancient Call, in last Presbyterian. Half the names to it are my kindred. The pastor, Brown, was father of [James] Brown, formerly American Minister to France. The Archibald Alexander in the list, is my great-grandfather, an eminent saint. I trust the prayers of that day are now in remembrance. A great awakening is now in progress in Mr. Skinner's church in Lexington; 105 have been admitted. The McDowell on the same list is forefather of James McDowell, at present Governor of Virginia. Our college meetings are well attended; two on Sunday, and one of half an hour every evening at 6½. I never knew a more assiduous pastor than Professor Maclean: he daily talks with some of the youth; and is doing more good than any of us.

My old cook, Judy, came in just now to tell me of some inquirers in my black church; and, speaking of plain preaching, said, " There was *Jemmy Armstrong* that used to preach at Larrence, he didn't preach in the fear of man." She meant your and my predecessor, the Rev. J. F. A. The black Methodists here practise orgies. The other day or night a wench was brought into their church, on a bier, laid out, and *in a trance*. During the exorcism she sat up and spake. My mother's black maid speaks of it exactly as if it were a miracle. They have carried off a large portion of my congregation. I have, God willing, to preach on New Year's day P. M. in Lord's new church, [Seventh Church, Philadelphia,] then to be opened. The deficit of the A. B. C. F. M. since their extra effort is amazing: viz., $18,000 less for this, than for same quarter 1841! $5,000 less than average for five years! And this, when the complaint has just been that the American Board swallowed up all from the other societies. I am for using our existing machinery, while approved, to its utmost, for evangelical ends: yet *Quere* 1. Whether we do not sometimes account of the engine, (board or scheme,) as almost apostolic, and essential to church-progress? 2. Whether it is not probable that God will allow all our present enginery to decay, with the circumstances which reared it? 3. Whether the conversion of the world will not result, under God, from an action more *individual*, more cheap, and more flowing from great affections in every church and every member of it? 4. Whether such is not the New Testament missionary work, as we read it in Scripture? These views have always struck me; even while I abhor the malignant opposition to our Boards, which seem to me innocent, indispensable, and infinitely the best existing mode of doing the work thus *collectively*. But will the church keep up its zeal in the present mode? I own I never thought Irving's book on " Apostolical Missions" so foolish as it seemed to everybody. As I always welcome any hints about preaching, let me give you one. A good *plan* is invaluable, and may be turned to better account ten years after date, than when first used. I learned of Summerfield to preach extempore, and *then* to write out the skeleton, after trial. Now this is to introduce my hint, which is, that a good plan for a ten-minutes'-session-room-harangue, is an equally good plan for a sermon. Therefore, whenever a text or passage has *opened* well before the mind, in an exhortation, write down the skeleton on going home: it will some day hatch a discourse.

PRINCETON, *January* 6, 1843.

Dr. Baird is at this moment, I guess, discoursing to the seminarists on the things of Europe. Last evening I heard him for about an hour and a half. Dod, at this same hour, is holding forth, for a second time, at the Musical Fund, [Philadelphia.] I have read a letter from Paris, by the Rev. Otto von Gerlach, of Berlin, on his way home from England, whither he went in the cortège of the king of Prussia, and where he staid five months. I mention it because of the interest felt about the proposed reorganization of the "Evangelical Church," and because, since the consecration of my namesake Alexander to the see of Jerusalem, the Oxonians have alleged that their system was to be set agoing in Prussia. Von Gerlach is an intimate of the king, and brother of one of his first privy-councillors. He says there is no truth in the report; that Frederick William admires the regularity of the Anglicans, but is not for their hierarchy; that he is for a more synodal polity. He spent five days with Pusey at Oxford, and talks of him exactly as we do. The Sunday School Journal is quite an anti-popery paper. There are four Romish priests in the Theological Seminary at Geneva. Burtt and [E. S.] Ely have both come back from the West. Ely's whiskers are as white as his shirt. Walsh writes with as much vigour and pith as ever for the National Intelligencer. He gave Baird a grand feu-de-joie in his last. His health is quite good. While there is not a grain of snow in Philadelphia or at Cranbury, it is a foot deep north of us, and in some parts of Orange Co., where Sam is, three feet deep. Delavan's "colossal stomachs" [illustrating effects of alcohol] are displayed in the Seminary. Quere: whether a good Madonna is not as fine an altar-piece as any entrails whatsoever? Maclean's house providentially saved from fire, on the 4th; attic caught from an ill-jointed stove-pipe of coal-stove below. Baird thinks that Providence has given to French Protestants the ablest defender of their liberties that they have had for a century, in young Count Gasparin, master of requests to the king, and member of the chamber of Deputies. There are about sixteen of my little African flock who seem to be seeking conversion. I perceive an increasing number in our ambitious students every year who babble the nonsensical dialect of transcendentalism. The chief lecturers on the Newark programme this winter are Bancroft, Brownson, Emerson, John Neale, Burritt, Bellows, Furness, and Emerson: I name the majority. Yankee Hill had the Dutch church (on dit) at Newark. You perceive a strong tendency towards catholic union, on the part of the suffering Scotch Presbyterians. God grant that we may see the same at home, to counteract the divisive fanaticism of the ultras! The strength of Presbyterianism, its tendency to increase, has, I think, always been in proportion to its keeping clear of polemic preaching, sectarian propagandism, and supplanting and proselyting ways; and in times when its direct aim was at converting souls. After oscillations to one side and the other, this is the resting-point of my opinion. If I have not wished you a happy-new-year, I do so now; and if I have, I doubly wish it, for you and yours. May our houses be Christian houses, and their inmates objects of special grace and mercy. If you have any coughing propensities, pray do as you would advise another, and subtract from your meetings; for you know well enough that the real good done is not always in the ratio of the number of preachings. I am in sorry condition as to strength.

PRINCETON, *January* 23, 1843.

Your Indians are here. If you have not Merle's History of the Reformation, mention to me your deficit. By all means circulate it, and by all means Carter's edition. I heard my good old father say yesterday that no book in our day he thought was doing more good. He puts the Reformation on its true ground, *i. e.* Luther made his great business the declaring of *saving doctrines*, (we lack a phrase here; I mean the truths which the soul converses with in the article of conversion,) and these went on triumphant, destroying popery, till (—when? for this is the great point) in every country the Reformers took another way, either controversy about minors, or political agitation. The difficulty you mention, of reaching certain people out of our congregations, τοῖς ἔξω, often occurs to me. It is the greatest argument I know of for new measures: an excitement brings them within the orbit of attraction. Hence I have known revivals in which Papists, Quakers, and infidels, who had not heard the gospel for years, have been awakened. Qu. Could not lay-people be the means of saving multitudes, if each would fix on an individual who never goes to church, and never cease till he brought him? if only once? Preach on John i. 46, and context. I would put such a book as the "Saints' Rest" into the hands of a Quaker; the affections must be gained over. Somebody, the other day, in ――'s study, saw a MS. sermon on his table, marked "No. 2500." There is some excellent writing in the close of the Annual Report of the American Board of Foreign Missions.

――, in a letter to me, some time ago, says, that the only preaching which will meet the demands of the awakened public mind, is the *metaphysical*. You and I may as well shut up shop. He argues the point, but I am less than ever convinced. I did not consider his preaching metaphysical, but I deny his proposition. In every age, the interest has attached to just that preaching which most directly reached the affections and passions of souls inquiring what must we do to be saved. This I think historically incontestable. A mix of Baxter and Flavel would be my highest wish as a preacher. I took my children to a private audience with the Indians; they were bivouacking and in dishabille. Secretary Ross did the honours. I am to lose the Hares from next door, but to be indemnified by the Crabbes, on t'other: Capt. Crabbe, U. S. N. What a beautiful euphemism is the following, in Rep. A. B. C. F. M., page 44, (speaking of 80 returned missionaries:) "Fifty were males, and thirty of these came home bereaved, or else in consequence of the sickness of their wives. About one-half of the bereaved missionaries have returned to their work with new partners." The Psalmodists, whom the Assembly "set over the service of song," [a committee for new hymn-book,] have resolved to go on and print. Some fine stanzas of Watts will soon be obsolete, *e. g.*:

> "Till God in human flesh I see,
> My thoughts no comfort find," etc.

I do not know a book of Scripture so consolatory as 2 Cor. Lately I culled the passages in it describing the writer's troubles, and was amazed; but the consolation is like sunshine over all, and everywhere the same—Christ. Cheerful religion is most like Scripture, and, as Dr. Hodge says, joy is an oil to every wheel of the machine. Hence I look with all but envy on such writers as Flavel, Bates, Philip and Matthew Henry, Romaine, and John Newton; they put me into working gear sooner than Brainerd, Payson, and the American school. The enclosed hymns by a valued friend of mine are better than sundry by Mrs. A., and Mrs. B., and Mrs. G., and Professor H., &c. Keep them for me. The author was a recluse "stickit minister," but a true scholar. He wrote a 12mo history of Virginia, which is the best I know, and of which Bancroft speaks highly; and a school reader the "Columbian Reader," better than any I know, except Pierpoint's.

When are you going to set up the "New Jersey Magazine," with Dr. Ewing for Editor? If you do not hurry, you will be anticipated, and surely the capital is the place. You might make it a religious and moral as well as a literary organ. I will contribute my quota; so will you. Dr. Beasley would send pieces abundantly. Trenton gentry would be glad of such an organ. I know your editorial fingers itch to paragraph a little. The records will furnish material for history. Music will find its place. Dr. ——— will embellish your pages. Poetesses will spring up, bland and numerous as poppies. The "children's department" will be attended to. The temperance-reform will have due notice.

The last Biblical Repository has an article on the Wife's Sister. He is driven to take the ground, that no church-court can declare evil that which the law of the land approves. "It is not decent," says he, "to suppose the law of the land against the law of God." Under Tiberius and Nero, Christ made no such supposition. Forsooth, the poor martyrs under Nero, who disobeyed his laws against Christianity, might have escaped martyrdom, if this second Daniel had come to judgment a few centuries earlier. Such is innovation in morals. What a pity 2 Cor. vii. 1 is torn away from the foregoing context! There is wonderful force lost in our version of 2 Cor. ix. 8; and observe it is about *giving:* Δυνατὸς δὲ ὁ Θεὸς πᾶσαν χάριν περισσεῦσαι εἰς ὑμᾶς, ἵνα ἐν παντὶ πάντοτε πᾶσαν αὐτάρκειαν, &c. Symmes Henry told a good thing about his ways of managing the Methodists when they made inroads. There were two or three Methodist families, in whose houses the preachers held meetings. "This will never do," said Henry, "you shall have my session-house," so the bell was rung, and he sat in the pulpit. Of course, the "rider" could not say any thing uncivil. After a few trials they dropped it.

Princeton, February 7, 1843.

[Rev. C. F.] Worrell was received [by Presbytery] and called to 2d Upper Freehold, (what confusion worse confounded among the Freeholds! we have a 2d *Upper* Freehold and no 1st do.—"Freehold," and "Freehold village.")[1] So the "first church Trenton" is in Ewing, [since called Ewing.] There is a revival at Nottingham Square, [now Hamilton Square.] I came

---

[1] Mr. Worrell's is now called "Millstone;" and "Freehold" is called "the Tennent Church;" leaving the village church the only "Freehold."

from Cranbury yesterday in a sleigh, in the teeth of the worst N.W. drift I ever faced. Symmes Henry has a delightful manse, the best I know. He is a truly hospitable, friendly man in his house. There are great revivals reported in Middle Pennsylvania: Carlisle, Chambersburg, Lewisburg, &c. You see Krummacher, of Elberfeld, is elected to succeed Rauch at Mercersburg. A man may write very popular books and yet not be a good president. Some say the Duane St. church will be a collegiate church, [in connexion with a proposed new organization.] I suppose we shall never see another General Assembly, without proposals to alter our book. I am disposed to praise the bridge that has brought us safe over.

Though I should not have vetoed ——'s admission, I think every Presbytery has a right to refuse entrance, without reasons stated; a man might be litigious, abusive, erratic, &c. The day may come when this Presbyterial right shall be very dear to us.

Don't you think our cities are rather feebly manned? O that our country-ministers would only aim at more learning and piety! Most of the great Puritans were in the provinces. So it was in old New England. But our country-pastors think themselves exempt from all scriptural research. I have turned schoolmaster, and teach Henry at home: I wish at least that he may know the Bible. I have been studying 2 Corinthians for a week or two, and have come at some little discoveries which please me a good deal. The heart of Paul breaks forth wonderfully in that epistle. Does not the spirit of the scriptural teaching go against female-prayer-meetings? As to Maternal Associations—why not Parental Associations, where *men* might lead in prayer? Look carefully at the Greek of 1 Tim. ii. 8, τοὺς ἄνδρας—not ἀνθρώπους—and mark the antithesis, afterwards, ὡσαύτως καὶ τὰς γυναῖκας, etc. Read over the whole passage in connexion, and see how, immediately after enjoining on *the men* to pray, he subjoins "let the woman learn in silence," &c.

PRINCETON, *February* 14, 1843.

Henry goes to-morrow to Trenton on some business, by whom I hope to send this valuable missive. My old and poor black kitchen-woman gives $12\frac{1}{2}$ cents a month to Foreign Missions. This is nearly twice as much as the pro rata of our Presbyterial-demand.

Come up and see the mortified, schirrous, and cancerous stomachs in the oratory [p. 362;] they are magnified, so as to tally with the statistics. An article on our national debt to two races, the black and the red, would do good. I wish I had some paper or magazine in which to insert literary scraps, which turn up in my reading, with an interspersion of religious remark. In regard to the Newark Daily, as I am the only one who writes in this line for it, I am found out and accosted about every thing I pen.

I think it likely my notes on 2 Corinthians will grow into something like an informal commentary. Much as we laugh at Rous's version, some of the psalms are wonderfully fine; and if we would only make the allowance which we do in regard to the old English ballads, we should find them noble, *e. g.* Ps. xxiii. Then they stick so close to the original. I do not wonder that those who have been brought up on them should be loth to give them up. A young Quaker from Bucks, graduated last year, who seemed only moral, writes that his being at College was blessed, he thinks, to his becoming acquainted with the grace of the gospel. Two youths, room-mates, eminent scholars, have been hopefully converted this winter. I don't see why everybody should not learn Greek enough to read the New Testament. It would be worth ten times as much as the nonsensical boarding school French, which never does any good to anybody.

PRINCETON, *February* 20, 1843.

I am reading very steadily on 2 Corinthians, and could easily make a book, if I could only satisfy myself as to what sort of a one. Three plans occur to me: 1. A critical exposition, analyzing the Greek text, and discussing the various opinions. If our clergy would read such a book, I believe it would be far the best. 2. A current, running comment, by way of *text*, with abundant notes of critical and contested points, by way of *marginal notes*. 3. A commentary, *all text*, without critical notices or authors cited, so written as to be readable straight ahead, for common readers, giving simply but fully my view of the sense. The more I meditate the more difficult does it seem; I mean to choose a plan. Hodge's method [Romans] chops up the matter too much into bits and compartments. Is it not better to put in the text after the Henry, than after the Scott method? Of all the commentaries I have examined, there is the most constant glow of piety in Calvin, and this without setting his pious remarks by themselves. I mean to send you a specimen chapter, for I wish sharp criticism, and the aid of other eyes. —— is the most laborious Bible student I know. I never saw a man who comes so near reading nothing but the Bible. He has whole paragraphs of the Hebrew in his head. His method is to hang over a single portion for days and weeks. He never reads cursorily. Yet he does not produce any thing interesting in the pulpit. He has no history, no science, no literature, no news. I think he is singularly devoid of *constructive* power; like one who quarries tons of stone, but builds nothing. I think him one of the most devout, serious, reverent men, but strangely blind to every thing like evangelical *privilege*.

Our trials and apprehensions, personal and domestic, ought to drive or draw us to greater spirituality, and more devotion to the best things. Let us pray for one another. Here is a paragraph of beautiful latinity, from Calvin, ad 2 Cor. i. 10, "Tametsi autem" [&c.]

PRINCETON, *March* 3, 1843.

I mean to send you Borrow's two books, ["Bible in Spain" and "The Zincali."] You will find them after-dinner reading of the best. You will devour them, always having your granum salis on the edge of your plate. His religion is of a peculiar kind, but his genius, chivalry, and good-nature will delight you; and whatever good he may have done in Spain, his adventures will suggest to you a hundred thoughts about the value of individual daring and apostolic missions among the Popish peasantry.

In a wood near this place are four old chestnut trees, the only ones of that species; so planted as to form a square. A few weeks ago, a deep hole was discovered between them, newly opened, with marks and remnants of two boxes, which have been taken out. Nobody can explain it. I hear a good deal about Millerism among the lowest sort of people; who, unfortunately, are those who become the prey, in such cases. ―— has bought, for the aisle of the Library, a Cashmere carpet, which Runjeet Singh gave to John C. Lowrie.

PRINCETON, *March* 27, 1843.

It is snowing again; what a March! For the improvident poor, it is really a serious matter. The comet seems to grow dim, but my namesake Stephen has had observations enough to derive elements for a very satisfactory calculation. From these he constructs an ephemeris, and if the thing's place every night answers to the ephemeris, the calculation is conceived to be verified. He will publish it. I attended a soirée of select observers in a case of Mesmerism, the other night. Further than the apparent sleep of the patient, I saw nothing wonderful.

Matt. xii. 30 is often quoted, with a very edifying sense, but how can it be made, in such sense, to cohere at all with what goes before and after? The ancients thought it referred to the devil. The connexion is certainly difficult. Our session is running down rapidly to a close; it ends April 13. Davidson has arrived at New Brunswick. If, as —— demands, we must have Scripture injunction for every thing in our polity, I think we must go vastly further than his present move. I see no title of Scripture for the life-long continuance of ministerial character, or against electing elders every other year, as the Dutch do, or for the power of a majority to govern, or for synods and general-assembly, or for the principle of representation. Where does the Bible say that ruling-elders are representatives of the people, or that they may not be chosen by the pastor? The whole of his arguments are from the jure-divino mint. I have no doubt that the majority of American Presbyterians stand on lower ground than this. Archbishop Whately's book ["Kingdom of Christ Delineated"] is of great value in this respect. It settles some principles about the freedom of the church, within certain limits, to organize itself, which are very comfortable to my mind. But for these, I should have to unchurch the Baptists, as much as they unchurch us, as they are ordained in many cases by laymen. It strikes me with great force, that when the apostle Paul is defending his apostolical claims in his epistles to the Corinthians, he never founds any of them on his external connexion, or succession, or any rites, (which might easily have been verified,) but in every instance, on his doctrine, spirit, and life; 1 Cor. iv. 1, and 9—15; ix. 1, 2, "the *seal* of mine apostleship are *ye*." 2 Cor. vi. 4, "approving ourselves as the ministers of God"—how?—"in much patience," &c.; xi. 23, "Are they ministers of Christ? I am more;" then he gives his proofs, xii. 12. He gives "the signs of an apostle," with no breath of rituality. And so much does he make of *doctrine* as a criterion, that though an angel preach otherwise, he is to be accursed, Gal. i. 8.

Princeton, *March* 30, 1843.

I send herewith a couple of catalogues, which you will please give to Capt. Ewing, (I suppose you know your elder is a miles emeritus, once a captain of horse.) In reperusing Foster's inimitable essays, I am much struck with the fitness of the last, to be put into the hands of a thoughtful, literary man, who feels a sort of contempt for the vulgar manifestations of religion, with which many are offended. Yesterday to my extreme surprise I received a call from Natchez. I am truly and only grieved, for, as I cannot live in that climate, that suffering people have again compassed a denial. The least hint of it beforehand would have led to my preventing such a step. I congratulate you on some symptoms of spring. We have had to boat it, from and to the depôt. Stephen Alexander has been delivering a public lecture on the comet, which gave much satisfaction. Gen. Jackson gives a recommendation (very religious too) of Pease's candy. A very decent Irishman told me yesterday he had been five months out of work. Great revivals and protracted meetings among the Seceders, at Newburgh. I see the Edinburgh Review bepraises Borrow as much as the Quarterly. Lowrie's Travels is a very good book, and worth reading. Dr. somebody in Albany has come out, giving the lie to Sewell's stomach-pictures, which, he says, are caricatures. Moffatt speaks of whole tribes as living for weeks on locusts in Africa. My regards to your "familiares," and am yours.

PRINCETON, April 8, 1843.

The languors of spring have come upon me with a witness. I know not many feelings worse than that of feeling no just cause for activity, and yet being unable to do any thing. If Providence permit, we shall be in Philadelphia next Thursday; probably at our former lodgings, Ninth and Spruce. I congratulate you on the accession of shad, a favourite Trenton dish. College duties are substantially over. There are to be 150 trees set out next week in the Library lot. You will find in the Repertory some things which I said in a late letter, [March 27,] but which, nevertheless, I did not get from the author of the article on "Ruling Elders." I am pleased to see a Layman in Virginia giving $525 as a "thank-offering." I should like to know from ———, what master of literature or art can produce a work, like his who made the lizard or the crow. Will any man compare the Venus de Medici with a living organization, having reproductive powers? I have no doubt that there was high civilization immediately before the deluge. Allison, the Scotchman, has resigned his charge at Paterson. The new school Psalm and Hymn book is out; compiled by Beman. The Methodists are going to have a meeting-house about halfway between us. You know, perhaps, that a second Dutch church is hatching in New Brunswick. There is a man in the Seminary, who is said to have been an actor in Philadelphia. One of Shakspeare's daughters married a John Hall, M. D., whose arms were, " Or on a bend sable," &c. Her epitaph ran thus:

> "Witty above her sex; but that's not all:
> Wise to salvation was good Mistress Hall.
> Something of Shakspeare was in *that*: but this
> *Wholly of him*, with whom she's now in bliss,"

Your next son should be called William S. The death of

poor —— [an idiot] must be a relief to his afflicted mother; though in such cases the very wen seems to involve some of the vital circulation. This year the months of April and Nisan begin together, which makes the passover fall on Good-Friday; this is worth putting into the papers. I must try to get to the synagogue. I do not expect to be among you until the Council of Trent, [meeting of Presbytery at Trenton.] I have a resolution to propound, recommending sturdy folks not to sit during prayer. I wish in my heart our church had adopted kneeling in prayer, and standing in song. The comet has entirely absented itself. Only two lecturers-errant this week. ——, so I hear since I began, has taken advisement with —— about the Hebrew letters going to make up 666. If you wish to know, I will find out. Vinegar is now said to be a fine thing for the teeth.

PHILADELPHIA, *April* 18, 1843.

Your friends here are well. We are 163 South 9th. Quaker Yearly Meeting, which accounts for the rain.[1] I attended a grand Concert of the Blind, yesterday, in full force; it was passing fine. I saw six elephants walking two and two, up Spruce Street. In a proof of ——'s, instead of "and when Abraham drew near the camp, *he heard a shout,*" it had "*he tore his shirt.*" I did not think the church very well filled on Sunday, considering the eminence of the divine. [himself] who preached. Next Sunday I am caught for St. Louis le Grand's, Penn Square, [an elegant new church.] Dr. Tyng's lectures are very largely attended. The rain has kept me from going about much. The Episcopal churches are much thronged; there is good policy in laying so much stress on the "service," which is, like potatoes, always present, whatsoever the other dishes may be. The cheapness of goods is wonderful. I bought very good white pocket handkerchiefs for 25 cents.

PHILADELPHIA, *April* 24, 1843.

My visit to Philadelphia, from which I anticipated much pleasure, has proved somewhat Tantalic, as I have had to be supine most of the time, with a complaint which has rendered locomotion excruciating. Otherwise I am well. Confined to the house, I have little news. I saw McCalla going by, looking like a general officer; hair as before. Leeser has started a magazine, "The Occident." The spring display of city-flowers is very charming. I bought a razor-strop from the celebrated "Strop-man," who harangues in front of the State House; I

[1] This is a common saying in Philadelphia.

got it for 25 cents, more for fun than any thing else, and I find it excellent. The "converted thief," Munday, goes about, rain or shine, bare-headed, but chin covered with an abundant shag. Odenheimer is out with a new book, "The True Churchman no Romanist." Bp. Kenrick lectures statedly, on the controverted points. There is a schism among the Jews in this country about instrumental music in the synagogue; Leeser thinks it "labour," and so forbidden; I think their yelling and eructation much more laborious.

PRINCETON, *May* 11, 1843.

The green fields, trees, birds, &c., are beyond all praise. I am glad to get back to my cabbage-garden. The Seminary examination is "being" made. I have been very busy, since my return, on a piece of writing, which has to be ready by Assembly-times.[1] On dit, that they will certainly have a tramontane Assembly next year.[2] Allan Mackenzie, who digs my garden, is afraid the troubles in the Kirk will lead to the "bringing in of episcopacy *and* prelacy." A crazy man lives next door; perhaps we shall have "vegetable marrows" thrown over the fence; vide Nicholas Nickleby "by Mr. Dickens of South Britain," as —— calls him in his newest series of letters. —— has left young ——, a half-converted Jew-lad, here, to study.[3] If you want some okra-seed, I raised a bushel last year. The giant, the dwarf, and the harpers have been here, but the "razor-strop" man has not yet got on so far. I hear of direful mercantile failures among some of the wealthiest of my acquaintances in Virginia. Our students begin to return; I see a few new faces. My old uncle Maj. John Alexander is to be in the Assembly; and D. v., my father will return with him to Virginia.[4] I hope he may be prospered in this, probably his last, visit to his native county. Never can I be sufficiently grateful for the preservation of my honoured parents to an old age of cheerfulness, health, and activity. The last British Critic is out in favour of auricular confession. Dr. McElroy is still at Santa Cruz. Dr. Chalmers says, in a speech, which I know not whether our papers have extracted, that the Scotch clergy are preparing for their change of circumstances, by going into smaller houses. Dr. Gordon, leaving one of the

---

[1] I cannot discover from the Minutes, or otherwise, what this paper was.
[2] The Assembly of 1844 met at Louisville, Kentucky.
[3] The conversion proved to be even less than half.
[4] For an account of this visit see "The Life of Archibald Alexander, D. D.," Chap. xviii.

finest mansions in Edinburgh, goes into a house of £35 rent. The new body will be called " the Free Presbyterian Church."

PRINCETON, *May* 24, 1843.

The Occidentals will, I have no doubt, have the next Assembly at Louisville. The New-School folks are in the expected trouble about abolition; and it will not be strange if their Southern members fall off. In this case, I confidently expect that the most of the latter will join us. Before this reaches you, I suppose the ruling-elder question will have been decided; perhaps to be reversed at Louisville.[1] Dr. McElroy has returned from St. Croix, in good health. During Maclean's absence [at General Assembly] I conduct a daily prayer-meeting at half-past five. I was at the communion at Dutch Neck last Sunday; 12 accession. I am suffering a most painful languor and debility; the cause must be latent disease, yet my ordinary functions are as usual. It is itself a disease, and one for which one can ask no sympathy, and which is not sufficiently prononcée to absolve the conscience from the obligation to work. I often feel that the effort of rising from my chair is a labour. Too soon has the grasshopper become a burden. Œconomos, one of our late Greeks, [in College,] died of consumption, in Fairfax co., Va., on the 9th inst. There is a young Jew here, [mentioned in last letter,] injudiciously sent by ———, one ———, of Posen, Germany, æt. 20, who has excited my strong commiseration. He is speculatively a Christian, and convinced of his sinfulness, but as blind as Pharisaism itself as to the plan of grace, and so distressed at being rejected by his parents, that he told me the other evening he had not been in bed for four nights. He speaks German, Polish, and English, and is a thorough Hebrew and Chaldee scholar, has read all the Talmud, and understands French. He is a " puer ingenui vultûs," and certainly of fine capacity; but unless he obtains some relief he will go mad. He showed me his phylacteries. His change of views was occasioned by the simple perusal of a New Testament, seen first by him since he grew up, and given him by a clergyman in Germany. John Miller is going to Richmond to assist Plumer in the redaction of the Watchman, and in preaching. A late drunkard of our town once said that the soil about Dutch Neck was like self-righteousness; the more a man had of it, the worse he was off. Young Wadsworth, late of the Seminary, now of Troy, is said to be a phœnix of eloquence; he is in Philadelphia.[2]

[1] The decision, by a vote of 83 to 35, was that three ministers (though without a ruling elder) constitute a quorum of Presbytery.
[2] Now pastor of the Fifth church there.

PRINCETON, *May* 30, 1843.

My father and uncle set out this week for "the old Colony and Dominion of Virginia." I am not well, but potter about in my garden on the few clear days; my truck looks promising, and it is a great amusement to me. [Jos. B.] Stratton is gone to supply Natchez, [now the Pastor.] Dr. Lindsly and Dr. Edgar both have sons, physicians, coming to the Seminary. I have had two visits from an old man who was in the battle of Princeton. My weight is just 132 lbs.

TYLERTON,[1] *June* 12, 1843.

You will judge from the papers that we have all been Tyler-mad; sundry of us have been so. I feel anxious that it should be generally known, that the programme of the part to be enacted by the Faculty of the College, was printed and posted, and the appointment made on our grounds, without consultation with us. As a faculty we did nothing. Several of us were present in the throng. The President and suite, viz., Wickliffe, wife and two daughters, Spencer, &c., went to the Episcopal church in the morning, and to the Presbyterian at night. Between services a grand dinner. They left us, with music and a great cortège, about 8 this morning. A large number of naval and some army officers were at Com. Stockton's in uniform. As the cavalcade passed [Mr. J. S.] Green's, departing, [Rev.] Dr. [Ashbel] Green came out; on which Tyler rapidly dismounted from his chariot and four and uncovered himself to the old man: the only impressive scene in the melodrama.

PRINCETON, *June* 15, 1843.

All your malignant evil speaking concerning ———, may be accounted for from the chagrin you experience at not being invited to orate. Notwithstanding what you say, I must honour the King: not that I did much for King John III.: but I am opposed to all ultra-democracy, of which the very extreme, I take it, is to make our tribute of respect dependent on mere popular like or dislike. [After referring to a medical friend, for whom he wished to find some public employment.] His mildness, reading, &c., would make him a good principal of an Insane Asylum. Could he not be spirited up to an agitation of the public in behalf of such an institution in Trenton? He might write a lecture and deliver it in our chief towns.[2] My father is heard from as far on as Waynesborough. He preached four or five

---

[1] The President of the United States had just been visiting at Princeton.

[2] This suggestion was made two years before the Legislature of New Jersey established the Insane Asylum near Trenton.

times at Charlottesville, and, from Dr. Cabell's letter, must have been in his very best mood. The college tee-total society, of which Maclean is the soul, has more than a hundred pledges: exclusive of an eminent professor, [himself,] who is suspected of daily potations of Oporto. I preached last evening from Prov. i. 32. Dr. —— [in New York] is down again, and uttering the Macedonian cry. I can certify, of personal observation this morning, that some toads are still found in Princeton: "Personally appeared before me," &c., &c. Give our kind regards to —— and circumjacent friends. A new pamphlet on the sister-question sent to me from Natchez. It has some hard arguments in it, some quite puzzling ones.

PRINCETON, *June* 24, 1843.

A little tropical weather after all. Dr. O'Shaughnessy, of Calcutta, (Prof. Phys.,) has been here. Brisbane, the Fourierist, and some aids, are looking out for a farm of a thousand acres in this neighbourhood, whereon to exemplify their socialism. The following is from the Leipsic Acta Eruditorum: "Jacobi Alexandri paradoxam opinionem de motu terræ circa lunam, ceu planetæ secundarii circa primarium, recensuimus in Actis, A. 1728, p. 127." I write a fresh lecture every week on Latin literature, which I read to the Sophomores, over and above their regular recitations. Musgrave has published an 8vo volume against the Methodists. Henry Van Dyck picked 50 quarts of strawberries yesterday morning: I have none worth naming. —— has become a regular hack, and writes on every topic which promises to catch the million: this may do for a laureat, but it is not the plan of a poet. There are some things often mentioned but seldom seen: yesterday, for the first time, I saw the death of a cow. At the present rate every family ought to take the Sunday School Journal. I propose, next Friday, to publish, with my name, a card in the Princeton Whig, calling attention to it. Suppose you do the same, simultaneously. I acknowledge the seven [Acts vi.] are not called deacons, but I suppose no one ever doubted that these are they; the duties being so much the same. It is a case where universal, uncontradicted tradition goes far with me, as in the case of the change of the Sabbath.

PRINCETON, *July* 19, 1843.

I am sorry that I cannot render you the assistance you ask on the next Lord's day. Not only have I to preach for Dr. Rice, but early next morning I have to examine a class, at our Quarterly Examination, to which I could not be back in time. I have been very much debilitated this summer, and lately, for the first time in my life, had to sit down in the midst of a sermon, from a sudden affection of the head.

There is more of the influenza within a few days, than we have had. Of ecclesiastical news there seems to be none. Last Sunday afternoon Dr. Green preached to my Africans. Though his voice laboured, the sermon was excellent, and towards the close very impressive. My father, when last heard from, was in Bath co., Va. Sam has gone on to accompany him home. Mr. Rogers, of Northern India, has been here. Mr. Walsh, late of the Seminary, is about to go to that mission. Smyth's new work on Presbyterianism is out. Joseph Tracy is making an abridgment of his former one. If —— should follow the example of some of the Oxonians, and turn Romanist, it would lower his dignity very much to be ordained sub-deacon, deacon, &c. A short-hand teacher is enlightening us at this time. I begin to need spectacles to read long-hand. It is not one of the agreeables of our college arrangements, that our hardest work and heaviest examinations come in the heat of summer: our terrible "Final" begins on the 7th of August. Do you hear of any colleges about to doctor us this fall? What a grand method it would be to sell D.D.s as they do commissions in the British army! They would then be sure to fall on such of us as long for them, while others who care not for them might be spared all trouble. Some painters have been pottering about the outside of our house for more than a month; what with ladders, daubing, and smell, it is decidedly worse than house-cleaning. I never, in my craziest moments, feel the slightest desire to share the greatness or fame of kings, grandees, poets, grand authors, orators, or the like; but I often feel a sort of envy for quiet folks, whom I see, far from all publicity, carrying on some humble household labour. These Fourier-systems would make every one live in public, and obliterate little family-circles, and all that we call Home. One of my neighbours lately caught a bull-frog, which had a whole cat-bird in his insides; he also caught a pike, with a sucker six inches long in its stomach. These marvels you will report to your Lyceum. Judge Tucker, of the University of Va., had for many years a periodical rheumatism in one knee, recurring with perfect accuracy every 13th day: it has for a year past been exchanged for a syncope, returning for some months at the same interval, but now oftener. The legislature of Virginia gave the widow of Prof. Davis $12,000 for the copyright of a work of his on Criminal Law.[1]

---

[1] The death of Professor Davis is mentioned on page 315.

PRINCETON, *August*, 1843.

My father has returned. He was gone sixty-four days, and in that time delivered thirty-two public discourses. So Pusey was really suspended: Vide his letter of the 2d inst. A man came last week into the office of the Board of Foreign Missions [New York] with a bag of money, laid it on the table, and said it was for the China Mission, on condition no questions should be asked: the contents were $10,000. Such an event ought to be laid before our people, to show them, by a scale they all too well understand, how some Christians rate the Mission work.

PRINCETON, *Sept.* 5, 1843.

I am truly glad to hear that your resort to the hill-country has done you good. My stay at the Cape [May] was very delightful, but very short; I arrived there on Monday evening, and came away on Saturday morning of the same week. Yet my spirits were much refreshed, and I think, if I could have stayed three weeks, I should have been made quite well. The Seminary has opened with a larger accession than is usual at this point of time. More are expected, as several commencements are yet to come off. The "Princeton" [a Navy Steam-ship] is to be launched this week. We had Dr. May of Alexandria [Episcopal Theological Seminary] at Cape ditto; a very agreeable man; as near being a low churchman as any I have seen. When called on by me, he made an extempore prayer at a meeting. I also made myself acquainted with Judge Stroud [of Philadelphia] formerly of our college. I see all connexion between Bokum and the Jews' Society is dissolved by proclamation. Did I ever tell you of a little quarrel I had this summer with Bokum? It arose from my "accusing him of injudiciousness." Thereupon ensued a correspondence, &c. I have been honoured with a picture of Husteecoluck-chee, alias John Douglass Bemo. He is on his way back to the Seminoles. Eleven of the last class, Andover, have agreed to go together to Iowa. Quere: whether all missionary enterprises among us ought not to yield precedence to the work of evangelizing the Southern slaves? Ministers ought to be among them, in sufficient numbers, even if they were to be emancipated to-morrow; so that the question has no limitation from that of Abolition. Next in order, I think, come the Indians, whose condition is now more favourable than that of any heathen tribes on earth, for receiving the gospel. The préstige, however, of this mission = 0 Will —— go to ——? No, I guess. If he does, he will go away from home. There is nothing in a professoral place at all resembling the worship which a popular city-pastor receives.

PRINCETON, *Sept.* 15, 1843.

I have read Young's sermon, [afterwards a "Campbellite Baptist:"] he must be an Arian. His fundamental articles make no mention of Trinity, Atonement, or even Incarnation. He objects to such terms as Trinity, Triune, three in one, coessential and coeternal. When a man objects to creeds, he always has a reason for it. I perceive he is out upon the Corn-laws. I hope to re-open my house on the 1st prox. Beds, stabling, the choicest wines, (in part of the stock of the late —— Esq.,) omnibuses passing twice a day, &c. Dr. Rice thinks he has a disease of the heart. He is like to go to Augusta, Ga., for the winter. I have, for a rarity, to marry a couple on Saturday night. Our venerable friend Mr. John McMullin has been released at last: all my thoughts of him are pleasant.[1] Mrs. Smith, relict of Dr. John B. Smith, is dead in Indiana, æt. 82. Capt. Stockton is ordered out for a four-months' cruise in the " Princeton." What a difference between us and the English, in regard to school-books! They still use, in all their great schools, the grammar of Edward VI. I have a copy of it. It is full of forms, and primary rules, but few observations. Our American Bibles vary exceedingly from the standard British ones, in small points, especially of orthography. Dr. Hodge's organ has come.

PRINCETON, *Sept.* 20, 1843.

I am conscious of no indebtedness in regard of letters, but being more good for nothing than common, I shall vent the contents of noddle on you. On Monday, a very ingenuous-looking young man, calling himself McMana, applied with much humility for aid to get to Albany. He offered to leave books in pawn, &c., and showed a certificate of church-membership from Mr. W. S. Potts of St. Louis. In the evening, Prof. Henry, going to the depot, happened to get into the same hack with this man, and (it being dark) shortly heard the fellow take great liberties with his name, asserting that he had dined with Prof. H., and moreover declaring that he was on his way to *Philadelphia.* At the depot he saw Prof. H., and tried to hide behind a platform. My brother Sam pulled him out, and H. extracted from him the money he had begged, and the certificate of church-membership. The Hon. Mr. ———, in the Quarterly Register, in a piece lamenting the decay of classic learning, recommends the Bible as "corpus juris *divinæ.*" This is the eventful day at

---

[1] Mr. McMullin was an elder of the Third Church of Philadelphia, when Dr. A. Alexander was pastor, and afterwards, and until his death, of the Sixth Church.

Easton: visions of gigantic Ds float before my mind. "Between the acting of a dreadful thing, &c.," v. Shakspeare. Our annual Examination is now being holden. I wish I had a number of the Christian Mirror to show you. There is a piece in it about Princeton, lauding every thing to the skies. Inter alia, much as follows; (I don't pretend to give exact words:) speaking of Dod:—"whose colloquial powers are no less extraordinary than those reported of Johnson, Sir James McIntosh, and Coleridge . . . The profound metaphysician, mathematician, divine—pupil of Sir Christopher Wren and Palladio." This, as Sam Slick says, is cutting it very fat.

PRINCETON, *September* 25, 1843.

I neglected to say to you that we will give you a bed during Commencement times, and a napkin at my father's. Do not imagine, my dear sir, that any elevation of rank on my part will prevent me from exercising all the condescension which is seemly towards my humbler friends. Come freely, and lay aside all the dread which the circumstances are fitted to inspire.[1]

TRENTON, *October* 2, 1843.

I am disposed to make a stand on this position, viz., that wherever our church has made great advances, it has been by the pressing of *converting truth*. The following words are uniformly spelled thus, in standard English Bibles; I mean certain places in all editions: 'Ax, horseleach, morter, brasen, throughly, whiles, Rahel, Judæa, houshold, enquire, sope, jubile, intreat, asswage, pluckt, caterpiller, lothe." Dr. Brownlee has had a paralytic stroke, from which he is not expected to recover.[2] We are hereafter to have Commencement in June, and a summer vacation. The faculty, who are most interested in not going wrong in such a matter, are unanimously for it. It was opposed by only four Trustees. In order to bring it about, we have to make the next nine months equal to twelve, by working double tides, and having only a fortnight of vacation, from opening of next term till the close of the succeeding one. Your friend, Dr. Kidd,[3] was a crony of old Mr. Potts's, and dedicated one of his works to him, in connexion, I think, with Dr. Green. He published, about 1815, a large octavo, on the Trinity; a

---

[1] The sportive allusion is to his having received the degree of Doctor of Divinity from Lafayette College. This honour was doubled upon him, in 1854, by Harvard University.

[2] Dr. Brownlee survived until February, 1860.

[3] I had inquired of him concerning a Professor Kidd, of Aberdeen, who had received the degree of D. D. from Princeton in 1818.

very heavy and abstruse work, in which he endeavoured to derive a metaphysical argument from mere reason.

PRINCETON, *October* 24, 1843.

When I parted with you on the 16th, I did not expect to go to Synod; but that night I repented and went. I got to Newark about 10 P. M. Next morning I awoke early, and finding it clear and frosty, I traversed the streets and surveyed the markets. I breakfasted at the Park House with Kinney and McDonald, and their wives. At 9 I ascended the cars for Morristown, and found myself in company with Mr. Helm of Salem. I have seen no cars more agreeable. We arrived at Morristown about half-past 10, having gone through a rolling country; fertile looking; snug houses, clean hamlets, signs of comfort; in a word, a little New England. Morristown is a pleasant but irregular village, on high ground, in sight of hills. Mr. Johnson, elder of Mr. Kirtland, here joined us, and we three went together to Newton. Dr. Rice, Maclean, and Talmage had lodged in Morristown, and taken an extra. Mr. Kirtland was detained by a funeral, and Mr. Dumont by the illness of his wife. We took a four-horse stage-coach, and began to climb the hills; and from this to Newton we had a perpetual succession of ups and downs. Yet even among the mountains the roads are smooth; often however mere galleries, cut around precipitous ledges. The inequalities, and the zig-zag of the trail, made it eight hours before we got to Newton at 7. It was 35 miles. We had passed through places called Denville, Dover, Rockaway, Sparta, (a pleasant village, where Torrey, formerly of Rio, is New-School minister.) I was enchanted all the way with the mountain and valley prospects. Like the Virginia valley, but not so much distant mountain range, and of course less bold than the Alleghany. Many iron-works, and much limestone. Millions of loose rocks in the fields; yet settlements close together, and many fine houses. The Synod had been four hours in session. Gray had preached, and McLean was in the chair: Rodgers and Imbrie clerks. We went in, and found a missionary meeting in progress. Morrison from India had spoken; Lowrie was speaking; then followed Dr. Janeway. Davidson prayed, and the choir (though a good one) balked in a tune. Perhaps you would like the names of the bishops: From the *North-west*, Foster, Hand, and Colton; from *Elizabethtown Pby.*, Williamson, Hunt, Ogden, Murray, (Kirtland, 2d day,) Cochrane, J. Cory, B. Cory, Street, and Imbrie; from *New Brunswick*, Comfort, Janeway, Rice, Rodgers, Deruelle, Maclean, Davidson, McLean, Vandoren, Mahon, Hale, Worrell, and Schenck; from *Raritan*,

Kirkpatrick, Studdiford, Hunt, Olmstead, Hull, Williams, and Sherwood; from *Newton*, Shafer, Castner, Longmore, Gray, Yeomans, Nassau, Johnston, Webster, Junkin, Lewers, Irwin, Worrell, Tully, McGee, McWilliam, Mack, and Lowrie; from *West Jersey*, Beach Jones, Helm, and Lawrence. I lodged at Dr. Shafer's. We were treated with great kindness. They live well in Sussex; it is a land of milk and honey, and their buckwheat cakes are unrivalled. Their butter equals Goshen, and is their chief export. Every thing went on pleasantly at Synod. There was no judicial business; there were no angry words. There was much conversation on the progress of religion and of our benevolent church-schemes. A uniform plan of raising money was reported, adopted, and recommended. The Synod yielded assent to the proposal for a new synod in Pennsylvania. On Wednesday Morrison spoke an hour on Foreign Missions. Though a very Moses in elocution, he deeply affected every one with his statements. I never before had such a notion of the missionary's contact with thousands of the heathen. Murray followed with a very spirited and effective speech. In the evening there was a meeting for domestic missions; full house and pulpit. Deruelle prayed, and —— and.—— orated: the one as fine as silk, the other as coarse as cordage: —— is a splendid declaimer; his organ is incomparable. —— abused the Episcopalians beyond aught I ever heard in public: many of them were there. Inter alia, he called (horresco referens) the sign of the cross, "the sign of the beast." On Thursday 19th, some resolutions for the Free Church passed, *nem. contradicente*. Our presbytery-minutes occasioned much mirth, by the Latin of the recorded exegeses: it was horrible indeed; and was pounced upon by some of the Newtonian Latinists. They must have been penned by some Bunyan among us: "the Latin I borrow." *e. g.* "An opera bona necessaria *sit?*" The next meeting to be at New Brunswick; where Dr. D. is effecting a painting in distemper back of the pulpit. He introduced a resolution assertory of what is falsely called the *strict* mode of baptism. He withdrew it, after satisfying himself that his view was the popular one. The business was all done at 1 P. M. on Thursday. We spent the afternoon, however, in devotion; addresses by Dr. Rice, Maclean, Vandoren, and McLean: and there was preaching at night by "P. P. clerk of this parish" [himself].

I found a number of former pupils in Synod, and there were residing in Newton, Martin Ryerson, Geo. Ryerson, Thomas Ryerson, Shafer, Thomson, (the surrogate,) and McCarter; all students of ours; from whom I received much attention. Friday, the 20th, was a fine day, but I saw quite thick ice, under the shade of a mountain, as late as half-past nine. Father Comfort offered me a seat in his vehicle, and the journey homeward was truly delightful. The old man fought all his battles o'er again, and was fine company. He knew every cross-road, and almost every house. We passed several little crystal lakes, and abundance of hills and valleys. We had in company, in other carriages, McLean, Vandoren, and Schenck. Our way was through Hackettstown, Schooley's Mountain, where we drank of the waters; German valley, where we dined; Germanstown, in Hunterdon; Lamington, Pluckamin, Somerville, Harlingen, and Kingston. We passed the natal spots of the McDonnells, I. V. Brown, and S. C. Henry. We lodged at Major Talmage's near Somerville, where we had profuse hospitality. I saw Dominie Messler, and called on Dominie Chambers and Dominie Labagh of Harlingen. I was, by a kind Providence, returned home in safety by 4 P. M. on Saturday, after a very delightful week. I passed through nine counties, viz., Mercer, Middlesex, Essex, Morris, Sussex, Warren, Hunterdon, Passaic, and Somerset. Not a word was said about Elders' impositions, [of hands in ordaining Ruling Elders,] Wife's sister, or the Psalm Book. I believe every member of the Synod went away with a pleasant feeling. Old Dr. Shafer is a most affectionate and pious man. I have volunteered to preach for Helm on the 5th of November, or Gunpowder-day. I learn from Mr. Lowrie, who got here on Saturday, that the Philadelphia Synod were in the trenches, and like to be some days, on the elder and quorum question.

PRINCETON, *November* 2, 1843.

I shall not be able to stop on my return from Salem, as the opening of our term will be so near. The awakening among the Jews, at Pesth, see last Missionary Herald, is a striking event. There have been two more deaths by small-pox, but it has not extended beyond the family, nor to any vaccinated subject. Gov. Haines [of New Jersey] was my classmate. Dr. Miller speaks of his mother as an eminent Christian. Rich. Johnson is expected here, to be fêted. John Owen, in his famous work on Congregationalism, after declaring that there is no such thing as a minister, who has no congregation, asserts expressly, that the church has no power to send men to preach to the heathen, or to any people not gathered into a church. This is a corollary, to be sure. He, as were all the New England pilgrim fathers, was stiff for ruling elders. All the early New England churches had them. He (O.) argues plausibly, that the Bible knows no visible organized church, except a particular congregation. This was also the New England tenet. I trust those members of legislature who profess godliness, will do something to bring their unconverted colleagues to church, &c. Morrison preached and spoke here on Sunday. Four young men of the Seminary are assigned to China. One of these and another during the long vacation, paid two thousand family-visits in the pines; everywhere giving advice, books, &c. One of the four, Culbertson, [Rev. M. S. C., now at Shanghai,] was an army-officer, and highly honoured at West Point; chosen to go on some military mission to France. I have a black synonyme or homonyme in Africa, [in one of the Mission Schools.] Nevins has published a pamphlet intituled "The Anxious Seat." The Western [Theological] Seminary [Alleghany city] has forty students. Clow, our college steward, is lord-mayor, and I am yours, with much sleepiness.

PRINCETON, *November* 21, 1843.

I preached on Sunday for ——. He is the best specimen I know of a country pastor, for demeanour, piety, and sound learning; a good theologian, and a ripe Hebraist and classical scholar. None but a Hercules should attempt three services. At his house I met Dr. ——, a surgeon in the army. He has been several years in the south and west; his last post being Fort Gibson. Last summer he went far into the Indian prairies, with a command of mounted dragoons, under Capt. Boon, a son of the famous hunter of Kentucky. Their business was the protection of the Santa Fe traders. He showed me specimens of the salt-rock, with which extensive tracts of that country are covered. He has been constantly among the Indians. He ridicules the notion of savage life being favourable to health, and says he never saw more disease among any people. Thousands die in infancy. They have perpetual coughs and pleurisies. Their doctors have scarcely any remedies, no knowledge of herbs, and little credit among the people, except as conjurers. They had a sorry fellow for chaplain, at Fort Gibson. He found a soldier with a bottle of rum, ordered him to deliver it, and on refusal drew a pistol on him. On one occasion, preaching, he chose to expound the phrase "fear and trembling." "Fear, my brethren," said he, "is—is—is—the emotion which fills your breast upon the approach of an enemy." This is like the New England parson, who, in preaching before a court, prayed "that all their decisions might be *overruled*." You will seldom find a more enchanting drive than the upper end of the river-road to Lambertville; I mean in summer. Studdiford has an English MS. of a tract of Wiclif's in good preservation, on vellum, which is at least four hundred years old. You should see it. A work of thrilling interest has appeared, intituled "Letters to a very young Lady:" it is not certain whether by Chalmers or Macaulay.[1] It is likely to move both hemispheres. I fear a church can never be supported at Titusville; the district is too small, and nobody is likely to attend from Pennsylvania.[2] Dr. Phillips's people [Wall Street Church, New York] have bought ground up town, [Fifth Avenue.] I am told that Merle d'Aubigné makes nothing beyond expenses by his original work, few copies of the French being sold. Suppose you and I get him to send us a copy in advance, and give him part proceeds of the translation, which would have a great sale. We have admitted more than seventy students, of whom more than twenty are communicants. From a concurrence of causes, my teaching labours are trebled this year. In Charlotte Elizabeth's Magazine, this dashing woman declares Cowper's melancholy to have been a judgment on him for translating Homer: an odd prolepsis, surely, inasmuch as he tried to hang himself shortly after he was of age, and never thought of his translation until he was more than fifty. All she ever will write will do less for the gospel than Cowper's Task, Truth, Charity, Expostulation, and Hymns. His translation, like his other works, was the refuge from a madness, which but for this would have driven him to suicide, or at least to the cells. Though he is not our only Christian poet, he is certainly (of the great ones) our only evangelical one. The cruelty of the aspersion is affecting. The woman is deaf herself. When Charles the Second taunted Milton with losing his sight, as a judgment, Milton reminded him that his majesty's father had lost his head. And when Warburton, in a like vein, told old Quin, that all the regicide judges came to a bloody end, the actor replied, "The same, your lordship may observe, is true of the twelve apostles." Missionary Morrison preached on Sunday at Pennington. Dr. Hare departs tomorrow, [for Philadelphia;] he does not abandon his school scheme.

PRINCETON, *December* 11, 1843.

I send you a catalogue of the Seminary. The commercial turn of the Seminary is evident from the accession of "Byers" and "Sellers." Mr. Webber has been a Texan major. Thomas Thomas is a Welshman. Mr. Byers is a Nova-Scotian licentiate. W. Scudder is a Ceylonese. I do not know any thing which I ever read so much from a sense of duty, as the

---

[1] A work of his own, published by the Sunday School Union, pp. 251.

[2] This proved a groundless fear. The enterprise has flourished so well that a handsome church edifice has already succeeded the one first occupied.

"Message:" it teaches one nothing, and gives no amusement. On Thanksgiving Day, I preached on the blessing of Peace. We were providentially prevented by the storm from having our parents to dine with us, as projected, but through divine favour we had the whole remainder of our large family. It was an event to be recorded with thanksgiving, as it has not occurred for many years, nor is likely ever to occur again; at least at such a season. We endeavoured to rejoice and be merry, and ate and drank: 2 Sam. vi. 19. We cannot in English compress like the Latins: this morning I read with my class Juvenal's *nemo malus felix*. My father has a severe catarrh; so has Dod; so has Dr. Miller; so has Dr. Hodge. The latest Oxford Bibles contain the following orthographic anomalies: "subtil, sycomore, agone, goodman, intreat, injoin, subtilly, sneesed, fetcht, ringstraked, scrowl, Nicolaitanes, vallies." I have a serious request to make of you, in which my feelings are very much interested. There ought to appear an article in our Princeton paper on Drinking and drinking-houses; and I wish not to be the writer. Do me the favour to send me such a piece on the following, brief, sharp, and short: "Beer-houses; danger even of fermented liquors; groups of young men at doors of such places; effect on good name; the *kind* of men who frequent; the sudden fall of many not reputed drunkards; delirium tremens, &c." The whole intended to warn young men, and to show that *such persons attract public attention.* Chalmers, in a written report, has a sentence much like this: "there are other channels, the foundations of which are connectable with our object." Prof. Dod begins this evening a course of lectures on Architecture in the Seminary, ladies to be admitted; Monday and Wednesday evenings. So [Daniel] O'Connell, lawyer like, is going to slip through the meshes of the law. There are said to be 30,000 witnesses on his side. Dr. Chalmers has sent for the Repertory, and requests a review of his Romans.[1] [Professor] Stuart ought to understand the Revelation; he has been lecturing on it 25 years. In Den's Theology, the Roman Catholic text-book, high Predestinarianism is taught, exactly as Turretine teaches it. I see Sydney Smith writes common-shore [sewer] exactly as it is pronounced. The probable withdrawing of Calhoun from the presidential race, will greatly brighten up Van Buren's prospect. I pray against the annexation of Texas; it would spread slavery over Mexico, and I fear add a century

---

[1] The theological works of Dr. Chalmers were reviewed by Mr. Alexander, in the Repertory of January, 1841, and those on education and ecclesiastical economy in the number for October, 1842. Part of the first article was by his father.

to its existence in the United States. Nothing but the opening of new cotton and sugar lands within twenty years has prevented the abolition of slavery (at least in regard to post-nati) in Maryland, Virginia, Kentucky, and Tennessee. If a wall were built around these States, the slaves would eat their own heads off in a twelvemonth.

Princeton, *December* 30, 1843.

Dr. Cunningham has been here for several days; but this is not his main visit. He is altogether the most satisfactory foreigner I have seen. By the Scotch papers I perceive he ranks among the first four or five in the Free Church. Height about 6 ft., and large in proportion; a stout but finely formed man; very handsomely dressed, and in an eminent degree the gentleman, in every thing but excess of snuff. Age, I reckon, about 41; spectacles. A shock of thick curly hair. He has no airs of patronage. Powerful reasoning and sound judgment seem to be his characteristics; and he is a walking treasury of facts, dates, and ecclesiastical law. I heard him for an hour, on Friday, in a speech to the students. Indescribable Scotch intonation, (but little idiom,) and convulsion of body, but flowing, elegant language, and amazing power in presenting argument. Though his manner is rugged and uncouth, and he has no sign of imagination, yet when he gets on tender topics of religion, he is so scriptural, and so sound, that one is affected by what he says. I have seldom listened to a man with more instruction. New and Old School in New York have joined in regard to him, and he has preached for both sides. On Sunday he is to preach for Drs. Phillips and Potts. On the 26th and 27th I was in Brunswick—visitation, [of committee of Presbytery.] Rodgers and I were the only foreign bishops. Good assemblies. Three weeks ago McClelland preached in the Second Dutch church, on profane swearing. He said that on a recent occasion he had gone to Rahway in the cars, and had counted seventy oaths. Also "It was once customary to rend the garments on hearing a false oath: if this were customary here, we should all go naked." "The sin prevails from the President in his bed, to the beggar on his dunghill." My father's address at Lexington [College] is printed; but the fashion of sending a copy to the author has not been introduced there. On Christmas day we were favoured of Providence to meet, all of us, at my father's, with three distant relations. My father preached an Advent sermon. New Year's day is the New York saints' day. I am concerned at having to say that good old Dr. Miller is quite ill, with pleurisy. The loss of him would be a sad blow to us. I think him one of the most conscientious and pious men I ever knew. His behaviour in a parlour-controversy is an example to every one, and has often put me to shame. According to the New England decision about incest, a man may now marry his step-mother; thus it is likely to be no longer so odd a thing "that one should have his father's wife." Cunningham says the prejudice against reading sermons is still very general in Scotland, and that committing to memory is the prevalent method; the Moderates have always read. Cunningham is to be professor of Church-polity, &c., with Chalmers, Welsh, and Duncan, in their new college, which is already in operation. I have had a file of "the Witness," which gives all the speeches in October. The men I should like to hear are five, three ministers and two elders: 1. Chalmers; 2. Guthrie; 3. Crichton; 4. Gordon; 5. Dunlop. My wife and I desire to wish you and yours every blessing in the new-year. For a motto, I will give you "Is any thing too hard for the Lord?"

PRINCETON, *January* 25, 1844.

Did you observe how distinctly Dr. Cunningham said *juty* for *duty?* He says, *Lighton*, (*Leighton*,) and so I find it written in old Scotch books. We have about $500 subscribed in Princeton, [for Free Church.] Potts, I think, is gaining on Wainwright, [in newspaper controversy on Episcopacy.] The latter has no more logic than a pudding. Our present plan of Presbyterial visitation is a great waste of labour. If the committee were all together, they might confer, and stir one another up. As it is, the visit becomes a simple protracted meeting, and that of the least profitable sort. Poor Dr. Rice, who is a most affectionate father, has heard of the death of his second daughter, wife of the Rev. Ezekiel Forman, of Versailles, Ky. The Dr. has some good signs in his congregation. From eight to twelve seeming conversions within a week or two. I have taken some pains to examine the series of texts preached on by Whitefield and Wesley: few of them are odd, or even uncommon; they are the familiar, evangelical, everlasting verses, which God has owned in all ages. I have been reading, with great delight, the Life of Dr. Waugh, a Scotch minister who died about fifteen years ago in London. He was a man of great eloquence, and a leader in the London Missionary Society. The average of his sermons for forty-six years was three a sabbath, and about 400 over. I have consulted several Scotch and one English copy of the catechism,

[1] Dr. Alexander for a long time followed the Moravian custom of adopting a "year-word," or text for the year; and while a pastor in New York, gave a sermon upon it to his congregation on the first Lord's-day of every year.

and find in all, scriptures in the plural. Wines is coming back here. A student in the Seminary lives on bread and water. I have heard that [Lyman] Coleman, (brother of the cross-banneret) [Editor of "The Banner of the Cross," an Episcopal periodical in Philadelphia,] is about to issue an anti-prelatic book, composed by him at Berlin, under the guidance of Neander. ["The Apostolic and Primitive Church," with Introduction by Neander.] Mrs. ——, an excellent old lady, but not a respecter of Priscian's head, being once at my father's, when two of our Greeks were there, turned round and said, "Am they Scotch?" I have heard an affecting story of poor Nordheimer. He foresaw his death, and, calculating pretty well when it would come, gave *double recitations* as long as he could sit up, so that his class might lose nothing. His Grammar is lauded in Gesenius's last edition of Lexicon. There is a great stir among the Baptists at Penn's Neck, on the straight turnpike from Trenton to Brunswick. Dr. Scudder is to be here this week. Dod is lecturing twice a week to crowds of Seminarists and ladies, on Architecture. He has reached his tenth lecture. I wonder if Cunningham will wake up the Philadelphians much. He is a powerful fellow; and a noble instance of what may be done without any pathos or any decoration. How I rejoice that Father Pollock [page 200] has had the hearing of him! —— has one good quality—he is afraid of nobody. I believe him also to be absolutely ignorant of personal rancour in controversy: he would be the first man in town to ask his enemy to dinner, after oceans of abuse; and that not of policy, but out of real good will. Dr. Miller, after a sore attack, begins to walk about the house. Grace seems to work in him, under this trial. I have a book (some 150 pp.) nearly ready for Sunday School Union, ["Good—Better—Best."] It is a narrative, but not aimed at children. Subject: the three methods of relieving human misery; to show that doing good to men's souls brings other relief in its train.

PRINCETON, *February* 20, 1844.

The Scotch delegates thicken upon us: we have had [Rev. Dr.] Burns and [Elder] Fergusson, and are daily expecting Lewis, who has arrived at New York. Burns, you know, is in Witherspoon's pulpit, at Paisley: he has been settled there thirty-three years. He is one of the most learned men in Scotland—has edited Halyburton's works, Wodrow's history, and is author of Memoirs of Prof. McGill. Burns's manner in the pulpit (gesture excepted) is more outré than Cunningham's. But his sermon was noble, rich, original, scriptural, and evangelical, and in diction elegant: and his closing prayer was seraphic. Fergusson is a smallish man, about 37 : about the dress and ways of a common weaver ; no apparent shirt. I was thunderstruck—especially when I found that Chalmers had picked him out. But my wonder ceased when I heard him, on the evening of the 18th. He spoke an hour and three-quarters by the watch—I wish it had been twice as long. In the first half of his speech he erred, by causing too much laughter. His *vis comica* is amazing. In the latter part he arose to a height of passion such as I have seldom witnessed. A critic would have condemned every thing in the elocution and gesture—but the eloquence was penetrating and transporting. I found Addison affected precisely as I was. In a word, it is utterly vain for me to communicate to you any idea of the degree of his power. As he rose, his diction became elegant and sublime. And yet he is only a merchant of Dundee.

A bad sore-throat prevails here. My father *has been* seriously, perhaps dangerously, ill with it. There is certainly a more general attention to religion here than I have ever known, but nothing like excitement. Scores of persons, who have neglected ordinances for years, come to every thing. Some of our most substantial men and women are affected. I suppose a hundred copies of the " Way of Life," [by Dr. Hodge,] and the " Great Change," [by Dr. Redford,] have been sold here within a few weeks. The latter has been blessed to the awakening of a number. A most visible effect has taken place on our tavern-haunters. In college we have little appearance of revival. Deruelle preached a very good sermon here last week. Burns thinks *Chammers* (so they all call him) will be out in the summer. Dr. Miller has recovered. I went to the African church on Sunday to hear [Elymas P.] Rogers, and heard a black named ———. He preached on Saving Faith, from the text, " In your *faith* possess ye your souls." Happily, he did not name chapter and verse. With a lecture of an hour every morning, a recitation every afternoon, and once or twice a week a sermon at night, I am kept in pretty good tension. Burns says he preaches four times on Sunday, a good part of his time. I am told Fergusson failed in speaking in Philadelphia.

PRINCETON, *March* 7, 1844.

Mr. Lewis of Dundee spoke twice here this week. He is a gentlemanly man, and gave us a delightful gospel-sermon. On leap-day [Feb. 29] I married a black couple : the bridegroom and bridemaid were both one-eyed.

Since I began this letter, a mournful event has occurred—the death of Mrs. [B. H.] Rice. She was ill about seventeen days. Her fever was violent and unyielding from the beginning. It left her, for several days before her death, in a state of extreme prostration.

Her mind was all peace, without a single cloud or anxiety, and she declared her triumph in Christ. Her friends, though deeply grieved, are filled with a sense of divine grace as displayed in her remarkable faith and hope. Poor Dr. Rice will feel his loss more hereafter. I know no man who leaned more upon a wife, nor any woman more remarkably fitted to cheer a desponding husband. She was as pious, open-hearted, benevolent, and self-sacrificing a person as I ever saw; and it is a general expression in town, that every one has lost a personal friend. Thus my good old father has, within a month, lost the oldest and the youngest of his brothers and sisters. He has one brother and two sisters surviving. I was at Worrell's [Monmouth co.] visitation on Saturday and Sunday, and had some hard work. Next Sunday is our Communion. About thirty will make profession of faith. The seriousness is not abated. It is a remarkable fact, that no one means of awakening has been so much blessed here, as the putting of books into people's hands; especially, "The Great Change," and "The Way of Life." We have had no inquiry-meetings, and latterly no increase of preaching. Domestic prayer-meetings have been a good deal multiplied. My father has not regained his strength, though he passes for well.

PRINCETON, *March* 16, 1844.

Dr. Cunningham is here again; chiefly to gather some hints about theological instruction. He has been laid up with lumbago. He grows in my esteem as a man of knowledge, piety, and consummate prudence.—(*Sunday*.) I heard Cunningham this morning, in the Seminary chapel. Text, 2 Cor. v. 14, 15. He explained the text, as I have for twenty years found myself constrained to understand it: "if one died ($\mathring{a}\pi\acute{e}\theta\alpha\nu\epsilon\nu$) for all—then all died," ($\mathring{a}\pi\acute{e}\theta\alpha\nu o\nu$.) The sermon was a most able one, uniting the highest degrees of plainness, argument, and unction. He read it, but exactly as he made his address. There was no ornament or illustration. In the evening Dr. C. preached; Heb. vii. 26, "Seeing he ever liveth to make intercession for us." Fifty minutes. I. The nature of the intercession. II. Practical application; in regard (1,) to the sins of believers; (2,) to the circumstances of believers; (3,) to their prayers; (4,) to their prospects and ultimate happiness. It was a noble sermon, as plain and unillustrated as before, but mighty in argument, and robustly eloquent. A very touching passage, seemingly for poor Dr. Rice. In his prayer he used that phrase of our excellent (Presbyterian) liturgy, "bless this *corner* of thy vineyard." Quære de hoc: how many corners has this polygon? are all the churches at the *cor-*

ners? He nevertheless prayed with great solemnity and devotion. In private, I am full of admiration for his considerate and discreet and gentlemanlike demeanour and words.—(*Monday.*) Sennakerim called here just now p. p. c., with a younger brother. He has been in America seven years, and goes back to Stamboul, as a naturalized citizen, and M.D. He has always behaved himself very well. None of our outlandishmen have been less offensive. Dr. Rice admitted 36 on profession of their faith. For the sake of a testimony for truth and godliness, I wish Frelinghuysen could be elected Vice President. I do not think I shall vote for Clay. I think Potts and Wainwright have been at it long enough, and should be choked off. A new periodical, (probably) to be called the Scottish Review, ["North British Review,"] will begin next month. The first number will have articles by Chalmers, Candlish, Sir David Brewster, Welsh, &c. It will not be merely religious. They want American articles, and will pay £15 a sheet. Reviews of American books of travel are specially mentioned. Dr. Chalmers says (in a note I heard read just now) that his class numbers 209: Dr. Lee's, (University of Edinburgh,) 30. A tract of my father's has been published in Armenian. The papers have given our late LL.D. to *John*, instead of *Alexander Dunlop*. They are very different men. The latter is the chief legal defender of the Free Church. His answer to the *Dean of Faculty* (Hope) is both a cogent and an elegant thing. Dunlop is lineally descended from two of the greatest leaders of the Scotch Kirk, (Dr. Carstairs, the friend of William III., and Dr. Robertson, the historian.)

PRINCETON, *March* 22, 1844.

Dr. Burns has been here; and, spite of my prejudices, I must say he preached, on Wednesday evening, one of the very noblest discourses I ever heard. The text was, Zec. xiii. 7, "Awake, O sword," etc. It was teeming with Scripture, but even the most familiar texts were made brilliant by their setting and connexion. I did not see him in private. You must read Webster's speech in the Girard College case: it is a noble defence of the Bible, the ministry, and religious training. I am to have a recitation four days in the week, at six o'clock in the morning, all summer. You see Dr. Potts has gone up town, [University Place Church.] Smyth's [of Charleston] sermon on the Free Church is out in Edinburgh. The Edinburgh *Witness* (of which I have had the reading lately) is conducted with great power. Plan of the Record; but the editor, Hugh Miller, is a genius, and a writer of extraordinary force and originality. He was a common mason at Cromarty, is now a leading geologist, and author. His severities are like those of Brougham ; who, by-the-bye, is coming out in a book against us.

PRINCETON, *April* 9, 1844.

If it had been in my power I should have hastened to Trenton upon receiving your note. But I was suffering from an attack of sore-throat and influenza. I am particularly glad to hear that your brother George is better; though from what you have said from time to time I gather that his case is serious. What you say of —— is really melancholy, if not alarming. His giving up music is like King Saul's flinging the javelin at David. The Rev. Tract Agent —— is here. He is a pleasant, scholarly, gentlemanly man, and made a fine impression, even on some among us who like few things from the pulpit. *Coal-porter* [Colporteur] is like to be a famous word in Anglo-American. You must be sure to attend the Methodist Conference in your city. When I was at the last one in Trenton, I thought it the most decorous ecclesiastical body I ever saw. So old Mr. Duponceau [of Philadelphia] is dead. Soon there will be none left of the magnates we used to look up to, and the great men will be our own coevals. Soon you will be startled with the compellation of "Father Hall,"—"the venerable father, who last addressed you,"—"the dear old man! I call him my spiritual father"—"years should speak," &c. You ought to follow up your piece in the Presbyterian, on Church-schools. It is a good string, and this is a good time. Only this morning I had a letter from Richmond, entreating for a man to set up a Female Seminary there; "what we want," he says, "is to get a first-rate Presbyterian school, and thus be relieved of the necessity of having our daughters *educated* Episcopalians."

You see the Abolitionists are out upon the Scotchmen, for fingering the wages of iniquity, [receiving donations for the Free Church from slaveholders.] They will learn a lesson as to the animus of American anti-slavery men. Having to go to College at 6½ A. M., I find my "matinal labours," as Walsh calls them, somewhat onerous. Dr. Yeomans wrote to me that they had 115 students in Lafayette College. Parke Godwin, the leading Fourierite, is an alumnus of the College and Seminary. Cooke represents the scheme as becoming formidable, from the numbers taken in. What a delightful book might be made about Philadelphia, if somebody would do what Watson ["Annals of Philadelphia"] tried to do:—antiquities, growth of city, views of all the old buildings, abundance of pictures, Penn, Benezet, Franklin, Morris, Rush, Wistar, White, Collin, Eastburn, Girard, Duponceau, Peale, &c. Could not you recall some of the incidents of your youth? Capt. Cox? David Allen? old Carswell? Mr. McElwaine? [all of his father's church in Pine street.] I am more and more convinced, that the greatest preparation for preaching extempore, is to know the English Bible by heart. An old black man, 78 years old, has learned to read, within six months, in this place. This being election-day, there has been not a little cursing of the " parsons," who all vote the Clay ticket, if any. You see that Pettit has made another speech in Congress, [against chaplains,] and again has had no echo. I wish old Adams would take him in hand. Hammit, of Congress, was a Methodist preacher in Virginia when I lived there. The Irish Catholics have been in treaty for an old stone house just back of my garden, for a mass-house. If they succeed, you are invited to the consecration.

PRINCETON, *April* 14, 1844.[1]

Though I thought a great deal about you, I did not dare to write until I received John's letter, which contained such comfortable statements, that I feel as if the opening were plain. I need scarcely say I sympathize with you and your mother, most deeply, under this affliction. It is true of your family, as of ours, that death has spared you long, only to make the blow of bereavement more severe. My recollection of George goes back to a very early period, and my renewed acquaintance with him, not many months ago, brought me into still nearer acquaintance with his kind and affectionate qualities. But I will not enlarge upon those considerations, which only serve to aggravate your loss. I know you feel it in your inmost soul. I know in some degree, what an interest you took in your brother's prosperity, and that his death must inflict a corresponding wound. And I think it very likely, that under the first impulse of the trial, you find yourself the subject of entirely new experience, and in danger of being " swallowed up of overmuch sorrow." And a certain time must elapse, before you can respond altogether to those statements of divine truth, which are applicable to your present condition, and which you will afterwards feel in all their force. It is my wish and prayer, that you, and your bereaved mother, and all the family, may be—not simply *comforted*—but what is infinitely better, *sanctified* by means of this affliction. For surely, if George is in heaven, as we are permitted to think he is, what have we more to wish for him? what have we more to wish for ourselves? Don't think of him

[1] I insert this letter of condolence on the death of a brother, notwithstanding it was first addressed to my sister.

as suffering, and dying—all that is past—it is no more to him than the suffering of your infancy is to you—think of him as "with Christ," "present with the Lord,"—adoring the infinite grace which saves sinners. The moment he departed, all the anxious prayers you ever put up for him were in an instant answered. Now let me very earnestly recommend to you, as a duty you owe to Christ, not to brood over the dark part of a dispensation which has so very bright a side. O that we may all be led to look more at the slightness of the hold we have on friends, and be prepared to go with them!

I have said these few words, not as believing there was any information to be given you, but as a testimony that you are not forgotten in your afflictions. And I beg that you will assure your mother and sister of my tender condolence. But how shall I speak of his widow? The Lord must comfort her; I trust He does; I am sure He will. I felt disposed to write to her, but did not feel that I had any call to intrude in this way, so soon after an unspeakable trial.

Every member of my father's family feels the blow which has fallen on yours. We have ourselves had a great loss, in the death of Aunt Rice. God grant that each of us may be prepared in the day of His coming!

I do not look for a reply until such time as you shall feel able to say something more calmly than you now can.

PRINCETON, *May* 6, 1844.

—— has written an article [for a religious paper] on the Elder Question, [the right of Ruling Elders to participate in the act of ordination.] The chief points are these: 1. The Scriptures ascribe to the *people* an important part in the government of the church. 2. Ruling Elders are the *representatives of the people*, in the exercise of this power, and are so called in our Standards. 3. The office is therefore of divine authority. 4. The power of elders is only that of the people whom they represent. 5. Ruling Elders are never said in our Standards to be the *Presbyters* of Scriptures; who (as we always contend against the prelatists) are bishops. (Turn to our Form of Government on this point.) 6. Ruling Elders, being representatives of the people, are not invested with the authority to ordain. This controversy is working great evil in the Southern churches. I would willingly give them the quorum-principle, if they would give up agitation on the other. David H. Bogart, a young lawyer of this place, was buried to-day. Dr. Rice preached, and Chaplain Starr read the Episcopal service, as part of the Odd Fellows' ceremony. What a poverty of invention among these

O. F., that they must needs borrow slavishly the cast-off sprig-throwing into the grave, from the Free-masons. Addison is about completing a bargain with Wiley & Putnam for the publication of his Commentary on Isaiah. He will print it in a very leisurely manner, as it is not fully written out. It will be chiefly for clerical readers, &c., and will make a large 8vo volume. He has laboured very much at it, and has gone over almost every part, repeatedly with pupils. I hear no word of my communication to the Christian Advocate and Journal [Methodist] about Summerfield. I can think of no reason why they should reject it. [It was published.] Oblige me by looking into two or three of the last numbers, as I do not see the paper.

PRINCETON, *May* 8, 1844.

I send you a catalogue of our college. You will find only five errors in Cortlandt Van Rensselaer's name.

Very much against my wish, I have to preach in New York [Duane Street Church] next Sunday. Some time ago they wrote to my father, to know whether I would entertain a call from them. I answered, through my father, very decidedly, in the negative. On the strength of this, I accepted, with others here, an invitation to preach for them. Now I learn, with regret, that they still mean to press the matter. I earnestly begged off, but they would not allow it.

I am now authorized to write a tract on Early Rising. I attend college prayers every morning, and spend an hour with a class before breakfast.

Shocking work in Philadelphia! [Destruction of a Roman Catholic Church by a mob.] I am afraid of the consequences of this Native American organization. Bishop Kenrick murders Scripture in a manner worth of the Anti-Bible party, in the end of his pacific proclamation.

One of our hens has eight ducklings. Three other hens are mothers, and two more will soon be. I never alighted on any home-attraction, which is so fertile in amusement for the children. Feeding, eggs, chicks, and ducklings, give them never-ending variety; especially as we have a regular Chicken College, roll-call, lectures on Clucking, Swimming, &c. Let me recommend a coop in your back-court. Capt. Crabb, U. S. N., my next-door neighbour, sometimes gets twenty-eight eggs per diem.

The new Pilgrim's Progress is elegant, but $4 will make it a book for the rich. The sumptuousness does not befit John Bunyan. Retzsch ought to illustrate it, in his outline way—broad and antique. The only picture in the book which pleases me, is Cruikshank's Vanity Fair. Charles Lamb has a capital letter to Bernard Barton, against the misplaced elegance of Southey's English edition. I see they have not followed Southey in retaining Bunyan's genuine street-English, such as "I thought you would *a* come in with violence."

A sloop, built on the canal, at Rocky Hill, passes by us, on regular trips, to and from Texas, (Galveston.)

There will be fine churches up town in New York, which will hear one another's organs. Duane Street will be left alone below.

PRINCETON, *June* 29, 1844.

I have had a disorder which has relaxed me a good deal. I have also had a call from Duane St. which has a similar effect.[1] I have to speak at New York the day after to-morrow, and Commencement is just over. These are reasons enough for not writing before, and for not writing eloquently now. The New York business I should settle very speedily, if it were left to my feelings; my friends, especially my father, warn me against a hasty determination. On the first vote (by ballot) when every one, without nomination, expressed his individual preference, I had 30; [scattering 21, blank 3.] On the fifth ballot, I had 47; [scattering 6, blank 3.] On the last (viva voce) I had 55 and there was 1 against. I have been reperusing Campbell's Gospels, with much pleasure. He directs one's attention to little variations of the common version from the Greek, which escape one even in reading the latter alone. Charlotte Elizabeth, who is one of the most influential writers of the age, has published a letter to Bishop Alexander [of Jerusalem] in which she remonstrates with him for not having his children circumcised. Charlotte should take the name of Zipporah. Quite a sect is rising in England, who think the Jews, when converted, should retain their ceremonies.

PRINCETON, *July* 4, 1844.

You perhaps have heard of certain matters, concerning which the true version may be welcome. The Duane people have agreed to call me. The vote was not unanimous. I spoke with none of them in New York. While there, I was visited by Mr. Greeley, a son-in-law of Dr. Tyler, and Mr. Dana, nephew of Dr. D. of Newburyport; both Bostonians, and introduced by John C. Green, with whom Mr. D. had been intimate in China. They are a deputation from the Committee of the

[1] He had preached in the Duane Street church as yet only on May 12th.

Bowdoin St. Church, formerly Dr. Beecher's, and more lately Mr. Winslow's. Their mission, to get me to candidate. On learning about the Duane business, they professed to be concerned, and returned, I believe, to Boston, requesting me not to decide the matter. We had a large assembly at the University chapel, but the heat and dyspnœa were terrible.[1] Burleigh pronounced a fine Christian poem, and was received with plaudits. Dr. Potts is to have a noble Gothic church; the walls are up. I heard Dr. Taylor in Grace church. His manner is very uncommon, sui generis, but, to me, exceedingly striking. I heard Andrews at the Tabernacle, and am not surprised at his great popularity. About 2,500 were out; I observed I was the only person who stood during prayer. I visited the Princeton and the North Carolina; and on the latter attended a party, at which I saw the officers of the two Mexican steamers in full dress; they danced; some of them are mulattoes. Bache says the prejudice of colour is absolutely gone, in Spanish America. I saw a party of Iowa Indians at the mission-rooms, in full dress; they were just about to embark for England. They are the party of "White Cloud." I became acquainted in New York with Sir Wm. Burnaby, an English proprietor in Bermuda; a pleasant, Roger de Coverley sort of man. We are all packed up for the Cape. This business of the call has given me unspeakable anxiety. The twofold solicitation, if I may so call it, makes me pause and ask, whether Providence does not mean to unsettle me from my semi-secular post. On examination, I do not find that I am drawn New Yorkward, so far as I know, by any attraction of a worldly nature. Ease, quiet, friends, retirement &c., are all *here*. I do feel a strong desire to preach. I am in a strait.

CAPE MAY, N. J., *July* 10, 1844.

Your acceptable letter came to hand last evening. By the same mail, two of same date, from Boston, about the church of St. Bowdoin. This island is the same which Thomson describes in his Castle of Indolence: "a dreamie land of drowsihede it was." The "salt-air" vindicates every thing; canine appetite, nakedness, sloth, and double naps. Mr. [now Bishop] Odenheimer is here; he and I at present *represent* the two parts of the church militant. Musicians abound. A troupe of Italians are very delightful. Dr. May of the Alexandria Seminary, who was my pleasant companion last summer, is not to be here till the 16th. My wife and children go in, of course, with me, and give me occupation enough in the surf. It has been uncom-

[1] On the 31st June he delivered the annual oration before the literary societies of the University of New York.

monly fine to-day. The number of visiters at present is about 1,000. There are a number of new houses, especially private cottages. One Capt. Hart and one Fotterall, have Chinese houses, very grand. We were on the steamboat Rob. Morris, when an accident befell the engine. The boat was detained at Newcastle from 11 on Saturday to 5 A. M., on Sunday. Five or six of us, out of 300, remained over the Sabbath. I was most hospitably entertained by Chancellor Johns, who is one of the principal persons there, and a very instructive host. His father, æt. 86, old Judge Johns, is as erect and merry as a bird, and has chewed tobacco enormously for seventeen years. He was chief justice for fifteen years, in which [Rev.] James P. Wilson was lawyer. I noted a number of anecdotes about him. I preached twice there, and have preached once here. Newcastle is like an old-world village —a sleepy hollow; but they have a regular sea-breeze, and good bathing. The air here is restorative in a high degree to me. I wish you were here, if only for a week.

I have had great anxieties about my duty in regard to Duane St. I have very earnestly wished to be fully employed in the work of the ministry; but I never thought of so responsible a charge. My visit to New York greatly impressed me with the mighty field on which even a moderate man might operate from that centre. I have no notion of abandoning the down-town, which, to me, is the city proper, in both New York and Philadelphia.

(*Thursday.*)—I failed to get this off yesterday. Politics here dull. The chief question is between Poverty Beach and the Light-House. Trade flourishes. The apple business rising. Ginger-bread dull. A handsome operation in straw hats has attracted attention. Oysters as per last quotation. Crabs rising.

My kind regards, and those of the " Capers " (sic in lingua insulari, verbo nempe pro hujus insulæ incolis usurpato) wait on you all. Yours very much.

CAPE MAY, N. J., *July* 15, 1844, 6 A. M.

Yesterday I preached twice, once at Cold Spring, once at the Mansion House, (Ludlam's.) There are many more opportunities of doing good than I could have imagined. I humbly trust that I have been enabled to gain the ear of a number of Quakers. What delightful inmates of a public house educated Friends are! You feel sure they will never swear, drink, or fight. They are too clannish; but to this they owe the maintenance of their peculiarities. Young Dr. Parrish, Dillwyn Parrish, their sister, and their wives, are here. They are highly educated and refined. ——— is here. It is a lesson to one, to observe how this good and really sensible man has coddled himself, and sacrificed to Fear, until the grass-hopper-burden is always on his back. I retract some of my opinions of ———; notwithstanding his intolerable manner and undeniable lack of *nous*, he is, I really think, one of the most God-fearing young men I ever saw. The care of a family makes me somewhat less free than on my former visits, but I have seldom passed a week of less trouble of mind than the last; and this notwithstanding the pendency of two serious questions. The Bowdoin St. *Church* have made me out a call; but the consent of the *Pew-proprietors* is awaited, and certain days' notice is required for this. The call from New York weighs more heavily on me. To go thither, I plainly see, will cut up by the roots my goodly tree of literary shade and family quiet, and deprive me of a support from parents, brothers, and elder ministers, on which I have leaned most pleasantly, but too long. I shall, if I go, seem to many to go for the gaud of a large stipend; this is of no weight, however, in the great account. If I go, it will be under this feeling, which I own grows upon me, *I dare not stay.*

CAPE ISLAND, *July* 17, 6 A. M., 1844.

Your very acceptable letter came to me by yesterday's mail in company with 269 new bathers. Three hundred are expected this evening. Three hundred sat down to tea at the Atlantic last evening. There cannot be less than 1,500 in all. Rooms are not to be had for love or money; people are sent several miles into the country, or laid out on dining-room floors. We have more than 100 here, chiefly Quakers. Our table is reputed the best. Three bands of music give us harmony to satiety. I preached twice on Sunday, once at Ludlam's to a very large audience. The New-School Elders and people seem as cordial with me as the others. I do hope that ugly wound is to be healed. It is a little Philadelphia down here, riots excepted. I wish you were here. A week would give you strength for all summer. Every evening I have to change my coat, and sleep under a blanket; nor have I had the feeling of unpleasant heat since I came, except when at some distance from the beach. Our head-waiter Brookes speaks French and Spanish fluently; and keeps all the accounts. Old Alexander Wilson (Quaker preacher) is here, and had an opportunity in our parlour. Mr. Eckel, of Barnes's church, is here, and, I fear, approaches his end. Though it is before breakfast, I hear a band of music playing on the strand. Chaplain Grier and son have arrived, also John K. Kane, Lapsley, Atwood, Dunton, Cleaveland. More letters from Boston. I am to be a Congregationalist; but New York claims rather preponderate.

PRINCETON, *August* 9, 1844.

The college opened yesterday. Thus far, about fifty matriculates. It is a sign of getting old, that I find numbers of my old college friends bringing sons on. All the *letters* I get from Boston indicate unanimous welcome. I do not think of turning Congregationalist, and they say nothing of turning Presbyterian; that settles the point, so far as I can see it with my present facts. Dr. Hodge, Prof. Henry, Mr. Packard, and Dr. Maclean, are the only persons who strenuously oppose my leaving Princeton. But, in my heart of hearts, I think they all, in their calculations, discount too liberally from the value of the *preached* word. Several of them are men whom I scarcely dare oppose, in a prudential question; yet, in my most solemn hours, I declare to you, their arguments have little weight with me, because I so profoundly believe *preaching* (including parochial teaching) to be God's great ordinance. O how much I need prayer and counsel! I am, after all, undecided. Give my love to ———. We shall welcome her at No. 499 Bowdoin St., or No. 1 Duane St., or No. 3 Steadman St., [Princeton,] as the case may be. Stilling's life, which everybody reads, was published at an obscure town in Pennsylvania, a number of years ago, and I then read it: it fell dead from the matrix. So much for having the entrée of the book-market. I think the book will do good among people who will not read an evangelical book.

PRINCETON, *August* 21, 1844.

I have asked myself repeatedly *ubi gentium* you are, that you do not reply to my last esteemed favour. Not to keep you in darkness, I now break through my silence, to say that I have accepted the call to New York. I feel, as you may imagine, almost terrified at what I have done. Yet I have no doubt as to the moral rightness of what I have done: success is a different thing. "Events are God's." The last two or three months have been a season of mental struggle. I have had to breast a current of advice and powerful reasoning, from some friends of ours, who are no mean argumentators, against my intimate convictions; and I have felt with them, that leaving Princeton is leaving *home*. At the same time, even in view of possible failure, I have quite a comfortable hope that God will not forsake me, and this sustains me more than usual. ——— says that the opinion is openly expressed, every day more and more, in his part of Virginia, that slavery is a curse, economically, and that the annexation of Texas is defended at the hustings, on the ground that it will tend to drain off the black race into that tropical region, in which the races are already mixed, and the prejudice of colour unknown. My father has been ill, but now goes about: so does Dr. Miller, though still feeble. We have matriculated about sixty-four new students, two from Massachusetts. I am very hard at work, giving my course to the Seniors before October 1st.

PRINCETON, *September* 3, 1844.

Several things have put me in the vocative, or case of O! 1. A catarrh, now in its 13th day; 2. Another disorder, in its 2d do.; and 3. A sermon, which has just been finished, after several days hammering at it. My good old father is unwell again. The difference between temperature of day and night, at this season, is a cause of many disorders; much more, I think, than even the abundance of fruit. The agitation of the public mind at our election-crises is a very injurious paroxysm. Democracy must be a cornucopia, to balance such evils; processions, rallies, torch-bearings, "yaller-kiver" minstrelsy, poles, coons, banners, lies, idle days and weeks, gaping for office by ten for one who gets it, rotation, absorption of mind in matters too high for such minds, endless restlessness, sacrifice of regular trades, &c., for temporary office, loquacity and debate, ending in alienation, disappointment, chagrin, and disaffection to lawful authorities. Such are the heads of my next political brochure. When you have opportunity, do not fail to talk with ——, on his own subject, on the general or fundamental principles. Half an hour with him is quite equal to any 8vo volume I ever read. He loves to be questioned, and never talks for display or argument. I rejoice that Walsh has the Consulship, [Paris;] his Americanism deserves it. I never tire of his *ana*, [in his letters to the Intelligencer,] which are copious during the vacation of Congress. By-the-bye, I think the National Intelligencer the very best of our papers, for dignity and honesty. It is wonderful how deep a Papist poor B. has become: I can liken it to nothing but a man's filling his eyes up with ounces of wax: it is part of his religion to see nothing and hear nothing; so I am told by those who know. The Seminary has more students than for ten years before. Watson's Annals [of Philadelphia] is fine, as to facts, but what a style! it is that of the youngest milliner's 'prentice. Dr. Green goes on with his autobiography. I prize his company: he is living on the verge of heaven. I always envied his most comfortable fixedness of opinion on all subjects. Several Princetonians enter the Seminary; my brother Samuel,

Archd. Rice, William A. Dod, and Frederick Kington. All have been law students, and the third a lawyer. [J. S] Green [Esq.] has sent at least seven pupils to the ministry. [George] Bush sends specimen-proofs of two works of his in the press. The one entitled *Anastasis* will, I fear, go against the catholic doctrine of resurrection. Did I speak to you about an article on the " New Jerusalem Church," in Rupp's new volume, on all the religions ? It is by a Virginia planter, and is the best article in the book, in point of style and scholarship. While I write, some one of the numerous bawling processions, with cheers and hip-hip-hurrahs, music, &c., is passing : cause unknown. I bid you good-night.

PRINCETON, *September* 11, 1844.

I am not shaken in any degree by what A.[1] says of the Free Church. I am aware that many seceders retain this old grudge, after all the causes are removed. The worst that can be said of the Free Church is that their retractation (it is such in effect) has been tardy, and that a false consistency makes them loth to eat up their old sayings. True it is, that they were truculent and absurd against Voluntaryism. I have a painful and threatening cough, now in its twenty-first day. I resisted all housing, &c., went to New York, Staten Island, &c ; but it is obstinate. I must stand ready to see the predictions of some verified, as to my capacity for pastoral labour. Staten Island is another Isle of Wight. I was altogether surprised and enchanted. A very gem : sea, bay, rivers, vales, mountains, incomparable verdure, villas, absence of all high-roads and noise. From one point, you see the Atlantic, New York, Brooklyn, Newark, Elizabethtown, Rahway, and immeasurable tracts of sea and land. Sunday morning I drove six miles to Richmond, the county-town, to hear Dr. Moore, eldest son of the old Bishop. Fancy the very ideal of an English country church ; on a green hill top, with a stretch of prospect over a narrow, sinuous valley, through which a pretty river flows towards the " Kills." It was well filled, and Mr. Peet of Rahway preached. In the P. M. I went to Fort Richmond, to worship with Brownlee's church, (Dutch:) here I heard James Romeyn ; and a more extraordinary man I never heard. Fulness of matter, every step sudden and unexpected, genius, strength, fire, terror, amazing and preposterous rapidity, contempt of rule and taste. It was an awful discourse ; 1 Thess. v. 3. It is one which I shall not

---

[1] A clergyman of the Scottish Relief Synod, who had spoken to his correspondent, in derogatory terms, of the newly professed liberality of the Free Church.

soon forget. In New York I overworked myself, looking for lodgings, and found none answering all conditions. Therefore, by urgent advice of my elders, I took a house, 83 White Street, east of Broadway, between Broadway and Elm Street, south side of White; two stories: look at a map of New York; you will see the yards are larger than usual there. But how unlike a Philadelphia house! $600 rent. After I had taken it, I learned that its first occupant had been the first pastor of our church, Dr. Romeyn. Installation probably Oct. 3. But not unless we hear from Moderator Webster pretty shortly.

END OF VOL. I.

INDEX TO VOL. I.

Abbott's Young Christian, 310.
Abeel, 253, 255.
Abelard, 117.
Adams, J., 125.
" J. Q., 73, 95, 96, 97, 99, 110, 112, 118, 124, 126.
Adams, N., 234.
Affliction, 142, 173, 184, 195, 218, 223, 245, 246, 257. (And see *Condolence*.)
Aiken, 59.
Aikman, 78, 176.
Alexander, A., 2, 10, 11, 12, 47, 148, 150, 156, 160, 167, 189, 228, 232, 238, 247, 251, 268, 279, 309, 310, 342, 343, 363, 372, 374, 376, 377, 386, 389, 390, 391.
Alexander, J. A., 66, 109, 111, 134, 135, 144, 148, 151, 167, 181, 188, 206, 219, 232, 268, 315, 346, 389, 395.
Alexander, Stephen, 217, 218, 368.
" W. C., 47, 73, 131, 132.
Alexanders, 41.
Alleine, 341.
Alward, 336.
America, Spanish, 72.
" South, 85, 113.
American Literature, 36.
Anagram, 306.
Anatomy, 74.
Anglomania, 233, 268.
"Ann Conover," 225.
Apostolic Succession, 283, 296, 369.
Apprentices, 225, 285.
Antinomians, 320.
Archives du Christianisme, 169.
Arm-chair, 258.
Arminians, 53, 54, 62.
Arminius, 243.
Armstrong, J. F., 199, 361.
" W. J., 12.
Assembly, General, 78, 103, 156, 166, 169, 188, 189, 238, 251, 252, 303, 357, 373.
Atonement, 149.

Babbage, 266.
Bache, 290, 293, 359.
Bacon, Lord, 77, 210.
Baird, 124, 362.
Ballads, Christian, 319.
Baltimore, 89, 172, 185.
Baptism, 296.
Barber, 89.
Barlow, 122.
Barnes, 134, 149, 154, 155, 161, 166, 170, 177, 237.
Barrow, 137, 214, 215.

Baxter, Richard, 77, 214, 284, 303, 320.
" Robert, 209.
Bayard, 251, 273, 287.
Beecher, 255.
Bellamy, 87.
Belleville, 125.
Benton, 72.
Berkeley, 70.
Berrien, 129, 137.
Bethune, 322.
Beza, 206.
Bible, 30, 54, 62, 64, 220, 233, 249, 255, 256, 325, 378.
Bible in education, 217, 219, (and above.)
" at family worship, 285, 288.
" Natural History, 153, 208.
" Charts, 308.
Bickersteth, 184, 190, 237.
Bile, 129.
Binney, 234.
Biography, 85.
Blacks, 162, 227, 260, 263, 289, 294, 295, 296, 297, 301, 307, 334, 340, 355. (See *Slavery* and *Colonization*.)
Blackwood's Magazine, 266, 310, 320.
"Blood on Door Post," 191.
Boccacio, 128.
Bonaparte, Napoleon, 105, 306, 322.
" Joseph, 12, 82, 125, 132, 146, 150.
Borrow, 368, 370.
Borsieri, 247, 251.
Bossuet, 70, 216.
Boston. (See *Bowdoin Street*.)
Boston Recorder, 241.
Boswell, 78.
Bourdaloue, 70, 216.
Bound Brook, 253.
Bouquet, Lines with, 59.
Bowdoin St. Church, 396, 400.
Boyle, 210.
Brainerd, David, 53, 85, 166, 254.
" J. G. C., 46, 78.
Branch, Secretary, 140.
Brearley, 199.
Breckinridge, John, 211, 266, 279, 284, 296, 334.
Breckinridge, R. J., 240, 242.
Breviary, 260.
British Officer, 60.
Broussais, 147.
Brown's Philosophy, 67, 70.
" David, 22.
" I. V., 129, 130.
" Rezeau, 150, 157.

Brownlee, 379.
Brownson, 311.
Bruce, 97.
Bruen, 134.
Buchanan, Missionary, 54.
" Poet, 105, 127.
Bucknell, 35.
Burckhardt, 206.
Burke, 103, 107.
Burnett, 257.
Burns, 388, 391.
Burr, 236, 244.
Bush, 234, 274, 292, 402.
Butler's Reminiscences, 69, 78.
" French Church, 84.
" Lives of Saints, 218.
" Analogy, 73.
Buzzard, 103.
Byron, 10, 73, 312.
Bythner, 167.

Calhoun, J. C., 99, 158.
Calvin, 187, 212, 235, 243, 276, 342, 367, 368.
" an Indian, 184.
Calvinism, 32, 52, 61, 70, 169, 215, 224, 239, 253, 358.
Cambridge Journal, 69.
Camp at Trenton, 281, 282, 284.
Campbell's Gospels, 396.
Canal, Delaware and Raritan, 89, 119, 122, 138.
Candidates for pulpit, 329.
Carey, W., 54.
Carnahan, 328.
Caroline, boat, 262.
Carrington, 96, 97, 352.
Carter's Travels, 127.
Caruthers, 313.
Case, 125.
Cassels, 337, 338, 346.
Castanis, 286.
Castaway, 343.
Catechisms, 205.
Cecil, 165, 216.
Chalmers, 29, 68, 70, 74, 258, 385.
Charlotte County, 94.
" Court-house, 94, 115, 269, 313.
" Elizabeth, 384, 396.
Charnock, 256.
Chaucer, 67, 68.
Chemistry, 124.
Cherokees, 146.
Child "100 years old," 257.
Children, writing for, 225, 231.
Children, factory, 225.
Cholera, 190, 193, 195, 206, 217.
Christ, Life of, 205, 298, 338.
Christ, Genealogy, 151.
Christian Advocate, 23, 40, 48, 62, 115.
" Observer, 174, 216, 238, 290.
" Spectator, 150.
Christmas, Rev., 82, 134, 176.
Churchman, 359.
Cicero, 58, 106, 118, 169, 239, 328.
Clam-classes, 265.
Clark, John, 272.
Classical Studies, 5, 10, 78.
Class Meetings, 167.
Claude, 86.
Clay, 157, 219, 326.
Cleaveland, 81.
"Cleon," 258.
Cliosophic Society, 26, 71, 242.

Clubs, 2, 209.
Colden on Masonry, 129.
Coleman, 388.
Coleridge, 46, 129, 214, 217, 229, 234, 261.
College, 19, 42, 87, 207, 212, 239, 260, 300, 332, 341, 343, 400.
College, Girard, 241, 265, 293.
Colleges, 107, 262, 359.
Colonization, 279, 297, 301, 308.
Colossians, 345, 347.
Columbus, 122.
Comet, 3.
Comfort, Rev., 270, 382.
Commencements, 26, 144.
Commentary, 124, 134, 153.
Communion 163, 172.
Concordance, 187.
Condolence, 142, 246, 277, 393.
Confession of Faith, 32.
Congregationalism, 382.
Congress, 238.
Cornell, 321.
Controversy, 225, 226, 227, 234, 254.
Conversations-Lexicon, 132.
Conversion, 4, 20, 45.
Cooper's Novels, 34, 67.
Corinthians, 367.
Corneille, 129.
Court-day, 100.
Cowley, 73.
Cowper, 7, 8, 11, 48, 50, 53, 73, 117, 384.
Cox, 192.
Crabbe, 290, 297.
Cramp's Popery, 185.
Credit System, 288.
Creeds, 32.
Cromwell, 136.
Cuban, 67.
Cunningham, 386, 387, 388, 390.
Cuvier, 78.
Cyprian, 115.

Daillé, 294.
Dana, 335.
Danville College, 159.
Darwin, 213.
David's Psalms, 221.
Davidson, 381.
Davies, 53, 74, 77, 137, 235, 302, 304, 351.
Davis, 315, 376.
D. D., 376, 379.
Deaf and Dumb, 36, 89, 141.
Death, 27, 35, 64, 75, 107, 172, 175, 176, 224.
Decapolis, 342.
Decoration, Civic, 238.
Demasism, 275, 285.
Demmé, 290.
Democracy, 239.
Demosthenes, 58.
Deruelle, 381, 389.
Despondency, 17, 43, 47, 59.
Dick, 321.
Dickens, 372.
Dickey, 183.
Doane, 217, 324.
Dod, 217, 256, 274, 362, 379, 385, 388.
Doddridge, 138, 150, 176, 184.
Dort Synod, 169.
Drawing, 242.
Dryden, 73.
Duane, Wm., 140.
Duane Street Church, 365, 395, 396, 399, 400.

Duffield, 187.
Dunlop, 391.
" Roman Literature, 120, 127.
Duponceau, 392.
Durand, 86.
Dwight, 136.

Earthquake, 343.
Ecclesiasticus, 285.
Editing, 140.
Education, 9, 21, 219.
" "Annual," 211.
Edwards, 53, 70, 71, 77, 165, 186, 221.
Elder Question, 394.
Eliot, 54.
Elijah, Life of, 204.
Elocution, 268.
Ely, 51, 220.
Encyclopædia, Edinburgh, 69.
" Americana, 141.
English, Old, 106, 213, 300.
Episcopacy, 212, 213, 231, 294.
Epitaphs, 342.
Erasmus, 115, 117, 126, 243.
Erskine's Evidences, 24.
Euripides, 242.
Ewing, Chief Justice, 82, 120, 194, 198, 200.
" Dr. F. A., 200, 208, 265, 301, 320, 369.
Examination, College, 312.
Extempore Preaching, 37.

Facts, 297, 301.
Fenelon, 242, 244.
Fergusson, 388.
Ferrar, 204.
Fichte, 121, 212.
Finch, 80.
Finney, 164, 186.
Fire, 231.
Fisher, 69.
Flavel, 256.
Flechiere, 70.
"Flower Book," 194.
Foster, 369.
Fourierists, 375, 376.
Fox, 137, 181.
Francke, 157, 166.
Frederick of Prussia, 146.
Free Church, 373, 381, 386, 387, 402.
Freeholds, 365.
Frelinghuysen, 147.
French, 29, 36, 70, 113, 205, 242.
" Church, 169, 279.
" Croquis, 209.
" Infidelity, 309.
" Poetry, 123.
" Pun, 139.
" Revolution, 105, 147, 154.
Frontis, 86.
Fuller, 76, 85, 213.
Fyler, 21.

Gall, 205.
Gazette, London, 204.
" National, 40, 58, 61, 67, 69, 73, 127, 129, 131, 134, 135, 136, 141, 147, 247.
Geography of Bible, 134, 189, 344.
Geology, 80, 81.
Gerhardt, 151.
Gerlack, 222, 232, 262.
German Hymns, 151, 306, 323.
" Language, Literature, and Theology, 112, 113, 114, 115, 121, 136, 212, 221, 222, 223, 225, 242, 274, 290, 306.
Germantown, 171.
Gesenius, 164, 325, 388.
Gibbon, 47, 77, 78, 85, 125, 135.
"Gift to Afflicted," 238.
Giles, 93, 137.
Girard College, 241, 265, 293.
Gladstone, 283.
Gleanings, Bib. Antiq., 189, 205.
Glendy, 90.
"God Forbid," 305, 307.
Goethe, 132, 133.
"Good, Better, Best," 294, 388.
Goode, 238, 359.
Goodrich, 116.
Gordon, 69, 235, 304.
Gough's "History," 137.
Government, forms of, 125.
Grammar, 127, 242, 326.
Graves, Rev., 211.
"Great Change," 389, 390.
Greece, 33, 113, 245.
Greek, 304.
Green, Dr., 21, 23, 284, 337, 374, 376, 401.
Grimke, 147.
Griscom, 89.
Grotius, 115, 116.
Guericke, 212.
Gulick, 230.
Gurney, J. J., 280.
Guyon, 48.
Gymnastics, 130.

Haines, 382.
Haldeman, 129.
Halifax, Va., 97
Hall, Basil, 134.
" Robert, 36, 137, 155, 216.
Halle, 105.
Halsey, 31, 80, 81.
Halyburton, 70.
Hampden Sydney, 107, 116, 302, 303.
Hamilton, 198.
Handel, 70.
Hanover Church, 302, 303.
" College, (South) 244.
Hare, 348, 384.
Hargous, 129, 139, 238.
Harlan, 339.
Harold, 86.
Harris, Peter, 295, 297, 328.
" Mammon, 310.
Harrison, 326, 329.
Hart, 148, 217.
Hartley's Evidences, 73.
"Harvest," 195.
Hayden's Geology, 81.
Hayley, 117.
Health, 6, 43, 46, 107, 108, 114, 168, 172, 182, 188, 228, 236, 238, 239, 256, 373, 375.
Heat, 83.
Heber, 109.
Hebrew, 141, 163, 166, 180, 182, 212, 347.
" Questions, 245, 246, 249.
Hegel, 212, 223.
"Help to Gospels," 167.
Hengstenberg, 138, 223, 260.
Henry, Matthew, 168.
" Patrick, 351, 353.
" Philip, 342.
" Professor, 205, 222, 227, 318, 319, 378.

Henry, S. C., 244, 365, 366.
Herder, 61.
Hexameter, 66.
Hicksites, 137, 182.
Hillyer, 313.
History, Ecclesiastical, 85.
Hoby, 242.
Hodge, 11, 15, 65, 71, 104, 109, 112, 113, 150, 156, 217, 223.
Hodgson, 41.
Hogan, 82.
Holland's Summerfield, 139.
Homer, 5, 97, 127.
Hooker, Mrs., 323.
Hopkinsians, 72, 149, 250.
Hopkinson, 86, 110, 156.
Horace, 10, 40, 71, 78, 83, 345.
Horne, 347, 348.
Horsley, 86.
Hosack, 81.
How, 155.
Howe, 137, 155, 158.
Howell, 233, 244.
Hug, 238, 347, 348.
Hume, 85.
Hundredth Letter, 127.
Hurlbut, 239.
Hurley, 49.
Hunt, 129.
Hunter, 78.
Huss, 324.
Hutton, 36.
Hypocrite, 185.

Imputation, 221.
Inconsistency, 174.
India, 247, 358.
India Rubber Shoes, 71.
Indians, 184, 377, 383, 397.
"Infant's Library," 219, 263.
Infidelity, 149, 323.
Ingleside, 348, 350, 352.
Intemperance, 120, 144, 150, 155, 229, 237, 243, 286, 299, 308, 323, 335, 346, 347, 350, 385.
Installations, 99, 119.
Introductions to Bible, 190, 222, 233, 255, 256, 347.
Irving, Edward, 35, 56, 65, 68, 181, 209.
" Washington, 109, 122, 124.
Italian, 125, 247, 251.

Jackson, 46, 73, 95, 107, 112, 113, 114, 158, 190.
"Jacob and Joseph," 217, 247.
Jacotot, 192, 194.
Jahn, 189.
James, H., 273.
James River, 104.
Jamestown, 104.
Janeway, 26, 28.
Jarratt, 302, 304.
Jay, 184.
Jenkyn, 230.
Jews, 214, 263, 287, 316, 346, 372, 373.
Job, 290.
Johlson, 181.
Johns, 398.
Johnson, 67, 127, 235, 323.
Jones, C. C., 337.
" J. H., 252.
" Sir W., 81.
Josephus, 247.

Julius, 225.
July 4th, 81, 130.
Justification, 387.
Juvenal, 324, 385.
Juvenile Letters, 1-12.

Kant, 121.
Kate Hall, 342.
Kemble, 240.
Kenrick, 185.
Kent, 231.
Kidd, 379.
Kilpin, 230.
Kinney. (See *Newark Advertiser.*)
Kirchenfreund, 151.
Kirk, Rev., 110, 118, 128, 157, 219, 279, 344.
Kollock, 328.
Krebs, 13.

Lafayette, 66, 82, 105, 128.
" College, 324.
Lake Poets, 46.
Lambertville, 383.
"Lame John," 309, 318.
Lane's Egypt, 276.
Lang, 300, 321.
Languages, 126. (See *Hebrew, Latin,* etc.)
Laryngitis, 269.
Latin, 69, 70, 105, 118, 120, 381, 385.
Laussat, 89.
Law, The, 37, 38, 39, 108.
Law's " Call," 76.
Lawrenceville, 129.
Leavitt, 231.
Lee's Grammar, 166, 206.
Leeser, 180, 182, 371.
Le Grand, 102, 349.
Legislature of New Jersey, 141, 248.
Leighton, 150, 180, 277.
Lenox, 81.
Letter-Writing, 7, 40, 43.
"Letters to Young Lady," 384.
" Younger Brother," 208.
" Russell's, 214, 273.
Lewis, 389.
Lexicon, 221, 346.
Library of Knowledge, 193.
Licensure, 84, 88.
Lightfoot, 153.
Limonade, 239.
Lindsly, 15, 24, 31.
Liturgy, 238.
Livingston, 74, 135.
Lizars, 74.
Locke, 6, 212, 219, 324.
Lockhart, 255.
Long Branch, 24.
Longfellow, 316.
Lowrie, 346, 370.
Lucian, 233.
Lunatic Asylum, 374.
Luther, 53, 56, 134, 194, 288, 299, 317.
Lybrand, 12.
Lyttelton, 329.

Macaulay, 309.
Magazines, 36, 37, 106, 108, 115, 149, 214, 215, 238, 242, 327.
Magee on Atonement, 86, 149.
Magie, David, 275.
"Man of Sin," 287.
Mania a potu, 155.
Manual Labor School, 113.

March, 265.
Marion College, 240, 244, 270.
Marriage, 143.
Marshall, Mungo, 83.
Marshman, 54.
Martin, artist, 139.
Martyn, Henry, 50, 53, 85, 167, 174.
Mason, J. M., 221.
Massillon, 70, 216.
Mastodon, 25.
Mathematics, 52.
Maxwell, 103, 355.
May, Cape, 132, 377, 397.
" Rev., 39, 51, 377, 397.
McCalla, 154, 177, 360, 371, 377.
McCarrier, 51, 52.
McClelland, 386.
McIlvaine, 191, 217, 238.
McLeod, 159.
McMullen, 378.
McNeely, 198.
Meade, 349.
"Measures," 186, 227.
Mechanic, American, 146, 283. (See *Quill*.)
Melancthon, 56, 115.
Memoirs, 243.
Merle D'Aubigne, 363.
Mesmerism, 368.
Metaphysics, 54, 121, 359, 364.
Methodists, 149, 150, 186, 204, 236, 278, 320, 336, 349, 375.
Middleton, 85, 174.
Milledoller, 74.
Millennium, 258.
Miller, Dr., 109, 155, 204, 206, 344, 386.
" Hugh, 391.
Milner, 236, 325.
Milton, 32, 73, 107, 114, 115, 116, 124, 125, 126, 173.
Mineralogy, 80.
Miniature, 95.
Ministry, 72, 79, 83, 196, 228, 247.
"Misadelphia," 160.
Misca, 238.
Missions, 157, 161, 206-211, 212, 215, 232, 236, 283, 361.
Missions, A. B. C. F., 150, 157, 236, 276.
" Map and Manual, 221, 222.
" Home, 241.
Mitchelmore, 210.
Mocking-bird, 98, 103, 269, 332.
Moffat, 264.
Molière, 113.
Money, 232.
Monk, Maria, 238.
"Monkey," 194.
Monteith, 113.
Moon Hoax, 231.
Moravians, 57.
More, Hannah, 117, 220, 240.
Mormons, 320.
"Morning Journal," 140.
Morristown, 380.
Mottoes, 243, 298.
Mulberries, 279, 285.
Murray, 381.
Music, 214, 218.

Names, 260.
Nasmith, 160.
Natchez, 369.
National Intelligencer, 322.
" Gazette. (See *Gazette*.)

Nature, 188.
Neander, 113, 213, 222, 230, 239.
Nesbit, 253, 256.
Nestorians, 317.
Nettleton, 115, 164, 167, 186, 227, 318.
Nevin, 189, 255.
Nevins, 90, 219, 383.
Newark, 234, 244.
Newark Advertiser, 146, 238, 246, 258, 262, 266, 269, 285, 367.
Newark College, 284.
New Brunswick, 88, 253.
Newcastle, 398.
New Haven Theology, 135, 168.
New Jersey, 120.
Newspaper, 140, 285, 338.
Newton, J., 48, 53, 117, 165, 176, 189, 300.
Niagara, 46, 76, 78, 79.
Nichol, 321.
Nordheimer, 276, 325, 388.
Norfolk, 104, 328.

Observer, N. Y., 232, 284.
Odenheimer, 372, 397.
Odd Fellows, 394.
"O. K.," 315.
Old Age, 255.
Onderdonk, 123, 231.
"Only Son," 205.
Ordination, 99.
Orthography, 274, 379, 385, 396.
Outram, 86.
Ovid, 8, 328.
Owen, 150, 221, 230, 382.
Oxford Tracts, 260, 289, 294, 296, 335.

Packard, 164, 217, 219, 225, 241, 290, 292, 306.
Paine, 122.
Paley, 117, 216.
Panama Mission, 124.
Paris, 105.
Parker, 222.
Parnell, 156, 358.
Parr, 239.
Pastor at Charlotte, 94, 98, 118.
" Trenton, 119, 202.
Paterson, 116.
Patton, 65, 88, 112.
Payson, 166.
Pearce, 85.
Penn, 210.
Penn-square Church, 371.
Penny Magazine, 213, 327.
" Paper, 254.
Persia, 109.
Petersburg, 91, 114.
Philadelphia, 3, 4, 14, 96, 109, 132, 370.
Philadelphian, 320.
Philological Society, 112.
Phrases, Incorrect, 306.
Piety, 73.
Pike, 174.
"Pilot," 34.
Planters, 127.
Playfair, 73.
Plumer, 354, 373.
Pocahontas, 104.
Poetry, by J. W. A., 59, 158, 258, 262, 315, 317.
Polemics, 40.
Poles, 160.
Politics, 358, 401.

Pollock, James, 199, 248, 388.
Pollok, 111, 157.
Pope, 22, 117, 126, 310, 312, 346.
Popery, 185, 192, 208, 226, 239, 247, 287, 322.
Potts, George, 47, 250.
" Wm., S., 328, 378.
Powhatan, 104.
Prayer, 173, 174, 184, 261, 311.
" Meetings, 366.
Preaching, 71, 74, 86, 94, 215, 268, 333, 334, 362, 364, 387. (See *Sermons*.)
Presbytery, 278, 284, 302.
"Presbyterian," The, 160, 161, 197, 203-207, 209, 278.
Presbyterian Church, 183, 206, 223, 226, 251, 268, 327, 359, 363, 369. (See *Barnes, General Assembly*, etc.)
Prescott, 266.
Priestley, 86.
Princeton, *passim*.
" Press, 45, 51, 65, 73, 77, 194.
Prison, 162.
Professor in College, 207, 208, 403.
Professors of Religion, 57.
"Progress," 213.
Pronunciation, 212, 242, 266, 286, 353, 385.
Proselytes, 239.
Protestants, 255.
Protevangelium, 345.
Proudfit, 209.
Pupils, Private, 335.

Quakers, 36, 37, 137, 181, 182, 292, 296, 320, 371.
Quakers' Trial, 182.
Queenston, 220.
Question Books, 284, 292.
Quill, Charles, 146, 266, 268, 271, 279.

Raleigh, 115, 125.
Randolph, 93, 94, 95, 96, 98, 99, 101, 114, 131, 270, 350, 356.
"Rase-corss," 141.
Rauch, 327.
"Record," 312.
Redemptioners, 325.
Redwood, 67.
Red-bird, 103.
Reed, 40, 47.
Reformation, 363.
Religious Counsels, 14, 18, 25, 27, 29, 34, 38, 62, 64, 74, 75, 77, 84, 85, 94, 165.
Repertory, Biblical, 65, 71, 73, 117, 126, 128, 138, 140, 143, 150, 151, 156, 157, 158, 160, 161, 176, 177, 181, 184, 186, 205, 208, 209, 221, 235, 246, 250, 255, 268, 275, 287, 312, 323, 370, 385.
"Remember me," 111, 115.
"Retirement," 95.
Review, American Quarterly, 96, 102, 105, 113, 115, 135, 213, 247.
Review, Edinburgh, 72, 283, 370.
" " (Presbyterian), 215.
" Literary and Theological, 250.
" North American, 34, 102.
" North British, 391.
" Quarterly, (London) 69, 72, 102, 325, 370.
Revival of Letters, 122.
Revivals, 116, 160, 162, 163, 172, 176, 177, 185, 204, 226, 237, 252, 253, 301, 336, 346, 361, 370.
Revolution, 154.

Révue Encyclopédique, 132.
Rheinwald, 212.
Rice, B. H., 92, 174, 228, 244, 387, 389.
" J. H., 183, 234, 293.
" Mrs., 186, 201.
Richardson's Dictionary, 240.
Richter, 290.
Ridgely, 96.
Ringseis, 223.
Rives, 314.
Rivet, 174.
Robertson, Dr., 85.
" Noah, 116.
Robinson, 337, 344.
Romeyn, 74, 403.
Roscoe, 85.
Rose, 167.
Rosenmuller, 117, 126, 190.
Ross, 14.
Rotteck, 323.
Round-Table, 68.
Rowan, 159.
Roy, 186.
Russell's Letters, 214, 273.

"Sacramental Discourses," 325.
Sandemanians, 273.
Sandwich Islands, 266, 277, 327.
Saratoga, 170, 171, 229.
Sartori, 119, 138.
Savage, 2, 237.
Saxe Weimar, 115.
Scaliger, 106.
Schaff, 151.
Schiller, 113, 128, 129, 130, 136, 141, 309.
Scholz, 126.
Schools, Public, 122, 123.
Schwartz, 54.
Sciot, 286.
Scott, Dr., 56, 85.
" Sir W., 105, 111, 255, 264.
" " Jane," 205.
Scougal, 77.
"Scripture Guide," 190.
Searle, 47.
Sectarism, 240.
Seixas, 89.
Self-denial, 50.
"Semeur," 326.
Sem.-centenary, 287.
Seneca, 328.
Sennakerim, 391.
Separatists, 295.
Sermons (and see *Preaching*), 189, 203.
" Barrow, 137, 214, 215.
" Baxter, 214, 364.
" Bossuet, 70, 216.
" Bourdaloue, 70, 86, 216
" Cecil, 216.
" Chalmers, 68, 74.
" Charnock, 256.
" Davies, 53, 74, 77, 137, 216.
" Edwards, 77, 216.
" English, 215.
" Episcopal, 216.
" Flavel, 256, 364.
" Flechière, 70.
" Griffin, 293.
" Hall, 36, 137, 214, 216.
" Hare, 304.
" Howe, 137.
" Irving, 35, 56, 68.
" Jay, 216.

Sermons, Massillon, 70, 216.
" Nevins, 90.
" Melville, 275.
" Newton, 216.
" Paley, 216.
" Sherlock, 214, 216.
" Taylor, 68, 214, 215.
" Tholuck, 231, 233.
" Wolfe, 216.
Servetus, 235.
Shakespeare, 8, 10, 47, 71, 79, 213.
Sharpe, 2.
Shelley, 112.
Sherlock, 214, 216.
Sigourney, 218.
Simeon, 211.
Simpson, 218.
Sioux, 79.
Skinner, 75, 124, 275, 289.
Skipwith, 356.
"Slatted over," 132.
Slavery, 88, 93, 117, 272, 306, 351, 352, 353, 354, 377, 385, 400.
Socinians, 53, 86, 149, 168, 290, 311.
Southard, 120, 128, 144, 201.
Southey, 305.
South Hanover College, 244.
Spaulding, 226.
Spanish beggars, 146.
Spectator, 310.
Spencer, 99.
Spenser, 86.
Spite-hall, 343.
Sprague's Ode, 36.
Spring, 289.
"Spy," Wirt's, 210.
Stael, De, 74, 105, 117, 233.
Staten Island, 402.
Staudlin, 121.
Steel-pens, 82.
Stephens, 335.
Stewart, C. S., 62.
" Dugald, 69, 70, 72.
Stilling, 400.
Stockton, Betsey, 294.
" Commodore, 309, 359, 374, 378.
Stone, 134, 234.
Stoves, 243, 315, 317, 340.
Stuart, J., 2.
" Prof., 385.
"Student's Notes," 43, 47.
Study, course of, 15, 106, 121, 249.
Stump Speeches, 99.
Studdiford, 385.
Style, 195.
Summerfield, 71, 81, 139, 362, 395.
Sunday-Schools, 189, 205, 206, 235, 243, 244, 251, 257, 291. (See *S. S. Union*.)
Sunday-School Journal, 160, 189, 191, 192, 193, 196, 209, 217, 276, 280, 286, 375.
Survilliers. (See *Bonaparte*.)
Suydam, 318, 327.
Swedish Churches, 338.
" Translation, 263.
Synod, 177, 270, 340, 380.
Systems of Theology, 186, 236.

Tabernacle, Broadway, 250.
Talmage, 45.
Tariff, 266.
Tauchnitz, 259.
Taylor, Isaac, 187, 195.
" Jeremy. 67, 68, 214, 215, 277, 306.

Temperance. (See *Intemperance*.)
Temporal Charity, 142.
Tennents, 165, 304.
"Ten Thousand a Year," 318, 321.
Terence, 126, 127, 136.
"Terror of Lord," 245.
Texas, 137.
Texts, 387.
" illustrated—
Gen. 3 : 15, 345.
Exod. 2 : 6, 325.
2 Sam. 23 : 5–17, 307.
Ezra 7 : 1–5, 153.
Job, 290.
Psalms 6, 175.
" 77 : 7, 204.
" 104, 188.
" 116, 175.
Isaiah 7 : 14, 158.
" 7 : 3, 151.
" 8 : 3, 151.
" 8 : 4, 151.
" 9 : 6, 152.
" 37, 175.
" 65 : 20, 257.
Ezekiel 39–40, 263.
Matthew 1, 151.
" 1 : 23, 151.
" 12 : 30, 368.
Luke 3 : 23–38, 153.
Luke 13 : 24, 63.
John, (Gospel,) 65.
Acts 6 : 1–6, 375.
" 8 : 37, 32.
Romans 3 : 4, 305.
" 5, 221.
" 9 : 15, 32.
1 Cor. 1 : 13–15, 296.
" 3 : 22–23, 357.
" 4 : 1–9, 15, 369.
" 7 : 29–31, 168.
" 9 : 27, 343.
" 10 : 2, 296.
" 14 : 35, 287.
2 Cor., 364.
" 1 : 9, 173.
" 4–5, 173.
" 4 : 7, 28.
" 5 : 11, 245.
" 5 : 14–15, 390.
" 6 : 4, 369.
" 7 : 1, 365.
" 9 : 1–2, 369.
" 9 : 8, 365.
" 11 : 23, 369.
Gal. 3 : 18–19, 62.
Eph. 1 : 4, 55.
Phil. 2 : 2–3, 158.
" 3 : 10, 165.
" 4 : 13, 165.
Col. 3 : 1–2, 345.
" 3 : 17, 165.
1 and 2 Thess., 287.
1 Tim., 2 : 8, 366.
2 Tim., 1 : 9, 55.
Hebrews 13 : 5, 176.
James 5 : 14, 174.
2 Peter 3 : 13, 257.
1 John 2 : 26–27, 326.
Rev. 16, 191.
Thanksgiving, 139, 385.
Thelwall, 89.
Theological Course, 178.

Theological Dictionary, 145.
" Seminary, (Princeton,) 12, 13, 41, 45, 177, 228, 368, 384.
" Seminary, (Western,) 353.
" Study, 5.
Tholuck, 231, 233, 242.
Thomas, 26.
Thomson, 215.
Thomson's Seasons, 8, 110.
Thorwaldsen, 241.
Ticknor, 127.
Tilghman, 234.
Titles, 262.
Tobacco, 73, 105.
Todd's Manual, 230.
Torrey, 342.
Townley, 82.
Townsend's Bible, 190.
Tract Society, 310.
Trades' Unions, 237, 240.
Transcendentalism, 274, 363.
Translations, 116.
Travels, 33, 82, 110, 131.
Trenton, 11, 112, 119, 202, 206, 255, 329, 331, 333, 356.
Trevelyan, 247.
Tucker, 107, 376.
Turretine, 71, 181, 187, 221.
Tutor, 42, 87.
Tyler, 374.

Union, Am. Sunday-School, 154, 157, 169, 171, 190, 196, 197, 203, 232, 233, 240, 241, 243, 247, 251, 292, 296, 314.
Unitarians. (See *Socinians*.)
University of New York, 397.
" Virginia, 107, 116, 305, 314.
Urquhart, 160.
Usher, 287.

Van Buren, 243, 341.
Velocipede, 3.
Venable, 352.
Ventilation, 319.
Vermont Chronicle, 240.
Vertot, 135.
Vethake, 137, 148, 169.
Vielleville, 130.
"Views in Palestine," 190.
Vineyard, Corner of, 390.
Virgil, 126.
Virginia, 33, 79, 86, 89, 91, 269.
Visiting, Pastor's, 128.
Vitringa, 242.
"Vivian Grey," 112.
Voltaire, 70, 146, 233, 256.
Voorhees, 199.
Vroom, 219.

Waddel, 83, 210, 235, 353.
Wadsworth, 373.

Wales, New South, 300.
Walker's Dictionary, 242.
Walpole, 343.
Walsh, 123, 126, 156, 226, 246, 247, 310, 314, 322, 325, 326, 343, 362, 401. (See *Gazette and Amer. Quarterly Review*.)
War, 236.
Ward, 54.
Washington, 138, 139.
" Judge, 125.
Waterbury, 14, 82, 128.
Watkins, 101.
Watson, Annals, 392, 401.
" Bishop, 31, 73.
" Divinity, 181, 187.
Watts, 238, 316.
" John, 157.
Waugh, 387.
Waverley Novels, 71, 111.
"Way of Life," 389, 396.
Wayland, 229.
Weatherby, 43.
Webster, Daniel, 33, 154, 261.
" Noah, 120, 132, 240.
Werter, Sorrows of, 133.
Wesley, 72, 123, 167, 187, 387.
Wharfs, 221.
Whately, 369.
Whig Society, 22, 26, 71, 242, 257.
Whip-poor-will, 103.
White, Bishop, 135, 217, 242, 263, 294.
Whitefield, 56, 165, 235, 387.
Wilberforce, 267, 268, 273.
Williams, J. W., 247.
Wilson, Bishop, 184.
" J. P., 35, 75, 109, 184, 263, 339.
Winchester, 139, 337.
Wirt, 144, 182, 210, 339, 348.
Witherspoon, 82.
Wiseman, 347.
"Witness," Edinburgh, 391.
Witsius, 221.
Wolfe, 216.
Wolff, 257, 260, 264, 339.
Women, Sufferings, 163.
" Name, 240.
Woodsons, 355.
Woolsey, 81.
Wordsworth, 46, 60, 131, 213, 234.
Working Man, 146, 283.
Wyatt, 101.

Yale College, 237.
Year-word, 387.
Yeomans, 206, 248, 251, 279, 301.
Young, 378.
"Youth's Friend," 243

Zealand, New, 300.
Zinzendorff, 236.
Zoology, 226.
Zuingle, 323, 324, 325.

END OF VOL. I.

www.ingramcontent.com/pod-product-compliance
Lightning Source LLC
Chambersburg PA
CBHW060937230426